Scriptures of the World's Religions

SECOND EDITION

edited by

James Fieser
University of Tennessee at Martin

John Powers
Australian National University

Mc Graw Hill

Boston Burr Ridge, IL Dubuque, IA Madison, WI New York
San Francisco St. Louis Bangkok Bogotá Caracas Kuala Lumpur
Lisbon London Madrid Mexico City Milan Montreal New Delhi
Santiago Seoul Singapore Sydney Taipei Toronto

Higher Education

SCRIPTURES OF THE WORLD'S RELIGIONS, SECOND EDITION

Published by McGraw-Hill, a business unit of The McGraw-Hill Companies, Inc., 1221 Avenue of the Americas, New York, NY 10020. Copyright © 2004 by The McGraw-Hill Companies, Inc. All rights reserved. Previous edition(s) 1998. All rights reserved. No part of this publication may be reproduced or distributed in any form or by any means, or stored in a database or retrieval system, without the prior written consent of The McGraw-Hill Companies, Inc., including, but not limited to, in any network or other electronic storage or transmission, or broadcast for distance learning.

This book is printed on acid-free paper containing 10% postconsumer waste.

2 3 4 5 6 7 8 9 0 DOC/DOC 0 9 8 7 6 5 4

ISBN 0-07-286522-9

Vice president and editor-in-chief: *Thalia Dorwick*
Publisher: *Chris Freitag*
Sponsoring editor: *Jon-David Hague*
Marketing manager: *Lisa G. Berry*
Project manager: *Richard H. Hecker*
Production supervisor: *Enboge Chong*
Design coordinator: *Mary Kazak*
Cover images: © *Getty Images,* © *Corbis*
Compositor: *Shepherd, Inc.*
Typeface: *10/12 Palatino*
Printer: *R. R. Donnelley/Crawfordsville, IN*

Library of Congress Cataloging-in-Publication Data

Scriptures of the world's religions/edited by James Fieser, John Powers—2nd ed
    p. cm
  Includes bibliography references.
  ISBN 0-07286522-9 (softcover : alk. paper)
   1. Sacred books. I. Fieser, James. II. Powers, John, 1957–

BL70.S37 2004
291.8'82--dc21

                                 2003048748

www.mhhe.com

About the Authors

JAMES FIESER is an assistant Professor of Philosophy at the University of Tennessee at Martin. He received his BA from Berea College (1980), and his MA and PhD from Purdue University's Department of Philosophy (1983, 1986). He is author, co-author, and editor of seven books, including *A Historical Introduction to Philosophy* (Oxford University Press, 2003) and *Socrates to Sartre and Beyond* (McGraw-Hill, 2003). He as edited and annotated the ten-volume *Early Responses to Hume* (Thoemmes Press, 1999–2003) and the five-volume *Scottish Common Sense Philosophy* (Thoemmes Press, 2000). He has published articles on the topics of David Hume, moral skepticism, rights theory, environmental ethics, business ethics, virtue theory, and natural law. He is founder and general editor of the *Internet Encyclopedia of Philosophy* web site.

JOHN POWERS is Reader in the Faculty of Asian Studies, Australian National University. He received his PhD from the University of Virginia in Buddhist Studies. His research interests include Indo-Tibetan Mahayana Buddhism, Indian philosophy, and contemporary human rights issues. He is the author of 7 books and 35 articles, including *Introduction to Tibetan Buddhism* (Ithaca: Snow Lion, 1995) and *Hermeneutics and Tradition in the Samdhinirmocana-sutra* (Leiden: E J Brill, 1993). He teaches courses on Asian Religions, Methodology, and Contemporary India.

Contents

Christianity   322

Preface

Several avenues are open for understanding the world's religions. One could dialog with believers of the various religions, visit their sacred sites and temples, or attend classes for converts. A more practical approach would be to read surveys of the various religions, some written by believers defending their faith, others by critics, and even more by academic historians, anthropologists, psychologists, and philosophers. Yet another avenue is to examine the collected sacred texts revered by these religions. Each of these approaches offers only a single perspective on one of the most complex phenomena of world civilization, and none alone can claim primacy.

This book introduces the world's religions through selections from their scriptures. There are special benefits to this avenue of exploration. In most cases the sacred texts are the oldest written documents in the tradition, and we gain a sense of immediate connection by studying the same documents that followers have been reading for millennia. The texts are also foundational to a religion's most important doctrines, rituals, social and ethical positions. Thus, they explain the authoritative basis of traditions that might otherwise seem incomprehensible, or even groundless. Finally, the texts have become the most sacred symbols of these traditions, implying that we are on holy ground each time a sentence is read.

We have prepared our selection of scriptures in three formats. The volume titled *Scriptures of the East* contains the sacred writings of Hinduism, Jainism, Buddhism, Sikhism, Confucianism, Daoism, Shinto, and Australian Aboriginal religions of the East. *Scriptures of the West* contains those of Zoroastrianism, Judaism, Christianity, Islam, the Baha'i Faith, and indigenous religions of the West. The volume titled *Scriptures of the World's Religions* contains all the material in the East and West volumes.

Since very few scriptures were originally written in the English language, these are selections of *translated* scriptures. Efforts have been made to find the most recent and readable translations available. A few scriptures are still available only in older translation, such as the Shinto Nihongi, and therefore are the default choice. We modernized some of these translations in view of recent scholarship. We have also been sensitive in our selection among competing translations. For example, in the Judaism chapter we opted for the

Jewish Publication Society's translation of the *Tanakh* rather than translations of the Old Testament that are more associated with Christianity. Similarly, in the Christianity chapter we used the Scholars Version of the New Testament gospels, a new translation that was prepared free of ecclesiastical and religious control. Unique to this anthology are several scriptures in Asian languages newly translated by John Powers.

An exhaustive collection of world scriptures would be over a thousand volumes in length. Selectivity, therefore, is inevitable. The first difficult choice was to confine the texts to those of religions that are practiced today. This excludes dead traditions that are mainly of academic interest, such as ancient Greek, Mesopotamian, and Egyptian religions. Second, preference is given to texts that discuss the lives and teachings of religious founders and present central doctrines. These are not only of greater intrinsic interest, but assure that the essential differences between religions emerge. Third, the scriptures selected are those accessible to lay practitioners, and not those intended mainly for theologians. Finally, emphasis is placed on religions that have a wide sphere of influence, specifically Hinduism, Buddhism, Judaism, Christianity, and Islam. Less influential religions, specifically Jainism, Shinto, Sikhism, Zoroastrianism, and the Baha'i Faith, are covered more briefly.

In spite of the above boundaries of inclusion, the notion of *scripture* used here is sufficiently broad to include three strata of religious texts. The first stratum involves texts that the religions themselves deem most sacred. The term *protocanonical* is typically used in reference to this level, which includes the Buddhist *Pali Canon*, the Muslim *Qur'an*, and the Jewish *Tanakh*. The second stratum involves more peripheral sacred texts, often termed *deuterocanonical*, that are usually derived from oral tradition. This includes collections of oral law, such as the Jewish *Talmud* and the Muslim *Hadith*, as well as texts on the lives of religious founders, such as the Sikh *Janam-sakhi*. The third stratum involves sectarian texts that at some time in the history of that religion were considered scripture by members of that sect. This final category allows for a broader range of texts than is found in most scripture anthologies, and includes sacred writings from sectarian movements and mystical traditions. Examples are the Christian *Book of Mormon* and the Jewish *Zohar*.

A high priority was placed on including material that supports the interests of women, presents women in positions of leadership, or is written by women. Some of these are Judaism's *Song of Deborah* in the *Tanakh*, the Christian *Gnostic Gospel of Mary*, the mystical sayings of Rabi'a in Islam, Buddhism's *Liberation Songs of the Nuns*, and the Jain debates on enlightenment of women.

The readings within each religion are categorized according to the inherent structure of the scriptural canons themselves, following a sequence of historical narrative or their dates of composition. This is preferred over topical arrangement, influenced by anthropological studies of religion, which eliminates narrative and historical context. We believe that our arrangement is more harmonious with the way each religion understands its own canon and that it is more consistent with how religious studies scholars understand a given religion's scriptures. In addition, it allows readers to gain a sense of the historical development of ideas and practices. This is important since all religious traditions are dynamic systems that create new paradigms in response to changing social conditions and religious ideals, while striving to maintain a perceived connection with their origins. The dynamic relation between tradition and innovation is critical to understanding and interpreting living religious systems. It is hoped that through our arrangement of texts in a roughly chronological sequence, readers will gain a sense of the relations between the origins of religions as reported in early canonical works and subsequent developments.

The most visible change to this second edition is the inclusion of two new sections: Australian Aboriginal Religions of the East, and Indigenous Religions of the West. Transliteration of Chinese terms now follows the Pinyin system, rather than the older Wade-Giles one. In the section on Judaism, new selections are added from the Talmud and on statements of faith. In the Christianity section, new selections are added on early Church fathers, Protestant statements of faith, and recent sectarian movements. In the Islam section, new selections are added from the Hadith and statements of faith.

We thank friends and colleagues who have generously offered advice on this book. Alphabetically, they are Stephen Benin, Ronald C. Bluming, Christopher Buck, Stevan L. Davies, Richard Detweiler, Richard Elliot Friedman, Charles Johnson, Habib Riazati, Norman Lillegard, William Magee, Rochelle Millen, Moojan Momen, Randall Nadeau, Joseph H. Peterson, Richard Pilgrim, Kenneth Rose, Betty Rosian, Aziz Sachedina, Chaim E. Schertz, Robert Stockman, Mark Towfiq, and Mark Tyson.

Hinduism

INTRODUCTION

Contemporary Hindus commonly refer to their tradition as the "universal truth" (*sanatana-dharma*), implying that it is a meta-tradition which is able to embrace the truths of all other systems of thought while transcending them through its expansive ability to embrace truth in multiple manifestations. Hinduism is the dominant religious tradition of the Indian subcontinent, and currently over 700 million people consider themselves to be Hindus.

Hinduism is, however, a difficult tradition to define. Its dominant feature is diversity, and its adherents are not required to accept any doctrine or set of doctrines, to perform any particular practices, or to accept any text or system as uniquely authoritative. Many Hindus, for example, are monotheists and believe that there is only one God, despite the proliferation of gods in Hinduism. They assert that God has many manifestations, and that God may appear differently to different people and different cultures.

Other Hindus are polytheists who believe that the various gods they worship are distinct entities, while pantheistic Hindus perceive the divine in the world around them, as a principle that manifests in natural phenomena, particular places, flora and fauna, or other humans. Some Hindus consider themselves to be agnostic, contending that God is in principle unknown and unknowable. Other Hindus are atheists who do not believe in the existence of any gods, but this position does not lead to their excommunication by their fellow Hindus. Even more confusing, in daily practice it is common to see one person or community sequentially manifesting combinations of these attitudes in different circumstances.

Hinduism has a plethora of doctrines and systems, but there is no collection of tenets that could constitute a universally binding Hindu creed, nor is there any core belief that is so fundamental that it would be accepted by all Hindus. Hinduism has produced a vast collection of sacred texts, but no one has the authority of the Christian Bible, the Jewish Torah, or the Muslim Qur'an. Perhaps the most widely revered sacred texts are the Vedas ("Wisdom Texts"), most of which were written over 2,000 years ago, but despite their generally accepted authoritativeness, few Hindus today are even able to read them, and the *brahmins* (priests) whose sacred task is to memorize and recite them generally are unable to explain what they mean.

In searching for a way to define the boundaries of Hinduism, the term "Hindu" may provide some help. It was originally coined by Persians who used it to refer to the people they encountered in northern India. Thus, the term "Hindu" originally referred to the inhabitants of a geographical area, and in later centuries it was adopted by people of India who identified themselves with the dominant religious tradition of the subcontinent.

Contemporary Hinduism is still delimited more by geography than by belief or practice: a Hindu is someone who lives on the Indian subcontinent or is descended from people of the region, who considers himself or herself to be a Hindu, and who is accepted as such by other Hindus. There are no distinctive doctrines whose acceptance would serve as a litmus test of orthodoxy, no ecclesiastical authority that is able to declare some to be Hindus in good standing or label others as heretics, and no ceremony whose performance would serve as a definitive rite of passage into the tradition. There is no founder of the tradition; it has no dominant system of theology or single moral code. Contemporary Hinduism embraces groups whose respective faiths and practices have virtually nothing in common with each other.

This is not to say, however, that Hinduism lacks distinctive doctrines, practices, or scriptures; in fact, the exact opposite is the case. Hinduism has developed a plethora of philosophical schools, rituals, and sacred texts, and its adherents commonly assert a belief in a shared heritage, historical continuity, and family relationships between the multiple manifestations of their tradition. The selections given below represent only a small sampling of the vast corpus of Hindu religious literature. In addition, it should be noted that this literature represents only a tiny part of the Hindu tradition, and primarily reflects the views and practices of a small intellectual elite. The vast majority of Hindus have been—and continue to be—primarily illiterate agricultural workers with little if any knowledge of the sacred scriptures. Their practices are generally derived from local cults and beliefs that often have little in common with the religion and philosophy of the authors of the scriptures. Furthermore, these texts do not form a coherent system, but are as diverse as Hinduism itself. They were written over the course of millennia and reflect shifting paradigms and political, religious, and social agendas, geographical differences, and varying ideas about how people should worship, think, live, and interact.

History of Hinduism and Hindu Scriptures

Hinduism may be compared to a complex symphony in which new themes are introduced as the piece develops, while old ones continue to be woven into its texture. Nothing is ever truly lost, and elements of the distant past often return to prominence at unexpected times, although often in forms that are altered in accordance with the intellectual and religious currents of a particular time and place. The scriptures of Hinduism reflect its diversity and its complex history. They include ancient hymns to anthropomorphic gods and liturgical texts detailing how priests should prepare sacrifices, mystical texts that speculate on the nature of ultimate reality, devotional literature to a variety of deities, philosophical texts of great subtlety and insight, and combinations of these and related themes.

The earliest stratum of Indian sacred literature that is accessible today is found in the Vedas, which evolved into their present form between 1400 and 400 B.C.E. The earliest of these were brought to India around 1300 B.C.E. by seminomadic tribes who referred to themselves as Aryans, meaning "noble" or "wise." Upon their arrival, the newcomers encountered indigenous inhabitants, who were dubbed "slaves" (*dasa* or *dasyu*).The Vedas are referred to by Hindus as "revelation" (*shruti*, literally "what is heard"), in contrast to other scriptures referred to as "tradition" (*smriti*, literally "what is remembered"). Both classes are regarded as canonical, but the latter is not considered to have the same level of authoritativeness as the Vedas. The Vedas, being completely transcendent, are not subject to human imperfections, but are products of direct revelation.

There are four Vedas: (1) the *Rig Veda,* so named because it is composed of stanzas (*rik*); (2) the *Sama Veda* (composed mostly of hymns taken from the *Rig Veda* and set to various melodies, or *saman*); (3) the *Yajur Veda* (composed of *yajus,* selected ritual prayers, mostly taken from the *Rig Veda*); and (4) the *Atharva Veda* (a collection of ritual texts named after the sage Atharvan). The Vedas contain several primary types of literature: (1) chants or hymns (*samhita*), generally directed toward the gods (*deva*) of the Vedic pantheon; (2) ritual texts (*brahmana*), which detail the sacrifices performed by brahmins; (3) mystical texts concerned with the quest for ultimate truth (*aranyakas* and *upanishads*). According to tradition, the Vedas are not the product of human composition (*apaurusheya*), but are a part of the very fabric of reality. They were directly perceived by "seers" (*rishi*), whose mystical contemplations—aided by ingestion of an intoxicating beverage called *soma*—enabled them to intuit primordial sounds reverberating throughout the universe, and rendered into human language as the books of the Vedas.

Aryan Religion and Society

Contemporary scholars commonly refer to the indigenous people of the subcontinent as Dravidians, and recent archeological evidence suggests that they attained a high degree of social development prior to the arrival of the Aryans, although their society was probably in decline by the time the Aryans began to enter India. The Aryans were of European stock, and described themselves as tall, fair-skinned, blond-haired, and civilized, while they characterized the indigenous people as short, snub-nosed, curly-haired, barbaric, and immoral. They viewed their coming as a positive development that introduced righteousness and civilization to the region, and during the next several centuries they gradually subjugated the Dravidians, who were generally relegated to the lowest levels of Aryan society.

From an early period, the Aryans and their descendants propounded the idea that human society should ideally be stratified, with each social class having clearly defined functions and duties. At the top of the hierarchy were the brahmins, the priestly class, whose sacred duty was to perform sacrifices to the gods described in the Vedas. Many of these gods were personifications of natural phenomena, such as the sun and moon, wind, and so forth. Many gods were believed to have dominion over a particular natural force or phenomenon, and the rituals of the Vedas were commonly directed to either one god or a small group of gods who were considered to have the ability to affect a particular sphere of divine provenance.

The role of the priests was central in this system: They were expected to remain ritually pure and to preserve the sacred texts, along with the sacred lore of priestcraft. Their social function prevented them from engaging in manual labor, trade, agriculture, or other nonpriestly occupations, since these were considered polluting. In exceptional circumstances occasioned by special need they were allowed to earn a living by other means, but ideally their lives should be devoted to study of the sacred Vedas and performance of Vedic rituals. This was crucial to the maintenance of the system of "upholding the world" (*loka-samgraha*), which was a core concern of Vedic religion. In this system, the brahmins performed a pivotal function in offering sacrifices to the gods. The sacrifices were generally transmuted into smoke through the agency of Agni, god of fire (who is manifested in the ritual fire, as well as other forms of combustion). Smoke converted the material of the sacrifice into a subtle essence suitable for the gods' consumption, and the process required that the brahmins remain ritually pure, since any pollution they acquired was passed on to their sacrifices. The gods would naturally be insulted if offered unclean food and would respond by denying the requests the brahmins made on behalf of the sponsors of the sacrifices.

The Vedic system was based on a symbiosis of gods and humans: The gods required the sacrificial offerings, and humans needed the gods to use their supernatural powers to maintain cosmic order (*rita*). The system assumed that humans only prosper in a stable and ordered cosmos, an idea that is reflected in the story of the slaying of the demon Vritra ("Obstructer") by Indra, the king of the gods in the Vedas. Demons thrive in chaos, and at the beginning of time Vritra rules over a chaotic cosmos until Indra, after a mighty battle, slays him and thus makes it possible for the gods to establish order. This primordial battle reflects the crucial role played by the gods in establishing and maintaining cosmic law.

The concerns of Vedic literature are primarily practical and this-worldly. They focus on particular pragmatic goals, such as bountiful crops, fertility, peace, stability, wealth, and so forth. The results of the sacrifices are believed to accrue in the present life, and although a world of the dead is mentioned, it does not play a major role in the early Vedic tradition.

The Upanishads and Yoga

The focus shifts in the later Vedic period, in which texts of speculative philosophy and mysticism begin to appear. Referred to as Aranyakas and Upanishads, they were written by sages who often expressed dissatisfaction with the ritualism and this-worldly focus of the early Vedic texts. Their authors sought the ultimate power behind the sacrifices, the force that gives rise to gods, humans, and all the other phenomena of the universe. They found this through a process of inward-looking meditation that sought an unchanging essence beyond the transient phenomena of existence. The present life was no longer viewed as the beginning and end of one's existence; rather, living beings were said to be reborn in successive lives in accordance with their actions (*karma*). The actions of the present result in opposite and equal reactions in the future, and one's present life was said to be a result of the karma accrued in the past. The cycle of existence (*samsara*) was said by the sages of the Upanishads to be beginningless, but it may be ended. It is perpetuated by a basic misunderstanding of the true nature of reality (*avidya*, "ignorance"), but one may escape it by attaining correct understanding of truth, which is found only by people who shift their attention from external things to find the truly real.

By following the path of wisdom that correctly discriminates the real from the unreal, the truly important from the merely pleasant, and the changeless from the transitory, the sage eventually discovers that within everyone is an eternal, unchanging essence, an immortal soul referred to as the "self" (*atman*). The Upanishads declare that this essence alone survives death, that it has been reborn countless times in an infinite variety of different bodies, while itself remaining unchanged by the multiple identities we all develop in successive lifetimes. It is characterized by three qualities: being, consciousness, and bliss (*sat cit ananda*), meaning that it is pure, unchanging being, and its nature is never altered, despite the changing external circumstances of our lives; it is pure consciousness that takes no notice of the vicissitudes of our lives; and it remains unaffected by our joys, sorrows, hopes, disappointments, pleasures, or pains, and so it is in a continuous state of equanimity. Moreover, the Upanishadic sages identified the self with the cosmic ultimate, something supremely mysterious, hidden from ordinary perception but all-pervasive, supremely subtle, the essence of all that is. This ultimate was said to be beyond words or conceptual thought, and was referred to as "Brahman," because it is the purest and most sublime principle of existence, just as in human society brahmins are the purest and holiest class.

According to this system, the perceptions of ordinary beings are profoundly distorted by ignorance, and the only way to attain correct knowledge is through a process of discipline (*yoga*) in which one's thoughts and body are gradually brought under control, and one's attention is turned away from sense objects and directed within. These premises are shared with the system outlined in the *Yoga Aphorisms* (*Yoga-sutra*) of Patanjali, who is credited with gathering together the principal practices and premises of the yoga system. Patanjali's system, however, differs in significant ways from that of the Upanishads, although both use the term "yoga" to describe their respective training programs. The Upanishads outline a monistic system in which the sole reality is said to be Brahman, while everything else is based on mistaken perceptions. Patanjali, by contrast, contends that both matter (*prakriti*) and spirit (*purusha*) are real entities, and the goal of his system is separation (*kaivalya*) of spirit from matter, while the Upanishads aim at a final apotheosis in which all dualities are transcended and one realizes the fundamental identity of the self and Brahman. The final goal of the Upanishads is expressed in the greatest of the "great statements" (*mahavakya*) that sum up the central insights of the Upanishadic sages: "That is you" (*tat tvam asi*), which expresses the identity of the individual soul and Brahman. Patanjali's goal, by contrast, is separation that liberates one's spiritual essence from matter.

The goal of both systems is liberation (*moksha*) from the cycle of existence, but each conceives release differently. Both consider yoga to be the primary practice for attaining the final goal, and for both yoga is a program of introspective meditation that begins with physical discipline, control of random, ignorant thoughts, and development of insight into unchanging truth, but the ontological presuppositions and ultimate goals of the two systems differ in significant details.

Social Structure

The Upanishads and Patanjali's yoga system represent a shift from the primacy of sacrifices to the gods in the early Vedic period to a general acceptance of the idea that the final goal of the religious path is *moksha*. As final liberation from cyclic existence came to be viewed as the supreme goal, sacrifices aimed at maintaining the order of the world and the acquisition of mundane benefits were consequently devalued as inferior to the pursuit of knowledge of truth. As an apparent reaction to this trend, orthodox elements began to stress the importance of performing one's social duties (*dharma*). Texts like the *Laws of Manu* and the *Bhagavad-gita* emphasized the importance of selfless, devout adherence to the duties of one's social class (*varna*): the brahmins, the warriors and rulers (*kshatriya*), the merchants and tradespeople (*vaishya*), and the servants (*shudra*). Both texts asserted that if people ignore their sacred duty the world will fall into chaos, society will crumble, and essential social functions will not be performed. The *Laws of Manu* delineate a system in which people should eventually renounce the world and pursue final liberation, but only after first performing the duties assigned to their social class. In its system of "duties of social classes and stages of life" (*varnashrama-dharma*), there are specific duties for each class, and these should be performed diligently in order to maintain the world. The system assumes that only in an ordered universe will some people have the leisure and resources to pursue liberation.

The ideal life begins with the student stage, in which a man finds a spiritual preceptor (*guru*), who teaches him the lore appropriate to his class. The three highest classes (brahmins, kshatriyas, and vaishyas) are said to be "twice-born" (*dvija*) because they undergo a ceremony (the *upanayana*) that initiates them into adulthood and is considered a "second birth." Only these three classes are permitted to study the Vedas or participate in Vedic rituals (but officiating in Vedic ceremonies is the special duty of brahmins).

After a period of study (which varies in length and content among the four classes), a man should marry, produce male heirs to continue the lineage and perform sacrifices for him and his ancestors after his death, and support the brahmins whose rituals maintain the whole cosmos. According to Manu, after a man has successfully performed his duty, and when he sees his grand-son born (assuring that the lineage will continue) and gray hairs on his head, he may withdraw from society (often with his wife) and begin to sever the ties that he cultivated during his life in the world. As a "forest dweller" (*vanaprastha*), he should be celibate and detached from worldly enjoyments, cultivate meditation on ultimate truth, and pursue liberation. When he knows that his attachment to mundane things has ceased, he may take the final step of becoming a "world renouncer" (*samnyasin*), completely devoted to the ultimate goal, wandering from place to place and subsisting on alms, intent on final liberation from cyclic existence.

In this system, everything has its time and place, and while liberation is recognized as the ultimate goal of the religious life, it is not allowed to be pursued in a way that might destabilize society. When the demands of dharma have been met, one may pursue one's own ends, but Manu declares that renouncing the world too soon would lead to a degeneration of the whole society, and the resulting chaos would make the attainment of liberation difficult, if not impossible, for anyone.

The Path of Devotion

Another important path to liberation lies in the "yoga of devotion" (*bhakti-yoga*), in which one finds salvation through completely identifying oneself with God. The yoga of devotion requires that one focus one's attention so completely on God that all thoughts of ego are transcended in a pure experience of union. There are a variety of ways of conceiving devotion: Sometimes it takes the form of a love affair in which the devotee experiences an ecstatic union surpassing any human love; for others devotion takes the form of selfless service to an omnipotent master. Often Hindu devotionalism exhibits elements of both, along with a feeling of an intensely personal relationship between a human being and God.

The selections presented below are arranged in a roughly chronological order and are taken from a wide range of Hindu scriptures. Of necessity many important scriptures have been omitted from this survey, and the ones that have been included were chosen because they exemplify central themes of contemporary and traditional Hindu religious thought.

VEDAS

CREATION OF THE UNIVERSE

The following selections are taken from the Rig Veda, *and are hymns and ritual texts devoted to the worship of the Vedic gods. These verses describe the attributes of the gods, recounting the mythos of each god and his or her particular sacrificial functions and associations. The first hymn depicts the creation of the universe as beginning with the sacrifice of Purusha ("Man"), a giant god whose body formed the raw material for the formation of the stars, the planets, and living things. According to the story, the four social classes (varna) of Hinduism were also created through this sacrifice, thus providing a scriptural justification for the stratification of Indian society.*

1. The Man had a thousand heads, a thousand eyes, a thousand feet. He pervaded the earth on all sides and extended beyond it as far as ten fingers.
2. It is the Man who is all this, whatever has been and what ever is to be. He is the ruler of immortality, when he grows beyond everything through food.
3. Such is his greatness, and the Man is yet more than this. All creatures are a quarter of him; three quarters are what is immortal in heaven.
4. With three quarters the Man rose upwards, and one quarter of him still remains here. From this he spread out in all directions, into that which eats and that which does not eat. . . .
6. When the gods spread the sacrifice with the Man as the offering, spring was the clarified butter, summer the fuel, autumn the oblation.
7. They anointed the Man, the sacrifice born at the beginning, upon the sacred grass. With him the gods, Sadhyas, and sages sacrificed.
8. From that sacrifice in which everything was offered, the melted fat was collected, and he made it into those beasts who live in the air, in the forest, and in villages.
9. From that sacrifice in which everything was offered, the verses and chants were born, the metres were born from it, and from it the formulas were born.
10. Horses were born from it, and those other animals that have two rows of teeth; cows were born from it, and from it goats and sheep were born.
11. When they divided the Man, into how many parts did they apportion him? What do they call his mouth, his two arms and thighs and feet?
12. His mouth became the Brahmin; his arms were made into the Warrior (*kshatriya*), his thighs the People (*vaishya*), and from his feet the Servants (*shudra*) were born. . . .
15. The moon was born from his mind; from his eye the sun was born. Indra and Agni came from his mouth, and from his vital breath the Wind was born.
14. From his navel the middle realm of space arose; from his head the sky evolved. From his two feet came the earth, and the quarters of the sky from his ear. Thus they set the worlds in order. . . .
16. With the sacrifice the gods sacrificed to the sacrifice. These were the first ritual laws (*dharma*). These very powers reached the dome of the sky where dwell the Sadhyas, the ancient gods.

Source: *Rig Veda* I0.90: *Purusha-Sukta*, from *The Rig Veda*, tr. Wendy Doniger O'Flaherty (New York: Penguin, 1981), pp. 30–31.

ORIGIN OF THE GODS

This passage offers another view of creation. It indicates that originally existence arose from nonexistence and that the gods later were produced by a goddess "who crouched with legs spread," an image with obvious anthropomorphic overtones. It suggests that the creation of the gods was similar to a human birth, but the position described may also suggest that creation is linked with the practice of yoga, which is believed to produce energy that may be used in the generation of life.

1. Let us now speak with wonder of the births of the gods—so that some one may see them when the hymns are chanted in this later age.
2. The lord of sacred speech, like a smith, fanned them together. In the earliest age of the gods, existence was born from nonexistence.
3. In the first age of the gods, existence was born from nonexistence. After this the quarters of the sky were born from her who crouched with legs spread.
4. The earth was born from her who crouched with legs spread, and from the earth the quarters of the sky were born. From Aditi, Daksha was born, and from Daksha Aditi was born.
5. For Aditi was born as your daughter, O Daksha, and after her were born the blessed gods, the kinsmen of immortality.
6. When you gods took your places there in the water with your hands joined together, a thick cloud of mist arose from you like dust from dancers.
7. When you gods like magicians caused the worlds to swell, you drew forth the sun that was hidden in the ocean.
8. Eight sons are there of Aditi, who were born of her body. With seven she went forth among the gods, but she threw Martanda, the sun, aside.
9. With seven sons Aditi went forth into the earliest age. But she bore Martanda so that he would in turn beget offspring and then soon die.

Source: *Rig Veda* 10.72, from *The Rig Veda*, pp. 38–39.

INDRA, THE PARADIGMATIC WARRIOR

In Vedic mythology, Indra is said to be the king of the gods, and he embodies the warrior virtues valued by the Aryans. He is fearless in battle, always victorious over his enemies and, although he is sometimes portrayed as proud and boastful, these qualities do not detract from his prowess as a warrior. This hymn recounts the greatest of his mighty deeds, the slaying of the demon Vritra, a powerful serpentlike creature that was wreaking havoc throughout the universe, holding back the rain waters that are essential to the prosperity of living things, and obstructing the establishment of cosmic order, which is required for a stable and harmonious world. Wielding his mighty thunderbolt, Indra slays the demon, splits open his body, cuts off his limbs, and thus eliminates the threat he poses.

1. Let me now sing the heroic deeds of Indra, the first that the thunderbolt-wielder performed. He killed the dragon and pierced an opening for the waters; he split open the bellies of mountains.

2. He killed the dragon who lay upon the mountain; Tvashtri fashioned the roaring thunderbolt for him. Like lowing cows, the flowing waters rushed straight down to the sea.

3. Wildly excited like a bull, he took the Soma for himself and drank the extract from the three bowls in the three-day Soma ceremony. Indra the Generous seized his thunderbolt to hurl it as a weapon; he killed the first-born of dragons.

4. Indra, when you killed the first-born of dragons and overcame by your own magic the magic of the magicians, at that very moment you brought forth the sun, the sky, and dawn. Since then you have found no enemy to conquer you.

5. With his great weapon, the thunderbolt, Indra killed the shoulderless Vritra, his greatest enemy. Like the trunk of a tree whose branches have been lopped off by an axe, the dragon lies flat upon the ground.

6. For, muddled by drunkenness like one who is no soldier, Vritra challenged the great hero who had overcome the mighty and who drank Soma to the dregs. Unable to withstand the onslaught of his weapons, he found Indra an enemy to conquer him and was shattered, his nose crushed.

7. Without feet or hands he fought against Indra, who struck him on the nape of the neck with his thunderbolt. The steer who wished to become the equal of the bull bursting with seed, Vritra lay broken in many places.

8. Over him as he lay there like a broken reed the swelling waters flowed for man. Those waters that Vritra had enclosed with his power—the dragon now lay at their feet.

9. The vital energy of Vritra's mother ebbed away, for Indra had hurled his deadly weapon at her. Above was the mother, below was the son; Danu lay down like a cow with her calf.

10. In the midst of the channels of the waters which never stood still or rested, the body was hidden. The waters flow over Vritra's secret place; he who found Indra an enemy to conquer him sank into long darkness.

11. The waters who had the Dasa for their husband, the dragon for their protector, were imprisoned like the cows imprisoned by the Panis. When he killed Vritra he split open the outlet of the waters that had been closed.

12. Indra, you became a hair of a horse's tail when Vritra struck you on the corner of the mouth. You, the one god, the brave one, you won the cows; you won the Soma; you released the seven streams so that they could flow.

13. No use was the lightning and thunder, fog and hail that he had scattered about, when the dragon and Indra fought. Indra the Generous remained victorious for all time to come.

14. What avenger of the dragon did you see, Indra, that fear entered your heart when you had killed him? Then you crossed the ninety-nine streams like the frightened eagle crossing the realms of earth and air.
15. Indra, who wields the thunderbolt in his hand, is the king of that which moves and that which rests, of the tame and of the horned. He rules the people as their king, encircling all this as a rim encircles spokes.

Source: *Rig Veda* 1.3, from *The Rig Veda*, pp. 149–151.

PRAYER TO AGNI, THE GOD OF FIRE

Agni is one of the most important gods of the Vedas. As the god of fire, he transmutes sacrificial offerings into smoke, which is consumed by the gods. Thus he serves as the intermediary between the divine and human realms and is a paradigm for the brahmin priests.

1. I pray to Agni, the household priest who is the god of the sacrifice, the one who chants and invokes and brings most treasure.
2. Agni earned the prayers of the ancient sages, and of those of the present, too; he will bring the gods here.
3. Through Agni one may win wealth, and growth from day to day, glorious and most abounding in heroic sons.
4. Agni, the sacrificial ritual that you encompass on all sides—only that one goes to the gods.
5. Agni, the priest with the sharp sight of a poet, the true and most brilliant, the god will come with the gods.
6. Whatever good you wish to do for the one who worships you, Agni, through you, O Angiras, that comes true.
7. To you, Agni, who shine upon darkness, we come day after day, bringing our thoughts and homage.
8. To you, the king over sacrifices, the shining guardian of the Order, growing in your own house.
9. Be easy for us to reach, like a father to his son. Abide with us, Agni, for our happiness.

Source: *Rig Veda* 1.1, from *The Rig Veda*, p. 99.

BURNING DEAD BODIES

This hymn invokes Agni in his role as transporter of the dead. He is asked to burn the corpse of a dead man and to ensure that he is brought to the land of the dead. The concept of afterlife is rather vague in the early Vedas. There are references to a world of the dead, ruled by Yama, who was the first human to die. He found the way to the land of the dead, and now he brings others there. At the end of the ritual the pyre is soaked so thoroughly with water that a small pool is formed, and plants, frogs, and other living things will grow there, symbolizing the renewal of life from the ashes of death.

[To Agni:] Do not burn him entirely, Agni, or engulf him in your flames. Do not consume his skin or his flesh. When you have cooked him perfectly, O knower of creatures, only then send him forth to the fathers. When you cook him perfectly, O knower of creatures, then give him over to the fathers. When he goes on the path that leads away the vital breath, then he will be led by the will of the gods.

[To the dead man:] May your eye go to the sun, your vital breath to the wind. Go to the sky or to earth, as is your nature; or go to the waters, if that is your fate. Take root in the plants with your limbs.

[To the funeral fire:] The goat is your share; burn him with your heat. Let your brilliant light and flame burn him. With your gentle forms, O knower of creatures, carry this man to the world of those who have done good deeds. Set him free again to go to the fathers, Agni, when he has been offered as an oblation in you and wanders with the sacrificial drink. Let him reach his own descendants, dressing himself in a life-span. O knower of creatures, let him join with a body.

[To the dead man:] Whatever the black bird has pecked out of you, or the ant, the snake, or even a beast of prey, may Agni who eats all things make it whole, and Soma who has entered the Brahmins. Gird yourself with the limbs of the cow as an armor against Agni, and cover yourself with fat and suet, so that he will not embrace you with his impetuous heat in his passionate desire to burn you up.

[To the funeral fire:] O Agni, do not overturn this cup, that is dear to the gods and to those who love Soma, fit for the gods to drink from, a cup in which the immortal gods carouse. I send the flesh-eating fire far away. Let him go to those whose king is Yama, carrying away all impurities. But let that other (form of fire), the knower of creatures, come here and carry the oblation to the gods, since he knows the way in advance.

[To the dead man:] The flesh-eating fire has entered your house, though he sees there the other, the knower of creatures; I take that god away to the sacrifice of the fathers. Let him carry the heated drink to the farthest dwelling place. . . .

[To the new fire:] Joyously would we put you in place, joyously would we kindle you. Joyously carry the joyous fathers here to eat the oblation. Now, Agni, quench and revive the very one you have burnt up. Let water plants grow in this place. O cool one, bringer of coolness; O fresh one, bringer of freshness; unite with the female frog. Delight and inspire this Agni.

Source: *Rig Veda* 10.16, from Wendy Doniger O'Flaherty, *Textual Sources for the Study of Hinduism*, (Chicago: University of Chicago Press, 1988), p. 7.

THE BENEFICIAL EFFECTS OF DRINKING SOMA

Soma is an intoxicating drink that plays a major role in Vedic literature. It was made from a creeping plant that was crushed and strained to make a whitish beverage that apparently produced visions and ecstatic states of mind. The plant used is a matter of current debate, and a number of theories have been proposed, none of which is considered definitive by contemporary scholars. As this passage indicates, those who drank it experienced a feeling of exaltation and expansion of consciousness. The writer of this hymn claims that drinking it has also made him immortal.

1. I have tasted the sweet drink of life, knowing that it inspires good thoughts and joyous expansiveness to the extreme, that all the gods and mortals seek it together, calling it honey.

2. When you penetrate inside, you will know no limits, and you will avert the wrath of the gods. Enjoying Indra's friendship, O drop of Soma, bring riches as a docile cow brings the yoke.

3. We have drunk the Soma; we have become immortal; we have gone to the light; we have found the gods. What can hatred and the malice of a mortal do to us now, O immortal one?

4. When we have drunk you, O drop of Soma, be good to our heart, kind as a father to his son, thoughtful as a friend to a friend. Far-famed Soma, stretch out our lifespan so that we may live.

5. The glorious drops that I have drunk set me free in wide space. You have bound me together in my limbs as thongs bind a chariot. Let the drops protect me from the foot that stumbles and keep lameness away from me.

6. Inflame me like a fire kindled by friction; make us see far; make us richer, better. For when I am intoxicated with you, Soma, I think myself rich. Draw near and make us thrive.

7. We would enjoy you, pressed with a fervent heart, like riches from a father. King Soma, stretch out our lifespans as the sun stretches the spring days.

8. King Soma, have mercy on us for our well-being. Know that we are devoted to your laws. Passion and fury are stirred up. O drop of Soma, do not hand us over to the pleasure of the enemy.

9. For you, Soma, are the guardian of our body; watching over men, you have settled down in every limb. If we break your laws, O god, have mercy on us like a good friend, to make us better.

10. Let me join closely with my compassionate friend [Soma] so that he will not injure me when I have drunk him. O lord of bay horses, for the Soma that is lodged in us I approach Indra to stretch out our lifespan.

11. Weaknesses and diseases have gone; the forces of darkness have fled in terror. Soma has climbed up in us, expanding. We have come to the place where they stretch out lifespans.

12. The drop that we have drunk has entered our hearts, an immortal inside mortals. O fathers, let us serve that Soma with the oblations and abide in his mercy and kindness.

13. Uniting in agreement with the fathers, O drop of Soma, you have extended yourself through sky and earth. Let us serve him with an oblation; let us be masters of riches.

14. You protecting Gods, speak out for us. Do not let sleep or harmful speech seize us. Let us, always dear to Soma, speak as men of power in the sacrificial gathering.
15. Soma, you give us the force of life on every side. Enter into us, finding the sunlight, watching over men. O drop of Soma, summon your helpers and protect us before and after.

Source: *Rig Veda* 8.48, from *The Rig Veda*, pp. 134–136.

SEX AND THE YOGIN

This hymn depicts a struggle between a husband and wife named Agastya and Lopamudra. Lopamudra has just successfully seduced Agastya, who was trying to avoid sexual intercourse in order to store up the vital energy he acquired as a product of yogic exertions. It captures a common theme in classical Indian literature: woman as temptress, whose unrestrained sexual desire and physical charms distract male yogins from their ascetic practice and cause them to dissipate the power they have painstakingly gained through meditation and self-restraint.

1. [Lopamudra:] 'For many autumns past I have toiled, night and day, and each dawn has brought old age closer, age that distorts the glory of bodies. Virile men should go to their wives.
2. For even the men of the past, who acted according to the Law and talked about the Law with the gods, broke off when they did not find the end. Women should unite with virile men.'
3. [Agastya:] 'Not in vain is all this toil, which the gods encourage. We two must always strive against each other, and by this we will win the race that is won by a hundred means, when we merge together as a couple.'
4. [Lopamudra:] 'Desire has come upon me for the bull who roars and is held back, desire engulfing me from this side, that side, all sides.'
5. [The poet:] Lopamudra draws out the virile bull: the foolish woman sucks dry the panting wise man.
6. [Agastya:] 'By this Soma which I have drunk, in my innermost heart I say: Let him forgive us if we have sinned, for a mortal is full of many desires.'
7. Agastya, digging with spades, wishing for children, progeny, and strength, nourished both ways, for he was a powerful sage. He found fulfillment of his real hopes among the gods.

Source: *Rig Veda* 1.179, from *The Rig Veda*, pp. 250–251.

A CLEVER WOMAN

This hymn is spoken by a woman who has managed to eliminate her rivals and emerge victorious over her husband, who now submits to her will.

1. There the sun has risen, and here my good fortune has risen. Being a clever woman, and able to triumph, I have triumphed over my husband.
2. I am the banner; I am the head. I am the formidable one who has the deciding word. My husband will obey my will alone, as I emerge triumphant.
3. My sons kill their enemies and my daughter is an empress, and I am completely victorious. My voice is supreme in my husband's ears.
4. The oblation that Indra made and so became glorious and supreme, this is what I have made for you, O gods. I have become truly without rival wives.
5. Without rival wives, killer of rival wives, victorious and pre-eminent, I have grabbed for myself the attraction of the other women as if it were the wealth of flighty women.
6. I have conquered and become pre-eminent over these rival wives, so that I may rule as empress over this hero and over the people.

Source: *Rig Veda* 10.159, from *The Rig Veda*, p. 291.

THE HORSE SACRIFICE

The horse sacrifice served to establish the dominion of a king by demonstrating how large an area he controlled. For a year prior to the sacrifice, a horse would be set free to wander wherever it wished, indicating the hegemony of the king. To the extent that other rulers were unable to turn the horse away, it served notice of the areas a particular ruler effectively controlled. At the end of the year the horse was offered as a sacrifice to the gods, but although it was killed it is stated in the ritual that it would enjoy a future in heaven.

[To the priests:] The invoker, the officiant, the overseer, the fire-kindler, the holder of the pressing-stones, the cantor, the sacrificial priest—fill your bellies with this well-prepared, well-sacrificed sacrifice. The hewers of the sacrificial stake and those who carry it, and those who carve the knob for the horse's sacrificial stake, and those who gather together the things to cook the charger—let their approval encourage us. The horse with his smooth back went forth into the fields of the gods, just when I made my prayer. The inspired sages exult in him. We have made him a welcome companion at the banquet of the gods.

[To the horse:] The charger's rope and halter, the reins and bridle on the head, and even the grass that has been held up to the mouth—let all that stay with you even among the gods. Whatever of the horse's flesh the fly has eaten, or whatever stays stuck to the stake or the axe, or to the hands or nails of the slaughterer—let all of that stay with you even among the gods. Whatever food remains in the stomach, sending forth gas, or whatever smell there is from the raw flesh—let the slaughterers make that well done; let them cook the sacrificial animal until he is perfectly cooked.

Whatever runs off your body when it has been placed on the spit and roasted by the fire, let it not lie there in the earth or on the grass, but let it be given to the gods who long for it.

[To the priests:] Those (priests) who see that the racehorse is cooked, who say, 'It smells good! Take it away!,' and who wait for the doling out of the flesh of the charger—let their approval encourage us. The testing fork for the cauldron that cooks the flesh, the pots for pouring the broth, the cover of the bowls to keep it warm, the hooks, the dishes—all these attend the horse.

[To the horse:] The place where the horse walks, where he rests, where he rolls, and the fetters on the horse's feet, and what he has drunk and the fodder he has eaten—let all of that stay with you even among the gods. Let not the fire that reeks of smoke darken you, nor the red-hot cauldron split into pieces. The gods receive the horse who has been sacrificed, worshipped, consecrated, and sanctified with the cry of 'Vashat!' The cloth that they spread beneath the horse, the upper covering, the golden trappings on him, the halter and the fetters on his feet—let these things that are his own bind the horse among the gods.

[To the horse:] If someone riding you has struck you too hard with heel or whip when you shied, I make all these things well again for you with prayer, as they do with the ladle for the oblation in sacrifices.

[To the priests:] The axe cuts through the thirty-four ribs of the racehorse who is the companion of the gods. Keep the limbs undamaged and place them in the proper pattern. Cut them apart, calling out piece by piece. One (priest) is the slaughterer of the horse of Tvashtri; two (priests) restrain him. This is the rule.

[To the horse:] As many of your limbs as I set out, according to the rules, so many balls I offer into the fire. Let not your dear soul burn you as you go away. Let not the axe do lasting harm to your body. Let no greedy, clumsy slaughterer hack in the wrong place and damage your limbs with his knife. You do not really die through this, nor are you harmed. You go to the gods on paths pleasant to go on. The two bay stallions, the two roan mares are now your chariot mates. The racehorse has been set in the donkey's yoke.

[To the gods:] Let this racehorse bring us good cattle and good horses, male children and all nourishing wealth. Let Aditi make us free from sin. Let the horse with our offerings achieve sovereign power for us.

Source: *Rig Veda* 1.162, from *Textual Sources for the Study of Hinduism*, pp. 9–10.

TO THE FIRE ALTAR

This hymn is used to help the sacrificer mentally prepare prior to performance of the sacrifice. He visualizes the fire altar as the entire universe and views the sacrifice as a way to attain spiritual knowledge. It is notable in that it shows the increasingly cosmic significance given to the rituals: they were no longer merely localized sacrifices performed for particular ends, but instead microcosmic expressions of macrocosmic forces and processes. The sacrificer meditates on the greater ramifications of the sacrifice about to be performed, its cosmic repercussions, and its transformative effects on the person who performs it. It also shows an expanding view of the cosmos and a corresponding expansion in the religious vision of brahmin priests, who are no longer content simply to perform sacrifices for limited goals, but increasingly interested in the effects they will have beyond this world and in the mind of the sacrificer.

1. The fire altar built here is this world. The stones surrounding it are the waters. Its Yajushmati bricks are humans. Its Sudadohas [a drink of immortality] are cows. Plants and trees are its cement, offerings, and fuel. Agni is its connecting bricks. Thus this constitutes all of Agni. Agni pervades space. Whoever knows this becomes all of Agni, the pervader of space.
2. Moreover, the fire altar is also the air. The horizon is its surrounding circle of bricks. . . .The birds are its Yajushmati bricks. . . .
3. Moreover, the fire altar is also the sky. . . .
4. Moreover, the fire altar is also the sun. . . .
5. Moreover, the fire altar is also the stars. . . .
7. Moreover, the fire altar is also the meters [of verses]. . . .
10. Moreover, the fire altar is also the year. . . .
12. Moreover, the fire altar is also the body. . . .
14. Moreover, the fire altar is also all beings and all gods. All the gods and all beings are the waters, and the constructed fire altar is the same as the waters. . . .
16. Referring to this, the verse states:
    By way of wisdom they ascend to the place where desires disappear.
    Neither sacrificial gifts nor the devoted performers of sacrifices who lack wisdom go there.
    One who is ignorant of this does not go to that world either by sacrificial offerings or devout actions.
    It belongs to those with wisdom.

Source: *Shatapatha Brahmana* 10.5.4.1–16.

WHAT IS THE ORIGIN OF THE WORLD?

This poem represents an early speculative tendency from the Vedic period. The writer of the poem is considering what, if anything, existed before the world as we know it, before creation, and even before the birth of the gods.

There was neither nonexistence nor existence then; there was neither the realm of space nor the sky which is beyond. What stirred? Where? In whose protection? Was there water, bottomlessly deep? There was neither death nor immortality then. There was no distinguishing sign of night nor of day. That one breathed, windless, by its own impulse. Other than that there was nothing beyond. Darkness was hidden by darkness in the beginning; with no distinguishing sign, all this was water. The life force that was covered with emptiness, that one arose through the power of heat.

Desire came upon that one in the beginning; that was the first seed of mind. Poets seeking in their heart with wisdom found the bond of existence in nonexistence. Their cord was extended across. Was there below? Was there above? There were seed-placers; there were powers. There was impulse beneath; there was giving-forth above.

Who really knows? Who will here proclaim it? Whence was it produced? Whence is this creation? The gods came afterwards, with the creation of this universe. Who then knows whence it has arisen? Whence this creation has arisen—perhaps it formed itself, or perhaps it did not—the one who looks down on it, in the highest heaven, only he knows—or perhaps he does not know.

Source: *Rig Veda* 10.129, from *Textual Sources for the Study of Hinduism*, p. 33.

VEDANTA: THE UPANISHADS AND THEIR COMMENTARIES

YAMA'S INSTRUCTIONS TO NACIKETAS

The Katha Upanishad *presents the story of a brahmin boy named Naciketas. His father, Aruni, is performing a sacrifice in which he is required to give away all his possessions, but Naciketas notices that he is not complying with the spirit of the sacrifice. Naciketas asks his father, "To whom will you give me?", to which his father angrily replies, "I give you to Yama [the god of death]." Unfortunately for both Naciketas and his father, words spoken in the context of a sacrifice have great power, and so Naciketas is immediately sent to the palace of Yama.*

Yama, however, is not in the palace when Naciketas arrives and does not return for three days. When Yama returns and sees that Naciketas has been waiting for a long while and has not been given the courtesy due to a brahmin, he apologizes and offers to make restitution by granting Naciketas three wishes. Being a dutiful son, Naciketas first asks that he be able to return to his father and that his father receive him with happiness and love instead of anger.

His next wish is significant: He asks Yama to teach him about the Naciketas fire for which he is named. This is significant because it shows that in this text the traditional values and practices of brahmins are not being questioned. Naciketas does not doubt the efficacy of the sacrifices; instead, he wishes to learn more about them, and only after this does he make his third request, in which he asks Yama to tell him what happens to a human being after death.

Yama responds by testing Naciketas in order to determine his sincerity in asking about this. He offers Naciketas worldly goods instead, things like wealth, land, power, long-lived sons and grandsons, fame, etc., but none of these things interest Naciketas. He understands that such things are transitory and fleeting, and he wishes instead for knowledge of the atman (the self), which is truly valuable. Having tested his resolve, Yama praises him for choosing the good (shreyas) over the pleasant (preyas). Yama then teaches Naciketas about the atman, the essence of each individual, the eternal, unchanging reality that exists forever, unaffected by the circumstances and events of a person's countless rebirths. The atman, *he declares, cannot be known through the senses or the intellect: it must be known through direct, intuitive realization. The culmination of the teaching is Yama's revelation that the* atman *is not only a personal essence; it is also said to be identical with the cosmic Ultimate, called* Brahman.

2.1.1. Yama said: "The good is one thing, and the pleasant another. Both of these different goals blind a person. From among the two, it is better for one who chooses the good. A person who chooses the pleasant does not fulfill his goals.

   2. "A person receives both the good and the pleasant. Thoroughly examining the two, a wise person distinguishes them. The wise person chooses the good rather than the pleasant. The stupid person, due to grasping, chooses the pleasant. . . ."

   14. Naciketas asked Yama: "Tell me what you see beyond righteousness and unrighteousness, beyond what is done and not done, and what is beyond what was and what will be."

   15. Yama said: "I will briefly explain to you all that is taught in the Vedas, all that asceticism declares, and that which sages seek through religious practice: It is Om.

   16. "This syllable truly is Brahman, it is the supreme syllable. Whoever knows it obtains all wishes.

   17. "This is the best support, this is the supreme support. Knowing this support, a person attains happiness in the world of Brahma.

   18. "The wise one is not born, does not die; it does not come from anywhere, does not become anything. It is unborn, enduring, permanent; this one is not destroyed when the body is destroyed.

   19. "If someone thinks to destroy and if the destroyed thinks of being destroyed, then neither understands. This [atman] neither destroys nor is it destroyed.

   20. "The *atman* hidden in the heart of all living beings is smaller than the smallest and greater than the greatest. A person who does not act with desire and is free from sadness sees it and its greatness through the purity of mind and senses. . . .

   23. "The self is not gained through study, nor by the intellect, nor by much learning; it is gained only by whomever it chooses: to such a person the self reveals itself.

   24. "Not to one who has not renounced wrongdoing, nor by one who is not tranquil, nor to one who is not calm, nor to one whose mind is not at peace: They cannot gain it through intelligence (*prajna*)."

2.3.1. "You should know that the *atman* is like the rider of a chariot, and the body is like the chariot. You should know that the intellect (*buddhi*) is like the chariot driver, and the mind is like the reins. . . .

   4. "The senses are said to be the horses, and sense-objects are the area in which they travel. The self, together with senses and mind, are termed 'enjoyer' by the wise.

5. "If one lacks understanding and does not constantly control the mind, then one's senses become uncontrolled like the bad horses of a charioteer.

6. "If one is wise and constantly controls the mind, then one's senses remain controlled like the good horses of a charioteer.

7. "If one lacks understanding, lacks mental control, and is impure, then one can never reach the goal, but continues in cyclic existence (*samsara*).

8. "If one is wise, however, with a fully disciplined mind, then one reaches the goal and will not be reborn again. . . .

13. "The wise should restrain speech and mind, mind should be restrained in the understanding self, understanding should be restrained in the great self, and that should be restrained in the tranquil *atman*.

14. "Arise, awaken, go and attain your wishes; understand them! The poets say that the path is like the sharp edge of a razor, difficult to travel, difficult to obtain.

15. "It is soundless, intangible, formless, inexhaustible. In the same way, it is tasteless, eternal, and odorless, beginningless, endless, beyond the great, unchanging. By understanding it, one escapes the jaws of death."

4.1. Yama said: The Self-Existent opened the senses outward; thus humans look outward, not toward the inner *atman*. But a wise person, seeking immortality, turns in the reverse direction and sees the inner *atman*.

2. "Childish people go after outward pleasures. They walk into the net of death that is spread everywhere. But the wise, knowing immortality, do not seek the permanent among the impermanent.

3. "One knows color, taste, smell, sounds, touches, and sexual pleasures only through this (*atman*). What else remains? This indeed is That.

4. "By recognizing the great, all-pervading *atman*, by which one perceives both sleeping and dream states, the wise overcome sorrow. This indeed is That.

5. "One who knows this experiencer, the living *atman* that is nearest to one, which is lord of the past and the future, is never afraid of it. This indeed is That. . . .

9. "The sun arises from it and sets into it. All gods are based in it, and none ever move beyond it. This indeed is That. . . .

11. "Through it the mind attains [realization]. There is absolutely no difference here. If one perceives difference here, one goes from death to death."

6.1. Yama said: Its root is above, its branches below, this eternal tree. That [root] is the Pure. That is Brahman. That is called the Immortal. All worlds rest on it, and none go beyond it. This, indeed, is That.

2. "The whole world, whatever exists, was created from and moves in life. The great fear, the raised thunderbolt: those who know That become immortal.

3. "From fear of It fire burns, from fear of It the sun gives off heat. From fear of It Indra and Vayu, and Yama the fifth, speed along.

9. "One cannot see its form, and no one ever sees it with the eye. It is framed by the heart, by thought, by the mind: those who know That become immortal.

10. "When one stops the five knowledges [derived from the senses], together with the mind, and the intellect is still, that is said to be the highest path.

11. "This is said to be yoga, the firm restraint of the senses. Then one becomes undistracted. Yoga, truly, is the beginning and the end.

12. "It is not perceived through speech, through mind, nor by sight. How can it be understood other than by saying, 'It is'?"

Source: *Katha Upanishad* selections.

SACRIFICES CANNOT LEAD TO THE ULTIMATE GOAL

This passage expresses a somewhat different opinion of the value of sacrifices: It calls them "unsteady boats" that should not be relied on by a person wishing to leave cyclic existence. It does not, however, urge brahmins to stop performing sacrifices, but instead warns them not to rely on them exclusively and instead advises them to remove themselves from the world and practice asceticism and devotion in the forest in order to work at achieving a tranquil mind that knows truth.

1.2.1. This is the truth: The sacrificial rites that the sages saw in the hymns are variously elaborated in the three [Vedas]. Perform them constantly, O lovers of truth. This is the path to the world of good deeds.

2. When the flame flickers after the offering fire has been kindled, then between the offerings of the two portions of clarified butter one should give one's main oblations—an offering made with faith. . . .

7. These sacrificial rituals, eighteen in number, are, however, unsteady boats, in which only the lesser work is expressed. The fools who delight in this as supreme go again and again to old age and death.

8. Abiding in the midst of ignorance, wise only according to their own estimate, thinking themselves to be learned, but really dense, these deluded men are like blind men led by one who is himself blind.

9. Abiding variously in ignorance, childishly they think, "We have accomplished our aim." Since the performers of actions do not understand because of desire, therefore, they, the wretched ones, sink down [from heaven] when their worlds are exhausted.

10. Regarding sacrifice and merit as most important, the deluded ones do not know of anything better. Having enjoyed themselves only for a

time on top of the heaven won by good deeds, they re-enter this world or a lower one.

11. Those who practice austerities (*tapas*) and devotion in the forest, the tranquil ones, the knowers of truth, living the life of wandering beggars: they depart, freed from desire, through the door of the sun, to where the immortal Person (*purusha*) lives, the imperishable Atman.

12. Having examined the worlds won by actions, a brahmin should arrive at nothing but indifference. The world that was not made is not won by what is done [i.e., by sacrifice]. For the sake of that knowledge, one should go with sacrificial fuel in hand to a spiritual teacher (*guru*) who is well-versed in the scriptures and also firm in the realization of Brahman.

13. Approaching the wise [teacher] properly, one with tranquil thoughts, who has attained peace, is taught this very truth, the knowledge of Brahman by means of which one knows the imperishable Person, the only Reality.

Source: *Mundaka Upanishad*, ch. 1.

INSTRUCTIONS ON RENOUNCING THE WORLD

This passage instructs the aspiring world renouncer (samnyasin) *on the proper motivation for leaving society. It indicates that one should give up performance of the Vedic rituals and leave family, friends, and occupation behind, focusing one's attention on the final goal of realization of the* atman. *In a special ritual, one takes into oneself the sacred fire that one had maintained as a householder, which now becomes identified with the fire of the digestive processes. One discards the sacred thread that one has worn since the initiation* (upanayana) *ceremony, which designates one as a member of one of the three "twice-born" classes. After this one has no caste identity, and can wander anywhere—and take food from anyone—without fear of ritual pollution.*

Aruni went to the realm of Prajapati and, approaching him, said: "Lord, by what means does one completely renounce religious activities?" Prajapati said: "One should forsake sons, brothers, relatives, and so forth; one should give up the topknot, the sacred string, sacrifices, ritual codes, and Vedic recitation. . . . One should have a staff and a garment; and renounce everything else.

"A householder or a student (*brahma-carin*) or a forest hermit should discard his sacred string on the ground or in water. He should place the external fires in the fire of his stomach and the *gayatri* in the fire of his speech. . . ."

"From that point on, he should live without mantras. He should bathe at the start of the three periods of the day and, deeply immersed in meditation, he should realize his union with the Self."

Source: *Aruni Upanishad* 1–2.

SELF-EFFORT AND LIBERATION

The following passage comes from the Crest Jewel of Discrimination, *attributed by Hindu tradition to Shankara, one of the greatest expositors of the thought of the Upanishads and the primary exponent of the nondualist* (advaita) *school of commentary. The author contends that the path to liberation is a solitary one. He states that every person must win salvation alone, and that no one else can help. Even the scriptures are only guideposts, but one who becomes attached to them will remain enmeshed in cyclic existence. They point the way, but the goal is reached only by those who transcend all mundane supports and actualize direct, nonconceptual understanding of the* atman.

Children may free their father from his debts, but no other person can free a man from his bondage: he must do it himself. Others may relieve the suffering caused by a burden that weighs upon the head; but the suffering which comes from hunger and the like can only be relieved by one's self. The sick man who takes medicine and follows the rules of diet is seen to be restored to health—but not through the efforts of another. A clear vision of the Reality may be obtained only through our own eyes, when they have been opened by spiritual insight—never through the eyes of some other seer. Through our own eyes we learn what the moon looks like: how could we learn this through the eyes of others? Those cords that bind us, because of our ignorance, our lustful desires and the fruits of our karma—how could anybody but ourselves untie them, even in the course of innumerable ages? Neither by the practice of Yoga or of Sankhya philosophy, nor by good works, nor by learning, does liberation come; but only through a realization that Atman and Brahman are one—in no other way. . . .

Erudition, well-articulated speech, a wealth of words, and skill in expounding the scriptures—these things give pleasure to the learned, but they do not bring liberation. Study of the scriptures is fruitless as long as Brahman has not been experienced. And when Brahman has been experienced, it is useless to read the scriptures. A network of words is like a dense forest which causes the mind to wander hither and thither. Therefore, those who know this truth should struggle hard to experience Brahman. When a man has been bitten by the snake of ignorance he can only be cured by the realization of Brahman. What use are Vedas or scriptures, charms or herbs? A sickness is not cured by saying the word "medicine." You must take the medicine. Liberation does not come by merely saying the word "Brahman." Brahman must be actually experienced. Until you allow this apparent universe to dissolve from your consciousness—until you have experienced Brahman—how can you find liberation just by saying the word "Brahman?" The result is merely a noise.

Source: *Viveka-chudamani,* from *Shankara's Crest-Jewel of Discrimination,* tr. Swami Prabhavananda and Christopher Isherwood (Hollywood: Vendanta Press, 1975), pp. 40–41]

MAYA

Maya *plays a central role in Shankara's interpretation of the Upanishads. The term literally means "magic" or "illusion," and he claims that it is the power by which Brahman hides the truth from ordinary beings. It is a creative power that causes the apparent phenomena of cyclic existence to be superimposed on the unitary Brahman.*

Maya, in her potential aspect, is the divine power of the Lord. She has no beginning. She is composed of the three qualities (*guna*), subtle, beyond perception. It is from the effects she produces that her existence is inferred by the wise. It is she who gives birth to the whole universe. She is neither being nor nonbeing, nor a mixture of both. She is neither divided nor undivided, nor a mixture of both. She is neither an indivisible whole, nor composed of parts, nor a mixture of both. She is most strange. Her nature is inexplicable. Just as knowing a rope to be a rope destroys the illusion that it is a snake, so Maya is destroyed by direct experience of Brahman—the pure, the free, the one without a second.

Source: *Viveka-chudamani,* from *Shankara's Crest-Jewel of Discrimination,* p. 49.

THAT IS YOU

The Upanishadic statement "That is you" (tat tvam asi) *is viewed by exponents of nondualist Vedanta as a statement of the nondifference of* atman *and* Brahman. *The following excerpt discusses this statement from the nondualist perspective.*

The scriptures establish the absolute identity of Atman and Brahman by declaring repeatedly: "That is you." The terms "Brahman" and "Atman," in their true meaning, refer to "That" and "you" respectively. In their literal, superficial meaning, "Brahman" and "Atman" have opposite attributes, like the sun and the glow-worm, the king and his servant, the ocean and the well, or Mount Meru and the atom. Their identity is established only when they are understood in their true significance, and not in a superficial sense.

"Brahman" may refer to God, the ruler of Maya and creator of the universe. The "Atman" may refer to the individual soul, associated with the five coverings which are effects of Maya. Thus regarded, they possess opposite attributes. But this apparent opposition is caused by Maya and her effects. It is not real, therefore, but superimposed. These attributes caused by Maya and her effects are superimposed upon God and upon the individual soul. When they have been completely eliminated, neither soul nor God remains. If you take the kingdom from a king and the weapons from a soldier, there is neither soldier nor king. The scriptures repudiate any idea of a duality in Brahman. Let a man seek illumination in the knowledge of Brahman, as the scriptures direct. Then those attributes, which our ignorance has superimposed upon Brahman, will disappear. . . .

Then let him meditate upon the identity of Brahman and Atman, and so realize the truth. Through spiritual discrimination, let him understand the true inner meaning of the terms "Brahman" and "Atman," thus realizing their absolute identity. See the reality in both, and you will find that there is but one. . . .

Just as a clay jar or vessel is understood to be nothing but clay, so this whole universe, born of Brahman, essentially Brahman, is Brahman only—for there is nothing else but Brahman, nothing beyond That. That is the reality. That is our Atman. Therefore, "That is you"—pure, blissful, supreme Brahman, the one without a second.

Source: *Viveka-chudamani*, from *Shankara's Crest-Jewel of Discrimination*, pp. 72–74.

QUALIFIED NONDUALISM: RAMANUJA'S INTERPRETATION

Ramanuja disagress with the nondualist system of Upanishadic interpretation. In this passage, he contends that it is absurd to completely equate the absolute Brahman *with the individual* atman. *As an exponent of devotinalism, Ramanuja rejects the nondualist system, since it would make devotion absurd. If* atman *and* Brahman *were one, there would be no real basis for worship. Ramanuja contends that the Upanishadic statement "That is you" does not mean what nondualists think it does; rather, it indicates that there are two separate entities,* atman *and* Brahman, *and that the former is wholly dependent upon the latter, like a wave in relation to the ocean. The wave appears to stand apart from the ocean, but its substance and being derive from the ocean, although it has at least a qualifiedly separate identity. Similarly, the* atman *derives from* Brahman *but because the history of each atman is distinctly its own, it contradicts reason and actual experience to claim that* atman *is completely identical with* Brahman.

1.1.1. The word "Brahman" refers to the highest Person, in whom all faults are naturally eliminated, who possesses all the most auspicious qualities, is unlimited, unsurpassed, and incalculable. Everywhere the word Brahman is associated with the quality of magnitude. . . . [Brahman] is the "Lord of All.". . .

Our [nondualist Vedantin] opponents say: 'Brahman is only consciousness, is completely opposed to all particularity, and is the highest reality; all difference—such as different types of knowers, objects of knowledge, different knowledge produced by them, and anything beyond that is false when posited of [Brahman].'

[We reply:] Brahman, which is to be understood by means of its distinctive characteristics, has a nature distinguished from all objects other than itself, and those contradictions are eliminated by these three words: The word "truth" excludes anything that is "non-truth," that which is amenable to modification. The word "knowledge" indicates what is excluded from non-sentient things whose illumination depends upon others. And the word "limitless" indicates what is excluded from anything that is circumscribed by space, time or matter. This exclusion is not a positive or negative quality, but [indicates] Brahman itself as distinguished from everything that is other than itself. . . . The ramification of this is that Brahman is self-luminous, with all contradictions excluded. . . .

Those who propound the doctrine of a substance devoid of all difference cannot legitimately assert that there is a proof for such a substance, because all means of valid cognition have for their objects things that are affected by difference. . . . All consciousness implies difference. All states of consciousness have for their objects things that are marked by some difference, as we see in the case of judgements like, "I saw this.". . . It therefore must be admitted that reality is affected with difference, which is well established by valid proofs. . . .

Instead, what all these scriptures deny is only plurality in the sense of contradicting the unity of the world which is utterly dependent on Brahman as an effect and which has Brahman as the inner controlling principle that is its true Self. They do not deny plurality on the part of Brahman in the sense of deciding to become manifold. . . .

Moreover, in texts like the one that states, "That is you" the connection between the constituent parts does not indicate an absolute unity of undifferentiated substance. Instead, the words "that" and "you" indicate that Brahman is distinguished by difference. The word "that" refers to Brahman, which is omniscient and so forth. . . . Moreover, it is impossible that ignorance could belong to Brahman, whose essential nature is knowledge, which is free from all imperfections, omniscient, and contains within itself all auspicious qualities; nor [is it possible that Brahman] could be the basis of the faults and afflictions that arise from ignorance.

Source: Ramanuja, *Sribhasya*, ch. 1.

YOGA

THE MEANING OF YOGA

The following excerpts are taken from the Yoga Aphorisms, *attributed to Patanjali, and an explanatory text entitled the* Yoga Commentary, *attributed to Vyasa. The verses of the Aphorisms are given in boldface, and the Commentary is given in plain text.*

As the text indicates, the term [yoga] *may be used to refer to a range of practices for disciplining mind and body. In Patanjali's system the focus is on developing progressively greater control over the agitations and fluctuations of mind and body in order to arrive at a state of perfect equanimity. One accomplishes this by turning the attention inward, away from sense objects, which leads to detachment and wisdom.*

A person who becomes detached from external things has no basis for continued existence, and thus becomes liberated from the cycle of birth and death. Unlike the system of the Upanishads, however, Patanjali does not understand liberation as a union of the individual atman with the cosmic ultimate Brahman, but as separation of one's spiritual essence (purusha) *from insentient matter* (prakriti). *In the yoga system, both are considered to be real, and the association of the two is said to be beginningless. Because matter's tendency is to procreate and acquire, and because it is transitory and prone to decay, beings whose spirits are associated with matter necessarily experience suffering. This suffering can, however, be transcended by following the path of the "eight limbs" of physical and mental discipline, which culminate in a state of perfect mental equipoise.*

1. **Here is an instruction on yoga.**
   Yoga is meditative concentration (*samadhi*), and it is a characteristic of the mind pervading all its states. . . . The five states of the mind are: (1) wandering; (2) deluded; (3) distracted; (4) one-pointed; and (5) cut off.
2. **Yoga is the cessation of states of mind.**
   Since the mind has the three functions of perception, movement, and rest, it is constituted by the three qualities of purity (*sattva*), lightness (*rajas*), and heaviness (*tamas*). . . .
3. **Then the seer abides in his own nature.**
5. **The states are of five types, and are afflicted and nonafflicted.**
   The afflicted are those that are based on afflictions like ignorance and so forth and serve as the basis of latencies. The nonafflicted are those that have conceptuality for their object and that oppose the operation of the qualities. . . .
12. **The [states of mind] are restrained by practice and detachment.**
   The stream of mind flows both ways: it flows toward good and it flows toward evil. That which flows on to separation down the plane of discriminative knowledge moves toward happiness. That which leads to rebirth flows down the plane of nondiscrimination and moves toward wrong-doing.
17. **Meditative concentration is attained with the help of conceptual understanding, analytical thought, bliss, and self-awareness.**
   Conceptual understanding is the mind's coarse direct experience when it is directed toward an object. Analytical thought is subtle [cognition]. Joy is happiness. Self-awareness is consciousness pertaining to the self. . . . All these states have an object of observation (*alambana*).
30. **Sickness, laxity, doubt, carelessness, laziness, worldliness, wrong views, failure to attain any level [of concentration], instability: these distractions of mind are the obstacles.**
31. **Pain, despair, unsteadiness of the body, inspiration, and expiration are the companions of these distractions.**
32. **In order to prevent them, one should become familiar with one entity.**

33. **By cultivating friendliness, compassion regarding suffering, joy regarding merit, and indifference toward demerit, one [attains] a calm, undisturbed mind.**

Source: *Yoga-sutras* and *Yoga-bhashya*, ch. 1.

YOGIC TECHNIQUES

In section two Patanjali describes the process by which one develops one's powers of concentration through disciplining thoughts, bringing mind and body under control, and weaning oneself from attachment to external objects.

2.1. **Asceticism (*tapas*), study, and devotion to God constitute the yoga of action.**
  3. **The afflictions are ignorance, self-cherishing, desire, aversion, and love of life.**

Ignorance is simply misconception. Self-cherishing and the others are also based on ignorance and, since they cannot exist without it, they are ignorant. Thus when ignorance is destroyed, their destruction also follows.

  5. **Ignorance is taking the impermanent, the impure, the painful, and the not-self to be permanent, pure, pleasurable, and the self.**
  6. **When one views the appearances of a unitary self through the power of perception, this is self-cherishing.**
  7. **Attachment is abiding in pleasure.**
  8. **Aversion is abiding in revulsion toward pain.**
  9. **Love of life, moving along by its own potency, exists even in the wise.**
11. **Their mental states are destroyed by meditation.**

As the gross dirt of clothes is at first shaken off, and then the fine dirt is washed off by effort and work, so the coarse essential mental states need only slight counteracting efforts, whereas the subtle mental states need very powerful counteragents.

17. **The conjunction of the knower and the knowable is the cause of what is to be escaped.**
18. **The knowable has the nature of purity, lightness, and heaviness; it consists of the elements and the powers of sensation; its purposes are experience and liberation.**

Liberation is the ascertainment of the nature of the enjoyer, the self. Beyond the knowledge of these two there is no wisdom.

20. **The perceiver is only perception; even though pure, it perceives by way of conditions.**

"Only perception": This means that it is nothing other than the power of becoming conscious; that is to say, it is not touched by the qualities. This self cognizes the intellect by reflection. He is neither quite similar nor quite dissimilar to the intellect. "It is not quite similar." Why? The intellect, having for its sphere of action objects known and not yet known, is of course changeable. . . .

"It is not quite dissimilar." Why? . . . Since the self cognizes ideas as the intellect, grasped by consciousness, it is transformed into them; it appears by the act of cognition to be the very self of the intellect, although in reality it is not so. . . .

28. **With the diminution of impurity by the sustained practice of the limbs (*anga*) of yoga, the light of wisdom reaches up to discriminating knowledge.**

29. **Restraint, observance, posture, breath control, withdrawal [of the senses], mental stability, meditation, and meditative concentration are the eight limbs of yoga.**

30. **Of these, the restraints (*yama*) are: non-injury (*ahimsa*), truthfulness, not stealing, celibacy, and having few possessions.**

32. **The observances (*niyama*) are: cleanliness, contentment, asceticism, study, and devotion to God.**

Of these, cleanliness is brought about by earth and water, etc., and by eating clean things, etc. This is external. It is internal when it involves washing away impurities of the mind. Contentment is absence of desire to get more of the necessities of life than one already possesses. Asceticism involves bearing extreme conditions, hunger, thirst, cold, and heat, standing or sitting . . . or severe penances. Study is reading texts that are concerned with liberation, or the repetition of the sacred syllable *Om*. Devotion to God involves offering one's actions to the supreme Teacher.

33. **When thoughts of wrongdoing bother you, familiarize yourself with their antidotes.**

40. **By cleanliness is meant disgust with one's body and cessation of contact with others.**

46. **Posture is steadily relaxed.**

47. **By relaxation of effort and by limitless absorption.**

Posture is perfected when effort ceases, so that there may be no more agitation of the body. Or, when the mind achieves balance with regard to the infinite, it brings about the perfection of posture.

49. **Breath control (*pranayama*) involves restraining the inhalation and exhalation movements [of breath,] which follows when that [control of posture] has been achieved.**

54. **Withdrawal [of the senses] (*pratyahara*) is that by which the senses do not come into contact with their objects and follow the nature of the mind.**

Source: *Yoga-sutras* and *Yoga-bhashya*, ch. 2.

YOGIC ATTAINMENTS

In this section Patanjali discusses the results of yogic practice, which include unshakable mental stability, equanimity, dispassion, and eventually liberation from the cycle of birth and death.

3.1. Mental stability (*dharana*) is mental steadiness.

Mental stability involves the mind becoming focused on such places as the sphere of the navel, the lotus of the heart, the light in the brain, the tip of the nose, the tip of the tongue, and similar parts of the body; or on any other external object. . . .

49. Only one who fully understands the distinction between purity and the self attains supremacy over all states of being and becomes omniscient.

Omniscience refers to simultaneously discriminating knowledge of the "qualities"—which are of the nature of all phenomena—and showing forth as they do separately the quiescent, the disturbed, and the unpredictable characteristics. This attainment is known as the "sorrowless" (*vishoka*). Reaching this, the yogi moves omniscient and powerful, with all his afflictions ended.

50. When the seed of bondage has been destroyed by desirelessness even for those [attainments], absolute separation (*kaivalya*) results.

Then all the seeds of afflictions pass, together with the mind, into latency. When they have become latent, the self does not then suffer. . . . This state—in which the qualities manifest in the mind as afflictions, actions, and fruitions without having fulfilled their object and come back to action—is the final separation of consciousness from the qualities. This is the state of absolute separation, when the self remains consciousness alone, as in its own nature.

Source: *Yoga-sutras* and *Yoga-bhashya*, ch. 3.

PURANAS AND EPICS

THE FOUR AGES

In contemporary India the Puranas and Epics are among the most widely known of Hindu scriptures. The Puranas recount the mythologies of such popular gods as Shiva, Vishnu, and Devi (the Goddess). Rich in symbolism and containing a wide variety of divergent traditions, they describe the attributes of the gods and indicate how they should be worshiped.

The two great epics of Hinduism, the Ramayana *and the* Mahabharata, *are monumental stories that weave history, myth, and religion into complex, multifaceted tales that recount important historical and mythical events and indicate the lessons that should be drawn from them. The* Ramayana *tells the story of Rama—considered by tradition to be an incarnation (avatara) of Vishnu—who takes birth among humans in order to fight against evil forces and establish dharma in the world. Forced to leave his kingdom with his dutiful wife Sita, he wanders in the wilderness, establishing dharma wherever he goes. In a climactic battle he faces the demon Ravana, who has captured Sita. Rama slays Ravana, thus enabling dharma to be established in the demon's realm.*

The Mahabharata—*which contains the* Bhagavad-gita, *one of the most important religious texts in contemporary Hinduism—tells the story of a conflict between related clans for supremacy in northern India. Unlike the heroes of the* Ramayana, *the protagonists of the* Mahabharata *(the Pandavas) often make mistakes, question what is the right course of action, and regret wrong decisions.*

In this passage from the Linga Purana, *Indra teaches a human sage about the cyclical nature of time. According to this system, when the universe is first created a golden age begins. During this time beings have long lifespans, beautiful bodies, and great happiness. As time goes on, however, things begin imperceptibly to worsen, and eventually it becomes necessary to divide people according to their predispositions.*

First, you should know, comes the Golden Age, and then the Age of the Trey; and the Age of the Deuce and the Fourth Age come next: these are the four Ages, in brief. The Golden Age is the age of goodness (*sattva*); the Age of the Trey is the age of energy (*rajas*); the Age of the Deuce is a mixture of energy and darkness (*tamas*); and the Dark Age is the age of darkness; each age has its characteristic ways of behaving. Meditation is the main thing in the Golden Age; sacrifice in the Age of the Trey; worship in the Age of Deuce; purity and charity in the Dark Age. The Golden Age lasts for four thousand years, and is followed by a twilight of four hundred years. And the lifespan of living creatures lasts for four thousand human years in the Golden Age.

After the twilight of the Golden Age has passed, one of the four feet of the dharma of the Ages is gone in all of its aspects. The excellent Age of the Trey is one fourth less than the Golden Age; the Age of the Deuce lasts for half the time of the Golden Age, and the Dark Age lasts for one half the time of the Age of the Deuce. The last three twilights last for three hundred, two hundred, and one hundred years; this happens in aeon after aeon, Age after Age. In the first Age, the Golden Age, the eternal dharma walks on four feet; in the Age of Trey, on three feet; in the Age of Deuce, on two feet. In the Fourth Age it lacks three feet and is devoid of the element of goodness.

In (every) Golden Age, people are born in pairs; their livelihood consists in reveling in the taste of what exists right before one's eyes. All creatures are satisfied, always, and take delight in all enjoyments. There is no distinction between the lowest and the highest among them; they are all good, all equal in their lifespan, happiness, and form, in the Golden Age. They have no preferences, nor do they experience the opposing pairs of emotions; they do not hate or get tired. They have no homes or dwelling-places, but live in the mountains and oceans; they have no sorrow, but consist mostly of goodness and generally live alone. They go wherever they wish, constantly rejoicing in their minds; in the Golden Age, people do not engage in any actions, good or bad.

At that time there was no system of separate classes and stages of life, and no mixture (of classes or castes). But in the course of time, in the Age of the Trey, they no longer reveled in the taste (of existence). When that fulfillment was lost, another sort of fulfillment was born. When water reaches its subtle state, it is transformed into clouds; from thundering clouds, rain is emitted. As soon as the surface of the earth was touched by that rain, trees appeared on it, and they became houses for the people, who used those trees for their livelihood and all their enjoyments. People lived off those trees at the beginning of the Age of the Trey.

But then, after a long time, people began to change; the emotions of passion and greed arose, for no apparent cause, as a result of a change in the people that arose out of time. Then all the trees that they regarded as their houses vanished, and when they had vanished, the people who were born in pairs became confused. They began to think about their fulfillment, considering the matter truthfully, and then the trees that they regarded as their houses appeared again. These trees brought forth clothing and fruits and jewelry; and on the very same trees there would grow, in bud after bud, honey made by no bees, powerful honey of superb aroma, color, and taste. People lived on that honey, lived happily all their life long, finding their delight and their nourishment in that perfection, always free from fever.

But then, as another time came, they became greedy. They lopped off the limbs of the trees and took by force the honey that no bees had made. As a result of that crime that they committed in their greed, the magic trees, together with their honey, vanished, first here, then there, and as time exerted its power, very little of that fulfillment was left. As the Age of the Trey came on, the opposing pairs of emotions arose, and people became quite miserable as a result of the sharp cold and rain and heat. Tortured by these opposing pairs, they began to cover themselves; and then they made houses on the mountain to ward off the opposing pairs. Formerly, they had gone wherever they wished, living without fixed dwellings; now they began to live in fixed dwellings according to their need and their pleasure. . . .

Then, by the force of that Age, all the people were so crazy with rage that they seized one another and took their sons, wives, wealth, and so forth, by force. When he realized all this, the lotus-born (Brahma) created the Kshatriyas to protect people from getting wounded (*kshatat-tratum*), in order to establish a firm support for the moral boundaries. Then by means of his own brilliance, the god who is the soul of all established the system of the classes and stages of life, and he himself established the livelihood for each profession to live on. Gradually, the institution of sacrifice evolved in the Age of the Trey, but even then some good people did not perform animal sacrifices. For eventually Vishnu, who sees everything, performed a sacrifice by force, and then as a result of that the Brahmins prescribed the non-violent sacrifice.

But then, in the Age of the Deuce, men began to have differences of opinion, to differ in mind, action, and speech, and to have difficulty making a living. Then, gradually, as a result of the exhaustion of their bodies, all creatures became subject to greed, working for wages, working as merchants, fighting, indecision about basic principles, lack of interest in the schools of the Vedas, confounding of dharmas, destruction of the system of the classes and stages of life, and, finally, lust and hatred. For in the Age of the Deuce, passion, greed, and drunkenness arise.

And in (every) Age of the Deuce, a sage named Vyasa divides the Veda into four. For it is known that there was a single Veda, in four parts, in the Ages of the Trey; but as a result of the shrinking of the lifespan, it was divided up in the Ages of the Deuce. And these divisions were further divided by the sons of the (Rig Vedic) seers, according to their deviant opinions; they transposed the order of the (Rig Vedic) mantras and the Brahmanas, and they changed the accents and the syllables. Wise men compiled the collections of the *Rig Veda, Yajur Veda*, and *Sama Veda;* though they were composed in common, they have been (subsequently) separated by people of various opinions, divided into *Brahmanas, Kalpasutras,* and explications of the mantras. . . .

Drought, death, disease, and other plagues cause sufferings born of speech, mind, and action, and as a result one becomes numb. From this numbness people begin to think about release from suffering. From this thinking there arises detachment, and from detachment they begin to see their faults. As a result of seeing their faults, knowledge arises in the Age of the Deuce. Now, it will be recalled that the behavior characteristic of the Age of the Deuce was a mixture of energy and darkness. But there was dharma in the first age, the Golden Age, and that dharma still functions in the Age of the Trey; in the Age of the Deuce, however, it becomes disturbed, and in the Dark Age it vanishes.

In the Fourth Age, men's senses are disturbed by darkness and they fall prey to illusion and jealousy; they even kill ascetics. In the Dark Age, there is always carelessness, passion, hunger, and fear; the terrible fear of drought pits one country against another. Scripture has no authority, and men take to the violation of dharma; they act without dharma, without morality; they are very angry and not very smart. . . . When scripture is destroyed, and the dharma that is known from the Shastras, then people will kill one another, for they will have no moral boundaries, no check to their violence, no affection, and no shame. When dharma is destroyed, and people attack one another, they will become stunted and live only twenty-five years; their senses will become confused with arguing, and they will abandon their sons and wives. When they are struck by drought, they will abandon agriculture; they will leave their own countries and go to lands beyond their borders, seeking water in rivers, oceans, wells, and mountains.

Suffering greatly, they will live on honey, raw meat, roots, and fruits; they will wear garments of bark, leaves, and antelope skins; they will perform no rituals and have no possessions. They will fall away from the system of classes and stages of life and fall prey to the terrible mingling of classes. Then there will be very few people left, caught up in this calamity. Afflicted by old age, disease, and hunger, their minds will be numbed by suffering. But from this numbness there will arise thought, and thought makes the mind balanced. Understanding comes from a balanced mind, and from understanding comes a dedication to dharma. The people who are left at the end of the Dark Age will have a kind of formless mental peace. Then, in a day and a night, the age will be transformed for them, deluding their wits as if they were dreaming or insane. And then, by the power of the goal of the future, the Golden Age will begin. And when the Golden Age has begun again, the people left over from the Dark Age become the people born in the Golden Age. . . .

Source: *Linga Purana* 1.39.5–34, 48–70; 1.40.1–3, 66cd–76, from *Textual Sources for the Study of Hinduism*, pp. 69–71.

THE LINGAM OF SHIVA

In this passage, Vishnu tells a human sage about the origin of the lingam, *the phallus of Shiva. The* lingam *symbolizes both his procreative force and the energy he stores through asceticism. The story begins with a conversation between Brahma, said to be the creator of the universe in Hindu mythology, and Vishnu, who is the creator of Brahma. Brahma believes himself to be supreme, self-created, and omnipotent, but Vishnu informs him that he is in fact his creature. Both gods are then amazed to see a huge flaming* lingam *that stretches out of sight. They agree to try to find its top and bottom, but after one thousand years flying respectively up and down are unable to fathom its dimensions. At this point they realize that there is a greater power than themselves, which turns out to be Shiva.*

Once upon a time, when the whole triple world was unmanifest, in darkness, swallowed up by me, I lay there alone, with all the creatures in my belly. I had a thousand heads and a thousand eyes, and a thousand feet; I held in my hands the conch shell, discus, and mace, as I lay in the immaculate water. Then, all of a sudden, I saw from afar the four-headed (Brahma), the great yogi, the Person with golden luminosity, infinitely luminous, as bright as a hundred suns, blazing with his own brilliance. The god was wearing a black antelope skin and carrying a water-pot; and in the space of the blinking of an eye, that supreme Person arrived. Then Brahma, to whom all people bow, said to me, 'Who are you? And where do you come from? And why are you staying here? Tell me, sir. I am the maker of the worlds, self-created, facing in all directions.' When Brahma had spoken like that to me, I said to him: 'I am the maker of the worlds, and also the one who destroys them, again and again.' As the two of us were talking together in this way, each wishing to surpass the other, we saw a flame arising in the northern quarter. As we looked at that flame we were amazed, and its brilliance and power made us cup our hands in reverence and bow to that light from Shiva. The flame grew, a surpassing marvel, and Brahma and I hastened to run up to it. It broke through heaven and earth with its halo of flame, and in the middle of the flame we saw a lingam of great lustre, measuring just a handsbreadth, unmanifest and full of supreme light. In the middle, it was neither gold nor stone or silver; it was indescribable, unimaginable, visible and invisible again and again. It had a thousand garlands of flames, amazing, miraculous; it had great brilliance, and kept getting much bigger. It was covered with a halo of flame, terrifying all creatures with its monstrous form, excessive, bursting through heaven and earth.

Then Brahma said to me, 'Quickly, go down and find out the (bottom) end of this noble lingam. I will go up until I see its (top) end.' We agreed to do this, and went up and down. I kept going down for a thousand years, but I did not reach the end of the lingam; and then I became afraid. In the very same way, Brahma did not find its end above, and came back to join me right there in the expanse of water. Then we were amazed and frightened of the noble one; deluded by his power of illusion, we lost our wits and became confused. But then we meditated on the lord who faces in all directions, the origin and resting place of the worlds, the unchanging lord. Cupping our hands in reverence, we paid homage to Shiva, the trident-bearer, who makes the great, terrifying sound, who has a frightening form, and fangs, who is manifest, and great:

'We bow to you, O lord of the gods and people; we bow to you god, noble lord of all creatures. We bow to you, the eternally successful yogi, the support of all the universe, the highest ruler, the highest ultimate reality, the undying, the highest place. You are the eldest, the lovely god, the ruddy one, the jumper, the lord Shiva . . . you are the sacrifice, the vows, and the observances; the Vedas, the worlds, the gods, the true god everywhere. You are the quality of sound in space; you are the origin and dissolution of creatures. You are the perfume in the earth, the fluidity of the waters, the brightness of fire, great lord. You are the touch of the wind, lord of gods, and the form of the moon. You are the knowledge in intelligence, lord of gods, and the seed in nature. You destroy all the worlds; you are Time, the Ender, made of death. You alone maintain the three worlds, and you alone create them, O lord. . . . We bow to you who have the power of a million million suns, who are as white as a thousand moons; we bow to you who hold the thunderbolt and the bow called Pinaka; we bow to you who hold the bow and arrows in your hand. We bow to you whose body is adorned with ashes; we bow to you who destroyed the body of Kama (the god of erotic love); we bow to you, god of the golden embryo, the golden robe, the golden womb, the golden navel, the golden semen, variegated with a thousand eyes; we bow to you, god of the golden color and the golden hair, you the golden hero and the giver of gold; we bow to you, god, master of gold with the sound of gold. We bow to you with the Pinaka bow in your hand, Shankara, the blue-necked.'

When he had been praised like that, he became manifest, the one of great intellect, the god of gods, womb of the universe, shining as bright as a million suns; and filled with pity, the great god, the great light, spoke to us, as if he would swallow up the sky with his thousands of millions of mouths. His neck was shaped like a conch shell; his belly was lovely; he was adorned with various kinds of jewels; his body was variegated with all sorts of gems, and he wore various kinds of garlands and unguents. The lord had the Pinaka bow in his hand and he held the trident; he was fit to be worshipped by the gods. He wore a great serpent for his sacred thread, but he did not frighten the gods.

He sent forth a great laugh, with the noise of the sound of the *dundubhi* drum, like the roar of thunder, a laugh that filled the entire universe. The two of us were terrified by that great sound, but then the great god said, 'I am satisfied with you two, best of the gods. See my great yoga, and lose all your fear. Both of you, eternal, were born from my limbs in the past; Brahma here, the grandfather of all people, is my right arm, and Vishnu is my left arm, always unconquered in battles. I am satisfied with the two of you, and so I will give you a boon, whatever you ask.' Then the two of us were ecstatic, and we bowed to the feet of the lord, and we said to the great god, who was standing there inclined to favor us, 'If you are really satisfied, and if you are going to give us a boon, then let the two of us always have devotion for you, O god, lord of the gods.' The god of gods said, 'So be it, fortunate ones. Create masses of progeny.' And when he had said this, the lord god vanished.

Source: *Brahmanda Purana* 1.2.26.10–61, from *Textual Sources for the Study of Hinduism*, pp. 85–87.

RAMA, A GOD AMONG HUMANS

The opening section of the Ramayana *contains a synopsis of the main events of the story. The following verses tell of how prince Rama was banished from his kingdom through the machinations of his stepmother Kaikeyi, who had been told by his father Dasharatha that she could ask him for anything she wished. Kaikeyi requested that Rama, the rightful ruler, not assume the throne, and that her son Bharata would instead become king. As a righteous king, Dasharatha could not refuse, and so reluctantly he acceded to the request.*

Kaikeyi knew that the people of the kingdom wanted Rama to rule, and so to ensure that Bharata would remain king she asked that Rama be banished in order that popular opinion would not undermine her son's authority. The king agreed, but as a result he died of a broken heart soon after.

Accompanied by his brother Lakshman and Sita, the model of a devout Hindu wife, Rama went off to the forest. During his travels he was beset by a horde of demons (rakshasa), but he defeated them all. This angered the demon lord Ravana, who captured Sita and imprisoned her in his city of Lanka. Ravana then fell in love with Sita and tried to convince her to renounce Rama and become his queen, but Sita spurned his advances.

With the help of Hanuman, lord of monkeys, Rama eventually located Sita, slew Ravana, and rescued her. He then returned in triumph to his kingdom, and Bharata eagerly abdicated in Rama's favor, since he had never wished to usurp Rama.

Following Rama's return, however, his subjects began to gossip about Sita, insinuating that while she was in Ravana's castle she may have succumbed to his advances.

Rama knew that Sita was innocent, but reluctantly realized that the gossip could undermine his moral authority, which is closely connected to his wife's conduct. Following the dictates of dharma, Rama was forced to banish Sita from the Kingdom. Rama was heartbroken knowing that her love for him kept her chaste in the castle of Ravana, but his royal duty required him to maintain his reputation for righteousness. The following verses describe how he left the kingdom, joined forces with Hanuman, and then defeated Ravana.

8. There is a famous king named Rama . . . who is self-controlled, very powerful, radiant, resolute, and illustrious.

9. Wise and established in good conduct, he is eloquent and regal. He vanquishes his enemies. He has wide shoulders and powerful arms. . . .

12. He understands dharma and always keeps his promises. He always thinks of his subjects welfare. He is famous, pure, disciplined, and contemplative (*samadhiman*).

13. Protector of all living beings, guardian of dharma, he knows the essence of the Vedas and their subsidiary lore and is equally skilled in the science of combat. . . .

18–19. His generosity is equal to that of Kubera, the provider of wealth, and his devotion to truth is like that of Dharma [the god of righteousness]. Dasharatha, the lord of the earth, loved him and wanted to name Rama, his eldest son, as his successor. . . .

20. As Queen Kaikeyi, the king's wife, watched the coronation preparations, she [decided] to ask for a wish that had been promised long ago. She demanded that Bharata [her son] be crowned instead and that Rama be exiled.

21. Dasharatha was a man who kept his promises, and so, caught in the trap of his own righteousness, he had to exile his beloved son Rama.

22. To please Kaikeyi, the hero Rama honored the promise made by his father and went into the forest. . . .

37–38. Then in battle Rama killed all the *rakshasas*: . . . About fourteen thousand *rakshasas* were killed while he resided in Dandaka.

39–42. Then Ravana, king of *rakshasas*, heard of the massacre of his relatives, and flew into a rage and . . . he lured the king's sons far away. Then he kidnapped Rama's wife. . . .

47. Then [Rama] met the monkey Hanuman on the shores of Lake Pampa. . . .

56. This bull among monkeys wished to find Janaka's daughter [Sita] and sent all the monkeys searching in all directions. . . .

58. When he reached the city of Lanka, which was ruled by Ravana, he saw Sita pensive and sad in a grove of *ashoka* trees. . . .

62. The great monkey burned the city of Lanka, but spared Sita, and then returned to tell Rama the good news. . . .

65. Then the god of the ocean appeared before Rama, and Rama followed his advice by having Nala build a bridge [to Lanka].

66. Using this [bridge], he went to the city of Lanka, and after killing Ravana in battle he crowned Vibhishana as lord of the *rakshasas* in Lanka.

67. One who reads the story of Rama, which brings merit and purity, will be freed from all sin. One who reads it with devotion and faith will ultimately be worshipped, together with his sons, grandsons, and servants after death.

Source: *Ramayana*, ch. 1.

THE *BHAGAVAD-GITA*: ARJUNA'S REFUSAL TO FIGHT

The following passages are taken from the Bhagavad-gita, *one of the most influential of Hindu religious texts. A part of the monumental epic* Mahabharata, *it tells the story of a climactic battle between the Pandavas and the Kauravas, two rival clans contending for supremacy in northern India. As the story opens, the Pandava Arjuna, perhaps the greatest warrior of his generation, decides to scout the opposition. He asks his charioteer Krishna (who, unbeknownst to him, is really an incarnation of the god Vishnu) to drive the chariot in front of the enemy lines. As he rides past the Kauravas, however, he experiences a crisis of conscience: He recognizes that many of his opponents are relatives, friends, and teachers, and that killing them would result in a great deal of negative karma.*

It is important to note that Arjuna is not concerned with killing per se; as a warrior he has killed many people in the past, but these particular people are linked to him by close karmic bonds, and so he perceives a contradiction between the demands of his warrior's duty (dharma) and the dictates of the law of karma. He decides that the only solution is to opt out of the conflict altogether and become a world renouncer.

In response, Krishna lectures him on the necessity of correctly performing dharma and indicates that Arjuna will receive more negative karma by dereliction of duty than by killing. Furthermore, Krishna asserts, his opponents have already assured their own destruction by their evil deeds, and so Arjuna is merely the instrument through which God will exact punishment. Then Krishna gives Arjuna a solution to the problem he faces, which involves a mental reorientation. Arjuna's problem, as explained by Krishna, is that he sees himself as an agent and is attached to the results of his actions. If, however, he learns the technique of "disciplined action" (karma-yoga), he can develop the ability to act without involving the false sense of ego. Arjuna is told to act selflessly, perceiving himself as an impersonal agent of dharma who is simply following God's will. If he offers all of his actions to God as an act of devotion and cultivates complete detachment, then Arjuna may act without acquiring any negative karma. Moreover, Krishna tells him, such a mental perspective is the mind-set of the true world renouncer, and this alone leads to liberation from cyclic existence.

20. Arjuna, his war flag a rampant monkey, saw Dhritarashtra's sons assembled as weapons were ready to clash, and he lifted his bow.

21. He told his charioteer: "Krishna, halt my chariot between the armies! . . ."
26. Arjuna saw them standing there: fathers, grandfathers, teachers, uncles, brothers, sons, grandsons, and friends.
27. He surveyed his elders and companions in both armies, all his kinsmen assembled together.
28. Dejected, filled with strange pity, he said this: "Krishna, I see my kinsmen gathered here, wanting war.
29. "My limbs sink, my mouth is parched, my body trembles, the hair bristles on my flesh.
30. "The magic bow slips from my hand, my skin burns, I cannot stand still, my mind reels.
31. "I see omens of chaos, Krishna; I see no good in killing my kinsmen in battle.
32. "Krishna, I seek no victory, or kingship or pleasures. What use to us are kingship, delights, or life itself? . . .
36. "What joy is there for us, Krishna, in killing Dhritarashtra's sons? Evil will haunt us if we kill them, though their bows are drawn to kill.
37. "Honor forbids us to kill our cousins, Dhritarashtra's sons; how can we know happiness if we kill our own kinsmen? . . .
40. "When the family is ruined, the timeless laws of family duty perish; and when duty is lost, chaos overwhelms the family.
41. "In overwhelming chaos, Krishna, women of the family are corrupted; and when women are corrupted, disorder is born in society. . . .
44. "Krishna, we have heard that a place in hell is reserved for men who undermine family duties. . . .
46. "If Dhritarashtra's armed sons kill me in battle when I am unarmed and offer no resistance, it will be my reward."
47. Saying this in the time of war, Arjuna slumped into the chariot and laid down his bow and arrows, his mind tormented by grief.

2.2. [Krishna:] "Why this cowardice in time of crisis, Arjuna? The coward is ignoble, shameful, foreign to the ways of heaven.
3. "Don't yield to impotence! It is unnatural to you! Banish this petty weakness from your heart. Rise to the fight, Arjuna! . . .
11. "You grieve for those beyond grief, and you speak words of insight; but learned men do not grieve for the dead or the living.
12. "Never have I not existed, nor you, nor these kings; and never in the future shall we cease to exist. . . .
16. "Nothing of nonbeing comes to be, nor does being cease to exist; the boundary between these two is seen by men who see reality.
17. "Indestructible is the presence that pervades all this; no one can destroy this unchanging reality.
18. "Our bodies are known to end, but the embodied self is enduring, indestructible, and immeasurable; therefore, Arjuna, fight the battle!

19. "He who thinks this self a killer and he who thinks it killed, both fail to understand; it does not kill, nor is it killed.

20. "It is not born, it does not die; having been, it will never not be; unborn, enduring, constant, and primordial, it is not killed when the body is killed. . . .

22. "Just as a man discards worn-out clothes to put on new and different ones, so the embodied self discards its worn-out bodies to take on other new ones. . . .

30. "The self embodied in the body of every being is indestructible; you have no cause to grieve for all these creatures, Arjuna!

31. "Look to your own duty; do not tremble before it; nothing is better for a warrior than a battle of sacred duty.

32. "The doors of heaven open for warriors who rejoice to have a battle like this thrust on them by chance.

33. "If you fail to wage this war of sacred duty, you will abandon your own duty and fame only to gain evil.

34. "People will tell of your undying shame, and for a man of honor shame is worse than death.

35. "The great chariot warriors will think you deserted in fear of battle; you will be despised by those who held you in esteem.

36. "Your enemies will slander you, scorning your skill in so many unspeakable ways—could any suffering be worse?

37. "If you are killed, you win heaven; if you triumph, you enjoy the earth; therefore, Arjuna, stand up and resolve to fight the battle!

38. "Impartial to joy and suffering, gain and loss, victory and defeat, arm yourself for the battle, lest you fall into evil. . . .

47. "Be intent on action, not on the fruits of action; avoid attraction to the fruits and attachment to inaction!

48. "Perform actions, firm in discipline (*yoga*), relinquishing attachment; be impartial to failure and success—this equanimity is called discipline. . . .

50. "Wise men disciplined by understanding relinquish the fruit born of action; freed from these bonds of rebirth, they reach a place beyond decay. . . .

55. "When he gives up desires in his mind, is content with the self within himself, then he is said to be a man whose insight is sure, Arjuna.

56. "When suffering does not disturb his mind, when his craving for pleasures has vanished, when attraction, fear, and anger are gone, he is called a sage whose thought is sure. . . .

61. "Controlling all [the senses], with discipline he should focus on me; when his senses are under control, his insight is sure. . . .

71. "When he renounces all desires and acts without craving, possessiveness, or individuality, he finds peace.

72. "This is the place of the infinite spirit (Brahman); achieving it, one is freed from delusion; abiding in it even at the time of death, one finds the pure calm of infinity. . . .

4.6. "Though myself unborn, undying, the lord of creatures, I fashion nature, which is mine, and I come into being through my own magic.

7. "Whenever sacred duty decays and chaos prevails, then I create myself, Arjuna. . . .

13. "I created mankind in four classes, different in their qualities and actions; though unchanging, I am the agent of this, the actor who never acts!

14. "I desire no fruit of actions, and actions do not defile me; one who knows this about me is not bound by actions. . . .

6.2. "Know that discipline, Arjuna, is what men call renunciation; no man is disciplined without renouncing willful intent. . . .

4. "He is said to be mature in discipline when he has renounced all intention and is detached from sense objects and actions. . . .

20. "When his thought ceases, checked by the exercise of discipline, he is content within the self, seeing the self through himself.

21. "Absolute joy beyond the senses can only be grasped by understanding; when one knows it, he abides there and never wanders from this reality. . . .

9.27. "Whatever you do—what you take, what you offer, what you give, what penances you perform—do as an offering to me, Arjuna!

28. "You will be freed from the bonds of action, armed with the discipline of renunciation, your self liberated, you will join me."

Source: *Bhagavad-gita* selections, from *The Bhagavad-gita: Krishna's Counsel in Time of War*, tr. Barbara Stoler Miller (New York: Columbia University Press, 1986), pp. 23–27, 29, 31–34, 36, 37, 39, 50, 52, 86.

DEVOTIONAL LITERATURE

PRAISE OF THE GODDESS

This passage declares that the goddess is the real source of all creation. All the male deities of Hinduism—as well as all that exists—has its origin in her. It also indicates how she should be worshiped: with all one's heart, as the Divine Mother who protects her devotees as a mother protects her children.

This blessed goddess Mahamaya, having forcibly seized the minds even of men of knowledge, leads them to delusion.
Through her is created the entire three-tiered universe, that which both does and does not move.
Just she is the gracious giver of boons to men, for the sake of (their) release.
From bondage to mundane life; she is indeed the queen (governing) all who have power. . . .
Brahma said:
By you is everything supported, by you the world created;

By you is it protected, O Goddess, and you always consume (it) at the end (of time). . . .
Terrible with your sword and spear, likewise with cudgel and discus,
With conch and bow, having arrows, sling, and iron mace as your weapons,
Gentle, more gentle than other gentle ones, exceedingly beautiful,
You are superior to the high and low, the supreme queen.
Whatever and whenever anything exists, whether it be real or unreal, O you have everything as your very soul,
Of all that, you are the power; how then can you be adequately praised?

Source: *Devi-Mahatmya* I.42–I.63, from *Encountering the Goddess*, tr. Thomas B. Coburn (Albany: State University of New York Press, 1991), pp. 35–37.

PRAYER FOR IDENTITY WITH THE GODDESS

The Goddess is described as both fearful and benevolent, indicating that she is connected with both the pleasant and unpleasant aspects of existence. This poem, traditionally attributed to Shankara, asks for her help in attaining perfect identification with her in a state of perfect devotion in which notions of separateness and personality are transcended.

If Shiva is united with Shakti, he is able to exert his powers as lord; if not, the god is not able to stir.
Hence to you, who must be propitiated by Hari [Vishnu], Hara [Shiva], Virarnchi [Brahma], and the other [gods],
How can one who has not acquired merit be fit to offer reverence and praise? . . .

For the ignorant you are the island city of the sun, for the mentally stagnant you are a waterfall of streams of nectar [flowing] from a bouquet of intelligence,
For the poor you are a rosary of wishing-jewels; for those who in the ocean of birth are submerged, you are the tusk of that boar who was the enemy of Mura, O Lady.

Banded with a tinkling girdle, heavy with breasts like the frontal lobes of young elephants,
Slender of waist, with face like the full moon of autumn, bearing on the palms of her hands bow, arrows, noose, and goad,
Let there be seated before us the pride of him who shook the cities [Shiva]. . . .

May you, O Blessed Lady, extend to me, your slave, a compassionate glance!
When one desiring to praise you utters the words "you, O Lady" [which also mean, "May I be you"],
At that moment you grant him a state of identity with you.
With your feet illuminated by the crests of Mukunda, Brahma, and Indra.

Source: *Saundaryalahari*, attributed to Shankara, tr. W. N. Brown (Cambridge: Harvard University Press, 1958), pp. 48, 50, 56.

MIRABAI'S MYSTICAL MARRIAGE TO KRISHNA

Mirabai remains one of the most popular devotional poets of medieval India. She was probably born around 1550 and is said to have been the wife of a Rajput prince who was the son of the ruler (Rana) of Mewar. According to legend, before her marriage she had fallen in love with Krishna and refused to consummate her marriage to the prince because her relationship with the Lord took precedence. One story that is told of her relates that one time she was exchanging words of love to a visitor on the other side of a locked door. Her father-in-law, the ruler, overheard her and, outraged by the shame she had brought on his family, threatened to kill her. She told him that the person to whom she was speaking was the Lord Krishna, and not a human lover, and her life was spared. In this poem she alludes to an incident in which the Rana tries to poison her, but she believes that she was saved by Krishna. She indicates that her devotion to the Lord has caused her to leave behind her family, friends, and the privileged life she led in the palace, and to seek the company of fellow devotees.

> My love is reserved for Gopal, the Mountain Lifter
> and for no one else.
> O saints and ascetics,
> I have seen the world and its ways.
> I left my brothers and relatives
> And all my possessions.
> Abandoning worldly shame,
> I came to sit with ascetics.
> Together with devotees [of Krishna,] I was happy.
> [But] when I looked at the world, I wept.
> I planted the vine of love
> And watered it with my tears.
> I churned curds
> And extracted the ghee;
> I threw out the buttermilk.
> The King sent me a cup of poison,
> And I gladly drank it all.
> Mira's love is deeply rooted;
> She accepts whatever comes to her.

Source: Poem from *Mirabai ki Padavali*.

CHEATING ON HER HUSBAND

Mahadeviyakka was an important poet of the iconoclastic Virashaiva tradition. In her poetry, her devotion to Shiva was often expressed in sexual terms. This led to conflicts with traditional mores and values, particularly those regarding the proper conduct of women. In the following verses, she indicates that her intense devotion to Shiva prevented her from the devotion to her husband required of a traditional Hindu wife. She compares her apparently loveless marriage with her husband to her devotion to Shiva and indicates how little she values the former relationship in comparison with her devotional love affair with the Lord.

> I have Maya for mother-in-law; the world for father-in-law;
> three brothers-in-law, like tigers;
> And the husband's thoughts are full of laughing women: no god, this man.
> And I cannot cross the sister-in-law.
> But I will give this wench the slip and go cuckold my husband with Hara, my Lord.
> My mind is my maid: by her kindness, I join my Lord, my utterly beautiful Lord from the mountain-peaks, my lord white as jasmine,
> and I will make Him my good husband.

Source: poem by Mahadeviyakka, from *Speaking of Siva,* tr. A. K. Ramanujan (Baltimore: Penguin Books, 1973), p. 141.]

TREATISES ON DHARMA

ACTIONS AND THEIR RESULTS

The Laws of Manu *codify the hierarchy of medieval Indian society and outline the duties of the four primary social groups: (1)* brahmins, *the priests; (2)* kshatriyas, *the warriors and rulers; (3)* vaishyas, *tradespeople and merchants, and (4)* shudras, *or servants. Each of them is said to have a role to play in creating a stable and ordered society. Manu also outlines the duties for four stages of life: the student, the householder, the forest-dweller, and the world renouncer. According to this scheme, liberation is recognized as the supreme goal of the religious life, but its pursuit should be postponed until the proper time, which is said to be when one has seen a grandson born (indicating that one's lineage will continue) and gray hairs have appeared on one's head (indicating that one has lived long enough to fulfill the requirements of dharma).*

4.97. It is better (to discharge) one's own (appointed) duty (*dharma*) incompletely than to perform completely that of another; for he who lives according to the law of another (caste) is instantly excluded from his own. . . .

12.3. Action, which springs from the mind, from speech, and from the body, produces either good or evil results; by actions are caused (the various) conditions of men, the highest, middling, and the lowest.

4. Know that the mind is the instigator here below, even for [actions] that are connected with the body. . . .

40. Those endowed with Goodness (*sattva*) reach the state of gods, those endowed with Activity (*rajas*) the state of men, and those endowed with Darkness (*tamas*) always sink to the condition of beasts; that is the threefold course of transmigrations. . . .

95. All those traditions (*smriti*) and all those despicable systems of philosophy, which are not based on the Veda, produce no reward after death; for they are declared to be founded on darkness. . . .

104. Austerity and sacred learning are the best means by which a brahmin gains supreme happiness; by austerity he destroys guilt, by sacred learning he obtains the cessation of (births and) deaths. . . .

173. If (the punishment falls) not on (the offender) himself, (it falls) on his sons, if not on the sons, (at least) on his grandsons; but an iniquity (once) committed never fails to produce consequences for him who wrought it.

174. He prospers for a while through unrighteousness, then he gains great good fortune, next he conquers his enemies, but (at last) he perishes (branch and) root. . . .

240. Single is each being born; single it dies; single it enjoys (the reward of its) virtue; single (it suffers the punishment of its) sin. . . .

31. For the sake of the prosperity of the worlds, he (the Lord) caused the brahmin, the kshatriya, the vaishya, and the shudra to proceed from his mouth, his arms, his thighs, and his feet. . . .

87. But in order to protect this universe He, the most glorious one, assigned separate (duties and) occupations to those who came from his mouth, arms, thighs, and feet. . . .

10.1. The three twice-born castes, carrying out their (prescribed) duties, study (the Veda); but among them the brahmin (alone) shall teach it, and not the other two; this is an established rule. . . .

3. On account of his pre-eminence, on account of the superiority of his origin, on account of his observance of restrictive rules, and on account of his particular sanctification, the brahmin is the lord of (all) castes.

4. The brahmin, the kshatriya, and the vaishya castes are the twice-born ones, but the fourth, the shudra, has one birth only; there is no fifth (caste).

5. In all castes those (children) only which are begotten in the direct order on wedded wives, equal (in caste and married as) virgins, are to be considered to belong to the same caste (as the fathers). . . .

45. All those tribes in this world, which are excluded from the (community of) those born from the mouth, the arms, the thighs, and the feet (of Brahman), are called Dasyus ["slaves"], whether they speak the language of the barbarians (*mleccha*) or that of the Aryans. . . .

Source: *The Laws of Manu*, chs. 4, 12, 10.

The Four Stages of Life

6.87. The student, the householder, the forest dweller, and the world renouncer: these constitute the four separate orders. . . .

89. And in accordance with the precepts of the Veda and of the traditional texts, the householder is declared to be superior to all of them, because he supports the other three. . . .

7.352. Men who commit adultery with the wives of others, the king shall cause to be marked by punishments which cause terror, and afterwards banish.

353. For by (adultery) is caused a mixture of the castes among men; from that (follows) sin, which cuts up even the roots and causes the destruction of everything. . . .

2.36. In the eighth year after conception, one should perform the initiation (*upanayana*) of a brahmin, in the eleventh (year) after conception (that) of a kshatriya, but in the twelfth that of a vaishya. . . .

69. Having performed the (rite of) initiation, the teacher must first instruct the (pupil) in (the rules of) personal purification, conduct, of the fire sacrifice, and of the twilight (morning and evening) devotions. . . .

176. Every day, having bathed and being purified, he must offer libations of water to the gods, sages . . . worship the gods, and place fuel (on the sacred fire).

177. He should abstain from honey, meat, perfumes, garlands, substances (used for) flavoring (food), women, all substances turned acid, and from doing injury to living creatures, . . .

179. From gambling, idle disputes, backbiting, and lying, looking at and touching women, and from hurting others. . . .

199. Let him not pronounce the mere name of his teacher (without adding an honorific title), behind his back even, and let him not mimic his gait, speech, and deportment. . . .

201. By censuring (his teacher), though justly, he will become a donkey (in his next birth); by falsely defaming him, a dog; he who lives on his teacher's substance will become a worm, and he who is envious (of his merit), a (larger) insect. . . .

3.1. The vow (of studying) the three Vedas under a teacher must be kept for thirty-six years, or for half that time, or for a quarter, until the (student) has perfectly learned them.

3.2. (A student) who has studied in due order the three Vedas, or two, or even one only, without breaking the (rules of) studentship, shall enter the order of the householders. . . .

4. Having bathed, with the permission of his teacher, and performed according to the rule the rite on homecoming, a twice-born man shall marry a wife of equal caste who is endowed with auspicious (bodily) marks. . . .

75. Let (every man) in this (second order, at least) daily apply himself to the private recitation of the Veda, and also to the performance of the offering to the gods; for he who is diligent in the performance of sacrifices supports both the movable and the immovable creation. . . .

78. Because men of the three (other) orders are daily supported by the householder with (gifts of) sacred knowledge and food, therefore (the stage of) householder is the most excellent stage. . . .

2. A brahmin must seek a means of subsistence which either causes no, or at least little, pain (to others), and live (by that) except in times of distress.

3. For the purpose of gaining bare subsistence, let him accumulate property by (following those) irreproachable occupations (which are prescribed for) his (caste), without (unduly) fatiguing his body. . . .

11. Let him never, for the sake of subsistence, follow the ways of the world; let him live the pure, straightforward, honest life of a brahmin. . . .

Source: *The Laws of Manu*, chs. 6, 7, 3.

Leaving Home Life

6.1. A twice-born *snataka*, who has thus lived according to the law in the order of householders, may, taking a firm resolution and keeping his organs in subjection, live in the forest, duly [observing the rules given below].

2. When a householder sees his (skin) wrinkled, and (his hair) white, and the sons of his sons, then he may resort to the forest.

3. Abandoning all food raised by cultivation, and all his belongings, he may depart into the forest, either committing his wife to his sons, or accompanied by her. . . .

8. Let him be always industrious in privately reciting the Veda; let him be patient in hardships, friendly, of collected mind, ever liberal, and never a receiver of gifts, and compassionate towards all living creatures. . . .

26. Making no effort (to procure) things that give pleasure, chaste, sleeping on the bare ground, not caring for any shelter, dwelling at the roots of trees. . . .

33. Having thus passed the third part of his life in the forest, he may live as an ascetic during the fourth part of his existence, after abandoning all attachment to worldly objects.

34. He who after passing from order to order, after offering sacrifices and subduing the senses, becomes, tired with (giving) alms and offerings of food, an ascetic, gains bliss after death. . . .

36. Having studied the Vedas in accordance with the rule, having begat sons in accordance with the sacred law, and having offered sacrifices according to his ability, he may direct his mind to (the attainment of) final liberation.

37. A twice-born man who seeks final liberation, without having studied the Vedas, without having begotten sons, and without having offered sacrifices, sinks downwards.

38. Having performed the *Ishti*, sacred to the Lord of Creatures, where (he gives) all his property as a sacrificial fee, having deposited the sacred fires in himself, a brahmin may depart from his house (as an ascetic). . . .

41. Departing from his house fully provided with the means of purification, let him wander about absolutely silent, and caring nothing for enjoyments that may be offered (to him). . . .

45. Let him not desire to die, let him not desire to live; let him wait for (his appointed) time, as a servant (waits) for the payment of his wages. . . .

49. Delighting in what refers to the Self, sitting (in yogic meditation), independent (of external help), entirely abstaining from sensual enjoyments, with himself for his only companion, he shall live in this world, desiring the bliss (of final liberation). . . .

65. By deep meditation let him recognize the subtle nature of the Supreme Self, and its presence in all organisms. . . .

85. A twice-born man who becomes an ascetic, after the successive performance of the above-mentioned acts, shakes off sin here below and reaches the highest Brahman.

Source: *The Laws of Manu*, ch. 6.

Duties of the Four Social Classes

i. The Brahmin

4.74. Brahmins who are intent on the means (of gaining union with) Brahman and firm in [discharging] their duties shall live by correctly performing the following six acts in their (proper) order.

75. Teaching, studying, sacrificing for oneself, sacrificing for others, making gifts and receiving them are the six acts of a brahmin. . . .

79. To carry arms for striking and for throwing (is prescribed) for kshatriyas as a means of subsistence; to trade, (to raise) cattle, and agriculture for vaishyas; but their duties are liberality, study of the Vedas, and performance of sacrifices.

80. Among the several occupations, the most commendable are: teaching the Veda for a brahmin, protecting (the people) for kshatriya, and trade for a vaishya.

81. But a brahmin, unable to subsist by his peculiar occupations just mentioned, may live according to the law applicable to kshatriyas, for the latter is next to him in rank.

82. If it is asked, "What should he do if he cannot maintain himself by either (of these occupations," the answer is), he may adopt the vaishya's mode of life, employing himself in agriculture and raising cattle.

83. But a brahmin, or a kshatriya, living by a vaishya's mode of subsistence, shall carefully avoid agriculture, (which causes) injury to many beings and depends on others. . . .

92. By (selling) flesh, salt, and lac a brahmin at once becomes an outcaste; by selling milk he becomes (equal to) a shudra in three days.

93. But by willingly selling in this world other (forbidden) commodities, a brahmin assumes after seven nights the character of vaishya. . . .

95. A kshatriya who has fallen into distress may subsist by all these (means); but he must never arrogantly adopt the mode of life of his betters. . . .

102. A brahmin who has fallen into distress may accept (gifts) from anybody; because according to the law it is not possible that anything pure can be sullied.

ii. The Kshatriya

18. Punishment alone governs all created beings, punishment alone protects them, punishment watches over them while they sleep; the wise declare punishment to be the law (*dharma*).
19. If (punishment) is properly inflicted after consideration it makes all people happy; but inflicted without consideration, it destroys everything.
20. If the king did not, without tiring, inflict punishment on those worthy to be punished, the stronger would roast the weaker, like fish on a spit. . . .
22. The whole world is kept in order by punishment, for a guiltless man is hard to find; through fear of punishment the whole world yields enjoyments. . . .
88. Not to turn back in battle, to protect the people, to honor the brahmins is the best means for a king to secure happiness.
89. Those kings who, seeking to slay each other in battle, fight with the utmost exertion and do not turn back, go to heaven. . . .
144. The highest duty of a kshatriya is to protect his subjects, for the king who enjoys the rewards just mentioned is required to do that duty. . . .
198. He should, (however), try to conquer his foes by conciliation by (well-applied) gifts and by creating dissension, used either separately or conjointly, never by fighting (if it can be avoided).
199. For when two (princes) fight, victory and defeat in the battle are, as experience teaches, uncertain; he should therefore avoid an engagement.

iii. The Vaishya

9.326. After a vaishya has received the sacraments and has taken a wife, he shall be always attentive to the business whereby he may subsist and to (that of) cattle.
327. For when the Lord of Creatures created cattle, he gave them to vaishyas; to the brahmins and to the king he entrusted all created beings.
328. A vaishya must never wish, "I will not keep cattle"; and if a vaishya is willing (to keep them), they must never be kept by other (castes).
329. (A vaishya) must know the respective value of gems, of pearls, of coral, of metals, of (cloth) made of thread, of perfumes, and of spices.
330. He must know how to plant seeds and the good and bad qualities of fields, and he must perfectly know all measures and weights. . . .
333. Let him exert himself to the utmost in order to increase his property in a righteous manner, and he should zealously give food to all created beings.

iv. The Shudra

8.334. Serving brahmins who are learned in the Vedas, who are householders, and who are famous (for virtue) is the highest duty of a shudra,
which leads to beatitude.

335. [A shudra who is] pure, the servant of his betters, gentle in his speech,
free from pride, and who always seeks a refuge with brahmins, attains
(in his next life) a higher caste. . . .

413. But a shudra, whether bought or unbought, he may compel to do
servile work; for he was created by the Self-existent to be the slave of
brahmins.

414. A shudra, even though emancipated by his master, is not released
from servitude; since that is innate in him, who can set him free from
it? . . .

128. The more a (shudra), keeping himself free from envy, imitates the
behavior of the virtuous, the more he gains . . . in this world and the
next.

Source: *The Laws of Manu*, chs. 4, 9, 8.

How Women Should Live

3.55. Women must be honored and adorned by their fathers, brothers, husbands, and brothers-in-law, who desire (their own) welfare.

56. Where women are honored, there the gods are pleased; but where
they are not honored, no sacred rite yields rewards.

57. Where the female relations live in grief, the family soon wholly perishes; but that family where they are not unhappy ever prospers.

58. The houses on which female relations, not being duly honored, pronounce a curse, perish completely, as if destroyed by magic. . . .

60. In that family where the husband is pleased with his wife and the wife
with her husband, happiness will assuredly be lasting. . . .

67. The nuptial ceremony is stated to be the Vedic sacrament for women
(and to be equal to the initiation), serving the husband is (equivalent
to) the residence in (the house of the) teacher, and household duties
are (the same) as the (daily) worship of the sacred fire. . . .

5.147. By a girl, by a young woman, or even by an aged one, nothing must
be done independently, even in her own house.

148. In childhood a female must be subject to her father, in youth to her
husband, when her lord is dead to her sons; a woman must never be
independent. . . .

150. She must always be cheerful, clever in household affairs, careful in
cleaning her utensils, and economical in expenditure.

151. Him to whom her father may give her, or her brother with her father's
permission, she shall obey as long as he lives, and when he is dead,
she must not insult (his memory). . . .

154. Though destitute of virtue, or seeking pleasure (elsewhere), or devoid of good qualities, a husband must be constantly worshipped as a god by a faithful wife.

155. No sacrifice, no vow, no fast must be performed by women apart (from their husbands); if a wife obeys her husband, she will be exalted for that (reason alone) in heaven.

156. A faithful wife, who desires to dwell (after death) with her husband, must never do anything that might displease him who took her hand, whether he be alive or dead.

157. At her pleasure let her emaciate her body by (living on) pure flowers, roots, and fruit; but she must never even mention the name of another man after her husband has died. . . .

160. A virtuous wife who after the death of her husband constantly remains chaste, even if she has no sons, reaches heaven, just like those chaste men. . . .

164. By violating her duty towards her husband, a wife is disgraced in this world; (after death) she enters the womb of a jackal, and is tormented by diseases for her sin.

165. She who, controlling her thoughts, words, and deeds, never fights her lord, lives (after death) with her husband (in heaven) and is called virtuous. . . .

167. A twice-born man, versed in the sacred law, shall burn a wife of equal caste who conducts herself thus and dies before him with (the sacred fires used for) the Agnihotra and with the sacrificial implements.

168. Having thus, at the funeral, given the sacred fires to his wife who dies before him, he may marry again, and again kindle (the fires).

Source: *The Laws of Manu*, chs. 3, 5.

MANU'S INSTRUCTIONS ON FINDING THE RIGHT MATE

Marriage is a matter of great concern in classical Hindu texts, since stable marriages are thought to be essential to the proper ordering of society. According to Manu, marriage should occur only within one's caste, and he provides a number of other criteria for men to consider when looking for a wife.

When, with the permission of his teacher, he has bathed and performed the ritual for homecoming (at the end of his studies) according to the ritual rules, a twice-born man should take a wife who is of the same class and has the right marks. A woman who does not come from the same blood line on her mother's side, nor belong to the same ritual line on her father's side, is considered proper as a wife and a sexual partner for a twice-born man. When it comes to relations with a woman, a man should avoid the ten following families, even if they are great or prosperous with cattle, rich in sheep, or possessing other wealth: a family that has abandoned the rituals, one that does not have boys, or a family that does not chant the Veda; and those families in which they have hairy bodies, piles, consumption, weak digestion, bad memories, and families with white leprosy, or black leprosy. A man should not marry a maiden who is a redhead or has an extra limb or is sickly or who is bald or too hairy or talks too much or is sallow or who is named after a constellation, a tree, or a river, who has a low caste name, who is named after a mountain, a bird, a snake, or has a slave name, or who has a fearsome name. He should have nothing to do with a woman who is too fat or too thin, too tall or too dwarfish, who is past her prime or lacks a limb, or who is fond of quarreling.

He should take a woman whose limbs are complete and who has a pleasant name, who walks like a swan or an elephant, whose body hair and hair on the head are fine and whose teeth are not big, with delicate limbs. A wise man, out of concern for the dharma of daughters, will not marry a woman who has no brother or whose father is unknown.

Taking a woman of the same class is recommended to twice-born men for the first marriage; but for men in whom sexual desire has arisen, these should be the choices, listed in order: according to the tradition, only a Shudra woman can be the wife of a Shudra; she and one of his own class can be the wife of a Vaishya; these two and one of his own class for a Kshatriya; and these three and one of his own class for the high-born (Brahmin). A Shudra woman is not mentioned as the wife of a Brahmin or a Kshatriya even when they are under duress, even in a story. Twice-born men who are so infatuated as to take as wives women of low caste quickly reduce their families, including the children, to the status of Shudras. . . . A Brahmin who beds a Shudra woman goes to hell; if he begets a child on her, he forsakes the status of Brahmin. The ancestors and the gods do not eat the offerings to the gods, to the ancestors, and to guests made by such a man, and so he does not go to heaven. No expiation is ordained for a (twice-born) man who drinks the froth from the lips of a Shudra woman or who is tainted by her breath or who begets a son on her.

Now listen to the summary of these eight marriage rituals for the four classes, that are both for good and for ill, in this life and after death. Now, the eight are the marriages named after Brahma, the gods, the sages, Prajapati, the demons, the Gandharvas, the ogres, and the ghouls. I will tell you all about which one is within the dharma of each class, and the faults and qualities of each, and their merits and demerits when it comes to offspring. It should be understood that the first six as they are listed above are within the dharma of a Brahmin, the last four are for a Kshatriya, and these same four, with the exception of the ogre marriage, are for a Vaishya or a Shudra. . . .

A marriage is known as following the dharma of a Brahma marriage when a man dresses his daughter and adorns her and summons a man who knows the Vedas and is moral, and himself gives her to him as a gift.

They say a marriage is in the dharma of the gods when a man adorns his daughter and gives her as a gift to a sacrificial priest, in the course of a properly performed sacrifice. . . .

It is called a demonic dharma when the maiden is given to a man because he desires her himself, when he has given as much wealth as he can to her relatives and to the maiden herself. The ritual is known as a Gandharva marriage when the bride and her groom unite with one another because they want to, as a result of the desire for sexual intercourse. The wedding is called the rule of the ogres when a man forcibly carries off a maiden out of her house, screaming and weeping, after he has killed, wounded, or beaten (her and/or her relatives). The lowest and most evil of marriages, known as that of the ghouls, takes place when a man secretly seduces a girl who is asleep, drunk, or out of her mind. . . .

A man should approach his wife sexually during her fertile period, and always find his sexual pleasure in his own wife; and when he desires sexual pleasure he may go to her to whom he is vowed, except on the days at the junctures. The natural fertile season of a woman lasts for sixteen nights, according to the tradition. . . . On the even nights, sons are conceived, and on the uneven nights, daughters; therefore, a man who wants sons should unite with his wife during her fertile season on the even nights. A male child is born when the seed of the man is greater (than that of the woman), and a female child when the seed of the woman is greater (than that of the man); if both are equal, a hermaphrodite is born, or a boy and a girl; and if the seed is weak or scanty, there will be a miscarriage.

Source: *The Laws of Manu*, ch. 3, from *Textual Sources for the Study of Hinduism*, pp. 101–103.

GLOSSARY

Agni God of fire in the Vedas, who transmutes sacrificial offerings into food for the gods.

Aryan The European tribes that settled in India in the second millennium B.C.E.

Atman "Soul," the divine essence of every individual.

Avidya "Ignorance," the primary factor that enmeshes living beings in the cycle of birth, death, and rebirth.

Bhagavad-gita "*Song of God*," a section of the epic *Mahabharata* that describes the ethical dilemma of Arjuna, who is torn between the demands of karma and dharma.

Bhakti Selfless devotion to God.

Brahman The ultimate reality described in the Upanishads.

Brahmin The priestly caste of traditional Hinduism.

Deva The gods of Hinduism.

Devi The Goddess, who manifests in various female forms.

Dharma "Duty," "Law," the occupational, social, and religious roles required of individuals as a result of their places in society.

Dravidian   Term coined by Western scholars for the indigenous inhabitants of India, who were displaced and conquered by the Aryans.

Harijan   "Children of God," a term coined by Mahatma Gandhi for groups of Hindus traditionally viewed as being outside the caste system (commonly referred to as "untouchables").

Hindu   An adherent of Hinduism.

Indra   King of the gods in the Vedic stories, and the paradigmatic warrior.

Karma   "Actions," which bring about concordant results.

Kshatriya   The caste whose members were traditionally warriors and rulers.

Loka-samgraha   "Upholding the World," the goal of the sacrifices enjoined by the Vedas.

Maya   "Magic" or "illusion," the creative power of Brahman that manifests as the phenomena of the world.

Moksha   "Release" from the cycle of birth, death, and rebirth.

Ramayana   Epic story of the heroic deeds of Rama, believed by tradition to be an incarnation of the god Vishnu.

Rishi   "Seers" who revealed the Vedas.

Rita   Cosmic order, which is maintained by the gods.

Samnyasin   One who renounces the world in order to seek liberation from cyclic existence.

Samsara   "Cyclic Existence," the beginningless cycle of birth, death, and rebirth in which ignorant beings are trapped.

Sanatana-dharma   "Universal Truth," a term for Hinduism, implying that it is able to embrace the limited "truths" of other religions and philosophies.

Shankara   Most influential of traditional commentators on the Upanishads.

Shiva   God who exemplifies yogic practice, who will destroy the world at the end of the present cosmic cycle.

Shudra   The caste whose traditional duty was to serve the castes above them.

Upanishads   Mystical texts that speculate on the nature of human existence and the ultimate reality.

Vaishya   The caste whose members traditionally were merchants and skilled artisans.

Varna   The four main social groupings of traditional Indian society (brahmins, kshatriyas, vaishyas, and shudras).

Veda   The four early sacred texts of Hinduism, which describe the gods and rituals connected with them.

Vedanta   Tradition of commentary on the Upanishads.

Vishnu   God whose traditional role is to protect dharma.

Yoga   System of meditative cultivation involving physical and mental discipline.

FURTHER READINGS

AVALON, ARTHUR (Sir John Woodroffe). *Shakti and Shakta*. New York: Dover, 1978.

BASHAM, A. L. *The Wonder That Was India*. London: Sidgwick & Jackson, 1967.

DANIÉLOU, ALAIN. *The Myths and Gods of India*. Rochester, VT: Inner Traditions International, 1985.

DASGUPTA, SURENDRANATH. *A History of Indian Philosophy*. 5 vols. Delhi: Motilal Banarsidass, 1975.

ELIADE, MIRCEA. *Yoga: Immortality and Freedom*. Princeton: Princeton University Press, 1969.

HIRIYANA, M. *Essentials of Indian Philosophy*. London: Unwin, 1949.

HOPKINS, THOMAS J. *The Hindu Religious Tradition*. Belmont, CA: Wadsworth, 1971.

KAELBER, WALTER O. *Tapta Marga: Asceticism and Initiation in Vedic India*. New York: State University of New York Press, 1989.

KINSLEY, DAVID R. *Hindu Goddesses: Visions of the Divine Feminine in the Hindu Religious Tradition*. Delhi: Motilal Banarsidass, 1987.

——. *Hinduism: A Cultural Perspective*. Englewood Cliffs, NJ: Prentice-Hall, 1982.

MINOR, ROBERT. *Modern Indian Interpreters of the Bhagavad Gita*. Albany: State University of New York Press, 1986.

POTTER, KARL H. *Encyclopedia of Indian Philosophies, Vol I: Bibliography*. Princeton: Princeton University Press, 1983.

——. *Encyclopedia of Indian Philosophies, Vol. III: Advaita Vedānta up to Śaṃkara and His Pupils*. Delhi: Motilal Banarsidass, 1981.

——. *Presuppositions of India's Philosophies*. Delhi: Motilal Banarsidass, n.d.

RAMANUJAN, A. K. *Speaking of Śiva*. Baltimore: Penguin, 1973.

SIVARAMAN, KRISHNA. *Saivism in Philosophical Perspective: A Study of the Formative Concepts, Problems and Methods of Śaiva Siddhānta*. Delhi: Motilal Banarsidass, 1973.

ZAEHNER, R. C. *Hindu and Muslim Mysticism*. New York: Schocken, 1969.

ZIMMER, HEINRICH. *Philosophies of India*. Princeton: Princeton University Press, 1951.

Jainism

INTRODUCTION

The contemporary Jaina tradition traces itself back to Vardhamana Jnatriputra, an ascetic who was born in the northern part of modern-day Bihar in the sixth century B.C.E. This was also the area in which the Buddha lived, and the two religious leaders were said to have been familiar with each other's reputations and teachings. Both traditions rejected key elements of the dominant brahamanical system, including the sacrifices enjoined by the Vedas and the caste system, and both emphasized the goal of final liberation from cyclic existence, although they differed significantly in their paths.

Jainism's founder, referred to by his followers as Mahavira ("Great Hero"), advocated a path of strict asceticism and noninjury (*ahimsa*) to all living things as the keys to liberation (*moksha*). By controlling desires, restraining the wandering of the senses, and limiting consumption to the minimum needed to sustain life, Mahavira eliminated all attachments to material enjoyments, wandered naked from place to place (symbolizing his dispassion toward mundane norms and possessions), and through rigorous spiritual discipline eventually overcame any possibility of return to cyclic existence. In recognition of his hard-won victory over the temptations of the world, his followers commonly refer to him as Jina, meaning "Victor." The term *Jaina* means "Followers of the Victor."

Mahavira did not claim to be a religious innovator or to have discovered a new path to salvation; rather, he asserted that he was one of many who have discovered the way. According to Jaina tradition, he was the twenty-fourth Tirthankara, or "Ford-Maker," a name given by Jainas to the great ascetics who not only find the path to liberation, but also show it to others.

The most distinctive features of Jainism are its extreme asceticism, together with its emphasis on personal effort, and its strict adherence to the doctrine of noninjury. The Jaina path to liberation involves renunciation of material things, coupled with ascetic practices aimed at purifying the soul (*jiva*), cleansing it of the karmic accretions that have colored it and bound it to matter (*ajiva*). In this process, one can depend only upon oneself and one's own effort. In Jainism there is no creator God and no higher power that can aid one in reaching salvation, which in Jainism is attained by first ridding oneself of all karma, both good and bad, and by attaining "liberating wisdom" (*kevala-jnana*), which allows one to separate oneself from matter.

Jain metaphysics divides the universe into two main categories, *jiva* and *ajiva*. *Jiva* refers to the life-principle that is found in all things, while *ajiva* is insentient matter, along with the categories of time and space. It is the main impediment to the release of individual *jivas*. According to Jainism, all things, even material entities, have a life force. *Jiva* is an eternal substance that adjusts in size and shape to the physical body it inhabits. Matter is nonsentient, and because of its connection with the life force, living beings inevitably suffer as a result of the fact that matter is prone to change and decay.

The *jiva's* natural purview is universal—it is omniscient, but the senses place restrictions on it. To bring the soul to its natural omniscience, one needs to overcome the limitations imposed upon it by matter, to let the soul perceive without the constraints placed on it by the senses, which serve as blinders for the naturally omniscient *jiva*. This leads to full and direct knowledge of all things in all aspects.

God is unnecessary in Jainism, because the soul by itself is capable of knowing everything and accomplishing the highest goal of liberation. Furthermore, karma operates according to its own laws and does not require or permit the intervention of a higher power that can alleviate or erase its effects. Each being must suffer the results of his or her actions, and no god can change this. It is up to the individual to work out his or her own salvation.

In Jain metaphysics, the universe is filled with life—everything possesses a soul, even plants and such apparently unliving things as stones, which are at such a low level of sentience, and so oppressed by matter, that they appear to be devoid of life. The soul is considered to be permeable, and all of one's actions lead to influxes of karma, which is seen as subtle matter that pervades the soul (as opposed to merely covering or obscuring it). Karmic matter varies in color in accordance with the relative goodness or evil of the act committed. For instance, killing a living being, even inadvertently, leads to an influx of very dark karma (this is why many Jaina monks wear masks over their noses and mouths and carry brooms to sweep in front of themselves, in order to avoid inadvertently killing living beings). Beings who engage in occupations that involve a great deal of killing, such as butchers, have jet black *jivas*, which can be cleansed only through prodigious amounts of asceticism and physical mortification. Because of this, Jainas are strictly prohibited from engaging in occupations that involve the taking of life, which has kept them from being, for instance, hunters and fishermen.

Jainas also hold that each *jiva* has eternally been associated with *ajiva*, and there has never been a time when they were separated, and no "fall" through which *jiva* became associated with *ajiva*. *Jiva's* association with *ajiva* is begin-ningless, but it is possible to terminate it. In addition, there is no creator deity that made the world as it is—it has always been as it is and always will be, although it does go through cycles of relative degeneration and regeneration.

All actions lead to karmic influx, but evil actions color the *jiva* with very dark karma that is difficult to eliminate, while good or meritorious actions color the *jiva* with light karma that is easily cleansed. Elimination of karma occurs naturally, and in every moment beings are working off the effects of past actions. Most beings, however, are simultaneously creating new karma, and so the process is self-perpetuating.

The only way to burn off more karma than one creates is to dedicate oneself to a program of asceticism and meditation. The karma accumulated in the *jiva* will burn off naturally, but this is a slow process. It can be aided through fasting, celibacy, and various types of ascetic practices aimed at developing *tapas* (literally "heat," the energy one acquires through self-restraint and asceticism). This may be used to burn off karma.

The first step of the Jaina path to liberation involves halting the influx of new karma (*samvara*), which is followed by a program of cleansing the karma one has already acquired (*nirjara*). When this process is completed one attains liberation (*moksha*).

Because of past karma that has not yet been eradicated, one may still have a physical body, but this too will pass away when its past karma is exhausted. At this point, the soul is freed of its bondage to matter, and is luminous, omniscient, and completely free. It then rises toward the top of the universe (which in traditional Jaina cosmology is pictured as a giant human), and comes to rest at the base of the cranium of the universe in a realm called "World of Saints" (*siddha-loka*), where it dwells forever with the other perfected beings, completely beyond any future suffering and eternally removed from the world.

No outside force or power can aid the individual in this process. Only one's own effort can cleanse one's *jiva* of the effects of accumulated karma. Gods and other human beings are unable to help the individual, since they are similarly enmeshed in the process. Even the Tirthankaras are unable to help (beyond providing instruction and guidance during their lifetimes), since their liberation has removed them from any concern with the world, and so they are beyond the reach of prayers and supplications.

Liberation is only possible in the realm in which humans live, which is said to be a small disk in the middle of the universe. Below this realm are various painful destinies, such as hells, and above it are the realms of demigods and gods. Humans are in a position superior to that of the gods, who live a long and blissful existence, and thus are unaware that when their good karma is exhausted they will inevitably sink back to the lower levels of rebirth.

Jaina Scriptures

Jainism today has two main sects, the Digambaras ("Sky Clad") and the Shvetambaras ("White Clad"). The former group believes that liberation requires renunciation of all possessions, including clothes. Digambara monks, following Mahavira's example, are expected to be completely naked, their only permitted possession a small broom used to whisk away insects before they sit or lie down.

The Shvetambaras agree that Mahavira wore no clothes, but assert that the present time is one of degeneration, and so nudity is inappropriate today. Their monks and nuns wear simple white robes, but this practice is denounced by Digambaras as indicating that they have attachments to worldly things. As a result, Digambaras hold that Shvetambara monastics are actually no more advanced spiritually than laypeople who follow the Jaina precepts.

These differences in monastic discipline parallel the divergences in their respective scriptural traditions. Each school has its own canon, and for the most part they do not accept the authority of the other's scriptures (although the doctrinal contents of the their texts are generally in accord). One reason for the disagreement is the fact that the first Jaina synod was held about two centuries after Mahavira's death. The canon that resulted from this forms the core of the Digambara canon, but since it was held well after the death of the founder many texts had become lost or forgotten, and there were differing recensions of many works. In the fifth century the Shvetambaras held a council that resulted in their authoritative texts being written down and distributed to the Jaina community.

The oldest texts of the Jaina canon were written in Prakrits, languages that were related to Sanskrit but that contained numerous grammatical forms and vocabulary from local dialects. In later times Jaina writers began composing texts in local vernaculars, and sometimes in Sanskrit. The most widely accepted scriptures are named "Early Texts" (*Purva*), but these are no longer extant. Jaina scholars contend that elements of these texts are incorporated into the present canons. The Digambaras, for example, contend that one of the branches of their canon, the twelfth "Limb" (*Anga*), contains portions of the Early Texts.

The Shvetambara canon is referred to as "Tradition" (*Agama*) or "Doctrine" (*Siddhanta*), and contains 45 texts that are arranged into six divisions: (1) the Limbs; (2) Sub-Limbs (*Upanga*); (3) Miscellaneous Texts (*Prakirnaka*); (4) Treatises on Cutting (*Chedasutra*), which mostly focus on matters of discipline; (5) Appendices (*Culikasutras*); and (6) Basic Texts (*Mulasutras*). This canon contains a variety of texts of different ages and in different languages, and some texts contain material in different dialects.

The primary texts for Digambaras are scholastic works written by authors who lived around the first century C.E., the most important of whom are Vattakera, author of the *Basic Conduct* (*Mulacara*), Kundakunda, author of the *Essence of Doctrine* (*Samayasara*), and Shivarya, who wrote the *Accomplishment* (*Aradhana*). Both Digambaras and Shvetambaras accept the authority of the *Treatise on Attaining the Meaning of the Principles* (*Tattvarthadhigama Sutra*), a text that summarizes the key points of Jaina doctrine in 350 stanzas. In addition, both schools have extensive collections of didactic and expository works called *Supplements* (*Anuyoga*), which cover a wide range of subjects, including rules for right living and dialectical debate, poetry, uplifting stories, and hymns.

The following passages are drawn from texts of the two main sects of Jainism and touch on most of the important themes of Jaina religious practice and the path to liberation. They stress the total responsibility of the individual for his or her own actions and indicate that salvation is won or lost by oneself alone. The Jaina path begins with renunciation of worldly things, conjoined with avoidance of any action that injures another living being. These practices are also linked to yogic meditation, which allows a person to discipline the senses and emotions and to eliminate desire. They also allow one to generate *tapas*, a spiritual energy that can burn up karma and thus cleanse the *jiva*.

JAINA SCRIPTURES

MAHAVIRA, THE ASCETIC PARADIGM

Jaina scriptures contain a number of descriptions of the life and liberation of Mahavira. These emphasize his extreme asceticism, his self-control, his unshakable patience and equanimity, and his final victory. Due to his years of fighting the desires of the flesh, he gradually weaned himself of all physical desires and separated his spiritual essence from the bonds of material existence.

Even in places crowded with ordinary people, Mahavira remained in profound concentration. Even when people spoke to him, he would not answer, but would quietly move away. In all situations he remained undisturbed. . . . He did not pay any attention to harsh words or vicious insults, but remained immersed in religious pursuits. He had no interest in stories, plays, songs, fights, or other entertainments. . . . He did not do any harm to any living beings, nor did he cause others to do so. . . . He did not own any clothes, nor did he accept any from anyone else. . . . He knew exactly how much food and drink was needed [to sustain life], and he had no interest in delicious food. He did not even care what sort of food [he ate]. He did not even wipe his eyes, nor did he scratch his body when it itched. When he walked, he moved in silence, not looking to the side, nor backwards. He only spoke when spoken to, and even then only very little. Always fully aware of the dangers of harming living beings, his gaze was fixed on the path ahead of him. He had forsworn the use of clothing, and in winter would walk with his hands outspread, rather than [warming himself by] folding his arms under his shoulders. . . . He endured many terrible hardships when he stopped. He might be bitten by a snake, a mongoose, or a dog; he was sometimes attacked by ants who made his flesh bleed, and he was often tormented by flies, mosquitoes, bees, and wasps. . . . Mahavira endured all of the many hardships and difficulties caused by humans and other beings. . . . Even in times of bitter cold, he did not even consider [finding shelter], but would stand near a shed and bear the cold with equanimity. When the night grew cold, he would go outside for a while, and in this way he endured the torments of cold with perfect calm and correct conduct. . . . Indifferent to all sensual delights, he cheerfully wandered from place to place, speaking very little. In the winter he would meditate in the shade, and in summer he would expose himself to the blazing heat of the sun. . . . Thoroughly purifying himself, disciplining his mind, body, and speech, Mahavira became completely calm and equanimical. During the time [he practiced meditation], he remained in perfect equipoise and peace.

Source: *Acaranga-sutra* and *Kalpa-sutra* selections.

WOMEN CANNOT ATTAIN LIBERATION

Digambara and Shvetambara texts disagree on the spiritual aptitude of women. The Digambaras contend that women should not be permitted to go without clothing, and that since nudity is a precondition for liberation, women are unable to attain the supreme religious goal. A woman's best hope is to follow the precepts and work toward a future rebirth as a man.

The Shvetambaras reject this idea and assert that women are able to attain liberation. Nudity, while commendable during Mahavira's time, is inappropriate today, and the wearing of simple clothes is no hindrance to liberation. Interestingly, both sects agree on the point that women should not be permitted to renounce clothing, since a woman's body is inherently sexual, and a naked woman would attract unwanted sexual desire.

The following passage is perhaps the earliest example of the Digambara doctrine that women are unable to attain liberation because of their gender. They cannot renounce clothing, they are fickle and emotional, their bodies are breeding grounds for small organisms, and their bodily processes lead to the destruction of these creatures, which is a violation of the dictates of noninjury.

10. [Going] without clothes and [using] the hands as a bowl for receiving alms have been taught by the supreme lords of the Jinas [as] the sole path to liberation (moksha); all other [ways of mendicant behavior] are not [valid] paths.

19. [Worldly behavior,] the outward sign of which is the accepting of possessions—be they small or great—is condemned in the teaching of the Jinas; [only] one without possessions is free from household life.

20. One endowed with the five great vows (*mahavrata*) and the three protections (*gupti*) is restrained [i.e. is a mendicant]. He [alone] is on the path to liberation free from bonds and is worthy of praise.

21. The second outward sign is said to be that of the higher and lower "listeners" [i.e. lay people: the lower, holding] the bowl, wanders for alms silently, with well controlled movement and speech.

22. The [third] outward sign is that of women: a nun eats food only once per day and wears one piece of cloth [while a female novice who wears two pieces of clothing] eats wearing [only] one.

23. In the teaching of the Jina no person who wears clothes attains [liberation], even if he is a Tirthankara. The path to liberation is that of nakedness, and all other [paths] are wrong paths.

24. It is taught [in the scriptures] that in the genital organs of women, in the area between their breasts, and in their navels and armpits are

extremely small (sukshma) living beings, so how can women be ordained [since their bodies make them unable to keep the first vow of non-violence]?

25. If there is purity because of right-view, then she too is said to be associated with the path. [However, even if] she has practiced severe [ascetic] practices it is said in the teaching that there is no ordination for women.

26. Women do not have purity of mind, and by nature their minds are slack, women get their period each month, [and therefore] they have no meditation free from anxiety.

Source: Kundakunda, *Sutraprabrita;* tr. Royce Wiles.

WOMEN CAN ATTAIN LIBERATION

2. There is liberation for women, because women possess all the causes [necessary for liberation]. The cause of liberation is fulfillment of the three jewels (*ratna-traya*), and this is not incompatible [with womanhood].

    [Commentary:] The cause of liberation from the sickness of cyclic existence is the non-deficiency of the [three jewels:] correct view, knowledge, and conduct. There is liberation from cyclic existence for those who perfect them. Furthermore, because women do not lack the causes of nirvana, it is not reasonable [to assert] that any of the three jewels are incompatible with womanhood, and so it is not the case that there is no liberation for women. . . .

4. Nuns are able to understand the Jina's words, have faith in them, and practice them faultlessly.

    [Commentary:] Correct knowledge is the proper understanding of the Jina's words. Correct view is faith in [the Jina's words]. . . . Correct conduct involves applying them appropriately. And this is just what the three jewels are said to be. Release [from cyclic existence] is characterized by complete freedom from all karmas, [which occurs when the three jewels] are perfected. . . . All of these are found in women.

    [A Digambara opponent] might assert that women cannot attain release because they have clothes. People like householders, who are bound by possessions, cannot attain release. If it were not the case [that people who own clothes have possessions], then even male [monks] could wear clothes, and renouncing them would be irrelevant [to the attainment of release]. . . .

    If [as the opponent claims] liberation cannot be attained by those who [wear] clothes, and if one could attain liberation by renouncing them, then certainly it would be acceptable for [women] to renounce [clothing]. Clothes are not necessary for life, and since even life itself may be abandoned [in order to attain liberation], then it goes without saying that [one may renounce] mere clothes! If release were attained simply due to the absence of those [clothes], then what fool seeking release would lose it just through wearing clothes?

The Lord Arhats, the guides for the path to release, taught that women must wear clothes and prohibited them from renouncing clothes, and so it follows that clothes are necessary for release, like a whisk broom [that is used to sweep away small creatures]. . . .

If women were to give up clothing, this would result in their abandoning the whole corpus of monastic rules. As is well known, women are overpowered by [men who] are excited due to seeing their naked bodies and limbs, in the same way that mares—who naturally have clothing—are overpowered by stallions. . . . Furthermore, women from good families are naturally very shy, and if they [were required to] abandon clothing [in order to become nuns], then they would refuse to do so. Clothes are a possession, and so there is some demerit in wearing them, but still by this all of the monastic rules are maintained. Therefore, having ascertained that there is greater benefit and lesser demerit in wearing clothes, rather than renouncing them, the holy Arhats declared that nuns must wear clothes and prohibited them from abandoning them.

Source: *Strinirvana-pariccheda;* tr. Royce Wiles.

BONDAGE AND LIBERATION

This passage states some of the most important themes of Jaina philosophy and religious practice: the importance of overcoming desire for worldly things, the importance of noninjury, and how negative actions result in negative consequences.

One should understand the causes of the soul's bondage [to cyclic existence], and through knowing them, one should overcome them. . . .

A person who owns even a little property—of either living or nonliving things—or who acquiesces to others' owning it, will not be released from suffering. Those who kill living beings, or who cause others to kill them, or who consent to their being killed, will have increasing demerit.

A person who is emotionally attached to relatives or friends is a fool who will suffer greatly, because the numbers of those to whom one is attached always increase. Wealth and relatives cannot protect one [from suffering]. Only by understanding this and [the nature of] life will a person overcome karma.

Source: *Sutrakritanga* 1.1.1.

THE WORTHLESSNESS OF POSSESSIONS, FRIENDS, AND RELATIVES

This passage looks at the things that most people value—possessions, friends, family, etc.—and dismisses them as transitory things that ultimately lead to suffering. In addition, it warns people not to put off religious practice until a future time: the best time to begin is right now, since one's faculties will diminish over time. Thus, a wise person will recognize the tenuousness of the things of the world and renounce them in order to pursue a life of religious practice and asceticism, which alone can lead to salvation.

1.2.2 Oppressed by great suffering and deluded, worldly people [think,] "My mother, father, sister, wife, sons, daughters, daughters-in-law, friends, relatives, and associates, my things, transactions, food, and clothes [are all important]." Infatuated by strong attachments to these things, they are immersed in them.

[Such people] live constantly tormented by greed. In season and out of season, they strive [to amass wealth]; desiring money and fortune, they become thieves who rob and steal. Their minds are always engrossed [in accumulating wealth], and they repeatedly become killers.

In this [world], some lives are short, and their hearing, sight, sense of smell, sense of touch, and tactile sense degenerate [and so they die young and unfulfilled]. Realizing that life is moving [toward its end, they become depressed]. Then eventually they are overcome by senility.

Then, at a certain time, the members of their families begin to grumble at them, and then they begin to grumble [at their families]. They will be unable to protect or give refuge [to their aging relative], and [the old person] will be unable to protect them or give them refuge. An old person is not fit for laughter, nor play, nor sexual intercourse, nor adornment. Thus, one should make effort in asceticism. Having considered the opportunity [that the present life presents for those intent on liberation], the wise will not relax in their efforts, even for a short while. The years are passing by, and youth is fading away.

Source: *Acarangasutra* 1.2.1–12.

THE IMPORTANCE OF EQUANIMITY

In Jaina practice, asceticism serves to discipline body and mind and is also used to burn off one's karma. Since in Jainism karma has a physical manifestation, it is not enough simply to gain knowledge: A person must also perform physical austerities in order to eradicate the physical effects of karma. In practicing monastic discipline, self-control is important, and a monk should gain firm control over his emotions and never lose his temper. No matter what others do to him—whether they speak harshly to him, injure him, or disturb him—he should never become angry at them and should always remain in control, because a moment of anger can destroy hard-won self-discipline and can lead to negative mental states and harmful actions.

If someone abuses a monk, he should not become angry. Losing one's temper is foolish, and so a monk does not become heated [with anger]. When [a monk] hears cruel and harsh words that prick his senses like thorns, he remains perfectly silent and does not take them to heart.

When he is beaten, he does not become angry, nor does he have malicious thoughts. Understanding that patience is the supreme good, a monk should meditate on dharma. If someone hurts a restrained and equanimical monk, he should think, "The soul (*jiva*) is eternal," and bear his torment with a smile. . . .

A monk should seek a bit of food after a householder has finished cooking but, whether or not he receives food, he does not care in either case, [thinking,] "I received no food today, but tomorrow I may get some." For a monk who thinks thus, success and failure are equal.

Realizing that he had encountered suffering, if he is oppressed by pain, he should steady his mind cheerfully and bear all the ills that afflict him. . . . Though the monk is physically oppressed by sweat or dust, or the rays of the summer sun, he does not yearn for comfort. A monk who desires liberation bears [all this, practicing] the unsurpassed, noble dharma, bearing untold filth on his body until the body expires.

Source: *Uttaradhyayanasutra* 2.24–37.

THE WORLD IS FULL OF SUFFERING

This passage is spoken by a prince named Mrigaputra to his parents. He wishes to convince them to allow him to renounce household life and become a monk. He tells them that since according to the Jaina doctrine of transmigration he has been reborn an infinite number of times, he has suffered excruciating torments in many lives. He recounts various painful types of physical suffering and death and concludes that he no longer wishes to be a part of the cycle of birth and death.

From clubs and knives, stakes and maces, breaking my limbs,
An infinite number of times I have suffered without hope.
By sharp-edged razors, by knives and shears,
Many times I have been drawn and quartered, torn apart and skinned.
Helpless in snares and traps, a deer,
I have been caught and bound and fastened, and often I have been killed.
A helpless fish, I have been caught with hooks and nets;
An infinite number of times I have been killed and scraped, split and gutted.
A bird, I have been caught by hawks or trapped in nets,
Or trapped by birdlime, and I have been killed an infinite number of times.
A tree, with axes and saws by the carpenters
An infinite number of times I have been felled, stripped of my bark, cut up, and sawn into planks.
As iron, with hammer and tongs by blacksmiths an infinite number of times I have been struck and beaten, split and filed. . . .
Ever afraid, trembling, in pain and suffering, I have felt the greatest sorrow and agony. . . .
In every kind of existence I have suffered pains that have known no reprieve for a moment.

Source: *Uttaradhyayanasutra* 19.61–67, 71, 74: *Sources of Indian Tradition*, ed. Ainslie Embree (New York: Columbia University Press, 1988), pp. 62–63.

FASTING UNTO DEATH

This passage speaks of the Jaina practice of itvara *or* sallekhana, *in which an advanced practitioner may voluntarily starve to death. This practice is said to eliminate large amounts of negative karma and may even lead to final liberation. According to legend, Mahavira himself did this, since he knew that he would be released at the end of his life and that the fast unto death would be an effective means of eliminating the last subtle vestiges of his karma. Generally a monk will prepare for this practice through a gradu- ated program of fasting that may last for 12 years, but if he is sick he can begin the fast without this previous training. In this passage, it is described as a difficult discipline, but the end reward is seen as a glorious culmination of one's spiritual training.*

If a monk thinks, "Illness is causing my body to wither, and I am not able to perform my religious duties," he should gradually reduce his diet, and through this reduction should pare away his desires. . . . He should enter a village . . . and beg for straw. After receiving it, he should retire into seclusion somewhere outside [the village]. After thoroughly examin- ing and clearing the ground—where there are no eggs [of insects], nor insects, nor seeds, nor sprouts, nor dew, nor water, nor ants, nor mildew, nor marsh, nor cobwebs—he should spread the straw on it. Then he should observe [the religious fast until death] called *itvara*. . . .

The *itvara* is proper. The monk, remaining true [to his vows], devoid of desires, successfully crosses over the ocean of cyclic existence, never doubting his ability to fulfill the fast, happily accomplishing [his goal], unaffected by circumstances, understanding that the body is mortal, over- coming various hardships and troubles, understanding that body and soul are separate, accomplishing the formidable (*bhairava*) task [of *itvara*]. This is not a miserable or untimely death. It may even lead to attainment of final liberation. Such a death is a peaceful haven for all monks who are completely free from craving for life. It is beneficial and leads to happi- ness; it is proper, salutary, and meritorious.

Source: *Acarangasutra* 1.7.105.

THERE IS NO CREATOR GOD

This passage considers various arguments for the existence of a creator of the universe and rejects them. This reflects a fundamental Jaina emphasis on the individual: There is no other power that is able to help the individual escape from cyclic existence—we are on our own, and every person's present position is the result of his or her own past actions. No outside power can change the results of one's karma, nor can anyone other than oneself effect one's salvation. The law of karma is absolute and operates according to its own laws, and no deity can abrogate the workings of karma.

Some foolish men declare that a Creator made the world.
The doctrine that the world was created is ill-advised, and should be rejected.
If God created the world, where was he before creation?

If you say he was transcendent then, and needed no support, where is he now?

No single being had the skill to make this world—

For how can an immaterial god create that which is material?

How could God have made the world without any raw material?

If you say he made this first, and then the world, you are faced with an endless regression.

If you say that this raw material arose naturally you fall into another fallacy,

For the whole universe might thus have been its own creator and have arisen naturally in the same way.

If God created the world by an act of his own will, without any raw material,

Then it is just his will and nothing else—and who will believe this nonsense?

If he is ever perfect and complete, how could the will to create have arisen in him?

If, on the other hand, he is not perfect, he could no more create the universe than a potter could.

If he is formless, actionless, and all-embracing, how could he have created the world?

Such a soul, devoid of all modality, would have no desire to create anything.

If he is perfect, he does not strive for the three aims of humanity,

So what advantage would be gained by creating the universe?

If you say that he created for no purpose, because it was his nature to do so, then God is pointless.

If he created in some kind of sport, it was the sport of a foolish child, leading to trouble. . . .

If out of love for living things and need of them he made the world,

Why did he not make creation wholly blissful, free from misfortune?

If he were transcendent he would not create, for he would be free;

Nor if involved in transmigration, for then he would not be almighty.

So the doctrine that the world was created by God makes no sense at all.

And God commits great sin in killing the children that he himself created.

If you say that he kills only to destroy evil beings, why did he create such beings in the first place? . . .

Good men should combat the believer in divine creation, maddened by an evil doctrine.

Know that the world is uncreated, as time itself is, without beginning and end. . . .

Uncreated and indestructible, it endures through the compulsion of its own nature,

Divided into three sections—hell, earth, and heaven.

Source: *Mahapurana* 4.16–31, 38–40: *Sources of Indian Tradition*, pp. 80–82.

EXCERPTS FROM *THE SUTRA ON UNDERSTANDING THE MEANING OF THE CATEGORIES*

This text is accepted as canonical by both Shvetambaras and Digambaras. It contains a concise overview of the primary categories of the Jaina philosophical system and a summary of the path to liberation.

  1.1. Right belief, [right] knowledge, [right] conduct: these [together constitute] the path to liberation.

    2. Belief or conviction in things ascertained as they are [is] right belief.

    3. This is attained by insight or understanding.

    4. The categories (*tattva*) are: (1) soul (*jiva*); (2) non-soul (*ajiva*); (3) inflow [of karmic matter into the soul: *asrava*]; (4) bondage (*bandha*); (5) stopping [inflow of karmic matter: *samvara*]; (6) elimination [of karmic matter: *nirjara*]; and (7) liberation (*moksha*) [of the soul from matter]. . . .

  2.7. The soul's [essence] is life, the capacity to be liberated, and the incapacity to be liberated.

    8. The distinctive characteristic of the soul is attention. . . .

   10. Souls are [of two kinds]: worldly and liberated.

   11. [Worldly souls] are [of two kinds]: with mind and without mind.

   12. Worldly souls are again [of two kinds]: moving and unmoving. . . .

   14. Moving souls have two senses, etc.

   15. There are five senses. . . .

   23. Worms, ants, bumblebees, and humans each have one more than the one preceding. . . .

 5.16. Due to expansion or contraction of its enclosure, [the soul occupies space] in the same way that light from a lamp does. . . .

   18. [The function] of space is to give place [to all the other substances].

   19. [The function] of matter is [to form the basis of] bodies, speech, mind, and breath.

   20. [The function] of matter is also to make possible worldly enjoyment, pain, life, and death.

   21. [The function] of souls is to support each other.

   22. And [the function] of time is [to explain] continued existence, change, movement, and long or short duration. . . .

 6.1. Yoga is activity of body, speech, and mind.

    2. It [is concerned with] inflow [of karmic matter].

    3. [Inflow is of two kinds]: good, which is [inflow] of meritorious [karmas]; and bad, which is [inflow] of negative [karmas]. . . .

   12. Compassion for living beings, compassion for those who have taken vows, charity, self-control with some attachment, etc., yoga, patience, and contentment: these are [the causes of inflow] of pleasant karmic matter. . . .

 7.1. The vows involve avoidance of harming (*himsa*), lying, stealing, non-celibacy, and attachment. . . .

    3. In order to establish these [in the mind], there are five meditations for each.

    4. The five [meditations for the vow against harming] are carefulness of speech, carefulness of mind, care in walking, care in lifting and laying down things, and thoroughly seeing to one's food and drink.

    5. And the five [meditations for the vow against lying] are avoiding anger, greed, cowardice and frivolity, and speaking in accordance with scriptural injunctions.

6. The five [meditations for the vow against stealing] are living in a solitary place, living in a deserted place, living in a place where one is not likely to be interfered with by others and where one is not likely to interfere with others, purity of alms, and not disputing with followers of the true doctrine [as to "mine" and "yours"].

7. The five [meditations for the vow against non-celibacy] are renunciation of hearing stories inciting desire for women, renunciation of seeing their beautiful bodies, renunciation of remembrance of past enjoyments, renunciation of aphrodisiacs, and renunciation of beautifying one's own body.

8. The five [meditations for the vow against worldly desire] are giving up love and hatred for the pleasing and displeasing objects of the senses. . . .

12. In order [to develop] detachment toward the tribulations [of the world, one should consider] the nature of the world and the body. . . .

8.1. The causes of bondage are wrong belief, non-renunciation, carelessness, passions, and union [of the soul with the mind, body, and speech].

2. The soul, due to its having passion, assimilates matter which is fit to form karmas. This is bondage. . . .

9.1. Stopping [of karmic inflows] is destruction of inflows.

2. It is [brought about by] discipline, carefulness, observances, meditation, overcoming suffering, and good conduct.

3. Due to asceticism, one eliminates [karmic matter].

4. Discipline is proper control [over mind, speech, and body].

5. Carefulness is [taking proper care] when walking, speaking, eating, lifting and laying down, and in excreting.

6. Observances are: forgiveness, humility, honesty, contentment, truth, restraint, asceticism, renunciation, non-attachment and celibacy, all to the highest degree.

7. The meditations are: impermanence, vulnerability, cyclic existence, aloneness, separateness, inflow, stopping [of inflows], elimination [of inflows], [the nature of] the world, the difficulty of attaining enlightenment, and the nature of the true doctrine. . . .

19. External austerities are: fasting, eating less than one's fill, taking a vow to accept food from a householder, renunciation of delicacies, sleeping in a lonely place, and mortification of the body.

20. The others, that is, internal austerities, are: expiation, discipline, service, study, giving up attachment, and concentration. . . .

10.1. Separation [results from] destruction of delusion and by simultaneous destruction of what obscures wisdom and perception.

2. Liberation is complete freedom from all karma due to the non-existence of the causes of bondage and to the eradication [of karmic matter].

4. After [attainment of] separation, there remain perfect correct wisdom, perfect correct perception, and the state of ultimate accomplishhment (*siddhatva*).

Source: *Tattvarthadhigama-sutra* selections.

GLOSSARY

Ajiva   Lifeless, insentient matter.

Digambara   "Sky-Clad," one of the two sects of contemporary Jainism, whose monks abjure the wearing of clothes.

Jaina   "Follower of the Conqueror (Mahavira)."

Jina   "Victor," an epithet of Mahavira, symbolizing his victory over ignorance.

Jiva   "Soul," the life force that inheres in all beings.

Karma   "Actions," which bring about concordant results.

Kevala-jnana   "Liberating Wisdom," which breaks the bonds of ignorance and leads to release from the cycle of birth, death, and rebirth.

Mahavira   "Great Hero," title of the founder of Jainism.

Moksha   "Release" from the cycle of birth, death, and rebirth.

Samsara   "Cyclic Existence," the beginningless cycle of birth, death, and rebirth in which ignorant beings are trapped.

Shvetambara   "White-Clad," one of the two sects of contemporary Jainism, whose monks and nuns wear simple white robes.

Siddha-loka   Supramundane realm in which liberated souls reside.

Tapas   "Heat," the energy generated by ascetic practices, which burns up accumulated karma.

Tirthankara   "Ford Maker," an epithet of Mahavira and his legendary predecessors, who are said to have found the path to liberation and taught it to others.

FURTHER READINGS

ALSDORF, LUDWIG. "What Are the Contents of the Drstavāda?" *German Scholars on India*. Varanasi: Chowkambha Sanskrit Series, 1973, vol. 1, pp. 1–5.

BHARGAVA, DAYANAND. *Jaina Ethics*. Delhi: Motilal Banarsidass, 1968.

BRONKHORST, JOHANNES. "On the Chronology of the *Tattvārtha Sūtra* and Some Early Commentaries." *Archiv für Indische Philosophie*, 29 (1985), pp. 155–184.

BUHLER, GEORG. "On the Authenticity of the Jaina Tradition." *Wiener Zeitschrift für die Kunde des Morganlandes*, 1 (1887), pp. 165–180.

——. *The Indian Sect of the Jainas*. Calcutta: Gupta [India] Private Ltd., 1963.

BURCH, GEORGE BOSWORTH. "Seven-Valued Logic in Jain Philosophy." *International Philosophical Quarterly*, 3 (1964), pp. 68–93.

CHATTERJEE, A. K. *A Comprehensive History of Jainism*. 2 vols. Calcutta: Firma KLM, 1978–84.

CORT, JOHN. "Models of and for the Study of the Jains." *Method of Theory in the Study of Religion*, 2 (1990), pp. 42–71.

FISHER, EBERHARD, AND JAIN, JYOTINDRA. *Art and Rituals: 2500 Years of Jainism in India*. New Delhi: Sterling, 1877.

FOLKERT, KENDALL W. *Scripture and Community: Collected Essays on the Jains*. Atlanta: Scholars Press, 1993.

GLASENAPP, HELMUTH VON. *The Doctrine of Karman in Jain Philosophy* (tr. Barry Gifford). Bombay: Bai Vijbai, 1942.

JAINI, PADMANABH S. *Gender and Salvation: Jaina Debates on the Spiritual Liberation of Women.* Berkeley: University of California Press, 1991.

——. *The Jaina Path of Purification.* Berkeley: University of California Press, 1979.

MEHTA, MOHAN LAL. *Jaina Philosophy.* Varanasi: P.V. Research Institute, 1971.

SANGAVE, VILAS ADINATH. *Jaina Community: A Social Survey.* Bombay: Popular Prakashan, 1980.

TALIB, G. S., ed. *Jainism.* Patiala: Punjabi University, 1975.

TATIA, NATHMAL. *Studies in Jaina Philosophy.* Banaras: Jain Cultural Research Society, 1951.

ZYDENBOS, ROBERT I. *Mokṣa in Jainism, According to Umāsvāti.* Wiesbaden: Franz Steiner Verlag, 1983.

Buddhism

INTRODUCTION

Nearly 2,500 years ago, according to Buddhist tradition, a young man sat under a tree in northern India, determined to find a way to transcend the sufferings that he recognized as being endemic to the world. Born a prince named Siddhartha Gautama in a small kingdom in what is today southern Nepal, he had renounced his royal heritage in order to escape the cycle of birth, death, and rebirth that inevitably leads to suffering, loss, and pain. As he sat under the tree, he recognized that all of the world's problems begin with a fundamental ignorance (*avidya*) that causes beings to misunderstand the true nature of reality. Because of this, they engage in actions that lead to their own suffering and fail to recognize what leads to happiness.

Siddhartha remained in meditation throughout the night, and during this time the veils of ignorance lifted from his perception. He came to understand how the lives of all beings in the world are constantly influenced by the effects of their own actions (*karma*), and that seeking happiness within the changing phenomena of the mundane world is a fundamental mistake. He saw everything in the world as impermanent (*anitya*) and understood that because of the fact of constant change even things that seem to provide happiness—such as wealth, fame, power, sex, relationships—are in fact sources of suffering (*duhkha*).

In addition, he perceived that everything comes into being in dependence upon causes and conditions—a doctrine referred to in Buddhism as "dependent arising" (*pratitya-samutpada*)—and he understood that because phenomena are in a constant state of flux there is no enduring essence underlying them. Nor is there a supreme being who oversees the process of change and decides the fates of beings. Rather, every being is responsible for its own destiny, and the entire system of universal interdependent causation is driven by its own internal forces. Individual beings are what they are because of the actions they performed in the past.

Moreover, beings lack an enduring self or soul. This doctrine is referred to in Buddhist literature as "selflessness" (*anatman*), which is a denial of the sort of permanent, partless, and immortal entity that is called *"atman"* (literally "I" or "self") in Hinduism and "soul" in Christianity. This doctrine is connected with the idea that all phenomena lack substantial entities, and are characterized by an "emptiness" (*shunyata*) of inherent existence (*svabhava*, literally "own-being").

At dawn of the following morning, full awareness arose in him, and all traces of ignorance disappeared. He had become a *"buddha,"* a term derived from the Sanskrit root word *budh,* meaning to wake up or to regain consciousness. Thus he was now fully awakened from the sleep of ignorance in which most beings spend life after life. At first he thought to remain under the tree and pass away without revealing what he had understood, since he knew that the teachings of an awakened being are subtle and difficult for ordinary beings to comprehend. As he sat there in blissful contemplation, however, the Indian god Brahma came to him, bowed down before him, and begged him to teach others. Brahma pointed out that there would be some intelligent people who would derive benefit from his teachings and that many people would find true happiness by following the path that he had discovered.

Feeling a sense of profound compassion for suffering beings, Buddha agreed to share his wisdom with them, and so embarked on a teaching career that would last for about 40 years. He traveled around India, teaching all who wished to listen, and many people recognized the truth of his words and became his disciples. According to Buddhist tradition, he was an accomplished teacher who was able to perceive the proclivities and mind-sets of his listeners and who could skillfully adapt his teachings for each person and group while still retaining the essential message. He had many lay disciples, but he emphasized the centrality of a monastic lifestyle for those who were intent on liberation. According to his biography, he died in a grove of trees near the town of Vaishali at the age of 80.

Shortly after his death his followers convened a council to codify the teachings of the Buddha. According to tradition, the council met in Rajagriha, a place in which Buddha had delivered many discourses. The participants were five hundred of his closest disciples who had become *arhats* (meaning that they had eradicated mental afflictions and transcended all attachment to mundane things). Such people, it was believed, would not be afflicted by faulty memories or biased by sectarian considerations.

The members of the assembly recounted what they had heard Buddha say on specific occasions, and they prefaced their remarks with the phrase, "Thus have I heard: At one time the Exalted One was residing in. . . ." This formula indicated that the speaker had been a member of the audience, and it provided the context and background of the discourse. Other members would certify the veracity of the account or correct minor details, and at the end of the council all present were satisfied that the Buddha's words had been definitively recorded. The canon of Buddhism was declared closed, and the council issued a pronouncement that henceforth no new teachings would be admitted as the "word of the Buddha" (*buddha-vacana*).

Despite the intentions of the council, however, new teachings and doctrines continued to appear in the following centuries, and the Buddhist community developed numerous divisions. The most significant of these was the split into two schools termed "Hinayana," or "Lesser Vehicle" and "Mahayana," or "Greater Vehicle." These names were obviously coined by the latter group, which considered itself to be superior to its rivals because it propounded a goal of universal salvation, while the Hinayana emphasized the importance of working primarily for one's own emancipation. The Hinayana ideal is the *arhat,* a being who overcomes all ties to the phenomenal world and so attains *nirvana,* which is said to be a state beyond birth and death. It is also described as perfect bliss.

Their Mahayana rivals condemned this as a selfish and limited goal. The Mahayana ideal is the *bodhisattva* (a being—*sattva*—whose goal is awakening—*bodhi*), who seeks to attain the state of buddhahood in order to help others to find the path to final happiness. This form of Buddhism later predominated in Central and East Asia—countries such as Tibet, Mongolia, Korea, Japan, Vietnam, and China—while Hinayana schools took hold in Southeast Asia—in such countries as Sri Lanka, Thailand, Burma, Cambodia, and Laos.

Buddhists in these countries do not accept the designation of their tradition as a "Lesser Vehicle." Rather, they contend that the dominant Theravada tradition (the only one of the numerous schools collectively designated by the term "Hinayana" that survives today) is in fact the true teaching of Buddha. They further believe that the Mahayana *sutras* (discourses believed by Mahayanists to have been spoken by the historical Buddha) are in fact forgeries that proclaim practices and doctrines that the Buddha never taught, but which were actually falsely propounded by others long after his death.

The oldest distinctively Mahayana literature is a group of texts that discuss the "perfection of wisdom" (*prajna-paramita*). The earliest of these is probably the *Perfection of Wisdom in 8,000 Lines, the* oldest version of which may have been composed as early as the first century B.C.E. The Perfection of Wisdom texts do not make their appearance until several centuries after the death of the Buddha, but they claim to have been spoken by him during his lifetime. Mahayana tradition explains the chronological discrepancy by contending that they were indeed taught by the Buddha to advanced disciples, but that he ordered that they be hidden in the underwater realm of *nagas* (beings with snakelike bodies and human heads) until the time was right for their propagation.

The legend further reports that the second-century philosopher Nagarjuna (fl. ca. 150 C.E.) was the person preordained by Buddha to recover and explicate the Perfection of Wisdom texts. After one of his lectures, some *nagas* approached him and told him of the texts hidden in their kingdom, and so Nagarjuna traveled there and returned with the sutras to India. He is credited with founding the Madhyamaka (Middle Way) school of Buddhist philosophy, which emphasized the centrality of the doctrine of emptiness. Nagarjuna and his commentators (the most influential of whom was Candrakirti, ca. 550–600) developed the philosophical ramifications of this doctrine, which is closely connected with the notion of dependent arising. Since all phenomena come into being as a result of causes and conditions, abide due to causes and conditions, and pass away due to causes and conditions, everything in the universe is empty of a substantial entity. Ordinary beings, however, perceive them as existing in the way that they appear—that is, as real, substantial things that inherently possess certain qualities. Nagarjuna declared that a failure to understand emptiness correctly leads to mistaken perceptions of things, and that erroneous philosophical views are the reifications of such notions.

The Madhyamaka philosophers applied this insight not only to mistaken perceptions but also to the doctrines of rival schools, which they contended were founded on self-contradictory assumptions. Through a process of dialectical reasoning, Madhyamaka thinkers exposed both Buddhist and non-Buddhist systems of thought to a rigorous critique, the goal of which was to lead people to recognize the ultimate futility of attempting to encapsulate truth in philosophical propositions.

Approximately two centuries after Nagarjuna, a new Mahayana school arose in India, which is commonly known as the Yogic Practice School (*Yogacara*). The main scriptural source for this school is the *Sutra Explaining the Thought* (*Samdhinirmocana-sutra*), which consists of a series of questions put to the Buddha by a group of bodhisattvas.

The name "Yogic Practice School" may have been derived from an important treatise by Asanga (ca. 310–390) entitled the *Levels of Yogic Practice* (*Yogacara-bhumi*). Along with his brother Vasubandhu (ca. 320–400), Asanga is credited with founding this school and developing its central doctrines. Yogacara emphasizes the importance of meditative practice, and several passages in Yogacara texts indicate that the founders of the school perceived other Mahayana Buddhists as being overly concerned with dialectical debate while neglecting meditation.

The Yogacara school is commonly referred to in Tibet as "Mind Only" (*sems tsam*; Sanskrit: *citta-matra*) because of an idea found in some Yogacara texts that all the phenomena of the world are "cognition-only" (*vijnapti-matra*), implying that everything we perceive is conditioned by consciousness.

In the following centuries, a number of syncretic schools developed. They tended to mingle Madhyamaka and Yogacara doctrines. The greatest examples of this syncretic period are the philosophers Shantarakshita (ca. 680–740) and Kamalashila (ca. 740–790), who are among the last significant Buddhist philosophers in India.

In addition to these developments in philosophy, sometime around the sixth or seventh century a new trend in practice developed in India, which was written down in texts called *tantras*. These texts purported to have been spoken by the historical Buddha (or sometimes by other buddhas), and while they incorporated the traditional Mahayana ideal of the bodhisattva who seeks buddhahood for the benefit of all beings, they also proposed some radically new practices and paradigms. The central practices of *tantra* include visualizations intended to foster cognitive reorientation, the use of prayers (*mantra*) to buddhas that are intended to facilitate the transformation of the meditator into a fully enlightened buddha, and often elaborate rituals.

In the tantric practice of deity yoga (*devata-yoga*), meditators first visualize buddhas in front of themselves (this is referred to as the "generation stage," *utpanna-krama*), and then they invite the buddhas to merge with them, a process that symbolically transforms them into buddhas (this is referred to as the "completion stage," *nishpanna-krama*). The practice of deity yoga is intended to help meditators to become familiar with having the body, speech, and mind of buddhas, and with performing the compassionate activities of buddhas. Because meditators train in the desired effect of buddhahood, the path of tantra is said by its adherents to be much shorter than that of traditional Mahayana, which was said to require a minimum of three "countless eons" (*asamkhyeya-kalpa*) to complete. With the special practices of tantra, it is said to be possible to become a buddha in as little as one human lifetime.

Following this last flowering of Buddhist thought in India, Buddhism began to decline. It became increasingly a tradition of elite scholar-monks who studied in great monastic universities like Nalanda and Vikramashila in northern India. Buddhism failed to adapt to changing social and political circumstances, and apparently lacked a wide base of support. Thus, when a series of invasions by Turkish Muslims descended on India in the 9th through 12th centuries, after the invaders had sacked the great north Indian monastic universities and killed many prominent monks, Buddhism was dealt a death blow from which it never recovered.

The Spread of Buddhism Outside of India

During the third century B.C.E. the spread of Buddhism was furthered by Ashoka (270–232), the third of the Mauryan kings who created the first pan-Indian empire. Ashoka was converted to Buddhism by a Theravada monk and, after a bloody war of conquest against the neighboring state of Kalinga, he recognized that such aggression violated the principles of Buddhism. From this point on he renounced war as an instrument of foreign policy. He began to implement Buddhist principles in the administration of the kingdom and, in order to inform the populace of his political and ruling philosophy, he had edicts inscribed on stone pillars and placed throughout his kingdom. A number of them still survive today. His reign is considered by Buddhists to have been a model of good government, one that was informed by Buddhist principles of righteousness and respect for life.

His advocacy of Buddhism was one of the primary reasons for the spread of the tradition into Southeast Asia. He sent teams of missionaries all over the Indian subcontinent, and to Sri Lanka, Burma, and other neighboring areas. Due to Ashoka's influence and personal power, the missionaries were generally well received in the countries they visited, and they were often successful in convincing people to convert to Buddhism. One of the most successful of the missions he sponsored was led by his son Mahinda, who traveled to Sri Lanka along with four other monks and a novice. According to Buddhist tradition, the mission was so successful that the king of Sri Lanka became a Buddhist, and Mahinda then supervised the translation of the Theravada canon (written in the Pali language) into Sinhala. He also helped to found a monastery that was named the Mahavihara, which became the main bastion of Theravada orthodoxy on Sri Lanka for over 1,000 years.

It is unclear exactly when Buddhism first arrived in East Asia. China was the first country in the region to record contact with Buddhism: A royal edict issued in 65 C.E. reports that a prince in what is now northern Kiangsu Province performed Buddhist sacrifices and entertained Buddhist monks and laypeople. The earliest Buddhists in China were probably from Central Asia, and for centuries Buddhism was widely perceived as a religion of foreigners.

In 148 C.E. a monk named An Shigao, from the Central Asian kingdom of Kusha, began translating Indian Buddhist texts into Chinese in Loyang, which was to become the capital of the later Han dynasty. An Shigao and a number of other monks (mostly from Central Asia) translated about 30 Buddhist texts during the next three decades. The early translators used a translation system termed "matching concepts" (*keyi*), which was to have important ramifications for the development of Chinese Buddhism. Realizing that China had a highly developed culture and that Chinese tended to view people from other countries as uncouth barbarians, the early translators used indigenous terminology—particularly Daoist terminology—to translate Sanskrit technical terms. One result of this practice was that it made many foreign ideas more palatable to Chinese readers, but it also inevitably colored the translations to such an extent that for the first few centuries after Buddhism's arrival in China, many Chinese believed it to be another version of Daoism.

In later centuries, Chinese Buddhism developed its own identity, and from China Buddhism was passed on to Korea and Japan. In 552, according to the *Nihonshoki,* the Korean state of Paekche sent Buddhist texts and images to Japan, hoping to persuade the Japanese emperor to become an ally in its war with the neighboring state of Silla. Some members of the Soga clan wanted to worship the buddha as a powerful foreign god (*kami*), hoping by this to gain influence by associating themselves with what they believed to be a deity of the powerful Chinese empire. The early Japanese interest in Buddhism was mostly connected with purported magical powers of buddhas and Buddhist monks, but after the emperor Yomei (r. 585–587) converted to Buddhism, Japanese began to travel to China in order to study with Buddhist teachers there, and indigenous Buddhist schools developed in Japan.

Yomei's son Prince Shotoku (574–622) enthusiastically propagated Buddhism. He is credited with building numerous Buddhist temples and with sponsoring Japanese monks to travel to China for study. He is also the author of commentaries on three Buddhist texts. In later times he was viewed in Japan as an incarnation of the bodhisattva Avalokiteshvara.

During the reign of the Tibetan king Trisong Detsen (740–798), the Indian scholar Shantarakshita traveled to Tibet, but opposition from some of the king's ministers forced him to leave. Before departing, he urged the king to invite the tantric adept Padmasambhava. Upon his arrival in Tibet, Padmasambhava claimed that Shantarakshita's efforts had been frustrated by the country's demons. Padmasambhava then challenged the demons to personal combat, and none were able to defeat him. This so impressed the king and his court that Shantarakshita was invited back at Padmasambhava's urging, and the first monastery in Tibet was built at Samye. This marked the beginning of the "first dissemination" of Buddhism to Tibet, which ended when the devout Buddhist king Relbachen (815–836) was assassinated.

His death in 836 marked the beginning of an interregnum period for Tibetan Buddhism, which ended in 1042 when Atisha (982–1054), one of the directors of the monastic university of Nalanda, traveled to Tibet. This is considered by Tibetan historians to mark the beginning of the "second dissemination" of Buddhism to Tibet. Atisha was so successful in bringing the dharma to Tibet that Buddhism quickly became the dominant religious tradition in the country.

Today Buddhism continues to flourish in Asia, despite such setbacks as the suppression of religion in China since the inauguration of the People's Republic of China. The current government follows Karl Marx's notion that religion is "the opiate of the masses" and an impediment to social development. In recent years government persecution of Buddhism has eased somewhat, and currently it is enjoying increased support from the Chinese populace. The government is also allowing young people to become ordained as Buddhist monks and nuns.

Buddhism is becoming increasingly popular in Western countries, and a number of prominent Buddhist teachers have established successful centers in Europe and North America. The Dalai Lama, Thich Nhat Hanh, Sogyal Rinpoche, a number of Zen masters (*roshi*), and Theravada meditation teachers have attracted substantial followings outside of Asia, and books and articles about Buddhism are appearing with increasing frequency in Western countries.

Buddhist Scriptures

The early Buddhist canon is traditionally referred to as the "Three Baskets" (*tripitaka*; Pali: *tipitaka*), consisting of (1) *vinaya*: rules of conduct, which are mainly concerned with the regulation of the monastic order; (2) *sutras*: discourses purportedly spoken by the Buddha, and sometimes by his immediate disciples; and (3) *abhidharma,* which includes scholastic treatises that codify and interpret the teachings attributed to the Buddha. According to Buddhist tradition, this division was instituted at the first council. This canon was written in a language called Pali, which is believed to have been derived from a dialect used in the region of Magadha. A second council introduced some modifications to the rules of monastic discipline, and later councils added other texts to the canon.

At first the canon was transmitted orally, but after a time of political and social turmoil King Vattagamani of Sri Lanka ordered that it be committed to writing. This was accomplished between 35 and 32 B.C.E. The *sutras* and *vinaya* were written in Pali, but some of the commentaries were in Sinhala. The Sinhala texts were translated into Pali in the fifth century C.E.

The *Vinaya* section of the Pali canon consists of rules of conduct, most of which are aimed at monks and nuns. Many of these are derived from specific cases in which the Buddha was asked for a ruling on the conduct of particular members of the order, and the general rules he promulgated still serve as the basis for monastic conduct.

The *Sutra* (Pali: *Sutta*) section of the Pali canon is traditionally divided into five "groupings" (*nikaya*): (1) the "long" (*digha*) discourses; (2) the "medium length" (*majjhima*) discourses; (3) the "grouped" (*samyutta*) discourses; (4) the "enumerated" (*anguttara*) discourses, which are arranged according to the enumerations of their topics; and (5) the "minor" (*khuddaka*) discourses, which constitute the largest section of the canon and the one that contains the widest variety of materials. It includes stories of the Buddha's former births (*Jataka*), which report how he gradually perfected the exalted qualities of a buddha; accounts of the lives of the great disciples (*apadana*); didactic verses (*gatha*); an influential work entitled the *Path of Truth* (*Dhammapada*); and a number of other important texts.

The *Abhidharma* (Pali: *abhidhamma*) section includes seven treatises, which organize the doctrines of particular classes of Buddha's discourses. The *Abhidharma* writers attempted to systematize the profusion of teachings attributed to Buddha into a coherent philosophy. Their texts classify experience in terms of impermanent groupings of factors referred to as *dharma* (Pali: *dhamma*), which in aggregations are the focus of the doctrine (*dharma*) taught by Buddha. They are simple real things, indivisible into something more basic. Collections of *dharmas* are the phenomena of experience. Everything in the world—people, animals, plants, inanimate objects—consists of impermanent groupings of *dharmas*. Thus nothing possesses an underlying soul or essence. The collections of *dharmas* are changing in every moment, and so all of reality is viewed as a vast interconnected network of change and interlinking causes and conditions.

Other early schools developed their own distinctive canons, many of which have very different collections of texts, although the doctrines and practices they contain are similar. Some schools, such as the Sarvastivadins, used Sanskrit for their canons, but today only fragments of these collections exist, mostly in Chinese translations. Although Mahayana schools developed an impressive literature, there does not seem to have been an attempt to create a Mahayana canon in India. The surviving Mahayana canons were all compiled in other countries.

Canons compiled in Mahayana countries contain much of the material of the Pali canon, but they also include Mahayana sutras and other texts not found in the Pali canon. The Tibetan canon, for example, contains a wealth of Mahayana sutras translated from Sanskrit, treatises (*shastra*) by important Indian Buddhist thinkers, *tantras* and tantric commentaries, and miscellaneous writings that were deemed important enough to include in the canon. The Chinese canon also contains Mahayana sutras, Indian philosophical treatises, and a variety of other texts, but its compilation was much less systematic than that of the Tibetan canon. The Tibetan translators had access to a much wider range of literature, due to the fact that the canon was collected in Tibet many centuries after the Chinese one. In addition, Buddhist literature came to China in a rather haphazard way. The transmission of Buddhist texts to China occurred over the course of several centuries, and during this time the tradition in India was developing and creating new schools and doctrines.

The Chinese canon was transmitted to Korea and Japan. Tibet and Mongolia both follow the Tibetan canon, which according to tradition was redacted and codified by Pudön (1290–1364). The Theravada countries of Southeast Asia follow the Pali canon and generally consider the texts of Mahayana to be heterodox.

In addition to this canonical literature, each school of Buddhism has created literature that it considers to be authoritative. In the selections below we provide examples of such texts from a wide range of schools and periods of Buddhist literature, but the vast scope of canonical and extracanonical literature prevents us from including many important works. The selections are intended to present a representative sampling of early texts that contain central doctrines or that recount important events in the history of Buddhism, along with statements by Buddhist thinkers of later times that represent influential developments in Buddhist thought and practice.

PALI CANON

THE LIFE OF THE BUDDHA

According to traditional accounts, the Buddha was born a prince named Siddhartha Gautama in a small kingdom in what is today southern Nepal. His final incarnation was a culmination of a training program that spanned countless lifetimes, during which he gradually perfected the exalted qualities that would mark him as a buddha. Shortly after his birth, his father consulted a number of astrologers, all of whom declared that the newborn prince would become a great king and that he would rule the whole world with truth and righteousness. One astrologer, however, declared that if the prince were to see a sick person, an old person, a corpse, and a world-renouncing ascetic, he would become dissatisfied with his life and become a wandering mendicant in order to seek final peace. These four things became known in Buddhism as the "four sights." The first three epitomize the problems inherent in the world, while the fourth points to the way out of the endless cycle of birth, death, and rebirth, which is characterized by suffering and loss.

According to the Extensive Sport Sutra (Lalitavistara-sutra), *Siddhartha's father, king Shuddhodana, decided to prevent his son from encountering any of the four sights and surrounded him with pleasant diversions during his early years. The prince, however, eventually convinced his father to let him visit a part of the city that lay outside the palace gates.*

Before allowing the prince to ride out in his chariot, Shuddhodana first ordered that the streets be cleared of all sick and old people, and that the prince not be allowed to see any corpses or world renouncers. Despite the king's efforts, however, at one point the path of the royal chariot was blocked by a sick man. Siddhartha had never before encountered serious illness, and he turned to Candaka, his charioteer, and asked,

> O charioteer, who is this man, weak and powerless?
> His flesh, blood, and skin withered, his veins protruding,
> With whitened hair, few teeth, his body emaciated,
> Walking painfully and leaning on a staff?

Candaka informed the prince that the man had grown old and that such afflictions were the inevitable result of age. He added,

> O prince, this man is oppressed by age
> His organs are weak; he is in pain, and his strength and vigor are gone.
> Abandoned by his friends, he is helpless and unable to work,
> Like wood abandoned in a forest. . . .
> Lord, this is not unique to his race or his country.
> Age exhausts youth and the entire world.
> Even you will be separated from the company
> Of your mother and father, friends and relatives.
> There is no other fate for living beings.

Siddhartha was amazed to find that most people see such sights every day but persist in shortsighted pursuits and mundane affairs, apparently unconcerned that they will inevitably become sick, grow old, and die.

In three subsequent journeys outside the palace, Siddhartha saw an old man and a corpse, and when he learned that eventually his young, healthy body would become weak and decrepit he fell into a profound depression. On a fourth trip, Siddhartha saw a world renouncer, a man who stood apart from the crowd, who owned nothing and was unaffected by the petty concerns of the masses, and who radiated calm, serenity, and a profound inner peace. This sight lifted Siddhartha's spirits, since it revealed to him that there is a way to transcend the vicissitudes of mundane existence and find true happiness. Intrigued by the ascetic, Siddhartha asked Candaka what sort of man he was, and the charioteer replied,

> Lord, this man is one of the order of bhikshus [mendicants].
> Having abandoned sensual desires,
> He has disciplined conduct.
> He has become a wandering mendicant.
> Who views himself and the external world with the same regard.
> Devoid of attachment or emnity, he lives by begging.

Realizing the folly of remaining in the palace, Siddhartha resolved to renounce the world and find inner peace.

> Candaka, for countless ages I have enjoyed sensual objects
> Of sight, sound, color, flavor, and touch, in all their varieties;
> But they have not made me happy. . . .
> Realizing this, I will embark on the raft of dharma, which is steadfast,
> Endowed with the range of austerities, good conduct,
> Equanimity, effort, strength, and generosity,
> Which is sturdy, made of the firmness of effort, and strongly held together.

Siddhartha then declared his desire to become awakened in order to show other suffering beings a way to end suffering:

> I desire and wish that,
> After attaining the level of awakening,
> Which is beyond decay and death,
> I will save the world.
> The time for that has arrived.

Siddhartha left the palace and subsequently practiced meditation with several teachers, but none could show him a path leading to the cessation of suffering. At one point he fell in with five spiritual seekers who told him that the way to salvation lies in severe asceticism. He followed their practices, and eventually was eating only a single grain of rice per day. After swooning due to weakness, however, Siddhartha realized that extreme asceticism is just as much a trap as the hedonistic indulgence of his early years.

Thus he left his ascetic companions behind and resolved to find a path leading to the cessation of suffering. He recognized that he would have to discover the truth for himself. Before embarking on his final quest for truth Siddhartha made a solemn vow,

> As I sit here, my body may wither away,
> My skin, bones, and flesh may decay,
> But until I have attained awakening—
> Which is difficult to gain even during many ages—
> I will not move from this place.

Siddhartha stood in a spot that is now known as "the Circle of Awakening," located in modern-day Bodhgaya. Sitting under a tree, during the night Siddhartha entered into progressively deeper meditative states, in which the patterns of the world fell into place for him, and thus he came to understand the causes and effects of actions, why beings suffer, and how to transcend all the pains and sorrows of the world.

By the dawn of the next morning he had completely awakened from the misconceptions of ordinary people, and at this point Buddhist texts refer to him as "buddha," indicating that he was now fully awake and aware of the true nature of all things. Scanning the world with his heightened perception, the Buddha recognized that his realization was too profound to be understood by the vast majority of beings in the world, and so initially he decided to remain under the tree in profound equanimity, and to pass away without teaching what he had learned.

> Profound, peaceful, perfectly pure,
> Luminous, uncompounded, ambrosial
> Is the dharma I have attained.
> Even if I were to teach it,
> Others could not understand
> Thus, I should remain silent in the forest.

After the Buddha had made this statement, however, the Indian god Brahma appeared before him and begged him to teach what he had learned for the benefit of those few beings who could understand and profit from his wisdom. Moved by compassion for the sufferings of beings caught up in the round of cyclic existence, the Buddha agreed, and for the next 40 years he traveled around India, teaching all who cared to listen.

Source: *Lalita-vistara* selections.

THE FIRST SERMON

Shortly after making the decision to teach, Buddha surveyed the world in order to choose a place to begin his teaching career. He decided to travel to Sarnath, where his five former companions were still practicing pointless austerities, hoping in this way to find happiness.

The following excerpt purports to be Buddha's first public teaching. It is referred to as the "Sutra Turning the Wheel of Doctrine" because it set in motion the Buddha's teaching career. In this passage, he lays out some of the themes that would be central to his later teachings, such as the importance of following a "middle way" that avoids the extremes of sensual indulgence and extreme asceticism, and the "four noble truths": (1) that all mundane existence involves suffering; (2) that suffering is caused by desire; (3) that there can be a cessation of suffering; and (4) the eightfold noble path that leads to this cessation.

Thus have I heard: At one time, the Exalted One was living near Varanasi, at Isipatana near the Deer Park. Then the Exalted One spoke to the group of five monks: These two extremes, O monks, should not be practiced by one who has gone forth [from the household life]. What are the two? That which is linked with sensual desires, which is low, vulgar, common, unworthy, and useless, and that which is linked with self-torture, which is painful, unworthy, and useless. By avoiding these two extremes the Tathagata [Buddha] has gained the knowledge of the middle path which gives vision and knowledge, and leads to calm, to clair-voyances, to enlightenment, to nirvana.

O monks, what is the middle path, which gives vision. . . ? It is the noble eightfold path: right views, right intention, right speech, right action, right livelihood, right effort, right mindfulness, right concentration. This, O monks, is the middle path, which gives vision. . . .

1. Now this, O monks, is the noble truth of suffering: birth is suffering, old age is suffering, death is suffering, sorrow, grieving, dejection, and despair are suffering. Contact with unpleasant things is suffering, not getting what you want is also suffering. In short, the five aggregates of grasping are suffering.
2. Now this, O monks, is the noble truth of the arising of suffering: that craving which leads to rebirth, combined with longing and lust for this and that—craving for sensual pleasure, craving for rebirth, craving for cessation of birth. . . .
3. Now this, O monks, is the noble truth of the cessation of suffering: It is the complete cessation without remainder of that craving, the abandonment, release from, and non-attachment to it.
4. Now this, O monks, is the noble truth of the path that leads to the cessation of suffering: This is the noble eightfold path. . . .

Now monks, as long as my threefold knowledge and insight regarding these noble truths . . . were not well purified, so long, O monks, I was not sure that in this world . . . I had attained the highest complete awakening.

But when my threefold knowledge and insight in these noble truths with their twelve divisions were well purified, then, O monks, I was sure that in this world . . . I had attained the highest complete awakening. Now knowledge and insight have arisen in me, so that I know: My mind's liberation is assured; this is my last existence; for me there is no rebirth.

Source: *Samyutta-nikaya* 5.420–423.

THE BUDDHA'S GOOD QUALITIES

From a Buddhist perspective, the Buddha is not only important as a person who taught a corpus of texts. The events of his life serve as an inspiration to devout Buddhists, who see him as the supreme example of how meditative realization should be put into practice in daily life. The following passage describes how he lived and related to people and things around him.

Renouncing the killing of living beings, the ascetic Gotama abstains from killing. He has put down the club and the sword, and he lives modestly, full of mercy, desiring in his compassion the welfare of all living beings.

Having renounced the taking of what is not given, the ascetic Gotama abstains from grasping after what does not belong to him. He accepts what is given to him and waits for it to be given; and he lives in honesty and purity of heart. . . .

Having renounced unchastity, the ascetic Gotama is celibate and aloof and has lost all desire for sexual intercourse, which is vulgar.

Having renounced false speech, the ascetic Gotama abstains from lying, he speaks the truth, holds to the truth, is trustworthy, and does not break his word in the world. . . .

Having renounced slander, the ascetic Gotama abstains from libel. When he hears something in one place he will not repeat it in another in order to cause strife . . . but he unites those who are divided by strife and encourages those who are friends. His pleasure is in peace, he loves peace and delights in it, and when he speaks he speaks words that make for peace. . . .

Having renounced harsh speech, the ascetic Gotama avoids abusive speech. He speaks only words that are blameless, pleasing to the ear, touching the heart, cultured, pleasing to people, loved by people. . . .

Having renounced frivolous talk, the ascetic Gotama avoids gossip. He speaks at the right time, in accordance with the facts, with meaningful words, speaking of the truth (*dhamma*), of the discipline (*vinaya*). His speech is memorable, timely, well illustrated, measured, and to the point.

The ascetic Gotama has renounced doing harm to seeds or plants. He takes only one meal per day, not eating at night, nor at the wrong time. He abstains from watching shows or attending fairs with song, dance, and music. He has renounced the wearing of ornaments and does not adorn himself with garlands, scents, or cosmetics. He abstains from using a large or high bed. He abstains from accepting silver or gold, raw grain or raw meat. He abstains from accepting women or girls, male or female slaves, sheep or goats, birds or pigs, elephants or cows, horses or mares, fields or property. He abstains from acting as a go-between or messenger, from buying and selling, from falsifying with scales, weights, or measures. He abstains from crookedness and bribery, from cheating and fraud. He abstains from injury, murder, binding with bonds, stealing, and acts of violence.

Source: *Digha-nikaya* 1.4–10.

CRITERIA FOR ASSESSING VALID TEACHINGS AND TEACHERS

Although there are many passages in Buddhist literature in which faith is extolled as an important virtue, this faith should ideally be based on evidence and valid reasoning. In addition, there are several places in Buddhist literature in which Buddha exhorts his listeners to examine teachers and teachings closely before putting trust in them. In the following passage, Buddha addresses a group of people collectively referred to as Kalamas, who are confused by the conflicting claims of the religious systems of their day. Buddha advises them to verify all claims themselves by examining which doctrines lead to positive results, and which lead to negative ones. The former should be adopted, and the latter rejected.

Do not be [convinced] by reports, tradition, or hearsay; nor by skill in the scriptural collections, argumentation, or reasoning; nor after examining conditions or considering theories; nor because [a theory] fits appearances, nor because of respect for an ascetic [who holds a particular view]. Rather, Kalamas, when you know for yourselves: These doctrines are non-virtuous; these doctrines are erroneous; these doctrines are rejected by the wise, these doctrines, when performed and undertaken, lead to loss and suffering—then you should reject them, Kalamas.

Source: *Anguttara-nikaya* 1.189.

NIRVANA

Nirvana is said to be the final cessation of suffering, a state beyond the cycle of birth and death. As such, it could be said to be the ultimate goal of the path taught by the Buddha, whose quest was motivated by a concern with the unsatisfactoriness of cyclic existence and a wish to find a way out of the round of suffering that characterizes the mundane world. Despite its importance, however, there are few descriptions of nirvana in Buddhist literature. The selection below is one of the most detailed analyses of what nirvana is and how one attains it.

Monks, there exists something in which there is neither earth nor water, fire nor air. It is not the sphere of infinite space, nor the sphere of infinite consciousness, nor the sphere of nothingness, nor the sphere of neither perception nor non-perception. It is neither this world nor another world, nor both, neither sun nor moon.

Monks, I do not state that it comes nor that it goes. It neither abides nor passes away. It is not caused, established, arisen, supported. It is the end of suffering. . . .

What I call the selfless is difficult to perceive, for it is not easy to perceive the truth. But one who knows it cuts through craving, and for one who knows it, there is nothing to hold onto. . . .

Monks, there exists something that is unborn, unmade, uncreated, unconditioned. Monks, if there were not an unborn, unmade, uncreated, unconditioned, then there would be no way to indicate how to escape from the born, made, created, and conditioned. However, monks, since there exists something that is unborn, unmade, uncreated, and unconditioned, it is known that there is an escape from that which is born, made, created, and conditioned. . . .

There is wandering for those who are attached, but there is no wandering for those who are unattached. There is serenity when there is no wandering, and when there is serenity, there is no desire. When there is no desire, there is neither coming nor going, and when there is no coming nor going there is neither death nor rebirth. When there is neither death nor rebirth, there is neither this life nor the next life, nor anything in between. It is the end of suffering.

Source: *Udana*, ch. 8.80.

DEPENDENT ARISING

After attaining awakening, the Buddha indicated that he had come to realize that all the phenomena of the universe are interconnected by relationships of mutual causality. Things come into being in dependence upon causes and conditions, abide due to causes and conditions, and eventually pass away due to causes and conditions. Thus, the world is viewed by Buddhists as a dynamic and ever-changing system. The following passage describes the process of causation in relation to human existence, which is said to proceed in a cyclical fashion. Because of a basic misunderstanding of the workings of reality (referred to as "ignorance"), people falsely imagine that some worldly things can bring them happiness, and thus they generate desire and try to acquire these things. Such attitudes provide the basis for the arising of negative mental states, and these states in turn provide a basis for beings to return to the world in a future birth. This next life will begin with the conditioning of the last, and so the entire cycle will repeat itself unless a person recognizes the folly of conventional wisdom and chooses to follow the Buddhist path, which is designed to provide a way out of the trap of cyclic existence.

[Ananda, quoting Buddha, said:] 'Kaccana, on two things the world generally bases its view: existence and non-existence. Kaccana, one who perceives with correct insight the arising of the world as it really is does not think of the non-existence of the world. Kaccana, one who perceives with correct insight the cessation of the world as it really is does not think of the existence of the world. Kaccana, the world in general seizes on systems and is imprisoned by dogmas. One who does not seek after, seize on, or fixate on this seizing on systems, this dogma, this mental bias does not say, "This is my self." One who thinks, "Whatever arises is only suffering; whatever ceases is suffering" has no doubts or qualms. In this sense, knowledge not borrowed from others comes to one. This, Kaccana, is right view.

'Kaccana, "Everything exists" is one extreme; Kaccana, "Nothing exists" is the other extreme. Not approaching either extreme, Kaccana, the Tathagata teaches you a doctrine in terms of a middle path: ignorance depends on action; action depends on consciousness; consciousness depends on name and form; name and form depend on the six sense spheres; the six sense spheres depend on contact; contact depends on feeling; feeling depends on attachment; attachment depends on grasping; grasping depends on existence; existence depends on birth; birth depends on aging and death. Suffering, despair, misery, grief, and sorrow depend on aging and death. In this way, the whole mass of suffering arises. But due to the complete eradication and cessation of ignorance comes a cessation of karmas and so forth. This is the cessation of this whole mass of suffering.

Source: *Samyutta-nikaya* 3.90.

QUESTIONS THAT SHOULD BE AVOIDED

The following passage contains a series of questions about metaphysical topics posed to the Buddha by a wandering ascetic named Vacchagotta. The Buddha's response is interesting: He does not even try to provide answers, nor does he indicate that he does not answer because of ignorance on his part. Rather, he tells Vacchagotta that there is no point in answering the questions, since they are irrelevant to the goal of salvation. He indicates that people who spend their time pondering such questions and arguing about philosophical conundrums are unlikely to find release from suffering, and so the wisest course of action is to avoid such questions as a waste of time.

Thus have I heard: At one time the Exalted One was staying near Savatthi in the Jeta Grove in Anathapindika's hermitage. . . . Then the wanderer Vacchagotta approached the Exalted One . . . and said, 'Gotama, does the reverend Gotama have this view: "The world is eternal; this is the truth, and all else is falsehood"?'

'Vaccha, I do not have this view. . . .'

'Then, Gotama, does the reverend Gotama have this view: "The world is not eternal; this is the truth, and all else is falsehood"?'

'Vaccha, I do not have this view. . . .'

'Now, Gotama, does the reverend Gotama have this view: "The world is finite; this is the truth, and all else is falsehood"?'

'Vaccha, I do not have this view. . . .'

'Then, Gotama, does the reverend Gotama have this view: "The world is not finite; this is the truth, and all else is falsehood"?'

'Vaccha, I do not have this view. . . .'

'Now, Gotama, does the reverend Gotama have this view: "The soul (*jiva*) and the body are the same; this is the truth, and all else is falsehood"?'

'Vaccha, I do not have this view. . . .'

'Then, Gotama, does the reverend Gotama have this view: "The soul is one thing and the body is another; this is the truth, and all else is falsehood"?'

'Vaccha, I do not have this view. . . .'

'Now, Gotama, does the reverend Gotama have this view: "After death, the Tathagata exists; this is the truth, and all else is falsehood"?'

'Vaccha, I do not have this view. . . .'

'Then, Gotama, does the reverend Gotama have this view: "After death, the Tathagata does not exist; this is the truth, and all else is falsehood"?'

'Vaccha, I do not have this view. . . .'

'Now, Gotama, does the reverend Gotama have this view: "After death, the Tathagata both exists and does not exist; this is the truth, and all else is falsehood"?'

'Vaccha, I do not have this view. . . .'

'Then, Gotama, does the reverend Gotama have this view: "After death, the Tathagata neither exists nor does not exist; this is the truth, and all else is falsehood"?'

'Vaccha, I do not have this view. . . .'

'Gotama, what is the danger that the reverend Gotama sees that he does not hold any of these views?'

'Vaccha, thinking that "the world is eternal" is going to a [wrong] view, holding a view, the wilderness of views, the writhing of views, the scuffling of views, the bonds of views; it is accompanied by anguish, distress, misery, fever; it does not lead to turning away from [the world], to dispassion, cessation, calm, clairvoyances, awakening, nor to nirvana. . . . Vaccha, contending that this is dangerous, I do not approach any of these views.'

'But does Gotama have any views?'

'Vaccha, holding to any view has been eliminated by the Tathagata . . . so I say that through destruction, dispassion, cessation, abandoning, getting rid of all imaginings, all supposings, all latent pride that "I am the doer, mine is the deed," a Tathagata is released without desire.'

'But Gotama, where is a monk whose mind is thus released reborn?'

'Vaccha, the term "reborn" does not apply.'

'Then, Gotama, is he not reborn?'

'Vaccha, the term "not reborn" does not apply.'

'Then, Gotama, is he both reborn and not reborn?'

'Vaccha, "both reborn and not reborn" does not apply.'

'Then, Gotama, is he neither reborn nor not reborn?'

'Vaccha, "neither reborn nor not reborn" does not apply.' . . .

'I am confused at this point, Gotama; I am bewildered, and I have lost all the satisfaction from the earlier conversation I had with Gotama.'

'You should be confused, Vaccha, you should be bewildered. Vaccha, this doctrine *(dhamma)* is profound, difficult to see, difficult to understand, peaceful, wonderful, beyond argumentation, subtle, understood by the wise; but it is difficult for you, who hold another view, another allegiance, another goal, having different practices and a different teacher. Well, then, Vaccha, I will now question you in return. . . . If a fire were burning in front of you, would you know, "This fire is burning in front of me'?"

'Gotama . . . I would know.' . . .

'Vaccha, if the fire in front of you were put out, would you know, "This fire that was in front of me has been put out"?'

'Gotama . . . I would know.'

'But, Vaccha, if someone were to ask you—"Regarding that fire that was in front of you and that has been put out, in which direction has the fire gone from here: to the east, west, north, or south"—what would you reply to this question, Vaccha?'

'Gotama, it does not apply. Gotama, the fire burned because of a supply of grass and sticks, but due to having totally consumed this and due to a lack of other fuel, it is said to be put out since it is without fuel.'

'Vaccha, in the same way, the form by which one recognizing the Tathagata would recognize him has been eliminated by the Tathagata, uprooted, made like a stump of a palm tree that has become non-existent and will not arise again in the future. Vaccha, the Tathagata is released from designation by form, he is profound, immeasurable, unfathomable like the great ocean. "Reborn" does not apply; "not reborn" does not apply. The feelings . . . discriminations . . . compositional factors . . . consciousness by which one recognizing the Tathagata might recognize him have been eliminated by the Tathagata, uprooted . . . and will not arise again in the future. Vaccha, the Tathagata is released from all designation by consciousness; he is profound, immeasurable, unfathomable as the great ocean. "Reborn" does not apply; "not reborn" does not apply; "both reborn and not reborn" does not apply; "neither reborn nor not reborn" does not apply.'

Source: *Majjhima-nikaya* 3.72.

SELFLESSNESS

Buddhism denies that there is anything corresponding to the common idea of a soul or self. Instead, the Buddha taught that the soul is a false notion imputed to a collection of constantly changing parts. These are referred to as the five "aggregates" (skandha): form, feelings, discriminations, consciousness, and compositional factors. Form refers to one's physical form, and feelings are our emotional responses to the things we experience. Discriminations are classifications of these experiences into pleasant, unpleasant, and neutral. Consciousness refers to the functioning of the mind, and compositional factors are other aspects connected with the false sense of self, such as one's karmas.

[Buddha:] 'Monks, form is selflessness. Monks, if form were the self, then form would not be involved with sickness, and one could say of the body: "Let my form be thus; let my form not be thus." Monks, because form is selfless, it is involved with sickness, and one cannot say of form: "Let my form be thus; let my form not be thus."

'Feeling is selfless . . . discrimination is selfless . . . the aggregates are selfless . . . compositional factors are selfless . . . consciousness is selfless. Monks, if consciousness were the self, then consciousness would not be involved with sickness, and one could say of consciousness: "Let my consciousness be thus; let my consciousness not be thus. . . ."

'What do you think monks: Is form permanent or impermanent?'

'Impermanent, sir.'

'And is the impermanent suffering or happiness?'

'Suffering, sir.'

'And with respect to what is impermanent, suffering, naturally unstable, is it proper to perceive it in this way: "This is mine; I am this; this is my self?"'

'Definitely not, sir.'

'It is the same way with feelings, discriminations, compositional factors, and consciousness. Therefore, monks, every single form—past, future, or present; internal or external; gross or subtle; low or high; near or far—should be viewed in this way, as it really is, with correct insight: "This is not mine; this is not I; this is not my self."'

'Every single feeling, every single discrimination, every single compositional factor . . . every single consciousness [should be viewed in this way].

'Perceiving [these] in this way, monks, the well-taught, wise disciple feels disgust for form, feels disgust for feeling, feels disgust for discrimination, feels disgust for compositional factors, and feels disgust for consciousness. Feeling disgust in this way, one becomes averse; becoming averse, one is liberated. Awareness that the liberated person is liberated arises, so that one knows: "Birth is destroyed; the virtuous life has been lived; my work is done; for such a life there is nothing beyond [this world]."'

Source: *Samyutta-nikaya* 3.59.

INSTRUCTIONS ON MEDITATION

Following the example of the Buddha, Buddhism emphasizes the importance of meditation as a means for attaining clarity of perception, eliminating mental afflictions, and escaping from cyclic existence. The following passage, attributed to Ashvaghosha (ca. second century C.E.*), is believed to contain instructions given by Buddha to his half-brother Nanda.*

Now after having closed the windows of the senses with the shutters of mindfulness, you should know the proper measure of food in order to meditate properly and maintain good health. For too much food impedes the intake of breath, makes one lethargic and sleepy, and saps one's strength. Furthermore, just as too much food leads to distraction, eating too little makes one weak. . . . Thus as a practitioner of yoga you should feed your body simply in order to overcome hunger, and not out of desire for food or love of it.

After spending the day in self-controlled mental concentration, you should shake off sleepiness and spend the night engaged in the discipline of yoga. And do not think that your awareness is properly aware when drowsiness manifests itself in your heart. When you are overcome by sleepiness, you should apply your attention to exertion and steadfastness, strength and courage. You should clearly recite the texts you have been taught, and you should teach them to others and ponder them yourself. In order to remain awake, splash water on your face, look around in all directions, and look at the stars. . . .

During the first three watches of the night, you should practice [meditation], but after that you should lie down and rest on your right side, remaining awake in your heart, your mind at peace, keeping your attention on the idea of light. In the third watch, you should get up and, either walking or sitting, continue to practice yoga, with a pure mind and controlled senses. . . .

Sit cross-legged in a solitary place, keep your back straight, and direct your mindfulness in front of you, [focusing] on the tip of the nose, the forehead, or the space between the eyebrows. Keep the wandering mind focused completely on one thing. If a mental affliction—a desirous thought—arises, you should not hold to it, but should brush it off like dust on your clothes. Even if you have eliminated desires from your mind, there is still an innate tendency toward them, like a fire smoldering in ashes. My friend, this should be extinguished by meditation, in the way that fire is extinguished by water. Unless you do this, desire will arise again from the innate tendency, as plants arise from a seed. Only by destroying [the tendencies] will they finally be eradicated, like plants whose roots have been destroyed. . . .

When one washes dirt from gold, one first gets rid of the largest pieces of dirt, and then the smaller ones, and having cleaned it one is left with pieces of pure gold. In the same way, in order to attain liberation, one should discipline the mind, first washing away the coarser faults, and then the smaller ones, until one is left with pure pieces of dharma.

Source: *Saundarananda* chs. 14, 15.

ORDINATION OF WOMEN

When Buddha began his teaching career, his first disciples were monks, but eventually some women became followers and began to desire ordination as nuns. The woman who put the request to Buddha was Mahapajapati Gotami, who had raised him after his mother died. Buddha first refused her request, but after she obtained the support of Ananda, Buddha's personal assistant, he eventually agreed, but added that the decision to admit nuns into the order would shorten the period of "true dharma" by 500 years. It seems clear from the passage, however, that this is not due to any inherent inferiority on the part of women, since Buddha asserts that women are capable of following the spiritual path and attaining the fruits of meditative training. Some commentators speculate that the reason for his refusal may have been that his early followers were homeless wanderers, and so there were no adequate facilities for separating men and women. Because of the pervasiveness and strength of sexual desire, groups of men and women in close proximity inevitably develop attractions and tensions, which lead to conflict. Whatever the reasons for his initial reluctance, Buddha did eventually ordain women, but he added the condition that nuns must observe eight additional rules.

> Then Mahapajapati Gotami approached the Lord and, having paid obeisance to him, stood to one side. And Mahapajapati Gotami said this to the Lord:
> "Lord, it would be good if women could be initiated into the order, in the doctrine and discipline taught by the Tathagata."
> [Buddha replied:] "Gotami, do not request the initiation of women into the order. . . ."

She made her request two more times, but after being refused she despondently concluded that Buddha would not allow the ordination of women.

> Then Mahapajapati Gotami, having cut off her hair, putting on saffron robes, went to Vesali . . . and when she arrived, her feet were swollen, her body covered with dust, tears covered her face, as she stood outside the grove [where Buddha was staying].
> When the venerable Ananda saw Mahapajapati Gotami standing there . . . he asked, "Gotami, why are you standing there, your feet swollen, your body covered with dust, and crying?"
> "Venerable Ananda, it is because the Lord does not allow women to be initiated into the order, in the doctrine and discipline taught by the Tathagata."

On hearing this, Ananda offered to intercede on her behalf and approached the Buddha, asking why he had refused her.

> Then the venerable Ananda approached the Lord and, having paid obeisance to him, stood to one side. . . . And he said this to the Lord:
> "Lord, Mahapajapati Gotami is standing outside the grove, her feet swollen, her body covered with dust, tears on her face, and crying, and she says that the Lord will not allow women to be initiated into the order,

in the doctrine and discipline taught by the Tathagata. Lord, it would be good if women were to be initiated into the order. . . ."

"Ananda, do not request the initiation of women into the order, in the doctrine and discipline taught by the Tathagata."

Then the venerable Ananda thought, "The Lord does not allow the initiation of women into the order . . . but perhaps I can ask in another way. . . ." Then the venerable Ananda said to the Lord: "Lord, are women who have been initiated into the order, in the doctrine and discipline taught by the Tathagata, able to attain the fruit of a stream-enterer, or the fruit of a once-returner, or the fruit of a non-returner, or arhathood?"

"Ananda, women who have been initiated into the order . . . are able to attain the fruit of a stream-enterer, or the fruit of a once-returner, or the fruit of a non-returner, or arhathood."

"So, Lord, women who have been initiated into the order are able to attain [these fruits], and Mahapajapati Gotami was very helpful to the Lord: she was the Lord's aunt, foster mother, and nurse, she suckled him when his mother died [and he should repay her kindness]."

[Hearing this, Buddha said:] "Ananda, if Mahapajapati Gotami accepts eight cardinal rules she may receive initiation into the order. . . ." Then Ananda . . . went to Mahapajapati Gotami and said, "Gotami, if you will accept eight cardinal rules, you may receive initiation into the order. . . ." [She replied:] "Honored Ananda, I accept these eight cardinal rules and will never transgress them during my entire life."

Ananda then informed Buddha that Mahapajapati had accepted these rules, to which he replied:

"Ananda, if women had not been given the opportunity to receive initiation into the order, in the doctrine and discipline taught by the Tathagata, then, Ananda, the monastic system would have lasted longer, and the true doctrine would have endured for one thousand years. But, Ananda, since women may now receive ordination . . . the monastic system will only endure for five hundred years."

Source: *Vinaya-pitaka, Cullavagga,* ch. 10, from the *Rules of Discipline for Nuns* (*Bhiksuni Vinaya*): tr. John Strong, *The Experience of Buddhism* (Belmont, CA: Wadsworth, 1995), pp. 52–56.

THE CESSATION OF SUFFERING

After the Buddha agreed to create an order of nuns, a number of women took monastic vows, and some were eventually recognized as advanced meditators. The verses below were written by the nun Patacara after she became an arhati (a female arhat). Her early biography is recounted in the Songs of the Nuns (Therigatha), *and it graphically illustrates the problems of cyclic existence. Her entire family is killed one by one under tragic circumstances, and she is driven to the brink of madness. In a state of utter despair, she meets the Buddha, who counsels her and allows her to become a nun.*

After years of meditative practice, she severs all attachments to worldly things, recognizing them as a source of suffering.

> Ploughing their fields, sowing seeds in the ground,
> Men care for their wives and children and prosper.
> Why is it that I, endowed with morality and adhering to the teachings,
> Do not attain nirvana? I am neither lazy nor conceited.
> After washing my feet, I observed the water; watching the water flow downwards,
> I focused my mind as one [trains] a noble thoroughbred horse.
> Then I took a lamp and entered my cell. After observing the bed, I sat on the couch.
> Holding a pin, I pulled out the wick.
> The lamp goes out: nirvana. My mind is free!

Source: *Therigatha*, psalm 47.

MY TEACHER

The Songs of the Nuns *collection contains a wealth of information on the religious lives of the early Buddhist nuns. Their biographies describe their struggles and tribulations, and many indicate that they saw monastic ordination as a way to escape the drudgery of household work and loveless marriages. The following passage was written by an anonymous nun who celebrates her liberation from sorrow, and it praises her teacher, a fellow nun who showed her the path.*

> Four or five times I went from my cell
> Without having attained peace of mind or control over my mind.
> I approached a nun whom I could trust, and she taught me about the doctrine,
> The aggregates, the sense spheres, and the elements.
> Having listened to her doctrinal instructions, I sat cross legged for seven days,
> Possessed of joy and bliss.
> On the eighth day I stretched out my feet,
> Having eliminated the mass of darkness (of ignorance).

Source: *Therigatha*, psalm 38.

THE JOY OF RELEASE

The following poem was written by the mother of Sumangala (a monk who became an arhat). She was the wife of a poor umbrella maker who left her home and became a nun. Later she attained the level of arhathood, which she celebrates in these verses.

> Free, I am free!
> I am completely free from my kitchen pestle!
> [I am free from] my worthless husband and even his sun umbrella!
> And my pot that smells like a water snake!
> I have eliminated all desire and hatred,

Going to the base of a tree, [I think,] 'What happiness!'
And contemplate this happiness.

Source: *Therigatha*, psalm 22.

THE BUDDHA'S LAST DAYS
AND FINAL INSTRUCTIONS

*After a long and successful teaching career, Buddha's body had become old and
wracked with constant pain. Realizing that his mission had been accomplished,
Buddha decided to enter final nirvana* (parinirvana). *He first asked his disciples if
they had any final questions, and then told them that they should rely on the teachings
they had already received. Buddha further informed them that he had told them everything of the path and the true doctrine that could be put into words, holding nothing
back, and so it was now up to them to put these teachings into practice.*

[Buddha:] 'Ananda, I have taught the doctrine without distinguishing
"inner" and "outer." As to this, the Tathagata is not a "closed-fisted
teacher" with reference to the doctrine [i.e., he does not hold anything
back]. If anyone thinks, "I should watch over the order," or "The order
should refer to me," then let him promulgate something about the order.
The Tathagata does not think in such terms. Thus the Tathagata does not
promulgate something about the order. . . .

Ananda, I am now aged, old, an elder, my time has gone, I have
arrived at the age of eighty years. Just as an old cart is made to go by tying
it together with straps, so the Tathagata's body is made to go by strapping
it together. Ananda, during periods when the Tathagata, by withdrawing
his attention from all signs, by the cessation of some emotions, enters into
the signless concentration of thought and stays in it, on such occasions the
Tathagata's body is made comfortable.

'Therefore, Ananda . . . you should live with yourselves as islands,
with yourselves as refuges, with no one else as refuge; with the doctrine as
an island, with the doctrine as a refuge, with no one else as refuge. . . .

'It might be that you will think, Ananda, "The Teacher's word has
ceased, now we have no teacher!" You should not perceive things in this
way. The doctrine and discipline that I have taught and described will be
the teacher after I pass away.'

*He then told Ananda that after his death it would be permissible for monks to
abolish the minor rules of monastic discipline, but Ananda neglected to ask him which
these were. Buddha again exhorted his followers to rely on the teachings he had
already taught them, and Ananda informed him that none of the monks present had
any doubts about the doctrine, the path, or monastic discipline. Buddha then delivered
his final teaching to his disciples:*

'Monks, all compounded things are subject to decay and disintegration. Work out your own salvations with diligence.' These were the Tathagata's last words.

Source: *Digha-nikaya, Mahaparinibbana-sutta.*

THE QUESTIONS OF KING MILINDA

According to Buddhist tradition, the Bactrian king Menander (Pali: Milinda) engaged the Buddhist sage Nagasena in a series of philosophical discussions in which Nagasena convinced him of the truth of Buddha's teachings. The following dialogue concerns the Buddhist doctrine of selflessness, which holds that there is no enduring self, no soul, no truly existent personal identity. The king at first expresses disbelief, pointing out that he is clearly speaking to Nagasena, who seems to be a concretely existing person. Nagasena convinces the king by using the analogy of a chariot, which is composed of parts that separately are incapable of performing the functions of a chariot, but which when assembled are given the conventional designation "chariot." Similarly, human beings (and all other phenomena) are merely collections of parts that are given conventional designations, but they lack any enduring entity.

Then King Milinda said to the venerable Nagasena: 'What is your reverence called? What is your name, reverend sir?'

'Sire, I am known as Nagasena; my fellow religious practitioners, sir, address me as Nagasena. But although [my] parents gave [me] the name of Nagasena . . . still it is only a designation, a name, a denotation, a conventional expression, since Nagasena is only a name because there is no person here to be found. . . .'

'If, reverend Nagasena, there is no person to be found, who is it that gives you necessities like robe material, food, lodging, and medicines for the sick, who is it that uses them, who is it that keeps the precepts, practices meditation, actualizes the paths, the fruits, nirvana; who kills living beings, takes what is not given, commits immoral acts, tells lies, drinks intoxicants, and commits the five types of immediate karmas? In that case, there is no virtue; there is no non-virtue; there is no one who does or who makes another do things that are virtuous or non-virtuous; there is no fruit or ripening of good or bad karma. Reverend Nagasena, if someone kills you, there will be no demerit. Also, reverend Nagasena, you have no teacher, no preceptor, no ordination. . . .

'Is form Nagasena?'

'No, sire.'

'Is feeling Nagasena?'

'No, sire.'

'Is discrimination Nagasena?'

'No, sire.'

'Are compositional factors Nagasena?'

'No, sire.'

'Is consciousness Nagasena?'

'No, sire.'

'Then, reverend sir, are form, feelings, discriminations, compositional factors, and consciousness together Nagasena?'

'No, sire.'

'Then, reverend sir, is there something other than form, feelings, discriminations, compositional factors, and consciousness that is Nagasena?'

'No, sire.'

'Reverend sir, although I question you closely, I fail to find any Nagasena. Nagasena is only a sound, sir. Who is Nagasena? Reverend sir, you are speaking a lie, a falsehood: there is no Nagasena.'

Then the venerable Nagasena said to king Milinda: '. . . Your majesty, did you come here on foot, or riding?'

'Reverend sir, I did not come on foot; I came in a chariot.'

'Sire, if you came in a chariot, show me the chariot. Is the pole the chariot, sire?'

'No, reverend sir.'

'Is the axle the chariot?'

'No, reverend sir.'

'Are the wheels . . . the frame . . . the banner-staff . . . the yoke . . . the reins . . . the goad the chariot?'

'No, reverend sir.'

'Then, sire, are pole, axle, wheels, frame, banner-staff, yoke, reins, goad together the chariot?'

'No, reverend sir.'

'Then, sire, is something other than the pole, axle, wheels, frame, banner-staff, yoke, reins, goad together the chariot?'

'No, reverend sir.'

'Sire, although I question you closely, I fail to find any chariot. Chariot is only a sound, sire. What is the chariot? . . .'

'Reverend Nagasena . . . it is because of the pole, axle, wheels, frame, banner-staff, yoke, reins, and goad that "chariot" exists as a designation, appellation, denotation, as a conventional usage, as a name.'

'Good: sire, you understand the chariot. It is just like this for me, sire: because of the hair of the head and because of the hair of the body . . . and because of the brain of the head, form, feelings, discriminations, compositional factors, and consciousness that "Nagasena" exists as designation, appellation, denotation, as a conventional usage, as a name. But ultimately there is no person to be found here. . . .'

'Wonderful, reverend Nagasena! Marvelous, reverend Nagasena! The replies to the questions that were asked are truly brilliant. If the Buddha were still here, he would applaud. Well done, well done, Nagasena!'

Source: *Milinda-panho*, 2.25–28.

MAHAYANA SCRIPTURES

THE *HEART OF PERFECT WISDOM SUTRA*

The passage below is the entire text of the Heart of Perfect Wisdom Sutra, *one of the shortest texts of the Perfection of Wisdom corpus. It is said by Mahayanists to contain the essence of the teachings of this voluminous literature.*

Thus have I heard: At one time the Exalted One was dwelling on the Vulture Peak in Rajagriha together with a great assembly of monks and a great assembly of bodhisattvas. At that time, the Exalted One was immersed in a meditative absorption (*samadhi*) on the enumerations of phenomena called "perception of the profound." Also at that time, the bodhisattva, the great being, the superior Avalokiteshvara was considering the meaning of the profound perfection of wisdom, and he saw that the five aggregates (*skandha*) are empty of inherent existence. Then, due to the inspiration of the Buddha, the venerable Shariputra spoke thus to the bodhisattva, the great being, the superior Avalokiteshvara: 'How should a son of good lineage train if he wants to practice the profound perfection of wisdom?'

The bodhisattva, the great being, the superior Avalokiteshvara spoke thus to the venerable Shariputra: 'Shariputra, sons of good lineage or daughters of good lineage who want to practice the profound perfection of wisdom should perceive [reality] in this way: They should correctly perceive the five aggregates also as empty of inherent existence. Form is emptiness; emptiness is form. Emptiness is not other than form; form is not other than emptiness. In the same way, feelings, discriminations, compositional factors, and consciousness are empty. Shariputra, in that way, all phenomena are empty, without characteristics, unproduced, unceasing, undefiled, not undefiled, not decreasing, not increasing. Therefore, Shariputra, in emptiness there is no form, no feelings, no discriminations, no compositional factors, no consciousness, no eye, no ear, no nose, no tongue, no body, no mind, no form, no sound, no odor, no taste, no object of touch, no phenomenon. There is no eye constituent, no mental constituent, up to and including no mental consciousness constituent. There is no ignorance, no extinction of ignorance, up to and including no aging and death and no extinction of aging and death. In the same way, there is no suffering, no source [of suffering], no cessation [of suffering], no path, no exalted wisdom, no attainment, and also no non-attainment.

'Therefore, Shariputra, because bodhisattvas have no attainment, they depend on and abide in the perfection of wisdom. Because their minds are unobstructed, they are without fear. Having completely passed beyond all error, they go to the fulfillment of nirvana. All the buddhas who live in the three times [past, present, and future] have been completely awakened into unsurpassable, complete, perfect awakening through relying on the perfection of wisdom.

'Therefore, the *mantra* of the perfection of wisdom is the *mantra* of great knowledge, the unsurpassable *mantra,* the *mantra* that is equal to the unequaled, the *mantra* that thoroughly pacifies all suffering. Because it is not false, it should be known to be true. The *mantra* of the perfection wisdom is as follows:

Om gate gate paragate parasamgate bodhir svaha [*Om* gone, gone, gone beyond, gone completely beyond; praise to awakening.]

'Shariputra, bodhisattvas, great beings, should train in the profound perfection of wisdom in that way.'

Then the Exalted One arose from that meditative absorption and said to the bodhisattva, the great being, the superior Avalokiteshvara: 'Well done! Well done, well done, son of good lineage, it is just so. Son of good lineage, it is like that; the profound perfection of wisdom should be practiced just as you have indicated. Even the Tathagatas admire this.' When the Exalted One had spoken thus, the venerable Shariputra, the bodhisattva, the great being, the superior Avalokiteshvara, and all those around them, and those of the world, the gods, humans, demigods, and *gandharvas* were filled with admiration and praised the words of the Exalted One.

Source: *Prajnaparamita-hridaya-sutra.*

EXCERPTS FROM THE *DIAMOND SUTRA*

Perfection of Wisdom texts contain many warnings against holding too rigidly to doctrines, even Buddhist doctrines. In the following passage, Buddha warns his disciple Subhuti against conceiving sentient beings as truly existing, and then applies the reasoning of emptiness to other Buddhist categories.

[Buddha:] 'Subhuti, due to being established in the bodhisattva vehicle, one should give rise to the thought, "As many sentient beings there are that are included among the realms of sentient beings . . . whatever realms of sentient beings can be conceived, all these should be brought by me to nirvana, to a final nirvana that is a realm of nirvana without remainder; but, although countless sentient beings have reached final nirvana, no sentient being whatsoever has reached final nirvana." Why is this? Subhuti, if a discrimination of a sentient being arises in a bodhisattva [literally, "awakening-being"], he should not be called an awakening-being. Why is this? Subhuti, one who gives rise to the discrimination of such a self, the discrimination of a sentient being, the discrimination of a soul, or the discrimination of a person should not be called a bodhisattva. . . .

'Subhuti, all of them produce and acquire an immeasurable and incalculable store of merit. Why is this? Subhuti, it is because these bodhisattvas, great beings, do not give rise to the discrimination of a self, the discrimination of a sentient being, the discrimination of a soul, or the discrimination of a person. Also, Subhuti, these bodhisattvas, great beings, do not give rise to discriminations of phenomena, nor do they give rise to discriminations of non-phenomena, nor do they give rise to discrimination or to non-discrimination. Why is this? Subhuti, if these bodhisattvas, great beings, gave rise to discriminations of phenomena, this would be grasping a self, grasping a sentient being, grasping a soul, grasping a person. If they gave rise to discriminations of non-phenomena, this also would be grasping a self, grasping a sentient being, grasping a soul, grasping a person. Why is this? Subhuti, in no way should a bodhisattva, a great being, grasp either phenomena nor non-phenomena. Therefore, this has been said by the Tathagata with hidden intent: "For those who understand the teaching of *dharma* that is like a raft, *dharma* should be abandoned, and still more non-*dharma.*"'

Source: *Vajracchedika-prajnaparamita-sutra* selections.

WHY BODHISATTVAS
ARE SUPERIOR TO HEARERS

Some early Mahayana texts have a distinctly sectarian tone, particularly when they compare the ideals of the arhat and the bodhisattva. In the following passage from the 8,000 Line Perfection of Wisdom Sutra, *Buddha describes to Subhuti the differences between the attitudes of Hinayanists and Mahayanists.*

[Buddha:] 'Subhuti, bodhisattvas, great beings, should not train in the way that persons of the hearer vehicle and solitary realizer vehicle train. Subhuti, in what way do persons of the hearer vehicle and the solitary realizer vehicle train? Subhuti, they think thus, "[I] should discipline only myself; [I] should pacify only myself; [I] should attain nirvana by myself." In order to discipline only themselves and pacify themselves and attain nirvana, they begin to apply themselves to establishing all the virtuous roots. Also, Subhuti, bodhisattvas, great beings, should not train in this way. On the contrary, Subhuti, bodhisattvas, great beings, should train thus, "In order to benefit all the world, I will dwell in suchness; and, establishing all sentient beings in suchness, I will lead the immeasurable realms of sentient beings to nirvana." Bodhisattvas, great beings, should begin applying themselves in that way to establishing all virtuous roots, but should not be conceited because of this. . . .

'Those who say, "In this very life, having thoroughly freed the mind from contamination, without attachment, [I] will pass beyond sorrow" are "at the level of hearers and solitary realizers." With respect to this, bodhisattvas, great beings, should not give rise to such thoughts. Why is this? Subhuti, bodhisattvas, great beings, abide in the great vehicle and put on the great armor; they should not give rise to thoughts of even a little elaboration. Why is this? These supreme beings thoroughly lead the world and are a great benefit to the world. Therefore, they should always and uninterruptedly train well in the six perfections.'

Source: *Ashtasahasrika-prajnaparamita-sutra* (*'Phags pa shes rab kyi pha rol tu phyin pa brgyad stong pa'i mdo*), ch. 11]

ON THE DIFFERENCES
BETWEEN MEN AND WOMEN

The dialogue below applies the doctrine of emptiness to the commonly accepted differences between men and women. When these are closely examined, they are found to be merely the results of misguided conceptuality, since there is no inherently existent difference between the sexes.

The dialogue occurs in the house of Vimalakirti, a lay bodhisattva who is pretending to be sick in order to initiate a discourse on the dharma. The Buddha's disciples follow Manjushri—an advanced bodhisattva who is said to embody wisdom—to Vimalakirti's house in order to hear the two discuss the perfection of wisdom.

The interchange is so profound that a young goddess who lives in Vimalakirti's house rains down flowers on the assembly. The Hinayana monks who are present try frantically to brush them off, because monks are forbidden in the Vinaya to wear flowers or adornments. The bodhisattvas in the audience, however, are unaffected by such rigid adherence to rules, and so the flowers fall from their robes.

This causes Shariputra—described in Pali texts as the most advanced of Buddha's Hinayana disciples in the development of wisdom—to marvel at the attainments of the goddess and the bodhisattvas. She chides him for viewing the fruits of meditative training as things to be acquired, and in response Shariputra asks her why she does not change from a woman into a man. The question appears to be based on traditional Indian perceptions of authority, according to which wisdom is associated with elder males. The goddess violates these principles, because she is young and female. But it is clear from the dialogue that she is very advanced in understanding the perfection of wisdom.

The goddess responds to Shariputra's challenge by turning him into a woman and herself into a man. This leads to one of the most poignant scenes in the sutra, in which Shariputra experiences discomfort in his new body, apparently because of the Vinaya injunctions preventing monks from physical contact with women. Shariputra, now in a woman's body, is unable to avoid such contact, and tells the goddess that he is a woman without being a woman. The goddess replies that all women are women without being women, because "woman" is merely a conventional designation with no ultimate referent.

A goddess who lived in the house of Vimalakirti, having heard the doctrinal teaching of the bodhisattvas, the great beings, was very pleased, delighted, and moved. She took on a material form and scattered heavenly flowers over the great bodhisattvas and great hearers. When she had thrown them, the flowers that landed on the bodies of the bodhisattvas fell to the ground, while those that fell on the bodies of the great hearers remained stuck to them and did not fall to the ground. Then the great hearers tried to use their supernatural powers to shake off the flowers, but the flowers did not fall off. Then the goddess asked the venerable Shariputra: 'Venerable Shariputra, why do you try to shake off the flowers?'

'Goddess, flowers are not fitting for monks; that is why we reject them.'

'Venerable Shariputra, do not speak thus. Why? These flowers are perfectly fitting. Why? The flowers are flowers and are free from conceptuality; it is only yourselves, the elders, who conceptualize them and create conceptuality toward them. Venerable Shariputra, among those who have renounced the world to take up monastic discipline, such conceptualizations and conceptuality are not fitting; it is those who do not conceive either conceptualizations nor conceptuality who are fit.

'Venerable Shariputra, take a good look at these bodhisattvas, great beings: the flowers do not stick to them because they have abandoned conceptuality. . . . Flowers stick to those who have not yet abandoned the defilements; they do not stick to those who have abandoned them. . . .'

'Well done! Well done, Goddess! What have you attained, what have you gained that enables you to have such eloquence?'

'It is because I have not attained anything nor gained anything that I have such eloquence. Those who think that they have attained or gained something are deluded with respect to the well-taught disciplinary doctrine. . . .'

'Goddess, why do you not change your womanhood?'

'During the twelve years [that I have lived in this house], I have looked for womanhood, but have never found it. Venerable Shariputra, if a skillful magician created an illusory woman through transformation, could you ask her why she does not change her womanhood?'

'Every illusory creation is unreal.'

'In the same way, venerable Shariputra, all phenomena are unreal and have an illusory nature; why would you think of asking them to change their womanhood?'

Then the goddess performed a supernatural feat that caused the elder Shariputra to appear in every way like the goddess and she herself to appear in every way like the elder Shariputra. Then the goddess who had changed into Shariputra asked Shariputra who had been changed into a goddess: 'Why do you not change your womanhood, venerable sir?'

[Shariputra:] 'I do not know either how I lost my male form nor how I acquired a female body.'

[Goddess:] 'Elder, if you were able to change your female form, then all women could change their womanhood. Elder, just as you appear to be a woman, so also all women appear in the form of women, but they appear in the form of women without being women. It was with this hidden thought that the Exalted One said: "Phenomena are neither male nor female."'

Then the goddess cut off her supernatural power and the venerable Shariputra regained his previous form. Then the goddess said to Shariputra: 'Venerable Shariputra, where is your female form now?'

[Shariputra:] 'My female form is neither made nor changed.'

[Goddess:] 'Well done! Well done, venerable sir! In the same way, all phenomena, just as they are, are neither made nor changed. Saying that they are neither made nor changed is the word of the Buddha. . . .'

[Shariputra:] 'Goddess, how long will it be before you reach awakening?'

[Goddess:] 'Elder, when you yourself return to being a worldly person, with all the qualities of a worldly person, then I myself will reach unsurpassed, perfect awakening.'

[Shariputra:] 'Goddess, it is impossible that I could return to being a worldly person, with all the qualities of a worldly person; it cannot occur.'

[Goddess:] 'Venerable Shariputra, in the same way, it is impossible that I will ever attain unsurpassed, perfect awakening; it cannot occur. Why? Because unsurpassed, perfect awakening is founded on a non-foundation. Thus, since there is no foundation, who could reach unsurpassed, perfect awakening?'

[Shariputra:] 'But the Tathagata has said: "Tathagatas as innumerable as the sands of the Ganges river attain, have attained, and will attain unsurpassed, perfect awakening."'

[Goddess:] 'Venerable Shariputra, the words, "buddhas past, future, and present" are conventional expressions made up of syllables and numbers. Buddhas are neither past, nor future, nor present, and their awakening transcends the three divisions of time. Tell me, elder, have you already attained the level of arhat?'

[Shariputra:] 'I have attained it because there is nothing to attain.'

[Goddess:] It is the same with awakening: it is attained because there is nothing to attain.

Source: *Vimalakirti-nirdesha-sutra* (*'Phags pa dri ma med par grags pas bstan pa'i mdo*), ch. 6.

THE *LOTUS SUTRA:*
PARABLE OF THE BURNING HOUSE

The parable of the burning house is a famous allegory for the practice of "skillful means" (upaya-kaushalya), *which is one of the important abilities of bodhisattvas and buddhas. It involves adapting the dharma to the interests and proclivities of individual listeners, telling them things that will attract them to the practice of Buddhism. The question posed in the dialogue concerns whether such tactics should be considered underhanded or dishonest. The answer, not surprisingly, is no: The means used are for the good of the beings, and benefit them greatly in the long run. Moreover, with beings who are thoroughly enmeshed in the concerns of the world it is necessary to draw their attention away from mundane pleasures toward the dharma, which can lead to lasting happiness.*

[Buddha:] "Shariputra, let us suppose that in a village somewhere . . . there was a householder who was . . . very wealthy. Suppose that he owned a great mansion, lofty, spacious, built long ago, inhabited by hundreds of living beings. The house had one door and was covered with thatch, its terraces were collapsing, the bases of its pillars were rotting, and the plaster and coverings of the walls were falling apart. Now suppose that all of a sudden the whole house burst into flames and that the householder managed to get himself out, but that his little boys [were still inside]. . . ."

[He thought:] "I was able to get out of the burning house through the door safely, without being touched by the flames, but my children remain in the house, playing with their toys, enjoying themselves. They do not realize . . . that the house is on fire, and so are not afraid. Even though they are caught up in the fire and are being scorched by flames, though they are actually suffering, they are unaware of it, and so they do not think to come out. . . ."

"So he called to the boys: 'Come, my children, the house is burning with a mass of flames! Come out, so that you will not be burned in the inferno and come to disaster!'

"But the ignorant boys paid no attention to the man's words, even though he only wished for their well-being. . . . They did not care, and did not run from the house, did not understand, and did not comprehend even the meaning of the word 'inferno.' Instead, they continued to run and play here and there, occasionally looking at their father. Why? Because they were ignorant children.

"So then, Shariputra, the man thought: . . . 'I should use a skillful method to cause the children to come out of the house.' The man knew the mental dispositions of his children and clearly understood their interests. He knew of the kinds of toys they liked. . . . So he said to them: 'Children, all the toys that you like . . . such as little ox carts, goat carts, and deer carts, which are pleasing and captivating to you, have all been put outside by me, so that you can play with them. Come, run out of the house! I will give each of you what you want! Come quickly! Come and get these toys!

"Then the boys, hearing him mentioning the names of the toys they liked . . . quickly ran from the burning house, not waiting for each other, and calling, 'Who will be first? Who will be foremost?'

"Then the man, seeing that his children had come out of the house safely, knowing that they were out of danger . . . gave his children . . . ox carts only. They were made of seven precious metals, and had railings, were hung with strings of bells, were high and lofty, adorned with wonderful and precious jewels, illuminated by garlands of gems, decorated with wreaths of flowers. . . .

"Now what do you think, Shariputra, did that man lie to his children by first promising them three vehicles and then later giving them only great vehicles, the best vehicles?"

Shariputra said: "No indeed, Lord! Not at all! There is no reason to think that in this case the man was a liar, because he was using skillful means in order to cause his children to come out of the burning house, and because of this he gave them the gift of life. Moreover, Lord, in addition to keeping their lives, they also received those toys. But, Lord, even if the man had not given them a single cart, he would still not have been a liar. Why is this? Because, Lord, that man first thought, 'By using skillful means, I will liberate those children from a great mass of suffering. . . . '"

"Well said, Shariputra, well said! You have spoken well! In the same way, the Tathagata also . . . is the father of the world, who has attained the supreme perfection of understanding of great skillful means, who is greatly compassionate, who has a mind that is unwearied, who is concerned for the well-being of others. He appears in this triple world, which is like a burning house blazing with the whole mass of suffering and despair . . . in order to liberate from desire, aversion, and obscuration those beings who remain trapped in the mists of ignorance, in order to liberate them from the blindness of ignorance, birth, old age, death, sorrow, grief, suffering, sadness, and dissatisfaction, in order to awaken them to supreme, perfect awakening. . . . In this triple world, which is like a burning house, they enjoy themselves and run here and there. Even though they are afflicted by a great deal of suffering, they do not even think that they are suffering. . . .

"Therefore, Shariputra, the Tathagata, who is just like that strong-armed man who . . . employed skillful means to coax his children from the burning house . . . speaks of three vehicles: the hearers' vehicle, the solitary realizers' vehicle, and the bodhisattvas' vehicle. . . .

"So the Tathagata is not a liar when he uses skillful means, first holding out the prospect of three vehicles and then leading beings to final nirvana by means of a single great vehicle."

Source: *Saddharma-pundarika-sutra*, ch. 3; tr. John Strong, *The Experience of Buddhism*, pp. 135–137.

EVERYTHING IS
CONTROLLED BY THE MIND

The passage below comes from the Cloud of Jewels Sutra. *It indicates that all phenomena are productions of mind and that everything is created by mind. Ordinary beings allow the mind to wander at will, thus enmeshing them in confused and harmful thoughts, but bodhisattvas are advised to train the mind in order to bring it under control.*

All phenomena originate in the mind, and when the mind is fully known all phenomena are fully known. For by the mind the world is led . . . and through the mind karma is piled up, whether good or bad. The mind swings like a firebrand, the mind rears up like a wave, the mind burns like a forest fire, like a great flood the mind carries all things away. Bodhisattvas, thoroughly examining the nature of things, remain in ever-present mindfulness of the activity of the mind, and so do not fall into the mind's power, but the mind comes under their control. And with the mind under their control, all phenomena are under their control.

Source: *Ratnamegha-sutra,* from the *Shiksha-samuchchaya,* ch. 6.

THE BASIS CONSCIOUSNESS

The passage below from the Sutra Explaining the Thought *is one of the earliest descriptions of the "basis consciousness"* (alaya-vijnana), *a doctrine that was central to the Indian Yogacara school and that was also influential in other Mahayana countries, particularly Tibet and China. The basis consciousness is the most fundamental level of mind, and it is said to be comprised of the "seeds" of past actions and mental states.*

The seeds become part of the continuum of the basis consciousness, which is moved along by their force. If one cultivates positive actions and thoughts, for example, one's mind will become habituated to positive actions and thoughts. The converse is true of those who engage in negative actions and thoughts.

Under appropriate conditions, the seeds give rise to corresponding thoughts and emotions, and these are the phenomena of ordinary experience. Mind and its objects are said to arise together, and so there is no substantial difference between subject and object. Because of this, phenomena are said to be "cognition-only" (vijnaptimatra), *meaning that all we ever perceive are mental impressions, and not things in themselves.*

[Buddha:] 'Initially in dependence upon two types of appropriation—the appropriation of the physical sense powers associated with a support and the appropriation of predispositions which proliferate conventional designations with respect to signs, names, and concepts—the mind which has all seeds ripens; it develops, increases, and expands in its operations. . . .

'Consciousness is also called the "appropriating consciousness" because it holds and appropriates the body in that way. It is called the "basis consciousness" because there is the same establishment and abiding within those bodies. . . . It is called "mind" because it collects and accumulates forms, sounds, smells, tastes, and tangible objects.

Source: *Samdhinirmochana-sutra,* ch. 5.

NAGARJUNA ON EMPTINESS

Nagarjuna, founder of the Madhyamaka school of Indian Mahayana, emphasized the centrality of the doctrine of emptiness in his philosophy. In the following verses he indicates that concepts are empty because language is simply an interconnected system of terms that do not capture actual things. They simply relate to other words.

One who fully recognizes this fact becomes freed from the snares of language and attains correct realization, an important part of the path to liberation.

1. Through the force of worldly conventions, buddhas
    Have spoken of duration, arising, disintegration, existence, non-existence,
    Inferior, middling, and superior,
    But they have not spoken [of these] in an ultimate sense.
2. Self, non-self, and self-non-self do not exist,
    And so conventional expressions do not [really] signify.
    Like nirvana, all expressible things are empty of inherent existence.
3. Since all things completely lack inherent existence—either in causes or
    conditions, [in their] totality, or separately—they are empty.
4. Because it exists, being does not arise;
    Because it does not exist, non-being does not arise.
5. Because they are discordant phenomena, being and non-being
    [together] do not arise.
    Thus they neither endure nor cease. . . .
7. Without one, many does not exist; without many, one is not possible.
    Thus, dependently arisen things are indeterminable. . . .
56. In dependence upon the internal and external sense spheres (*ayatana*)
    Consciousness arises.
    Thus, just like mirages and illusions, consciousness is empty.
57. In dependence upon an apprehendable object, consciousness arises.
    Thus, the observable does not exist [in itself].
    [The subject of consciousness] does not exist without the apprehend-
    able and consciousness.
    Thus, the subject of consciousness does not exist [by itself]. . . .
65. Due to correctly perceiving that things are empty, one becomes
    non-deluded.
    Ignorance ceases, and thus the twelve limbs [of dependent arising]
    cease. . . .
67. Nothing exists inherently, nor is there non-being there.
    Arising from causes and conditions, being and non-being are empty.
68. All things are empty of inherent existence,
    And so the incomparable Tathagata teaches dependent arising with
    respect to things. . . .
72. One with faith who seeks the truth, who considers this principle with
    reason,
    Relying on the dharma that is free of supports, is liberated from exis-
    tence and non-existence [and abides in] peace.
73. When one understands that "this is a result of that," the net of wrong
    views is eradicated.
    Due to abandoning attachment, obscuration, and hatred, undefiled,
    one attains nirvana.

Source: Nagarjuna, *Shunyata-saptati,* tr. Christian Lindtner, in *Master of Wisdom: Writings of the Buddhist Master Nagarjuna* (Berkeley: Dharma Publishing, 1986), pp. 95–119.

THE BODHISATTVA'S
VOWS OF UNIVERSAL LOVE

The following verses, written by Shantideva, are among the most eloquent expressions in Mahayana literature of the ideal mind-set of bodhisattvas, who should dedicate all of their energies to helping other beings in every possible way.

16. May those who malign me, or harm me, or accuse me falsely, and others all be recipients of awakening.
17. May I be a protector of the helpless, a guide for those on the path, a boat, a bridge, a way for those who wish to cross over.
18. May I be a lamp for those who need a lamp, a bed for those who seek a bed, and a slave for those who desire a slave.
19. May I become a wish-fulfilling jewel, an inexhaustible jar, a powerful mantra, a cure for all sickness, a wish-fulfilling tree, and a cow of plenty for all creatures.
20. As earth and the other elements are enjoyed in various ways by innumerable beings living throughout space,
    So may I be the sustenance for various kinds of beings in all the realms of space for as long as all are not satisfied.

Source: Santideva, *Bodhicaryavatara, "Bodhicitta-parigraha"* tr. Marion Matics, *Entering the Path of Enlightenment* (London: Macmillan, 1970), pp. 154–155.

TANTRIC SKILL IN MEANS

Tantric texts claim that the system of tantra skillfully uses aspects of reality that cause bondage for people who are enmeshed in mundane conceptuality—things like desire and other negative emotions. The following excerpt from the Hevajra Tantra *indicates that these may serve as aids to the path of liberation if the proper means are used.*

Those things by which evil men are bound, others turn into means and gain thereby release from the bonds of existence. By passion the world is bound, by passion too it is released, but by heretical Buddhists this practice of reversals is not known.

Source: *Hevajra-tantra* I.ix.2–3, tr. David Snellgrove, *Indo-Tibetan Buddhism* (Boston: Shambhala, 1987), vol. I, pp. 125–126.

THE STAGE OF COMPLETION

The tantric practice of deity yoga involves first creating a vivid image of a buddha in front of one, and then visualizing the buddha as merging with oneself. One views oneself as a buddha—with the body, speech, and mind of a buddha—and as performing the activities of an awakened being. The first procedure is called the "generation stage," and the second, which is described in the following passage from the Guhyasamaja Tantra, *is termed the "completion stage." In order to avoid becoming attached to the visualization, one should be aware that both the buddha and oneself are empty of inherent existence. Thus at the end of the session, one dissolves both oneself and the buddha into emptiness.*

> Everything from the crown of the head to the feet dissolves into the heart; you engage in the perfect yoga (meditation on emptiness). . . . All sentient beings and all other phenomena dissolve into clear light and then dissolve into you; then you yourself, as the deity, dissolve into your heart. . . . Just as mist on a mirror fades toward the center and disappears, so does everything—the net of illusory manifestation—dissolve into the clear light of emptiness. Just as fish are easily seen in clear water, so does everything—the net of illusory manifestation—emerge from the clear light of emptiness.

Source: *Guhyasamaja-tantra;* quoted in Khenpo Könchog Gyaltsen *The Garland of Mahamudra Practices* (Ithaca: Snow Lion, 1986), pp. 56–57.

WOMEN SHOULD BE HONORED

One of the notable features of the tantric movement is an emphasis on the spiritual capacities of women. Classical Indian literature indicates that exetreme misogyny was prevalent in the society, which makes this aspect of tantra even more significant. An example of the emphasis on the equality of women is the fact that one of the basic vows required of all tantric practitioners is a pledge not to denigrate women, "who are the bearers of wisdom." The following passage from the Chandamaharoshana Tantra *expresses a similar sentiment in its praises of women.*

> When women are honored,
> They provide instant accomplishments (*siddhi*)
> To those who wish for the welfare of all beings.
> Thus one should honor women.
> Women are heaven, women are dharma,
> Women are also the supreme asceticism (*tapas*).
> Women are Buddha, women are the sangha;
> Women are the perfection of wisdom.

Source: *Candamaharosana-tantra,* 8.27–30.

SAMSARA AND NIRVANA ARE ONE

The following excerpts from the Hevajra Tantra *discuss the tantric idea that there is no fundamental difference between cyclic existence and nirvana. Buddhas perceive them as undifferentiable, but ordinary beings, because of their delusions, think in terms of dichotomies, and so imagine that the path and goal are separate.*

Then the essence is declared, pure and consisting in knowledge, where
there is not the slightest difference between cyclic existence and
nirvana.
Nothing is mentally produced in the highest bliss, and no one
produces it,
There is no bodily form, neither object nor subject,
Neither flesh nor blood, neither dung nor urine,
No sickness, no delusion, no purification,
No passion, no wrath, no delusion, no envy,
No malignity, no conceit of self, no visible object,
Nothing mentally produced and no producer,
No friend is there, no enemy,
Calm is the Innate and undifferentiated. . . .
The Enlightened One is neither existence nor non-existence; he has a form
with arms and faces and yet in highest bliss is formless.
So the whole world is the Innate, for the Innate is its essence.
Its essence too is nirvana when the mind is in a purified state.

Source: *Hevajra-tantra*, ch. I.x.32–34, II.ii.43–44, tr. David Snellgrove, *The Hevajra Tantra: A Critical Study* (London: Oxford University Press, 1959), vol. I, p. 92.

USING DESIRE TO ERADICATE DESIRE

Tantric adepts claim that the fact that tantra uses emotions like desire as means in the path is an example of the skillful practices of the system. The following passage from Viryavajra's Commentary on the Samputa Tantra *contends that there are four levels of the use of desire: visualizing a man and woman looking at each other; laughing with each other; holding hands; and sexual union. Each of these represents a progressively higher level of desire. One should engage in these practices, however, in order to utilize the energy of desire as a force that can be used to eradicate mental afflictions. The skillful use of desire is said in some texts to be like rubbing two sticks together to make a fire, which then consumes the sticks themselves. In this case, the process is compared to the way that insects are born in wood, and then later consume the wood.*

Within the sound of laughter non-conceptual bliss is generated; or it is generated from looking at the body, the touch of holding hands and the embrace of the two; or from the touch [of union] . . . just as an insect is generated from the wood and then eats the wood itself, so meditative stabilization is generated from bliss [in dependence on desire] and is culti-vated as emptiness [whereupon desire is consumed].

Source: Viryavajra's *Commentary on the Samputa Tantra;* quoted in *Sngags rim chen mo*, II.7.

THE STATE OF PURE AWARENESS

The following passage from the Hevajra Tantra *describes the state of mind of one who has transcended all discursive and dichotomizing thought through direct, intuitive awareness of the boundless clarity of mind.*

From self-experiencing comes this knowledge, which is free from ideas of self and other; like the sky it is pure and void, the essence supreme of non-existence and existence, a mingling of wisdom and method, a mingling of passion and absence of passion. It is the life of living things, it is the Unchanging One Supreme; it is all-pervading, abiding in all embodied things. It is the stuff the world is made of, and in it existence and non-existence have their origin. It is all other things that there are. . . . It is the essential nature of all existing things and illusory in its forms.

Source: *Hevajra-tantra* I.x.8–12, tr. David L. Snellgrove, *The Hevajra Tantra*, p. 81.

THE IMPORTANCE OF THE GURU

The special techniques of tantra are said to be very powerful, but they can also be dangerous. Thus tantric texts warn meditators to find qualified spiritual guides (guru) who can help them to avoid possible pitfalls. One of the central practices of tantra is "guru yoga," in which one visualizes one's guru as a fully awakened buddha. One who does this successfully is said to move quickly toward actualization of buddhahood. In the following passage the tantric master Tilopa teaches that finding a qualified guru is a prerequisite for successful tantric practice.

The ignorant may know that sesame oil—the essence—exists in the sesame seed, but because they do not know how, they cannot extract the oil. So also does the innate fundamental wisdom abide in the heart of all migrators; but unless it is pointed out by the guru, it cannot be realized. By pounding the seeds and clearing away the husks, one can extract the essence—the sesame oil. Similarly, when it is shown by the guru, the meaning of suchness is so illuminated that one can enter into it.

Source: Tilopa, quoted in *The Garland of Mahamudra Practices*, p. 58.

TIBETAN BUDDHIST SCRIPTURES

ULTIMATE REALITY

The "great completion" (dzogchen) tradition of Tibetan Buddhism is practiced by all of the four main schools—Nyingma, Kagyu, Sakya, and Geluk—but most closely associated with the Nyingma. In this system all phenomena are said to be creations of mind that, like mind, are a union of luminosity and emptiness. In the following passage, meditators are instructed on the nature of ultimate reality, in which phenomena spontaneously appear to the mind although they have no real substance.

Since [things exist] only in the manner of mirages, dreams, and delusions, you should abandon [false appearances] and adopt [virtuous practices], work for the sake [of others], avoid [non-virtue] and practice [virtue]. Wash away the afflictions of desire, anger, and obscuration with the waters of their antidotes: [meditation on] repulsiveness, love, and dependent arising. Because ultimate reality is non-arisen and pure, it is free from elaborations (*spros pa, prapanca*) such as the duality of samsara and nirvana. . . . All phenomena merely appear naturally to your own mind on the mandala that is the sphere of the foundation, the buddha nature. They are falsities, not really things, empty, and only appear as forms, as the aggregates, realms, spheres, and so forth. . . . The unsurpassed, supreme, secret great completion directly actualizes the sphere of the spontaneously existent. This foundational sphere is unchanging, like space. [All good] qualities [reside] in it spontaneously, as the sun, moon, planets, and stars [reside] in the sky. There is no need to seek it, since it has existed since beginningless time. No work or effort [is necessary,] as this path is naturally manifest.

Source: Longchen Rapjampa, *Chos bzhi rin po che'i phreng ba* (*Four Themed Precious Garland*).

BARDO, THE STATE BETWEEN LIVES

The following excerpts are drawn from a Tibetan classic on death and dying entitled Liberation through Hearing in the Intermediate State, *attributed to Padmasambhava. According to the tradition, it was hidden by Padmasambhava and rediscovered by the "treasure finder" Karma Lingpa in the fourteenth century. The book describes the "intermediate state" (bardo; translated here as "the between") that all beings are said to enter after death.*

During the process of dying, the physiological changes that occur are accompanied by mental changes in which the coarser levels of mind drop away, revealing progressively more subtle aspects of consciousness. At the moment of death, the most subtle level of mind dawns. This is called the "mind of clear light," and compared to it all other minds are adventitious.

At this point one enters the intermediate state and experiences strange and terrifying sights. These are all said to be aspects of one's own mind, and they include visions of mild and terrifying beings, deafening sounds, and other intense sense experiences. The intermediate state is a time of great opportunity, however, and if one is able to maintain awareness and focus on the clear light nature of mind and perceive all experiences as merely aspects of mind, one may become a buddha, or at least attain rebirth in the pure land of a buddha. In such places the conditions are optimal for beings who seek buddhahood. If one is unable to maintain mindfulness, one will be reborn in accordance with one's accumulated karma.

> Hey! Now when the life between dawns upon me,
> I will abandon laziness, as life has no more time,
> Unwavering, enter the path of learning, thinking, and meditating,
> And taking perceptions and mind as a path,
> I will realize the Three Bodies of enlightenment! . . .

Conscious of dreaming, I will enjoy the changes as clear light.
Not sleeping mindlessly like an animal,
I will cherish the practice merging sleep and realization! . . .
Now when the death-point between dawns upon me,
I will give up the preoccupations of the all-desiring mind,
Enter unwavering the experience of the clarity of the precepts,
And transmigrate into the birthless space of inner awareness;
About to lose this created body of flesh and blood,
I will realize it to be impermanent illusion! . . .
I will . . . enter into the recognition of all objects as my mind's own visions,
And understand this as the pattern of perception in the between;
Come to this moment, arrived at this most critical cessation,
I will not fear my own visions of deities mild and fierce! . . .
Now courage and positive perception are essential.

Source: *Bardo thos grol* from *Bar do thos grol: The Tibetan Book of the Dead: Liberation through Understanding in the Between,* tr. Robert A. F. Thurman (New York: Bantam, 1994), pp. 115–116.

MILAREPA ON MEDITATION

Milarepa, one of the most influential figures in Tibetan Buddhism, was born into a fairly well-to-do family, but his greedy aunt and uncle took everything away from him, his mother, and sister. Overcome by rage, his mother coerced Milarepa into learning black magic and sending a curse on the aunt and uncle, with the result that a number of people died, but not the primary objects of his revenge.

Milarepa, terrified of the consequences of his evil deeds, searched for a spiritual guide (lama) who could help him escape the consequences of his actions. He eventually found Marpa, who gave Milarepa a series of difficult and dispiriting tasks, which cleansed his negative karma. After this Milarepa spent many years living in a cave and practicing solitary meditation, which culminated in his attainment of awakening. He is considered in Tibet to be the supreme example of the attainment of buddhahood in one lifetime through tantric practice.

Look up into the sky, and practice meditation free from the fringe and center.
Look up at the sun and moon, and practice meditation free from bright and dim.
Look over the mountains, and practice meditation free from departing and changing.
Look down at the lake, and practice meditation free from waves.
Look here at your mind, and practice meditation free from discursive thought.

Source: *Rje btsun mi la ras pa'i rnam thar,* (*Religious Biography of the Master Milarepa*), pp. 49bff.

NIGUMA ON MAHAMUDRA

Niguma is said by Tibetan tradition to have been the founder of the Shangpa lineage of the Kagyu tradition. In the following passage she describes the view of mahamudra *(literally, "great seal"), which is said by the Kagyu school to be the supreme form of*

Buddhist practice. In mahamudra, one dispenses with the visualizations and rituals of tantra and focuses on the natural state of mind, which is said to be a union of clear light and emptiness. All phenomena are viewed as the spontaneous play of mind, and by cultivating this awareness it is said that the meditator moves quickly toward the attainment of buddhahood.

Do nothing at all with the mind;
Abide in a non-artificial and natural state.
Your own unwavering mind is the truth body (*dharma-kaya*).
The important thing for meditation is an unwavering mind.
You should realize the great [reality] that is free from extremes.
The afflictions, desires, aversions, and conceptualizations
That arise like bubbles on the ocean of cyclic existence
Should be cut off with the sharp sword of non-production
That is not different from the nature of things.
When you cut off the trunk and roots,
The branches will not grow.
Just as in the clear ocean
Waves pop up and sink into the water,
So conceptualizations are not really different from reality.
So don't look for faults, remain at ease.
Whatever arises, whatever materializes,
Don't hold on to it, but immediately let it go.
Appearances, sounds, and phenomena are one's own mind;
There are no other phenomena apart from mind.
Mind is free from the elaborations of arising and cessation.
The nature of mind, awareness,
Enjoys the five qualities of the Desire Realm, but
Does not wander from reality. . . .
In the great realm of reality (*dharma-dhatu*)
There is nothing to abandon or adopt,
No meditative equipoise or post-meditation period.

Source: Niguma, *Rang grol phyag rgya chen po* (*Individual Liberation of the Great Seal*).

INSTRUCTIONS FROM MANJUSHRI

The following verses, according to the Sakya tradition of Tibetan Buddhism, were spoken to Günga Nyingpo (1092–1158). They are a summary of the entire Buddhist path, including the renunciation of the world, the development of compassion, and the importance of avoiding extreme views.

If you cling to this life, then you are not a dharma practitioner.
If you cling to existence, then you do not have renunciation.
If you are attached to your own interests, then you do not have the mind of awakening.
If you hold to [a position], then you do not have the correct view.

Source: Drakpa Gyeltsen, *Zhen pa bzhi bral* (*Parting from the Four Attachments*).

THE TRIPLE APPEARANCE

The Sakya school teaches that there are three main levels of awareness, which are summarized in the following stanzas from Virupa's Vajra Verses. *The first verse refers to the perceptions of ordinary beings, which are colored by ignorance and mental affliction. The second verse describes the perceptions of people on the path, who have some experience with meditation and thus have overcome some of their mental afflictions. The final verse indicates that buddhas perceive the world unafflicted by ignorance, hatred, desire, etc., and so are at the level of the "pure appearance." The Sakya tradition stresses that although they appear to be incompatible, the three appearances are fundamentally non-different.*

> For sentient beings with the afflictions is the impure appearance.
> For the meditator with transic absorption is the appearance of experience.
> For the ornamental wheel of the Sugata's [Buddha's] inexhaustible awakened body, voice and mind is the pure appearance.

Source: *Rdo rje tshigs rkang, (Vajra Verses)* ch. 1, quoted in Ngorchen Konchog Lhundrub, *The Beautiful Ornament of the Three Visions* (Ithaca: Snow Lion, 1991), p. xvi.

DEVELOPING THE MIND OF AWAKENING

Ordinary beings are consumed by self-centered desires and think primarily of their own narrow interests. Bodhisattvas spend countless eons working toward buddhahood for the benefit of all beings, cheerfully accepting all the tribulations that occur along the path. Given the vast gulf between the attitudes of bodhisattvas and ordinary beings, it is difficult for people enmeshed in mundane concerns to imagine making the transition to true altruism.

The following passage by Tsong Khapa (the founder of the Gelukpa school of Tibetan Buddhism) outlines a seven-step program for developing the "mind of awakening," which marks the beginning of the bodhisattva path. It begins by recognizing that because one has been reborn in an infinite variety of situations since beginningless time, one has been in every possible relationship with every other sentient being. Thus, every sentient being has been one's mother, and has been a nurturing and caring friend.

One should reflect on the kindness of one's own mother, and then think that every other being has been equally kind. One then resolves to repay this kindness, and generates a feeling of love toward others, wishing that they have happiness and the causes of happiness. One then develops compassion for sentient beings, since they are experiencing suffering as a result of contaminated actions and afflictions.

In the next stage one attains the "unusual attitude," which involves vowing to work to free all beings from suffering and establish them in buddhahood. The final step is attainment of the mind of awakening, which is a resolve to do whatever is necessary to attain buddhahood in order to help all sentient beings.

From one's own viewpoint, since one has cycled beginninglessly, there are no sentient beings who have not been one's friends hundreds of times. Therefore, one should think, 'Whom should I value?' 'Whom should I hate?' . . .

Imagine your mother very clearly in front of you. Consider several times how she has been your mother numberless times, not only now, but from beginningless cyclic existence. When she was your mother, she protected you from all danger and brought about your benefit and happiness. In particular, in this life she held you for a long time in her womb. Once you were born, while you still had new hair, she held you to the warmth of her flesh and rocked you on the tips of her ten fingers.

She nursed you at her breast . . . and wiped away your filth with her hand. In various ways she nourished you tirelessly. When you were hungry and thirsty, she gave you drink, and when you were cold, clothes, and when poor, money. She gave you those things that were precious to her. Moreover, she did not find these easily. . . . When you suffered with a fever she would rather have died herself than have her child die; and if her child became sick, from the depths of her heart she would rather have suffered herself than have her child suffer. . . .

Source: *Lam rim chen mo*, (*Great Exposition of the Stages of the Path*), pp. 572.5, 575.1.

CHINESE AND JAPANESE BUDDHIST SCRIPTURES

WHY BUDDHISM IS SUPERIOR TO DAOISM AND CONFUCIANISM

The following passage, by Jizang (549–623), is an example of the sectarian debates between Buddhists and Daoists in China. Drawn from the Profound Meaning of the Three Treatises, *it compares the teachings of Buddhism to those of Laozi and Zhuangzi.*

Shi Sengzhao (374–414) says, 'Every time I read Laozi and Zhuangzi, it causes me to lament and say: 'It is beautiful, but as for the technique of abiding with the spirit, of quieting the mental ties [that bind us to life and death], they have not yet mastered [them]. . . .'

Kumarajiva long ago heard that the three mysteries, together with the nine teachings of Buddhism, were both definitive. Laozi, together with Shakyamuni [Buddha], were [held to be] comparable in actions. So [Kumarajiva] lamented thus, and lamenting said, 'Lao[zi] and Zhuang[zi] have entered the profound. Therefore, they certainly do lead astray the ears and eyes.' This is the wisdom of the ordinary person. These are reckless words [claiming that Buddhism and Daoism are comparable]. In saying this, it appears to be the ultimate, and still has not yet begun to approach it. . . .

Non-Buddhists are not yet able to consider the ultimate, and still wander among the myriad things. Buddhist teachings, without moving away from absolute truth, teach, still establishing the various phenomena. Non-Buddhists reside in the teachings of gain and loss. Buddhists vanquish the two extremes in the principle of negation. Non-Buddhists have not yet extinguished both the knower and known. Buddhists have extinguished both subject and object.

If we take these [two, Buddhists and non-Buddhists], and further examine them in detail, it is like comparing a small bird's wings to the wings of a *peng* bird, or comparing a well to the ocean. [These metaphors] are not yet sufficient to explain their difference. Kumarajiva doubted the final teachings [of the Daoists]. What more can I say?

Source: Jizang, *Sanlun Xuanyi* (*The Profound Meaning of the Three Treatises*) ch. 1.

THE *PLATFORM SUTRA* OF THE SIXTH PATRIARCH

The Chan (Japanese: Zen) school developed in China. Asserting that the teachings of the school were a "special transmission outside of the scriptures," Zen masters claimed that their tradition represents the authentic teaching of the Buddha, who is said to have passed on the essence of his awakened mind to his disciple Mahakashyapa. He in turn passed it on to his main disciple, and so it continued in India through an unbroken chain of transmission until Bodhidharma, the last Indian "patriarch," traveled to China.

Bodhidharma, a semilegendary figure, is said to have arrived at the Shaolin monastery in China, where he sat in silent meditation in front of a wall for several years. At the end of this period, he began teaching the tradition to Chinese disciples, one of whom became the first Chinese patriarch.

The following passage was spoken by Hui Neng, the sixth patriarch, to a group of disciples. It contains many of the important doctrines of the developed Chan tradition, including the doctrine of "sudden awakening," which holds that buddhas become awakened in a flash of insight, and not gradually, as traditional Indian Buddhism taught. According to Indian Buddhist meditation texts, meditators should enter into concentrated meditative states called samadhi, *and these states lead to the awakening of wisdom* (prajna). *Hui Neng, however, declared that such ideas impose a false dualism onto the path to buddhahood. He contended that both concentration and wisdom are present in every moment of thought and that they cannot legitimately be separated.*

He also opposed the goal-oriented practices of traditional Mahayana, and said that one becomes awakened by eliminating discursive thought. When all conceptual thoughts drop away and one attains the state of "no-thought" (wu nian), *the mind flows freely and unimpededly, in harmony with the rhythms of the world. This is the state of mind characteristic of buddhahood, and any notions of "path" and "goal," or "cultivation" and "attainment," are products of dualistic thinking that will impede one's progress toward awakening.*

The Master Hui Neng called, saying: 'Good friends, awakening (*bodhi*) and intuitive wisdom (*prajna*) are from the outset possessed by men of this world themselves. It is just because the mind is deluded that men cannot attain awakening to themselves. They must seek a good teacher to show them how to see into their own natures. Good friends, if you meet awakening, [Buddha]-wisdom will be achieved.

13. 'Good friends, my teaching of the dharma takes meditation (*ding*) and wisdom (*hui*) as its basis. Never under any circumstances say mistakenly that meditation and wisdom are different; they are a unity, not two things. Meditation itself is the substance of wisdom; wisdom itself is the function of meditation. At the very moment when there is wisdom, then meditation exists in wisdom; at the very moment when there is meditation, then wisdom exists in meditation. Good friends, this means that meditation and wisdom are alike. Students, be careful not to say that meditation gives rise to wisdom, or that wisdom gives rise to meditation, or that meditation and wisdom are different from each other. . . .

16. 'Good friends, in the Dharma there is no sudden or gradual, but among people some are keen and others dull. The deluded recommend the gradual method, the awakened practice the sudden teaching. To understand the original mind of yourself is to see into your own original nature. Once awakened, there is from the outset no distinction between these two methods; those who are not awakened will for long *kalpas* [eons] be caught in the cycle of transmigration.

17. 'Good friends, in this teaching of mine, from ancient times up to the present, all have set up no-thought as the main doctrine, non-form as the substance, and non-abiding as the basis. Non-form is to be separated from form even when associated with form. No-thought is not to think even when involved in thought. Non-abiding is the original nature of humanity.

'Successive thoughts do not stop; prior thoughts, present thoughts, and future thoughts follow one after the other without cessation. If one instant of thought is cut off, the Dharma body separates from the physical body, and in the midst of successive thoughts there will be no place for attachment to anything. If one instant of thought clings, then successive thoughts cling; this is known as being fettered. If in all things successive thoughts do not cling, then you are unfettered. Therefore, non-abiding is made the basis.

Source: Hui Neng, *Platform Sutra* 12–16, tr. Philip Yampolsky, *The Platform Sutra of the Sixth Patriarch* (New York: Columbia University Press, 1967), pp. 135–138.

KUKAI: EXOTERIC AND ESOTERIC BUDDHISM

Kukai (774–835), posthumously known as Kobo Daishi, was one of the most influential thinkers of the Heian period (794–1185). He traveled to China in 804 to study Buddhism, and learned the doctrines and practices of Esoteric Buddhism (Chinese: Zhenyan; Japanese: Shingon) with the Chinese master Hui Guo. This school is a branch of Vajrayana ("Vajra Vehicle"), which is based on the tantras of Indian Buddhism.

Like its counterparts in South Asia, East Asian Esoteric Buddhism emphasizes the importance of visualizations, mantras, and rituals for bringing about a cognitive transformation of one's mind into the mind of a buddha.

In the following passage, Kukai compares the path of Esoteric Buddhism to that of Exoteric Buddhism. He contends that Esoteric Buddhism is far superior to the Exoteric teachings and practices and that it is more effective in bringing about mundane benefits as well as final awakening. Kukai believed that human beings have the capacity to become "awakened in this very body" (sokushin jobutsu) and that the rituals and symbols of Esoteric Buddhism appeal directly to their basic nature of buddha-potential and enable them quickly to attain the state of buddhahood. These practices bring the body, speech, and mind of the meditator into concordance with those of the truth body, and thus allow the primordial buddha Mahavairocana to communicate directly with advanced practitioners.

I have heard that there are two kinds of preaching of the Buddha. One is shallow and incomplete while the other is esoteric. The shallow teaching is comprised of the scriptures with long passages and verses, whereas the esoteric teaching is the *dharani* [esoteric prayers thought to have magical properties] found in the scriptures.

The shallow teaching is, as one text says, like the diagnoses of an illness and the prescription of a medicine. The esoteric method of reciting *dharani* is like prescribing appropriate medicine, ingesting it, and curing the ailment. If a person is ill, opening a medical text and reciting its contents will be of no avail in treating the illness. It is necessary to adapt the medicine to the disease and to ingest it in accordance with proper methods. Only then will the illness be eliminated and life preserved.

However, the present custom of chanting the *Sutra of Golden Light* at the Imperial Palace is simply the reading of sentences and the empty recital of doctrine. There is no drawing of buddha images in accordance with proper technique nor the practice of setting up an altar for offerings and for the ceremonies of empowerment. Although the reading of the *Sutra* may appear to be an opportunity to listen to the preaching of the nectar-like teachings of the Buddha, in actuality it lacks the precious taste of the finest essence of Buddhist truth.

I humbly request that from this year on, fourteen monks skilled in esoteric ritual and fourteen novices be selected who, while properly reading the *Sutra*, will for seven days arrange the sacred images, perform the requisite offerings, and recite *mantra* in a specially adorned room. If this is done, both the exoteric and esoteric teachings, which express the Buddha's true intent, will cause great happiness in the world and thereby fulfill the compassionate vows of the holy ones.

Source: Kukai, *Petition to Supplement the Annual Reading of Sutra in the Imperial Palace;* tr. David Gardiner.

DOGEN'S MEDITATION INSTRUCTIONS

Dogen (1200–1253), founder of the Soto *(Chinese: Zaodong) school of Zen, traveled to China in 1223 and studied with Rujing, a Chinese Chan master. One day during meditation practice, another monk fell asleep, and Rujing woke him up, admonishing* him to practice meditation diligently in order to "drop off body and mind" (Japanese: shinjin datsuraku), an idea that became a cornerstone of Dogen's system of meditative practice. The following passage contains instructions on meditation practice (zazen), which in Dogen's system is based on the experience of "not thinking" (hishiryo).

In the state of not thinking, a meditator moves beyond discursive and dichotomizing thought (shiryo), transcends the tendency to stop ordinary thought by suppressing it (fushiryo), and thus enters into a spontaneous awareness of reality in which thoughts flow along of their own accord. In this state of spontaneous mindfulness, the meditator experiences his or her own "buddha nature," an inherent propensity toward awakening that is shared by all beings.

Once you have settled your posture, you should regulate your breathing. Whenever a thought occurs, be aware of it; as soon as you are aware of it, it will vanish. If you remain for a long period forgetful of objects, you will naturally become unified. This is the essential art of *zazen*. Zazen is the dharma gate of great ease and joy. . . .

Having thus regulated body and mind, take a breath and exhale fully. Sitting fixedly, think of not thinking. How do you think of not thinking? Nonthinking. This is the art of *zazen*. Zazen is not the practice of *dhyana* [meditation]. It is the dharma gate of great ease and joy. It is undefiled practice and verification.

Source: Dogen, *Shobogenzo* selections, from *Dogen's Manual of Zen Meditation,* tr. Carl Bielefeldt (Berkeley: University of California Press, 1988), p. 181.

THE MU KOAN

The Rinzai (Chinese: Linji) school of Zen is renowned for its use of koan, riddles that cannot be answered by rational or discursive modes of thought. The following passage contains the koan that is generally given to beginning students, referred to as the "Mu koan." It reports that a monk asked the Zen master Joshu if a dog has the buddha nature, to which Joshu answered, "Mu!" Mu may be translated as "not," but in the koan Joshu's answer is not a denial, but rather an indication that the question makes no sense from the point of view of awakening.

The dilemma behind the question is based on traditional Japanese Buddhist ideas about the path. It is widely accepted in Japanese Buddhism that all beings—including dogs—have the buddha nature, an inherent potential for buddhahood. Thus, from the point of view of tradition, Joshu's answer should be "Yes." But since Zen claims to transcend blind adherence to tradition, this would be an unacceptable answer. On the other hand, if Joshu were to state that dogs do not have the buddha nature, he could be accused of contravening Buddhist doctrine and setting himself above the buddhas.

Thus Joshu's answer is an invitation to move beyond tradition and conceptualization to a direct perception of truth. The Zen tradition refers to this koan as the "closed opening" or the "gateless barrier," because once a meditator perceives the meaning behind Joshu's statement, this marks the first dawning of realization that will eventually culminate in full awakening, referred to in Zen as "satori." It is intended to cause *a cognitive crisis as the meditator attempts to solve the riddle by means of conceptual thought, but finds all such attempts utterly frustrated. This leads to the development of the "great doubt" (daigi), which is said to burn inside of one like a red-hot ball of iron. When the koan is solved, however, the pain and frustration disappear, and are replaced by a serene, nonconceptual awareness.*

A monk once asked Master Joshu, 'Has a dog the Buddha Nature or not?' Joshu said, 'Mu!'

Mumon's commentary: In studying Zen, one must pass the barriers set up by ancient Zen Masters. For the attainment of incomparable satori, one has to cast away his discriminating mind. Those who have not passed the barrier and have not cast away the discriminating mind are all phantoms haunting trees and plants.

Now Tell me, what is the barrier of the Zen Masters? Just this 'Mu'—it is the barrier of Zen. It is thus called 'the gateless barrier of Zen.' Those who have passed the barrier will not only see Joshu clearly, but will go hand in hand with all the Masters of the past, see them face to face. . . . Wouldn't it be wonderful? Don't you want to pass the barrier? Then concentrate yourself into this 'Mu,' with your 360 bones and 84,000 pores, making your whole body one great inquiry. Day and night work intently at it. Do not attempt nihilistic or dualistic interpretations. It is like having swallowed a red hot iron ball. You try to vomit it but cannot. . . .

You kill the Buddha if you meet him; you kill the ancient Masters if you meet them. On the brink of life and death you are utterly free, and in the six realms and the four modes of life you live, with great joy, a genuine life in complete freedom.

Source: From *Zen Comments on the Mumonkan,* tr. Zenkei Shibayama (New York: Mentor, 1974), pp. 19–20.

PURE LAND: SHINRAN ON AMIDA'S VOW

The Pure Land (Chinese: Jingdu; *Japanese:* Jodo) *tradition focuses on a buddha named Amitabha ("Limitless Light") or Amitayus ("Limitless Life"), who as a merchant named Dharmakara is said to have made a series of vows concerning the sort of "buddha-land" he would create after his attainment of buddhahood. In the* Sutra on the Array of the Joyous Land (Sukhavativyuha-sutra), *Dharmakara indicates that his land will be especially wonderful, a place in which the conditions for buddhahood are optimal. Beings fortunate enough to be born into this land will receive teachings from buddhas and bodhisattvas, and they will quickly progress toward awakening.*

Amitabha also teaches that beings may be reborn in his land if they have sincere faith in him. The Japanese Pure Land teacher Shinran (1173–1262) stated that anyone may be reborn in Amitabha's paradise, regardless of past actions. Previous teachers had contended that birth in Sukhavati required good moral character and constant repetition of the formula, "Praise to Amida Buddha" (Namu Amida Butsu), but Shinran declared that all that is necessary is one moment of sincere belief (shinjin, literally "believing mind"). Shinran makes a distinction between "self-power," which characterizes the practices of early Buddhism, and "other-power," in which one relies completely on the saving power of Amitabha. Shinran contends that the former practice was appropriate in the Buddha's day, but that the present age is one of degeneration, and human beings have become so depraved that their only hope is to rely on Amitabha. The Tannisho *was written by a direct disciple of Shinran, probably Yuien (d. 1290) in the decades after Shinran's death, and it remains a respected record of Shinran's teachings.*

When our hearts are moved to invoke the name of Amida, believing that we can achieve rebirth in His Pure Land through the workings of the wondrous power of His vow—at that very moment we are saved by Amitabha Buddha, and we become recipients of the benefits that He bestows without exception upon all living beings. Amida's primal vow [to save all living beings by enabling them to be reborn in his Pure Land] does not discriminate between young and old, or between doers of good or evil. All that is necessary is for us to put our faith in His vow. This is because Amida's vow was made with the intention to save all living beings, caught up as they are in their evil deeds and worldly desires. For this reason, putting our faith in Amida's primal vow does not require us to perform any other good deeds, because there can be no greater merit than that which is attained by calling on Amida's name. Neither should we fear doing evil: there is no act so evil as to be able to obstruct the workings of Amida's vow. . . .

Even a good person can be reborn in the Pure Land. How much easier it is for an evil person to achieve this! Contrary to this fact, lay people generally say: "Even an evil person can achieve rebirth in the Pure Land. It goes without saying that it is much easier for a good person." While at first glance there may seem to be some reason for this view, it goes against the purpose of Amida's vow, which is based on the saving power of reliance on the Other. Why is this? Those who practice good deeds, relying on their own power, are not of a mind to wholeheartedly avail themselves of the Other Power of Amida, and are therefore not acting in accord with His vow. If, however, they let go of their reliance on their own power, and place their trust in the Other Power of Amida, they will be able to achieve rebirth in the Pure Land.

Source: Shinran, *Tannisho* selections, from *Tannisho: A Primer,* tr. Dennis Hirota (Kyoto, Ryukoku University, 1982), pp. 22–24.

TRUTH DECAY: NICHIREN ON THE TITLE OF THE *LOTUS SUTRA*

Nichiren (1222–1282) was one of the most charismatic figures of Japanese Buddhism. Initially trained in the Tendai school, he became disenchanted with its doctrines and practices, considering them to be inappropriate to the current age, which he believed to be the "age of degenerate dharma" (Japanese: mappo) *that the Buddha had predicted would begin 1,500 years after his death. Many Japanese Buddhists of the Kamakura period (1185–1333) believed that the turmoils of the time indicated that the final age of dharma had arrived, and a number of teachers believed that in such a time new models and practices were required.*

Since in the final age people become progressively more degenerate, Nichiren contended that the practices of the past—including intensive meditation practice and adherence to monastic vows—were no longer possible for most people, and thus simpler and more effective practices, appropriate to mappo, were required. Nichiren focused on the Lotus Sutra (Saddharma-pundarika-sutra) *as the only viable teaching for mappo, and he counseled his followers to place all of their faith in it. Its teachings, however, were deemed too profound for most people to understand, and so Nichiren developed the practice of chanting the title of the sutra (Namu Myohorengekyo in Japanese) and trusting to the saving power of the sutra to bring worldly benefits and final salvation.*

> Question: If someone did not know the real meaning of the *Lotus Sutra* and did not understand its import, but merely recited the words 'Namu Myohorengekyo' once a day or once a month or once a year or once in ten years or once in a lifetime, without being tempted by evil deeds, great or small, would that person not only avoid the four evil realms but also achieve that stage from which there is no return?
>
> Answer: He would. . . .
>
> The words 'Myohorengekyo' . . . include all the beings of the nine worlds and of the Buddha world. Since they include the ten worlds, they include all the conditions one may be born into in the ten worlds. If the words 'Myohorengekyo' include all dharmas, one word of the scripture is lord of all scriptures. It embodies all scriptures.

Source: Nichiren, *Hokke Damokushii* selections, from *Hokke Damokushii*, tr. Lauren Rodel, in *Nichiren: Selected Writings* (Honolulu: University of Hawaii Press, 1980), pp. 82, 85.

GLOSSARY

Anatman   "Selflessness," the doctrine that there is no permanent, partless, substantial essence or soul.

Arhat   The ideal of "Hinayana" Buddhism, who strives to attain a personal nirvana.

Avidya   "Ignorance," the primary factor that enmeshes living beings in the cycle of birth, death, and rebirth.

Bodhisattva   A compassionate being who resolves to bring other beings to liberation.

Buddha   "Awakened One," epithet of those who successfully break the hold of ignorance, liberate themselves from cyclic existence, and teach others the path to liberation.

Chan/Zen   A school that developed in East Asia, which emphasized meditation aimed at a non-conceptual, direct understanding of reality.

Completion Stage   *(nishpanna-krama)* Tantric practice in which one visualizes oneself as being transformed into a buddha.

Deity Yoga *(devata-yoga)* The tantric practice of visualizing oneself as a buddha.

Dependent Arising *(pratitya-samutpada)* Doctrine that phenomena arise and pass away in dependence upon causes and conditions.

Dharma Buddhist doctrine and practice.

Duhkha "Suffering," the first "noble truth" of Buddhism, which holds that cyclic existence is characterized by suffering.

Eightfold Noble Path Fourth of the "four noble truths," which involves cultivation of correct views, actions, and meditative practices in order to bring an end to suffering.

Five Aggregates The components of the psycho-physical personality, and the factors on the basis of which unawakened beings impute the false notion of a "self": (1) form; (2) feelings; (3) discriminations; (4) consciousness; (5) compositional factors.

Four Noble Truths Basic propositions attributed to the Buddha: (1) suffering; (2) the cause of suffering; (3) the cessation of suffering; (4) the eightfold noble path.

Generation Stage *(utpanna-krama)* Tantric practice of visualizing a vivid image of a buddha in front of oneself.

Hinayana "Lesser Vehicle," a term coined by Mahayanists to describe their opponents, whose path they characterized as selfish and inferior to their own.

Karma "Actions," which bring about concordant results.

Keyi "Matching Concepts," a translation style adopted for early Chinese versions of Buddhist texts, which involved using indigenous Chinese terms for Sanskrit words.

Madhyamaka "Middle Way School," one of the most influential systems of Indian Buddhism.

Mahayana "Greater Vehicle," the school of Buddhism that emphasizes the ideal of the bodhisattva.

Nirvana Liberation from cyclic existence.

Pure Land A school of Buddhism popular in East Asia whose adherents strive for rebirth in the realm of the Buddha Amitabha.

Samsara "Cyclic Existence," the beginningless cycle of birth, death, and rebirth in which ignorant beings are trapped.

Shakyamuni "Sage of the Shakyas," an epithet of the historical Buddha, whose name at birth was Siddhartha Gautama.

Shunyata "Emptiness," the lack of inherent existence that characterizes all persons and phenomena.

Skill in Means *(upaya-kaushalya)* The ability to adapt Buddhist teachings and practices to the level of understanding of one's audience.

Sutra Discourses attributed to the historical Buddha.

Tantra Discourses attributed to the historical Buddha, which appeared sometime around the seventh century and that advocate practices involving visualizing oneself as a buddha.

Yogacara "Yogic Practice School," a system of Indian Buddhism whose main early exponents were the brothers Asanga and Vasubandhu

Zen See **Chan**

FURTHER READINGS

BECHERT, HEINZ AND GOMBRICH, RICHARD. *The World of Buddhism.* New York: Thames and Hudson, 1984.

BIELFELDT, CARL, tr. *Dogen's Manuals of Zen Meditation.* Berkeley: University of California Press, 1988.

CH'EN, KENNETH. *Buddhism in China: A Historical Survey.* Princeton: Princeton University Press, 1984.

COLLINS, STEVEN. *Selfless Persons: Imagery and Thought in Theravāda Buddhism.* Cambridge: Cambridge University Press, 1982.

DUMOULIN, HEINRICH. *Zen Buddhism: A History,* 2 vols. New York: Macmillan, 1988.

GOMBRICH, RICHARD. *Theravāda Buddhism: A Social History from Ancient Benares to Modern Columbo.* London: Routledge & Kegan Paul, 1988.

GREGORY, PETER N., ed. *Sudden and Gradual: Approaches to Enlightenment in Chinese Thought.* Honolulu: University of Hawaii Press, 1987.

GRIFFITHS, PAUL J. *On Being Mindless: Buddhist Meditation and the Mind-Body Problem.* La Salle, IL: Open Court, 1986.

HUNTINGTON, C.W. *The Emptiness of Emptiness: An Introduction to Early Indian Mādhyamika.* Honolulu: University of Hawaii Press, 1989.

KIYOTA, MINORU, ed. *Mahāyāna Buddhist Meditation.* Honolulu: University of Hawaii Press, 1978.

LAMOTTE, ÉTIENNE. *History of Indian Buddhism.* Sara Webb-Boin, tr. Louvain: Peeters Press, 1988.

MATSUNAGA, DAIGAN AND ALICIA. *Foundation of Japanese Buddhism,* 2 vols. Los Angeles: Buddhist Books International, 1974.

MURCOTT, SUSAN. *The First Buddhist Women: Translations and Commentary on the Therigatha.* Berkeley: Parallax Press, 1991.

NAKAMURA, HAJIME. *Indian Buddhism: A Survey with Bibliographical Notes.* Delhi: Motilal Banarsidass, 1987.

PAUL, DIANA. *Women in Buddhism: Images of the Feminine in Mahāyāna Tradition.* Berkeley: Asian Humanities Press, 1979.

POWERS, JOHN. *Introduction to Tibetan Buddhism.* Ithaca: Snow Lion, 1995.

PREBISH, CHARLES S., ed. *Buddhism: A Modern Perspective.* University Park: The Pennsylvania State University Press, 1975.

RAHULA, WALPOLA. *What the Buddha Taught.* New York: Grove Press, 1959.

ROBINSON, RICHARD. *The Buddhist Religion.* Encino, CA: Dickenson Publishing, 1977.

RUEGG, DAVID S. *The Literature of the Madhyamaka School of Philosophy in India.* Wiesbaden: Otto Harrassowitz, 1981.

SNELLING, JOHN. *The Buddhist Handbook: A Complete Guide to Buddhist Schools, Teaching, Practice, and History.* Rochester, VT: Inner Traditions, 1991.

WILLIAMS, PAUL. *Mahāyāna Buddhism: The Doctrinal Foundations.* London and New York: Routledge, 1989.

WRIGHT, ARTHUR F. *Buddhism in Chinese History.* Stanford: Stanford University Press, 1959.

Sikhism

INTRODUCTION

Early one morning in 1499 Nanak (1469–1539), the founder of the Sikh tradition, went to a river to perform his daily religious ablutions. When he failed to return, search parties were sent out, but all they found were his clothes on the bank of the river. Assuming that the current had carried Nanak away, they returned to town and reported the news. Several days later, however, Nanak reappeared, and after refusing to speak for three days he told his friends and family that he had been taken to the presence of God and given a mission: to teach Hindus and Muslims that both groups in fact worship the same God. God, he said, was distressed by the sectarian violence perpetrated in His name in India and wanted Nanak to call his followers from rigid adherence to dogmas and the performance of empty rituals to the true essence of religion, which is known only by those who move beyond external observances like ceremonies, prayers, pilgrimages, and study to the rich inner life of true spirituality. This is characterized by selfless devotion (*bhakti*) to God.

Nanak summarized God's message with the statement, "There is neither Hindu nor Muslim, so whose path should I follow? I will follow God's path, and God is neither Hindu nor Muslim." These words were the cornerstone of his later speeches and writings, in which he stressed the unity of God and the idea that the differences in how religions characterize Him are merely due to human failure to grasp the divine essence. Nanak further contended that there is no reason for religious groups to fight each other, since any system is necessarily limited, and all theological ideas are inadequate.

After his meeting with God, Sikh texts refer to Nanak as "Guru," a teacher and devotee of God. Throughout his life he worked to reconcile Hindus and Muslims, to teach them that God is everywhere and continually calls His creatures to experience Him directly and intuitively. This cannot be accomplished by those who rely on external religious observances, and God is found only by practitioners of pure devotion who open themselves to the divine call and experience mystical union.

Nanak taught that devotion is the highest form of religious practice, but also the most difficult. The ego is a powerful force in human beings, and it causes us to recoil from the experience of union, in which all sense of individuality is swept away by a transcendent vision of the divine presence.

Nanak belonged to a widespread but unorganized group of mystics known as Sants, whose members stressed the unity of God and criticized both

Hindus and Muslims for being overly concerned with the external aspects of their traditions, while failing to recognize that all theistic religions worship the same ultimate source of all being. The greatest early exponent of this tradition was Kabir, a weaver from Varanasi. He was born into a Muslim family that converted from Hinduism, but his writings indicate that he saw himself as having transcended any sectarian affiliation.

In his poetry he accuses both Muslim and Hindu religious leaders of hypocrisy and of failing to grasp the true essence of religion. Hindu *pandits* (religious scholars) are portrayed as being mainly concerned with profit and position, with empty ceremonies and merely external observances. Muslim clerics, he contends, tend to be caught up in systems and words and so do not understand that God is one and that all religious traditions have their source in the same ultimate reality. This reality is beyond the reach of human thought; it cannot be grasped by words or doctrines, and is only truly understood by those who abandon external religious observances and devote themselves wholeheartedly to meditation and worship.

The poetry of Nanak stresses similar themes. He denounces idol worship and indicates that such practices as pilgrimages, ritual bathing, and ceremonies tend to keep the individual far from God. Nanak, like Kabir, views God as having two aspects: God is both immanent (*saguna*, literally, "having qualities") and transcendent (*nirguna*, "without qualities"). In essence God is completely transcendent, and any qualities imputed to God are merely human attempts to grasp the ultimate reality in terms that we are able to understand. God in essence is completely other, unknowable, and ineffable, but may still be experienced by those who empty themselves of ego and open themselves to the divine presence.

Nanak died in 1539 after founding and guiding a small group of followers he referred to as "Sikhs," or students. His students were both Hindus and Muslims, who saw Nanak as a great religious leader whose mystical experiences transcended their sectarian divisions. According to Sikh legends, he continually worked to help them to overcome their limitations of religious vision.

Nanak's final teaching was given on his deathbed. When it became clear that death was near, a dispute arose between Hindu and Muslim Sikhs. The former group wanted to cremate him in accordance with their traditions, while the latter argued for burying his body. Nanak settled the dispute by telling them that each group should place a garland of flowers on one side of his body, and that the group whose garland remained unwilted after three days would be able to dispose of his corpse in accordance with its traditions. The next morning the shroud was removed, but his body was gone. All that remained were two garlands of unwilted flowers. Thus even in death Nanak taught his followers the importance of overcoming sectarian differences.

Before Nanak died, he designated his disciple Guru Angad (1504–1552) as his successor. According to Sikh tradition, this event marks the inauguration of the Sikh path (*panth*). The office of Guru was in turn passed on to Amar Das (1479–1574), and then to Guru Ram Das (1534–1581). The fifth Guru, Arjan (1563–1606), worked to mold the Sikhs into a cohesive religious, social, and economic community. He initiated construction of the Golden Temple at Amritsar, which is today the holiest shrine of the Sikhs, and he directed the compilation of the *Adi Granth,* the holiest scripture of the tradition. This text contains writings by Nanak and the other early Gurus, as well as works by Kabir and other devotional poets. Today the *Adi Granth* is the center of the religious life of the community. Ornate copies of the text are placed on special pedestals in the center of each Sikh temple (*gurdvar,* literally, "door to the Guru"), and portions of it are chanted almost constantly while the temple is open.

Arjan's tenure marks a change of direction for the Sikh community. During the reigns of the first four Gurus the Panth had enjoyed generally amicable relations with the Muslim Mughal rulers who controlled northern India, but with the ascension of the emperor Jehangir the situation changed. Hearkening back to the militancy of the early Muslim conquerors, Jehangir actively persecuted other religious groups, including the Sikhs. He had Arjan captured, and tortured him with the intention of forcing the Guru to renounce his faith. Arjan refused to submit to the emperor's demands, and he eventually died in prison. Shortly before his death, he advised his son Hargobind (1595–1664) to "sit fully armed upon the throne," since Arjan recognized the threat the new Mughal ruler posed for his community.

Guru Hargobind followed the wishes of his father, Guru Arjan, and began wearing two swords at all times, one symbolizing his religious authority, and the other his temporal authority. His tenure marks the beginning of the transition of the Panth from a group of devotional mystics concerned with reconciling the differences between Hindus and Muslims into a tradition stressing the importance of combat readiness and willingness to fight—and die if necessary—in order to defend the faith.

The seventh Guru, Hari Rai (1630–1661) ruled during a time of increasing tensions between the Sikhs and the Mughal emperor. The eighth, Hari Krishan (1656–1664), died as a child, and was succeeded by Tegh Bahadur (1621–1675), who became another Sikh martyr as a result of his opposition to the emperor's imposition of a tax on all non-Muslims in his empire. Intending to make an example of the Guru, the emperor had him imprisoned and tortured. He was ordered to renounce his faith and his opposition to the tax. When he refused, Tegh Bahadur was executed.

His son Gobind Singh (1666–1708) became the tenth and last Guru. Realizing that the position made its holder a target, as the Guru lay dying from wounds inflicted by a Muslim assassin he declared that henceforth the *Adi Granth* would be the Guru. He told the community to view the text as the condensation of the inspired words of the Gurus, the mouthpieces of God, which should guide them in their religious lives.

Gobind Singh's other major contribution to the development of Sikhism was his institution of the Khalsa, the community of Sikh believers. He recognized that survival of the faith required that Sikhs become fully committed to preparing themselves to defend the community against attacks by its enemies, and in a special ceremony he called on the faithful to step forward if they were truly prepared to die for their religion. Five stepped forward, and they became the first members of the new community. The Guru then instructed his followers to adopt five distinctive marks symbolic of their new commitment, which are referred to as the "Five Ks" because their names in the Punjabi language all begin with the letter K. These are (1) *kesh,* hair, which refers to the Sikh practice of not cutting the hair; (2) *kangha,* a comb used to keep the hair neat; (3) *kirpan,* a short sword, symbolizing the warrior ethos of the Khalsa; (4) *kara,* a steel wristband; and (5) *kachch,* short pants. Many male members of the community also began wearing turbans as a way of managing their hair, and most males also changed their family name to Singh, meaning lion, as a symbol of their devotion to the Guru. Women changed their names to Kaur, meaning princess, and all Sikhs were declared by the Guru to be members of the warrior caste (*kshatriya*), symbolizing both their emphasis on combat readiness and the equality of all believers.

Nanak had established the Panth as a community dedicated to reconciling Hindus and Muslims, but Gobind Singh realized that peaceful relations with the Mughal emperor were no longer possible. In order to maintain its survival, the community would have to defend itself against attacks, and it would have to develop into a cohesive and well-trained military force in order to protect itself from its neighbors. It is ironic that Sikhism began as a movement dedicated to reconciling different faiths but was pushed by historical circumstances to become a tradition that stressed the differences of its members from other religious groups and that was determined to defend itself from hostile opponents.

Sikh Doctrines and Practices

Sikh theology contends that God is one without a second, the transcendent ultimate that cannot be grasped by human intelligence or described by language. God is commonly referred to by such negative terms as Timeless (*akal*) and Unproduced (*ajuni*), but is also described positively as Truth or Being (*sat*). God is both utterly transcendent and accessible to His creatures through grace. God chooses some beings to draw near to Him through devotion, and He speaks to all beings through the words of the Gurus.

Sikhs commonly refer to God as *Akal Purakh,* "Timeless Being." He creates and sustains the universe, and is known only by those who approach Him with devotion. God reveals Himself through the Divine Name (*nam*), which expresses aspects of the divine Reality as understood by the limited intellects of His creatures. All of creation reflects the glory and activity of God, and so in this sense everything is an expression of the Name. People are able to approach God through meditation on the Name, through which they may transcend ordinary understanding and approach the Divine Presence. The Name is said in Sikh texts to be "the total expression of all that God is," and those who open themselves to the Name through selfless devotion may come to know God in a way that transcends ordinary knowing.

One of the most important of Sikh meditative practices is "remembering the Name" (*nam simaran*), in which the devotee contemplates various epithets of God, along with the adumbrations of the divine essence that are found throughout creation. In this practice, the meditator generally repeats a particular word or *mantra,* or chants the songs of the Gurus, in order to bring about intuitive understanding of God.

Sikhism teaches that there is only one God, although He is known in various guises by different religions. In essence, however, God transcends all creeds and systems. Sikhism rejects the idea that God takes physical incarnations (*avatara*). God is utterly transcendent and cannot be contained within the limited form of a created being. Like Hinduism, however, Sikhism contends that living creatures are reborn in a beginningless cycle (*samsara*) and that each being's situation is a result of past actions (*karma*). The ultimate goal of Sikhism is liberation (*moksha*) from cyclic existence, but this can be attained only through God's grace, and not by personal effort.

The primary factor preventing the attainment of liberation is self-reliance (*haumai*), which causes beings falsely to imagine that they are independent and autonomous, that their fates are within their own control, and that salvation may be attained through actions. In order to combat self-reliance, one must cultivate proper attitude (*hukam*), which involves recognizing one's utter dependence upon God. Humble and devoted repetition of the Name helps one to develop humility and to recognize the transcendent glory of God.

God is within everyone, and so rituals are unnecessary, according to Sikhism, nor is there any point in making pilgrimages, since God is everywhere. One may worship God anywhere and at any time, and Sikhism urges its followers to strive toward realization of the Divine Presence all around them. Sikhism contends that ignorance (*avidya*) is the primary factor preventing one from knowing God, and that ignorance is eliminated only by those who humbly submit themselves to the divine will and listen to God's message as revealed by the words of the Gurus and other inspired devotional mystics.

Since God is the ultimate source of everything, all is really God, although ignorant beings fail to realize this fact. God's presence is hidden from us by the power of illusion (*maya*), a process of projection that causes beings mistakenly to imagine that they have an existence apart from Him. In reality, however, everything is a part of Him, and nothing can exist apart from Him. When one wakes up to the reality behind this illusion (which can occur only through God's grace), one realizes the unity of God and gradually comes to perceive God in everything. Sikhism's formulation of the doctrine of *maya* differs from that of Advaita Vedanta in that in Sikh philosophy *maya* is not an objective reality projected by God, but a subjective error resulting from a wrong point of view, a belief in duality rather than unity. This causes the mirage of the world to be seen as an end in itself. It is eliminated by devotion and meditation on the divine Name. One who is wholeheartedly immersed in this practice may through the grace of God escape the cycle of birth and death and attain final liberation, which Sikhism contends is an eternally blissful state of union with the Ultimate.

Sikh Scriptures

The first attempt to create a collection of authoritative Sikh texts was made during the tenure of the third Guru, Amar Das (1552–1574), who supervised a compilation of works by his predecessors. The fifth Guru, Arjan, began the collection of texts that became the *Adi Granth,* the most revered scripture of the tradition. Sikhs consider it to be the Guru, since it contains the collected wisdom of the early Gurus and their Sant predecessors.

There are three known recensions of the *Adi Granth:* (1) one believed to be the original text written by Bhai Gurdas and owned by a Sikh family in Kartarpur; (2) the "Damdama Recension," which was compiled during the 17th century and which includes works by Guru Tegh Bahadur; and (3) the "Banno Recension," which is widely regarded by Sikhs as noncanonical. The Damdama Recension is the standard text for all copies of the *Adi Granth* published in modern times. Modern published texts of the *Adi Granth* follow this version, even to the extent of adopting its pagination. Thus, all copies of the *Adi Granth* have 1,430 pages, and every individual page mirrors the contents of the original Damdama text.

The *Adi Granth* is divided into three main portions: (1) Introductory Material (pp. 1–13); (2) Ragas (pp. 14–1353); and (3) Miscellaneous Works (pp. 1353–1430). The introductory section begins with the *Mul Mantra,* the basic statement of Sikh faith. The next portions are the works of the *Japji* of Guru Nanak, which is regarded as containing his quintessential teachings. The introductory material ends with works by Guru Angad, Nanak's immediate successor. The second portion of the introductory section is referred to as the *Sodar,* so named because the first word of the first hymn is *sodar.* This section contains four poems by Guru Nanak, three by Guru Ram Das, and two by Guru Arjan. The third section of the introduction is named *Sohila* or *Kirtan Sohila.* It contains three works by Guru Nanak, one by Guru Ram Das, and one by Guru Arjan.

The term *Raga* refers to various metres used in the works of the second section of the *Adi Granth.* This is the largest portion of the text, and is divided into 31 sections, each of which contains hymns of a particular type. Within each *Raga,* works are arranged according to length and content. Hymns in four stanzas are placed at the beginning, followed by hymns in eight stanzas. The last part of the *Ragas* contains poems by predecessors of Sikhism whose religious visions are considered to be consonant with that of Guru Nanak and his successors. Works by Kabir and the devotional poets Namdev and Ravidas are found in this section.

The section containing Miscellaneous Works has more writings by Kabir, and some compositions by the Sufi teacher Sheikh Farid. The final portion of the *Adi Granth* consists of 57 verses by Guru Tegh Bahadur, two works by Guru Arjan, and the *Rag-mala,* which summarizes the contents of the *Ragas.*

The language of the *Adi Granth* is referred to as "*Sant Bhasa,*" the language of the Sants. Linguistically similar to modern Punjabi, it was the language adopted by the devotional Sant poets of the 15th and 16th centuries in northern India. The words of the *Adi Granth* are recorded in the Gurmukhi script, which is also used for modern Punjabi.

Another important scriptural source for Sikhism is the *Dasam Granth*, the compilation of which is associated with the tenth Guru, Gobind Singh. Like the *Adi Granth*, it is referred to as "Guru," and is widely regarded as an authoritative text, but it is far less important for the tradition than the *Adi Granth*. It contains a range of literature, including extensive portions of stories from Hindu literature, many of which are written in different dialects.

The compositions of the mystic poets Bhai Gurdas and Bhai Nand Lal are also highly regarded by Sikhs and have the status of scriptures. The former writer lived during the tenure of the third through sixth Gurus, and the latter was a follower of Guru Gobind Singh. Along with the *Adi Granth* and the *Dasam Granth*, their writings are the only works approved for recitation in Sikh temples.

Mention should also be made of the *janam-sakhis*, which are hagiographical stories of Guru Nanak's life; they stress the themes of the unity of God, the pointlessness of sectarianism, and the worthlessness of external religious observances. They were probably composed during the 16th century, and although they have not been granted the status of scriptures, these stories are widely popular.

SIKH SCRIPTURES

NANAK, THE FIRST GURU

According to the Sikh tradition, Guru Nanak was born in the northern Punjab in an area that today is part of Pakistan. In this region Muslims and Hindus frequently came into conflict, which deeply troubled Nanak. As a member of the Sant tradition, he believed that both groups worship the same God, and so they should not fight. Even as a child Nanak was drawn to religious contemplation, and as he grew up his interest in the divine Reality became so intense that he cared little for mundane things.

One day he went to a nearby river to perform his ritual ablutions, but he disappeared. A search was conducted, but all that was found of Nanak were his clothes. After three days he reappeared, but he refused to discuss where he had been. After three days he told his friends and relatives that he had been taken to the presence of God and given a special mission. God had informed him that Hindus and Muslims both worship Him and that He wished that they join together in faith and not fight against each other. Guru Nanak was to be the prophet of the message of reconciliation, and he spent the remainder of his life working to bring the two groups together.

Baba Nanak was born in Talvandi, the son of Kalu, who was a Bedi Khatri by caste. In this Age of Darkness he proclaimed the divine Name and founded his community of followers, the Panth. Baba Nanak was born in the year S. 1526 on the third day of the month of Vaisakh [April 15, 1469 A.C.]. . . . Celestial music resounded in heaven. A mighty host of gods hailed his birth, and with them all manner of spirit and divinity. 'God has come to save the world!' they cried. . . .

As he grew older he began to play with other children, but his attitude differed from theirs in that he paid heed to the spiritual things of God. When he turned five he began to give utterance to deep and mysterious thoughts. Whatever he uttered was spoken with profound understanding, with the result that everyone's doubts and questions were resolved. The Hindus vowed that a god had taken birth in human form. The Muslims declared that a follower of divine truth had been born. . . .

After returning home in the evening Baba Nanak would devote his nights to singing hymns, and when it came to the last watch of the night he would go to the river and bathe. One morning, having gone to bathe, he entered the waters of the Vein stream but failed to emerge. His servant looked for him until mid-morning and then taking his clothes returned home to tell Jai Ram what had happened. . . . [A] thorough search was made, but to no avail.

Eventually, however, Baba Nanak did return. After three days and three nights had passed he emerged from the stream, and having done so he declared: 'There is neither Hindu nor Muslim. . . .'

Source: *Janam-Sakhi* selections, tr. W. H. McLeod, *Textual Sources for the Study of Sikhism* (Chicago: University of Chicago Press, 1984), pp. 18–21.

GURU NANAK'S DEATH

Although Hindus and Muslims became Nanak's followers, members of each group often retained strong ties to their original religion, despite Nanak's efforts to wean them of sectarianism. As he was preparing to die, members of each group proposed to dispose of his physical remains in accordance with their respective burial customs. Nanak's final lesson to his followers gently chided them for this behavior.

Guru Baba Nanak then went and sat under a withered acacia which immediately produced leaves and flowers, becoming verdant again. . . . Baba Nanak's wife began to weep and the various members of his family joined her in her grief. . . . The assembled congregation sang hymns of praise and Baba Nanak passed into an ecstatic trance. While thus transported, and in obedience to the divine will, he sang the hymn entitled *The Twelve Months*. It was early morning and the time had come for his final departure. . . . 'Even the Guru's dogs lack nothing, my sons,' he said. 'You shall be abundantly supplied with food and clothing, and if you repeat the Guru's name you will be liberated from the bondage of human life.'

Hindus and Muslims who had put their faith in the divine Name began to debate what should be done with the Guru's corpse. 'We shall bury him,' said the Muslims. 'No, let us cremate his body,' said the Hindus. 'Place flowers on both sides of my body,' said Baba Nanak, 'flowers from the Hindus on the right side and flowers from the Muslims on the left. If tomorrow the Hindus' flowers are still fresh let my body be burned, and if the Muslims' flowers are still fresh let it be buried.'

Baba Nanak then commanded the congregation to sing. . . . Baba Nanak then covered himself with a sheet and passed away. Those who had gathered around him prostrated themselves, and when the sheet was removed they found that there was nothing under it. The flowers on both sides remained fresh, and both Hindus and Muslims took their respective shares. All who were gathered there prostrated themselves again.

Source: *Puratan Janam-Sakhi*, pp. 111–115: from *Textual Sources for the Study of Sikhism*, p. 25.

THE *MUL MANTRA*: THE BASIC STATEMENT

Guru Arjan placed the Mul Mantra, *the basic Sikh statement of faith, at the beginning of the holiest book of the Sikhs, the* Adi Granth. *It expresses the primary attributes of the Sikh conception of God, His absolute unity and absolute transcendence.*

There is one God, Eternal Truth is His Name.
Maker of all things, fearing nothing and at enmity with nothing, timeless is His image.
Not begotten, being of His own Being: by the grace of the Guru, made known to humanity.

Source: *Adi Granth* 1.1.

JAP: THE MEDITATION

As He was in the beginning: The truth, so throughout the ages, He ever has been the truth, so even now He is truth immanent, so forever and ever He shall be truth eternal.

Source: *Adi Granth* 1.1–2: from *Selections from the Sacred Writings of the Sikhs*, tr. Dr. Trilochan Singh et al. (London, George Allen & Unwin, 1960), p. 28.

THE DIVINE NAME

*The divine Name (*nam*) is an important motif in the* Adi Granth. *The nature of God is intimated through the various epithets used to call and describe Him, and although none of these is able adequately to convey God's essence, each provides some insight into what God is.*

If in this life I should live to eternity, nourished by nothing save air; if I should dwell in the darkest of dungeons, sense never resting in sleep; yet must your glory transcend all my striving; no words can encompass the Name.

He who is truly the Spirit Eternal, immanent, blissful, serene; only by grace can we learn of God's goodness, only by grace can we tell.

If I were slain and my body dismembered, pressed in a hand-mill and ground; if I were burnt in a fire all-consuming, mingled with ashes and dust; yet must your glory transcend all my striving; no words can encompass the Name.
If as a bird I could soar to the heavens, a hundred such realms in my reach; if I could change so that none might perceive me and live without food, without drink; yet must your glory transcend all my striving; no words can encompass the Name.

Listening to the Name bestows truth, divine wisdom, contentment.
To bathe in the joy of the Name is to bathe in the holy places.
By hearing the Name and reading it one attains to honor;
By listening, the mind may reach the highest blissful poise of meditation on God.
Nanak says, the saints are always happy;
By listening to the Name sorrow and sin are destroyed.

Source: *Adi Granth*, "Siri Raga" selections, from *Textual Sources for the Study of Sikhism*, p. 40, and *Selections from the Sacred Writings of the Sikhs*, p. 34.

MEDITATION ON THE NAME

In this passage Nanak indicates that the writings of Hindus and Muslims fail to capture the true essence of God. All the scholars of these traditions are grasping futilely for what cannot be grasped.

Pilgrimages, penances, compassion and almsgiving bring a little merit, the size of a sesame seed.
But one who hears and believes and loves the Name will bathe and be made clean in a place of pilgrimage within.
All goodness is Yours, O Lord, I have none;
Though without performing good deeds none can aspire to adore You.
Blessed are You, the Creator and the Manifestation, You are the word, You are the primal Truth and Beauty, and You are the heart's joy and desire.
When in time, in what age, in what day of the month or week, in what season and in what month did you create the world?
The pundits do not know or they would have written it in the *Puranas;*
The Qazis do not know, or they would have recorded it in the *Qur'an;*
Nor do the yogis know the moment of the day;
Nor the day of the month or the week, nor the month nor the season.
Only God who made the world knows when He made it.
Then how will I approach You Lord?
In what words will I praise You?
In what words will I speak of You?
How will I know You?
Nanak, all humanity speaks of Him, and each would be wiser than the next one;
Great is the Lord, great is His Name,
What He ordains comes to pass,
Nanak, a person puffed up with his own wisdom
Will get no honor from God in the life to come.

Source: *Adi Granth*, "Siri Raga" 1: from *Selections from the Sacred Writings of the Sikhs*, pp. 39–40.

NUDITY DOES NOT MAKE ONE A SAINT

In this poem Kabir stresses the need for true devotion to God, referred to here as Ram (an incarnation of Vishnu). Kabir indicates that asceticism is useless, since one only reaches liberation through ecstatic love of God, in which all sense of self is eliminated and one is consumed by pure love.

> Whether you are naked or clothed, what does it matter
> If you have not recognized the inward Ram (*atmaram*)?
> If one could achieve yoga by wandering naked,
> Then would not deer in the forest achieve liberation?
> If by shaving one's head one could have spiritual mastery (*siddhi*)
> Then would sheep also not go to heaven?
> My brother, if by holding back your seed you could be saved,
> Then surely eunuchs would attain the highest place in heaven.
> Kabir says: Listen brother, without the name of Ram
> Who has ever achieved liberation?

Source: *Kabir Granthavali, pad* 174.

BOOKS AND LEARNING ARE OF NO USE

A central theme of Kabir's poems is a rejection of the value of study and prayer as performed by the religious leaders of his day, who are characterized as holding to the letter of the scriptures without grasping the true meaning.

> Pundit, why are you so foolish?
> You don't speak of Ram, you fool!
> Carrying your Vedas and Puranas, moving like a donkey loaded with sandalwood,
> Unless you learn about the name of Ram,
> You will come to grief.
> You slaughter living beings and call it dharma;
> What then, brother, would non-dharma be?
> You refer to each other as "Great Saint"; whom, then, should I call "Butcher"?
> Your mind is blind, your understanding dull.
> Brother, how can you preach to others?
> You sell your knowledge for money, and spend your human life in vain.

Source: *Kabir Granthavali, pad* 191.

EXTERNAL OBSERVANCES ARE OF NO USE

Like their Sant predecessors, Sikhs denounced the practice of external religious observances. Far from bringing people closer to God, Sikhs believe that such practices tend to obscure the divine presence, which is all around us, in all things, and directly accessible to human intuition.

He cannot be installed like an idol,
Nor can humans shape His likeness.
He made Himself and maintains Himself
On His heights sustained forever;
Honored are they in His shrine who meditate upon Him.
Sing, Nanak, the psalms of God as the treasury of sublime virtues.
If one sings of God and hears of Him, and lets love of God sprout within,
All sorrow will depart; in the soul, God will create abiding peace.
The word of the Guru is the inner music;
The word of the Guru is the highest scripture;
The word of the Guru is all-pervading.
The Guru is Shiva, the Guru is Vishnu and Brahma, the Guru is the mother Goddess.
If I knew Him as He truly is
What words could utter my knowledge?
Enlightened by God, the Guru has unraveled one mystery
There is only one Truth, one bestower of life;
May I never forget Him.

Source: *Adi Granth,* "Japji" 5: from *Selections from the Sacred Writings of the Sikhs,* pp. 31–32.

ON *HUKAM*

Hukam *is central to Sikh meditative practice. It literally means propriety, putting things where they belong. It involves understanding one's relation to God and God's place in the universe. Cultivating hukam is necessary to overcoming self-reliance* (haumai), *the false notion that one is an autonomous individual independent of God's grace.*

Hukam is beyond describing, [but this much we can understand:] that all forms were created by *hukam,* life was created through *hukam,* greatness is imparted in accordance with *hukam.* Distinctions between what is exalted and what is lowly are the result of *hukam,* and in accordance with it suffering comes to some and joy to others. Through *hukam* one receives blessing and another is condemned to everlasting transmigration. All are within *hukam;* no one is beyond its authority. Nanak, if anyone comprehends *hukam,* his self-centeredness is purged.

Source: *Adi Granth,* "Japji" 2: from *Adi Granth: Guru Nanak and the Sikh Religion,* tr. W. H. McLeod (Oxford: Clarendon Press, 1968), p. 200.

ON *HAUMAI*

Haumai *is born of ignorance, which is the root cause of continued transmigration. It is a perceptual error in which one mistakenly believes that one is independent and autonomous, although the fact of the matter is that everything in the universe is created and sustained by God. Those who hold to mistaken views of separateness and individuality fail to recognize the omnipresence of God and their utter dependence upon his grace.*

Innumerable are the blind fools, sunk in folly;
Innumerable those living on thievery and dishonesty.
Innumerable the tyrants ruling by brute force;
Innumerable the violent cutthroats and murderers;
Innumerable those revolving in their own falsehood;
Innumerable the polluted living on filth;
Innumerable the slanderers bearing on their heads their loads of sin.
The sinner Nanak thus enumerates the evil-doers,
I who am unworthy even once to be made a sacrifice to You.
All that You will is good, Formless One, abiding in Your peace.

Source: *Adi Granth*, "Japji" 18.

THE TRUE GURU

Throughout Sikh literature the importance of the Guru is emphasized. In the early years of the tradition the Guru was human, and Sikhs believed that Nanak and his successors were mouthpieces through whom God revealed his message to humanity. Following the tenure of the 10th Guru, Gobind Singh, the Adi Granth *was designated as the Guru, since it contained the inspired messages of the human Gurus and their Sant predecessors. The Gurus are believed to provide essential guidance, since their words are the signposts provided by God to call His devotees to mystical realization of truth.*

If the True Guru is gracious, trust becomes complete.
If the True Guru is gracious, no one ever yearns.
If the True Guru is gracious, trouble is a thing unknown.
If the True Guru is gracious, God's pleasure is acclaimed.
If the True Guru is gracious, how could there be fear of death?
If the True Guru is gracious, lasting happiness is granted.
If the True Guru is gracious, one finds life's greatest treasures.
If the True Guru is gracious, one mingles with the Truth.

Source: *Var majh Pauri*, 25: *Sources of Indian Tradition,* ed. Ainslie Embree (New York: Columbia University Press, 1988), p. 505.

THE ECSTASY OF MYSTICAL UNION

Kabir's poetry contains a wealth of striking metaphors and images intended to convey nuances of the experience of mystical union that cannot be expressed through ordinary language. In this poem he describes the bliss of devotional union experienced by one who abandons ego and ritual and is granted the transcendent experience of union with God.

2. The radiance of the Supreme Brahman (*parabrahm*) cannot be imagined;
   Its beauty is ineffable, and seeing it is the only real evidence.
3. The fortunate hail fell to earth, and so lost its selfhood;
   When it melted, it became water and flowed into the lake.

4. I found the one I sought just where I was,
   And it has now become me, though I previously spoke of it as "Other."
5. Light shines in the Unapproachable, the Inaccessible.
   Kabir has brought his worship there, beyond the realm of "merit" and "sin.". . .
7. Love illuminated the cage [of physical existence], an eternal flame arose,
   My doubts disappeared, and happiness dawned when I encountered my Beloved. . . .
9. Water turned into ice, and then the ice melted;
   Everything that was has become It, and so what more can be said? . . .
12. Kabir has found the One, the Unapproachable, whose radiance is indescribable,
   The Luminous wife who is a *paras* [a stone that brings immortality]
   The god whom I now see. . . .
19. Sun and moon have become merged, and both dwell in one house.
   My mind has attained the goal of its search due to my past actions.
20. Transcending all limitations, I entered into the Boundless,
   Dwelling in Emptiness (*sunni*).
   I now reside in the palace that the sages cannot find.

Source: Kabir, *Sakhi* 9.

GUIDELINES FOR A HAPPY MARRIAGE

Guru Gobind Singh advises married couples to view themselves as one entity and to avoid deceit in their relationship. Wives are urged to remain faithful and to be subservient to their husbands, while husbands are warned of the negative consequences of mistreating their wives.

When husband and wife sit side by side why should we treat them as two?
Outwardly separate, their bodies distinct, yet inwardly joined as one.
Comply with whatever your Spouse may desire, never resisting, spurning deceit. . . .
Obey his commands in total surrender, this is the fragrance to bring. . . .
Abandon self-will, the Beloved draws near; no cunning will ever avail.
Be humble in manner and practice restraint, let sweetness of speech be your prayer.
If these are the garments adorning a bride the husband she seeks will be found.
Sweet is her speech, approved by the Loved One; grant that the joy may endure evermore.
Filled with the spirit of truth and contentment, the family's pride and joy.
The one who is constant in goodness and virtue is cherished and loved by the Spouse.
Behind closed doors and a forest of curtains he lies with another's wife.

When the angels of Death shall demand your account how then can the truth
be concealed?
This is the message the Guru has brought; let this be your vow while your
body has breath.
Bestow your affection on none save your wife; spurning temptation, avoid
other beds.
Watchful, untainted, even in dreams.

Source: *Sukhamani* 4.5: *Textual Sources for the Study of Sikhism*, pp. 117–118.

FORMATION OF THE *KHALSA*

*This passage tells the story of how the 10th Guru, Gobind Singh, inaugurated the
institution of the Sikh* Khalsa *(community). Besieged by Muslim rulers who wanted
to eliminate the Sikhs, the Guru realized that in order to survive his followers would
have to develop into a military force. In a move that permanently changed the character of the Sikh community, he gathered the faithful together and asked if any were
willing to die for their faith. Five men stepped forward, and the Guru led them one by
one to a tent, and then emerged with his sword dripping blood. Many of the people in
attendance believed that the Guru had gone mad, but Gobind Singh later showed them
that the five men were actually unharmed. He had killed five goats, and the blood they
had witnessed had been that of the animals. The following day the Guru completed the
process of transforming the community into a warrior group by declaring that henceforth the Sikhs would adopt external signs differentiating them from other communities. They would consider themselves to be members of the* Khalsa, *and membership
would henceforth be exclusive.*

On the day before . . . the Guru [Gobind Singh] arranged for a large
tent made of fine woolen fabric to be pitched on the area known as Kesgarh.
Earlier he had given instructions for a large dais to be erected at the edge of
the area. At that place he held a magnificent reception attended by five
thousand Sikhs, all with eyes for none save the Guru. While they were
gazing with rapture the Guru rose from his throne and in order to test them
addressed the mighty assembly as follows. 'I want the heads of five Sikhs to
offer as a sacrifice to God,' he proclaimed. 'Those Sikhs, beloved of the
Guru, who cheerfully give their heads will enjoy in the eternal hereafter all
the happiness that their hearts desire.'

Terror gripped the hearts of all who heard him. All fell silent, the
blood draining from their faces. The Guru drew his sacred sword and
called them again. 'Why are you silent?' he cried. 'Who amongst you sincerely believes his body to be of no account? Let him stand up.'

Hearing this Daya Singh, a pious Khatri from Lahore, stood with
hands respectfully joined. The Guru conducted him into the tent where
five goats were secretly tethered. He felled one of them, letting its blood
gush out. When he returned to the assembly the people were stunned by
the sight of his bloodstained sword. When he proceeded to demand the
head of another Sikh they stood petrified. 'He must have been bewitched

by the goddess,' they said. 'Why else should he demand the heads of Sikhs?' Some said one thing, some another. . . . [The Guru repeated the procedure with four other Sikhs.]

All were faithful disciples, pious men wholly given to worship and meditation who valued true wisdom and principle more than their own lives. When the Guru called for heads to be sacrificed these five Sikhs offered theirs. Faint-hearted Sikhs . . . tricked by the goat ruse into believing that men were really being killed, whispered anxiously to each other, desperately wanting to flee. This they were unable to do. Overpowered by the radiant presence of the Guru, each was firmly rooted to the spot.

Although many more Sikhs, faithful and brave, were by this time clamoring to give their heads the Guru demanded only five. . . . To those who responded, the Cherished Five, he gave new garments and fine weapons so that their appearance should resemble his own. Then he led them from the tent, back to his assembled Sikhs. All were thunderstruck, believing that the Guru had restored to life those whom he had previously slain. . . .

[The Guru said:] "Now it is clear for all to see that the Panth will win renown, that it will strike down the enemies of this land while it spreads abroad the message of the Sikh faith. All this will happen because God has made himself manifest in these five. . . . We give thanks to God that he has destroyed the religion of Muhammad and his successors, replacing it with the supremacy of the Guru's chosen five. . . ."

On the morning following this momentous event. . . . After pouring water from the Satluj river into a large iron vessel the Guru gave instructions for the Cherished Five to be clad in white garments together with a sword and other symbolic forms. He then had them stand before him and commanded them to repeat the divine name 'Vahiguru,' fixing their minds on God as they did so. This they were to continue doing while he stirred the sanctified water (*amrit*) in the iron vessel with a double-edged sword held vertically. . . .

The Guru then used the tip of his sword to take a small quantity of amrit from the iron vessel. This he did five times, letting each portion run from his sword on to his face. Then he applied amrit to each of the Cherished Five. . . . Finally he promulgated the code of conduct which they were to observe. . . . Thus did the Guru lay the foundations of the Khalsa, determine its form, and define the obligations of its members.

Sources: *Tavarikh Guru Khalsa* selections: from *Textual Sources for the Study Sikhism*, pp. 34–37.

JUSTIFICATION FOR USE OF FORCE

This poem, written by Guru Gobind Singh to the Mughal emperor Aurangzeb, accuses him of treachery and argues that Sikhs should fight to defend themselves against the unjust attacks of India's Muslim rulers. These verses stand in obvious contrast to the vision of religious harmony articulated by Nanak, who looked for ways to bring Hindus and Muslims together in a religious community that transcended their differences and emphasized the essential unity of religions.

> What could forty starving men do when they were suddenly attacked by ten thousand?
> The violators of solemn oaths came suddenly and began attacking.
> Then I was forced to do battle, using arrows and gunfire in self-defence.
> When all attempts at negotiation have failed, one is justified in unsheathing the sword.
> You tell me that I can rely on your oaths on the Qur'an,
> But if I had not done so earlier, this would not have come to pass. . . .
> One should know that it is evil to deviate from the truth. . . .
> You should not wield the sword carelessly in order to draw blood from anyone.
> God will shed your blood in the same way.
> You should not be indifferent, but should know that God cares nothing for human praise.
> He is the Lord of the earth and the sky, the Fearless,
> Creator of the universe and of all that is in it. . . .
> If you are strong, do not harm the poor,
> And do not renege on your promises with axes and clubs.
> When God is on one's side, what can an enemy do, even if he uses many tricks?
> Even if the enemy attacks thousands of times,
> He cannot harm one who has God on his side
> And who is protected by His benevolence.

Source: Guru Gobind Singh, *Japharnama.*

GOD, THE SWORD SUPREME

Gobind Singh realized that the continued existence of his religion required that Sikhs learn to defend themselves. In this poem he indicates that military preparedness is a sacred duty and that God requires his followers to become warriors in order to fight for the truth.

> Sword, that strikes in a flash, that scatters the armies of the wicked in the great battlefield; you symbol of the brave.
> Your arm is irresistible, your brightness shines forth the blaze of the splendor dazzling like the sun.
> Sword, you are the protector of saints, you are the scourge of the wicked; scatterer of sinners I take refuge in You.
> Hail to the Creator, Savior and Sustainer, hail to You: Sword supreme.

Source: Guru Gobind Singh, *Bachiter Natak, 1: Selections from the Sacred Writings of the Sikhs,* p. 270.

GLOSSARY

Adi Granth *"First Book,"* the holiest book of the Sikhs, which contains writings of Guru Nanak and his successors, along with poems of Sants.

Akal Purakh "Timeless Being," one of the Sikh names of God.

Avidya "Ignorance," the basic factor that enmeshes beings in the cycle of birth, death, and rebirth.

Bhakti Selfless devotion to God.

Five Ks Distinctive marks of Sikh believers, instituted by Guru Gobind Singh: (1) *kesh,* unshorn hair; (2) *kangha,* comb; (3) *kirpan,* short sword; (4) *kara,* steel wristband; (5) *kachch,* short pants.

Gobind Singh The 10th Guru, founder of the khalsa (1666–1708).

Guru "Teacher," a designation for Nanak and his successors, and later for the *Adi Granth.*

Haumai Self-reliance, the false notion that one is independent of God.

Hukam An attitude of humility, brought about by the realization of one's utter dependence on God.

Karma Actions that lead to concordant results.

Khalsa The Sikh community, founded by Guru Gobind Singh.

Maya "Illusion," a falsehood caused by ignorance, which causes beings to perceive multiplicity instead of the unitary truth of God.

Moksha "Release" from the cycle of birth, death, and rebirth, which is brought about by God's grace.

Mul Mantra "Root Prayer," the fundamental statement of Sikh doctrine.

Nam "Divine Name," which refers both to the various epithets of God and to His manifestations in the world.

Nam Simaran "Remembering the Name," the practice of contemplating God's attributes and actions.

Nanak The founder of the Sikh tradition (1469–1539).

Nirguna "Without Qualities," a designation of God's essential nature.

Samsara "Cyclic Existence," the beginningless cycle of birth, death, and rebirth in which ordinary beings are trapped.

Sant Indian mystics who advocated pure devotion to God and who denounced religious sectarianism.

Sikh "Disciple," a term coined by Guru Nanak to designate his followers.

FURTHER READINGS

ANAND, BALWANT SINGH. *Guru Nanak: His Life Was His Message.* New Delhi: Guru Nanak Foundation, 1983.

BARRIER, N. GERALD. *The Sikhs and Their Literature: A Guide to Tracts, Books, and Periodicals, 1849–1919.* Delhi: Manohar, 1985.

COLE, W. OWEN and PIARA SINGH SAMBHI. *The Sikhs: Their Religious Beliefs and Practices*. London: Routledge & Kegan Paul, 1978.

GANDHI, SURJIT SINGH. *History of the Sikh Gurus: A Comprehensive Study*. Delhi: Gur Das Kapur, 1978.

JUERGENSMEYER, M. and BARRIER, N. G. (eds.). *Sikh Studies: Comparative Perspectives on a Changing Tradition*. Berkeley: Berkeley Religious Studies Series, 1979.

KOHLI, SURINDAR SINGH. *A Critical Study of the Adi Granth*. New Delhi: Punjabi Writers' Cooperative Society, 1961.

LOEHLIN, C. H. *The Sikhs and Their Scriptures*. Lucknow: Lucknow Publishing House, 1958.

MANSUKHANI, GOBIND SINGH. *Aspects of Sikhism*. New Delhi: Punjabi Writers' Cooperative Industrial Society, 1982.

MCLEOD, W. H. *The Sikhs: History, Religion and Society*. New York: Columbia University Press, 1989.

SETHI, AMARJIT SINGH. *Universal Sikhism*. New Delhi: Hemkunt Press, 1972.

SHACKLE, C. *An Introduction to the Sacred Language of the Sikhs*. London: School of Oriental and African Studies, 1983.

SINGH, HAKAM. *Sikh Studies: A Classified Bibliography of Printed Books in English*. Patiala: Punjab Publishing House, 1982.

Confucianism

INTRODUCTION

Of all the traditions discussed in this book, Confucianism probably has the least in common with what most contemporary Westerners associate with "religion." Confucius (ca. 551–479 B.C.E.), the founder of Confucianism, did not assert the existence of a creator God, although he did mention an impersonal force called "Heaven" (*tian*) that watches over human affairs and confers a mandate on rulers that legitimates their power. Confucianism has no churches and no ecclesiastical hierarchy, and Confucius never clearly articulated any vision of the afterlife or a path to salvation. The focus of Confucius was squarely on human beings and their social relations with others. Confucius's philosophy articulated his vision of the Way (*dao*) of the "superior person" (*junzi*), who embodies the qualities of a truly good human being. When asked about "religious" topics such as the nature of Heaven, the existence and propitiation of spirits, and so forth, Confucius generally cautioned his audiences to focus on the present life and on their personal conduct, and not to waste time on idle speculation.

Confucius is the latinate form of Kong Fuzi, or "Master Kong." According to Chinese tradition, he lived during the fifth century B.C.E. He was born in the small state of Lu, in modern-day Shandong Province. Some accounts claim that he was a descendant of the royal house of the Shang Dynasty (1751–1122 B.C.E., the earliest authenticated dynasty of China), but his family had become impoverished by Confucius's time. His father is said to have been a soldier, and his mother was not the first wife. According to later tradition, when Confucius was born dragons appeared in his house and a unicorn was sighted in his village.

His father died when Confucius was young, and his mother died while he was still a child. According to Sima Qian, when Confucius was a boy he had little interest in the games of other children, and instead preferred to arrange sacrificial implements and pretend to be performing rituals. Apparently Confucius did not have a formal education, but through independent study managed to become renowned for his learning.

In his twenties he began to attract students. He married young and held a minor government position that required him to keep records of stores of grains and animals used for official sacrifices. According to some accounts, his interest in rituals led him to visit Laozi to seek advice on the performance of sacrifices, but Confucius was admonished for being excessively concerned with external observances and thus neglecting the Dao.

Confucius was married around the age of 19 to a woman from Bin Guan in the state of Song. They had a son and a daughter. Fearing the onset of social disruption in Lu, he traveled to the state of Qi, hoping to gain a position of influence. He was well received but failed to achieve his primary objective, and so returned to Lu at the age of 51. There he was appointed minister of justice, and according to Confucian accounts he instituted a period of good government. Records of his tenure claim that articles left on the road were returned to their owners, and people could travel freely without fear of crime. He became an advisor to the duke of Lu, but reportedly resigned in disgust after the duke received a present of 80 dancing girls from the rival duke of Qi, after which he no longer attended to his duties in the morning.

Confucius lived during a time of social and political turmoil, and this had a powerful effect on his thinking. The Zhou dynasty (1111–249 B.C.E.), which had unified China and fostered the development of Chinese culture, was losing control, and China was in the process of breaking up into fiefdoms that were vying with each other for territory and power. Confucius lamented this social disintegration and hoped to guide his country back to the norms and practices of the early days of the Zhou dynasty as reported in The *Book of Poetry* and the *Book of History,* both of which extolled the superior qualities of sage-emperors of the Shang and Zhou dynasties. Confucius hoped to find a position of political power that would allow him to help the rulers of his time to rediscover the traditions of the past, which he believed would help China to correct its problems and reestablish good government.

Unable to find a suitable position in Lu, at the age of 53 Confucius began a trek through China in search of a ruler who would allow him to put his ideas into practice. During the course of 13 years he journeyed to nine states. Some received him warmly and asked his advice, but in one state he was surrounded and threatened, and he was made a target of assassination in another, and detained by government authorities in a third state.

He promised that any state that allowed him significant control of domestic matters and foreign affairs would soon enjoy prosperity and enhanced prestige, and that it would have a contented populace that fully supported the policies of the rulers, but his ideas of government by wise and humane rulers were considered dangerous at a time when most rulers controlled their domains by force. After realizing that no one would give him an opportunity to implement his ideas, he returned to Lu at the age of 68 and devoted himself to teaching, convinced that his life's mission had been a failure.

His fame as a teacher grew, however, and traditional sources report that young men came from far and wide to study with Confucius and that he never turned away a student who was unable to pay him. As a result, young men of humble origins had access to education, which was an important factor in finding employment in government.

Confucius taught his students to cultivate themselves and urged them to aspire to become "noble men." The noble man, according to Confucius, possesses an unwavering moral compass, and thus knows what is correct in all situations. He has the virtue of "human-heartedness" (*ren*), the coalescence of the moral qualities that characterize those who are truly good. A noble man is honest, is courageous, stands in awe of Heaven and constantly seeks to perfect himself, is learned but does not boast of his learning, does not set his mind "for" or "against" anything, holds to no particular political philosophy, but rather seeks to follow what is right in every situation. He has no needs of his own, and so is able to work selflessly for others. His unassuming manifestation of good qualities inspires others to become better. Society, according to Confucius, is perfected by such people, who set a moral standard that subtly motivates others to correct themselves in order to emulate them.

Although Confucius was unable to acquire the political power he desired during his lifetime, his students passed on his teachings, becoming teachers themselves. Some of them became influential educators and helped to install his notion of the superior person as a standard for conduct among the educated elite of China. In addition, Confucius introduced to China the idea that the primary criteria for holding public office should be intelligence, learning, and highly developed moral character rather than hereditary status. He believed that universal standards of ethical behavior are outlined in the classics, and so he urged his students to study these texts in order to develop their moral awareness.

The Confucian Revival

In the centuries following Confucius's death, many of his disciples became educators, and as a result Confucian philosophy became a part of the standard curriculum of educated Chinese. Despite its widespread influence, however, the vitality of the tradition languished from the 4th through 10th centuries. Most of the best minds of China were either Daoists or Buddhists, and although Confucianism was widely studied there were few notable interpreters of the tradition.

This situation changed dramatically in the 11th century, when several prominent Confucian philosophers began to revive the tradition. Many of them were influenced by Buddhism and Daoism, and several had been Buddhists in their early years, but they ultimately rejected Buddhism because they considered its doctrine of "emptiness" (*shunyata*) to be nihilistic. They also saw the Buddhist emphasis on monasticism as unnatural, but found that the Confucian tradition valued the family and the norms of traditional Chinese society. A growing number of Confucian thinkers characterized Buddhism as a religion of "barbarians," unsuited to refined Chinese sensibilities, and they found in Confucianism a tradition that accorded with the norms and values of cultured Chinese. Among the early figures of this revival—which is referred to in China as "Study of Nature and Propriety" (*xing li xue*) and by Western scholars as "Neo-Confucianism"—were such prominent philosophers as Zhou Dunyi (1017–1073), Shao Yong (1011–1077), Zhang Zai (1020–1077), and the two brothers Cheng Hao (1032–1085) and Cheng Yi (1033–1107).

The Neo-Confucian revival is divided by contemporary scholars into two streams, one rationalistic and one idealistic. The major figure of the rationalist tradition was Zhu Xi (1130–1200), while Wang Yangming (1427–1529) was the main exponent of the idealists. Confucians of the first group focused on the foundational principles (*li*) of the natural world, human behavior, and society, while the idealists were primarily concerned with how to develop a moral consciousness through training the mind (*xin*).

Confucian Scriptures

According to Confucian tradition, Confucius edited the texts that came to be regarded as the Confucian classics: the *Book of Poetry* (*Shijing*), the *Book of Changes* (*Yijing*), the *Book of History* (*Shujing*), the *Book of Rites* (*Liji*), and the *Spring and Autumn Annals* (*Qunqiu*). These are regarded as the primary canonical texts of the tradition, along with the "Four Books": the *Analects* (*Lunyu*), the *Centeredness* (*Zhongyong*), the *Great Learning* (*Daxue*), and the *Mencius* (*Mangzi*).

The *Book of Poetry* is the earliest anthology of Chinese poetry. It contains 305 poems dating from early times until the later part of the Zhou dynasty. Confucian tradition holds that Confucius selected these from an earlier collection of three thousand poems, choosing those written in the finest style and exhibiting a high level of moral consciousness. The poems in the collection are mostly written in a style using rhymed quatrains with four characters per line, which became the standard for Chinese poetic writing after the time of Confucius.

The *Book of Changes* discusses how natural systems change, and it has long been regarded as a manual for divination. It contains 64 hexagrams, along with explanations of the significance of each one and "ten wings" of commentary that indicate how they should be interpreted. According to Confucian tradition, the ten wings were composed by Confucius, but this attribution has been rejected by most contemporary scholars (although it is admitted that he may have had a hand in composing one of the wings).

The hexagrams are composed of two trigrams each, and the trigrams are composed of broken and unbroken lines. The lines signify interactions of *yin* and *yang*, the two opposing polarities whose movements govern the developments of natural systems. *Yin* is said to be passive, wet, yielding, and feminine, and is represented by broken lines, while *yang* is aggressive, dry, forceful, and masculine, and is represented by unbroken lines. The pattern of the lines of a hexagram is believed to provide indications of the directions of natural elements and forces.

The *Book of History* is a collection of historical records and speeches purportedly from the early dynasties of China. It is the earliest Chinese historical work, containing documents from 17 centuries, dating back to the time of the legendary sage kings (third millennium B.C.E.). According to tradition, it was compiled and edited by Confucius, who chose selections for their historical and moral import. Each selection reports an event in Chinese history and contains a colophon that indicates the moral judgments of the author.

The *Book of Rites* describes the implements used in state rituals, the rules of the royal court, and it contains ethical exhortations for women and children, discussions of education, descriptions of proper performance of funerals and sacrifices to ancestors, and how a scholar should behave.

The *Spring and Autumn Annals* are historical records from the state of Lu from the period between 722 to 481 B.C.E. It describes the behavior of rulers, and is composed in a way that indicates the moral judgment of the compiler, believed by tradition to be Confucius.

Confucian tradition also holds that Confucius edited the *Book of Music* (*Yuejing*), which is now lost. It was replaced in the 12th century by a ritual text entitled *Rites of Zhou* (*Zhouli*). During the Han period, these six texts came to be referred to as the "six disciplines" (*liu shu*), and later as the "six classics" (*liujing*). Modern scholarship questions whether or not Confucius actually had a hand in editing these texts, since no evidence exists for this, except for relatively late traditions. It is clear from accounts of his life that he was thoroughly familiar with these texts and that he taught them to his students, but contemporary scholars see little reason to accept the tradition that he edited them.

The *Analects* contains 492 chapters collected into 20 books, and it contains pithy instructions on the core concepts of Confucius's philosophy. The primary focus is the training and character of the noble man, who is morally upright, learned, and restrained in his appetites.

The *Centeredness* was originally chapter 42 of the *Book of Rites*. According to Confucian tradition it was authored by Zeng Can (ca. 505–436 B.C.E.), but Zhu Xi contended that the opening paragraph was written by Confucius and that the rest of the work was an explanation composed by Zeng Can. It outlines three goals for the noble man: "making luminous virtue shine" (*ming ming de*), "having sympathy for the people" (*qin min*), and "abiding in attainment of perfect goodness" (*zhiyu zhishan*). These are said to be the first steps toward ordering society and establishing good government.

The *Great Learning* was originally chapter 31 of the *Book of Rites*, but came to be regarded as a separate text by the Confucian tradition. Zisi, a grandson of Confucius, is traditionally held to be its author, but this attribution is rejected by most contemporary scholars. It discusses the Dao of Heaven, which is said to be a principle that transcends the world but is manifest in its workings.

The *Mencius* contains teachings of the Confucian scholar Mangzi. These were written down by his students. The writings of Mencius represented an influential commentary on the thought of Confucius concerning the conduct of the sage and the nature of good government. The text consists of seven chapters, divided into two parts each.

Qin Shihuangdi, the founder of the Qin dynasty (221–206 B.C.E.), ordered Confucian texts burned, and as a result some works were lost, but most of the important texts survived, hidden by scholars until the political climate changed. The emperor also ordered the execution of a number of Confucian scholars, since he viewed the Confucian ideals of benevolent government as being at odds with his own authoritarian style.

When the Qin was overthrown by the Han dynasty, Confucianism again became the state ideology, largely due to the efforts of the Confucian scholar Dong Zhongshu, who was an advisor to emperor Wudi (r. 140–87 B.C.E.). In 125 he created a university whose educational program was based on the study of the Five Classics (the *Book of Music* had been lost during the persecution of Confucianism) and the Four Books.

In the 12th century, Zhu Xi published an edition of the Four Books that became the primary text for Confucian studies, eclipsing the Five Classics. In his system, students were advised to read the *Great Learning* first in order to learn the basic patterns of Confucianism, and then to move on to the *Analects*, which developed the ideas contained in the *Great Learning*. After that they should study the *Mencius* for its ability to inspire thought, and finally they should study *Centeredness*, which he described as profound and subtle. Due to his influence, these texts formed the basis for topics of the imperial examination system until it was abolished in 1905.

Although Confucius himself seldom mentioned such topics as spiritual beings, the nature of Heaven, life after death, or spirituality in general, his teachings became the basis for the most influential tradition of philosophy in China, one that eventually developed religious characteristics. Later Confucians propounded elaborate cosmological theories, doctrines concerning death and afterlife, and cultic practices. The tradition spread into other parts of Asia, and has been an important influence in Korea, Japan, and Vietnam. Although officially proscribed by the current leadership of the People's Republic of China, the ideas and values of Confucianism continue to exert a powerful influence on the Chinese people today.

CONFUCIAN SCRIPTURES

SIMA QIAN'S ACCOUNT OF CONFUCIUS'S LIFE

Sima Qian's account of Confucius's life, compiled in the 2nd century B.C.E., is very influential in China, though considered to be rather unreliable by modern scholars. Written on the basis of legends that had arisen around the figure of Confucius, it purports to describe his early life and to provide a biography of his adult years. The admiration of the writer is evident throughout the account, and especially in the concluding remarks.

Confucius was born in Zou, a village in the region of Zhangbing in the state of Lu. . . . As a child, Confucius liked to play with sacrificial implements, arranging them as if for a ceremony. . . . Confucius was poor and humble. Growing up and working as keeper of the granaries for the Ji clan he measured the grains fairly; when he was keeper of the livestock the animals flourished, and so he was made minister of works. Subsequently he left Lu, was dismissed from Ji, driven out of Song and Wei and ran into trouble between Zhen and Zai. Finally he returned to Lu.

Well over six feet, Confucius was called the Tall Man, and everybody marveled at his height. He returned to the state of Lu as it had treated him well. . . .

All the men of Lu from the ministers down overstepped their rightful bounds and did not act correctly. This is why Confucius did not take an official position, and instead edited the *Book of Songs, Book of History, Book of Rites*, and the *Book of Music* in his retirement, and more and more pupils came even from distant places to study with him. . . .

When Confucius had spent three years in Zai, Wu attacked Zhen, and Zhu sent its army. . . . Hearing that Confucius was living between Zhen and Zai, the people of Zhu sent an invitation to him. Before he was able to accept it, however, the ministers of Zhen and Zai discussed the situation and said, 'Confucius is a worthy man who has correctly pointed out the failings of every state. He has spent a great deal of time between Zhen and Zai, and he disapproves of all our actions and policies. Now the powerful state of Zhu has invited him. If he serves Zhu, it will be bad for us.' They sent men to surround Confucius in the countryside, keeping him from leaving. His supplies ran out, his followers were too weak to move, but Confucius went on teaching and singing, accompanying himself on the lute.

Zi Lu came up to him and said with indignation, 'Must a noble man endure privation?'

Confucius answered, 'A noble man can withstand privation, but a small man who faces privation tends to go wrong.'

Zi Kong looked unhappy, and Confucius said to him, 'Do you consider me to be a learned and educated man?'

Zi Kong replied, 'Of course; aren't you?'

Confucius said, 'Not at all; I have merely grasped the thread that links the rest. . . .'

Confucius taught his students the old songs, records, rituals, and music. In all he had 3,000 pupils, and seventy-two of them were proficient in all of the six arts. Many other people, such as Yan Zhuozou, were taught by him. In his teachings, Confucius stressed four things: culture, good conduct, loyalty, and honesty. He avoided four things: rash judgments, arbitrary opinions, hardheadedness, and vanity. He advocated caution during sacrifices, war, and illness, and he only helped those who were sincere. If he provided one corner of a square and a student could not infer the other three corners, he would not repeat himself. . . .

He said to Zi Kong, 'The world has strayed from the true Dao, and no one is able to follow me. . . . He died seven days later at the age of seventy-three, on the *ji zhou* day of the fourth month of the sixteenth year of the reign of Duke Ye of Lu (479 B.C.E.). . . .

[Sima Qian comments:] Although I cannot reach him, my heart goes out to him. When I read the words of Confucius, I try to see the man himself, and when in Lu I visited his temple and saw his carriage, clothes, and sacrificial implements. . . . The world has seen countless princes and powerful people who found fame and praise during their lives but were forgotten after death, while Confucius, though a commoner, has been revered by scholars for more than ten generations. From the emperor, princes, and nobles on down, all regard him as the highest authority. He is appropriately called the Supreme Sage.

Source: Sima Qian, *Shiji* (*Records of the Historian*).

THE *BOOK OF HISTORY*

The Book of History *purports to record events from early Chinese history. It was an important source for Confucius in his understanding of the exalted qualities of the sage emperors Yao and Shun, who are described as exemplars of righteousness, wisdom, and benevolent government.*

Examining into antiquity, we find that the Emperor Yao was called Fang Xun. He was reverent, intelligent, accomplished, sincere, and mild. He was sincerely respectful and capable of modesty. His light covered the four extremities of the empire and extended to Heaven above and the earth below. He was able to make bright his great virtue, and bring affection to the nine branches of the family. When the nine branches of the family had become harmonious, he distinguished and honored the hundred clans. When the hundred clans had become illustrious, he harmonized the myriad states. The numerous people were amply nourished and prosperous and became harmonious.

Source: *Shujing* selections: *Sources of Chinese Tradition*, vol. I, ed. William Theodore deBary, Wing-tsit Chan, and Burton Watson (New York: Columbia University Press, 1964), pp. 8–9.

CONFUCIUS: SELECTIONS FROM THE ANALECTS

The following selections are excerpted from the Analects (Lunyu), *which record instructions given by Confucius to his students and events in his life. The title of the text literally means "conversations," and it received this name because it mainly contains conversations between Confucius and his students. They emphasize an interrelated set of themes, including the character and training of the "noble man," the idea that rulers should govern by moral persuasion and should treat their subjects as a loving father treats his children, the importance of following tradition, the role of rituals and sacrifices in establishing a harmonious state, and the importance of providing for the basic needs of the populace.*

Confucius believed that the righteousness of leaders is the key to social stability and told rulers that it is important scrupulously to practice the social rituals that help a society to function harmoniously. The noble man, he taught, has a strong sense of propriety (li), a general term for the day-to-day norms of social interaction as well as for state ceremonies.

In addition, the noble man speaks the truth as he understands it, and so is concerned with the "rectification of names" (zheng ming), *which involves calling things what they are and using terms in a nondeceptive manner. Rulers who equivocate and who use euphemisms that attempt to cloak the truth of things lose the confidence of the people as surely as those who are morally degenerate and who blunder in their decisions.*

According to his student Zeng Zi, there is "one thread" running through all of Confucius's teachings: an emphasis on the centrality of morality and cultivation of an ethical foundation, which leads the noble man to treat others like himself (shu). *Human beings are said to have a basically moral nature* (zhong), *which needs to be developed by education and contact with superior persons. Such people cultivate their own moral consciousness and seek to establish others in virtue.*

Confucius taught that a person with the virtue of human-heartedness (ren) *knows how to treat others and acts appropriately in all situations. A central virtue of such a person is filial piety* (xiao), *which is evidenced by respect for elders and persons in authority, as well as by proper performance of rituals for the ancestors. Such behavior accords with the dictates of Heaven.*

Confucius believed that Heaven watches over human affairs and confers a mandate to rule (tianming). *This concept was first developed by the founders of the Zhou dynasty to justify their conquest of the Shang rulers. According to this theory, the emperor is the "son of Heaven"* (tianzi), *appointed to oversee human affairs, but rulers who become lazy, corrupt, or despotic cause Heaven to withdraw the mandate, and so lose their legitimacy. Heaven first sends warnings in the form of natural disasters, internal turmoil, or personal crises, and those who reform themselves may again earn Heaven's favor. Those who persist in their immoral actions, however, are eventually deposed by Heaven, which appoints other rulers of better moral character.*

I. 1. The Master said, 'Is it not a pleasure, having learned something, to try it out at due intervals? Is it not a joy to have friends come from afar? Is it not gentlemanly not to take offense when others fail to appreciate your abilities?'

4. Zeng Zi said, 'Every day I examine myself on three counts. In what I have undertaken on another's behalf, have I failed to do my best? In my dealings with my friends have I failed to be trustworthy in what I say? Have I passed on to others anything that I have not tried out myself?'

6. The Master said, 'A young man should be a good son at home and an obedient young man abroad, sparing of speech but trustworthy in what he says, and should love the multitude at large but cultivate the friendship of his fellow men. If he has any energy to spare from such action, let him devote it to making himself cultivated.'

9. Zeng Zi said, 'Conduct the funeral of your parents with meticulous care and let not sacrifices to your remote ancestors be forgotten, and the virtue of the common people will incline towards fullness.'

10. Zi Qin asked Zi Kong, 'When the Master arrives in a state, he invariably gets to know about its government. Does he seek this information. Or is it given him?'

Zi Kong said, 'The Master gets it through being cordial, good, respectful, frugal and deferential. The way the Master seeks it is, perhaps, different from the way other men seek it.'

11. The Master said, 'Observe what a man has in mind to do when his father is living, and then observe what he does when his father is dead. If, for three years, he makes no changes to his father's ways, he can be said to be a good son.'

14. The Master said, "The noble man (*junzi*) seeks neither a full belly nor a comfortable home. He is quick in action but cautious in speech. He goes to men possessed of the Way (*dao*) to be put right. Such a man can be described as eager to learn.'

II. 2. The Master said, 'The *Odes* are three hundred in number. They can be summed up in one phrase, "Swerving not from the right path."'

3. The Master said, 'Guide them by edicts, keep them in line with punishments, and the common people will stay out of trouble but will have no sense of shame. Guide them by virtue, keep them in line with the rites, and they will, besides having a sense of shame, reform themselves.'

4. The Master said, 'At fifteen I set my heart on learning; at thirty I took my stand; at forty I came to be free from doubts; at fifty I understood the Decree of Heaven; at sixty my ear was attuned; at seventy I followed my heart's desire without overstepping the line.'

6. Mang Wubo asked about being filial. The Master said, 'Give your father and mother no other cause for anxiety than illness.'

13. Zi Kong asked about the noble man. The Master said, 'He puts his words into action before allowing his words to follow his action.'

20. Ji Kangzi asked, 'How can one inculcate in the common people the virtue of reverence, of doing their best and of enthusiasm?'

The Master said, 'Rule over them with dignity and they will be reverent; treat them with kindness and they will do their best; raise the good and instruct those who are backward and they will be imbued with enthusiasm.'

III. 5. The Master said, 'Barbarian tribes with their rulers are inferior to Chinese states without them.'

IV. 4. The Master said, 'If a man sets his heart on benevolence, he will be free from evil.'

10. The Master said, 'In his dealings with the world the noble man is not invariably for or against anything. He is on the side of what is moral.'

14. The Master said, 'Do not worry because you have no official position. Worry about your qualifications. Do not worry because no one appreciates your abilities. Seek to be worthy of appreciation.'

15. The Master said, 'The noble man understands what is moral. The small man understands what is profitable.'

17. The Master said, 'When you meet someone better than yourself, turn your thoughts to becoming his equal. When you meet someone not as good as you are, look within and examine your own self.'

25. The Master said, 'Virtue never stands alone. It is bound to have neighbors.'

V. 16. The Master said of Zi Chan that he had the way of the noble man on four counts: he was respectful in the manner he conducted himself; he was reverent in the service of his lord; in caring for the common people, he was generous and, in employing their services, he was just.

VII. 1. The Master said, 'I transmit but do not innovate; I am truthful in what I say and devoted to antiquity.'

2. The Master said, 'Quietly to store up knowledge in my mind, to learn without flagging, to teach without growing weary, these present me with no difficulties.'

4. During his leisure moments, the Master remained correct although relaxed.

6. The Master said, 'I set my heart on the Way, base myself on virtue, lean upon benevolence for support and take my recreation in the arts.'

7. The Master said, 'I have never denied instruction to anyone who, of his own accord, has given me so much as a bundle of dried meat as a present.'

21. The topics the Master did not speak of were prodigies, force, disorder, and gods.

22. The Master said, 'Even when walking in the company of two other men, I am bound to be able to learn from them. The good points of the one I copy; the bad points of the other I correct in myself.'

37. The Master said, 'The noble man is easy of mind, while the small man is always full of anxiety.'

38. The Master was cordial yet not stern, inspiring yet not fierce, and respectful yet at ease.

VIII. 2. The Master said, 'Unless a man has the spirit of the rites, in being respectful he will wear himself out, in being careful he will become timid, in having courage he will become unruly, and in being forthright he will become intolerant.

'When the noble man feels profound affection for his parents, the common people will be stirred to benevolence. When he does not forget friends of long standing, the common people will not shirk their obligations to other people.'

7. Zeng Zi said, 'A noble man must be strong and resolute, for his burden is heavy, and the road is long. He takes benevolence as his burden. Is that not heavy? Only with death does the road come to an end. Is that not long?'

13. The Master said, 'Have the firm faith to devote yourself to learning, and abide to the death in the good way. Enter not a state that is in peril; stay not in a state that is in danger. Show yourself when the Way prevails in the Empire, but hide yourself when it does not. It is a shameful matter to be poor and humble when the Way prevails in the state. Equally, it is a shameful matter to be rich and noble when the Way falls into disuse in the state.'

IX. 14. The Master wanted to settle amongst the Nine Barbarian Tribes of the east. Someone said, 'But could you put up with their uncouth ways?' The Master said, 'Once a noble man settles amongst them, what uncouthness will there be?'

   18. The Master said, 'I have yet to meet the man who is as fond of virtue as he is of beauty in women.'

XI. 12. Ji Lu asked how the spirits of the dead and the gods should be served. The Master said, 'You are not able even to serve man. How can you serve the spirits?'

   'May I ask about death?'

   'You do not understand even life. How can you understand death?'

XII. 1. Yan Yuan asked about benevolence. The Master said, 'To return to the observance of the rites through overcoming the self constitutes benevolence. If for a single day a man could return to the observance of the rites through overcoming himself, then the whole Empire would consider benevolence to be his. However, the practice of benevolence depends on oneself alone, and not on others.'

   4. Sima Niu asked about the noble man. The Master said, 'The noble man is free from worries and fears.'

   'In that case, can a man be said to be a noble man simply because he is free from worries and fears?'

   The Master said, 'If, on examining himself, a man finds nothing to reproach himself for, what worries and fears can he have?'

   7. Zi Kong asked about government. The Master said, 'Give them enough food, give them enough arms, and the common people will have trust in you.'

   Zi Kong said, 'If one had to give up one of these three, which should one give up first?'

   'Give up arms.'

   Zi Kong said, 'If one had to give up one of the remaining two, which should one give up first?'

   'Give up food. Death has always been with us since the beginning of time, but when there is no trust, the common people will have nothing to stand on.'

   11. Duke Jing of Qi asked Confucius about government. Confucius answered, 'Let the ruler be a ruler, the subject a subject, the father a father, the son a son.' The Duke said, 'Splendid! Truly, if the ruler is not a ruler, the subject not a subject, the father not a father, the son not a son, then even if there is grain, would I get to eat it?'

   16. The Master said, 'The noble man helps others to realize what is good in them; he does not help them to realize what is bad in them. The small man does the opposite.'

   22. Fan Chi asked about benevolence. The Master said, 'Love your fellow men.'

   He asked about wisdom. The Master said, 'Know your fellow men.' Fan Chi failed to grasp his meaning. The Master said, 'Raise the straight and set them over the crooked. This can make the crooked straight.'

XIII. 1. Zi Lu asked about government. The Master said, 'Encourage the people to work hard by setting an example yourself.' Zi Lu asked for more. The Master said, 'Do not allow your efforts to slacken.'

3. Zi Lu said, 'If the Lord of Wei left the administration of his state to you, what would you put first?'

The Master said, 'If something is to be put first, it is, perhaps, the rectification of names.'

Zi Lu said, 'Is that so? What a roundabout way you take! Why bring rectification in at all?'

The Master said, 'Yu, how boorish you are. Where a noble man is ignorant, one would expect him not to offer any opinion. When names are not correct, what is said will not sound reasonable; when what is said does not sound reasonable, affairs will not culminate in success; when affairs do not culminate in success, rites and music will not flourish; when rites and music do not flourish, punishments will not fit the crimes; when punishments do not fit the crimes, the common people will not know where to put hand and foot. Thus when the noble man names something, the name is sure to be usable in speech, and when he says something this is sure to be practicable. The thing about the noble man is that he is anything but casual where speech is concerned.'

13. The Master said, 'If a man manages to make himself correct, what difficulty will there be for him to take part in government? If he cannot make himself correct, what business has he with making others correct?'

18. The Governor of She said to Confucius, 'In our village there is a man named "Straight Body." When his father stole a sheep, he gave evidence against him.' Confucius answered, 'In our village those who are straight are quite different. Fathers cover up for their sons, and sons cover up for their fathers. Straightness is to be found in such behavior.'

20. Zi Kong asked, 'What must a man be like before he can be said truly to be a noble man?' The Master said, 'A man who has a sense of shame in the way he conducts himself and, when sent abroad, does not disgrace the commission of his lord can be said to be a noble man.'

XV. 37. The Master said, 'The noble man is devoted to principle but not inflexible in small matters.'

XVI. 8. Confucius said, 'The noble man stands in awe of three things. He is in awe of the Decree of Heaven. He is in awe of great men. He is in awe of the words of the sages. The small man, being ignorant of the Decree of Heaven, does not stand in awe of it. He treats great men with insolence and the words of the sages with derision.'

Source: *Lunyu* selections: excerpted from *The Analects*, tr. D. C. Lau (New York: Dorset Press, 1979; Chinese terms have been converted to Pinyin spellings).

THE GREAT LEARNING

According to Confucian tradition, the Great Learning *was composed by Zeng Can, a student of Confucius. It is a short work that contains a condensed blueprint for personal cultivation and the ordering of the state. It has been the focus of a debate between the Neo-Confucian schools of Zhu Xi and Wang Yangming. Zhu Xi contended that the text is concerned with propriety, while Wang Yangming believed that it accords with his theory of the unity of humanity and Heaven.*

The way of the Great Learning consists of making luminous virtue shine; this entails having sympathy for the people and abiding in attainment of perfect goodness. After knowing [where to] abide, one is settled; once one is settled, one is able to be calm; once one is calm, one is able to be tranquil; once one is tranquil, one is able to have foresight; once one has foresight, one is able to begin consideration. Only after beginning consideration will the goal be attained. Things have roots and branches. Affairs have beginnings and ends. Knowing what is first and later, one will thus be near the Dao.

The ancients who wished to make their luminous virtue shine in the world first ordered their own states. Wishing to order their states, they first put their families in order. Wishing to put their families in order, they first cultivated their persons. Wishing to cultivate their persons, they first rectified their hearts. Wishing to rectify their hearts, they first made their intentions sincere. Wishing to make their intentions sincere, they first perfected their knowledge to the highest level.

Perfecting one's knowledge to the highest level consists in examination of things. Once things are examined, knowledge is perfected. When knowledge is perfected, intentions are sincere. When intentions are sincere, the heart is rectified. When the heart is rectified, one's person is cultivated. When one's person is cultivated, families are put in order. When families are put in order, states are ordered. When states are ordered, the whole world is tranquil.

Source: *Daxue* (*The Great Learning*).

CENTEREDNESS

The following text, the title of which is often translated as "The Doctrine of the Mean," consists of 3,567 characters and contains teachings attributed to Confucius. It describes the workings of Heaven and how they affect human life. According to the text, the Dao is a transcendent principle that pervades the entire universe, setting a standard and paradigm that sages seek to understand and emulate in their thoughts and behavior.

1. That which is Heaven's decree is called innate, following nature is called the Way (Dao), and cultivating the Way is called education. One cannot deviate from the Way for a moment; if one could, it would not be the Way. Because of this, the noble man is wary of what he does not see and apprehensive of what he does not hear. Nothing is better seen than what is hidden, and nothing is more apparent than what is obscure. Hence the noble man guards over his private realm. When happiness, anger, sorrow and pleasure have not yet arisen, this refers to centeredness; when these arise and are all balanced, this refers to harmony. The great foundation of the world is centeredness, and its great Way is harmony. When centered harmony is realized, heaven and earth will thereby be correctly aligned and all things will be fully developed.

2. Zhongni [Confucius] said: "The noble man, in the round of his life, is centered, but the inferior man's life is contrary to centeredness. The centered life of the noble man comes from his persisting in that centeredness; the life of the inferior man's being contrary to centeredness comes from his lack of scruples."

3. The Master said: "Centeredness is of itself consummate, but few people have been adept in it for a long time now."

4. The Master said: "I know why the Way is not followed: Those who are wise exceed it, and those who are foolish do not reach it. And I know why the Way is not clear: Those who are worthy exceed it, and those who do not emulate it do not reach it. There is no one who does not eat and drink, yet few are able really to perceive flavors."

6. The Master said: "Shun was indeed a man of great wisdom. Shun liked to query people, liked to examine their most trivial words, putting aside the evil, exalting the good. He grasped the two extremes and employed centeredness in regard to the people. This is why he was Shun [the sage-emperor]."

12. The noble man's Way is extensive yet hidden. The most foolish of men and women may share in some knowledge of it, but when it reaches its utmost even sages are ignorant of it. The most worthless of men and women may be able to practice it, but when it reaches its utmost even sages are not adept in it. In all the greatness of heaven and earth, there are still things which people complain about. Nothing in the world has adequate capacity to bear what is large in the Way of the noble man; nothing in the world can split what is small in it. The noble man's Way originates in ordinary men and women; yet at its utmost reach it reveals all heaven and earth.

Source: *Zhongyong* (*Centeredness*); tr. Kurt Vall.

THE LIFE OF MENCIUS

According to Sima Qian's account of Mencius's life, he was born in the small state of Zou and followed the example of Confucius in seeking public office in order to put his ideas into practice. Like his predecessor, however, he was unable to realize his ambitions, and made his greatest impact as a teacher.

Mencius (Mangzi) was born in Zou and was taught by a student of Master Si. After mastering the Dao, he traveled abroad and served King Xuan of Qi (r. 342–324 B.C.E.). King Xuan was unable to use him, so he went to Liang. King Hui of Liang did not find his counsel helpful. He was considered impractical and removed from the reality of affairs. . . . Wherever he went, he did not fit in. He retired, and together with students such as Wan Zhang he discussed the *Songs* and *Documents* and elucidated the ideas of Confucius, composing [his text entitled] *Mencius* in seven sections.

Source: Sima Qian, *Shiji.*

SELECTIONS FROM THE MENCIUS

The Mencius *contains teachings attributed to the Confucian scholar Mangzi, the most influential early disciple of Confucius. Mencius believed that the first rule of "humane government" (ren zheng) is to provide for the basic needs of the people, and he agreed with Confucius that rulers should rectify their own behavior and cultivate moral awareness.*

He taught his students that human nature (xing) is basically good, but that people become corrupted through exposure to negative influences. No matter how depraved a particular person might become, however, the basic nature remains good, and through proper education one's fundamental goodness may be reawakened.

In one passage he compares human nature to the shoots of plants growing on a hill called Ox Mountain, on which cattle graze. Plants constantly send up shoots, but the cattle eat them, and so the plants are not able to grow. If the cattle leave, however, the plants will be able to grow, just as human nature will find its innate goodness if the conditions inhibiting its growth are removed. In order for this to happen, people must train their minds (xin), which provide guidance in the process of moral development. The mind provides a faculty of discernment that, when attuned to human nature, develops into an unwavering sense of right and wrong.

Like Confucius, Mencius believed that Heaven confers a mandate on rulers and that it acts to remove corrupt rulers, but Mencius also contended that the people may become instruments of Heaven's will. When rulers become cruel and oppressive, they lose all legitimacy, and thus it becomes permissible for their subjects to remove them from office. Such doctrines were viewed by the rulers of his day as dangerous, and not surprisingly he was unable to find anyone to give him a position of real power. The following selections are drawn from his collected teachings, entitled the Mencius.

Mencius went to see King Hui of Liang. 'Sir,' said the King, 'You have come all this distance, thinking nothing of [traveling] a thousand *li*. You must surely have some way of profiting my state?'

'Your majesty,' answered Mencius, 'What is the point of mentioning the word "profit"? All that matters is that there should be benevolence and rightness. If your Majesty says, "How can I profit my family?" and the noble man and commoners say, "How can I profit my person?" then those above and those below will be trying to profit at the expense of one another and the state will be imperiled. . . . [I]f profit is put before rightness, there is no satisfaction short of total usurpation. No benevolent man ever abandons his parents, and no dutiful man ever puts his prince last. Perhaps you will now endorse what I have said, "All that matters is that there should be benevolence and rightness. What is the point of mentioning the word "profit""?

King Hui of Liang said, 'I have done my best for my state. When crops failed in He Nei I moved the population to He Dong and the grain to He Nei, and reversed the action when crops failed in He Dong. I have not noticed any of my neighbors taking such pains over his government. Yet how is it the population of the neighboring states has not decreased and mine has not increased?'

'Your majesty is fond of war,' said Mencius. 'May I use an analogy from it? After weapons were crossed to the rolling of drums, some soldiers fled, abandoning their armor and trailing their weapons. One stopped after a hundred paces, another after fifty paces. What would you think if the latter, as one who ran only fifty paces, were to laugh at the former who ran a hundred?'

'He had no right to,' said the King. 'He did not quite run a hundred paces. That is all. But all the same, he ran.'

'If you can see that,' said Mencius, 'you will not expect your own state to be more populous than the neighboring states. If you do not interfere with the busy seasons in the fields, then there will be more grain than the people can eat; if you do not allow nets with too fine a mesh to be used in large ponds, then there will be more fish and turtles than they can eat; if hatchets and axes are permitted in the forests on the hills only in the proper seasons, then there will be more timber than they can use. When the people have more grain, more fish and turtles than they can eat, and more timber than they can use, then in the support of their parents when alive and in the mourning of them when dead, they will be able to have no regrets over anything left undone. For the people not to have any regrets over anything left undone, whether in the support of their parents when alive or in the mourning of them when dead is the first step along the Kingly way. . . .

Now when food meant for human beings is so plentiful as to be thrown to dogs and pigs, you fail to realize that it is time for collection, and when men drop dead from starvation by the wayside, you fail to realize that it is time for distribution. When people die, you simply say, "It is none of my doing. It is the fault of the harvest." In what way is that different from killing a man by running him through, while saying all the time, "It is none of my doing. It is the fault of the weapon?" Stop putting the blame on the harvest and the people of the whole Empire will come to you.'

Mencius said to King Xuan of Qi 'Suppose a subject of Your Majesty's, having entrusted his wife and children to the care of a friend, were to go on a trip to Chu, only to find, upon his return, that his friend had allowed his wife and children to suffer cold and hunger, then what should he do about it?'

'Break with his friend.'

'If the Marshal of the Guards was unable to keep his guards in order, then what should be done about it?'

'Remove him from office.'

'If the whole realm within the four borders was ill-governed, then what should be done about it?'

The King turned to his attendants and changed the subject.

King Xuan of Qi asked, 'Is it true that Tang banished Jie and King Wu marched against Zou?'

'It is so recorded,' answered Mencius.

'Is regicide permissible?'

'He who mutilates benevolence is a mutilator; he who cripples rightness is a crippler; and a man who is both a mutilator and a crippler is an "outcast." I have indeed heard of the punishment of the "outcast Zou," but I have not heard of any regicide.'

There was a border clash between Zou and Lu. Duke Mu of Zou asked, 'Thirty-three of my officials died, yet none of my people would sacrifice their lives for them. If I punish them, there are too many to be punished. If I do not punish them, then there they were, looking on with hostility at the death of their superiors without going to their aid. What do you think is the best thing for me to do?'

'In years of bad harvest and famine,' answered Mencius, 'close on a thousand of your people suffered, the old and the young being abandoned in the gutter, the able-bodied scattering in all directions, yet your granaries were full and there was failure on the part of your officials to inform you of what was happening. This shows how callous those in authority were and how cruelly they treated the people. Zeng Zi said, "Take heed! Take heed! What you mete out will be paid back to you." It is only now that the people have had an opportunity of paying back what they conceived. You should not bear them any grudge. Practice benevolent government and the people will be sure to love their superiors and die for them.'

'The will is commander over the *qi* (material force) while the *qi* is that which fills the body. Where the will arrives there the *qi* halts. Hence it is said, "Take hold of your will and do not abuse your *qi*" . . .'

'May I ask what your strong points are?'

'I have an insight into words. I am good at cultivating my "flood-like *qi*."'

'May I ask what this "flood-like *qi*" is?'

'It is difficult to explain. This is a *qi* which is, in the highest degree, vast and unyielding. Nourish it with integrity and place no obstacle in its path and it will fill the space between Heaven and Earth. It is a *qi* which unites rightness and the Way. Deprive it of these and it will collapse. It is born of accumulated rightness and cannot be appropriated by anyone through a sporadic show of rightness. Whenever one acts in a way that falls below the standard set in one's heart, it will collapse. . . . You must work at it and never let it out of your mind. At the same time, while you must never let it out of your mind, you must not forcibly help it grow either. You must not be like the man from Song. There was a man from Song who pulled at his seedlings because he was worried about their failure to grow. Having done so, he went on his way home, not realizing what he had done. "I am worn out today," said he to his family. "I have been helping the seedlings to grow." His son rushed out to take a look and there the seedlings were, all shriveled up. There are few in the world who can resist the urge to help their seedlings to grow. There are some who leave the seedlings unattended, thinking that nothing they can do will be of any use. They are the people who do not even bother to weed. There are others who help the seedlings to grow. They are the people who pull at them. Not only do they fail to help them but they do the seedlings positive harm.'

Mencius said, 'No man is devoid of a heart sensitive to the suffering of others. Such a sensitive heart was possessed by the former Kings and this manifested itself in compassionate government. With such a sensitive heart behind compassionate government, it was as easy to rule the Empire as rolling it in your palm.'

'My reason for saying that no man is devoid of a heart sensitive to the suffering of others is this. Suppose a man were, all of a sudden, to see a young child on the verge of falling into a well. He would certainly be moved to compassion, not because he wanted to get in the good graces of the parents, nor because he wished to win the praise of his fellow villagers or friends, nor yet because he disliked the cry of the child. From this it can be seen that whoever is devoid of the heart of compassion is not human, whoever is devoid of the heart of shame is not human, whoever is devoid of the heart of courtesy and modesty is not human, and whoever is devoid of the heart of right and wrong is not human. The heart of compassion is the germ of benevolence; the heart of shame, of dutifulness; the heart of courtesy and modesty, of observance of the rites; the heart of right and wrong, of wisdom. Man has these four germs just as he has four limbs. For a man possessing these four germs to deny his own potentialities is for him to cripple himself; for him to deny the potentialities of his prince is for him to cripple his prince. If a man is able to develop all these four germs that he possesses, it will be like a fire starting up or a spring coming through. When these are fully developed, he can bend the whole realm within the Four Seas. If he fails to develop them, he will not be able even to serve his parents.'

Gaozi said, 'Human nature is like whirling water. Give it an outlet in the east and it will flow east; give it an outlet in the west and it will flow west. Human nature does not show any preference for either good or bad just as water does not show any preference for either east or west.'

'It certainly is the case,' said Mencius, 'that water does not show any preference for either east or west, but does it show the same indifference to high and low? Human nature is good just as water seeks low ground. There is no man who is not good; there is no water that does not flow downwards.

'Now in the case of water, by splashing it one can make it shoot up higher than one's forehead, and by forcing it one can make it stay on a hill. How can that be the nature of water? It is the circumstances being what they are. That man can be made bad shows that his nature is no different from that of water in this respect.'

Source: Mangzi, *Mencius*, tr. D. C. Lau (Hong Kong: The Chinese University Press, 1979, vol. I), pp. 3ff. Chinese terms have been converted to Pinyin spellings.

XUNZI: THE NATURE OF HUMAN BEINGS IS EVIL

The most influential interpreter of Confucius prior to the Han dynasty was Xunzi (Xun Qing, d. 215 B.C.E.), a younger contemporary of Mencius who lived in the state of Zhao and who is best known today for his treatises on government and warfare. Unlike Mencius, Xunzi believed that human nature is basically evil and that rulers must employ strict controls in order to keep their subjects in line. He advocated strong centralized rule and the use of punishment to restrain the population, but he also believed that human beings can be taught to be good through discipline and education. He was reportedly a teacher of Han Fei, the exponent of the philosophy of Legalism that became the dominant ideology of the Qin dynasty.

Xunzi rejected Mencius's ideas about human nature, contending that humans have innate desires, which can never be fully satisfied. People naturally desire to possess things and envy others who have things that they do not, and these basic tendencies oppose the cultivation of virtue. Goodness is attained only through training that teaches people to restrain their urges and recognize higher goods. This training requires study of the classics and education in proper performance of rites. He also rejected Mencius's idea of Heaven as a moral force that oversees human affairs. For Xunzi, Heaven is simply nature, which is impersonal and has no ethical dimension, but operates in accordance with its own laws without regard to individual virtue or human desires.

Human nature is evil; any good in humans is acquired by conscious exertion. Now, the nature of man is such that he is born with a love of profit. Following this nature will cause its aggressiveness and greedy tendencies to grow and courtesy and deference to disappear. Humans are born with feelings of envy and hatred. . . .

This being the case, when each person follows his inborn nature and indulges his natural inclinations, aggressiveness and greed are certain to develop. . . . Thus it is necessary that man's nature undergo the transforming influence of a teacher and the model that he be guided by is ritual and moral principles. Only after this has been accomplished do courtesy and deference develop. Unite these qualities with precepts of good form and reason, and the result is an age of orderly government. If we consider the implications of these facts, it is plain that human nature is evil and that any good in humans is acquired by conscious exertion.

Source: *Xunzi*, III. 150–151: *Xunzi: A Translation and Study of the Complete Works*, vol. III, tr. John Knoblock (Stanford: Stanford University Press, 1994), pp. 150–151.

YANG XIONG: HUMAN NATURE IS A MIXTURE OF GOOD AND EVIL

The question of whether human nature is basically good or evil was an important one for the Confucian tradition after Confucius. Mencius declared that human nature is basically good, while Xunzi believed it to be basically evil. Confucius himself did not make a definitive statement on the matter, and only said that people are born alike but become different through training and practice. He did contend, however, that all men have the potential to become noble men, and so it seems clear that his view of human nature was probably closer to that of Mencius than to Xunzi's negative assessment.

In the following passage, Yang Xiong (53 B.C.E.–18 C.E.) stakes out a middle position, contending that human nature is a mixture of good and evil. He contends that people become either good or evil as a result of their training: the good cultivate good, while the evil cultivate evil. His treatise helped to focus the attention of Confucian thinkers on this issue, but was criticized by later Confucians for its contention that human nature is partially evil.

Human nature is a mixture of good and evil. If we cultivate goodness, we will be good people; if we cultivate evil, we will be evil people; substance (*qi*) is the horse on which we ride to good or evil. Because of this, the noble man strives hard in learning and exerts himself in practice. The consummate Way is for him to make his goods precious before selling them, to perfect his person before forming relations with other people, to complete his plans before acting.

Source: Fuyan 3.1a–b: tr. Kurt Vall.

HAN YU: ATTACK ON BUDDHISM AND DAOISM

Han Yu (768–824) was a public official who led a Confucian attack on Buddhism and Daoism and called on the emperor to suppress them. He described Buddhism as a religion of barbarians that is at odds with cultured Chinese sensibilities, and he denounced Daoism as a religion that panders to primitive superstition.

The following excerpt is from a letter he wrote to the emperor regarding the veneration of a relic of the Buddha. He advised the emperor to reconsider his decision to publicly view a fragment of bone believed to have been left over after the Buddha was cremated, on the grounds that this may seem to the common people to be lending imperial support to the Buddhist practice of relic veneration, which Han Yu considered barbaric.

Your servant begs leave to say that Buddhism is no more than a cult of the barbarian peoples which spread to China in the time of the Latter Han. It did not exist here in ancient times. . . . When Emperor Gaozu [founder of the Tang] received the throne from the House of Sui, he deliberated upon the suppression of Buddhism. But at that time the various officials, being of small worth and knowledge, were unable fully to comprehend the ways of the ancient kings and the exigencies of past and present, and so could not implement the wisdom of the emperor and rescue the age from corruption. . . .

Now Buddha was a man of the barbarians who did not speak the language of China and wore clothes of a different fashion. His sayings did not concern the ways of our ancient kings, nor did his manner of dress conform to their laws. He understood neither the duties that bind sovereign and subject, nor the affections of father and son. If he were still alive today and came to our court by order of his ruler, Your Majesty might condescend to receive him, but . . . he would then be escorted to the borders of the nation, dismissed, and not allowed to delude the masses. How then, when he has long been dead, could his rotten bones, the foul and unlucky remains of his body, be rightly admitted to the palace? Confucius said, 'Respect ghosts and spirits, but keep them at a distance, . . .' Now without reason Your Majesty has caused this loathsome thing to be brought in and would personally go to view it. . . . Your servant is deeply shamed and begs that this bone be given to the proper authorities to be cast into fire and water, that this evil may be rooted out, the world freed from its error, and later generations spared this delusion. . . . If the Buddha does indeed have supernatural power to send down curses and calamities, may they fall only upon the person of your servant, who calls upon High Heaven to witness that he does not regret his words.

Source: Han Yu, *Changli Xianshang Wenji*, 39.2b–42: *Sources of Chinese Tradition*, pp. 371–372.

ZHOU DUNYI: THE GREAT ULTIMATE

Zhou Dunyi (1017–1073) was one of the important early figures in the Neo-Confucian revival that took place during the Song dynasty (960–1279). His most significant text was The Diagram of the Great Ultimate Explained (Taiji tu shuo), *a short work that equates the "great ultimate" (taiji) with the "non-ultimate" (wuji), which he describes as a reality transcending space and time. Its movement generates yang, the active force in nature, and its rest gives rise to yin, the passive element of natural systems. Through the interaction of these two, the "five agents" or "five elements" (wuxing) are produced, and the combinations of these elements give rise to the phenomena of the world. Zhou conceives of the universe as a dynamic and holistic system in which natural forces and human conduct are interrelated.*

1. [It is] the non-ultimate, yet also the great ultimate.
2. The great ultimate moves and produces yang. Moving to the limit, it rests. Resting, it produces yin. Resting completely, it moves again. Movement and rest alternate: each is the other's root. It distinguishes yin and yang: the two modes are established by it.
3. Yang diversifies and yin harmonizes, producing water, fire, wood, metal, and earth. The five substances (*qi*) propagate accordingly, and the four seasons are brought about by it.
4. The five phases *(xing)* are the one yin and yang. Yin and yang are the one great ultimate. The great ultimate is based in the non-ultimate. As for the production of the five phases, each has its own nature.
5. The non-ultimate reality and the essence of the Two (yin and yang) and the Five Agents marvelously harmonize and integrate. The Way of *qian* [Heaven] becomes masculine, and the Way of *kun* [earth] becomes feminine. The two affect each other, the changes producing all things: producing and reproducing and changing endlessly.
6. Humans alone get the finest endowment, and are the most spiritually potent. It is thus that their physical form is produced, and their spirit obtains understanding. The five principles of their natures respond, good and evil are distinguished, and affairs thus proceed along their courses.
7. The sage settles these matters with centeredness and rectitude, humanity and righteousness (the Way of the sage is nothing but centeredness and rectitude, humanity and righteousness), makes tranquility dominant (he is without desire and thus tranquil). In this way he sets up a standard for human perfection. Thus the sage harmonizes his power with heaven and earth, his brilliance with the sun and the moon, his time with the four seasons, and his good and bad fortunes with the spirits.
8. The noble man cultivates these qualities and earns good fortune; the inferior man goes against them and suffers misfortune.

9. Thus it is said that yin and yang establish the Way of heaven, yielding and firmness establish the Way of earth, and humanity and righteousness establish the Way of humans. It is also said that by looking into the cycle of things the explanation of life and death will become known.

10. How great is the *Book of Changes!* This is where its utmost values lies!

Source: Zhou Dunyi, *Taiji tu shuo,* ch. 1: tr. Kurt Vall.

ZHU XI: NATURE AND HUMANITY

Zhu Xi's philosophy is sometimes referred to as "study of principle" (li xueh), because he was concerned with developing understanding of the principles underlying human behavior and social interaction. He believed that society can be rectified through diligent study of the patterns of organization and development that underlie both human civilization and nature. In 1313 Zhu Xi's interpretations of Confucius were officially recognized as the orthodox system of Confucianism and became the basis for civil examinations administered by the government. As a result, they exerted tremendous influence in Chinese education until the abolition of the system by the Nationalist government in 1905.

His philosophy was influenced by Zhou Dunyi's The Diagram of the Great Ultimate Explained. *Zhu Xi interpreted the "ultimate" (ji) as the furthest point that can be reached, and he defined the "great ultimate (taiji) as the sum total of the principles of all the phenomena of the universe and the highest principle of each individual thing. According to Zhu Xi, the entire universe is one principle, and he interpreted the notion of "investigation of phenomena" as described in the* Great Learning *as a procedure of examining things in order to become aware of how each phenomenon manifests principle.*

He also contended that principle and material force are separate factualities in phenomena, although they are inseparable. Principle is immaterial, unitary, eternal, changeless, and indestructible. He viewed it as constituting the essence of things and as being always good. Material force is the energy that sustains physical things and provides the impetus for their production and transformation. It is corporeal, manifold, changeable, differentiated, and impermanent. It can become either good or evil in accordance with the choices made by human beings.

Nature corresponds with the great ultimate, and mind corresponds with yin and yang. The great ultimate is just within yin and yang; it cannot be separated from it. Yet on fully considering the great ultimate, it is of itself the great ultimate, as yin and yang are of themselves yin and yang. Nature and mind are also this Way. It is what is meant by the [notion that] they are one and yet two, and yet one.

Though nature is insubstantial, it is a concrete principle; and though the mind is an actual thing, it is yet insubstantial; thus it can embrace all principle. This is something that comes to be grasped only when people examine their own being. Nature is thus the principles that the mind has, and the mind is where principles come together.

Nature is principle (*li*), and the mind is what embraces everything and applies it to things.

Nature is before movement, and feelings are when it has already moved. Mind embraces the already moving and the not yet moving. So, the mind before it moves is nature, and when it has already moved it is feelings. Desire is what comes out of feelings. Mind is like water: nature resembles the water's stillness; feelings, the water's flow; desire, its great waves. But great waves have both what is good and what is not good. The good desires are the kind that resemble the idea, "I desire humaneness." The ones that are not good persistently race forth as if they were billowing waves. When such desires are preponderate, then heavenly principle is excluded. It is like water rising to burst the levee: there is nothing that is not damaged.

Mind designates what is in command, the ruler. It rules over both movement and stillness. It is incorrect to say that it is not doing anything during stillness, so that only when we get to movement is there a ruler. To call it "the ruler" is to say that it is an all-pervasive presence in both movement and stillness. The mind brings together nature and feelings. Yet it is incorrect to say that it is one thing that is all of a piece with them, not something separate on its own.

Source: Zhu XI, *Xing qing xin yi deng mingyi* selections: tr. Kurt Vall.

WANG YANGMING: QUESTIONS ON THE GREAT LEARNING

Wang Yangming (1472–1529) was an important opponent of Zhu Xi who lived during the Ming dynasty (1368–1644). He was a government official and scholar, as well as an eminent military strategist whose real name was Wang Shouren. He became known as Wang Yangming because he maintained a retreat in Yangming Valley in Chekiang Province. His Inquiry on the Great Learning *was his most important work and was widely debated by other Chinese thinkers. In this text he rejects Zhu Xi's explanation of the* Great Learning, *which places the investigation of things* (kewu) *before making thoughts sincere. Wang placed primary emphasis on the study of mind* (xin xueh), *which focuses on developing moral awareness through education and ethical instruction.*

Understanding, Wang contended, comes from within and not through external actions. He believed that knowledge of the good is innate and that principle (li) *is a universal factor that is found in human beings as well as natural phenomena. He followed Mencius's idea that human beings are naturally good and that those who fully cultivate their nature are able to overcome selfish tendencies and embrace the truth of the Great Learning.*

Wang also rejected Zhu Xi's notion that the investigation of things is an examination of external phenomena. Wang contended that goodness is an innate quality of the mind and believed that it involves "eliminating what is incorrect in the mind in order to preserve the correctness of its original nature." For Wang, the investigation of things entails an ethical imperative to put moral standards into practice and cultivate one's character.

A previous scholar considered the *Great Learning* to be the learning of great men. I venture to ask why the *Great Learning* should consist in manifesting lucid character? Master Yangming said: The great man takes heaven and earth and all the things as one entity; he sees that the world is but one family, and that the Middle Country is an individual in it. Now, those who make entities separate and self and other distinct are petty people. The great man's ability to take heaven and earth and all things as one entity is not a result of his attention to it; but because the humanity of his mind is fundamentally thus: he becomes one with heaven and earth and all things. This is surely not confined to the great man: even in an inferior man's mind this is so. It is he himself who nevertheless makes it inferior, and that's all. Thus if he sees a child falling into a well, he cannot fail to have a concerned and compassionate mind towards it. This comes from his humanity and the child forming one entity. A child is still one of his own kind. Yet even if he sees a bird or animal shivering fearfully and calling pitifully, his mind cannot abide it. This comes from his humanity and the birds and animals forming one entity. This then is the mind which is capable of forming one entity with other things, and even though someone's mind may be that of an inferior man, it cannot but possess this capacity. And this has its root in heaven-decreed nature, which is inherently clear and unobscured. That is why it is called "lucid character."

So when unobscured by selfish desires, even an inferior man with an inferior man's mind—because of his humaneness which is capable of forming one entity with other things—is yet a noble man. But when obscured by selfish desire, even a noble man, because he cuts himself off from other beings, is nevertheless an inferior man. So, engaging in the learning of the noble man just means getting rid of the obscuration of selfish desires, thereby spontaneously manifesting lucid character and resuming essential oneness with heaven and earth and all things. It is not that there is something separate, something that can be added onto his basic being.

The utmost good is the ultimate principle of manifesting character and loving people. Heavenly decreed nature is purely of the utmost good. It is clear and unobscured, thus evincing its perfection. It is the substance of lucid character: it is what is called innate understanding. As the highest good is manifested, right and wrong are known by it, and it is affected and responds commensurately with the situation. There is nothing that does not inherently possess Heaven's centeredness: this is the unchanging principle of people and things.

The Teacher said: The endeavor of great learning is manifesting lucid character; manifesting lucid character is just making thought sincere; the endeavor of making thought sincere is just plumbing things and gaining understanding. So making dominant the task of making thought sincere and then going on to practice the endeavor of examining things and gaining understanding means that that endeavor will have results from the beginning. This is to say that being good and getting rid of evil are nothing but the task of making thought sincere. With [Zhu Xi's] new edition [of the *Great Learning*] exhaustively examining the principle *(li)* of things and affairs comes first; but this approach makes the task vast and hazy, so that there will be no result at all. In the main, the endeavor of centeredness is just making the self sincere. When making the self sincere reaches its furthest point, then it is consummate sincerity. When making thought sincere is at the utmost, then it is consummate good. All these endeavors are the same.

Source: Wang Yangming, Daxue wen, ch. 1: tr. Kurt Vall.

GLOSSARY

Confucius (ca. 551–479 B.C.E.; Chinese: Kong Fuzi): Founder of Confucianism and one of the great sages of China.

Dao "Way," a pattern of action that applies to all human societies and to natural forces.

Junzi "Noble Man," one who embodies the ideal qualities of a Confucian gentleman.

Li "Propriety," one of the primary Confucian virtues, involving proper social conduct and rituals.

Lunyu *(analects)* A collection of aphorisms attributed to Confucius.

Mencius (ca. 4th century B.C.E; Chinese: Mangzi): One of the most influential Confucian thinkers.

Neo-Confucianism A movement to revive Confucianism that began in the 11th century.

Rectification of Names *(zhengming)* The principle of using words nondeceptively, of saying what one actually means.

Ren "Human-heartedness," one of the primary Confucian virtues, evidenced by proper attitudes and actions toward others.

Tian "Heaven," an impersonal force that watches over human affairs.

FURTHER READINGS

CHEN, LI FU. *The Confucian Way: A New and Systematic Study of the 'Four Books.'* London: KPI, 1986.

FINGARETTE, HERBERT. *Confucius: The Secular as Sacred.* San Francisco: Harper Torchbooks, 1972.

HALL, DAVID L. and AMES, ROGER T. *Thinking Through Confucius.* Albany: State University of New York Press, 1987.

MCNAUGHTON, WILLIAM, ed. *The Confucian Vision.* Ann Arbor: Ann Arbor Paperbacks, 1974.

SCHWARTZ, BENJAMIN. *The World of Thought in Ancient China.* Cambridge, MA: Belknap Press, 1985.

WEI-MING, TU. *Centrality and Commonality: An Essay on Confucian Religiousness.* Albany: State University of New York Press, 1989.

Daoism

INTRODUCTION

For modern Chinese, religion is primarily a matter of participation in community activities and rituals connected with important transitions rather than adherence to doctrines and codes of conduct. Chinese rituals mark and celebrate the important rites of passage of human existence: birth, marriage, and death, as well as events in the agricultural calendar, such as planting and harvest. These rituals developed in a culture that is overwhelmingly agrarian and rural, in which the majority of people were (and still are) engaged in agricultural work. Underlying many Chinese religious practices is a deeply felt sense of the importance of promoting community solidarity and an emphasis on the rootedness of the individual and the collective in the natural world.

Another important feature of Chinese religious traditions is their eclecticism. The indigenous Chinese religious systems borrowed elements from each other and from traditions like Buddhism that were imported to China, and the foreign systems in turn adopted Chinese motifs and ideas in order to accommodate themselves to Chinese sensibilities. Among contemporary Chinese, sharp distinctions are seldom drawn between the major religious traditions of China: Daoism, Confucianism, and Buddhism; rather, they are viewed as harmoniously intersecting with each other to form a comprehensive system that is able to adapt itself to a wide spectrum of religious needs. The three traditions are collectively referred to as "lineage of teachings" (*zongjiao*) or "the three teachings" (*sanjiao*), indicating that they are not perceived as separate systems of doctrine and practice but as mutually complementary emphases.

Confucianism is viewed as being primarily concerned with the interactions of people in a social context. It outlines the norms and values that ensure social harmony, along with the rituals and duties that enable people to act appropriately when in the company of others. Daoism focuses on the connections between human beings and their natural environment, how natural processes and forces affect human existence, and how to predict the movements of these forces and manipulate them for the benefit of individuals and society. The purview of Buddhism is mainly life after death, since Buddhism brought to China a highly developed eschatology and a pantheon of compassionate buddhas and bodhisattvas who are willing and able to give aid both in the present life and after death.

173

The origins of Daoism lie in popular religious practices and ideas of ancient China. According to popular Daoist belief, the earliest codification of the central concepts of the tradition was set forth by Laozi, who according to legend was a sage who lived in the sixth century B.C.E. and who worked as an archivist in the state of Lu. Credited with the authorship of the classic work entitled *The Way and Virtue (Daodejing)*, Laozi became concerned with the degeneration of his society and decided to leave China and travel beyond the Western Gate that marked the border between Chinese civilization and the regions inhabited by non-Chinese peoples. As Laozi was leaving, the gate-keeper Yin Xi asked him to write a short outline of his philosophy for the benefit of posterity. Initially reluctant to commit his ideas to writing because words inevitably distort the truth, Laozi eventually agreed and summarized the essentials of what later came to be Daoist philosophy.

It should be noted that the text makes no claim to originality. Rather, Laozi stresses that his thoughts accord with those of the sages of the past and merely recapitulate the wisdom found by all who understand the subtle and profound workings of the universe. His text has two primary concerns: the Way (*dao*) and Virtue or Power (*de*), which is connected with its manifest operations. The Dao is described as a universal force, subtle and omnipresent, that gives rise to all things and provides their sustenance. It is the vital energy that makes all life possible, and it pervades the entire universe, providing a pattern for the growth and development of living things.

Transcending and embracing all dichotomies, the Dao is comprised of two opposite but complementary polarities, *yin* and *yang* Originally these terms seem to have referred to the shady and sunny sides of mountains, respectively. *Yin* is described as yielding, wet, passive, dark, and feminine, while *yang* is said to be aggressive, dry, active, light, and masculine. These distinctions reflect distinctive tendencies within natural systems, but they are not diametrically opposed. Rather, each contains elements of the other, and their interaction provides the creative and dynamic force behind the changes that occur in the natural world.

The Dao is ineffable. It transcends all sense experience and all thought. It may, however, be understood by the sage who becomes open to it and thus "becomes one with the Great Thoroughfare." The primary obstacle to this attainment is the senses, in combination with the intellect, which trick people into thinking that ordinary perceptions and cognitions provide a true picture of reality. Those who seek to become sages are counseled to empty themselves, to cast off learning, reasoning, words, and intellection. In this way they become open to direct experience of Dao, through which they can find true harmony with their environment and enjoy a long and tranquil life.

The workings of Dao tend toward harmony and balance, and whenever any part of a natural system develops extreme qualities, this imbalance triggers a corresponding backlash. This is true of natural phenomena and human beings. Imbalances in nature are corrected by automatic reactions, and the more extreme the imbalance, the more powerful will be the reaction. Similar principles operate in individual human lives and the actions of collectives.

Any person or group that develops extreme qualities or that disturbs the natural harmony of the world will reap corresponding consequences, which will inevitably right the balance of nature. Thus the Daoist sage goes along with the operations of the Dao, not forcing things, and so is able to live long and peacefully. Those who do not understand this principle are doomed to waste their vital energies in fruitless aggression and activity, like a strong swimmer who pushes against a current but eventually becomes exhausted and is carried downstream.

Laozi compares human beings at birth to uncarved blocks of wood (*pu*), with rough edges and unsymmetrical, like natural phenomena that have not been tampered with. Confucians shared this idea, but while they proposed to carve the block in order to properly socialize it, Laozi sees this notion as profoundly misguided. Humans at birth are supple and yielding, full of life energy, but through the process of acculturation they are placed into artificial molds and unnatural situations, which dissipate their energies in useless activities. Those who allow themselves to become caught up in the rat race inevitably wear themselves down and become like withered, dead branches—hard, stiff, and unyielding—and so shorten their lifespans.

According to Laozi, the operations of Dao may be compared to the movement of water. When water encounters a hard obstacle like a rock, it simply flows around it, rather than battering against it. Water, which is soft and yielding, does not contend against obstacles placed in its way, but instead moves around them, finding the path of least resistance. As it does this, however, it also slowly and inexorably wears down the resistance of even the hardest rock, and over the course of time overcomes all obstacles and may even create deep chasms in solid rock. Similarly, the sage avoids direct confrontation and goes along with the natural flow of Dao, practicing the Daoist virtue of "non-action" (*wuwei*). A person who perfects this technique appears to do nothing, but in reality moves with the natural rhythms of the world, thus working in accordance with the Dao to promote harmony and prosperity.

Zhuangzi, the other major figure of the early Daoist mystical tradition, shares similar views of the workings of Dao and the way of the sage. Where Laozi's text uses terse aphorisms to make its points, however, Zhuangzi tells stories that describe the way of the sage. Many of these have bizarre characters and strange situations, and they are pervaded by a subtle humor that gently mocks the ordinary ways of the world and the concerns of human society.

Zhuangzi also differs from Laozi in that he has little interest in applying Daoist principles in the political arena. The second half of Laozi's text is concerned with how rulers should act and the principles of good governance, while Zhuangzi repeatedly emphasizes his utter disinterest in becoming involved in such matters. Rather, Zhuangzi counsels his readers to cultivate uselessness, since things that are truly useless cannot be used by others and thus are left alone. The sage, according to Zhuangzi, moves unobtrusively among the hustle and bustle of the world, living at the margins of society, and is generally not even recognized as a sage by his or her contemporaries.

The establishment of Daoism as a distinctive religious tradition dates back to 142 C.E., when Zhang Daoling received the first of a series of revelations from Taishang Laojun, Lord Lao the Most High. This deity is the personification of the Dao and is believed by Daoist tradition to be Laozi, who in reality was a human form taken by the Dao in order to teach the truth to human beings. Zhang Daoling began to spread the teachings he had received and established the first organized Daoist system, named True Unity of Celestial Masters. Because of his connection with the first revelation, he was recognized as the first of the Celestial Masters, the patriarchs of the school.

The tradition continues today. The 64th Celestial Master currently resides in Taiwan and is considered to be the direct descendant of Zhang Daoling. The Celestial Masters tradition traces its philosophical roots back to the works of Laozi and Zhuangzi, and it has also developed into a communal religion that emphasizes rituals for purification and exorcism, along with teachings on morality.

Contemporary scholars commonly distinguish two main streams of Daoist thought: the system of the philosophers of the fourth and third centuries B.C.E. is termed "philosophical Daoism," and the later tradition that was concerned with techniques leading to immortality is termed "religious Daoism." While this division does capture an important distinction of emphases within the tradition, it is also overly simplistic. Daoism has a long and complex history that has produced numerous strands of thought and practice, and recent research has shown that elements of the "religious" strand may be found in the works of the early "philosophical" Daoists, and texts of "religious" Daoism are strongly influenced by the thought of "philosophical" Daoists.

In Zhuangzi's stories there are several mentions of the "immortals" (*xian*), who are said to live on a remote mountain (or, according to other accounts, on a hidden island). They avoid eating cereals, guard their vital energies, and are able to fly through the air. While most people dissipate their vital energies through involvement in mundane affairs, worry, and eating unhealthy foods, the immortals practice physical regimens that safeguard the life force (*qi*), while also avoiding activities and environments that weaken it. The search for immortality was an important concern of the developed Daoist tradition, which created elaborate systems of practice designed to promote long life. Among these were physical exercises that emulated the movements of long-lived animals (who were considered to be naturally adept at guarding vital energies), sexual techniques (*fang zhong*) that were believed to increase one's store of energy, special diets that were believed to promote the cultivation of energy, and chemical elixirs designed to replenish lost energy. Many of these elixirs contained cinnabar (mercuric sulfide), a red-colored liquid metal that was widely believed to contain a high concentration of vital energy.

Daoist masters also developed systems of meditative practices designed to promote longevity, such as "meditation on the One" (*shouyi*), in which one guards the vital energies, concentrating on the universal life force emanated by the Dao. This practice culminates in an ecstatic vision of multicolored light. Other techniques described five primary energy centers in the body, each of which was inhabited by a particular god. Meditators were advised to increase the energy levels in these centers by safeguarding the energy drawn into the body through breathing, by avoiding grains, by ingesting specific medicinal plants, and by medical techniques such as acupuncture and control of the pulse.

Daoist Scriptures

Given the long and varied history of Daoism and the range of concerns of Daoist authors, it is not surprising that the Daoist canon (*daozang*) contains a great variety of texts. All traditions of Daoism trace their origins back to the works of Laozi, Zhuangzi, and other early masters such as Liezi. Later developments incorporate their ideas and symbols, although they often diverge from their systems in significant ways. Moreover, despite the importance of these early masters for the later tradition, the development of the religion of Daoism took place many centuries after their deaths. The dawn of an organized religion of Daoism was the second century C.E., and it can be traced back to the movements of the Great Peace (Taiping) and the Celestial Masters, which formed around charismatic leaders and spread throughout China, among both common people and the cultural and political elite.

During the fourth and fifth centuries, Daoism became a widely popular tradition which appealed to all classes of Chinese society, and it is during this time that it began to develop a distinctive collection of scriptures. The earliest listing of Daoist texts was attempted by Ban Gu (32–92), in his *History of the Han* (*Han shu*), but it was not until the latter part of the fifth century that the first comprehensive catalogue of Daoist scriptures was prepared by Lu Xiujing (406–477). Sponsored by Song Mingdi (r. 465–477), he compiled the *Index to the Scriptures of the Three Caverns* (*Sandong Jingshu Mulu*), which he presented to the emperor in 471. Now lost, this massive compilation was said to have listed over 1,200 fascicles (*juan*), including philosophical texts, alchemical works, and descriptions of talismans.

The next important listing of Daoist literature was prepared by order of Emperor Tang Xuanzong (r. 713–756), who believed himself to be a direct descendant of Laozi (who by this time was widely regarded as a celestial deity). The emperor ordered a search throughout his empire for all existing Daoist literature, which was eventually brought together in a collection called *Sublime Compendium of the Three Caverns* (*Sandong Qiong gang*), which is said to have comprised 3,700 texts. He had a number of copies made of the collection, which were then stored in Daoist temples. Shortly after this, however, the imperial libraries of the capitals of Chang'an and Loyang were destroyed during the An Lushan and Shi Siming rebellions, with the result that much of this huge collection was also lost.

Another compilation was ordered during the Song dynasty (960–1279). Song Zhenzong (r. 998–1022) ordered his advisor Wang Qinruo (962–1025) to compile a catalogue of existing Daoist literature, and later Zhang Junfang (ca. 1008–1029) headed a team of Daoist priests who compiled a collection of Daoist scriptures called *Precious Canon of the Celestial Palace of the Great Song*

(*Song Tiangong Daozang*), which had 4,565 titles. This is regarded by the tradition as the first definitive edition of the Daoist canon.

During subsequent dynasties other compilations of the Daoist canon were prepared. The latest version of the canon was printed in 1926, with the sponsorship of the Nationalist government. Consisting of 1,120 fascicles, it is the largest collection of Daoist literature ever completed. Fu Zengxiang (1872–1950), a former minister of education, convinced President Xu Shichang (1855–1939) to allocate government funds to preserve this literature. Based on the collection of the White Cloud Abbey (Baiyun Guan) of Beijing, it is believed to be descended from an edition of the canon prepared in 1445, and later emended in 1845.

Since the compilation of the canon by Lu Xiujing in 471, editions of the *Daozang* have traditionally followed his division of Daoist texts into the "Three Caverns": (1) Cavern of Perfection (*dongzhen*), which derives from the Supreme Clarity (*shangqing*) texts; (2) Cavern of Mystery (*dongxuan*), which derives from the Numinous Treasure (*lingbao*) literature; and (3) Cavern of Spirit (*dongshen*), which is based on the texts collectively called "Three Kings" (*sanhuang*). This division appears to be patterned on the division of Buddhist teachings into the Three Vehicles.

In addition to this central division, the Daoist canon also contains other texts, such as the "Four Supplements" (*sifu*), which follow the Three Caverns, named respectively *Great Mystery* (*taixuan*), *Great Peace* (*taiping*), *Great Purity* (*taiqing*), and *True Unity* (*zhengyi*). The first three of these have traditionally been regarded as supplements to the Three Caverns, although in fact their origins are believed by contemporary scholars to have been composed in reference to other texts. The *Great Mystery* supplement is based on the *Daodejing*; the *Great Peace*, *Great Purity*, and *True Unity* collections appear to be based on the *Scripture on the Great Peace* (*Taipingjing*); the *Great Purity* (*Taiqing*) texts are based on alchemy, and the True Unity or Celestial Masters tradition.

As Daoist literature developed, other texts found their way into the canon that did not fit neatly into the early divisions, and as a result the canon was further subdivided. In the modern canon, each of the Three Caverns is divided into 12 sections: (1) original revelations; (2) celestial talismans; (3) commentaries; (4) sacred diagrams; (5) histories and genealogies; (6) codes of conduct; (7) rules for ceremonies; (8) outlines of rituals; (9) techniques for alchemy, geomancy, and numerology; (10) hagiographical works; (11) hymns and prayers; and (12) memorial addresses. Despite the apparently detailed nature of this division, individual sections contain a range of literature, and individual texts within a given division may not correspond to the general category.

In addition to the *Daozang*, another important compilation of Daoist scriptures should be mentioned, the *Edition of Essentials from the Daoist Canon* (*Daozang Jiyao*), a smaller collection of texts compiled during the Qing dynasty (1644–1912). The 1906 edition of this corpus contains 287 titles, including works attributed to Sun Buer, some of whose writings are excerpted below. These two collections of scriptures contain hundreds of rituals for renewal (*jiao*), funeral liturgies (*zhai*), philosophical texts, cosmological treatises, rituals for festivals and healing, discussions of external and internal alchemy, medical literature, meditation texts, descriptions for identification and preparation of healing herbs and roots, mythological stories and hagiographies of great Daoist masters and immortals, and a variety of other types of literature.

Due to the diffuse nature of the Daoist canon, it is possible to provide only a small cross-section of this literature. The following selections attempt to give a representative sampling of some of the most important texts and genres of literature in the canon and focus on developments that have had a significant impact on the development of Daoism.

DAOIST SCRIPTURES

A BRIEF ACCOUNT OF LAOZI'S LIFE

A number of contemporary scholars believe that Laozi (whose name means "Old Master") may not have been a historical figure. In addition, there is significant textual evidence that the work attributed to him actually comprises materials from different authors and was compiled centuries after he lived. His historicity is doubted because there is little solid evidence that he ever lived and considerable confusion among the sources that mention him. According to the record composed by the historian Sima Qian (154–80 B.C.E.), Laozi was reportedly born in a small village in southern China in the later period of the Zhou dynasty. His surname was Li, and his personal name was Er. He worked as an archivist for most of his life but, after becoming concerned with what he perceived as a degeneration of his society, Laozi decided to leave through the Western Gate, which marked the boundary of China. According to Sima Qian, he was not heard from again. In later times, however, numerous sightings of Laozi were reported, and a wealth of legends concerning this mysterious figure circulated throughout China.

Laozi cultivated the Dao and the Virtue. His teaching focused on remaining apart [from society] and avoiding fame. After living under the Zhou for a long time, he saw that the Zhou was in decline, and he decided to leave. When he reached the pass [on the western frontier of China], Yin Xi, the Guardian of the Pass, said, 'Since you are about to completely withdraw, I ask you to write a text for me.' Laozi thus composed a book in two sections which described the meaning of the Dao and the Virtue in more than five thousand characters. He then left. No one knows what became of him.

Source: Sima Qian, *Shiji*, p. 63.2142.

LAOZI INSTRUCTS CONFUCIUS

According to traditional sources, Laozi was an older contemporary of Confucius, and the two supposedly met on several occasions. When Daoist texts report their meetings, Laozi is portrayed as utterly surpassing Confucius in his understanding of Dao and as admonishing him to give up his attachment to rituals, propriety, and learning and embrace simplicity. Not surprisingly, Confucian sources portray Confucius as the victor. In the following selection, drawn from Sima Qian's history, Confucius comes to Laozi for instruction on the proper performance of rituals, but is advised instead to give up his rigidity and affectations and embrace Dao.

Confucius traveled to Zhou with the intention of questioning Laozi about rites. Laozi said, 'The people you mention have decomposed, both the people and their bones. Only their words remain here. Also, when the noble person attains his season, he will harness his horses. If he does not attain it, he will be pushed along like a tumbleweed moving with the wind. . . . Get rid of your arrogant manners and many desires, get rid of your artificial mannerisms and your grand ambitions. These all are of no benefit to you. This is all I have to tell you.'

Confucius left and told his disciples, 'I know that birds can fly, I know that fish can swim, and I know that animals can run. One may make traps for things that run, one may put out lines for that which swims, and one may make arrows with attached twine for that which flies. But regarding the dragon, I may never know how it flies in the wind and clouds and ascends into the sky. Today I have met Laozi. Is he like the dragon?'

Source: Sima Qian, *Shiji*, p. 63.2139.

LAOZI CONVERTS THE BARBARIANS

When Buddhism first arrived in China, many Daoists welcomed it as a kindred system, but over time rivalries between the two traditions developed, although they continued to borrow from each other. In the following passage, a Daoist author claims that the Buddha was really Laozi, who traveled to India after passing through the Western Gate. He intended to teach them the essence of Daoism, but soon realized that they were only capable of understanding the "Lesser Way," an inferior version of his teaching suitable for barbarians. The passage reflects traditional Chinese attitudes toward non-Chinese peoples, who are seen as savages.

Using his divine powers, [Laozi] then summoned all the barbarian kings. Without question they appeared from far and near. There were numerous kings and nobles. . . . They all came with their wives and concubines, families and other dependents. They crowded around the Venerable Lord, coming ever closer in order to hear the law.

At this time the Venerable Lord addressed the assembled barbarian kings:

'Your hearts are full of evil! You engage in killing and harm other beings! Since you feed only on blood and meat, you cut short manifold lives!

'Today I will . . . prohibit meat-eating among you and leave you with a diet of wheat and gruel. This will take care of all that slaughter and killing! Those among you who cannot desist shall themselves become dead meat!

'You barbarians are greedy and cruel! You make no difference between kin and stranger. You are intent only to satisfy your greed and debauchery! Not a trace of mercy or sense of social duty is within you!

'Look at you! Your hair and beards are unkempt and too long! How can you comb and wash them? Even from a distance you are full of rank smell! How awfully dirty your bodies must be!

'Now that you are made to cultivate the Dao all these things will be great annoyances to your practice. I therefore order all of you to shave off your beards and hair. . . . By teaching you the Lesser Way, I will, by and by, lead you to more cultivated manners. In addition, I will give you a number of precepts and prohibitions, so that you gradually get to exercise mercy and compassion. Each month on the fifteenth day, you shall repent your sins.'

Source: *Huahujing*, p. 1266b: *The Taoist Experience: An Anthology,* tr. Livia Kohn (Albany: State University of New York Press, 1993), pp. 76–77.

LAOZI BECOMES AN IMMORTAL

The following excerpt is taken from the Scripture of the Western Ascension, *which portrays Laozi as an immortal after his departure from China. The text reports that he traveled to India, where he became known as the Buddha. He taught the essentials of Daoism to his Indian audiences, and shortly before leaving human society forever he returned to China to impart a final instruction to Yin Xi.*

Suddenly Laozi was nowhere to be seen. The office building was illuminated by a brilliance of five colors, simultaneously dark and yellow. Yin Xi went into the courtyard, bowed down and said: 'Please, dear spirit man, let me see you once again. Give me one more rule, and I can guard the primordial source of all.'

He looked up and saw Laozi suspended in midair several feet above the ground. He looked like a statue. The image appeared and disappeared; it was vague and indistinct and seemed to waver between young and old.

Laozi said: 'I will give you one more admonition; make sure you get it right: Get rid of all impurity and stop all thoughts; calm your mind and guard the One. When all impurities are gone, the myriad affairs are done. These are the essentials of my Dao.'

Then the vision vanished. Yin Xi did not know where it had gone. He cried bitterly and worshipped it in remembrance. Then he retired from office on grounds of illness. He gave up all thinking and guarded the One, and the myriad affairs were done.

Source: *Xishengjing* selections: Livia Kohn, *Early Chinese Mysticism: Philosophy and Soteriology in the Taoist Tradition* (Princeton: Princeton University Press, 1992), p. 131.

LAOZI: THE *DAODEJING*

Regarded by Daoist tradition as the oldest text of the canon, the Daodejing is attributed to Laozi. Containing about five thousand characters, it is also popularly known as "The Five Thousand Character Classic." Modern versions of the text are divided into two sections, the first of which describes the Dao, while the second is concerned with how rulers should follow the way of Dao in order to rule wisely and well. Some contemporary scholars believe that the text we have today is not in fact a unitary work, but instead contains materials from various periods. It is widely believed to have been compiled during the Warring States Period, around 250 B.C.E., and the earliest known version of the text dates back to the beginning of the Han dynasty (202–220). It has also been the subject of numerous commentaries, many of which may still be found today in the Daoist canon.

1. The Dao that can be described
    Is not the eternal Dao.
    The name that can be spoken
    Is not the eternal name.
    The nameless is the origin of Heaven and Earth;
    The named is the mother of all things.
    Remain always free from desire,
    And you will see its subtlety.
    Always hold onto desires,
    And you will only see its results.
    The two develop together
    But have different names.
    They are deep and mysterious.
    Deeper and more mysterious, the gate of all wonders.

2. When beauty is recognized, ugliness is born.
    When good is recognized, evil is born.
    Is and is not give rise to each other;
    Difficult requires easy;
    Long is measured by short;
    High is determined by low;
    Sound is harmonized by voice;
    Back follows front.
    Therefore, the sage applies himself to non-action (*wuwei*),
    Moves without speaking,
    Creates the ten thousand things without hindrance,
    Lives, but does not possess,
    Acts, but does not presume,
    Accomplishes, but takes no credit.
    Since no credit is taken, his accomplishments endure.

3. Do not exalt heroes,
    And people will not quarrel.
    Do not value rare objects,
    And people will not steal.
    Don't display things of desire,
    And their hearts will not be troubled.
    Therefore, the sage governs by emptying their hearts and filling their stomachs,
    Discouraging their ambitions and strengthening their bones;
    Leads people away from knowledge and desire;
    Keeps the learned from imposing on others;
    Practices non-action, and the natural order is not disturbed.

4. Dao is empty.
   Use it, and it will never overflow;
   It is bottomless, the origin of all things.
   It blunts sharp edges,
   Unties knots, softens light,
   Merges with the dust.
   I do not know from where it comes,
   Its appearance precedes the Ancestor.

6. The spirit of the valley never dies.
   It is called the mysterious female.
   The gate of the mysterious female
   Is called the root of heaven and earth.
   It is continuous and exists forever;
   Use it and you will never wear it out.

8. It is best to be like water;
   Which benefits the ten thousand things and does not compete.
   It collects in the places in which humans disdain to live,
   Near the Dao.
   Live in goodness;
   Keep your mind deep;
   Treat others with kindness;
   Keep your word;
   Do what is right;
   Work at the proper time;
   If you do not contend, you cannot be blamed.

10. Can you balance your life force
    And embrace the One without differentiation?
    Can you gently control your breath like an infant?
    Can you purify your profound insight so it will become stainless?
    Can you love people and govern the state without [clinging to] knowledge?
    Can you open and shut the Gate of Heaven
    Without clinging to the earth? . . .
    Produce and cultivate
    Produce but not possess,
    Act without depending,
    Excel but do not try to master [others]:
    This is called profound virtue (*de*).

14. We look at it and do not see it;
    It is called the Invisible.
    We listen to it and do not hear it;
    It is called the Inaudible.
    We touch it and do not feel it;
    It is called the subtle. . . .
    Infinite and boundless, it cannot be named;
    It subsists in nothingness.
    It is shape without shape, form (*xiang*) without form.
    It is the vague and elusive. . . .

17. With the best rulers
     The people know that they exist.
     The next best they see and praise.
     The next they fear.
     And the next they revile.
     If you do not have basic trust
     There will be no trust at all,
     Be circumspect in the use of words.
     When your work is done,
     The people will say, "We have done it ourselves."

18. With the decline of the great Dao,
     The [doctrines of] humanity and righteousness appeared.
     When learning and cleverness are recognized,
     Great hypocrisy arises.
     When family relations are forgotten,
     Filial piety and affection arise.
     When a country falls into chaos,
     Loyal citizens come forth.

22. The crippled becomes whole.
     The crooked becomes straight.
     The hollow becomes filled.
     The worn becomes renewed.
     The meager becomes increased.
     The full becomes deluded.
     Therefore, sages embrace the One
     And maintain the world.
     Do not display themselves
     And are therefore luminous.
     Do not assert themselves
     And are therefore exalted.
     Do not boast
     And therefore succeed.
     Are not complacent
     And thus endure.
     Do not contend
     And so no one in the world
     Can contend against them.

28. One who knows the male and maintains the female
     Becomes the valley of the world.
     Being the valley of the world,
     Virtue will endure.
     Return to the state of infancy.
     Know the white, maintain the black,
     Become the model for the world.
     Being the model for the world,
     One will never deviate from virtue.
     Return to the state of the uncarved block (*pu*).

37. The Dao does nothing
    Yet through it everything is done.
    If kings and princes could hold to it,
    The world would be transformed of its own accord.
    When transformed, beings wish to engage in action.
    Still them through wordless simplicity.
    Then there will be no desire.
    Absence of desire is tranquillity,
    And the world becomes peaceful of its own accord.

41. When superior people hear of Dao
    They endeavor to live in accordance with it.
    When the mediocre hear of Dao
    Sometimes they are aware of it, and sometimes they are not.
    When the lowest type hear of Dao
    They break into loud laughter.
    If it were not laughed at, it would not be Dao.

43. The softest thing in the world overcomes the hardest.
    Non-being penetrates that which has no space.
    This indicates the benefit of non-action.
    Few in the world can understand wordless teaching and the benefit of
    non-action.

48. In pursuing knowledge, one gains daily;
    Pursuing Dao, one loses daily.
    Through losing and losing again,
    One arrives at non-action.
    By doing nothing everything is done.
    View the whole world as nothing.
    When one makes the slightest effort,
    The world is beyond one's grasp.

49. The sage has no fixed opinions,
    The opinions of ordinary people become his own.
    I am good to people who are good;
    I am also good to those who are not good:
    That is the goodness of virtue.
    I believe honest people;
    I also believe the dishonest:
    This is the trust of virtue.
    Sages create harmony in the world.
    They mingle their hearts with the world.
    Ordinary people fix their eyes and ears on them,
    But sages become the children of the world.

63. Act without acting.
    Serve without serving.
    Taste without tasting.
    Whether it is great or small, many or few,
    Repay hatred with virtue.

Deal with the difficult through what is easy;
Deal with the big through the small.
The difficulties of the world
Should be dealt with through the easiest;
The great things of the world
Should be accomplished through the smallest.

65. The rulers of old did not enlighten the people,
But kept them ignorant.
Therefore, ruling through cleverness
Leads to rebellion.
Not ruling through cleverness
Leads to good fortune.

76. When people are born, they are soft and weak;
At death, they are stiff and strong.
The ten thousand plants and trees are born soft and supple,
And at death are brittle and dry.
Hardness and strength are the companions of death,
And softness and weakness are the companions of life.
Therefore, the strongest armies do not seek to conquer.
The mightiest trees are cut down.
The strong and great sink down;
The soft and weak rise.

78. Nothing in the world is softer and weaker than water
But nothing is superior to it in overcoming the hard and strong;
Weakness overcomes strength
And softness overcomes hardness.
Everyone knows this, and no one practices it.

81. True words are not fine-sounding;
Fine-sounding words are not true.
Good people do not argue;
Argumentative people are not good.
Wise people are not learned;
The learned are not wise.
The sage does not accumulate things;
Has enough by working for others;
Gives to others and has even more.
The Dao of Heaven benefits and does not harm.
The Dao of the sage accomplishes, but does not contend.

Source: *Daodejing*, selections.

WANG BI: COMMENTARY ON THE *DAODEJING*

Wang Bi (226–249), author of the most influential commentary on the Daodejing, *is renowned in China as one of the foremost representatives of the Dark Learning (xuanxue) school of Chinese philosophy. This school is based on the "Three Dark Texts": the* Yijing, *the* Daodejing, *and the* Zhuangzi. *The philosophers of the Dark*

Learning school proposed to return to the ancient classics, whose ideas they mingled with Confucian notions about the ideal society and Daoist metaphysics. One of Wang Bi's original contributions to Chinese thought was the notion of "original non-being" (benwu), according to which prior to the creation of the universe there was only undifferentiated non-being. From this arose the One, another way of conceiving the Dao. From the One arose the Two, and from this came the myriad things of the universe.

All being originates from nonbeing. Therefore, the time before there were physical shapes and names is the beginning of the myriad beings. When shapes and names are there, [the Dao] raises them, educates them, adjusts them, and causes their end. It serves as their mother. The text [the *Daodejing*] means that the Dao produces and completes beings on the basis of the formless and the nameless. They are produced and completed but do not know how or why.

Source: *Laozi 1.1.1a: Early Chinese Mysticism*, p. 61.

VISUALIZING THE DAO

The following passage is an example of how Laozi's ideas became mingled with long life practices in later Daoist literature. It indicates techniques for visualization that will enable the meditator to harmonize vital energies and acquire esoteric wisdom.

These are the secret instructions of the Highest Lord.
First burn incense and straighten your robes, greet the ten directions with three bows each. Concentrate your mind inside and visualize Master Yin and the Master on the River, as well as Laozi, the Great Teacher of the Law. Then recite the following in your mind:
Mysterious, again mysterious, the origin of Dao,
Above, virtue incorporates chaos and the prime. . . .
In my room, the seven jewels come together,
Doors and windows open of themselves.
Utter in my purity, I strive for deeper truth,
Riding on bright light, I ascend the purple sky.
Sun and moon to my right and left,
I go to the immortals, and eternal life.
All seven ancestors arise, are reborn in heaven,
The world, how true, the gate to virtue and to Dao.

Finish this mental recitation, then clap your teeth and swallow the saliva thirty-six times each. Visualize the green dragon to your left, the white tiger to your right, the red bird in front of you, and the dark warrior at your back. . . .
On three sides you are joined by an attendant, each having a retinue of a thousand carriages and ten thousand horsemen. Eight thousand jade maidens and jade lads of heaven and earth stand guard for you.
Then repeat the formula, this time aloud, and begin to recite the five thousand words of the Scripture [the *Daodejing*]. Conclude by three times clapping your teeth and swallowing the saliva.

Source: *Laozi Daodejing Xuzhui: The Taoist Experience*, pp. 173–174.

THE DAO OF IMMORTALITY

According to legend, Heshang Gong, the Master on the River, lived during the reign of the Han emperor Wen (179–156 B.C.E.), but the earliest dated stories of his life come from the third century C.E. He is said to have lived near the Yellow River, where he studied the Daodejing *in solitude. Eventually he came to the attention of the emperor, who asked him to teach the essentials of Laozi's text. In the passage below, he indicates how the ideas of the* Daodejing *became mingled with immortality practices such as breathing exercises and gymnastics. In the system of Heshang Gong, people receive vital energy (*qi*) from Heaven, but they ordinarily dissipate it unless they practice special techniques to keep it stored in the vital organs.*

The Dao of prolonged life lies with the Mysterious Female. Mysterious is heaven, within human beings it is the nose. Female is earth, within human beings it is the mouth.

Heaven feeds people with the five energies. They enter the body through the nose and are stored in the heart. These five energies are clear and subtle, they form essence and spirit, intelligence and clear perception, sound and voice, as well as the five kinds of inner nature.

Heaven's manifest counterpart is the spirit soul. The spirit soul is male. It enters and leaves the human body through the nose. It is aligned with the Dao of heaven. Thus the nose is the Mysterious.

Earth nourishes people with the five tastes. They enter the body through the mouth and are stored in the stomach. The five tastes are turbid and coarse, they form the physical body, bones and flesh, blood and arteries, as well as the six kinds of emotions.

Earth's manifest counterpart is the material soul. The material soul is female. It enters and leaves the human body through the mouth. It is aligned with the Dao of earth. Thus the mouth is the female.

The nose and the mouth are the gateways by which the primordial energy that pervades Heaven and Earth comes and goes. Inhalation and exhalation through the nose and the mouth continue without interruption, subtly and miraculously. It is as if it would go on forever, yet seems not to be there at all. In your application of breathing, remain relaxed and comfortable. Never make haste or labor the exercise.

Source: *Laozi Daodejing Xuzhui* 6.1.5ab: *Early Chinese Mysticism*, p. 68.

PURITY AND TRANQUILLITY

*As the Daoist tradition developed, Laozi's successors developed techniques for incorporating his doctrines into religious practice. The following excerpt, which became popular during the Song dynasty (960–1260), was used as a guide to meditation practice by the Complete Perfection (*Quanzhen*) school of Daoism, and is still in use today in its religious services.*

The Great Dao has no form;
It brings forth and raises heaven and earth.
The Great Dao has no feelings;
It regulates the course of the sun and the moon.
The Great Dao has no name;
It raises and nourishes the myriad beings.
I do not know its name—
So I call it Dao.
The Dao can be pure or turbid, moving or tranquil.
Heaven is pure, earth is turbid;
Heaven is moving, earth is tranquil.
The male is moving, the female is tranquil. . . .
Always be pure and tranquil;
Heaven and earth
Return to the primordial.
The human spirit is fond of purity,
But the mind disturbs it.
The human mind is full of tranquillity,
But desires meddle with it.
Get rid of desires for good,
And the mind will be calm.
Cleanse your mind,
And the spirit will be pure.

Source: *Qingjing jing: The Taoist Experience,* pp. 25–26.

ZHUANGZI'S LIFE AND WORK

Zhuangzi, one of the two main figures of "philosophical Daoism," is believed to have lived during the fourth century B.C.E. *Little is known about his life except for the enigmatic descriptions found in his own works. Sima Qian reports that he lived in the southern country of Mang, in modern-day Henan, and that he died around 290* B.C.E. *He is said to have held a minor government post but refused any offers of higher office, preferring to retain his autonomy and personal freedom. According to his own account, he sought to live apart from his society, refusing honors and political involvement, and cultivated the virtue of "uselessness," which enabled him to move unmolested in the world and to attain a state of harmony with the Dao.*

Zhuangzi lived in Mang. His given name was Zhou. Zhou once worked as a functionary at Qiyuan in Mang. He was a contemporary of King Hui of Liang (r. 370–335 B.C.E.) and King Xuan of Qi (r. 342–324 B.C.E.). There was nothing his teachings did not consider, and their essence hearkened back to the words of Laozi. His texts, comprising more than 100,000 characters, all used allegories. . . . He mocked people like Confucius and elucidated the meanings of Laozi . . . and he was adept at creating texts with hidden allusions and analogies. He used them to attack the Confucians and followers of Mozi. Even the greatest scholars of his day could not defend themselves against him. His words flowed and swirled freely, at his whim, and powerful people could not use him, including kings, dukes, and others.

Source: Sima Qian, *Shiji*, 63.2144.

THE DAO IS IN EVERYTHING

In the following selection, Zhuangzi indicates that Dao is everywhere and in everything, and that those who truly know it understand that it pervades even the lowest and most despised parts of the world.

> Dong Guo asked Zhuangzi, "The thing called Dao: where does it exist?"
> Zhuangzi said, "There's no place it doesn't exist."
> "Come," said Dong Guo, "you must be more specific!"
> "It is in ants."
> "How can it be in something so low?"
> "It is in grass."
> "But that's even lower!"
> "It is in bricks and shards."
> "But that's even lower!"
> "It is in excrement."

Source: *Zhuangzi*, ch. 22.

THE VALUE OF KNOWING DAO

According to Zhuangzi, most people waste their energies striving and planning for the future, and so fail to live in the moment. Sages, however, learn to move with the flow of Dao, and so they lead long and peaceful lives.

'Dao is without beginning or end, but things have their life and death—you cannot rely upon their fulfillment. One moment empty, the next moment full—you cannot depend upon their form. The years cannot be held off; time cannot be stopped. Decay, growth, fullness, and emptiness end and then begin again. It is thus that we must describe the plan of the Great Meaning and discuss the principles of the ten thousand things. The life of things is a gallop, a headlong dash—with every movement they alter, with every moment they shift. What should you do and what should you not do? Everything will change of itself, that is certain!'

'If that is so,' said the Lord of the River, 'then what is valuable about Dao?'

Ruo of the North Sea said, 'One who understands Dao is certain to have command of basic principles. One who has command of basic principles is certain to know how to deal with circumstances. And one who knows how to deal with circumstances will not allow things to cause harm. When a person has perfect virtue, fire cannot burn him, water cannot drown him, cold and heat cannot afflict him, birds and beasts cannot injure him. . . .'

Source: *Zhuangzi*, ch. 17: *Chuang-tzu: Basic Writings*, tr. Burton Watson (New York: Columbia University Press, 1964), pp. 103–104.

THE PITFALLS OF WORDS AND CONCEPTS

A central theme of Zhuangzi's philosophy is the limitations of language. Those who become caught up in expressions and concepts inevitably fail to recognize truth, which cannot be captured in words.

Now I am going to make a statement here. I don't know whether it fits into the category of other people's statements or not. But whether it fits into their category or whether it doesn't, it obviously fits into some category. So in that respect it is no different from their statements. However, let me try making my statement.

There is a beginning. There is a not yet beginning to be a beginning. There is a not yet beginning to be a not yet beginning to be a beginning. There is being. There is nonbeing. There is a not yet beginning to be nonbeing. There is a not yet beginning to be a not yet beginning to be nonbeing. Suddenly there is being and nonbeing. But between this being and nonbeing, I don't really know which is being and which is nonbeing. Now I have just said something. But I don't know whether what I have said has really said something or whether it hasn't said something.

There is nothing in the world bigger than the tip of an autumn hair, and Mount Tai is little. No one has lived longer than a dead child, and Pengzu died young. Heaven and earth were born at the same time I was, and the ten thousand things are one with me.

We have already become one, so how can I say anything? But I have just said that we are one, so how can I not be saying something? The one and what I said about it make two, and two and the original one make three. If we go on this way, then even the cleverest mathematician can't tell where we'll end, much less an ordinary person. If by moving from nonbeing to being we get to three, how far will we get if we move from being to being? Better not to move, but let things be! . . .

If Dao is made clear, it is not Dao. If discriminations are put into words, they do not suffice. If benevolence has a constant object, it cannot be universal. If modesty is fastidious, it cannot be trusted. If daring attacks, it cannot be complete. These five are all round, but they tend toward the square.

Source: *Zhuangzi*, ch. 2: *Chuang-tzu: Basic Writings*.

THE VALUE OF UNLEARNING

Zhuangzi teaches that most problems come from entanglement with words and concepts. As an antidote, he advises that we "unlearn" the lessons that others have taught us "for our own good." Ideas of morality, justice, truth, etc. merely confuse people and make them think of doing the opposite. To counteract this, an important meditative practice is "sitting and forgetting" (zuowang), in which one simply lets thoughts flow freely, in harmony with Dao, and thus artificial concepts disperse of their own accord. A person who perfects this is able to attain the state of "free and easy wandering" in which one acts spontaneously, in accordance with the impulses of the moment. The following passage contains a section from Zhuangzi and a commentary by Guo Xiang, who compiled the edition that is the only extant version of the Zhuangzi.

> "What does 'sitting in oblivion' mean?" Confucius asked. "I smash up my limbs and body," Yan Hui replied, "drive out perceptions and intellect, get rid of physical shape and abandon all knowledge. Thus I merge with the Great Thoroughfare."
>
> Guo Xiang comments,
>
> Practicing this forgetfulness, how can there be anything not forgotten? First forget the traces, such as benevolence and righteousness; then put that which caused the traces out of the mind. On the inside, unaware of one's body, on the outside never know there is a universe. Only then will one be fully open, become one with the process of change and pervade everything.

Source: Guo Xiang, *Zhuangzi Zhu*, p. 8.39a: *Early Chinese Mysticism*, pp. 74–75.

THE SAGE IS GODLIKE

A person who is in harmony with Dao is able to move freely in the world, unharmed by things that injure ordinary people. The following passage was cited by the later Daoist tradition as evidence that Zhuangzi was interested in immortality practices, since his description of the sage indicates that understanding of Dao makes a person godlike, able to fly and to transcend death.

> Wang Ni said, "The Perfect Man is godlike. Though the great swamps blaze, they cannot burn him; though the great rivers freeze, they cannot chill him; though swift lightning splits the hills and howling gales shake the sea, they cannot frighten him. A man like this rides the clouds and mist, straddles the sun and moon, and wanders beyond the four seas. Even life and death have no effect on such a man, much less the rules of profit and loss!"

Source: *Zhuangzi*, ch. 2: *Chuang Tzu: Basic Writings*, pp. 41–42.

DREAMS AND REALITY

In the following passage, Zhuangzi falls asleep and dreams that he is a butterfly, but when he awakes he is unsure whether he is Zhuangzi or a butterfly dreaming of being Zhuangzi. The passage exemplifies the way that Zhuangzi merges dreams and waking "reality" while indicating that the boundaries between the two are not as rigid as ordinary people assume.

Once Zhuang Zhou dreamt that he was a butterfly, a butterfly flitting and flying around, content with himself and doing as he pleased. He didn't know he was Zhuang Zhou. Suddenly he woke up and there he was, solid and clearly Zhuang Zhou. But he didn't know if he was really Zhuang Zhou who had dreamt he was a butterfly, or a butterfly now dreaming he was Zhuang Zhou. Between Zhuang Zhou and a butterfly there must be some difference! These are the transformations of things.

Source: *Zhuangzi*, ch. 2: *Chuang-tzu: Basic Writings.*

WORLDLY FAME IS LIKE A DEAD RAT

Throughout his life, Zhuangzi avoided all attempts to make himself useful to his society. When offered important positions, he turned them down, preferring instead to live in the moment, unharried by the concerns of busy and important people.

When Huizi was prime minister of Liang, Zhuangzi set off to visit him. Someone said to Huizi, 'Zhuangzi is coming because he wants to replace you as prime minister!'

With this Huizi was filled with alarm and searched all over the state for three days and three nights trying to find Zhuangzi. Zhuangzi then came to see him and said, 'In the south there is a bird called the Yuanchu. . . . The Yuanchu rises up from the South Sea and flies to the North Sea, and it will rest on nothing but the Wutong tree, eat nothing but the fruit of the Lien, and drink only from springs of sweet water. Once there was an owl who had gotten hold of a half-rotten old rat, and as the Yuanchu passed by, it raised its head, looked up at the Yuanchu, and said, "Shoo!" Now that you have this Liang state of yours, are you trying to shoo me?'

Source: *Zhuangzi*, ch. 17: *Chuang Tzu: Basic Writings*, pp. 109–110.

SIMPLICITY AND NATURALNESS

According to Zhuangzi, the sage completely transcends the limitations felt by ordinary beings, and cares nothing for their judgments.

The sage leans on the sun and moon, tucks the universe under his arm, merges himself with things, leaves the confusion and muddle as it is, and looks on slaves as exalted. Ordinary men strain and struggle; the sage is stupid and blockish. He takes part in ten thousand ages and achieves simplicity in oneness. For him, all the ten thousand things are what they are, and thus they enfold each other.

Source: *Zhuangzi*, ch. 2: *Chuang Tzu: Basic Writings*, p. 42.

THE TRUE MAN

The sage moves in the world without becoming attached to anything. Living in the moment, he simply takes things as they come, and so is at peace. Ordinary people, by contrast, are full of desires, cares, and worries, and so fail to realize their potential.

One who knows what Heaven does and knows what humanity does has reached the peak. Knowing what Heaven does, one lives with Heaven. Knowing what humanity does, one uses the knowledge of what one knows to help out the knowledge of what one doesn't know, and lives out the years that Heaven provides without being cut off midway—this is perfect knowledge. . . .

What do I mean by a True Man? The True Man of ancient times did not rebel against poverty, did not grow proud in plenty, and did not plan affairs. Being like this, he could commit an error and not regret it, could meet with success and not make a show. Being like this, he could climb the high places and not be frightened, could enter the water and not get wet, could enter the fire and not get burned. His knowledge could climb all the way up to the Way like this.

The True Man of ancient times slept without dreaming and woke without care; he ate without savoring and his breath came from deep inside. The True Man breathes with his heels; the mass of men breathe with their throats. Crushed and bound down, they gasp out their words as though they were retching. Deep in their passions and desires, they are shallow in the workings of Heaven.

The True Man of ancient times knew nothing of loving life, knew nothing of hating death. He emerged without delight; he went back in without a fuss. He came briskly, went briskly, and that was all. He didn't forget where he began, didn't try to find out where he would end. He received something and took pleasure in it; he forgot about it and handed it back again. This is what I call not using the mind to repel the Way, not using man to help out Heaven. This is what I call the True Man.

Since he is like this, his mind forgets; his face is calm; his forehead is broad. This person is chilly like autumn, balmy like spring, and his joy and anger prevail through the four seasons. He goes along with what is right for things and no one knows his limit. . . . Therefore, he who delights in bringing success to things is not a sage; he who has affections is not benevolent; he who looks for the right time is not a worthy man; he who cannot encompass both profit and loss is not a noble man; he who thinks of conduct and fame and misleads himself is not a man of breeding. . . . This was the True Man of old: with bearing that was lofty and did not crumble; he appeared to lack but accepted nothing; he was dignified in his correctness but not insistent; he was vast in emptiness but not ostentatious. Mild and cheerful, he seemed to be happy; reluctant, he could not help doing certain things. . . .

Therefore his liking was one and his not liking was one. His being one was one and his not being one was one. In being one, he was acting as a companion of Heaven. In not being one, he was acting as a companion of man. When man and Heaven do not defeat each other, then he may be said to have the True Man.

Source: *Zhuangzi*, ch. 6: *Chuang Tzu: Basic Writings*, pp. 73–76.

WHAT THE SAGE KNOWS

Zhuangzi's friend, the logician Huizi, is a favorite target of the subtle humor for which Zhuangzi is famous. Portrayed as a philosopher who is fond of hair-splitting distinctions, Huizi is chided by his friend for becoming overly attached to logic and words and thus failing to embrace the myriad mysteries of the natural world.

Zhuangzi and Huizi were walking on a bridge over the Hao River. Zhuangzi said, 'Minnows moving about freely—that is what fish enjoy!'

Huizi said, 'You're not a fish. How do you know [how] fish [think]?'

Zhuangzi said, 'You're not me, so how do you know I don't know what fish enjoy?'

Huizi said, 'I'm not you, so I certainly don't know what you know. On the other hand, you're certainly not a fish, and so you certainly can't know what fish enjoy.'

Zhuangzi said, 'Let's go back to your original point. You said, "How do you know what fish enjoy," and so you already knew I knew when you asked me. I know it by being here above the Hao.'

Source: *Zhuangzi*, ch. 17: *Chuang Tzu: Basic Writings*.

A PERSON WITHOUT FEELINGS

In this passage, Huizi attempts to turn the tables on Zhuangzi, suggesting that despite his friend's emphasis on naturalness, what he advocates is really contrary to nature. Human beings naturally have feelings of attachment toward certain things and aversion toward others, and it is absurd to suggest that anyone can truly view all things as equal.

Huizi said to Zhuangzi, 'Can a person really be without feelings?'
'Yes.'
'But a person who has no feelings—how can you call him a person?'

'The Dao provided a face; Heaven provided a human form—why can't you call him a human?'

'But once you've called him a person, how can he be without feelings?'

'That's not what I mean by feelings. When I talk about having no feelings, I mean that a person doesn't allow preferences and aversions to enter and do harm. Instead, he always lets things be the way they are and doesn't try to push life along.'

'If he doesn't try to push life along, then how does he keep himself alive?'

'The Dao gave him a human face; Heaven gave him a human form. He doesn't let preferences or aversions enter and do harm. You, now—you place your spirit outside. You exhaust your energy, leaning on a tree and moaning, slumping at your desk and dozing—Heaven picked out a human body for you and you use it to babble about verbal sophistry!'

Source: *Zhuangzi*, ch. 5: *Chuang Tzu: Basic Writings*, p. 72.

AN OLD USELESS TREE

In his writings, Zhuangzi frequently extols the value of becoming useless. Those who make themselves useful are used by others, and so they dissipate their vital energies and die young. The sage, however, appears to be stupid and blockish, and so others believe that he is useless, and thus they leave him alone.

Carpenter Shi went to Qi and, when he got to Crooked Shaft, he saw a serrate oak standing by the village shrine. It was broad enough to shelter several thousand oxen and measured a hundred spans around, towering above the hills. The lowest branches were eighty feet from the ground, and a dozen or so of them could have been made into boats. There were so many sightseers that the place looked like a fair, but the carpenter didn't even glance around and went on his way without stopping. His apprentice stood staring for a long time and then ran after Carpenter Shi and said, 'Since I first took up my axe and followed you, Master, I have never seen timber as beautiful as this. But you don't even bother to look, and go right on without stopping. Why is that?'

'Forget it—say no more!' said the carpenter. 'It's a worthless tree! Make boats out of it and they'd sink; make coffins and they'd rot in no time. Use it for doors and it would sweat sap like pine; use it for posts and the worms would eat them up. It's not a timber tree—there's nothing it can be used for. That's how it got to be that old!'

After Carpenter Shi had returned home, the oak tree appeared to him in a dream and said, 'What are you comparing me with? Are you comparing me with those useful trees? The cherry apple, the pear, the orange, the citron, the rest of those fructiferous trees and shrubs—as soon as their fruit is ripe, they are torn apart and subjected to abuse. Their big limbs are broken off, their little limbs are yanked around. Their utility makes life miserable for them, and so they don't get to finish out the years Heaven gave them, but are cut off in midjourney. They bring it on themselves—the pulling and tearing of the common mob. And it's the same way with all other things.

'As for me, I've been trying a long time to be of no use, and now that I'm about to die, I've finally got it. This is of great use to me. If I had been of some use, would I ever have grown this large? Moreover, you and I are both of us things. What's the point of this—things condemning things? You, a worthless man about to die—how do you know I'm a worthless tree?' When Carpenter Shi woke up, he reported his dream. His apprentice said, 'If it's so intent on being of no use, what's it doing there at the village shrine?'

'Shhh! Say no more! It's only resting there. If we carp and criticize, it will merely conclude that we don't understand it. Even if it weren't at the shrine, do you suppose it would be cut down? It protects itself in a different way from ordinary people. If you try to judge it by conventional standards, you'll be way off!'

Source: *Zhuangzi*, ch. 4: *Chuang Tzu: Basic Writings*, pp. 60–61.

DRAGGING HIS TAIL IN THE MUD

In ancient China, rulers often asked renowned sages to be their advisors in order to receive wise counsel. In the following story, Zhuangzi is approached with such a job offer.

Once, when Zhuangzi was fishing in the Pu River, the king of Chu sent two officials to go and announce to him: 'I would like to trouble you with the administration of my realm.'

Zhuangzi held on to the fishing pole and, without turning his head, said, 'I have heard that there is a sacred tortoise in Chu that has been dead for three thousand years. The king keeps it wrapped in cloth and boxed, and stores it in the ancestral temple. Now would this tortoise rather be dead and have its bones left behind and honored? Or would it rather be alive and dragging its tail in the mud?'

'It would rather be alive and dragging its tail in the mud,' said the two officials.

Zhuangzi said, 'Go away! I'll drag my tail in the mud!'

Source: *Zhuangzi*, ch. 17: *Chuang Tzu: Basic Writings*, p. 109.

ZHUANGZI'S WIFE DIED

Since death is an inevitable part of life, the sage embraces it along with other aspects of the natural world. For most people, death is fearful and oppressive, but for the sage death is part of the cosmic mystery constantly unfolding around us.

Zhuangzi's wife died. When Huizi went to convey his condolences, he found Zhuangzi sitting with his legs sprawled out, pounding on a tub and singing. 'You lived with her, she brought up your children and grew old,' said Huizi. 'It should be enough simply not to weep at her death. But pounding on a tub and singing—this is going too far, isn't it?'

Zhuangzi said, 'You're wrong. When she first died, do you think I didn't grieve like anyone else? But I looked back to her beginning and the time before she was born. Not only the time before she was born, but the time before she had a body. Not only the time before she had a body, but the time before she had a spirit. In the midst of the jumble of wonder and mystery a change took place and she had a spirit. Another change and she had a body. Another change and she was born. Now there's been another change and she's dead. It's just like the progression of the four seasons, spring, summer, fall, winter.

'Now she's going to lie down peacefully in a vast room. If I were to follow after her bawling and sobbing, it would show that I don't understand anything about fate. So I stopped.'

Source: *Zhuangzi*, ch. 18: *Chuang Tzu: Basic Writings*, p. 113.

THE LADY OF GREAT MYSTERY

Although the position of women was well below that of men in classical China, there are many stories of female sages in the Daoist canon. These women managed to transcend the boundaries imposed on them by their society. Applying esoteric lore in secret, they became recognized as teachers, and sometimes even as immortals. The following selection, from a collection of stories of immortals from the Han dynasty, reports on the life of the "Lady of Great Mystery," who is said to have successfully practiced the secret arts of immortality and to have ascended to heaven in broad daylight, a sign of exceptional accomplishment.

The Lady of Great Mystery had the family name Zhuan and was personally called He. When she was a little girl she lost first her father and after a little while also her mother.

Understanding that living beings often did not fulfill their destined lifespans, she felt sympathy and sadness. She used to say: 'Once people have lost their existence in this world, they cannot recover it. Whatever has died cannot come back to life. Life is so limited! It is over so fast! Without cultivating the Dao, how can one extend one's life?'

She duly left to find enlightened teachers, wishing to purify her mind and pursue the Dao. She obtained the arts of the Jade Master and practiced them diligently for several years.

As a result she was able to enter the water and not get wet. Even in the severest cold of winter she would walk over frozen rivers wearing only a single garment. All the time her expression would not change, and her body would remain comfortably warm for a succession of days.

The Lady of Great Mystery could also move government offices, temples, cities, and lodges. They would appear in other places quite without moving from their original location. Whatever she pointed at would vanish into thin air. Doors, windows, boxes, or caskets that were securely locked needed only a short flexing of her finger to break wide open. Mountains would tumble, trees would fall at the pointing of her hand. Another short gesture would resurrect them to their former state. . . .

The Lady of Great Mystery perfectly mastered all thirty-six arts of the immortals. She could resurrect the dead and bring them back to life. She saved innumerable people, but nobody knew what she used for her dresses or her food, nor did anybody ever learn her arts from her. Her complexion was always that of a young girl; her hair stayed always black as a raven. Later she ascended into heaven in broad daylight. She was never seen again.

Source: *Biographies of Spirit Immortals*, "The Lady of Great Mystery": *The Taoist Experience*, pp. 291–292.

SUN BUER: IMMORTALITY PRACTICES FOR WOMEN

Sun Buer, known in Daoist literature as "Clear and Calm Free Human," lived during the 12th century. Perhaps the best-known of Daoist women immortals, externally she lived an unremarkable life, raising three children and performing the duties expected of a Chinese wife. At the age of 51 she undertook the training of Daoist immortality practices, and it is reported that she quickly mastered difficult esoteric techniques. She composed a number of texts on immortality, most of which focus on distinctive techniques for women. A central concern is harnessing the vital energy and causing it to move up along the spine through subtle energy channels, and thus to the top of the head. It then cascades down the front of the body, bringing indescribable bliss and restoring vitality. The verses are written in a code using the terminology of the Daoist immortalists, and so an explanatory commentary by Zhen Yangming, a 20th-century Daoist master, is included.

> Tie up the tiger and return it to the true lair;
> Bridle the dragon and gradually increase the elixir.
> Nature should be clear as water,
> Mind should be as still as a mountain.
> Tuning the breath, gather it into the gold crucible;
> Stabilizing the spirit, guard the jade pass.
> If you can increase the grain of rice day by day,
> You will be rejuvenated.

Commentary by Zhen Yangming

The tiger is energy, while the dragon is spirit. The "true lair" is the general area between the breasts. To tie up the tiger and return it to the true lair is what was explained by the Master of Higher Light, One Who Has Reached

Emptiness, in these terms: "When women cultivate immortality, they must first accumulate energy in their breasts."

This is the distinction between primal and acquired energy. Refinement of acquired energy uses the method of tuning the breath and freezing the spirit; to gather primal energy, you wait until there is living energy stirring in your body to start. To bridle the dragon simply means to freeze the spirit so as to join it to energy. When spirit and energy unite, the earthly soul and the celestial soul link, and the elixir is crystallized. One of the Celestial Teachers of the Zhang clan, the Empty Peaceful One, said, "Once the original spirit emerges, then gather it back in; when the spirit returns, energy in the body spontaneously circulates. Do this every morning and every evening, and eternal youth will naturally form a spiritual embryo." This is the meaning of bridling the dragon and gradually increasing the elixir. . . .

"Nature should be clear as water, mind should be as still as a mountain." Real Human Zhang Sanfeng said, "Freezing the spirit, tune the breath; tuning the breath, freeze the spirit. This should be done all at once, as one operation. Freezing the spirit means gathering the clarified mind within. When the mind is clear and cool, peaceful and light, then you can practice gathering it into the lair of energy. This is called freezing the spirit. After you do this, you feel as though you are sitting on a high mountain, gazing at the myriad mountains and rivers, or as though you have lit a heavenly lamp that lights up all dark realms. This is what is called freezing the spirit in the void. And tuning the breath is not hard; once mind and spirit are quiet, following the breath spontaneously, I keep this spontaneity. . . ."

The Real Human Zhang said, "When you sit, you should embrace energy with spirit, and keep your mind on breath, in the elixir field, with clear serenity, concentrating undistracted. The energy stored within combines with energy coming from outside to crystallize in the elixir field, filling it and growing stronger day by day and month by month, reaching the four limbs, flowing through the hundred channels, striking open the double pass at the middle of the spine, floating up to the nirvana chamber in the center of the brain. Then it turns and goes down to the heart and enters the field of elixir below in the abdomen. Spirit and energy keep to one another, resting on one another with each breath, and the course of the Waterwheel (the cycle of energy circulation) is opened. When the work reaches this point, the effective construction of the foundation is already half done. . . ."

"If you can increase the grain of rice day by day, you will be rejuvenated." In response to questions about what this "grain of rice" is, I can bring up an alchemical classic by Zhang Boduan. This classic . . . says, "The Undifferentiated encloses Space, Space encloses the worlds of desire, form, and formlessness. When you look for the root source of it all, it is a particle big as a grain." It also says, "A grain, and grain again; at first scarcely perceptible, it eventually becomes clearly evident."

This is the meaning of the statement "If you can increase the grain of rice day by day. . . ." Put simply, it is a matter of gradual culling and refinement of spirit and energy, gradually solidifying and combining them. It does not mean that this little ball of spirit and energy combined has a definite shape like a grain of rice that you can find.

Source: *Cultivating the Elixir;* from *Immortal Sisters,* tr. Thomas Cleary (Boston: Shambhala, 1989), pp. 34–37.

SEXUAL TECHNIQUES FOR MEN

The Daoist canon contains a wealth of information on long-life practices developed over the centuries by Daoists intent on extending their lifespans. Among these are various sexual techniques that are said to allow people to increase their energy level. Sexual practices for men often include ways to increase yang energy, while females are taught how to increase yin energy. Many of these describe a sort of sexual vampirism in which the energy of the partner is transferred to the practitioner. In other texts, it appears that the sexual practices awaken and augment one's natural energy. The following passage is written for men, who are advised to take as many sexual partners as possible, and that they should ideally be in their early teens, since young women have a greater store of energy. They are also counseled to avoid partners who are familiar with these techniques, since female adepts may turn the tables on them and take their energy.

The Master of Pure Harmony says: 'Those who would cultivate their yang energy must not allow women to steal glimpses of this art. Not only is this of no benefit to one's yang energy, but it may even lead to injury or illness. . . .'

According to Pengsu the Long-Lived, if a man wishes to derive the greatest benefit [from sexual techniques], it is best to find a woman who has no knowledge of them. He also had better choose young maidens for mounting, because then his complexion will become like a maiden's. When it comes to women, one should be vexed only by their not being young. It is best to obtain those between fourteen or fifteen and eighteen or nineteen. In any event, they should never be older than thirty. Even those under thirty are of no benefit if they have given birth. My late master handed down these methods and himself used them to live for three thousand years. If combined with drugs, they will even lead to immortality.

In practicing the union of yin and yang to increase your energy and cultivate long life, do not limit yourself to just one woman. Much better to get three, nine, or eleven: the more the better! Absorb her secreted essence by mounting the "vast spring" and reverting the essence upward. Your skin will become glossy, your body light, your eyes bright, and your energy so strong that you will be able to overcome all your enemies. Old men will feel like twenty and young men will feel their strength increase a hundredfold.

When having intercourse with women, as soon as you feel yourself aroused, change partners. By changing partners, you can lengthen your life. If you return habitually to the same woman, her yin energy will become progressively weaker and this will be of little benefit to you.

Source: *Yufang Bizhui,* "Sexual Instructions of the Master of Pure Harmony," 636: *The Taoist Experience,* pp. 155–156.

SEXUAL TECHNIQUES FOR WOMEN

The procedure for women is similar to that for men: they are advised to have as many partners as possible, and that they should ideally be young, since the young have a greater store of energy. Women should avoid becoming aroused, since orgasm dissipates the energies cultivated by sexual activity. Those who succeed in restraining themselves will acquire the energy dissipated by their partners through seminal emission.

The Master of Pure Harmony says: 'It is not only that yang can be cultivated, but yin too.' The Queen Mother of the West, for example, attained the Dao by cultivating her yin energy. As soon as she had intercourse with a man he would immediately take sick, while her complexion would be ever more radiant without the use of rouge or powder. She always ate curds and plucked the five-stringed lute in order to harmonize her heart and concentrate her mind. She was quite without any other desire.

The Queen Mother had no husband but was fond of intercourse with young boys. If this is not fit to be taught to the world, how is it that such an elevated personage as the Queen Mother herself practiced it?

When having intercourse with a man, first calm your heart and still your mind. If the man is not yet fully aroused, wait for his energy to arrive and slightly restrain your emotion to attune yourself to him. Do not move or become agitated, lest your yin essence become exhausted first. If this happens, you will be left in a deficient state and susceptible to cold wind illnesses. . . .

If a woman is able to master this Dao and has frequent intercourse with men, she can avoid all grain for nine days without getting hungry. Even those who are sick and have sexual relations with ghosts attain this ability to fast. But they become emaciated after a while. So, how much more beneficial must it be to have intercourse with men?

Source: *Yufang Bizhui* 635: *The Taoist Experience*, p. 156.

THE GREAT MAN

The Great Man (daren) is an important motif in Daoist literature. Described as a perfected sage, the Great Man is said to wander to the farthest reaches of the cosmos, visiting strange and mysterious realms and acquiring esoteric knowledge, along with substances that promote immortality. The following excerpt is from Ruanji's (210–263) poem "Biography of Master Great Man," which describes the Great Man as a natural ruler with sovereignty over the whole universe.

Heaven and earth dissolve,
The six harmonies open out,
Stars and constellations tumble,
Sun and moon fall down.

I leap up and farther up,
What should I cherish?
My clothes are not seamed, but I am beautifully dressed;
My girdle has no pendants but is ornate naturally.
Up and down I wander, fluttering about:
Who could fathom my eternity?

Source: *Daren Xiansheng Zhuang*, ch.1: *Early Chinese Mysticism*, p. 102.

THE VALUE OF DRUNKENNESS

The following poem was written by Liu Ling (ca. 265 C.E.), one of the "Seven Sages of the Bamboo Grove," a group of poet-philosophers who came together to discuss ultimate reality and engage in "pure conversation" (shingtan). In this poem he appears to refer to his own way of life. He was renowned for his fondness for wine, and is said to have traveled throughout the Chinese countryside accompanied by a servant who carried a shovel and a jug of wine. The wine enabled him to maintain a constant state of inebriation (which he believed helped him to harmonize with the Dao). The purpose of the shovel was to allow the servant to bury him on the spot when he died.

There is Master Great Man—

He takes heaven and earth as a single morning
A thousand years as one short moment.
The sun and the moon are windows for him,
The Eight Wilds are his garden.

He travels without wheels or tracks,
Sojourns without house or hearth.
He makes heaven his curtain and earth his seat,
Indulges in what he pleases.

Stopping, he grasps his wine-cup and maintains his goblet;
Moving, he carries a casket and holds a jar in his hand.
His only obligation is toward wine,
And of this he knows abundance. . . .

Utterly free he is from yearnings and from worries,
Always happy and full in his contentment.
Without ever moving he gets drunk,
Then, with a start he sobers up.

Listens quietly, but does not hear the rolling of thunder . . .
Unaware of the cold biting the flesh he is,
Unmoved by the afflictions of covetousness.
Looking down he watches the myriad beings bustling about
Like tiny pieces of duckweed that float on the Han and Jiang. . . .

Source: *Jiu Desong* 47: *Early Chinese Mysticism*, pp. 105–106.

TRANSCENDING THE WORLD

In the texts of Laozi and Zhuangzi there are suggestions that sages transcend the world and that its cares no longer burden them. This theme was developed in other Daoist texts that extol the prowess of the "Great Man," who is portrayed as a mighty figure traveling in the remote corners of the world—and the highest reaches of heaven—without obstruction, complete master of all things.

> Heat and cold don't harm me; nothing stirs me up.
> Sadness and worry have no hold on me; pure energy at rest.
> I float on mist, leap into heaven, pass through all with no restraint.
> To and fro, subtle and wondrous, the way never slants.
> My delights and happinesses are not of this world, how could I ever fight with it?

Source: *Yuan You: Early Chinese Mysticism*, p. 103.

THE MUSIC OF DAO

This excerpt is taken from the Scripture of the Western Ascension (Xishengjing), *a fifth-century text that brings together the "three traditions" of Daoism, Confucianism, and Buddhism into a harmonious religious vision. Most of the text reports oral teachings given by Laozi to Yin Xi, the guardian of the Western Gate and recipient of the* Daodejing. *In this text Laozi reveals that he is really a divinity, the manifestation of Dao, and he further describes its workings so that Yin Xi might merge with it and thus attain immortality. The text is notable for its description of Laozi's ascension into Heaven as an immortal and for its use of the Buddhist concepts of karma, rebirth, and selflessness. It also incorporates Buddhist meditation techniques, integrating them into the Daoist quest for immortality.*

> The Dao is nature.
> Who practices can attain [it]. Who hears can speak [about it].
> Who knows does not speak; who speaks does not know.
> Language is formed when sounds are exchanged.
> Thus in conversation, words make sense.
> When one does not know the Dao, words create confusion.
> Therefore I don't hear, don't speak; I don't know why things are.
> It can be compared to the knowledge of musical sound.
> One becomes conscious of it by plucking a string.
> Though the mind may know the appropriate sounds, yet the mouth is unable to formulate them.
> Similarly the Dao is deep, subtle, wondrous; who knows it does not speak.
> On the other hand, one may be conscious of musical sounds and melodies.
> One then dampens the sounds to consider them within.
> Then when the mind makes the mouth speak, one speaks but does not know.
> Laozi said: The Dao is deep and very profound, an abyss of emptiness and non-being.
> Though you may hear its doctrine, in your mind you don't grasp its subtlety.

Why is this so? The written word does not exhaust speech, and by relying on scriptures and sticking to texts your learning remains on the same [intellectual] level.

Rather, you must measure it: recollect it within, meditate on it and consider it carefully. . . .

Laozi said: Heaven, earth, people, and all beings originally contain the primordial source of the Dao.

They emerge together from the Grand Immaculate, from the first beginning of emptiness and non-being; they come from the radiance of essence, flickering softly, from supreme mystery, subtle and wondrous.

It can be compared to a dam ten thousand miles in height. It has gushing, gurgling streams beneath. Looking down they seem all turbid and confused; looking closer there are countless sand grains on the bottom.

Obscure in the extreme, utterly undifferentiated, we don't know where they come from: as in a person recently deceased one cannot see the numinous spirit soul:

It has merged with the engulfing power of yin, and yang can no longer shine forth to make it distinct.

Look at the past and the future as you look at the present.

If you can't even understand that, how will you know about not existing or being alive? . . .

Talented and analytical, you have a certain wisdom, receiving the teaching by word of mouth. But while you claim to have penetrated the innermost part of the Dao, you cannot intuit its true inner essence.

Therefore if you have lost the foundation of life, how could you know the primordial source of the Dao?

Source: *Xishengjing* selections: *Taoist Mystical Philosophy: The Scripture of the Western Ascension*, tr. Livia Kohn (Albany: State University of New York Press, 1991), pp. 235, 240.

GLOSSARY

Cinnabar   Mercuric sulfide, believed by Daoist alchemists to be the key to an elixir of immortality.

Dao   "Way," the impersonal force that sustains all life and dictates patterns of growth and development.

Daodejing   *The Way and Virtue*, a classic work of Daoism attributed to Laozi.

De   The power or virtue of Dao, which enables it to influence the movements of natural systems.

Immortals   (*xian*) Daoist sages and alchemists who have discovered the secrets of physical immortality.

Laozi   The legendary founder of Daoism, said to have lived during the sixth century B.C.E.

Philosophical Daoism   A term coined by Western scholars to designate the strand of Daoism represented by Laozi and Zhuangzi, which is concerned with the nature and activities of Dao.

Pu   "The Uncarved Block," a metaphor for human beings in their natural state before society distorts their true nature through training and education.

Qi   Vital energy or life force that sustains living beings.

Religious Daoism   A term coined by Western scholars to designate the strand of Daoism that was concerned primarily with the quest for immortality.

Wuwei   "Not Acting," the attitude of the Daoist sage, which involves allowing events to happen naturally, in accordance with the movements of Dao.

Yang   The active and aggressive aspect of Dao.

Yin   The passive aspect of Dao.

Zhuangzi   One of the most influential figures of early philosophical Daoism.

Zuowang   "Sitting and forgetting," a method of Daoist meditation involving dropping off the accumulated training that interferes with understanding of Dao.

FURTHER READINGS

AMES, ROGER T. "Is Political Taoism Anarchism?" *Journal of Chinese Philosophy*, 10 (1983), pp. 27–47.

——*The Art of Rulership: A Study in Ancient Chinese Political Thought*. Honolulu: University of Hawaii Press, 1983.

ANDERSEN, POUL. *The Method of Holding the Three Ones: A Taoist Manual of Meditation of the Fourth Century A.D.* London: Curzon Press, 1979.

BLOFELD, JOHN. *Taoism: The Quest for Immortality*. London, Boston: Mandala Books, Unwin Paperbacks, 1979.

CHANG, CHUNG-YAN. "The Philosophy of Taoism According to Chuang Tzu." *Philosophy East and West*, 27 (October 1977), pp. 409–422.

GIRARDOT, N. *Myth and Meaning in Early Taoism: The Theme of Chaos (hun-tun)*. Berkeley: University of California Press, 1983.

GRAHAM, A. C. *Disputers of the Tao: Philosophical Argument in Ancient China*. LaSalle: Open Court, 1989.

KOHN, LIVIA (ed.) *Taoist Meditation and Longevity Techniques*. Ann Arbor: University of Michigan, Center for Chinese Studies Publications, 1989.

LAGERWEY, JOHN. *Taoist Ritual in Chinese Society and History*. New York: Macmillan, 1987.

MAIR, VICTOR H. (ed.) *Experimental Essays on Chuang-tzu*. Honolulu: University of Hawaii Press, 1983.

SASO, MICHAEL. *Taoism and the Rite of Cosmic Renewal*. Pullman: Washington State University Press, 1972.

—— "The Taoist Tradition." *China Quarterly*, 41 (1979), pp. 83–102.

SCHWARTZ, BENJAMIN. *The World of Thought in Ancient China*. Cambridge, MA: Belknap Press, 1985.

STRICKMANN, MICHEL (ed.) *Tantric and Taoist Studies in Honour of R.A. Stein*, *Mélanges Chinois et Bouddhiques*, 21 (1983).

THOMPSON, LAURENCE G. *Chinese Religion: An Introduction*. Belmont, CA: Wadsworth Publishing, 1989.

WALEY, ARTHUR (tr.). *The Way and Its Power: A Study of the Tao Te Ching and Its Place in Chinese Thought*. London: Allen & Unwin, 1934.

WELCH, HOLMES. *Taoism: The Parting of the Way*. Boston: Beacon Press, 1957.

WELCH, HOLMES and SEIDEL, ANNA (eds.) *Facets of Taoism: Essays in Chinese Religion*. New Haven: Yale University Press, 1979.

YUNG-LAN, FUNG. *A History of Chinese Philosophy*. Princeton: Princeton University Press, 1953.

Shinto

INTRODUCTION

In ancient Japan there was no term for indigenous religious practices, but when Buddhism was introduced to the country in the sixth century the term Shinto, or "way of the *kami*," was coined in order to differentiate Japanese traditions from the foreign faith (which was labeled *butsudo,* or "way of the Buddha"). The *kami* are the indigenous gods of Japan, and Shinto is a general term referring to religious practices relating to them. Shinto has no founder, no organization based on believers' adherence to particular doctrines, and no beliefs or practices that are required of all. In contemporary Japan, Shinto is most visibly practiced at the many shrines found throughout the country, in popular festivals and pilgrimages, and in the continuing manifestations of reverence for the forces inhabiting the natural world that are celebrated in prayers and offerings to the kami.

The Japanese have traditionally believed that their country is the residence of many powerful beings and that these beings directly influence the lives of humans, as well as natural phenomena. Kami are commonly associated with natural forces such as wind and storms, with awe-inspiring places such as mountains, waterfalls, and rivers, and with spirits of deceased humans.

Most kami have a delineated sphere of influence, and their worship generally centers on a particular shrine or area. Other kami have a national significance and are venerated throughout Japan. The most prominent kami is the sun goddess, Amatarasu Omikami (Great Heavenly Illuminating Goddess), who in ancient myths is said to be the progenitor of the Japanese race. Amatarasu is also closely associated with the ruling house of Japan, which claims descent from her. This claim is a part of the official legitimation for the rule of the emperor, who was traditionally believed to be semidivine. This was expressed in the title of "Living Kami" (*Akitsukami*), which was given to the emperor and implied that he was a direct descendant of Amatarasu.

Shinto is not a unified system of beliefs and practices, but rather a general term that encompasses many different traditions dating from the earliest periods of Japanese history. Some of the elements and practices of Shinto may be derived from the religious lives of Japanese who lived thousands of years ago in prehistoric times, while others are influenced by the imported traditions of Daoism, Buddhism, and Confucianism, along with various indigenous practices and beliefs.

For the average contemporary Japanese, Shinto is not concerned primarily with doctrines. Rather, practicing Shinto involves performing actions expected of Japanese people who recognize the existence and power of the kami and who engage in actions traditionally associated with them. In the broadest sense, Shinto includes all the actions—festivals, rituals, prayers, offerings, pilgrimages, etc.—that pertain to the kami.

Because kami are believed to reside throughout the Japanese archipelago, there are shrines to local and national kami scattered throughout the islands, and these are an important focus of Shinto practice. There are between 78,000 and 79,000 Shinto shrines in Japan today, and traditional households generally have an altar to the clan deity (*uchigami*), at which regular offerings are presented.

In the modern period, Shinto can be classified into three broad categories, which although distinguishable are interrelated: Shrine Shinto (*Jinja Shinto*), Sectarian Shinto (*Kyoha Shinto*), and Folk Shinto (*Minzoku Shinto*). The first type includes rituals and other activities performed at Shinto shrines. It centers on the prayers and offerings addressed to the kami, which are generally expected to lead to specific concrete results, such as material success, health, academic accomplishments, or protection. It is believed that prayers and offerings make the kami positively predisposed toward the people who present them and that the kami in return may grant their requests. The most important deity of Shrine Shinto is Amatarasu, whose main shrine is at Ise. The deities worshiped in Shinto shrines are collectively referred to as "the gods of heaven and earth" (*tenshin chigi*). Rituals and prayers are also offered for the well-being of deceased ancestors and to ensure the peace, stability, and prosperity of the country.

Contemporary Shinto thought commonly contends that ritual actions must be combined with a pure mind, since the kami will positively respond only to people whose thoughts are sincere. In order to gain the blessing and aid of the kami, one must have the "heart of truth" (*makoto no kokoro*) or "true heart" (*magokoro*), which is characterized by reverence for the natural world, concordance between one's thoughts and actions, and, most important, an attitude of truthfulness that is the result of cultivating purity of heart.

Sectarian Shinto includes a number of Shinto groups that have developed into cohesive religious movements. Primarily composed of 13 sects officially recognized by the government during the Meiji era (1868–1911), Sectarian Shinto groups generally have a historical founder and tend to emphasize group solidarity. In addition, their religious centers are often churches rather than shrines.

Folk Shinto is a general term applied to the practices and beliefs of the mass of Japanese people who visit shrines and engage in activities relating to the kami but who do not feel a strong affiliation with any particular sect. Such practices emphasize reverence for natural forces, purification, and the idea that by performing certain actions one may gain access to the power of the kami in order to influence particular aspects of one's life.

Although many Japanese believe that Shinto is an enduring tradition of indigenous religious practices, contemporary Shinto practice is in fact an amalgamation of numerous influences, including Buddhism, Confucianism,

Daoism, and Chinese philosophy. The focus of Shinto practice is the natural world, and Shinto emphasizes the connection of individuals with their environment. In modern times the development of Shinto has been strongly influenced by revivalist movements that seek to link it with Japan's past. One particularly important movement has been the school of Revival Shinto (*Fukko Shinto*), which was linked to the National Learning (*Kokugaku*) movement of the early Edo period (late seventeenth century). This movement was an attempt to purge Shinto of the influence of Buddhism and other foreign traditions and return to a "pure" and "original" form of Shinto. The most important exponent of Revival Shinto was Motoori Norinaga, whose study of Japanese classics such as the *Tale of Genji* convinced him that there is a discernible Japanese character, which is based on awareness of, and reverence for, the natural environment. Norinaga stressed the polytheistic character of Shinto and contended that mundane affairs are shaped by the will of the kami.

During the Meiji period the nationalistic tendencies of Revival Shinto were highlighted and Shinto became the official state cult. The government stressed the divine origin of Japan and pointed out that no foreign invasion of the nation had ever succeeded. This was attributed to the actions of the kami, who protected Japan and worked to ensure its well-being. The government also emphasized the traditional connection between the emperor and Amatarasu Omikami, which was believed to confer on the emperor a divine right to rule.

Because these nationalistic notions were a part of the militaristic policies of Japan prior to and during World War II, State Shinto was outlawed during the Allied occupation, and the emperor publicly repudiated his divine status. With the removal of government patronage, Shinto again became the popular religion of the Japanese people, a position that it holds today. Throughout the Japanese archipelago, people worship at the numerous Shinto shrines, participate in Shinto festivals, purchase amulets empowered by kami and believed to bring success, protection, or good health, and pay reverence to their clan deities and the spirits of their ancestors. Shinto remains a diffuse tradition that incorporates elements of other systems but that is distinctively Japanese.

Shinto Scriptures

Shinto is a practice-oriented tradition that focuses on rituals, prayers, and attitudes associated with worship and veneration of the kami, and it has no distinct canon and few traditional texts. The earliest literary use of the term Shinto is found in the *Nihonshoki* (*Chronicles of Japan,* written in 720), which purports to be a record of the early history of Japan and which is an important source of information on ancient Japanese religious ideas and practices. The *Nihonshoki* (also referred to as the *Nihongi*) and the *Kojiki* (*Records of Ancient Matters*) are among the oldest sources available for pre-Buddhist Japanese religious practices and myths, and these two works are the oldest known sacred literature of Shinto.

According to the accounts of these texts, before the arrival of humans on the Japanese islands, two kami named Izanami and Izanagi stood on the "floating bridge of heaven" and stirred the primordial waters with a jeweled spear. When the water began to coagulate they gathered up the sediment and let drops fall to form the islands of Japan.

Izanami died after giving birth to Kagutsuchi, the fire god, and Izanami followed her to the netherworld hoping to ask her to return to the land of the living. She replied that she had already eaten the food of the dead and so could not return without special permission. She then instructed him not to follow her when she made the request, but after waiting for a long time he became impatient and went after her. When he found her, however, her flesh was putrefying and decomposed, which revolted him, and so he fled the netherworld, returned to the land of the living, and bathed in order to purify himself. When he washed his eyes, the dripping water gave rise to Amatarasu, the sun goddess, and her brother, Tsukiyomi the moon god.

Both the *Kojiki* and *Nihonshoki* indicate that Amatarasu is the divine ancestor of the emperor, an idea that played an important role in the legitimation of the royal line. In addition, their descriptions of Japan as a special place created and guarded by the kami have been influential in shaping Japanese ideas about themselves and their country. The legends of these two works link the origin of the Japanese people with the kami and indicate that humans and kami are intimately interrelated. Humans need the power of kami in order to achieve their goals, and the kami for their part require reverence and offerings from humans.

Other important Shinto texts include the *Fudoki* (*Records of Wind and Earth*), written in the eighth century, which is a collection of myths and legends; the *Man'yoshu* (*Collection of Ten Thousand Poems*), compiled in the late eighth century, which contains poems expressing the beliefs and practices of the common people; and the *Sendai Kujihongi* (*Narrative of Ancient Matters*), compiled in the ninth century, which contains accounts of the practices of the Mononobe clan.

SHINTO SCRIPTURES

BIRTH OF THE KAMI OF SUN AND MOON

The following passage describes the birth of Amatarasu Omikami, the sun goddess, and her brother, Tsukiyomi the moon god. It also indicates that Izanami and Izanagi produced various other kami of various temperaments, some of which were good, while others were malevolent.

> Izanagi no Mikoto and Izanami no Mikoto consulted together, saying: 'We have now produced the Great-Eight-Island Country [Japan], with the mountains, rivers, herbs, and trees. Why should we not produce someone who shall be lord of the universe?' They then together produced the Sun Goddess, who was called O-hiru-me no muchi.
>
> The resplendent luster of this child shone throughout all the six quarters. Therefore the two Deities rejoiced, saying: 'We have had many children,

but none of them have been equal to this wondrous infant. She ought not to be kept long in this land, but we ought of our own accord to send her at once to Heaven, and entrust to her the affairs of Heaven.' At this time Heaven and Earth were still not far separated, and therefore they sent her up to Heaven by the ladder of Heaven.

They next produced the Moon-god. His radiance was next to that of the Sun in splendor. This god was to be the consort of the Sun-goddess, and to share in her government. They therefore sent him also to Heaven.

Next they produced the leech-child, which even at the age of three years could not stand upright. They therefore placed it in the rock-camphor wood boat of Heaven, and abandoned it to the winds.

Their next child was Suso no o no Mikoto. This god had a fierce temper and was given to cruel acts. Moreover he made a practice of continually weeping and wailing. So he brought many of the people of the land to an untimely end. Again he caused green mountains to become withered. Therefore the two gods, his parents, addressed Susa no o no Mikoto, saying: 'You are exceedingly wicked, and it is not fitting that you should reign over the world. Certainly you must depart far away to the Nether-land.' So at length they expelled him.

Source: *Nihongi*, ch. 1: W. G. Aston, *Nihongi* (London: George Allen & Unwin, 1956) I, pp. 18–20; pp. 16–17.

THE BIRTH OF GREAT KAMI

According to the following account, the first beings to arise in the world were three kami. *They were followed by two more* kami, *and the five together became the progenitors of all the other* kami. *It then describes a confrontation between Amatarasu and her brother Susa no o, who is said to have a wicked and deceitful disposition. When he decided to ascend into Heaven, she stopped him and demanded to know what his intentions were. He assured her that he meant no harm, but she did not believe him. In order to ensure that he would remain true to his word, he proposed that both should swear and produce children, which apparently made Susa no o keep his promise.*

At the beginning of heaven and earth, there came into existence in the Plain of High Heaven the Heavenly Center Lord Kami, next, the Kami of High Generative Force, and then the Kami of Divine Generative Force.

Next, when the earth was young, not yet solid, there developed something like reed-shoots from which the Male Kami of Excellent Reed Shoots and then Heavenly Eternal Standing Kami emerged.

The above five kami are the heavenly kami of special standing. . . .

Then, there came into existence Earth Eternal Standing Kami, Kami of Abundant Clouds Field, male and female Kami of Clay, male and female Kami of Post, male and female kami of Great Door, Kami of Complete Surface and his spouse, Kami of Awesomeness, Izanagi (Kami-Who-Invites) and his spouse, Izanami (Kami-Who-Is-Invited). . . .

So thereupon His-Swift-Impetuous-Male-Augustness (Susa no o) said: 'If that be so, I will take leave of the Heaven-Shining-Great-August Deity (Amatarasu), and depart.' [With these words] he forthwith went up to Heaven, whereupon all the mountains and rivers shook, and every land and country quaked. So the Heaven-Shining-Deity, alarmed at the noise, said: 'The reason of the ascent hither of His Augustness my elder brother is surely no good intent. It is only that he wishes to wrest my land from me.' And she forthwith, unbinding her august hair, twisted it into august bunches; and both into the left and into the right august bunch, as likewise into her august head-dress and likewise on to her left and her right august arm, she twisted an augustly complete [string] of curved jewels eight feet [long] of five hundred jewels; and, slinging on her back a quiver holding a thousand [arrows], and adding a quiver holding five hundred [arrows], she likewise took and slung at her side a mighty and high [sounding] elbow-pad, and brandished and stuck her bow upright so that the top shook; and she stamped her feet into the hard ground up to her opposing thighs, kicking away [the earth] like rotten snow, and stood valiantly like a mighty man, and waiting, asked: 'Why do you ascend here?' Then Susa no o replied, saying: 'I have no evil intent. It is only that when the Great-August-Deity [our father] spoke, deigning to enquire the cause of my wailing and weeping, I said: "I wail because I wish to go to my deceased mother's land"; whereupon the Great-August-Deity said: 'You will not dwell in this land,' and deigned to expel me with a divine expulsion. It is therefore, solely with the thought of taking leave of you and departing, that I have ascended here. I have no strange intentions.'

Then the Heaven-Shining-Deity said: 'If that is so, how shall I know the sincerity of your intentions?' Thereupon Susa no o replied, saying: 'Let each of us swear, and produce children.' So as they then swore to each other from the opposite banks of the Tranquil River of Heaven, the august names of the Deities that were born from the mist [of their breath] when, having first begged Susa no o to hand her the ten-grasp saber which was girded on him and broken into three fragments, and with the jewels making a jingling sound and having brandished and washed them in the True-Pool-Well of Heaven, and having crunchingly crunched them, the Heaven-Shining Deity blew them away, were Her Augustness Torrent-Mist-Princess . . . next Her Augustness Lovely-Island-Princess . . . next Her Augustness Princess-of-the-Torrent.

Source: *Kojiki*, ch. 1: *Kojiki, Records of Ancient Matters*, ch. 1: *The Great Asian Religions: An Anthology* (New York: MacMillan, 1969), pp. 231–2.

THE CREATION OF JAPAN

When the earth was newly formed, the islands of Japan were still below the waters, and Izanami and Izanagi decided to create a special land. They thrust a spear into the waters, and the brine that dripped from it formed the islands of the Japanese archipelago. After this they united, and their union resulted in the birth of more kami.

Izanagi and Izanami stood on the floating bridge of Heaven, and held counsel together, saying: 'Is there not a country beneath?' Thereupon they thrust down the jewel-spear of Heaven, and groping about with it found the ocean. The brine which dripped from the point of the spear coagulated and became an island which received the name of Ono-goro-jima.

The two deities then descended and lived on this island. Accordingly they wished to become husband and wife together, and to produce countries. So they made Ono-goro-jima the pillar of the center of the land.

Now the male deity turning by the left, and the female deity by the right, they went round the pillar of the land separately. When they met together on the side, the female deity spoke first and said: 'How delightful! I have met with a lovely youth.' The male deity was displeased, and said: 'I am a man, and by right should have spoken first. How is it that on the contrary you, a woman, should have been the first to speak? This was unlucky. Let us go round again.' Upon this the two deities went back, and having met again, this time the male deity spoke first and said: 'How delightful! I have met a lovely maiden.'

Then he inquired of the female deity, saying: 'In your body is anything formed?' She answered, and said: 'In my body there is a place which is the source of femininity.' The male deity said: 'In my body again there is a place which is the source of masculinity. I wish to unite this source-place of my body to the source-place of your body.' Then the male and female first became united as husband and wife.

Now when the time of birth arrived, first of all the island of Ahaji was reckoned as the placenta, and their minds took no pleasure in it. Therefore it received the name Ahaji no Shima. Next was produced the island of O-yamato no Toyo-aki-tsu-sha (Rich-harvest Island of Yamato). Next they produced the island of Iyo no futa-na, and next the island of Tsukushi. Next the islands of Oki and Sado were born as twins. . . . Next was born the island of Koshi, then the island of O-shima, then the island of Kibi no Ko. Thus first arose the designation of the Great Eight-Island Country.

Source: *Nihongi*, ch. 1: *Nihongi*, pp. 10–17.

IZANAGI VISITS IZANAMI IN THE NETHERWORLD

This passage describes how Izanagi, longing for his deceased love, decided to visit her in the land of the dead and plead with her to return with him. When he saw her body putrefying and covered with maggots, however, he ran away in horror and purified himself by bathing. The drops of water from his eyes and nose produced three kami: *Amatarasu, Tsukiyomi (the moon god), and Susa no o.*

After giving birth to the land, they [Izanami and Izanagi] proceeded to bear kami [such as the kami of the wind, of the tree, of the mountain, and of the plains]. But Izanami died after giving birth to the kami of fire. . . .

Izanagi, hoping to meet again with his spouse, went after her to the land of Hades. When Izanami came out to greet him, Izanagi said, 'Oh my beloved, the land which you and I have been making has not yet been completed. Therefore, you must return with me.' To which Izanami replied, 'I greatly regret that you did not come here sooner, for I have already partaken of the hearth of the land of hades. But let me discuss with the kami of hades about my desire to return. You must, however, not look at me.' As she was gone so long, Izanagi, being impatient, entered the hall to look for her and found maggots squirming around the body of Izanami.

Izanagi, seeing this, was afraid and ran away, saying, 'Since I have been to an extremely horrible and unclean land, I must purify myself.' Thus, arriving at [a river], he purified and exorcised himself. When he washed his left eye, there came into existence the Sun Goddess, or Heavenly Illuminating Great Kami [Amatarasu], and when he washed his right eye, there emerged the Moon Kami [Tsukiyomi]. Finally, as he washed his nose there came into existence Valiant Male Kami [Susa no o].

Source: *Kojiki*, chs. 7, 9, 10, 11: *The Great Asian Religions*, pp. 232–233.

AMATARASU HIDES IN A CAVE

The passage below recounts a well-known Shinto myth in which Amatarasu decides to hide herself in a cave as a result of the misdeeds of Susa no o. When she enters the cave the world is plunged into darkness, and so the other kami *work together to draw her out again. When she leaves the cave, a sacred rope is placed across the entrance to ensure that she will never again conceal her radiance from the world.*

[At one time] the Sun Goddess [shocked by the misdeeds of her brother, Valiant Male Kami], opened the heavenly rock-cave door and concealed herself inside. Then the Plain of High Heaven became completely dark, and all manner of calamities arose.

Then the 800 myriads of kami gathered in a divine assembly, and summoned Kami of the Little Roof of Heaven and Kami of Grand Bead to perform a divination. They hung long strings of myriad curved beads on the upper branches of a sacred tree, and hung a large-dimensioned mirror on its middle branches. They also suspended in the lower branches white and blue cloth. These objects were held by Kami of Grand Bead as solemn offerings, while Kami of the Little Roof in Heaven intoned liturgical prayers (*norito*). Meanwhile, Kami of Heavenly Strength hid himself behind the entrance of the rock-cave, and Kami of Heavenly Headgear bound her sleeves with a cord of vine, and stamped on an overturned bucket which was placed before the rock-cave. Then she became kami-possessed, exposed her breasts and genitals. Thereupon, the 800 myriads of kami laughed so hard that the Plain of High Heaven shook with their laughter.

The Sun Goddess, intrigued by all this, opened the rock-cave door slightly, wondering why it was that the 800 myriads of kami were laughing. Then Kami of Heavenly Headgear said, 'There is a kami nobler than you, and that is why we are happy and dancing.' While she was speaking thus, Kami of the Little Roof and Kami of Grand Bead showed the mirror to the Sun Goddess. Thereupon, the Sun Goddess, thinking this ever more strange, gradually came out of the cave, and the hidden Kami of Grand Bead took her hand and pulled her out. Then as the Sun Goddess reappeared, the Plain of High Heaven was naturally illuminated.

Source: *Kojiki*, ch. 17: *The Great Asian Religions*, pp. 232–233.

THE SHRINE AT ISE

The Grand Shrine at Ise, dedicated to Amatarasu, is the most important Shinto shrine in Japan today. The following passage describes the events surrounding its inauguration and refers to the link between the emperor and Amatarasu.

25th year, Spring, and month, 8th day. The Emperor commanded the five officers, Takenu Kaha-wake, ancestor of the Abe no Omi; Hiko-kuni-fuku, ancestor of the Imperial Chieftains; O-kashima, ancestor of the Nakatome Deity Chieftains; and Tochine, ancestor of the Mononobe Deity chieftains . . . saying: 'The sagacity of Our predecessor on the throne, the Emperor Mimaki-iri-hiko-inie, was displayed in wisdom; he was reverential, intelligent, and capable. He was profoundly unassuming, and his disposition was to cherish self-abnegation. He adjusted the machinery of government, and did solemn worship to the Gods of Heaven and Earth. He practiced self-restraint and was watchful of his personal conduct. Every day he was heedful for that day. Thus the welfare of the people was sufficient, and the Empire was at peace. And now, under Our reign, will there be any remissness in the worship of the Gods of Heaven and Earth?'

3rd month, 10th day. The Great Goddess Amatarasu was taken from [the princess] Toyo-suki-iri-hime, and entrusted to [the princess] Yamato-hime no Mikoto. Now Yamato-hime sought for a place where she might enshrine the Great Goddess. So she proceeded to Sasahata in Uda. Then turning back from there, she entered the land of Omi, and went round eastwards to Mino, and so she arrived in the province of Ise.

Now the Great Goddess Amatarasu instructed Yamato-hime, saying: 'The province of Ise, of the divine wind, is the land in which the waves from the eternal world reside, the successive waves. It is a secluded and pleasant land. In this land I wish to reside.' In compliance, therefore, with the instruction of the Great Goddess, a shrine was erected to her in the province of Ise. Accordingly an Abstinence Palace was built at Kawakami in Isuzu. This was called the palace of Ise. It was there that the Great Goddess Amatarasu first descended from Heaven.

Source: *Nihongi*, ch. 5: *Nihongi*, p. 175.

WHY JAPAN IS SPECIAL

According to the legends of the Kojiki and Nihonshoki, Japan was created by the kami, *who continue to take an active interest in the Japanese islands and the people who inhabit them.*

Japan is the divine country. The heavenly ancestor it was who first laid its foundations, and the Sun Goddess left her descendants to reign over it forever and ever. This is true only of our country, and nothing similar may be found in foreign lands. That is why it is called the divine country.

Source: *Kitabatake Chikafusa*: *Sources of Japanese Tradition,* ed. Ryusaku Tsunoda, Wm. Theodore deBary, and Donald Keene (New York: Columbia University Press, 1958), p. 274.

PROTECTING THE STABILITY OF THE COUNTRY

The following passage reflects an idea that is common in East Asia, that natural calamities reflect on the personality and moral character of the ruler and serve as a sign of the displeasure of Heaven. It reports that when the ancient emperor Sujin experienced difficulties he asked the kami *to explain the cause, and he was informed that he had failed properly to venerate the* kami *Omononushi. The problems he was experiencing were a manifestation of the* kami's *displeasure, and the emperor was told that they would end when the emperor provided the appropriate offerings.*

During the reign of the tenth legendary emperor Sujin, there were many people who wandered away from their homes, and there were also some rebellions. The situation was such that the imperial virtue alone could not control the nation. Therefore, the emperor was penitent from morning till night, asking for divine punishment of the kami of heaven and earth upon himself. Prior to that time the two kami, the Sun Goddess and the Kami of Yamato, were worshipped together within the imperial palace. The emperor, however, was afraid of their potencies and did not feel at ease living with them. Therefore, he entrusted Princess Toyosukiri to worship the Sun Goddess at the village of Kasanui in Yamato, where a sacred shrine was established. Also he commissioned Princess Nunakiri to worship the Kami of Yamato.

[Then] the emperor stated, 'I did not realize that numerous calamities would take place during our reign. It may be that the lack of good rule might have incurred the wrath of the kami of heaven and earth. It might be well to inquire the cause of the calamities by means of divination.' The emperor therefore assembled the eighty myriads of kami and inquired about this matter by means of divination. At that time the kami spoke through the kami-possession of Princess Yamatotohimomoso, 'Why is the emperor worried over the disorder of the nation? Doesn't he know that the order of the nation would be restored if he properly venerated me?' The emperor asked which kami was thus giving such an instruction, and the answer was: 'I am the kami who resides within the province of Yamato, and my name is Omononushi-no-kami.' Following the divine instruction, the emperor worshipped the kami, but the expected result did not follow. Thus the emperor cleansed himself and fasted as well as purifying the palace, and addressed himself to the kami in prayer, asking, 'Is not our worship sufficient? Why is our worship not accepted? May we be further instructed in a dream as to the fulfillment of your divine favor toward us.'

That night a noble man who called himself Omononushi-no-kami appeared and spoke to the emperor in his dream, 'The emperor has no more cause to worry over the unsettled state of the nation. It is my divine wish to be worshipped by my child, Otataneko, and then the nation will be pacified immediately.' Upon learning the meaning of the dream, the emperor was greatly delighted and issued a proclamation throughout the country to look for Otataneko, who was subsequently found in the district of Chinu and was presented to the court. Whereupon the emperor asked Otataneko as to whose child he was, and the answer was: 'My father's name is the Great Kami Omononushi. My mother's name is Princess Ikutamayori.' The emperor then said, 'Now prosperity will come to us.' Thus, Otataneko was made the chief priest in charge of the worship of the Great Kami Omononushi. After that the emperor consulted divination as to the desirability of worshipping other kami, and found it desirable to do so. Accordingly he paid homage to the eighty myriads of kami. Thereupon the pestilence ceased and peace was restored in the nation, and good crops of the five kinds of grain made the peasantry prosperous.

Source: *Nihongi*, ch. 5, 6th and 7th years: *Nihongi*, pp. 239–240.

PRINCE SHOTOKU'S PROCLAMATION ON VENERATION OF KAMI

Prince Shotoku is a pivotal figure in Japanese history. He embraced Buddhism and propagated it throughout the country, but as the following passage indicates, he continued the ancient practices of venerating the indigenous kami.

[In 607 during the reign of Empress Suiko, r. 592–628] the following edict was issued [by the Prince Regent Shotoku, 573–621]: 'We are told that our imperial ancestors, in governing the nation, bent humbly under heaven and walked softly on earth. They venerated the kami of heaven and earth, and established shrines on the mountains and by the rivers, whereby they were in constant touch with the power of nature. Hence the winter (*yin*, negative cosmic force) and summer (*yang*, positive cosmic force) elements were kept in harmony, and their creative powers blended together. And now during our reign, it would be unthinkable to neglect the veneration of the kami of heaven and earth. May all the ministers from the bottom of their hearts pay homage to the kami of heaven and earth.'

Source: *Nihongi*, ch. 12: *Nihongi*, p. 241.

FESTIVAL OF THE GATES

This is a ritual prayer (norito) *recited to ask the* kami *to protect the imperial palace. It requests that they guard against evil spirits and safeguard the gates.*

We do most humbly invoke your hallowed names: Kushi-iha-mato, Toyo-iha-mato. For you dwell in all the inner and outer august gates of the four quarters, defending them like massive sacred rocks. For if from the four sides and the four quarters the hateful and unruly god Ame-no-maga-tsu-hi should appear, you are not enchanted by his wicked words, nor deceived into consenting to them. For if this evil should come from above you defend from above, and if it should come from below you defend from below, lying in wait to drive off and protect, and to exorcize with words. For you open the gates in the morning, and close the gates in the evening, and inquire and know the names of all who come in and of all who go out. For if there be any error or misdeed, you rectify it to the eye and to the ear as do the deities Kamu-naho-bi and Oho-naho-bi, and cause those in the service of the divine descendant to serve him in tranquility and peace. Thus do we most humbly praise your hallowed names, Toyo-iha-mato, Kushi-iha-mato. Thus humbly we speak.

Source: *Mikado Matsuri (Festival for the Imperial Palace Gates)*; tr. Meredith McKinney.

PRAYER TO AMATARASU DURING THE FESTIVAL OF THE SIXTH MONTH

This is a prayer spoken by the head priest of the Grand Shrine of Ise during a regular festival performed every six months. It asks Amatarasu to ensure that the emperor has a long life, to protect the country, and to promote the prosperity of the people.

By the solemn command of the Emperor,
[I pray] that you make his life a long life,
Prospering [his reign] as an abundant reign,
Eternal and unmoving as the sacred massed rocks,
That you favor also the princes who are born,
That you [protect] long and tranquilly the various officials,
As well as even the common people of the lands of the four quarters of the kingdom,
And that you cause to flourish in abundance
The five grains which they harvest.
With the prayer [I offer] the tribute threads habitually presented by the people of the Kamube
Established in the three counties and in the various lands and various places,

And the great wine and the great first fruits prepared in ritual purity,
Placing these in abundance like a long mountain range.
I, the great Nakatomi, abiding concealed behind the solemn *tama-gusi,*
On the seventeenth day of the sixth month of this year,
Do humbly speak your praises as the morning sun rises in effulgent glory.

Source: *Norito.*

PRAYER FOR MOVING THE SHRINE OF ISE

Every 20 years the grand shrine of Ise is rebuilt. There are two sites on which the shrines are constructed, and builders alternate between the two. When the time comes to construct a new shrine, the following prayer is spoken to the goddess in order to inform her that the time has come for her to move again.

By the solemn command of the Sovereign Grandchild,
I humbly speak in the solemn presence of the Great Sovereign Deity;
In accordance with the ancient custom,
The great shrine is built anew once in twenty years,
The various articles of clothing of fifty-four ages,
And the sacred treasures of twenty-one types are provided,
And exorcism, purification, and cleansing are performed.

Source: *Norito.*

MOUNT FUJI

Mount Fuji is widely viewed in Japan as a particularly sacred place and as the abode of powerful kami. *The following poem, contained in the* Manyoshi *collection, describes the grandeur of the mountain and the power of its* kami.

Between the provinces of Kai and Suruga
Stands the lofty peak of Fuji.
Heavenly clouds would not dare cross it;
Even birds dare not fly above it.
The fire of volcano is extinguished by snow,
And yet snow is consumed by fire.
It is hard to describe;
It is impossible to name it.
One only senses the presence of a mysterious kami. . . .
In the land of Yamato,
The land of the rising sun,
The lofty Mount Fuji is its treasure and its tutelary kami. . . .
One is never tired of gazing at its peak in the province of Suruga.

Source: *Manyoshi,* 3:319–321; *The Great Asian Religions,* p. 239.

LIFE IS TRANSITORY

A common theme in Shinto literature is the notion that things in the natural world are transitory. The following poem describes how the changes of the seasons are similar to the changes experienced by human beings.

> It has been told from the beginning of the world
> That life on earth is transitory. . . .
> Indeed we see even in the sky the moon waxes and wanes. . . .
> In the spring flowers decorate mountain-trees,
> But in the autumn with dew and frost
> Leaves turn colors and fall on the ground. . . .
> So it is with human life:
> Rosy cheek and black hair turn their color;
> The morning smile disappears in the evening
> Like the wind which blows away.
> Changes continue in life like the water passing away,
> And my tears do not stop over the uncertainty of life.

Source: *Manyoshi: The Great Asian Religions*, p. 239.

GLOSSARY

Amatarasu Omikami   The Sun Goddess, believed to be the divine progenitor of the imperial line.

Folk Shinto   (*minzoku shinto*) A term for popular practices connected with the kami.

Ise   The most prominent shrine of Shinto, dedicated to the Sun Goddess, Amatarasu Omikami.

Kami   The indigenous gods of Japan, often associated with particular places.

Makoto no kokoro   "Heart of Truth," an attitude of reverence toward the natural world and pure moral character.

Sectarian Shinto   (*kyoha shinto*) Distinctive schools of Shinto thought and practice.

Shinto   "Way of the Gods," believed by many traditional Japanese to be the native religious tradition of Japan.

Shrine Shinto   (*jinja shinto*) A form of Shinto that centers on ritual activities connected with shrines.

Uchigami   Clan deity.

FURTHER READINGS

Anesaki, Masaharu. *History of Japanese Religion*. London: Kegan Paul, 1930.
Geemers, Wilhelmus H. M. *Shrine Shinto after World War II*. Leiden: E. J. Brill, 1968.
Holtom, D. C. *The National Faith of Japan*. New York: Paragon, 1965.

KISHIMOTO, HIDEO. *Japanese Religion in the Meiji Era,* tr. John F. Howes. Tokyo: Obunsha, 1956.

KITAGAWA, JOSEPH M. *Religion in Japanese History.* New York: Columbia University Press, 1966.

MURAOKA, TSUNETSUGU. *Studies in Shinto Thought,* tr. Delmer M. Brown and James T. Araki. Tokyo: Japanese National Commission for Unesco, 1964.

Australian Aboriginal Religion

INTRODUCTION

Like many other aboriginal peoples, the earliest inhabitants of Australia developed complex religious systems that emphasized myth and ritual practices designed to explain how the world came to be as it is and describing techniques for manipulating natural forces. At the time of white settlement in Australia, there were an estimated 300,000 Aborigines, divided among around 500 tribes. There were more than 200 distinct Aboriginal languages, most of which were mutually unintelligible, and each tribal group had its own myth and ritual cycles. Thus the most significant aspect of Aboriginal religion was its diversity, although there are common themes and concerns that are still shared across the country.

Australian Aborigines have traditionally viewed themselves as custodians of the land, and much of their religious lore and practice is concerned with how the world came to be as it is and the role of humans in maintaining it. In Aboriginal culture, there is a strong sense that there is a common life force that pervades the entire world, and humans, animals, and spirits are all manifestations of it. They see themselves as fundamentally linked to the land they inhabit and as having a primordial connection with other humans and animals. Their ancestors were also aware of the fragility of their environment, and so they endeavored to avoid damaging it by their actions. This concern continues today among the Aboriginal peoples who maintain their traditions, but white settlement has led many to lose this sense of connection with the land.

During the early twentieth century, the Australian government pursued the now-discredited "White Australia" policy, which led to Aboriginal children being forcibly removed from their families and raised in orphanages or in white families in order to help them become part of "mainstream" Australia. The people of the "stolen generations," as they are now called, often suffered severe psychological scarring, and in its aftermath this policy has created pervasive problems among Aborigines. Among its legacies are high suicide rates and alcoholism, along with a common feeling among many contemporary Aborigines that they do not belong either in white society or among their own people. It has also virtually destroyed traditional religious practice in areas in which European culture is most dominant, particularly the southeastern parts of the country.

The Dreaming

Before Europeans landed in Australia, Aborigines had no writing systems; nor did they build permanent structures or monuments. Most tribes were nomadic, wandering from place to place in search of food and water, and many of their myths encoded information regarding where to find the necessities of life and instructions for the making of tools, temporary buildings, hunting, etc. The most pervasive shared aspect of Aboriginal religion is the "Dreaming," which is given different names in different areas. The Aranda people of the central desert region refer to it as "Alcheringa," the peoples of the western desert generally call it "Djugurba," and the Murngin word is "Wongar." For all Aboriginal peoples, the Dreaming is a primordial time during which things came to be as they now are. It has a beginning, but it has no real end, since it continues to affect and shape the present.

In Aboriginal mythology, there is no particular interest in the origin of the world; the stories of the Dreaming begin with the notion of the world already existing in an embryonic state, but still unformed. There was no light, because the sun and moon were slumbering beneath the surface of the earth, along with the ancestral beings whose actions are the focus of Dreaming stories. Many of these were the progenitors of the species that now inhabit Australia, and stories about them often relate how they came to have their distinctive shapes and characteristics. For example, there are a number of myths that tell why emus have no wings and spend all their time on the ground, unlike other birds. In several such myths, the emu ancestors were tricked into cutting off their own wings by other birds who were jealous of them. Beings took shape during the Dreaming, and events left permanent traces on the ancestors, which continue to be inherited by their descendants. In another myth, a lizard with a black patch on its tongue is said to have inherited this characteristic because its Dreaming ancestor once carried a burning coal in its mouth in order to bring fire to its tribe.

Aboriginal myths are overwhelmingly associated with the land, and each tribe's stories are connected with specific features of its territory. In Aboriginal religion there are no churches or other monuments in which religion is practiced; rather, certain areas are considered sacred, and rituals are performed in these places in accordance with their religious significance. One of the most fundamental problems for contemporary Aborigines who want to preserve their traditions is the fact that many sacred sites are now owned by the descendants of European settlers, who have fenced them off and regard Aborigines as trespassers. Most Aboriginal religious practice is connected to specific places in a tribe's traditional area, and once this link has been severed there is no possibility of recreating the ritual in another area because each place has its own specific Dreaming associations. Moreover, the patterns of traditional Aboriginal life were concerned with re-creating the events of the Dreaming, and their lands were crisscrossed by the tracks of their primordial ancestors. In their wanderings in search of food, they emulated the examples of these beings and maintained their sense of relatedness to them. This way of life is practiced today only by small tribal groups in isolated areas, and Aborigines living in urban areas face significant difficulties in attempting to adapt traditional religious myths and rituals to their present situations.

The overall concern in most myths of the Dreaming is how the world came to be inhabitable by humans, and the power of the ancestors is thought to be available still to those with the proper ritual knowledge. In some cases the ancestors were transformed into features of the landscape, and in others they died or passed beyond tribal lands, but in most cases their spirits survive, and they continue to be as alive as they were during the primordial Dreaming, though now in altered form. They are eternal, and many are said to be self-created. Unlike the gods of other peoples, however, the ancestors are portrayed as living much like humans: they hunt their food with spears or other hand weapons, they require water in order to survive, and even the most powerful build shelters in order to protect themselves from the elements.

Despite their great power and the cosmic significance of their actions, their lives parallel those of traditional Aborigines in most respects, and Aboriginal life was seen as replicating their paradigmatic actions in their daily activities. All of life was pervaded by a sense of sacredness, and for the traditional Aborigine the surrounding landscape contained the traces of the ancestors, and their actions had a sacred quality to the extent that they followed the models that had been initiated in the Dreaming. The events of the Dreaming have a primordial quality, and the Dreaming overlaps with conventional time. It continues to affect the present, and it is just as real as ordinary reality, and in fact is intimately conjoined with it.

In Dreaming stories, the ancestors are often shape-changers, and they physically adapt to changing circumstances. Some of these changes become permanent, while others are temporary. It is important to note that in Aboriginal religion the Dreaming does not merely reflect a past time, but is significant because it is also reflected in present reality. The beings of the Dreaming had great power and shaped both the land and its inhabitants, and they continue to exist as part of the world they formed. Their actions and conflicts altered the landscape, and they also laid the basis for tribal laws, customs, and rituals. The stories that were left behind provided examples of good and evil behavior, as well as answers to the problems that faced traditional people. In some cases the moral of a Dreaming myth is straightforward: "We do this because Baiame (the all-father in many Aboriginal myths) did so and commanded us to emulate him." In other cases, the ramifications of myths are deeply encoded in layers of meaning and may be differently interpreted in accordance with changing circumstances.

Although the Dreaming establishes the basis for human society and its laws, it is in no sense a golden age. The ancestors often act immorally, and in many stories humans learn not to emulate them because of the negative consequences of their actions. For example, in some myths of the Walmadjeri people of the central desert, the first men trick the first women and steal their sacred emblems and the magical powers associated with them. But even though the ancestors in such myths behave immorally, they are generally punished for their misbehavior, and so the moral order is upheld.

Religious Practice and Ritual Lore

Because there was no writing system for Aboriginal languages, the scriptures of their religion existed only in oral form. As noted previously, they mainly took the form of stories that recounted the deeds of ancestral beings, many of which contained prescriptions for present behavior. They also encoded often complex rituals, many of which were linked with the human life cycle. Surprisingly, birth does not figure very prominently in most Aboriginal religions, but puberty, tribal initiation, procreation, and death are central concerns. In some Aboriginal societies, death is seen as final, and there are a number of stories that recount how it first appeared during the Dreaming. But other tribes believe in a form of rebirth, in which the spirit of the deceased goes to another realm, which is generally said to be idyllic, though its main features reflect this world. In most cases the journey to the afterlife is fraught with peril, and many are unable to find their way, and so remain among the living as unhappy spirits. Those who successfully overcome the obstacles find a land inhabited by friends and relatives, in which game and water are plentiful, and in which life is much like that of our world, but better and happier.

Only those who live good lives have a chance to successfully make the journey to the afterlife. Good behavior requires adherence to the laws and norms of the tribe and submission to tribal authority. Traditional Aboriginal religion is profoundly conservative, and people are enjoined to strictly adhere to past paradigms and to obey the dictates of tribal authorities, who are generally old men. Deviation from tradition is viewed as a serious offence, and this conservatism is no doubt one of the reasons for the difficulties Aborigines have faced in adapting their traditions to modern Australian society. The myths and rituals of the Dreaming tell nomadic hunter-gatherers how to live in harmony with the natural environment, where to find food and water, and how to replicate the behavior of their ancestors, but provide few clues for how to live in fixed dwellings in urban areas or how to function within the modern economy.

Male dominance was a pervasive feature of traditional Aboriginal society. Male elders generally were the dominant figures, and most important rituals were performed by men. In recent years researchers have discovered that women also were involved in rituals, commonly referred to as "secret women's business," but these were generally seen as having significance only for female members of a tribe, while men's rituals were important for everyone. In tribal rituals, women played at most a subordinate role, as supporters of the men who led them. The inferior status of women is also reflected in Aboriginal myths: while there are a number of powerful and influential female characters, women are generally portrayed as submissive to men. Marriage is often the result of a man simply carrying a woman away and ordering her to become his wife, and male ancestors commonly disciplined their women through physical force, with beatings or physical deprivation. Female characters are often flighty and undependable, and firm male influence is needed in order to keep them in line. As in all traditional societies, however, religious paradigms reflect an ideal constructed by male elites, and the actual status of women probably varied considerably in Aboriginal societies. The following stories are drawn from a variety of tribes from different parts of the continent.

AUSTRALIAN ABORIGINAL MYTHS

THE FIRST DEATH

Death is a central concern of Aboriginal religion. There is a great deal of speculation regarding how it first entered the world and whether or not it is final. In this story from the Kamilroi tribe, Baiame, the all-father, finished creating the world, and after extensive travels around the land was well satisfied with his work. Subsequently he returned to his abode in the sky along with his wife Birrahgnooloo, who some tribes regard as the Mother-of-All and his partner in creation.

As Baiame walked the world, he fashioned various animals and plants, along with important features of the landscape such as rivers and mountains. Finally he created humans out of the dust of the mountains, intending that they would be custodians of the land. The first people began to reproduce, and Baiame's world became increasingly filled with various species. The sun and rain he provided sustained both plant and animal life, and sustenance was plentiful.

Long after his departure to heaven, however, the land was afflicted by the first great drought, which is still today a recurrent problem in Australia. Although humans had been ordered by Baiame not to eat certain species, a man driven to desperation began to kill and eat some of them and shared the food with his wife. They offered a forbidden kangaroo-rat to a friend who was afflicted by hunger, but mindful of Baiame's prohibition he refused the meat and went away.

As he walked he became steadily weaker, until he collapsed at the base of a large tree. The man and woman who had offered him food saw him from a distance and called out to him, but he was too weak to respond. As they watched, a large black shape emerged from the tree and picked up his dying body and carried it up into the high branches. The monster who carried him was Yowee, the spirit of death, and the man became the first human to die. Baiame had intended that his creation would be perfect and that all of his creatures would have plenty of food and water, but in his absence they experienced severe privation, which allowed death to enter the world and claim its first victim. Since that time death has been the fate of all creatures.

HOW FIRE BECAME WIDELY AVAILABLE

There are a number of Aboriginal myths concerning the origins of fire. In some the ancestors jealously guard the secrets of how to make and maintain fire, and there is a general sense that such a wondrous lore would not be freely shared. Fire is often obtained by trickery or theft, and those who get it generally want to keep it for themselves. In the following story from the Northern Territory, two men acquire the secret of fire and refuse to share it with their tribe.

Before fire was widely available, people made their food more edible by leaving it to dry in the sun. One day Bootoolgah the crane ancestor was rubbing two sticks together and noticed that this action produced a spark. He showed this to his wife Goonur the kangaroo rat, who realized that this technique could be used to make fire whenever they wanted. They fashioned two sticks that could be carried in a pouch, which they carried with them at all times. They first used fire to cook some fish they had caught, and marveled at how much better it tasted than sun-dried flesh.

They decided to keep the secret of fire for themselves, and they always went to hidden places to make their fires and cook their food. When other members of their tribe noticed that their meat looked different from theirs, Bootoolgah and Goonur claimed that they had dried it in the sun like everyone else, but the others became suspicious. One day Boolooral the night owl followed them silently and saw them making fire to cook their food, and he reported back to the elders of the tribe. Rather than try to take the secret by force, they decided to trick the two. They announced that a huge *corroboree* (tribal gathering) would be held, the largest in living memory, and that all the surrounding tribes would participate.

Each group arrived decorated with its distinctive symbols. Some painted their whole bodies, while others had elaborate costumes made with feathers. All performed dances unique to their tribes, and no one had ever seen such a wondrous display. During the celebrations Bootoolgah and Goonur became so entranced by the spectacle that they forgot to guard their fire sticks. When their guard was down a man who had been pretending to be sick grabbed the bag in which the fire sticks were hidden and brought them to the tribal elders. They learned how to use them to make fire, and subsequently shared the lore with the rest of the tribe, so that everyone could make use of it.

THE RAINBOW SERPENT

Different ancestors figure in myths of the various regions of Australia. One of the most widely dispersed ancestral characters is the Rainbow Serpent, named Ngaljod in Northern Arnhem Land and known by other names in other parts of the continent. He is said to be an enormous snake who commonly lives in lakes and rivers. When he moves from one place to another, he makes rivers and water holes. His voracious appetite often brings him into conflict with other ancestors. He is essentially an amoral character, whose actions created important aspects of the landscape, but he has no particular love for humans. Rather, he eats them whenever he can, and many myths about the Rainbow Snake focus on how dangerous he is.

Before going off to hunt, the men of a tribe in the Northern Territory warned their boys not to venture near the sea because a giant snake lived there, waiting to eat unwary children. After they left the boys began to play, but after becoming bored decided to follow the sound of the surf to the beach. As they drew near, they saw a beautiful rainbow in the sky, but they failed to realize that it was caused by the Rainbow Serpent, who had arched his coils up from the water. The colors of the rainbow were caused by the light reflecting off his scales.

When the boys reached the water, they were so enraptured by the beauty of the landscape that they failed to notice the serpent, who swam toward them swiftly and silently. He swallowed them whole. When the hunters returned to their camp, they immediately noticed that the boys had disappeared, and when they followed their tracks to the beach they found that they ended at the water's edge. There were two black rocks in the ocean that had not been there before, and the men realized that the rainbow serpent had swallowed the boys and turned them into rocks. There was nothing they could do about this situation, and so they sadly returned to their camp. The rocks are still visible today between Double Island Point and Inship Rock. When a rainbow appears in the sky, the elders of the tribe tell this story to the younger members in order to illustrate the importance of obedience and the dangers of wandering by themselves.

DIVISION OF LABOR BETWEEN THE SEXES

This story from tribes living near the Murray River in New South Wales tells of how men and women came to cohabit and describes how each has certain duties and obligations.

During the Dreaming the Raven ancestor wanted to cross a river, but since he could not swim he decided to build a canoe. After searching for suitable bark, he fashioned one and began to carry it to the water. As he walked, he began to hear a rhythmic tapping in the air above his head, and after searching around determined that it was coming from his canoe. He set it down and discovered to his surprise that a woman was sitting in it. He had never before seen a female, and so he stared at her, fascinated by the differences in their respective physiques.

The woman said nothing to him, but stepped from the canoe and helped him to carry it to the bank of the river. After they were both in the small craft, he handed her the paddle, but she shook her head and sat in the back of the canoe. Her actions indicated that she expected him to do the hard work of paddling. Because he had never before met a woman, he was unfamiliar with the proper relationships between the sexes, but she began to teach him his role and what sort of work was appropriate for her. He found many of her lessons difficult to accept, and the learning process was fraught with conflicts, but at the same time he realized that there were unexpected compensations. Many things he had had to do by himself were now shared, and they developed a mutually satisfactory partnership. Later they had children, and raising them presented more challenges and rewards. One day when the two were searching for food their young wandered from the tree in which they sheltered. When they reached the ground they adapted by taking on human form, and thus they became the first Aborigines. All of Australia's original people are descended from these two ancestors.

FURTHER READINGS

BERNDT, RONALD M. *Australian Aboriginal Religion*. Leiden: E. J. Brill, 1974.

COWAN, JAMES. *Aborigine Dreaming*. London: Thorsons, 2002.

KEEN, IAN. *Knowledge and Secrecy in an Aboriginal Religion*. Oxford: Clarendon Press, 1994.

REED, A. W. *Aboriginal Myths: Tales of the Dreamtime*. Sydney: Reed New Holland, 2000.

STAMMER, W. E. H. *On Aboriginal Religion*. Sydney: University of Sydney, 1989.

Zoroastrianism

INTRODUCTION

With little more than 100,000 followers, Zoroastrianism today is a shadow of its former self as a dominant religion of the Near East. Zoroastrianism developed in Iran and southern Russia around 1200 B.C.E., and at its height was the state religion of Persia's empires from the third century C.E. until the expansion of Islam in the seventh century. Although the face of Zoroastrianism changed over its long history, several doctrines have remained consistent: (1) Ahura Mazda is worshipped as the one supreme God. (2) Zarathushtra (or "Zoroaster" in Greek) is Ahura Mazda's prophet who delivers his unique revelation. (3) The universe is a battleground between opposing good and evil forces, and this cosmological dualism accounts for the presence of good and evil everywhere. Angra Mainyu, the primary evil spirit that embodies evil, is to be opposed. (4) Ahura Mazda created several divine beings, or Beneficent Immortals, who are to be venerated. (5) Humans will be judged in the afterlife for their good or evil deeds.

Background and Life of Zarathushtra

Between 2000 and 1500 B.C.E., there occurred a mass migration of Aryan people, perhaps from eastern Europe, to the region of what is now Iran. Over the next few centuries they successfully assimilated with the native people, as indicated by the name "Iran," which means home or land of the Aryans. The Aryan newcomers brought with them an ancient polytheistic religion that involved the worship of daevas, or divine beings. After some centuries, a group of these Aryans migrated farther to northern India, forming the basis of the early Hindu religion. Aryan culture had three principal social classes (priests, warriors, and cattle breeders), and different deities were associated with each. The gods of the priestly class included Mitra, Anahita, Varuna (the latter perhaps identified as Ahura Mazda). The priestly class also had religious rituals involving sacrificing oxen, imbibing the intoxicating juice of the haoma plant (*soma* in Sanskrit), and fire rituals, perhaps derived from Agni, the fire god of early India's religion.

Zarathushtra emerged as a religious reformer, reacting against both the polytheism and the rituals of the Aryan religion. Little historical information is available about the life of Zarathushtra, and scholars have variously placed him between 1500 and 500 B.C.E. The most plausible tradition places him around 1200 B.C.E. in the Azerbaijan province of Northwest Iran; some linguistic and archaeological evidence, however, suggest that he was from an oasis tribal setting in Eastern Iran, near what is now the Afghanistan border.

According to later Zoroastrian tradition, Zarathushtra began his mission at age 30, after having a series of visions in which he was escorted to Ahura Mazda's presence, where he received his divine message. The first ten years of his mission were especially unsuccessful, and his only convert was his cousin. His teaching antagonized a group of priests who conspired against him and threw him into prison. At age 42, when he was still in prison, his fortune changed with the conversion of King Vishtaspa (Hystaspes in Greek), an as yet unidentified monarch. Vishtaspa had an ill horse, and Zarathushtra healed it, leg by leg. During the process, the king was required to make certain concessions. The king was impressed, and the whole court accepted Zarathushtra's teachings.

Although Zarathushtra's life events remain hazy, there is greater knowledge about the content of his teachings and his role as a religious reformer. His foremost reform is advocating the supremacy of Ahura Mazda. The name *Ahura Mazda* means "Wise Lord," and Zarathushtra described him as holy, eternal, just, all knowing, and creator of all. Ahura Mazda is also said to be the source of all goodness, including success, glory, honor, physical health, and immortality. Zarathushtra condemned the *daevas* of the Indo-Iranian pantheon as subordinate devils, and their priests as devil followers. He also attacked many of the traditional Indo-Iranian religious rituals, especially the wasteful slaughter of great numbers of oxen, bulls, and cows in ritual sacrifices. Aspects of the haoma ritual were condemned, but Zarathushtra continued this tradition with some modifications. The traditional fire rituals were also modified so as to reflect worship of Ahura Mazda, who is symbolized by undying fire.

Zarathushtra emphasized the religious conflict between good and evil. This ethical emphasis is best described as dualistic insofar as all key players—human and divine—choose either good or evil. Ahura Mazda demands ethical and ritual purity and judges the souls of people after death. The principal evil force, called the Lie (*druj*), wages war against Ahura Mazda. To assist in the war against evil, Ahura Mazda created Beneficent Immortals (*Amesha Spentas*). Later Zoroastrian tradition sees them as guardians over areas of Creation. They are Asha Vahishta (Best Order, or Best Truth), associated with fire; Vohu Manah (Good Thought), associated with the ox; Khshathra Vairya (Desirable Dominion), associated with metals; Spenta Armaiti (Beneficent Devotion), associated with the earth; Haurvatat (Wholeness), associated with water; and Ameretat (Immortality), associated with plants. The theological status of the Beneficent Immortals is not entirely clear, and it is not certain whether they are distinct entities or merely different aspects of Ahura Mazda. Some scholars believe that their names and functions are derived from traditional Indo-Iranian deities, particularly the deities of the lower classes.

According to Zarathushtra, the cosmic ethical drama began when two twin spirits chose between good and evil. The spirit Spenta Mainyu (Beneficent

Spirit) allied himself with good, and Angra Mainyu (Destructive Spirit) chose evil. As Zoroastrianism developed over the centuries, Angra Mainyu became the embodiment of all evil, and even the rival of Ahura Mazda. Although his role is more limited in Zarathushtra's teachings, Zoroastrian tradition consistently describes Angra Mainyu as working for evil in the service of the Lie and is the source of misfortune, disaster, war, sickness, and death. To aid him in the assault on good, Angra Mainyu created several devils (*daevas*) which correspond with the Beneficent Immortals. The demon opposing Vohu Mano is Ako Mano (Bad Mind); against Asha Vahishta is Spozgar (Disorder); against Khshathra Vairya is Bushyasp (Sloth); against Spenta Armaiti is Asto Vidhatu (Death, literally, Bone Dissolver); against Haurvatat is Az (Greed); and against Ameretat is Tishn (Thirst). Angra Mainyu also counter-created demons/fiends which correspond to the other spiritual beings (*Yazads*).

The Rise and Decline of Zoroastrianism

Zarathushtra's new religion continued to spread after his death. During the Achaemenian Persian dynasty (550–330 B.C.E.), the first documented period of Zoroastrian influence, the religion was associated with the Magi. Although the identity and role of the Magi is unclear, they were experts in cultic ritual and claimed to be descendants of Zarathushtra's first converts. They may have originally been an early hereditary class of priests who allied themselves with Zarathushtra's teachings. When Mesopotamia was conquered by Alexander the Great, the impact of Greek culture caused a decline of Zoroastrianism. It was revived during the Parthian period (247 B.C.E.–237 C.E.), although there is little reliable information to indicate its character at this time.

Zoroastrianism peaked in influence during the Sasanian period (227–651 C.E.) when it became the state religion of Persia. Zoroastrian expansion throughout the empire was mostly the result of conversion, though at times adherents to rival forms of worship were punished. Sasanid theologians developed Zoroastrianism's great cosmological myths, dividing cosmic history into four 3,000-year periods. During the final period, Zarathushtra and his three descendant prophets appeared at 1,000-year intervals to wage war on Angra Mainyu. The world currently awaits the last prophet, Saoshyant, who will bring about final judgment and usher in a new world. The dead will then be resurrected, Ahura Mazda will judge all people according to their conduct as recorded in the book of deeds, and Angra Mainyu will be destroyed. Hell will also be dismantled, and the wicked (with few exceptions), having been purified, will be released.

Zoroastrianism gradually declined after 633 when the Muslims entered Persia and most of the population was forced to convert to Islam. Zoroastrianism was still tolerated for about three hundred more years, but persecution in the tenth century prompted many to leave Iran for India. Known as the Parsis, the immigrating Zoroastrians settled near Bombay and today total around 70,000. They are generally financially well off, and many help to support the remaining

Zoroastrians in Iran, who today number around 30,000. An additional 20,000 Zoroastrians live in other parts of the world.

Parallels between Zoroastrian beliefs and those of Judaism, Christianity, and Islam are striking, for example, the messianic figure of Saoshyant, the Armageddon-like final battle, bodily resurrection, final judgment, and heaven and hell. Many historians of religion believe that Zoroastrianism is the source of these beliefs. However, the complex web of Zoroastrian doctrines themselves developed over time, and precisely when certain doctrines first appeared is still unclear.

Zoroastrian Scriptures

The foundational and oldest Zoroastrian scripture is the *Avesta*, a compilation of liturgical texts composed over a 1,000-year period. The original *Avesta* probably comprised 22 books and included historical, medical, and legal information along with liturgical texts. Only a small part of the original *Avesta* has survived. Zoroastrian legend recounts that two official copies were destroyed by Alexander during his campaign in the Persian capital. Priests gathered the remaining orally transmitted fragments, which were regularly recited in liturgies. The *Avesta* was kept alive through recitation until about 400 C.E., when an official edition was ordered by the Sasanid rulers. It is written in an archaic language called Avestan, which is related to Sanskrit and uses a modified Pahlavi alphabet. The *Avesta* is the only surviving example of a text in this language.

In its current form, the *Avesta* is about 1,000 pages and written in different dialects from different periods of time. The most important division is the *Yasna*, a collection of prayers and liturgical formulas in 72 chapters. A 50-page section in the middle of the *Yasna*, called the *Gathas* (Chapters 28–34, 43–54), contains hymns in an older dialect, and is believed to have been written by Zarathushtra himself. The other key divisions of the *Avesta* are these:

Visparat (all the leaders): liturgical extension of the Yasna (22 chapters);

Vendidad (law against demons): instructions for ritual purification and moral practice to ward off evil powers, also containing myths and medical texts (22 chapters);

Khorde Avesta (*Smaller Avesta*): book of daily prayer used by the laity. Among other texts, it includes

- Yashts (songs of praise): long hymns to various divine beings, some paralleling those found in the Hindu Vedas, plus epic narratives about kings and heroes
- *Niyayeshs:* litanies to the Sun, Mithra, the Moon, the Waters, and Fire
- *Gahs:* dedications for each period of the day
- *Afrinagans:* blessings

The *Avesta* also includes several shorter fragments of lost books.

In addition to the *Avesta*, Zoroastrians have numerous scriptures from the Sasanian period which are written in a middle-Persian dialect called Pahlavi. Thus, the writings are typically called *Pahlavi texts*. Many are exegetical commentaries (called *Zand*) that translate, summarize, and explain the *Avesta*. The Pahlavi texts are more numerous than those of the *Avesta*. The primary ones are

> *Bundahishn (Original Creation)*: 36 chapters on cosmogony, mythology, and cosmic history

> *Denkard (Acts of the Religion)*: a collection of doctrines, customs, traditions, history, and literature, originally written in nine books, of which the first two are now lost

> *Datastan-i Denik:* religious opinions of the high priest Manushkihar in response to 92 questions

> *Zadsparam:* a collection by the high priest Zadsparam, younger brother of Manushkihar, which discusses cosmology and the life of Zarathushtra

In addition to the Pahlavi texts, several later Zoroastrian texts are written in a more modern Persian language. The most important of these is the *Sad Dar (One Hundred Doors)*, the first Zoroastrian text known to the West, being translated into Latin in 1700.

THE AVESTA

ZOROASTRIAN CREED

Most of the surviving texts of the Avesta *were used ceremonially. The following creed from* Yasna *Chapter 12 is among the oldest and most central Zoroastrian statements of faith, perhaps initially required of converts. In both thought and deed, the believer vows to reject all evil as associated with daevas and the Lie* (druj), *and instead adhere to the good of Ahura Mazda, and the Beneficent Immortals* (Amesha Spentas).

1. I curse the Daevas. I declare myself a Mazda-worshipper, a supporter of Zarathushtra, hostile to the Daevas, fond of Ahura's teaching, a praiser of the Amesha Spentas, a worshipper of the Amesha Spentas. I ascribe all good to Ahura Mazda, 'and all the best,' the Asha-owning one, splendid, xwarena-owning, whose is the cow, whose is Asha, whose is the light, 'may whose blissful areas be filled with light'.

2. I choose the good Spenta Armaiti for myself; let her be mine. I renounce the theft and robbery of the cow, and the damaging and plundering of the Mazdayasnian settlements.

3. I want freedom of movement and freedom of dwelling for those with homesteads, to those who dwell upon this earth with their cattle. With reverence for Asha, and (offerings) offered up, I vow this: I shall

nevermore damage or plunder the Mazdayasnian settlements, even if I have to risk life and limb.

4. I reject the authority of the Daevas, the wicked, no-good, lawless, evil-knowing, the most druj-like of beings, the foulest of beings, the most damaging of beings. I reject the Daevas and their comrades, I reject the demons (yatu) and their comrades; I reject any who harm beings. I reject them with my thoughts, words, and deeds. I reject them publicly. Even as I reject the head (authorities), so too do I reject the hostile followers of the druj.

5. As Ahura Mazda taught Zarathushtra at all discussions, at all meetings, at which Mazda and Zarathushtra conversed;

6. As Ahura Mazda taught Zarathushtra at all discussions, at all meetings, at which Mazda and Zarathushtra conversed—even as Zarathushtra rejected the authority of the Daevas, so I also reject, as Mazda-worshipper and supporter of Zarathushtra, the authority of the Daevas, even as he, the Asha-owning Zarathushtra, has rejected them.

7. As the belief of the waters, the belief of the plants, the belief of the well-made (Original) Cow; as the belief of Ahura Mazda who created the cow and the Asha-owning Man; as the belief of Zarathushtra, the belief of Kavi Vishtaspa, the belief of both Frashaostra and Jamaspa; as the belief of each of the Saoshyants (saviors)—fulfilling destiny and Asha-owning—so I am a Mazda-worshipper of this belief and teaching.

8. I profess myself a Mazda-worshipper, a Zoroastrian, having vowed it and professed it. I pledge myself to the well-thought thought, I pledge myself to the well-spoken word, I pledge myself to the well-done action.

9. I pledge myself to the Mazdayasnian religion, which causes the attack to be put off and weapons put down; which upholds khvaetvadatha (kin-marriage), which possesses Asha; which of all religions that exist or shall be, is the greatest, the best, and the most beautiful: Ahuric, Zoroastrian. I ascribe all good to Ahura Mazda. This is the creed of the Mazdayasnian religion.

Source: *Yasna* ch. 12, tr. Joseph H. Peterson.

DUALISM

The dualistic battle between good and evil forces is the most characteristic feature of Zoroastrianism during all phases of its history. The following is from a section of the Yasna *known as the* Gathas—*texts believed to have been written by Zarathushtra. In this Gatha, Zarathushtra describes the foundational moral conflict between Ahura Mazda and the Lie (druj). The conflict is carried on further by Ahura Mazda's twin sons, identified in other passages as the good Spenta Mainyu (Beneficent Spirit) and the evil Angra Mainyu (Destructive Spirit). This passage presents significant interpretive problems. On one interpretation, Spenta Mainyu is regarded as separate from Ahura Mazda; thus, both of these battling spirits—including Angra Mainyu— were created by Ahura Mazda. A second interpretation is that the twin sons are merely ethical concepts, not spiritual beings. Thus, Zarathushtra is retelling a tradi- tional myth that was familiar to his audience, and then reinterpreting it in the light of his own revelations. "Spenta Mainyu," then, is as a synonym for Ahura Mazda. In either interpretation, the cosmic dualism established between Spenta Mainyu and Angra Mainyu is paralleled by an ethical dualism between* Druj (*the lie, evil*) *and* Asha (*truth, righteousness*).

Now the two primal Spirits, who revealed themselves in vision as Twins, are the Better and the Bad in thought and word and action. Between these two the wise once chose aright, the foolish not so. When these two Spirits came together in the beginning, they established Life and Not-Life, and that at the last the Worst Existence [i.e., hell] shall be to the followers of the Lie [*druj*], but the Best Thought [i.e., heaven] to him that follows Truth [*asha*]. Of these two Spirits he that followed the Lie chose doing the worst things. The most beneficent Spirit chose Truth [*asha*], he that clothes him with heavy diamonds as a garment. So likewise they that are devoted to please Ahura Mazda by dutiful actions. Between these two, the *daevas* also chose not aright for delusion came upon them as they took counsel together, so that they chose the Worst Thought. Then they rushed together to Violence, that they might sicken the world of man.

To humankind came Dominion, Good Thought, and Truth [*asha*]. Piety gave continued life of their bodies, and indestructibility, so that by your retributions through the molten metal he may gain the prize over those others. So when there comes the punishment of these evil ones, then, Oh Mazda, at your command shall Good Thought establish the Dominion in the Consummation, for those who deliver the Lie, oh Ahura, into the hands of Truth [*asha*]. So may we be those that renovate the universe! Oh Mazda, and you other Ahuras, gather together the Assembly and you too the Truth [*asha*], that thoughts may meet where Wisdom is at home. Then truly on the [followers of] the Lie shall come the destruction of delight; but they that get the good name shall be partakers in the promised reward in the fair home of Good Thought, of Mazda, and of Truth [*asha*].

Source: *Yasna* ch. 30:3–10, adapted from James Hope Moulton, *Early Zoroastrianism*, (London: Williams and Northgate, 1913).

REMOVAL OF HAIR AND NAILS

The moral battle between good and evil touches not only the spiritual realm of thoughts and deeds, but the material realm as well. Things associated with contamination and death, for example, are deemed evil. Although no longer widely practiced today, Zoroastrian ritu- als concerning the removal of hair and nails vividly illustrate how physical things can be tainted by evil. The following purification rituals are from the Vendidad.

Zarathushtra asked Ahura Mazda: "Oh Ahura Mazda, most beneficent Spirit, maker of the material world, holy one! Which is the most deadly deed whereby a man increases most the baleful strength of the demons, as he would do by offering them a sacrifice?"

Ahura Mazda answered: "It is when a man here below combing his hair or shaving it off, or paring off his nails drops them in a hole or in a crack. Then for want of the lawful rites being observed, demons are produced in the earth. For want of the lawful rites being observed, those Khrafstras [i.e., vermin] are produced in the earth which men call lice, and which eat up the grain in the grain-field and the clothes in the wardrobe. Therefore, oh Zarathushtra, whenever here below you shall comb your hair or shave it off, or pare off your nails, you shall take them away ten paces from the faithful, twenty paces from the fire, thirty paces from the water, fifty paces from the consecrated bundles of *baresma* [i.e., grasses used in sacrifice]. Then you shall dig a hole, ten fingers deep if the earth be hard, twelve fingers deep if it be soft. You shall take the hair down there and you shall say aloud these fiend-smiting words: 'Out of him by his piety Mazda made the plants grow up.' Thereupon you shall draw three furrows with a knife of metal around the hole, or six furrows or nine, and you shall chant the *Ahuna-Vairya* three times, or six, or nine."

[Ahura Mazda continued:] "For the nails, you shall dig a hole, out of the house, as deep as the top joint of the little finger. You shall take the nails down there and you shall say aloud these fiend-smiting words: 'The words that are heard from the pious in holiness and good thought.' Then you shall draw three furrows with a knife of metal around the hole, or six furrows or nine, and you shall chant the *Ahuna-Vairya* three times, or six, or nine. And then [say], 'Look here, oh friend-of-Truth bird! Here are the nails for you, look at the nails here! May they be for you so many spears, knives, bows, falcon-winged arrows, and sling-stones against the Mazainya devils. If those nails have not been dedicated to the bird, they shall be in the hands of the Mazainya devils. All the Lie [*druj*] followers are the Lie incarnate; those who scorn a teaching scorn all teachings; those who disobey are entirely disobedient; those who are not Truth-owning are entirely Asha-disowning, and have forfeited their bodies [i.e., mortal sinners].

Source: *Vendidad*, 17:1–11, adapted from James Darmesteter, *The Zend-Avesta*, part 1 (Oxford: Clarendon Press, 1880).

REMOVAL OF THE DEAD

*The problem of physical things being contaminated by evil is most pronounced with dead human bodies. When one dies, a Corpse Demon (*druj nasu*) comes into the body and contaminates it and items that touch the body. Burial is not possible, since this* *contaminates the sacred earth, and cremation contaminates the fire. As described in the following selection from the* Vendidad, *the preferred method of corpse disposal is for dead bodies to be devoured by corpse-eating dogs and birds that frighten off the Corpse Demon. To facilitate this, Zoroastrians construct Towers of Silence (dakhmas), cylindrical walled structures that expose corpses to vultures. This practice has been frequently noted in literature and is one of the most distinctive aspects of Zoroastrian ritual.*

[Zarathushtra asked:] Oh Maker of the material world, holy one, to what place shall we bring, where shall we lay the bodies of the dead?

Ahura Mazda answered: On the highest summits, where corpse-eating beasts and birds can most readily find it. There shall the worshippers of Mazda fasten the corpse by the feet and by the hair, with brass, stones, or horn, lest the corpse-eating dogs and the corpse-eating birds shall go and carry the bones to the water and to the trees.

[Zarathushtra asked:] If they shall not fasten the corpse so that the corpse-eating dogs and the corpse-eating birds may go and carry the bones to the water and to the trees, what is the penalty that they shall pay?

Ahura Mazda answered: They shall be whipped: two hundred stripes. . . .

[Zarathushtra asked:] To what place shall we bring, where shall we lay the bones of the dead thereafter?

Ahura Mazda answered: The worshippers of Mazda shall erect a receptacle out of the reach of the dog, of the fox, and of the wolf, and wherein rain water cannot pool. Such a receptacle shall they erect, if they can afford it, with stones, chalk, and clay; if they cannot afford it, they shall lay down the dead man on the ground, with the earth as his bed, and the sunlight as his clothing.

Zarathushtra asked Ahura Mazda: When a man dies, at what moment does the Corpse Demon [i.e., *druj nasu*] rush upon him?

Ahura Mazda answered: Directly after death, as soon as conscious-ness has left the body, the Corpse Demon comes and rushes upon him, from the regions of the north, like the most ghastly vermin, with knees and tail sticking out, all stained with stains. . . .

[Zarathushtra asked:] If a man has been killed by a dog, or by a wolf, or by witchcraft, or by the artifices of hatred [i.e., poison], or by falling down a precipice, or by treachery, or by murderer, or by strangulation, how long after death does the Corpse Demon come and rush upon the dead?

Ahura Mazda answered: At the next watch [*gah*] after death [i.e., in a few hours], the Corpse Demon comes and rushes upon the dead. . . .

[Zarathushtra asked:] If there be a number of men resting in the same place, on adjoining bedding, on adjoining pillows, be there two men near one another, or five, or fifty, or a hundred, close by one another; and of those people one happens to die; how many of them does the Corpse Demon envelope with infection, pollution, and uncleanliness?

Ahura Mazda answered: If the dead one be a priest, the Corpse Demon rushes forth, she falls on the eleventh and defiles the ten. If the dead one be a warrior . . . she falls on the tenth and defiles the nine. If the dead one be a husbandman . . . she falls on the ninth and defiles the eight. If it be a shepherd's dog . . . she falls on the eight and defiles the seven. . . .

[Zarathushtra asked:] What part of his bedding and pillow does the Corpse Demon defile with infection, uncleanliness, and pollution?

Ahura Mazda answered: The Lie [*druj*] defiles with infection, uncleanliness, and pollution the upper sheet and the inner garment.

[Zarathushtra asked:] Can that garment be made clean that has been touched by the carcass of a dog or the corpse of a man?

Ahura Mazda answered: It can. . . . If, indeed, the garment has been defiled with semen, blood, feces, or vomit, the worshippers of Mazda shall cut it to pieces, and bury it [i.e., the defiled part] under the ground. But if it has not been defiled with semen, blood, feces, or vomit, then the worshippers of Mazda shall wash it with *gomez* [cow urine].

[Zarathushtra asked:] Can he be clean again who has eaten of the carcass of a dog or of the carcass of a man? . . .

Ahura Mazda answered: He cannot. . . . His burrow shall be dug out, his life shall be torn out, his bright eyes shall be put out; the Corpse Demon falls upon him, takes hold of him even to the end of the nails, and he is unclean, thenceforth, for ever and ever.

[Zarathushtra asked:] Can he be clean again, oh holy Ahura Mazda, who has brought a corpse with filth to either water or fire, and made either unclean?

Ahura Mazda answered: He cannot. . . . Those wicked ones it is, those men turned to Nasus [i.e., demons] that most increase spiders and locusts, those wicked ones it is, those men turned to Nasus, that most increase the grass-destroying drought. Those wicked ones it is, those men turned to Nasus, that increase most the power of the winter, produced by the demons [*daevas*], the cattle-killing, thick-snowing, overflowing, the piercing, fierce, mischievous winter. Upon them comes and rushes the Corpse Demon, she takes hold of them even to the end of the nails, and they are unclean, thenceforth, for ever and ever.

[Zarathushtra asked:] Can the wood be made clean, oh holy Ahura Mazda, to which dead matter has been brought from a dead dog, or from a dead man?

Ahura Mazda answered: It can. . . . If the Nasu has not yet been smitten by the corpse-eating dogs, or by the corpse-eating birds, they shall lay down, apart on the ground, the wood on the length of a *Vitasti* [i.e., five fingers] all around the dead matter, if the wood be dry; on the length of a *Frarathni* [i.e., fourteen fingers] all around, if it be wet; then they shall sprinkle it once over with water, and it shall be clean.

Source: *Vendidad*, 6:44–51; 7:1–8, 9–29, adapted from James Darmesteter, *The Zend-Avesta*, part 1 (Oxford: Clarendon Press, 1880).

THE DAILY PRAYER

The Khorde Avesta (Smaller Avesta) *is a book of the* Avesta *that contains daily prayer used by the laity. One such text is the* Nam Setayashne. *An interesting theological point of this devotional is the equation of Spenta Mainyu with Ahura Mazda.*

1. I praise the name of that Spenta Mainyu, the increaser, worthy to be praised, who always was, always is, and always will be; whose one name is Ahura Mazda, the God who is the greatest among all, wise, Creator, supporter, protector, endurer, the lord of Asha [truth/righteousness], forgiver, and dispenser of excellent and pure justice.

2. Thanks be to the exalted Lord of the world, who, of his own power and wisdom, created six Bounteous Immortals of high rank, numerous spiritual beings [*yazads*], the shining paradise Garothman, the surrounding heavens, the hot sun, the shining moon, the numerous stars, the wind, the atmosphere, the fire, the water, the earth, the trees, the cattle, the metals, and humankind.

3. Adoration and prayers to the righteous Lord who has given us speech and the power to think, thereby making us superior to other creatures of this world. He has done this so that we might rule over people and make people walk together to fight against the Daevas.

4. I bow in the presence of the omniscient and caretaking Lord, who has sent, through Zarathushtra Spitaman of the adorable farohar [i.e., guardian angel], the wisdom of the religion, for the purpose rendering people friendly towards Him. This wisdom we gain through natural intelligence and knowledge of science, and is the best guidance for all persons who are, were and will be. Through this wisdom the soul is freed from the pains of hell, and reaches into the shining, fragrant, ever-happy, and the highest mansions of the pure.

5. Oh Lord Protector! In obedience to your command I am firm in the pure religion and I promise to think and speak and do every righteousness. Forgive me of my many sins. May I keep my conduct pure and, in accordance with your wishes, keep my six powers of the soul uncontaminated: work, speech, thought, reasoning, memory, and intellect.

6. And, in order to obtain the riches of the next world through good thoughts, good words, and good deeds, I will worship you, that I may thus open for myself the path to the shining paradise. By this, the heavy punishment of hell will not be inflicted upon me and I may, passing over the Chinvat bridge, reach into the fragrant all-adorned and eternally happy mansions of paradise.

7. I praise the Lord of gifts, who gives to those who obey his commandments the reward of righteous wishes and who will at the end liberate transgressors from hell and adorn the world with purity.

Source: *Khorde Avesta, The Nam Setayashne 1–7*, adapted from Ratanshah E. Kohiyar, *The Dinkard* (Bombay, Printed at the Duftur Ashkara Press, 1874–1928).

PAHLAVI WRITINGS

THE CHINVAT BRIDGE, HEAVEN AND HELL

Zarathushtra taught that heaven awaits good people, and hell evil people. Entrance into heaven requires crossing the Chinvat Bridge which spans the abyss of hell below (Yasna 46:10, 11; 51:13). The details of this journey of the soul were worked out in later Pahlavi texts, such as the following by ninth-century Zoroastrian high priest Manushkihar from his Datastani Denik. *On the fourth day after death, our souls leave our bodies and we cross the Chinvat Bridge. If we sided with good during our lives, then the bridge is as wide as seven spears and we easily pass to heaven, which is filled with beauty, light, pleasant scents, and happiness. If we sided with evil during our lives, however, the bridge turns sideways and becomes as narrow as a razor's edge, and we plummet into hell, which is filled with stench, filth, and pain.*

20. The nineteenth question that you ask is this: To what place do the righteous and wicked go?

　　The reply is this. It is said that the souls of the dead are three nights on earth. The first night satisfaction comes to them from their good words and discomfort and punishment from their evil words. The second night come pleasure from their good words and discomfort and punishment from their evil words. The third night come exaltation from their good deeds and punishment from their evil deeds. That third night, in the dawn, they go to the place of account on Alburz [i.e., the mountain surrounding the world]. The account being rendered, they proceed to the [Chinvat] bridge. He who is righteous passes over the bridge on the ascent, and if belonging to Hamistagan [i.e., Purgatory] he goes there where their place is. If along with an excess of good works his habits are correct, he goes even to heaven; and if, along with an excess of good works and correct habits, he has chanted the sacred hymns, he goes even to the supreme heaven. He who is of the wicked falls from the lower end of the bridge, or from the middle of the bridge. He falls head-foremost to hell, and is precipitated to that grade which is suitable for his wickedness.

21. The twentieth question that you ask is this: How are the Chinvat bridge, the Daitih peak, and the path of the righteous and wicked; how are they when one is righteous, and how when one is wicked?

　　The reply is this, as the high-priests have said: the Daitih peak is in Eranwej, in the middle of the world. The beam-shaped spirit, the Chinvat bridge, reaches to the vicinity of that peak and is thrown across from the Alburz enclosure back to the Daitih peak. That bridge is like a beam of many sides, of whose edges there are some which are broad, and there are some which are thin and sharp. Its broad sides are so large that its width is twenty-seven reeds, and its sharp sides are so contracted that in thinness it is just like the edge of a razor. When the souls of the righteous and wicked arrive it turns to that side which is suitable to their needs, through the great glory of the creator and the command of him who takes the just account.

Moreover, the bridge becomes a broad bridge for the righteous, as much as the height of nine spears, and the length of those which they carry is each separately three reeds. It becomes a narrow bridge for the wicked, resembling the edge of a razor. Those who are righteous pass over the bridge. Their paths are filled with pleasantness, as when they eagerly and unweariedly walk in the golden-colored spring, and with the gallant body and sweet-scented blossom in the pleasant skin of that maiden spirit. Such is the price of goodness.

Those who are wicked, as they place their feet onto the bridge, because of distress and its sharpness, fall from the middle of the bridge, and roll over headmost. The unpleasantness of this path to hell is like the worldly one in the midst of the stinking and dying things. There numbers of the sharp-pointed darts are planted out inverted and point upwards, and they come unwillingly running. These do not allow him to stay behind or delay. This pleasantness and unpleasantness to the souls is much greater than their worldly likeness, since that which is fit for the spirit is greater than that fit for the world.

26. The twenty-fifth question that you ask is this: how are the nature of heaven and the comfort and pleasure which are in heaven?

The reply is this, that it is lofty, exalted, and supreme, most brilliant, most fragrant, and most pure, most supplied with beautiful existences, most desirable, and most good, and the place and home of the sacred beings. In it are all comfort, pleasure, joy, happiness, and welfare, more and better even than the greatest and most supreme welfare and pleasure in the world. There is no want, pain, distress, or discomfort at all in it. Its pleasantness and the welfare of the angels are from that constantly-beneficial place, the full and undiminishable space, the goodness and boundless world. The freedom of the heavenly from danger of evil in heaven is like their freedom from disturbance, and the coming of the good angels is like the heavenly ones' own good works provided. This prosperity and welfare of the spiritual existence is more than that of the world, as much as that which is unlimited and everlasting is more than that which is limited and demoniacal.

27. The twenty-sixth question that you ask is this: How are the nature of hell, and the pain, discomfort, punishment, and stench of hell?

The reply is this, that it is sunken, deep, and descending, most dark, most stinking, and most terrible, most supplied with wretched existences, and most bad, there is the place and cave of the demons and fiends. In it is no comfort, pleasantness, or joy whatever. In it are all stench, filth, pain, punishment, distress, profound evil, and discomfort. There is no resemblance of it whatever to worldly stench, filthiness, pain, and evil. Since there is no resemblance of the mixed evil of the world to that which is its sole-indicating good, there is also a deviation of it from the origin and home of evil.

So much more grievous is the evil in hell than even the most griev-ous evil on earth, as the greatness of the spiritual existence is more than that of the world. More grievous is the terror of the punishment on the soul than that of the vileness of the demons on the body. The punishment on the soul is from those whose home it has become, from the demons and darkness—a likeness of that evil to hell—the head of whom is Angra Mainyu the deadly.

The words of the high-priests are these, that where there is a fear of every other thing it is more than the thing itself. But hell is a thing worse than the fear of it.

Source: *Datastani Denik,* chs. 20, 21, 26, 27, adapted from E. W. West, *Pathlavi Texts,* part 2 (Oxford: Clarendon Press, 1882).

CREATION AND THE MILLENNIA

In later Pahlavi Zoroastrian writings, Angra Mainyu has a more elevated role in cosmic history. The following selection from the Bundahishn, *a Pahlavi text on cosmo-gony and cosmic history, describes the initial confrontation between Ahura Mazda and Angra Mainyu and their ensuing 12,000-year battle. During the first 3,000 years, Ahura Mazda created the Beneficent Immortals and the world. Angra Mainyu responded by creating helper demons. They then agreed to limit the struggle to an additional 9,000 years.*

As revealed by the religion of the Mazda Worshipers [i.e., Zoroastrians], so it is declared that Ahura Mazda is supreme in omniscience and good-ness, and unrivalled in splendor. The region of light is the place of Ahura Mazda, which they call "endless light," and the omniscience and goodness of the unrivalled Ahura Mazda is what they call "revelation."

Revelation is the explanation of both spirits together. One is he who is independent of unlimited time, because Ahura Mazda and the region, reli-gion, and time of Ahura Mazda were and are and ever will be. Meanwhile, Angra Mainyu in darkness, with backward understanding and desire for destruction, was in the abyss, and it is he who will not be. The place of that destruction, and also of that darkness, is what they call the "endlessly dark." Between them was empty space, that is, what they call "air," in which is now their meeting.

Both are limited and unlimited spirits, for the supreme is that which they call endless light, and the abyss that which is endlessly dark, so that between them is a void, and one is not connected with the other. Again, both spirits are limited as to their own selves. Secondly, on account of the omniscience of Ahura Mazda, both things are in the creation of Ahura Mazda, the finite and the infinite. For, this they know is that which is in the covenant of both spirits. Again, the complete sovereignty of the crea-tures of Ahura Mazda is in the future existence, and that also is unlimited forever and everlasting. The creatures of Angra Mainyu will perish at the time when the Final Body occurs, and that also is eternity.

Ahura Mazda, through omniscience, knows that Angra Mainyu exists, and whatever he schemes he infuses with malice and greediness till the end. Because he accomplishes the end by many means, he also produced spiritually the creatures which were necessary for those means, and they remained three thousand years in a spiritual state, so that they were unthinking and unmoving, with intangible bodies.

The evil spirit, on account of backward knowledge, was not aware of the existence of Ahura Mazda. Afterwards, he arose from the abyss, and came into the light which he saw. Desirous of destroying, and because of his malicious nature, he rushed in to destroy that light of Ahura Mazda unassailed by fiends. He saw its bravery and glory were greater than his own, so he fled back to the gloomy darkness, and formed many demons and fiends. The creatures of the destroyer arose for violence.

Ahura Mazda examined the creation of the Destructive Spirit, which were terrible, corrupt, and bad, and considered them not commendable. Afterwards, the evil spirit saw the creatures of Ahura Mazda. There appeared many creatures, and they seemed to him commendable. He commended the creatures and creation of Ahura Mazda. Then Ahura Mazda, with a knowledge of which way the end of the matter would be, went to meet the evil spirit, and proposed peace to him, and spoke thus: "Evil spirit! Bring assistance to my creatures and offer praise, so that, in reward for it, you and your creatures may become immortal and undecaying, without hunger and thirst."

The evil spirit shouted, "I will not depart, I will not provide assistance for your creatures, I will not offer praise among your creatures, and I am not of the same opinion with you as to good things. I will destroy your creatures forever and everlasting. Moreover, I will force all your creatures into disaffection to you and affection for myself." The explanation for this is that the evil spirit reflected that Ahura Mazda was helpless as regarded him. Therefore, Ahura Mazda offered peace, and Angra Mainyu did not agree, but continued on even into conflict with him.

Ahura Mazda spoke: "You are not omniscient and almighty, oh evil spirit, so that it is not possible for you to destroy me, and it is not possible for you to force my creatures so that they will not return to my possession. Through omniscience, Ahura Mazda knew if he did not grant a period of contest, then it would be possible for Angra Mainyu to seduce his creatures. As even now there are many of the intermixture of humankind who practise wrong more than right. Ahura Mazda spoke to the evil spirit: "Appoint a period so that the intermingling of the conflict may be for nine thousand years." For he knew that by appointing this period the evil spirit would be undone. Then the evil spirit, unobservant and through ignorance, was content with that agreement, just like two men quarrelling together, who propose a time thus: Let us appoint such-and-such a day for a fight.

Through omniscience, Ahura Mazda also knew that, within these nine thousand years, for three thousand years everything proceeds by the will of Ahura Mazda. In the next three thousand years, there is an intermingling of the wills of Ahura Mazda and Angra Mainyu. In the last three thousand years the evil spirit is made powerless, and they keep the adversary away from the creatures.

Afterwards, Ahura Mazda recited the *Ahunvar* [the Zoroastrians' most sacred prayer]. He also exhibited to the evil spirit his own triumph in the end, and the impotence of the evil spirit, the annihilation of the demons, and the resurrection and undisturbed future existence of the creatures forever and everlasting. The evil spirit, who perceived his own impotence and the annihilation of the demons became confounded, and fell back to the gloomy darkness. . . . He became confounded and impotent as to the harm he caused the creatures of Ahura Mazda, and he remained three thousand years in confusion.

Ahura Mazda created his creatures in the confusion of Angra Mainyu. First he produced Vohu Manah (Good Thought), by whom the movement of the creatures of Ahura Mazda was advanced. The evil spirit first created Mitokht (Falsehood), and then Akoman (Evil Thought). The first of Ahura Mazda's creatures of the world was the sky, and his good thought, by good procedure, produced the light of the world, along with which was the good religion of the Mazda Worshipers. This was because the resurrection which happens to the creatures was known to him. Afterwards arose Ardavahist, then Shatvairo, then Spendarmad, then Horvadad, and then Amerodad [the Beneficent Immortals]. From the dark world of Angra Mainyu were Akoman and Andar, then Sovar, then Nakahed, and then Tairev and Zairik. Of Ahura Mazda's creatures of the world, the first was the sky, the second water, the third earth, the fourth plants, the fifth animals, and the sixth mankind.

Source: *Bundahishn*, ch. 1, adapted from E. W. West, *Pahlavi Texts*, part 1 (Oxford: Clarendon Press, 1880).

LIFE OF ZARATHUSHTRA

During the second 3,000-year period of cosmic history, Angra Mainyu stays in darkness only to wage a full-scale assault on creation during the third 3,000-year period. The fourth and final 3,000-year period begins with the birth of Zarathushtra, who rallies humans to the cause of Ahura Mazda. The following describes the miraculous conception of Zarathushtra, attempts to kill him at an early age, his encounter with Vohu Manah and his call to prophethood at age 30. The selections are from the Pahlavi Denkard, *a Pahlavi compendium of Zoroastrian doctrine, and the* Zatspram, *a collection of doctrines from ninth-century* c.e. *Zoroastrian high priest Zatspram.*

One marvel before the birth of Zarathushtra is this which is declared, that the creator passed on that divine grace of Zarathushtra through the material existences of the creatures to Zarathushtra. When the command arose from Ahura Mazda, the coming of that glory from the spiritual existence to the worldly, and to the material substance of Zarathushtra, was manifested as a great wonder to the multitude. Just as revelation mentions it thus: "Thereupon, when Ahura Mazda had produced the material of Zarathushtra, the glory then, in the presence of Ahura Mazda, fled on towards the material Zarathushtra, on to the germ. From that germ it fled on, and to the light which is endless. From the light which is endless it fled on to that of the sun. From that of the sun it fled on to the moon. From that moon it fled on to those stars. From those stars it fled on to the wife which was in the house of Zoish. From that it fled on to the wife of Frahimrvana- Zoish, when she brought forth that girl who became the mother of Zarathushtra.

When the child had been born, Porushaspo [his father] called one of the five brothers of the race of Priests [*Karaps*], and spoke thus: "Fully observe the marks and specks of my son Zarathushtra."

The priest went and sat down before Zarathushtra, and the head of Zarathushtra was thereupon severely twisted by him, in order that he should be killed. But he, being fearless, watched the priests whose terror was distressing. As it was in those ten nights for hospitality, Ahura Mazda sent Spandarmad, Ardvisur, and Arda-frawash [i.e., the Holy Guardian Angel] down to the earth, by way of female care. Thereupon no marks (of evil) were observed on the child, and, further, the hand of that priest was withered, and that priest demanded the life of Zarathushtra from Porushaspo for the harm from him, which sprang upon himself from his own action.

At the same time Porushaspo took Zarathushtra, and gave him to the priest, that he might do with him according to his own will. He seized him and threw him out, at the feet of the oxen who were going on a path to the water. The leader of that herd of oxen stood still beside him, and 150 oxen, which walked behind it, were kept away from him thereby. Porushaspo took him, and carried him back to the house. . . .

The third day, firewood was gathered together by the priest, and Zarathushtra was deposited on it by him, the fire was stirred up by him, yet with the same result, the child was not burnt by it. . . .

On the completion of thirty years beyond his birth, the archangel Vohu Manah came on in commemoration of Ahura Mazda, when Zarathushtra was bringing his Haoma-water from the river Aevatak. . . . The words of Vohu Manah were: "O Zarathushtra, about what is your foremost distress? About what is your foremost endeavor? For what is the tendency of your desire?" Zarathushtra's reply was thus: "About Asha [truth/righteousness] I consider my foremost distress. About Asha [truth/righteousness] my foremost endeavor, and for Asha the tendency of my desire." The words of Vohu Manah were: "O Zarathushtra, that which is Asha is existing, so that whatever is that which is Asha is thus what is one's own." Zarathushtra spoke thus: "That which is Asha exists, and concerning that I am completely clear and aware. But where and how is the radiance which is that whose arrival is through Vohu Manah." Vohu Manah spoke to him thus: "O Zarathushtra, deposit this one garment which you carry, so that we may confer with him by whom you are produced and by whom I am produced, who is the most propitious of spirits, who is the most beneficent of existences, and who is he that I, who am Vohu Manah, am testifying." Thereupon, Zarathushtra thought thus: "Good is he who is the creator, who is better than this reminder." Then they proceeded in company, Vohu Manah and Zarathushtra, Vohu Manah first and Zarathushtra after.

Source: *Denkard,* book 7, ch. 2.2 ff.; *Zatspram,* ch. 16; *Denkard,* book 7, ch. 3:51, 56–63; adapted from E. W. West, *Pahlavi Texts,* part 5 (Oxford: Clarendon Press, 1897).

COMING OF SAOSHYANT

After Zarathushtra, three additional saviors are to come at 1,000-year intervals. They will be born from virgins who bathe in a lake guarded by 99,999 angels who preserve Zarathushtra's seed. The saviors are Hushedar, Aushedar-Mah, and Saoshyant. Saoshyant's coming marks the end of the 12,000-year cosmic struggle between Ahura Mazda and Angra Mainyu. The following, from the Pahlavi Denkard, *describes the birth of Saoshyant and his defeat of Angra Mainyu in the final battle.*

10. Thirty winters prior to the close of the tenth century [in the final millennium], the maiden Eredat-fedhri walks up to the waters. She is the mother of that testifying Saoshyant who is the guide to conveying away the opposition of the destroyer. . . . [Just as revelation states,] "That maiden whose title is All-overpowerer is thus all-overpowering. This is because through giving birth she brings forth him who overpowers all, both the affliction owing to demons, and also that owing to mankind." Then she sits in that water, when she is fifteen years old, and it introduces into the girl him whose name is the Triumphant Benefiter [i.e., Saoshyant], and his title is the Bodymaker. Such a benefiter as benefits the whole embodied existence, and such a bodymaker, alike possessing body and possessing life, as petitions about the disturbance of the embodied existences and mankind. Not before that has she associated with men; nor yet afterwards, when she becomes pregnant, has she done so before the time when she gives birth. When that man becomes thirty years old, the sun stands still in the zenith of the sky for the duration of thirty days and nights, and it arrives again at that place where it was appointed by allotment.

11. In his fifty-seventh year there occur the annihilation of the fiendishness of the two-legged race and others, and the subjugation of disease

and decrepitude, of death and persecution, and of the original evil of tyranny, apostasy, and depravity. There arise a perpetual verdant growth of vegetation and the primitive gift of joyfulness. For seventeen years everyone abstains from meat, then there are thirty years where people subsist on water alone, and then ten years where subsistence is on spiritual food alone.

All the splendor, glory, and power which have arisen in all those possessing splendor, glory, and power, are in him on whom they arrive together and for those who are his, when many inferior human beings are aroused splendid and powerful. Through their power and glory all the troops of the fiend are smitten. All mankind remain of one accord in the religion of Ahura Mazda, owing to the will of the creator, the command of that apostle, and the resources of his companions.

At the end of the fifty-seven years the fiend and Angra Mainyu are annihilated, the renovation for the future existence occurs, and the whole of the good creation is provided with purity and perfect splendor. Just as revelation states thus: "When that millennium has fully elapsed, which is the third of the religion of the Mazda-worshippers, that Mazda-worshipper whose name is so Triumphant then marches forward from the water Kasava with a thousand companions and also maidens of restrained disposition and blindly striving-behavior. He smites the wicked people who are tyrannical, and annihilates them."

Then those Mazda-worshippers smite, and none are smiting them. Then those Mazda-worshippers produce a longing for a renovation among the existences, one ever-living, ever-beneficial, and ever desiring a Lord. "Then I, who am Ahura Mazda, produce the renovation according to the longing among the existences, one ever-living, ever-beneficial, and ever desiring a Lord."

Source: *Denkard*, book 7, chs. 10.15 ff, 11.4 ff, adapted from E. W. West, *Pahlavi Texts*, part 5 (Oxford: Clarendon Press, 1897).

RESURRECTION OF THE DEAD, FINAL JUDGMENT

After the defeat of Angra Mainyu in the final battle, the dead will resurrect on the spot where they died, and Ahura Mazda will judge everyone. The evil of the world will be purged with molten metal, Angra Mainyu will be destroyed, and a new universe will come into being. These events are described in the following passage from the Pahlavi Bundahishn.

On the nature of the resurrection and future existence it says in revelation, that, whereas Mashya and Mashyang [Adam and Eve], who grew up from the earth, first fed upon water, then plants, then milk, and then meat, men also, when their time of death has come, first desist from eating meat, then milk, then from bread, till when they shall die they always feed upon water. So, likewise, in the millennium of Hushedar-mah, the strength of appetite will thus diminish, when men will remain three days and nights in superabundance through one taste of consecrated food. Then they will desist from meat food, and eat vegetables and milk. Afterwards, they abstain from milk food and abstain from vegetable food, and are feeding on water. For ten years before Saoshyant comes they remain without food, and do not die.

After Saoshyant comes they prepare the raising of the dead. . . . First, the bones of Gayomard [the primordial human] are roused up, then those of Mashya and Mashyang, then those of the rest of mankind. In fifty-seven years Saoshyant will raise all the dead. Whoever is righteous and whoever is wicked, every human creature, they rouse up from the spot where its life departs. Afterwards, when all material living beings assume again their bodies and forms, they will give them their protoplasm. Of the light accompanying the sun, one half will be given to Gayomard, and one half will give enlightenment among the rest of men, so that the soul and body will recognize that this is my father, and this is my mother, and this is my brother, and this is my wife, and these are some other of my nearest relations.

Then the assembly of Isat-Vastar will meet, where all mankind will stand at this time. In that assembly everyone sees his own good deeds and his own evil deeds. A wicked man becomes as conspicuous as a white sheep among those which are black. Whatever righteous man was friend of a wicked one in the world, and the wicked man complains of him who is righteous, thus, "Why did you not make me acquainted, when in the world, with the good deeds which he practised yourself?" If he who is righteous did not inform him, then it is necessary for him to suffer shame accordingly in that assembly.

Afterwards, they separate the righteous from the wicked. The righteous is carried to heaven, and they cast the wicked back to hell. Three days and nights they inflict punishment bodily in hell, and then he beholds bodily those three days' happiness in heaven. As it says that, on the day when the righteous man is parted from the wicked, the tears of everyone, thereupon, run down to his legs. When, after they separate sons from their fathers, a brother from his brother, and a friend from his friend, they suffer, everyone for his own deeds, and weep, the righteous for the wicked, and the wicked about himself. For there may be a father who is righteous and a son wicked, and there may be one brother who is righteous and one wicked. Those for whose peculiar deeds it is appointed . . . as those deserving death, undergo a punishment no other men undergo. They call it "the punishment of the three nights."

Among his producers of the renovation of the universe, those righteous men of whom it is written that they are living, fifteen men and fifteen damsels, will come to the assistance of Saoshyant. As Go-chihar [a meteor] falls in the celestial sphere from a moonbeam onto the earth, the distress of the earth becomes as that of a sheep when a wolf falls upon it. Afterwards, the fire and halo melt the metal of Shatvairo, in the hills and mountains, and it remains on this earth like a river. Then all men will pass into that melted metal and will become pure. When one is righteous, then it seems to him just as though he walks continually in warm milk. But when wicked, then it will seem to him as though he walks continually in world of melted metal.

Afterwards, with the greatest affection, all men come together, father and son and brother and friends ask one another: "Where were you these many years, and what was the judgment upon your soul? Have you been righteous or wicked?" The first soul of the body sees; it enquires of it with those words. All men become of one voice and administer loud praise to Ahura Mazda and the archangels.

Ahura Mazda completes his work at his time, and the creatures become so that it is not necessary to make any effort about them. Among those by whom the dead are prepared, it is not necessary that any effort be made. Saoshyant, with his assistants, will perform the rite for the restoration of the dead [*Yazishn*]. They slaughter the ox Hadhayos for this rite. From the fat of that ox and the white haoma they prepare the immortal beverage [*Hush*], and give it to all men, and all men become immortal forever and everlasting. Whoever had been an adult, they restore him then with an age of forty years. They who have been little when not dead, they restore them with an age of fifteen years. They give everyone his wife, and show him his children with the wife, so they act as now in the world, but there is no begetting of children.

Afterwards, Saoshyant and his assistants, by order of the creator Ahura Mazda, give every man the reward and recompense suitable to his deeds. . . . Afterwards, Ahura Mazda seizes on the evil spirits . . . and the dragon Go-chihr will be burnt in the melted metal, and the stench and pollution which were in hell are burned in that metal, and hell becomes quite pure. Ahura Mazda sets the hiding place into which the evil spirit fled, in that metal. He brings the land of hell back for the enlargement of the world. The renovation arises in the universe by his will, and the world is immortal forever and everlasting. This earth becomes an iceless, slopeless plain. Even the mountain, whose summit is the support of the Chinvat bridge, they keep down, and it will not exist.

Source: *Bundahishn* ch. 30, adapted from E. W. West, *Pahlavi Texts,* part 1 (Oxford: Clarendon Press, 1880).

SIX RITUAL OBLIGATIONS

Zoroastrians have a variety of rituals, such as seven holy days of obligation, rites of passage, including the navjote initiation ceremony for young adolescents, and rituals of cleansing and purification. Six primary ritual obligations are discussed in the following from the Sad Dar (Hundred Doors), *a text on a hundred subjects which is written in Persian.*

1. The sixth subject is this, that of the many good works there are those which, when they accomplish them, obtain great rewards; and if one does not perform them severe punishment seizes upon one at the head of the Chinvat bridge.

2. One is the celebration of the season festivals [*Gahambars*]. The second is keeping the days of the guardian spirits [fravashis, the last ten days of the religious year]. The third is attending to the souls of fathers, mothers, and other relations. The fourth is reciting the Sun Litany [*Khwarshed Nyaish*] three times every day. The fifth is reciting the Moon Litany [*Mah Nyayis*] three times every month, once when it becomes new, once when it becomes full, and once when it becomes slender. And the sixth is celebrating the Rapithwin ceremony once every year.

3. If not able to celebrate them oneself, it is requisite to order them, so that they may celebrate them every single time.

4. These six good works are things indispensable unto every one.

5. When any one of them is not performed—be it that which, if omitted at its own time, it is not possible to accomplish, or if it be that one time one omits an occasion, and another time they accomplish twice as much—one should consider that as an advantage, which occurs in retribution for it, or as atonement for the transgression.

6. Because they call the transgression of each of these six a bridge-sin; that is, every one through whom a transgression of these may have arisen they keep back, at the head of the Chinwad bridge, till punishment for it happens to him, and no good work is possible in this place, which is torment and punishment for him.

7. Therefore it is necessary to make an effort, that they may be performed each one at its own time, so that they may obtain a recompense, and not a severe punishment.

Source: *Sad Dar*, 6:1–7, adapted from E. W. West, *Pahlavi Texts*, part 3 (Oxford: Clarendon Press, 1885).

VIRTUES AND SOCIAL OBLIGATION

In addition to ritual obligations, Zoroastrians have strict codes of moral obligation that encourage virtues and condemn vices. Often these moral instructions are in the form of aphorisms (Andarz), such as the following from the Denkard.

23. There are five best things in religion. These are: truthfulness, generosity, being possessed of virtue, diligence, and advocacy. This truthfulness is best: one who acts (in such a manner) to the creatures of Ahura Mazda that the recipient of his action has so much more benefit when he acts like that to him. This generosity is best: One who makes a present to a person from whom he has no hope of receiving anything in reward in this world,

and he has not even this (hope), namely, that the recipient of his gift should hold him abundantly in gratitude and praise. This possession of virtue is best: One who makes battle against the non-material demons, whatever they may be, and in particular does not let these five demons into his body: Greed, Envy, Lust, Wrath, and Shame. This diligence is best: One who does the work which he is engaged in doing in such a manner that at every moment he has certainty in himself with regard to the following: were he to die at that hour it would not be necessary to do anything whatsoever in a way different from that in which he is doing it. That advocacy is best: One who speaks for a person who is inarticulate, who cannot speak his own misery and complaint; that person speaks out the voice of his own soul and of that of the poor and good person to the people of this world and these six Amesha Spentas.

24. They held this too: Wisdom is manifest in work, character in rule, friend in hardship.

C82. When food offerings [*myazd*], seasonal festivals [*gahambar*] and acts of charity to good people diminish, there is increase of evil government for men, pain for grain plants, bad husbandry, diminution of the fertility of the land and rains. When the virtue of consanguine marriage diminishes, darkness increases and light diminishes. When worship of the gods and the protection and advocacy of good people diminish, the evil government of rulers and unlawful action increase, and evil people gain the upper hand over good.

Source: *Denkard* 6:23, 24, C82, from *The Wisdom of the Sasanian Sages (Denkard VI)*, tr. Shaul Shaked (Boulder, Colorado: 1979), pp. 11, 173.

ZURVAN WRITINGS

ZURVAN AND HIS TWIN SONS

The Zurvan sect of Zoroastrianism flourished between the fifth and tenth centuries C.E. Zurvan, a minor deity mentioned in the Avesta, is the supreme God of the sect. Yasna 30 of the Avesta states that "Truly there are two primal Spirits, twins renowned to be in conflict. In thought and word, in act they are two: the better and the bad." The Zurvan sect interprets this literally and sees Ahura Mazda and Angra Mainyu as twin sons of Zurvan. The good and evil twins create the world and wage war on each other, and the evil twin is ultimately defeated. The following is a fragment from a lost fourth-century Pahlavi Zurvan text, as cited by Eznik of Kolb, an Armenian Christian apologist.

1. Behold what Zarathushtra said concerning the begetting of Ahura Mazda and Angra Mainyu. When nothing at all yet existed, neither heaven nor earth nor any other creature which is in heaven or on earth, there existed the great god Zurvan, whose name is to be interpreted as "fate" or "fortune." For one thousand years he offered sacrifice in order

that he might perhaps have a son who would be called Ahura Mazda, and who would make the heavens and earth and all which they contain.

2. For one thousand years he offered sacrifice. Then he pondered in his heart and said: "Shall I truly have profit of these sacrifices, and shall I have a son called Ahura Mazda? Or do I strive thus in vain?" And even while he reflected in this manner, Ahura Mazda and Angra Mainyu were conceived in the womb: Ahura Mazda through the offered sacrifice, Angra Mainyu through the doubt.

3. When he became aware of this, Zurvan said: "Lo, two sons are in the womb. Whichever of them appears swiftly before me, him I shall make king." Ahura Mazda, being aware of their father's purposes, revealed them to Angra Mainyu. . . .

4. And Angra Mainyu, having heard this, pierced the womb and came forth and presented himself to his father. And Zurvan, beholding him, knew not who he might be, and asked "Who are you?" And he said: "I am your son." Zurvan answered him: "My son is fragrant and bright, and you, you are dark and noisome." And while they spoke thus, Ahura Mazda, being born at the due time, bright and fragrant, came and presented himself before Zurvan. And Zurvan, beholding him, knew that he was his son, Ahura Mazda. And taking the rods which he held in his hand, and with which he had offered sacrifice, he gave them to Ahura Mazda and said: "Until now it is I who have offered sacrifice for you. Henceforth it is you who will offer it for me."

5. And while Zurvan was giving the rods to Ahura Mazda and blessing him, Angra Mainyu, having drawn near to Zurvan, said to him: "Have you not made this vow, that whichever of my two sons shall first come before me, him I shall make king? And Zurvan, that he should not violate his oath, said to Angra Mainyu: "Oh false and injurious one! The kingship shall be granted you for nine thousand years; and I shall establish Ahura Mazda as ruler over you. And after nine thousand years. Ahura Mazda shall reign and do all that he will wish to do."

6. Then Ahura Mazda and Angra Mainyu set to fashioning the creatures. And all that Ahura Mazda created was good and straight, and all that Angra Mainyu made was evil and crooked.

Source: Pahlavi fragment reported by Eznik of Kolb, from Mary Boyce, *Textual Sources for the Study of Zoroastrianism* (Chicago: University of Chicago Press, 1984), pp. 97–98.

GLOSSARY

Ahura Mazda (*Ohrmazd in Pahlavi*) Literally, "Wise Lord"; supreme God and originator of all good.

Amesha Spentas, or Beneficent Immortals Servant angels who assist Ahura Mazda in the battle against evil; alternatively, they are sometimes seen as aspects of Ahura Mazda.

Angra Mainyu   (*ahriman in pahlavi*) Literally, "Destructive Spirit" (antonym of "beneficent spirit"); the evil rival of Ahura Mazda in later Pahlavi texts.

Asha   Literally, "The Truth"; the good moral principle in opposition to the *druj* (the lie).

Avesta   Literally, "Basic Text"; the oldest and most sacred collection of Zoroastrian scriptures, written in the Avestan language.

Chinvat Bridge   Literally, "Separator Bridge"; bridge by which people enter heaven; it spans the abyss of hell below.

Daevas   Literally, "Heavenly Beings" in early Aryan religion; evil devils, demons in Zoroastrianism.

Druj   Literally, "The Lie"; evil spirit or spirits that wage war against Ahura Mazda, and are opposed to Truth (*Asha*).

Magi   Zoroastrian priests, or, perhaps, cult leaders who claimed to be descendants of Zarathushtra's first converts.

Pahlavi   An early form of the Persian language, in which later Zoroastrian scriptures were written.

Saoshyant   Literally, "Savior"; final descendant of Zarathushtra and the spiritual leader who will usher in the final judgment.

Spenta Mainyu   Literally, "Beneficent Spirit"; the good son of Ahura Mazda in the *Avesta,* or, perhaps, a synonym for Ahura Mazda.

Zurvan   Literally, "Time"; supreme God of the Zurvan sect, who is the father of Ahura Mazda and Angra Mainyu.

FURTHER READINGS

BOYCE, MARY A. *Zoroastrians: Their Religious Beliefs and Practices* (1979).

——. *Textual Sources for the Study of Zoroastrianism.* Chicago: University of Chicago Press, 1990.

——. *A History of Zoroastrianism,* 2 vol. Leiden: 1975–1982.

DHALLA, MANECKJI. *History of Zoroastrianism.* New York: 1977.

——. *Zoroastrian Theology from the Earliest Times to the Present Day.* New York: 1914.

DUCHESNE-GUILLEMIN, JACQUES. *Symbols and Values in Zoroastrianism.* Bombay: 1966.

——. *The Western Response to Zoroaster* (1958).

MALANDRA, WILLIAM W. *An Introduction to Ancient Iranian Religion: Readings from the Avesta and Achaemenid Inscriptions.* Minneapolis: University of Minnesota Press, 1983.

MOULTON, JAMES H. *Early Zoroastrianism.* London: 1913.

RANDERIA, JER D. *The Parsi Mind: A Zoroastrian Asset to Culture.* Munshiram Manoharlal Publishers, 1993.

SHAKED, SHAUL. *Wisdom of the Sasanian Sages.* Boulder, Colorado: 1979.

ZAEHNER, R. C. *The Dawn and Twilight of Zoroastrianism.* New York: Putnam, 1961.

——. *The Teachings of the Magi: A Compendium of Zoroastrian Beliefs* (1956).

Judaism

INTRODUCTION

Judaism, with its 3,000-year existence, is one of the world's oldest living religions. Like all religions, Judaism has evolved over time, but several key beliefs pervade its rich history. First and foremost is the belief that YHWH (usually pronounced Yahweh) is the only God and creator of all. Second, humans should obey God's law as found in both written and oral law. Third, God made a series of covenants with the Jews to designate their lineage as chosen. The most significant of these covenants are with Abraham, who received the promise of a nation, with Moses, who received the Law, and with David, who received the kingdom. Fourth is the belief that a coming King-Messiah will free the Jews from foreign domination. Unlike the other major monotheistic religions in the Western tradition—Christianity and Islam—Judaism is distinguished by being *this-worldly*. Although a doctrine of the afterlife can be found in its teachings, greater emphasis is placed on the nation, the land, and traditions.

Judaism's Beginnings

Judaism is inseparably tied to the history of the Jewish people; their scriptures, feasts, and worship practices recall events of the past. The earliest historical archaeological record derived from the period of Israel's settlement in its land is from the twelfth century B.C.E., during the period of the Judges. At this time the Israelites were occupied with capturing territory from the previous inhabitants of perhaps a thousand years, the Canaanites, and settling into agrarian life. The land, *Israel* to the Jews and *Canaan* to the Canaanites, is an area about the size of New Jersey, located on the southeast shore of the Mediterranean sea. Some of the Israelite stories defined their identity as a nation and entitled them to the land. In these stories, their lineage is traced back to Abraham, a Mesopotamian nomad from a few hundred years earlier. Abraham made a special pact with God whereby God would make him the father of a nation. Abraham and his clan migrated to Canaan, the land later given to him by God. Two generations later famine drove his descendants to Egypt. For a while all was fine, until the Pharaoh of Egypt resorted to forced labor for his building projects. Abraham's descendants were then enslaved for this purpose. Eventually, they were led by Moses out of Egypt and into the desert, where they wandered for 40 years. During the journey, Moses received detailed codes of law directly from God. The story further recounts that Moses' successors led the Israelites into Canaan to capture the land promised to Abraham.

Politically, Canaan was a decentralized collection of tiny independent kingdoms. Religiously, the Canaanites performed plant and animal sacrificial rites in temples and open-air places, and fertility rites of prostitution. Key deities of the Canaanites were El the creator, Asherah the consort of El, Baal the son of El and god of storm, and Anat daughter of El and goddess of war. The Israelites and Canaanites already shared a common ethnic and language family, which was Semitic. As the Israelites occupied the land and eventually controlled the region, many intermarried with the locals and adopted the Canaanite ways, including worship of their deities. Politically the Israelites were a loose confederation of twelve tribes. A political balance of power was held in Israel between the chosen tribal leaders, legal and military judges, prophets, and priests from a thirteenth and landless group or tribe, Levi. Geographically there was a more delicate balance of power between two southern tribes, Judah (the largest of the twelve) and Benjamin, and the remaining ten tribes located primarily in the north, who felt threatened by Judah's size and political dominance.

United and Divided Kingdoms

An unexpected influx of warring invaders from the northeast Mediterranean area forced the Israelites to unify politically. These invading Philistines had a special military advantage in iron weaponry. Bronze weapons were less effective, especially in the hands of an Israelite army of drafted civilians. The need for a monarchy arose to facilitate a more concerted effort to block the Philistine power. The first King, Saul, died in battle with the Philistines. The kingdom and military leadership passed to his son-in-law, David, who instituted a standing professional army. Equipped with iron weapons, David's army effectively put an end to the Philistine threat. Through military and diplomatic maneuvers, the Kingdom of Israel took control of territory as far south as Egypt, and as far north as Mesopotamia. At David's death, the throne passed to his young son, Solomon. Legendary for his wisdom and multiple diplomatic marriages, Solomon launched monumental building projects, including several fortified cities, a palace, and Israel's first permanent temple. Although Solomon taxed the entire country to fund his projects, benefits were seen primarily in Judah, which further alienated the northern tribes.

Solomon died about 922 B.C.E., and the throne passed to his son, Rehoboam. When Rehoboam announced that he would continue his father's policy of taxation, the northern tribes split from the south and proclaimed their own kingdom. The southern kingdom was thereafter referred to as *Judah*, while the northern kingdom retained the name *Israel*. During this period, both the northern and southern kingdoms continued to be influenced by Canaanite religious practices and efforts were made at monotheistic reform in both kingdoms by prophets and kings.

After a 200-year existence, the northern kingdom was conquered by the Assyrian empire. For several decades, the north had tried several strategies of resistance, but in 722 B.C.E. its kingdom was annexed as an Assyrian province. Some Israelites were deported, while others fled to Judah. Colonists from Mesopotamia settled in the region and intermarried with the remaining inhabitants, forming the group known as Samaritans, a remnant of which remains today. The southern kingdom escaped immediate annexation by becoming a vassal of the Assyrians. Two decades later, though, Judah's King Hezekiah broke with the Assyrians, prompting a military confrontation that ended in loss of territory for Judah and a return to vassal status. He, and later King Josiah, made valiant efforts at monotheistic reform, but each time the populus reverted to Canaanite practices.

Exile and Restoration

In Mesopotamia, the power structure shifted and the Babylonians overtook the Assyrians. The new Babylonian Empire invaded surrounding countries to bring them within its control, and in three separate invasions (596, 587, and 583 B.C.E.), two of which were provoked by the Judeans, Judah was crushed. Cities and homes were destroyed, thousands of skilled craftsmen and potential troublemakers were deported to Babylon, and thousands more fled to Egypt, some of whom went to the Island of Elephantine. Most significantly, Solomon's temple was destroyed.

Although records of events during the Babylonian captivity are sketchy, the trauma of the exile apparently forced the Israelites to reexamine and solidify their religious beliefs. In the absence of the temple, the *Torah,* or books of Moses, became more important. Their understanding of Yahweh may also have changed so that they now viewed him as sovereign authority over the universe. The term *Jew,* which means someone from Judah, became common at this time.

Yet again the power structure in Mesopotamia shifted. In 539 B.C.E., the Persian emperor Cyrus overthrew the Babylonians, returned 40,000 Jews to Judah, now known by its Greek pronunciation *Judea,* and authorized the rebuilding of the temple. Judea, however, remained a province of the Persian empire. The Jews who stayed in Babylon continued to prosper and populate, and their views may have been influenced by Zoroastrianism, the Persian religion at the time. Angelology and demonology become more prominent themes in post-exilic writings. Greater emphasis was placed on the resurrection of the dead, cataclysms of the end times, and the age of a redeemer or Messiah. In 458 B.C.E. an additional 17,000 people returned to the land under the leadership of the priest Ezra. He returned from Babylon with a complete *Torah* in the form we have today, which is the five books of Moses. He and governor Nehemiah instituted a theocratic state with power vested in the priests. The Jews were required to take an oath to observe the Torah, tithe, sacrifice, and attend feasts. Marriage with foreigners was condemned in order to assure cultural and religious survival. He also established a council called *The Great Synagogue* to formulate doctrine and perhaps compile the texts of the *Tanakh*. Indeed, Ezra's and Nehemiah's reforms set a new direction for the Jewish religion.

Maccabean Revolt and the Hasmonean Dynasty

The Persian Empire collapsed in 333 B.C.E. during Alexander the Great's campaign for world domination. The next year Judea also fell under his control. After Alexander's death, the empire was divided between four of his generals, whose dynasties were committed to Hellenization, that is, the propagation of Greek culture. Judea was passed back and forth between two dynasties of the divided empire: the Selucid Dynasty of Persia, and the Ptolemaic Dynasty of Egypt. From 301 to 198 B.C.E., life was peaceful under the Ptolemies. Then it changed hands to the Selucids. By 165 B.C.E., the extreme Hellenizing policies of Selucid King Antiochus Epiphanes reduced central Jewish religious rites to capital crimes. For many young Jews their heritage became an embarrassment, as evidenced by a frequently practiced surgical reversal of circumcision. The ultimate assault against the Jewish religion was the erection in the temple of an altar to Zeus upon which pigs were sacrificed. Further plans were made to confiscate land from Jews who followed their traditions. In revolt, an old priest named Mattathias killed a commissioner who had ordered him to sacrifice to Zeus. Gathering his five sons and followers, he fled to the desert. From there his son Judas Maccabeus launched a guerrilla attack, recapturing Jerusalem, and restored worship. Although the Selucid army responded to the revolt, the Selucids could not engage in a protracted guerrilla war, and ultimately recognized Judea as a semi-independent temple-state. The Maccabean leaders declared themselves a dynasty of Priest Kings, also called the Hasmonean Dynasty, and for the next hundred years engaged in relatively independent, although frequently despotic, rule.

The Hasmoneans greatly expanded Judea's borders and fortified key cities. It is probably during this time that synagogues emerged as centers for local religious education and worship. According to Josephus, noted Jewish historian of the first century C.E., three religious orders also emerged: the Pharisees, the Sadducees, and the Essenes. The Pharisees were priests and lay people who adopted a priestly life; they were proponents of oral tradition, purity rituals, a Messianic kingdom, and the resurrection of the dead. They were also dedicated teachers of these doctrines to the masses. The Sadducees were aristocratic and priestly rivals of the Pharisees, and denied many of their doctrines, especially those listed above. They also competed with the Pharisees for political influence in the Sanhedrin, the legislative assembly of Judea. The Essenes shared key doctrines with the Pharisees, such as food rituals, a Messianic kingdom, and the resurrection of the dead. However, they became disgusted with the tyrannical rule of the Hasmoneans and the quarreling religious leaders, and established a monastic community in the desert along the Dead Sea.

Roman Domination

Hasmonean rule of Judea ended in 63 B.C.E. when a civil war broke out between Jewish parties. Roman general Pompey was called in to arbitrate, but instead occupied Judea and declared it a Roman province. The first Roman governors were particularly brutal, enslaving or crucifying those who disobeyed. A cunning Jewish governor from Galilee, Herod the Great, was soon appointed King of the Jews in 37 B.C.E. Herod had non-Jewish ancestry and was never completely accepted by the Jews. Preoccupied with conspiracies against him, Herod built massive fortifications for protection. He also rebuilt Jerusalem and the temple on a grand scale. But taxation for these projects economically crippled the peasant population. After Herod's death in 4 B.C.E., the Romans appointed a series of governors who were insensitive to the religious practices and economic concerns of the people. Growing anti-Roman sentiment among the peasants led to revolts in which thousands of Jews were massacred. Incited by an oracle that a Jewish messiah would rule the world, a territory-wide peasant revolt finally erupted in 66 C.E. Although it was initially successful, the Romans marched on the rebellious Jewish territories, destroying everything in their path. Most important, the elaborate new temple in Jerusalem was destroyed, bringing an end to temple sacrifices in 70 C.E. Many Jews were sold as slaves, and the Jewish territories forfeited statehood status within the Roman Empire. With the temple in ruins for three generations, in 132 C.E. Jewish peasants and leaders were easily seduced by the messianic leader Simeon Bar Kokhba, who promised to restore the temple. His unsuccessful three-year revolt brought more destruction to the country and a massive dispersion, or Diaspora, of the Jews throughout Europe. Jerusalem became officially off limits to all Jews, and the country was ironically renamed *Palestine,* after the ancient Philistines, arch-enemies of the early Israelites.

Diaspora

With the Diaspora, the center of Judaism shifted from Jerusalem to Babylonia, where a large population of Jews had remained after the 586 B.C.E. exile. At its peak, one million Jews lived in Babylon in the years following the exile and restoration. The figure of the Rabbi emerged at this time as an authority in scriptural interpretation and Jewish law, culminating in the creation of the Babylonian *Talmud,* the ultimate repository of Jewish oral law and commentary. Babylonian Jews remained the dominant voice of Judaism until the Arab conquest of the region in the seventh century C.E.

In the centuries following, Jews of the Diaspora attempted to settle in communities throughout Europe, only to be forced out as host countries became intolerant of them. In the reshuffling, two distinct groups emerged, each with their own distinct language and religious rituals. The Saphardic Jews were expelled from Spain and Portugal and moved to the Ottoman Empire. The Ashkenasic Jews were expelled from other countries and moved to eastern Europe.

Beginning in the eighteenth century, Judaism evolved in several directions. In reaction to impersonal rabbinic legalism and widespread disillusionment in the absence of the expected Messiah, the Hasidic movement was founded by Baal Shem Tov. Hasidism offered a more mystical and joyous approach to Judaism, particularly for the laity. Although Hasidim were at first persecuted by traditional rabbinic schools, eventually half of the traditional rabbis joined them.

It was not until the eighteenth century Enlightenment that European countries finally granted civil rights to their Jewish citizens. As an outgrowth of their freedom, Reform Judaism was founded in Germany by Abraham Geiger in the nineteenth century. Geiger believed that Judaism should pertain more to the sphere of religion than to culture and that Jewish worship practices should be modified to parallel those of Protestant Christians. In reaction, the Orthodox denomination reaffirmed the traditional elements of Judaism. Mediating between the reformed and orthodox views, the Conservative denomination emerged as an attempt to "conserve" historical traditions that the Reform denomination had eliminated. Finally, in the twentieth century the Reconstructionist denomination was founded by Mordecai Kaplan as a development from the Conservative denomination. Reconstructionists offer a more pragmatic approach in the modern world, placing more emphasis on the cultural development of Judaism than on its religious elements.

The Tanakh

The most sacred collection of writings for Judaism is the *Tanakh*. The word "Tanakh" is an acronym coined in the middle ages from the initials of its three divisions: the Torah (Law), the Neviim (Prophets), and the Ketuvim (Writings). The 24 books of the *Tanakh* are traditionally categorized as follows:

Torah: Genesis, Exodus, Leviticus, Numbers, Deuteronomy

Neviim:

Former Prophets: Joshua, Judges, Samuel, Kings

Latter Prophets: Isaiah, Jeremiah, Ezekiel, The Twelve (Hosea, Joel, Amos, Obadiah, Jonah, Micah, Nahum, Habakkuk, Zephaniah, Haggai, Zechariah, Malachi)

Ketuvim: Psalms, Job, Proverbs, Ruth, Song of Songs, Ecclesiastes, Lamentations, Esther, Daniel, Ezra-Nehemiah, Chronicles

The books of the *Tanakh* were written and compiled over a period of 1,000 years, from approximately 1100 to 100 B.C.E. Each book has a detailed history of authorship, editing, and reediting. The writings appear in a variety of literary genres, including song lyrics, historical chronicles, wisdom literature, laws, prophecies, and apocalypses. The oldest stories and poems, such as the *Song of Deborah*, included here, may have been orally transmitted before taking written form. Much of the *Tanakh* bears the mark of post-exilic Judaism, either in composition or in editing. The books and main divisions of the *Tanakh* were in place when in 90 C.E. a Sanhedrin council in the Palestinian city of Jabneh gave the list its official stamp.

Of all writings within Judaism, the five books of the Torah have always been considered the most sacred. Thus, an understanding of its development is important. The term *Torah* means law, in the sense of instruction or teaching, which traces its authority to Moses. More specifically, *Torah* has come to mean the collection of writings consisting of Genesis, Exodus, Leviticus, Numbers, and Deuteronomy. Any account of the origin and authorship of the *Torah* must take place against the backdrop of a theory in biblical scholarship known as the Documentary Hypothesis, most famously articulated by Julius Wellhausen (1844–1918). According to this, the *Torah* is a fabric sewn from four distinct textual sources identified as J, E, P, and D. The J source acquired its name from its continued use of the word *Yahweh* (often mispronounced *Jehovah*) for God in early parts of the narrative (prior to the revelation of the divine name of God to Moses). The E source is so named for its pervasive use of the term *Elohim* for God. The D source refers to the bulk of the text of Deuteronomy, with its unique style. Finally, the P source derives its name from the priestly content of its text.

Since Wellhausen, biblical scholars have identified more precisely the authors and dates of the four sources. One interpretation is that the J source was written by an author of the southern kingdom and reflects the political interests of Judah. Sometimes this involves besmirching the north. The E source, by contrast, was written by an author of the northern kingdom, possibly a Levitic priest, who endorsed the north's political structure but attacked its religious establishment. Both J and E appear to have been written between 922 and 722 B.C.E. Shortly after the fall of the north to the Assyrians in 722 and during Hezekiah's reign in the south, J and E were spliced or *redacted* together into a single document as a conciliation to the northern Israelites who had migrated to Judah. In reaction to the influx of northern priests, the P source was created as an alternative to the J and E story. One hundred years later, during the reign of Josiah, the framework of the D source was written around an old law code as a catalyst for religious reform. The D source is the first part of a larger historical sequence encompassing Joshua, Judges, Samuel, and Kings, compiled and edited by a single historian. The complete sequence of texts, called the Deuteronomistic History, details God's covenant with David for an unbroken royal lineage and rejection of local altars in favor of a single sacrificial site at the temple in Jerusalem. Finally, all four sources (J, E, P, and D) were redacted together into the five books of Moses, the *Torah*, by a priest (possibly Ezra) during or shortly after the Babylonian exile.

Post-Exilic Writings

From 300 B.C.E. until about 200 C.E., the notion of an official Jewish canon of scriptures was fluid, even after the council of Jabneh in 90 C.E. Hundreds of religious texts appeared which were considered authoritative by many at this time. Although the authority of these texts was rejected by later Jewish scholars, even today they continue to have historical importance. These writings are classified into three collections: Apocrypha, Pseudepigrapha, and Dead Sea Scrolls.

The term *Apocrypha* is Greek for *concealed* and refers to 13 texts which at one time were associated with the Jewish canon but were officially rejected at the council of Jabneh. The original source of the Apocrypha is a Greek translation of the Jewish scriptures called the Septuagint (meaning "70"), so called because 72 Jewish scholars were brought to Egypt to create a Greek translation of Jewish scriptures between 285 and 246 B.C.E. Legend has it that each translated the first five books within 72 days, compared the various translations, and found them to be exactly the same. Completed around 100 B.C.E., the Septuagint contains the 13 Apocryphal books interspersed among the other books of the *Tanakh,* with no clear distinction in importance. The 13 books include Esdras 1 and 2, Tobit, Judith, the rest of the book of Esther, the Wisdom of Solomon, Ecclesiasticus (Sirach), Baruch, a Letter of Jeremiah, additions to the Book of Daniel (the Song of the Three Children, Susanna, and Bel and the Dragon), the Prayer of Manasseh, and Maccabees 1 and 2.

The term *Pseudepigrapha* means "writings with false subscriptions" and refers to a collection of 52 Jewish religious writings from 200 B.C.E. to 200 C.E., attributed to ideal figures in Jewish history such as Abraham and Moses. In literary styles paralleling those of the *Tanakh,* its four theological themes are the origins of sin and evil, God's transcendence, a coming Messiah, and the resurrection of the dead. The Pseudepigrapha is important in showing the diversity of Jewish theology at this time and the development of doctrines such as the Messiah, which are only hinted at in the *Tanakh.*

The Dead Sea Scrolls are a collection of writings and fragments discovered between 1947 and 1960 C.E. in the Qumran Valley area on the northwest shores of the Dead Sea. The religious community of Qumran was established around 200 B.C.E. as a desert haven against the oppressive political and religious realities of the time, and was destroyed in 70 C.E. by the Romans during the Jewish revolt. The Messianic community was preparing to be joined by angels for a final war against evil on earth. Although the Qumran community is often identified with the Essenes as described by Josephus, its association with that or any other sect is uncertain. Scriptures of the Qumran community were discovered in 1947, and made fully public in 1991. The writings include the earliest copies of many texts of the *Tanakh* as well as an array of previously unknown religious texts. When first discovered, the new documents were thought to represent the unique views of the post-exilic monastic community. More recently, however, some historians believe they originated in Jerusalem, the center of Jewish religious activity, and thus, like the Pseudepigrapha, reflect the breadth of Jewish scripture at the time.

Rabbinic Writings

During the first five centuries C.E., Judaism witnessed a dramatic flourishing of literary activity among Rabbis. One such was the composition of verse-by-verse commentaries on the *Tanakh*, known collectively and stylistically as *midrash*. Another and more important type of activity was the development of oral law, culminating in the texts of the *Mishnah* and the *Talmud*. Traditionally, the oral law of Judaism is believed to have been given to Moses by God at Mount Sinai, and orally transmitted for 1,500 years. In view of its divine origin, the oral law is on the same scriptural plane as the *Tanakh*. Historically, the foundation of the oral law tradition is thought to have been laid with Ezra's *Great Synagogue*, continuing through the Pharisees, and then extensively developed by the *Tannaim*, scholarly Rabbis who lived during the first two centuries C.E. Although the *Tannaim* resisted committing the oral traditions to writing, in 200 C.E. the Palestinian Rabbi Judah Ha-Nasi did just that. This work is the *Mishnah*, a collection of sayings attributed to specific *Tannaim* and Rabbinic schools from the first two centuries C.E. The sayings are stylistically rhythmic, which facilitated their early memorization. Much of its content derives from the legal codes in the Torah, although it rarely quotes the *Tanakh* directly. The text contains six key divisions: agricultural rules, laws governing the Sabbath and holidays, laws on marriage and divorce, the system of civil and criminal law, rules of temple sacrifices, and rules of purities and impurities.

Early Rabbis developed a tradition of commenting on the contents of the Mishnah. One collection, called the *Tosefta*, was written by the *Tannaim* themselves. After the Tannaim, two other groups of Rabbis continued commenting on the Mishnah: the *Amoraim* (200–500 C.E.), and the *Saboraim* (500–700 C.E.). Their comments became the basis of the *Talmud*, the grandest expression of this Rabbinic tradition. A first version of the *Talmud* appeared in 450 C.E. in Jerusalem, and a second and longer version in 500 C.E. in Babylon. Material was added to each version in the following century. Both the Jerusalem and Babylonian Talmuds have two parts: first, the text of the *Mishnah*, and second, the *Gemara*, which is a several-thousand-page collection of comments on the *Mishnah* written by the *Amoraim* and *Saboraim*. Both Talmuds are structured according to the main divisions of the *Mishnah*, although the Babylonian *Talmud* covers more divisions than its Jerusalem counterpart and, thus, is more definitive.

Medieval and Recent Writings

At the close of the Rabbinic period, Jewish writers continued penning commentaries on the Tanakh and Talmud. Only two of these writers can be mentioned here. First is the great philosopher Moses Maimonides (1135–1204 C.E.), whose family left Spain for North Africa to avoid persecution. When only 23, Maimonides began writing an extensive commentary on the Mishna, included in which is a statement of thirteen articles of faith that subsequently became a regular part of Jewish prayer services. Another influential author of the period was the thirteenth century Spaniard Moses de Leon, who, writing in the Jewish mystical tradition of Kabbala, composed the multivolume *Book of Splendor* (*Sefer ha-Zohar*). The hero of the book, Rabbi Shimon, a second-century C.E. *Tannaim*, presents to his followers a verse-by-verse mystical commentary on several books of the *Tanakh*. To gain a receptive audience and lend authenticity to its content, de Leon claimed that his work was a recently discovered ancient text written by Rabbi Shimon himself. For almost 600 years, Kabbalists took de Leon at his word. The various Jewish movements of the past few centuries—Hasidism, Reform Judaism, Orthodox Judaism, Conservative Judaism, Zionism—have each given birth to revered works in several genres, including commentaries, tales, statements of faith, and polemics.

BOOKS OF MOSES

CREATION

The first 11 books of the Tanakh *present a continuous historical narrative from the creation of the world until the Babylonian exile. Genesis opens with two creation stories, one from the P or Priestly source, and one from the J or Yahwist source. Central to both is the idea that humans are the pinnacle of God's creative activity. The P source creation story, presented below, emphasizes the cosmic structure of creation, as opposed to the earlier and perhaps agrarian-oriented account of the J source. Also, the writer sees creation involving three mandates. First, humans are to fill the earth and master it. Second, humans are to eat plants for food. Finally, the seventh day of the week is declared holy.*

When God began to create heaven and earth—the earth being unformed and void, with darkness over the surface of the deep and a wind from God sweeping over the water—God said, "Let there be light"; and there was light. God saw that the light was good, and God separated the light from the darkness. God called the light Day, and the darkness He called Night. And there was evening and there was morning, a first day.

God said, "Let there be an expanse in the midst of the water, that it may separate water from water." God made the expanse, and it separated the water which was below the expanse from the water which was above the expanse. And it was so. God called the expanse Sky. And there was evening and there was morning, a second day.

God said, "Let the water below the sky be gathered into one area, that the dry land may appear." And it was so. God called the dry land Earth, and the gathering of waters He called Seas. And God saw that this was good. And God said, "Let the earth sprout vegetation: seed-bearing plants, fruit trees of every kind on earth that bear fruit with the seed in it." And it was so. The earth brought forth vegetation: seed-bearing plants of every kind, and trees of every kind bearing fruit with the seed in it. And God saw that this was good. And there was evening and there was morning, a third day.

God said, "Let there be lights in the expanse of the sky to separate day from night; they shall serve as signs for the set times—the days and the years; and they shall serve as lights in the expanse of the sky to shine upon the earth." And it was so. God made the two great lights, the greater light to dominate the day and the lesser light to dominate the night, and the stars. And God set them in the expanse of the sky to shine upon the earth, to dominate the day and the night, and to separate light from darkness. And God saw that this was good. And there was evening and there was morning, a fourth day. God said, "Let the waters bring forth swarms of living creatures, and birds that fly above the earth across the expanse of the sky. God created the great sea monsters, and all the living creatures of every kind that creep, which the waters brought forth in swarms, and all the winged birds of every kind. And God saw that this was good. God blessed them, saying, "Be fertile and increase, fill the waters in the seas, and let the birds increase on the earth." And there was evening and there was morning, a fifth day.

God said, "Let the earth bring forth every kind of living creature: cattle, creeping things, and wild beasts of every kind." And it was so. God made wild beasts of every kind and cattle of every kind, and all kinds of creeping things of the earth. And God saw that this was good. And God said, "Let us make man in our image, after our likeness. They shall rule the fish of the sea, the birds of the sky, the cattle, the whole earth, and all the creeping things that creep on earth." And God created man in His image, in the image of God He created him; male and female He created them. God blessed them and God said to them, "Be fertile and increase, fill the earth and master it; and rule the fish of the sea, the birds of the sky, and all the living things that creep on earth."

God said, "See, I give you every seed-bearing plant that is upon all the earth, and every tree that has seed-bearing fruit; they shall be yours for food. And to all the animals on land, to all the birds of the sky, and to everything that creeps on earth, in which there is the breath of life, [I give] all the green plants for food." And it was so. And God saw all that He had made, and found it very good. And there was evening and there was morning, the sixth day.

The heaven and the earth were finished, and all their array. On the seventh day God finished the work that he had been doing, and He ceased on the seventh day from all the work that He had done. And God blessed the seventh day and declared it holy, because on it God ceased from all the work of creation that He had done. Such is the story of heaven and earth when they were created.

Source: Genesis 1:1–2:3, from *Tanakh: The Holy Scriptures* (Philadelphia: Jewish Publication Society, 1985).

COVENANT WITH NOAH

The first great covenant in the Tanakh is between God and Noah. The P text story relates how God finds all the earth's inhabitants wicked, except for Noah, and destroys the earth in a flood. When the water subsides, God promises that he will not again destroy the world by water and permits humans to eat animal flesh. The authors of the P text note later (in Exodus 40) that all slaughter of animals must be done in the context of a sacrificial rite conducted by a priest.

God blessed Noah and his sons, and said to them, "Be fertile and increase, and fill the earth. The fear and the dread of you shall be upon all the beasts of the earth and upon all the birds of the sky—everything with which the earth is astir—and upon all the fish of the sea; they are given into your hand. Every creature that lives shall be yours to eat; as with the green grasses, I give you all these. You must not, however, eat flesh with its life-blood in it. But for your own life-blood I will require a reckoning: I will require it of every beast; of man, too, will I require a reckoning for human life, of every man for that of his fellow man!

> Whoever sheds the blood of man,
> By man shall his blood be shed;
> For in His image
> Did God make man.

Be fertile, then, and increase; abound on the earth and increase on it."

And God said to Noah and to his sons with him, "I now establish My covenant with you and your offspring to come, and with every living thing that is with you—birds, cattle, and every wild beast as well—all that have come out of the ark, every living thing on earth. I will maintain My covenant with you: never again shall all flesh be cut off by the waters of a flood, and never again shall there be a flood to destroy the earth."

God further said, "This is the sign that I set for the covenant between Me and you, and every living creature with you, for all ages to come. I have set My bow in the clouds, and it shall serve as a sign of the covenant between Me and the earth. When I bring clouds over the earth, and the bow appears in the clouds, I will remember My covenant between Me and you and every living creature among all flesh, so that the waters shall never again become a flood to destroy all flesh. When the bow is in the clouds, I will see it and remember the everlasting covenant between God and all living creatures, all flesh that is on earth. That," God said to Noah, "shall be the sign of the covenant that I have established between Me and all flesh that is on earth."

Source: Genesis 9:1–17, from *Tanakh: The Holy Scriptures.*

COVENANT WITH ABRAHAM

The second great covenant of the Tanakh, *as it appears in the P text, is between God and Abraham, where Abraham is selected by God to be father of a multitude. God indicates that he will inherit the land of Canaan and that circumcision is to be the sign of that covenant. Circumcision is a rite to be performed by priests.*

When Abram was ninety-nine years old, the Lord appeared to Abram and said to him, "I am El Shaddai [God heeds]. Walk in My ways and be blameless. I will establish My covenant between Me and you, and I will make you exceedingly numerous."

Abram threw himself on his face; and God spoke to him further, "As for Me, this is My covenant with you: You shall be the father of a multitude of nations. And you shall no longer be called Abram, but your name shall be Abraham, for I make you the father of a multitude of nations. I will make you exceedingly fertile, and make nations of you; and kings shall come forth from you. I will maintain My covenant between Me and you, and your offspring to come, as an everlasting covenant throughout the ages, to be God to you and to your offspring to come. I assign the land you sojourn in to you and your offspring to come, all the land of Canaan, as an everlasting holding. I will be their God."

God further said to Abraham, "As for you, you and your offspring to come throughout the ages shall keep My covenant. Such shall be the covenant between Me and you and your offspring to follow which you shall keep: every male among you shall be circumcised. You shall circumcise the flesh of your foreskin, and that shall be the sign of the covenant between Me and you. And throughout the generations, every male among you shall be circumcised at the age of eight days. As for the homeborn slave and the one bought from an outsider who is not of your offspring, they must be circumcised, homeborn and purchased alike. Thus shall My covenant be marked in your flesh as an everlasting pact. And if any male who is uncircumcised fails to circumcise the flesh of his foreskin, that person shall be cut off from his kin; he has broken My covenant."

And God said to Abraham, "As for your wife Sarai, you shall not call her Sarai, but her name shall be Sarah. I will bless her; indeed, I will give you a son by her. I will bless her so that she shall give rise to nations; rulers of peoples shall issue from her." Abraham threw himself on his face and laughed, as he said to himself, "Can a child be born to a man a hundred years old, or can Sarah bear a child at ninety? And Abraham said to God, "O that Ishmael might live by Your favor!" God said, "Nevertheless, Sarah your wife shall bear you a son, and you shall name him Isaac; and I will maintain My covenant with him as an everlasting covenant for his offspring to come. As for Ishmael, I have heeded you. I hereby bless him. I will make him fertile and exceedingly numerous. He shall be the father of twelve chieftains, and I will make of him a great nation. But My covenant I will maintain with Isaac, whom Sarah shall bear to you at this season next year." And when He was done speaking with him, God was gone from Abraham.

Source: Genesis 17:1–22, from *Tanakh: The Holy Scriptures.*

PASSOVER AND EXODUS

Abraham's descendants migrate to Egypt to avoid famine in Canaan and, within a few generations, their population dramatically increases. Intimidated by their numbers, the Pharaoh enslaves the Israelites and issues an edict that male infants are to be drowned. To save her child, one woman places her toddler, Moses, in a basket and floats it down the Nile, where it is discovered and he is adopted by the Pharaoh's daughter. When Moses grows up, God appears to him and instructs him to lead his people out of Egypt and into Canaan. To break the Pharaoh's resistance in releasing the Israelites, God kills the first-born humans and cattle in Egypt. In preparation for the event, the Israelites are instructed to perform a series of activities as described below. Passover, one of Judaism's most sacred feasts, is in celebration of this event.

12. In the middle of the night the Lord struck down all the first-born in the land of Egypt, from the first-born of Pharaoh who sat on the throne to the first-born of the captive who was in the dungeon, and all the first-born of the cattle. And Pharaoh arose in the night, with all his courtiers and all the Egyptians—because there was a loud cry in Egypt; for there was no house where there was not someone dead. He summoned Moses and Aaron in the night and said, "Up, depart from among my people, you and the Israelites with you! Go, worship the Lord as you said! Take also your flocks and your herds, as you said, and be gone! And may you bring a blessing upon me also!"

    The Egyptians urged the people on, impatient to have them leave the country, for they said, "We shall all be dead." So the people took their dough before it was leavened, their kneading bowls wrapped in their cloaks upon their shoulders. The Israelites had done Moses' bidding and borrowed from the Egyptians objects of silver and gold, and clothing. And the Lord had disposed the Egyptians favorably toward the people, and they let them have their request; thus they stripped the Egyptians.

    The Israelites journeyed from Rameses to Succoth, about six hundred thousand men on foot, aside from children. Moreover, a mixed multitude went up with them, and very much livestock, both flocks and herds. And they baked unleavened cakes of the dough that they had taken out of Egypt, for it was not leavened, since they had been driven out of Egypt and could not delay; nor had they prepared any provisions for themselves.

    The length of time that the Israelites lived in Egypt was four hundred and thirty years; at the end of the four hundred and thirtieth year, to the very day, all the ranks of the Lord departed from the land of Egypt. That was for the Lord a night of vigil to bring them out of the land of Egypt; that same night is the Lord's, one of vigil for all the children of Israel throughout the ages.

14. When the king of Egypt was told that the people had fled, Pharaoh and his courtiers had a change of heart about the people and said,

"What is this we have done, releasing Israel from our service?" He ordered his chariot and took his men with him; he took six hundred of his picked chariots, and the rest of the chariots of Egypt, with officers in all of them. The Lord stiffened the heart of Pharaoh king of Egypt, and he gave chase to the Israelites. As the Israelites were departing defiantly, the Egyptians gave chase to them, and all the chariot horses of Pharaoh, his horsemen, and his warriors overtook them encamped by the sea, near Pihahiroth, before Baal-zephon.

As Pharaoh drew near, the Israelites caught sight of the Egyptians advancing upon them. Greatly frightened, the Israelites cried out to the Lord. And they said to Moses, "Was it for want of graves in Egypt that you brought us to die in the wilderness? What have you done to us, taking us out of Egypt? Is this not the very thing we told you in Egypt, saying, 'Let us be, and we will serve the Egyptians, for it is better for us to serve the Egyptians than to die in the wilderness'?" But Moses said to the people, "Have no fear! Stand by, and witness the deliverance which the Lord will work for you today; for the Egyptians whom you see today you will never see again. The Lord will battle for you; you hold your peace!"

Then the Lord said to Moses, "Why do you cry out to Me? Tell the Israelites to go forward. And you lift up your rod and hold out your arm over the sea and split it, so that the Israelites may march into the sea on dry ground. And I will stiffen the hearts of the Egyptians so that they go in after them; and I will gain glory through Pharaoh and all his warriors, his chariots and his horsemen. Let the Egyptians know that I am Lord, when I gain glory through Pharaoh, his chariots, and his horsemen."

The angel of God, who had been going ahead of the Israelite army, now moved and followed behind them; and the pillar of cloud shifted from in front of them and took up a place behind them, and it came between the army of the Egyptians and the army of Israel. Thus there was the cloud with the darkness, and it cast a spell upon the night, so that the one could not come near the other all through the night.

Then Moses held out his arm over the sea and the Lord drove back the sea with a strong east wind all that night, and turned the sea into dry ground. The waters were split, and the Israelites went into the sea on dry ground, the waters forming a wall for them on their right and on their left. The Egyptians came in pursuit after them into the sea, all of Pharaoh's horses, chariots, and horsemen. At the morning watch, the Lord looked down upon the Egyptian army from a pillar of fire and cloud, and threw the Egyptian army into a panic. He locked the wheels of their chariots so that they moved forward with difficulty. And the Egyptians said, "Let us flee from the Israelites, for the Lord is fighting for them against Egypt."

Then the Lord said to Moses, "Hold out your arm over the sea, that the waters may come back upon the Egyptians and upon their chariots and upon their horsemen." Moses held out his arm over the sea, and at daybreak the sea returned to its normal state, and the Egyptians fled at its approach. But the Lord hurled the Egyptians into the sea. The waters turned back and covered the chariots and the horsemen—Pharaoh's entire army that followed them into the sea; not one of them remained. But the Israelites had marched through the sea on dry ground, the waters forming a wall for them on their right and on their left.

Source: Exodus 12:29–41, 14:5–29, from *Tanakh: The Holy Scriptures.*

MOSAIC COVENANT

The third great covenant in the Tanakh *text consists of God giving the Law to Moses at Mount Sinai, a means by which the Israelites could become a holy people. Mosaic Law is articulated throughout the books of Exodus, Leviticus, Numbers, and Deuteronomy, interspersed with narratives about the Israelites' 40 years of wandering. Exodus 19, a JE text, describes the people's preparation for receiving the Law from God. Exodus 20, which is possibly a reworked version of an ancient P text, presents the best-known part of the Mosaic Law, the Ten Commandments.*

19. On the third new moon after the Israelites had gone forth from the land of Egypt, on that very day, they entered the wilderness of Sinai. Having journeyed from Rephidim, they entered the wilderness of Sinai and encamped in the wilderness. Israel encamped there in front of the mountain, and Moses went up to God. The Lord called to him from the mountain, saying, "Thus shall you say to the house of Jacob and declare to the children of Israel: 'You have seen what I did to the Egyptians, how I bore you on eagles' wings and brought you to Me. Now then, if you will obey Me faithfully and keep My covenant, you shall be My treasured possession among all the peoples. Indeed, all the earth is Mine, but you shall be to Me a kingdom of priests and a holy nation.' These are the words that you shall speak to the children of Israel."

Moses came and summoned the elders of the people and put before them all that the Lord had commanded him. All the people answered as one, saying, "All that the Lord has spoken we will do!" And Moses brought back the people's words to the Lord. And the Lord said to Moses, "I will come to you in a thick cloud, in order that the people may hear when I speak with you and so trust you ever after." Then Moses reported the people's words to the Lord, and the Lord said to Moses, "Go to the people and warn them to stay pure today and tomorrow. Let them wash their clothes. Let them be ready for the third day; for on the third day the Lord will come down, in the sight of all the people, on Mount Sinai. You shall set bounds for the people round about, saying, 'Beware of going up the mountain or touching the border of it. Whoever touches the mountain shall be put to death: no hand shall touch him, but he shall be either stoned or shot; beast or man, he shall not live.' When the ram's horn sounds a long blast, they may go up on the mountain."

Moses came down from the mountain to the people and warned the people to stay pure, and they washed their clothes. And he said to the people, "Be ready for the third day: do not go near a woman."

On the third day, as morning dawned, there was thunder, and lightning, and a dense cloud upon the mountain, and a very loud blast of the horn; and all the people who were in the camp trembled. Moses led the people out of the camp toward God, and they took their places at the foot of the mountain.

Now Mount Sinai was all in smoke, for the Lord had come down upon it in fire; the smoke rose like the smoke of a kiln, and the whole mountain trembled violently. The blare of the horn grew louder and louder. As Moses spoke, God answered him in thunder. The Lord came down upon Mount Sinai, on the top of the mountain, and the Lord called Moses to the top of the mountain and Moses went up. The Lord said to Moses, "Go down, warn the people not to break through to the Lord to gaze, lest many of them perish. The priests also, who come near the Lord, must stay pure, lest the Lord break out against them." But Moses said to the Lord, "The people cannot come up to Mount Sinai, for You warned us saying, 'Set bounds about the mountain and sanctify it.'" So the Lord said to him, "Go down, and come back together with Aaron; but let not the priests or the people break through to come up to the Lord, lest He break out against them." And Moses went down to the people and spoke to them.

20. God spoke all these words, saying:

I the Lord am your God who brought you out of the land of Egypt, the house of bondage: You shall have no other gods besides Me.

You shall not make for yourself a sculpted image, or any likeness of what is in the heavens above, or on the earth below, or in the waters under the earth. You shall not bow down to them or serve them for I the Lord your God am an impassioned God, visiting the guilt of the parents upon the children, upon the third and upon the fourth generations of those who reject Me, but showing kindness to the thousandth generation of those who love Me and keep My commandments.

You shall not swear falsely by the name of the Lord your God; for the Lord will not clear one who swears falsely by His name.

Remember the sabbath day and keep it holy. Six days you shall labor and do all your work, but the seventh day is a sabbath of the Lord your God: you shall not do any work—you, your son or daughter, your male or female slave, or your cattle, or the stranger who is within your settlements. For in six days the Lord made heaven and earth and sea, and all that is in them, and He rested on the seventh day; therefore the Lord blessed the sabbath day and hallowed it.

Honor your father and your mother, that you may long endure on the land that the Lord your God has assigned to you.

You shall not murder.

You shall not commit adultery.

You shall not steal.

You shall not bear false witness against your neighbor.

You shall not covet your neighbor's house; you shall not covet your neighbor's wife, or his male or female slave, or his ox or his ass, or anything that is your neighbor's.

All the people witnessed the thunder and lightning, the blare of the horn and the mountain smoking; and when the people saw it, they fell back and stood at a distance. "You speak to us," they said to Moses, "and we will obey; but let not God speak to us, lest we die." Moses answered the people, "Be not afraid; for God has come only in order to test you, and in order that the fear of Him may be ever with you, so that you do not go astray."

Source: Exodus 19, 20:1–17, from *Tanakh: The Holy Scriptures*.

HOLINESS CODE

The Mosaic Law contains a series of codes on social, ethical, and religious topics, such as the Covenant Code (Exodus 21–23), the Purity Code (Leviticus 11–16), the Holiness Code (Leviticus 17–27), and the Law Code (Deuteronomy 12–26). The literary and legal style of these codes is frequently compared to other codes of the ancient near east, such as the Code of Hammurabi, king of Ur. For example, on the issue of kidnapping, the Hammurabi code states, "If a man has stolen the young son of a freeman, he shall be put to death." By comparison, the Covenant Code in Exodus 21:16 states, "He who kidnaps a man—whether he has sold him or is still holding him—shall be put to death." The following is from the Holiness Code, a P text in the Book of Leviticus.

19. The Lord spoke to Moses, saying, Speak to the whole Israelite community and say to them: You shall be holy, for I, the Lord your God, am holy.

    You shall each revere his mother and his father, and keep My Sabbaths: I the Lord am your God.

    Do not turn to idols or make molten gods for yourselves: I the Lord am your God.

    When you sacrifice an offering of well-being to the Lord, sacrifice it so that it may be accepted on your behalf. It shall be eaten on the day you sacrifice it, or on the day following; but what is left by the third day must be consumed in fire. If it should be eaten on the third day, it is an offensive thing, it will not be acceptable. And he who eats of it shall bear his guilt, for he has profaned what is sacred to the Lord; that person shall be cut off from his kin.

When you reap the harvest of your land, you shall not reap all the way to the edges of your field, or gather the gleanings of your harvest. You shall not pick your vineyard bare, or gather the fallen fruit of your vineyard; you shall leave them for the poor and the stranger: I the Lord am your God.

You shall not steal; you shall not deal deceitfully or falsely with one another. You shall not swear falsely by My name, profaning the name of your God: I am the Lord.

You shall not defraud your fellow. You shall not commit robbery. The wages of a laborer shall not remain with you until morning.

You shall not insult the deaf, or place a stumbling block before the blind. You shall fear your God: I am the Lord.

You shall not render an unfair decision: do not favor the poor or show deference to the rich; judge your kinsman fairly. Do not deal basely with your countrymen. Do not profit by the blood of your fellow: I am the Lord.

You shall not hate your kinsfolk in your heart. Reprove your kinsman but incur no guilt because of him. You shall not take vengeance or bear a grudge against your countrymen. Love your fellow as yourself: I am the Lord.

You shall observe My laws.

You shall not let your cattle mate with a different kind; you shall not sow your field with two kinds of seed; you shall not put on cloth from a mixture of two kinds of material.

If a man has carnal relations with a woman who is a slave and has been designated for another man, but has not been redeemed or given her freedom, there shall be an indemnity; they shall not, however, be put to death, since she has not been freed. But he must bring to the entrance of the Tent of Meeting, as his guilt offering to the Lord, a ram of guilt offering. With the ram of guilt offering the priest shall make expiation for him before the Lord for the sin that he committed; and the sin that he committed will be forgiven.

When you enter the land and plant any tree for food, you shall regard its fruit as forbidden. Three years it shall be forbidden for you, not to be eaten. In the fourth year all its fruit shall be set aside for jubilation before the Lord; and only in the fifth year may you use its fruit—that its yield to you may be increased: I the Lord am your God.

You shall not eat anything with its blood. You shall not practice divination or soothsaying. You shall not round off the side-growth on your head, or destroy the side-growth of your beard. You shall not make gashes in your flesh for the dead, or incise any marks on yourselves: I am the Lord.

Do not degrade your daughter and make her a harlot, lest the land fall into harlotry and the land be filled with depravity. You shall keep my Sabbaths and venerate My sanctuary: I am the Lord.

Do not turn to ghosts and do not inquire of familiar spirits, to be defiled by them: I the Lord am your God.

You shall rise before the aged and show deference to the old; you shall fear your God: I am the Lord.

When a stranger resides with you in your land, you shall not wrong him. The stranger who resides with you shall be to you as one of your citizens; you shall love him as yourself, for you were strangers in the land of Egypt: I the Lord am your God.

You shall not falsify measures of length, weight, or capacity. You shall have an honest balance, honest weights, an honest *ephah,* and an honest *hin.* I the Lord am your God who freed you from the land of Egypt. You shall faithfully observe all my laws and all my rules: I am the Lord.

Source: Leviticus 19:1–37, from *Tanakh: The Holy Scriptures.*

CONQUEST AND UNITED KINGDOM

ENTRY INTO CANAAN

After 40 years of wandering, the Israelites enter Canaan under the leadership of Joshua, Moses' successor. This account is part of a larger text sequence called the Deuteronomistic History, edited just before the Babylonian exile, and encompasses the books of Deuteronomy through second Kings. The story emphasizes Deuteronomist themes, such as the importance of the Ark of the Covenant as the focus of God's presence, and the command to annihilate the present occupants of Canaan as a means of assuring religious purity.

After the death of Moses the servant of the Lord, the Lord said to Joshua son of Nun, Moses' attendant:

"My servant Moses is dead. Prepare to cross the Jordan, together with all this people, into the land that I am giving to the Israelites. Every spot on which your foot treads I give to you, as I promised Moses. Your territory shall extend from the wilderness and the Lebanon to the Great River, the River Euphrates [on the east]—the whole Hittite country—and up to the Mediterranean Sea on the west. No one shall be able to resist you as long as you live. As I was with Moses, so I will be with you; I will not fail you or forsake you.

Be strong and resolute, for you shall apportion to this people the land that I swore to their fathers to assign to them. But you must be very strong and resolute to observe faithfully all the Teaching that My servant Moses enjoined upon you. Do not deviate from it to the right or to the left, that you may be successful wherever you go. Let not this Book of the Teaching cease from your lips, but recite it day and night, so that you may observe faithfully all that is written in it. Only then will you prosper in your undertakings and only then will you be successful.

I charge you: Be strong and resolute; do not be terrified or dismayed, for the Lord your God is with you wherever you go."

Joshua thereupon gave orders to the officials of the people: "Go through the camp and charge the people thus: Get provisions ready, for in three days' time you are to cross the Jordan, in order to enter and possess the land that the Lord your God is giving you as a possession."

Then Joshua said the to Reubenites, the Gadites, and the half-tribe of Manasseh, "Remember what Moses the servant of the Lord enjoined upon you, when he said: 'The Lord your God is granting you a haven; He has assigned this territory to you.' Let your wives, children, and livestock remain in the land that Moses assigned to you on this side of the Jordan; but every one of your fighting men shall go across armed in the van of your kinsmen. And you shall assist them until the Lord has given your kinsmen a haven, such as you have, and they too have gained possession of the land that the Lord your God has assigned to them. Then you may return to the land on the east side of the Jordan, which Moses the servant of the Lord assigned to you as your possession, and you may possess it."

They answered Joshua, "We will do everything you have commanded us and we will go wherever you send us. We will obey you just as we obeyed Moses; let but the Lord your God be with you as He was with Moses! Any man who flouts your commands and does not obey every order you give him shall be put to death. Only be strong and resolute!"

Early next morning, Joshua and all the Israelites set out from Shittim and marched to the Jordan. They did not cross immediately, but spent the night there. Three days later, the officials went through the camp and charged the people as follows: "When you see the Ark of the Covenant of the Lord your God being borne by the levitical priests, you shall move forward. Follow it—but keep a distance of some two thousand cubits from it, never coming any closer to it—so that you may know by what route to march, since it is a road you have not traveled before."

And Joshua said to the people, "Purify yourselves, for tomorrow the Lord will perform wonders in your midst."

Then Joshua ordered the priests, "Take up the Ark of the Covenant and advance to the head of the people." And they took up the Ark of the Covenant and advanced to the head of the people.

The Lord said to Joshua, "This day, for the first time, I will exalt you in the sight of all Israel, so that they shall know that I will be with you as I was with Moses. For your part, command the priests who carry the Ark of the Covenant as follows: When you reach the edge of the waters of the Jordan, make a halt in the Jordan."

And Joshua said to the Israelites, "Come closer and listen to the words of the Lord our God. By this," Joshua continued, "you shall know that a living God is among you, and that He will dispossess for you the Canaanites, Hittites, Hivites, Perizzites, Girgashites, Amorites, and Jebusites: the Ark of the Covenant of the Sovereign of all the earth is advancing before you into the Jordan. Now select twelve men from the tribes of Israel, one man from each tribe. When the feet of the priests bearing the Ark of the Lord, the Sovereign of all the earth, come to rest in the waters of the Jordan, the waters of the Jordan—the water coming from upstream—will be cut off and will stand in a single heap."

When the people set out from their encampment to cross the Jordan, the priests bearing the Ark of the Covenant were at the head of the people. Now the Jordan keeps flowing over its entire bed throughout the harvest season. But as soon as the bearers of the Ark reached the Jordan, and the feet of the priests bearing the Ark dipped into the water at its edge, the waters coming down from upstream piled up in a single heap a great way off, at Adam, the town next to Zarethan; and those flowing away downstream to the Sea of the Arabah (the Dead Sea) ran out completely. So the people crossed near Jericho. The priests who bore the Ark of the Lord's Covenant stood on dry land exactly in the middle of the Jordan, while all Israel crossed over on dry land, until the entire nation had finished crossing the Jordan.

Source: Joshua 1, 3, from *Tanakh: The Holy Scriptures*.

SONG OF DEBORAH

After entry into Canaan, the Israelites fight to dislodge the Canaanites. Israel is then governed by a series of legal and military Judges, including Deborah, one of a few women leaders in Jewish history. With the aid of the military leader Barak, Deborah and a small group defeat the army of Jabin, King of Canaan. The Canaanite army, headed by Sisera, has an initial advantage of 900 chariots. Due to a sudden divinely caused cloudburst and flash flood, the Israelites gain the advantage. The Song of Deborah, which commemorates this victory, is one of the oldest passages of the Tanakh. *Composed about 1100 B.C.E., it is similar in structure to Canaanite poems of the period. Historically it denotes the Israelites' successful habitation of the hillsides, overshadowing Canaanite occupation of the valley regions.*

> When locks go untrimmed in Israel,
> When people dedicate themselves—
> Bless the Lord.
>
> Hear, O kings! Give ear, O potentates!
> I will sing, will sing to the Lord,
> Will hymn the Lord, the God of Israel.
>
> O Lord, when you came forth from Seir,
> Advanced from the country of Edom,
> The earth trembled;
> The heavens dripped,
> Yea, the clouds dripped water,
> The mountains quaked—
> Before the Lord, Him of Sinai,
> Before the Lord, God of Israel.
>
> In the days of Shamgar son of Anath,
> In the days of Jael, caravans ceased,

And wayfarers went
By roundabout paths.
Deliverance ceased,
Ceased in Israel,
Till you arose, O Deborah,
Arose, O mother, in Israel!
When they chose new gods,
Was there a fighter then in the gates?
No shield or spear was seen
Among forty thousand in Israel!

My heart is with Israel's leaders,
With the dedicated of the people—
Bless the Lord!
You riders on tawny she-asses,
You who sit on saddle rugs,
And you wayfarers, declare it!
Louder than the sounds of archers,
There among the watering places
Let them chant the gracious acts of the Lord,
His gracious deliverance of Israel.
Then did the people of the Lord
March down to the gates!
Awake, awake, O Deborah!
Awake, awake, strike up the chant!
Arise, O Barak;
Take your captives, O son of Abinoam!

Source: Judges 5:2–12, from *Tanakh: The Holy Scriptures*.

DAVIDIC COVENANT

In response to the need for a ruler who could unify the country against Philistine attacks, Saul is appointed the first king. The Deuteronomistic History relates how Saul's disobedience quickly puts him in disfavor with God, after which God selects David as Saul's more obedient successor. This reflects the most consistent theological theme throughout all seven books of the Deuteronomistic History: Obedience to God results in prosperity, disobedience results in hardship. The fourth and final great covenant in the Tanakh *is with King David, wherein a promise is given that David's house and kingship will be secure and his throne established forever.*

. . . Thus said the Lord of Hosts: I took you from the pasture, from following the flock, to be ruler of My people Israel, and I have been with you wherever you went, and have cut down all your enemies before you. Moreover, I will give you great renown like that of the greatest men on earth. I will establish a home for My people Israel and will plant them firm, so that they shall dwell secure and shall tremble no more. Evil men shall not oppress them any more as in the past, ever since I appointed chieftains over my people Israel. I will give you safety from all your enemies.

The Lord declares to you that He, the Lord, will establish a house for you. When your days are done and you lie with your fathers, I will raise up your offspring after you, one of your own issue, and I will establish his kingship. He shall build a house for my name, and I will establish his royal throne forever. I will be a father to him, and he shall be a son to Me. When he does wrong, I will chastise him with the rod of men and the affliction of mortals; but I will never withdraw My favor from him as I withdrew it from Saul, whom I removed to make room for you. Your house and your kingship shall ever be secure before you; your throne shall be established forever.

Source: 2 Samuel 7:8–16, from *Tanakh: The Holy Scriptures.*

PSALMS ASCRIBED TO DAVID

The Book of Psalms is a collection of 150 songs and prayers written over a 600-year period, many after the Babylonian exile. The book may have taken its final form under the editorship of Ezra, and is sometimes referred to as the hymn book of the second temple. Although the authorship of most of the psalms is uncertain, 73 are ascribed in the text to David and are traditionally said to reflect happy or troubled periods of his life. The psalms are classified as they relate to themes of deliverance, penitence, praise, pilgrimages, historical episodes, and messianic hope. The following is a selection of psalms of David.

8.

O Lord, our Lord,
How majestic is Your name throughout the earth,
You who have covered the heavens with Your splendor!
From the mouths of infants and sucklings
You have founded strength on account of Your foes,
to put an end to enemy and avenger.
When I behold Your heavens, the work of Your fingers,
the moon and stars that You set in place,
what is man that You have been mindful of him,
mortal man that You have taken note of him,
that You have made him little less than divine,
and adorned him with glory and majesty;
You have made him master over Your handiwork,
lying the world at his feet,
sheep and oxen, all of them,
and wild beasts, too;
the birds of the heavens, the fish of the sea,
whatever travels the paths of the seas.
O Lord, our Lord, how majestic is Your name throughout the earth!

23.

The Lord is my shepherd;
   I lack nothing.
He makes me lie down in green pastures;
    He leads me to water in places of repose;
    He renews my life;
    He guides me in right paths
    as befits His name.
Though I walk through a valley of deepest darkness,
    I fear no harm, for You are with me;
    Your rod and Your staff—they comfort me.
You spread a table for me in full view of my enemies;
    You anoint my head with oil;
    my drink is abundant.
Only goodness and steadfast love shall pursue me
    all the days of my life,
    and I shall dwell in the house of the Lord
    For many long years.

27.

The Lord is my light and my help;
    whom would I fear?
The Lord is the stronghold of my life,
    whom should I dread?
When evil men assail me
    to devour my flesh—
    it is they, my foes and my enemies,
    who stumble and fall.
Should an army besiege me,
    my heart would have no fear;
    should war beset me,
    still would I be confident.
One thing I ask of the Lord,
    only that do I seek:
    to live in the house of the Lord
    all the days of my life,
    to gaze upon the beauty of the Lord,
    to frequent His temple.
He will shelter me in His pavilion
    on an evil day,
    grant me the protection of His tent,
    raise me high upon a rock.
Now is my head high
    over my enemies roundabout;
    I sacrifice in His tent with shouts of joy,
    singing and chanting a hymn to the Lord.
Hear, O Lord, when I cry aloud;
    have mercy on me, answer me.

In Your behalf my heart says:
  seek My face!
O Lord, I seek Your face.
Do not hide Your face from me;
    do not thrust aside Your servant in anger;
    You have ever been my help.
Do not forsake me, do not abandon me,
    O God, my deliverer.
Though my father and mother abandon me,
    the Lord will take me in.
Show me Your way, O Lord,
    and lead me on a level path
    because of my watchful foes.
Do not subject me to the will of my foes,
    for false witnesses and unjust accusers have appeared against me.
    Had I not the assurance that I would enjoy the goodness of the Lord in the
    land of the living. . . .
Look to the Lord;
    be strong and of good courage!
O look to the Lord!

32.

Happy is he whose transgression is forgiven,
    whose sin is covered over.
Happy the man whom the Lord does not hold guilty,
    and in whose spirit there is no deceit.
As long as I said nothing,
    my limbs wasted away
    from my anguished roaring all day long.
For night and day
    Your hand lay heavy on me;
    my vigor waned
    as in the summer drought.
Then I acknowledge my sin to you;
    I did not cover up my guilt;
    I resolved, "I will confess my transgressions to the Lord,"
    and You forgave the guilt of my sin.
Therefore let every faithful man pray to You
    upon discovering [his sin]
    that the rushing mighty waters not overtake him.
You are my shelter;
    You preserve me from distress;
    You surround me with the joyous shouts of deliverance.
Let me enlighten you
    and show you which way to go;
    let me offer counsel; my eye is on you.
Be not like a senseless horse or mule
    whose movement must be curbed by bit and bridle,
    far be it from you!

Many are the torments of the wicked,
  but he who trusts in the Lord
  shall be surrounded with favor.
Rejoice in the Lord and exult, O you righteous;
  shout for joy, all upright men!

51.

Have mercy upon me, O God,
  as befits Your faithfulness;
  in keeping with Your abundant compassion,
  blot out my transgressions.
Wash me thoroughly of my iniquity,
  and purify me of my sin;
  for I recognize my transgressions,
  and am ever conscious of my sin.
Against You alone have I sinned,
  and done what is evil in Your sight;
  so You are just in Your sentence,
  and right in Your judgment.
Indeed I was born with iniquity;
  with sin my mother conceived me.
Indeed You desire truth about that which is hidden;
  teach me wisdom about secret things.
Purge me with hyssop till I am pure;
  wash me till I am whiter than snow.
Let me hear tidings of joy and gladness;
  let the bones You have crushed exult.
Hide Your face from my sins;
  blot out all my iniquities.
Fashion a pure heart for me, O God;
  create in me a steadfast spirit.
Do not cast me out of your presence,
  or take Your holy spirit away from me.
Let me again rejoice in Your help;
  let a vigorous spirit sustain me.
I will teach transgressors Your ways,
  That sinners may return to you.
Save me from bloodguilt,
  O God, God, my deliverer,
  that I may sing forth Your beneficence.
O Lord, open my lips,
  and let my mouth declare Your praise.
You do not want me to bring sacrifices;
  you do not desire burnt offerings;
True sacrifice to God is a contrite spirit;
  God, You will not despise
  a contrite and crushed heart.
May it please You to make Zion prosper;
  rebuild the walls of Jerusalem.

Then you will want sacrifices offered in righteousness,
　　burnt and whole offerings;
　　the bulls will be offered on Your altar.

Source: Psalms 8; 23; 27; 32; 51, from *Tanakh: The Holy Scriptures*.

SOLOMON'S TEMPLE

Israel's glory peaked during the reign of King Solomon, David's son. Its borders extended farther than they ever would again (though not as far as under David), and Israel was a key player in ancient near eastern politics. The jewel in the crown of Solomon's achievements was his temple, said to have taken 13 years to complete. According to the Deuteronomistic History, all sacrifices were to be performed only at the temple in Jerusalem; thus the temple became the focus of all religious activity in Israel. The following describes the extent and wealth of Solomon's kingdom, his wisdom, and his construction of the temple.

Judah and Israel were as numerous as the sands of the sea; they ate and drank and were content.

5. Solomon's rule extended over all the kingdoms of the Euphrates to the land of the Philistines and the boundary of Egypt. They brought Solomon tribute and were subject to him all his life. Solomon's daily provisions consisted of 30 *kors* of semolina, and 60 *kors* of [ordinary] flour, 10 fattened oxen, 20 pasture-fed oxen, and 100 sheep and goats, besides deer and gazelles, roebucks and fatted geese. For he controlled the whole region west of the Euphrates—all the kings west of the Euphrates, from Tiphsah to Gaza—and he had peace on all his borders roundabout. All the days of Solomon, Judah and Israel from Dan to Beer-sheba dwelt in safety, everyone under his own vine and under his own fig tree. Solomon had 40,000 stalls of horses for his chariotry and 12,000 horsemen.

All those prefects, each during his month, would furnish provisions for King Solomon and for all who were admitted to King Solomon's table; they did not fall short in anything. They would also, each in his turn, deliver barley and straw for the horses and the swift steeds to the places where they were stationed.

The Lord endowed Solomon with wisdom and discernment in great measure, with understanding as vast as the sands on the seashore. Solomon's wisdom was greater than the wisdom of all the Kedemites and than all the wisdom of the Egyptians. He was the wisest of all men: [wiser] than Ethan the Ezrahite, and Heman, Chalkol, and Darda the sons of Mahol. His fame spread among all the surrounding nations. He composed three thousand proverbs, and his songs numbered one thousand and five. He discoursed about trees, from the cedar in Lebanon to the hyssop that grows out of the wall;

and he discoursed about beasts, birds, creeping things, and fishes. Men of all peoples came to hear Solomon's wisdom, [sent] by all the kins of the earth who had heard of his wisdom.

King Hiram of Tyre sent his officials to Solomon when he heard that he had been anointed king in place of his father; for Hiram had always been a friend of David. Solomon sent this message to Hiram: "You know that my father David could not build a house for the name of the Lord his God because of the enemies that encompassed him, until the Lord had placed them under the soles of his feet. But now the Lord my God has given me respite all around; there is no adversary and not mischance. And so I propose to build a house for the name of the Lord my God, as the Lord promised my father David, saying, 'Your son, whom I will set on your throne in your place, shall build the house for My name.' Please, then, give orders for cedars to be cut for me in the Lebanon. My servants will work with yours, and I will pay you any wages you may ask for your servants; for as you know, there is none among us who knows how to cut timber like the Sidonians."

When Hiram heard Solomon's message, he was overjoyed. "Praised be the Lord this day," he said, "for granting David a wise son to govern this great people." So Hiram sent word to Solomon: "I have your message; I will supply all the cedar and cypress logs you require."

. . . King Solomon imposed forced labor on all Israel; the levy came to 30,000 men. He sent them to the Lebanon in shifts of 10,000 a month: they would spend one month in the Lebanon and two months at home. Adoniram was in charge of the forced labor. Solomon also had 70,000 porters and 80,000 quarriers in the hills, apart from Solomon's 3,300 officials who were in charge of the work and supervised the gangs doing the work.

The king ordered huge blocks of choice stone to be quarried, so that the foundations of the house might be laid with hewn stones. Solomon's masons, Hiram's masons, and the men of Gebal shaped them. Thus the timber and the stones for building the House were made ready.

. . . When Solomon had completed the construction of the House, he paneled the walls of the house on the inside with planks of cedar. He also overlaid the walls on the inside with wood, from the floor of the House to the ceiling. And he overlaid the floor of the House with planks of cypress. Twenty cubits from the rear of the House, he built [a partition] of cedar planks from the floor to the walls; he furnished its interior to serve as a Shrine, as the Holy of Holies. The front part of the House, that is, the Great Hall, measured 40 cubits. The cedar of the interior of the House had carvings of gourds and calyxes; It was all cedar, no stone was exposed. In the innermost part of the House, he fixed a Shrine in which to place the Ark of the Lord's Covenant. The interior of the Shrine was 20 cubits long, 20 cubits wide, and 20 cubits high. He overlaid it with solid gold; he similarly overlaid [its] cedar altar. Solomon overlaid the interior of the House with solid gold; and he inserted golden chains into the door of the Shrine. He overlaid [the Shrine] with gold, so that the entire House was overlaid with gold; he even overlaid with gold the entire altar of the Shrine. And so the entire House was completed.

Source: 1 Kings 4:20, 5:1–20, 27–33; 6:14–22, from *Tanakh: The Holy Scriptures.*

PROVERBS ATTRIBUTED TO SOLOMON

In the preceeding passage, Solomon is said to have been the wisest of all men and author of three thousand proverbs. The Book of Proverbs contains seven distinct collections of sayings, the first four of which are traditionally attributed to Solomon. Compiled during the time of Ezra, Proverbs contains sayings from throughout periods of the united and divided Kingdom, which are in the form of two-line sentences about an aspect of human experience, usually secular. Three literary styles are exhibited in the proverbs: synonymous parallelism, where the second line repeats the content of the first; antithetic parallelism, where good behavior in the first line is contrasted with bad behavior in the second line; and ascending parallelism, where the second line completes the train of thought in the first line. The following is from the second collection within Proverbs—thought to be the oldest part of the book—titled "The Proverbs of Solomon."

1. A gentle response allays wrath; A harsh word provokes anger.
2. The tongue of the wise produces much knowledge, But the mouth of dullards pours out folly.
3. The eyes of the Lord are everywhere, Observing the bad and the good.
4. A healing tongue is a tree of life, But a devious one makes for a broken spirit.
5. A fool spurns the discipline of his father, But one who heeds reproof becomes clever.
6. In the house of the righteous there is much treasure, But in the harvest of the wicked there is trouble.
7. The lips of the wise disseminate knowledge; Not so the minds of dullards.
8. The sacrifice of the wicked is an abomination to the Lord, But the prayer of the upright pleases Him.
9. The way of the wicked is an abomination to the Lord, But he loves him who pursues righteousness.
10. Discipline seems bad to him who forsakes the way; He who spurns reproof will die.
11. Sheol and Abaddon lie exposed to the Lord, How much more the minds of men!
12. The scoffer dislikes being reproved; He will not resort to the wise.
13. A joyful heart makes a cheerful face; A sad heart makes a despondent mood.

14. The mind of a prudent man seeks knowledge; The mouth of the dullard pursues folly.
15. All the days of a poor man are wretched, But contentment is a feast without end.
16. Better a little with fear of the Lord Than great wealth with confusion.
17. Better a meal of vegetables where there is love Than a fattened ox where there is hate.
18. A hot-tempered man provokes a quarrel; A patient man calms strife.
19. The way of a lazy man is like a hedge of thorns, But the path of the upright is paved.
20. A wise son makes his father happy; A fool of a man humiliates his mother.
21. Folly is joy to one devoid of sense; A prudent man walks a straight path.
22. Plans are foiled for want of counsel, But they succeed through many advisers.
23. A ready response is a joy to a man, And how good is a world rightly timed!
24. For an intelligent man the path of life leads upward, In order to avoid Sheol below.
25. The Lord will tear down the house of the proud, But he will establish the homestead of the widow.
26. Evil thoughts are an abomination to the Lord, But pleasant words are pure.
27. He who pursues ill-gotten gain makes trouble for his household; He who spurns gifts will live long.
28. The heart of the righteous man rehearses his answer, But the mouth of the wicked blurts out evil things.
29. The Lord is far from the wicked, But He hears the prayer of the righteous.
30. What brightens the eye gladdens the heart; Good news puts fat on the bones.
31. He whose ear heeds the discipline of life Lodges among the wise.
32. He who spurns discipline hates himself; He who heeds reproof gains understanding.
33. The fear of the Lord is the discipline of wisdom; Humility precedes honor.

Source: Proverbs 15, from *Tanakh: The Holy Scriptures*.

DIVIDED KINGDOM AND EXILE

ELIJAH VERSUS THE PRIESTS OF ASHERAH AND BAAL

After Solomon's reign, Israel divided into northern and southern kingdoms. The explanation given for this in the Deuteronomistic History is Solomon's continual worship of regional deities. Writers of the Tanakh condemn these worship practices and praise the Yahwist prophets and kings who challenge them. Israelite worship of the goddess Asherah is of particular interest. Asherah is the wife of the Canaanite high god, El, and in some popular Israelite religion may have been a consort of Yahweh. Worship rituals of Asherah center on sacred pillars, which in the Deuteronomistic History are strictly forbidden (Deuteronomy 16:21–22). The following story from the Deuteronomistic History dramatically presents a showdown between the prophets of Asherah and Baal on the one hand, and the prophet Elijah on the other hand. Elijah is the lone defender of Yahweh in the northern kingdom at this time.

16. . . . Ahab son of Omri became king over Israel in the thirty-eighth year of King Asa of Judah, and Ahab son of Omri reigned over Israel in Samaria for twenty-two years. Ahab son of Omri did what was displeasing to the Lord, more than all who preceded him. Not content to follow the sins of Jeroboam son of Nebat, he took a wife Jezebel daughter of King Ethball of the Phoenicians, and he went and served Baal and worshipped him. He erected an altar to Baal in the temple of Baal which he built in Samaria. Ahab also made a sacred post. Ahab did more to vex the Lord, the God of Israel, than all the kings of Israel who preceded him.

17. Elijah the Tisbite, an inhabitant of Gilead, said to Ahab, "As the Lord lives, the God of Israel whom I serve, there will be no dew or rain except at my bidding." . . .

18. Much later, in the third year, a word of the Lord came to Elijah: "Go, appear before Ahab; then I will send rain upon the earth." Thereupon Elijah set out to appear before Ahab. . . .

    When Ahab caught sight of Elijah, Ahab said to him, "Is that you, you troubler of Israel?" He retorted, "It is not I who have brought trouble on Israel, but you and your father's House, by forsaking the commandments of the Lord and going after the Baalim. Now summon all Israel to join me at Mount Carmel, together with the four hundred and fifty prophets of Baal and the four hundred prophets of Asherah, who eat at Jezebel's table.

    Ahab sent orders to all the Israelites and gathered the prophets at Mount Carmel. Elijah approached all the people and said, "How long will you keep hopping between two opinions? If the Lord is God, follow Him; and if Baal, follow him!" But the people answered him not a word. Then Elijah said to the people, "I am the only prophet of the Lord left, while the prophets of Baal are four hundred and fifty men. Let two young bulls be given to us. Let them choose one bull, cut it up, and lay it on the wood, but let them not apply fire; I will prepare the other bull, and lay it on the wood, and will not apply fire. You will then invoke your god by name, and I will invoke the Lord by name; and let us agree: the god who responds with fire, that one is God." And all the people answered, "Very good!"

    Elijah said to the prophets of Baal, "Choose one bull and prepare it first, for you are the majority; invoke your god by name, but apply no fire." They took the bull that was given them; they prepared it, and invoked Baal by name from morning until noon, shouting, "O Baal, answer us!" But there was no sound, and none who responded; so they performed a hopping dance about the altar that had been set up. When noon came, Elijah mocked them, saying, "Shout louder! After all, he is a god. But he may be in conversation, he may be detained, or he may be on a journey, or perhaps he is asleep and will wake up." So they shouted louder, and gashed themselves with knives and spears, according to their practice, until the blood streamed over them. When noon passed, they kept raving until the hour of presenting the meal offering. Still there was no sound, and none who responded or heeded.

Then Elijah said to all the people, "Come closer to me"; and all the people came closer to him. He repaired the damaged altar of the Lord. Then Elijah took twelve stones, corresponding to the number of the tribes of the sons of Jacob—to whom the word of the Lord had come: "Israel shall be your name"—and with the stones he built an altar in the name of the Lord. Around the altar he made a trench large enough for two *seahs* of seed. He laid out the wood, and he cut up the bull and laid it on the wood. And he said, "Fill four jars with water and pour it over the burnt offering and the wood." Then he said, "Do it a second time"; and they did it a second time. "Do it a third time," he said; and they did it a third time. The water ran down around the altar, and even the trench was filled with water.

When it was time to present the meal offering, the prophet Elijah came forward and said, "O Lord, God of Abraham, Isaac, and Israel! Let it be known today that You are God in Israel and that I am Your servant, and that I have done all these things at Your bidding. Answer me, O Lord, answer me, that this people may know that You, O Lord, are God; for You have turned their hearts backward."

Then fire from the Lord descended and consumed the burnt offering, the wood, the stones, and the earth; and it licked up the water that was in the trench. When they saw this, all the people flung themselves on their faces and cried out: "The Lord alone is God, The Lord alone is God!"

Source: 1 Kings 16:29–33; 17:1; 18:1–2, 17–40, from *Tanakh: The Holy Scriptures.*

ISAIAH'S WARNING TO JUDAH

In 722 the northern kingdom fell to the Mesopotamian superpower of the time, Assyria. Although the southern kingdom of Judah survived Assyrian encroachment, it was embroiled in foreign political conflicts. The prophet Isaiah was an advisor to two kings of the southern kingdom at the time: Ahaz and his successor Hezekiah. Under the leadership of King Hezekiah, the Kingdom of Judah survived the Assyrian attack and continued for another 150 years. His advice to both kings was the same: do not participate in anti-Assyrian conspiracies, but trust in God for deliverance. The Book of Isaiah is an anthology of prophetic writings from Isaiah's time through the

Babylonian exile. Of the book's 66 chapters, Isaiah's own words are confined to Chapters 1–11 and 28–32. Chapter 1 below expresses Isaiah's indictment against the people of Judah: They have forsaken God and risk being purged. Chapter 6 is Isaiah's call to prophethood.

1. The prophecies of Isaiah son of Amoz, who prophesied concerning Judah and Jerusalem in the reigns of Uzziah, Jotham, Ahaz, and Hezekiah, kings of Judah.

> Hear, O heavens, and give ear, O earth,
> For the Lord has spoken:
> I reared children and brought them up—
> And they have rebelled against Me!
> An ox knows its owner,
> An ass its master's crib:
> Israel does not know,
> My people takes no thought.
>
> Ah, sinful nation!
> People laden with iniquity!
> Brood of evildoers!
> Depraved children!
> They have forsaken the Lord,
> Spurned the Holy One of Israel,
> Turned their backs [on Him].
>
> Why do you seek further beatings,
> That you continue to offend?
> Every head is ailing,
> And every heart is sick.
> From head to foot
> No spot is sound:
> All bruises, and welts,
> And festering sores—
> Not pressed out, not bound up,
> Not softened with oil.
> Your land is a waste,
> Your cities burnt down;
> Before your eyes, the yield of your soil
> Is consumed by strangers—
> A wasteland as overthrown by strangers!
> Fair Zion is left
> Like a booth in a vineyard,
> Like a hut in a cucumber field,
> Like a city beleaguered. Had not the Lord of Hosts
> Left us some survivors,
> We should be like Sodom,
> Another Gomorrah. . . .
>
> "Come, let us reach an understanding,—says the Lord.
> Be your sins like crimson,
> They can turn snow-white;

Be they red as died wool,
They can become like fleece."
If, then, you agree and give heed,
You will eat the good things of the earth;
But if you refuse and disobey,
You will be devoured [by] the sword.
For it was the Lord who spoke.

6. In the year that King Uzziah died, I beheld my Lord seated on a high and lofty throne; and the skirts of His robe filled the Temple. Seraphs stood in attendance on Him. Each of them had six wings: with two he covered his face, with two he covered his legs, and with two he would fly.

And one would call to the other,
"Holy, holy, holy!
The Lord of Hosts!
His presence fills all the earth!"

The doorposts would shake at the sound of the one who called, and the House kept filling with smoke. I cried,

"Woe is me; I am lost!
For I am a man of unclean lips
And I live among a people of unclean lips;
Yet my own eyes have beheld
The King Lord of Hosts."

Then one of the seraphs flew over to me with a live coal, which he had taken from the altar with a pair of tongs. He touched it to my lips and declared,

Now that this has touched your lips,
Your guilt shall depart
And your sin be purged away.

Then I heard the voice of my Lord saying, "Whom shall I send? Who will go for us? And I said, "Here am I; send me." And He said, "Go say to that people:

'Hear, indeed, but do not understand;
See, indeed, but do not grasp'
Dull that people's mind,
Stop its ears,
And seal its eyes—
Lest, seeing with its eyes
And hearing with its ears,
It also grasp with its mind,
And repent and save itself."

I asked, "How long, my Lord?" And He replied:

"Till towns lie waste without inhabitants
And houses without people,

> And the ground lies waste and desolate—
> For the Lord will banish the population—
> And deserted sites are many
> In the midst of the land.

But while a tenth part yet remains in it, it shall repent. It shall be ravaged like the terebinth and the oak, of which stumps are left even when they are felled: its stump shall be a holy seed."

Source: Isaiah 1:1–9, 18–21; 6, from *Tanakh: The Holy Scriptures*.

BABYLONIAN CONQUEST AND EXILE

Around 610 B.C.E. a group of Semites in Babylon, the Chaldeans, overthrew the Assyrians and formed a new Babylonian Empire. At first Judah's king paid tribute to the Empire, but later rebelled, thinking that Egypt would come to his defense if necessary. In retaliation, the Babylonian army marched into Judah, looted the temple and royal treasury, and exiled the royal family and upper-class Israelites to Babylon. The Babylonians appointed Zedekiah as a puppet king but, when pressured by the Egyptians, he too rebelled. In 586 B.C.E., the Babylonian army again marched into Judah, this time destroying Jerusalem and the temple. The following recounts the tragedy of the exile.

24. . . . Jehoiachin was eighteen years old when he became king, and he reigned three months in Jerusalem; his mother's name was Nehushta daughter of Elnathan of Jerusalem. He did what was displeasing to the Lord, just as his father had done. At that time, the troops of King Nebuchadnezzar of Babylon marched against Jerusalem, and the city came under siege. King Nebuchadnezzar of Babylon advanced against the city while his troops were besieging it. Thereupon King Jehoiachin of Judah, along with his mother, and his courtiers, commanders, and officers, surrendered to the king of Babylon. The king of Babylon took him captive in the eighth year of his reign. He carried off from Jerusalem all the treasures of the House of the Lord and the treasures of the royal palace; he stripped off all the golden decorations in the Temple of the Lord—which King Solomon of Israel had made—as the Lord had warned. He exiled all of Jerusalem: all the commanders and all the warriors—ten thousand exiles—as well as all the craftsmen and smiths; only the poorest people in the land were left. He deported Jehoiachin to Babylon; and the king's mother and wives and officers and the notables of the land were brought as exiles from Jerusalem to Babylon. All the able men, to the number of seven thousand—all of them warriors, trained for battle—and a thousand craftsmen and smiths were brought to Babylon as exiles by the king of Babylon. And the king of Babylon appointed Mattaniah, Jehoiachin's uncle, king in his place, changing his name to Zedekiah.

Zedekiah was twenty-one years old when he became king, and he reigned eleven years in Jerusalem; his mother's name was Hamutal daughter of Jeremiah of Libnah. He did what was displeasing to the Lord, just as Jehoiakim had done. Indeed, Jerusalem and Judah were a cause of anger for the Lord, so that He cast them out of His presence.

25. Zedekiah rebelled against the king of Babylon. And in the ninth year of his reign, on the tenth day of the tenth month, Nebuchadnezzar moved against Jerusalem with his whole army. He besieged it; and they built towers against it all around. The city continued in a state of siege until the eleventh year of King Zedekiah. By the ninth day [of the fourth month] the famine had become acute in the city; there was no food left for the common people.

Then [the wall of] the city was breached. All the soldiers [left the city] by night through the gate between the double walls, which is near the king's garden—the Chaldeans were all around the city; and [the king] set out for the Arabah. But the Chaldean troops pursued the king, and they overtook him in the steppes of Jericho as his entire force left him and scattered. They captured the king and brought him before the king of Babylon at Riblah; and they put him on trial. They slaughtered Zedekiah's sons before his eyes; then Zedekiah's eyes were put out. He was chained in bronze fetters and he was brought to Babylon.

On the seventh day of the fifth month—that was the nineteenth year of King Nebuchadnezzar of Babylon—Nebuzaradan, the chief of the guards, an officer of the king of Babylon, came to Jerusalem. He burned the House of the Lord, the king's palace, and all the houses of Jerusalem; he burned down the house of every notable person. The entire Chaldean force that was with the chief of the guard tore down the walls of Jerusalem on every side. The remnant of the people that was left in the city, the defectors who had gone over to the king of Babylon—and the remnant of the population—were taken into exile by Nebuzaradan, the chief of the guards. But some of the poorest in the land were left by the chief of the guards, to be vinedressers and field hands.

The Chaldeans broke up the bronze columns of the House of the Lord, the stands, and the bronze tank that was in the House of the Lord; and they carried the bronze away to Babylon. They also took all the pails, scrapers, snuffers, ladles, and all the other bronze vessels used in the service. The chief of the guards took whatever was of gold and whatever was of silver: firepans and sprinkling bowls. The two columns, the one tank, and the stands that Solomon provided for the House of the Lord—all these objects contained bronze beyond weighing. The one column was eighteen cubits high. It had a bronze capital above it; the height of the capital was three cubits; and there was a meshwork [decorated] with pomegranates about the capital, all made of bronze. And the like was true of the other column with its meshwork.

Source: 2 Kings 24:8–20; 25:1–17, from *Tanakh: The Holy Scriptures.*

REMEMBERING ZION

Captive in Babylon, the psalmist in the following passage reflects nostalgically on the beauty of Zion, referring to the city of Jerusalem, possibly the Temple Mount.

> By the rivers of Babylon,
>   there we sat,
>   sat and wept,
>   as we thought of Zion.
> There on the poplars
>   we hung up our lyres,
>   for our captors asked us there for songs,
>   our tormentors, for amusement,
>   "Sing us one of the songs of Zion."
> How can we sing a song of the Lord
>   on alien soil?
> If I forget you, O Jerusalem,
>   let my right hand wither;
>   let my tongue stick to my palate
>   if I cease to think of you,
>   if I do not keep Jerusalem in memory
>   even at my happiest hour.
> Remember, O Lord, against the Edomites
>   the day of Jerusalem's fall;
>   how they cried, "Strip her, strip her
>   to her very foundations!"
> Fair Babylon, you predator,
>   a blessing on him who repays you in kind
>   what you have inflicted on us;
>   a blessing on him who seizes your babies
>   and dashes them against the rocks!

Source: Psalms 137, from *Tanakh: The Holy Scriptures.*

RETURN FROM EXILE AND RESTORATION

When Persian King Cyrus overthrew the Babylonian Empire in 539 B.C.E., he reversed the policy of exiling foreign captives as practiced by the Babylonians and, earlier, by the Assyrians. With his encouragement, 40,000 exiled Jews returned to their homeland. Cyrus encouraged the rebuilding of Jerusalem's temple and returned to the Jews the temple treasures which had been taken by the Babylonians.

1. In the first year of King Cyrus of Persia, when the word of the Lord spoken by Jeremiah was fulfilled, the Lord roused the spirit of King Cyrus of Persia to issue a proclamation throughout his realm by word of mouth and in writing as follows:

   "Thus said King Cyrus of Persia: The Lord God of Heaven has given me all the kingdoms of the earth and has charged me with building Him a house in Jerusalem, which is in Judah. Any one of you of all His people—may his God be with him, and let him go up to Jerusalem that is in Judah and build the House of the Lord God of Israel, the God that is in Jerusalem; and all who stay behind, wherever he may be living, let the people of his place assist him with silver, gold, goods, and livestock, besides the freewill offering to the House of God that is in Jerusalem."

So the chiefs of the clans of Judah and Benjamin, and the priests and Levites, all whose spirit had been roused by God, got ready to go up to build the House of the Lord that is in Jerusalem. All their neighbors supported them with silver vessels, with gold, with goods, with livestock, and with precious objects, besides what had been given as a freewill offering. King Cyrus of Persia released the vessels of the Lord's house which Nebuchadnezzar had taken away from Jerusalem and had put in the house of his God. The King Cyrus of Persia released through the office of Mithredath the treasurer, who gave an inventory of them to Sheshbazzar the prince of Judah. This is the inventory: 30 gold basins, 1,000 silver basins, 29 knives, 30 gold bowls, 410 silver doubled bowls, 1,000 other vessels, in all, 5,400 gold and silver vessels. Sheshbazzar brought all these back when the exiles came back from Babylon to Jerusalem.

3. When the seventh month arrived—the Israelites being settled in their towns—the entire people assembled as one man in Jerusalem. Then Jeshua son of Jozadak and his brother priests, and Zerubbabel son of Shealtiel and his brothers set to and built the altar of the God of Israel to offer burnt offerings upon it as is written in the Teaching of Moses, the man of God. They set up the Altar on its site because they were in fear of the peoples of the land, and they offered burnt offerings on it to the Lord, burnt offerings each morning and evening. Then they celebrated the festival of Tabernacles as is written, with its daily burnt offerings in the proper quantities, on each day as is prescribed for it, followed by the regular burnt offering and the offerings for the new moons and for all the sacred fixed times of the Lord, and whatever freewill offerings were made to the Lord. From the first day of the seventh month they began to make burnt offerings to the Lord, though the foundation of the Temple of the Lord had not been laid. They paid the hewers and craftsmen with money, and the Sidonians and Tyrians with food, drink, and oil to bring cedarwood from Lebanon by sea to Joppa, in accord with the authorization granted them by King Cyrus of Persia.

In the second year after their arrival at the House of God, at Jerusalem, in the second month, Zerubbabel son of Shealtiel and Jeshua son of Jozadak, and the rest of their brother priests and Levites, and all who had come from the captivity to Jerusalem, as their first step appointed Levites from the age of twenty and upward to supervise the work of the House of the Lord. Jeshua, his sons and brothers,

Kadmiel and his sons, the sons of Judah, together were appointed in charge of those who did the work in the House of God; also the sons of Henadad, their sons and brother Levites.

When the builders had laid the foundation of the Temple of the Lord, priests in their vestments with trumpets, and Levites sons of Asaph with cymbals were stationed to give praise to the Lord, as King David of Israel had ordained. They sang songs extolling and praising the Lord, "For He is good, His steadfast love for Israel is eternal." All the people raised a great shout extolling the Lord because the foundation of the House of the Lord had been laid. Many of the priests and Levites and the chiefs of the clans, the old men who had seen the first house, wept loudly at the sight of the founding of this house. Many others shouted joyously at the top of their voices. The people could not distinguish the shouts of joy from the people's weeping, for the people raised a great shout, the sound of which could be heard from afar.

Source: Ezra 1, 3, from *Tanakh: The Holy Scriptures*.

ESTHER

The Book of Esther is one of two books of the Tanakh focusing on the life of a Jewish heroine (the book of Ruth is the other). Esther is queen to Persian King Ahasuerus (Xerxes I), one of Cyrus's successors, reigning from 486 to 465 B.C.E. Unknown to the King, Esther is a Jew. When her cousin Mordecai refuses to bow to the King for religious reasons, Haman, a member of the court, is incensed and plots to have Mordecai, along with the rest of the Jews in the region, executed. The King sanctions Haman's plan. When Mordecai pleads with Esther to speak to the King on behalf of the Jews, she plans a banquet for the King during which she reveals Haman's plot. Haman is hanged on the very gallows he had prepared for Mordecai. The Jews are granted the right to defend themselves against their anti-Jewish enemies. The story of Esther is the basis for the Jewish feast Purim.

3. Some time afterward, King Ahasuerus promoted Haman son of Hammedatha the Agagite; he advanced him and seated him higher than any of his fellow officials. All the king's courtiers in the palace gate knelt and bowed low to Haman, for such was the king's order concerning him; but Mordecai would not kneel or bow low. Then the king's courtiers who were in the palace gate said to Mordecai, "Why do you disobey the king's order?" When they spoke to him day after day and he would not listen to them, they told Haman, in order to see whether Mordecai's resolve would prevail; for he had explained to them that he was a Jew. When Haman saw that Mordecai would not kneel or bow low to him, Haman was filled with rage. But he

disdained to lay hands on Mordecai alone; having been told who Mordecai's people were, Haman plotted to do away with all the Jews, Mordecai's people, throughout the kingdom of Ahasuerus.

In the first month, that is, the month of Nisan, in the twelfth year of King Ahasuerus, *pur*—which means "the lot"—was cast before Haman concerning every day and every month, [until it fell on] the twelfth month, that is, the month of Adar. Haman then said to King Ahasuerus, "There is a certain people, scattered and dispersed among the other peoples in all the provinces of your realm, whose laws are different from those of any other people and who do not obey the king's laws; and it is not in Your Majesty's interest to tolerate them. If it pleases Your Majesty, let an edict be drawn for their destruction, and I will pay ten thousand talents of silver to the stewards for deposit in the royal treasury." Thereupon the king removed his signet ring from his hand and gave it to Haman son of Hammedatha the Agagite, the foe of the Jews. And the king said, "The money and the people are yours to do with as you see fit.". . .

7. So the king and Haman came to feast with Queen Esther. On the second day, the king again asked Esther at the wine feast, "What is your wish, Queen Esther? It shall be granted you. And what is your request? Even to half the kingdom, it shall be fulfilled." Queen Esther replied: "If Your Majesty will do me the favor, and if it pleases Your Majesty, let my life be granted me as my wish, and my people as my request. For we have been sold, my people and I, to be destroyed, massacred, and exterminated. Had we only been sold as bondmen and bondwomen, I would have kept silent; for the adversary is not worthy of the king's trouble."

Thereupon King Ahasuerus demanded of Queen Esther, "Who is he and where is he who dared to do this?" "The adversary and enemy," replied Esther, "is this evil Haman!" And Haman cringed in terror before the king and the queen. The king, in his fury, left the wine feast for the palace garden, while Haman remained to plead with Queen Esther for his life; for he saw that the king was resolved to destroy him. When the king returned from the palace garden to the banquet room, Haman was lying prostrate on the couch on which Esther reclined. "Does he mean," cried the king, "to ravish the queen in my own palace?" No sooner did these words leave the king's lips than Haman's face was covered. Then Harbonah, one of the eunuchs in attendance on the king, said, "What is more, a stake is standing at Haman's house, fifty cubits high, which Haman made for Mordecai— the man whose words saved the king." "Impale him on it!" the king ordered. So they impaled Haman on the stake which he had put up for Mordecai, and the king's fury abated.

Source: Esther 3:7–11; 7, from *Tanakh: The Holy Scriptures.*

EZRA AND THE LAW

The concluding events of the Tanakh *focus on the activities of Ezra and Nehemiah, found in the books which bear their names. Ezra was a Babylonian-born Jewish priest devoted to the Law of Moses. In 458 B.C.E., he petitioned Artaxerxes, the reigning King of the Persian Empire, to lead another migration of Jews back to their homeland. Artaxerxes agreed and empowered him to make political and religious reforms as Ezra saw fit. On arrival, he was distressed to see that the returning Jews before him had intermarried, and he proclaimed that 114 priests and laymen should have their marriages annulled. Thirteen years after Ezra's return, Nehemiah, a Jewish cupbearer to the Persian King, was granted permission by the King to rebuild the walls of Jerusalem, still in ruins from the Babylonian invasion. A gifted administrator, Nehemiah completed the project in 52 days, even in the face of opposition from neighboring provinces. Shortly after completion of the walls, the Jews celebrated a series of feasts, during which Ezra publicly read and interpreted the scrolls of Moses. The following recounts Ezra's reading of the scrolls.*

When the seventh month arrived—the Israelites being [settled] in their towns—the entire people assembled as one man in the square before the Water Gate, and they asked Ezra the scribe to bring the scroll of the Teaching of Moses with which the Lord had charged Israel. On the first day of the seventh month, Ezra the priest brought the Teaching before the congregation, men and women and all who could listen with understanding. He read from it, facing the square before the Water Gate, from the first light until midday, to the men and the women and those who could understand; the ears of all the people were given to the scroll of the Teaching.

Ezra the scribe stood upon a wooden tower made for the purpose, and beside him stood Mattithaih, Shema, Anaiah, Uriah, Hilkiah, and Maaseiah at his right, and at his left Pedaiah, Mishael, Malchijah, Hashum, Hashbaddanah, Zechariah, and Meshullam. Ezra opened the scroll in the sight of all the people, for he was above all the people; as he opened it, all the people stood up. Ezra blessed the Lord, the great God, and all the people answered, "Amen, Amen," with hands upraised. Then they bowed their heads and prostrated themselves before the Lord with their faces to the ground. Jeshua, Bani, Sherebiah, Jamin, Akkub, Shabbethai, Hodiah, Maaseiah, Kelita, Azariah, Jozabad, Hanan, Pelaiah, and the Levites explained the Teaching to the People, while the people stood in their places. They read from the scroll of the Teaching of God, translating it and giving the sense; so they understood the reading.

Nehemiah the Tirshatha, Ezra the priest and scribe, and the Levites who were explaining to the people said to all the people, "This day is holy to the Lord your God: you must not mourn or weep," for all the people were weeping as they listened to the words of the Teaching. He further said to them, "Go, eat choice foods and drink sweet drinks and send portions to whoever has nothing prepared, for the day is holy to our Lord. Do not be sad, for your rejoicing in the Lord is the source of your strength." The Levites were quieting the people, saying, "Hush, for the day is holy; do not be sad." Then all the people went to eat and drink and send portions and make great merriment, for they understood the things they were told.

On the second day, the heads of the clans of all the people and the priests and Levites gathered to Ezra the scribe to study the words of the Teaching. They found written in the Teaching that the Lord had commanded Moses that the Israelites must dwell in booths during the festival of the seventh month, and that they must announce and proclaim throughout all their towns and Jerusalem as follows: "Go out to the mountains and bring leafy branches of olive trees, pine trees, myrtles, palms and [other] leafy trees to make booths, as it is written." So the people went out and brought them, and made themselves booths on their roofs, in their courtyards, in the courtyards of the House of God, in the square of the Water Gate and in the square of the Ephraim Gate. The whole community that returned from the captivity made booths and dwelt in the booths— the Israelites had not done so from the days of Joshua son of Nun to that day—and there was very great rejoicing. He read from the scroll of the Teaching of God each day, from the first to the last day. They celebrated the festival seven days, and there was a solemn gathering on the eighth, as prescribed.

Source: Nehemiah 8, from *Tanakh: The Holy Scriptures.*

POST-EXILIC WRITINGS

GREEK RULE AND THE COMING OF THE MESSIAH

Although the final events reported in the Tanakh *take place around 430* B.C.E., *the religious drama of the Jewish people continues in post-exilic writings, considered scriptural in many Jewish circles at the time. The extreme Hellenizing policies of Selucid King Antiochus Epiphanes created a crisis for traditional Jews, intensified further by the advocacy of these policies by Jewish High Priests themselves. Loyal Jewish writers sought a divine explanation for this crisis, which threatened their very existence. They wrote apocalyptic texts reporting visionlike revelations about a Messianic deliverer, a cataclysmic end to the empires of their oppressors, topped by final divine judgment. The Book of Daniel in the* Tanakh *is thought to be an apocalyptic work from this period. The following is from the First Book of Enoch, one of the most well-known apocalyptic texts of the Pseudepigrapha. The work, written by several authors between 200* B.C.E. *and 100* C.E., *reflects traditional apocalyptic themes.*

46. *The Son of Man.* There I saw one who was the Ancient of Days, and His head was white like wool. With Him was another being who had the appearance of a man; and his face was full of graciousness, like one of

the holy angels. I asked the angel who went with me and showed me all the hidden things, concerning that Son of Man, who he was, from where he was, and why he went with the Ancient of Days. He answered and said to me: "This is the Son of Man who has righteousness, with whom dwells righteousness, and who reveals all the treasures of that which is hidden because the Lord of Spirits has chosen him, and whose lot has the preeminence before the Lord of Spirits in uprightness forever. This Son of Man whom you have seen will raise up the kings and the mighty from their seats, and the strong from their thrones. He will loosen the reins of the strong, and break the teeth of the sinners. He will put down the kings from their thrones and kingdoms because they do not extol and praise Him, nor humbly acknowledge from what source the kingdom was bestowed upon them. He will put down the countenance of the strong, and will fill them with shame. Darkness will be their dwelling, and worms will be their bed. They will have no hope of rising from their beds, because they do not extol the name of the Lord of Spirits, raise their hands against the Most High, and tread upon the earth and dwell upon it. All their deeds manifest unrighteousness and their power rests upon their riches. Their faith is in the gods that they have made with their hands. They deny the name of the Lord of Spirits, and they persecute the houses of His congregations and the faithful who hang upon the name of the Lord of Spirits."

48. In that place I saw the fountain of righteousness which was inexhaustible. Around it were many fountains of wisdom: all the thirsty drank of them and were filled with wisdom. Their dwellings were with the righteous and holy and elect. At that hour that Son of Man was named in the presence of the Lord of Spirits, and his name before the Ancient of Days. Even before the sun and the signs were created, before the stars of the heaven were made, his name was named before the Lord of Spirits. He will be a staff to the righteous whereon to stay themselves and not fall. He will be the light of the Gentiles, and the hope of those who are troubled of heart. All who dwell on earth will fall down and worship before him, and will praise and bless and celebrate with song the Lord of Spirits. For this reason he has been chosen and hidden before Him, before the creation of the world and for evermore. And the wisdom of the Lord of Spirits has revealed him to the holy and righteous. For he has preserved the lot of the righteous, because they have hated and despised this world of unrighteousness, and have hated all its works and ways in the name of the Lord of Spirits. For in his name they are saved, and according to his good pleasure it has been in regard to their life. In these days will the kings of the earth become shamed because of the works of their hands—the strong who possess the land. For on the day of their anguish and affliction they will not be able to save themselves. I will

give them over into the hands of My elect. As straw in the fire, so will they burn before the face of the holy. As lead in the water, so will they sink before the face of the righteous, and no trace of them will any more be found. On the day of their affliction there will be rest on the earth, and before them they will fall and not rise again. There will be no one to take them with his hands and raise them. For they have denied the Lord of Spirits and His Messiah. The name of the Lord of Spirits be blessed.

51. *Resurrection of the Dead.* In those days the earth will also give back that which has been entrusted to it. Sheol also will give back that which it has received, and hell will give back that which it owes. In those days the Elect One will arise, and he will choose the righteous and holy from among them [i.e., the risen dead]. The day has drawn near that they should be saved. The Elect One will in those days sit on My throne, and his mouth will pour forth all the secrets of wisdom and counsel. For the Lord of Spirits has given them to him and has glorified him. In those days the mountains will leap like rams, the hills will also skip like lambs satisfied with milk, and the faces of all the angels in heaven will be lighted up with joy. The earth will rejoice, the righteous will dwell upon it, and the elect will walk thereon.

54. *Judgment.* I looked and turned to another part of the earth, and saw there a deep valley with burning fire. They brought the kings and the mighty, and began to throw them into this deep valley. There my eyes saw how they made instruments, iron chains of immeasurable weight. I asked the angel of peace who went with me, saying: "For whom are these chains being prepared?" He said to me: "These are being prepared for the hosts of [the demon] Azazel, so that they may take them and throw them into the abyss of complete condemnation, and they will cover their jaws with rough stones as the Lord of Spirits commanded. Michael, Gabriel, Raphael, and Phanuel will take hold of them on that great day, and throw them on that day into the burning furnace. The Lord of Spirits may then take vengeance on them for their unrighteousness in becoming subject to Satan and leading astray those who dwell on the earth." In those days will punishment come from the Lord of Spirits. He will open all the chambers of water that are above the heavens, and of the fountains which are beneath the earth. All the waters will be joined with the waters: that which is above the heavens is the masculine, and the water that is beneath the earth is the feminine. They will destroy all who dwell on the earth and those who dwell under the ends of the heaven. When they have recognized their unrighteousness which they have created on the earth, then by these they will die.

Source: First Enoch, 46, 48, 51, 54, adapted from R. H. Charles, *The Apocrypha and Pseudepigrapha of the Old Testament*, Oxford: Clarendon Press, 1913.

MACCABEAN REVOLT

The Book of Maccabees chronicles the clash between Hellenistic and Jewish culture, and culminates in the Maccabean revolt and rise to power. The Book of Maccabees, written about 100 B.C.E. and included in the Septuagint, is the primary source of information for this period of Jewish history. The following describes the Hellenizing policies of Antiochus Epiphanes and the initial revolt launched by Mattathias.

1. After Alexander the Macedonian, Philip's son, who came from the land of Kittim, had defeated Darius, king of the Persians and Medes, he became king in his place, having first ruled in Greece. He fought many campaigns, captured fortresses, and put kings to death. He advanced to the ends of the earth, gathering plunder from many nations; the earth fell silent before him, and his heart became proud and arrogant. He collected a very strong army and conquered provinces, nations, and rulers, and they became his tributaries. But after all this he took to his bed, realizing that he was going to die. He therefore summoned his officers, the nobles, who had been brought up with him from his youth, to divide his kingdom among them while he was still alive. Alexander had reigned twelve years when he died.

    So his officers took over his kingdom, each in his own territory, and after his death they all put on royal crowns, and so did their sons after them for many years, causing much distress over the earth.

    There sprang from these a sinful offshoot, Antiochus Epiphanes, son of King Antiochus, once a hostage at Rome. He became king in the year one hundred and thirty-seven of the kingdom of the Greeks.

    In those days there appeared in Israel men who were breakers of the law, and they seduced many people, saying: "Let us go and make an alliance with the Gentiles all around us; since we separated from them, many evils have come upon us." The proposal was agreeable; some from among the people promptly went to the king, and he authorized them to introduce the way of living of the Gentiles. Thereupon they built a gymnasium in Jerusalem according to the Gentile custom. They covered over the mark of their circumcision and abandoned the holy covenant; they allied themselves with the Gentiles and sold themselves to wrongdoing.

    When his kingdom seemed secure, Antiochus proposed to become king of Egypt, so as to rule over both kingdoms. He invaded Egypt with a strong force, with chariots and elephants, and with a large fleet, to make war on Ptolemy, king of Egypt. Ptolemy was frightened at his presence and fled, leaving many casualties. The fortified cities in the land of Egypt were captured, and Antiochus plundered the land of Egypt.

    After Antiochus had defeated Egypt in the year one hundred and forty-three, he returned and went up to Israel and to Jerusalem with a strong force. He insolently invaded the sanctuary and took away the golden altar, the lampstand for the light with all its fixtures, the offering table, the cups and the bowls, the golden censers, the curtain, the crowns, and the golden ornament on the facade of the temple. He stripped off everything, and took away the gold and silver and the precious vessels; he also took all the hidden treasures he could find. Taking all this, he went back to his own country, after he had spoken with great arrogance and shed much blood. . . .

Two years later, the king sent the Mysian commander to the cities of Judah, and he came to Jerusalem with a strong force. He spoke to them deceitfully in peaceful terms, and won their trust. Then he attacked the city suddenly, in a great onslaught, and destroyed many of the people in Israel. He plundered the city and set fire to it, demolished its houses and its surrounding walls, took captive the women and children, and seized the cattle. Then they built up the City of David with a high, massive wall and strong towers, and it became their citadel. There they installed a sinful race, perverse men, who fortified themselves inside it, storing up weapons and provisions, and depositing there the plunder they had collected from Jerusalem. And they became a great threat. . . .

Then the king wrote to his whole kingdom that all should be one people, each abandoning his particular customs. All the Gentiles conformed to the command of the king, and many Israelites were in favor of his religion; they sacrificed to idols and profaned the Sabbath.

The king sent messengers with letters to Jerusalem and to the cities of Judah, ordering them to follow customs foreign to their land: to prohibit holocausts, sacrifices, and libations in the sanctuary, to profane the sabbaths and feast days, to desecrate the sanctuary and the sacred ministers, to build pagan altars and temples and shrines, to sacrifice swine and unclean animals, to leave their sons uncircumcised, and to let themselves be defiled with every kind of impurity and abomination, so that they might forget the law and change all their observances. Whoever refused to act according to the command of the king should be put to death.

Such were the orders he published throughout his kingdom. He appointed inspectors over all the people, and he ordered the cities of Judah to offer sacrifices, each city in turn. Many of the people, those who abandoned the law, joined them and committed evil in the land. Israel was driven into hiding, wherever places of refuge could be found.

On the fifteenth day of the month Chislev, in the year one hundred and forty-five, the king erected the horrible abomination upon the altar of holocausts, and in the surrounding cities of Judah they built pagan altars. They also burnt incense at the doors of houses and in the streets. Any scrolls of the law which they found they tore up and burnt. Whoever was found with a scroll of the covenant, and whoever observed the law, was condemned to death by royal decree.

So they used their power against Israel, against those who were caught, each month, in the cities. On the twenty-fifth day of each month they sacrificed on the altar erected over the altar of holocausts. Women who had had their children circumcised were put to death, in keeping with the decree, with the babies hung from their necks; their families also and those who had circumcised them were killed. But many in Israel were determined and resolved in their hearts not to eat anything unclean; they preferred to die rather than to be defiled with unclean food or to profane the holy covenant; and they did die. Terrible affliction was upon Israel.

2. In those days Mattathias, son of John, son of Simeon, a priest of the family of Joarib, left Jerusalem and settled in Modein. He had five sons: John, who was called Gaddi; Simon, who was called Thassi; Judas, who was called Maccabeus; Eleazar, who was called Avaran; and Jonathan, who was called Apphus. When he saw the sacrileges that were being committed in Judah and in Jerusalem, he said: "Woe is me! Why was I born to see the ruin of my people and the ruin of the holy city, and to sit idle while it is given into the hands of enemies, and the sanctuary into the hands of strangers? . . ."

Then Mattathias and his sons tore their garments, put on sackcloth, and mourned bitterly.

The officers of the king in charge of enforcing the apostasy came to the city of Modein to organize the sacrifices. Many of Israel joined them, but Mattathias and his sons gathered in a group apart. Then the officers of the king addressed Mattathias: "You are a leader, an honorable and great man in this city, supported by sons and kinsmen. Come now, be the first to obey the king's command, as all the Gentiles and the men of Judah and those who are left in Jerusalem have done. Then you and your sons shall be numbered among the King's Friends, and shall be enriched with silver and gold and many gifts." But Mattathias answered in a loud voice: "Although all the Gentiles in the king's realm obey him, so that each forsakes the religion of his fathers and consents to the king's orders, yet I and my sons and my kinsmen will keep to the covenant of our fathers. God forbid that we should forsake the law and the commandments. We will not obey the words of the king nor depart from our religion in the slightest degree."

As he finished saying these words, a certain Jew came forward in the sight of all to offer sacrifice on the altar in Modein according to the king's order. When Mattathias saw him, he was filled with zeal; his heart was moved and his just fury was aroused; he sprang forward and killed him upon the altar. At the same time, he also killed the messenger of the king who was forcing them to sacrifice, and he tore down the altar. Thus he showed his zeal for the law, just as Phinehas did with Zimri, son of Salu.

Then Mattathias went through the city shouting, "Let everyone who is zealous for the law and who stands by the covenant follow after me!" Thereupon he fled to the mountains with his sons, leaving behind in the city all their possessions.

Source: First Maccabees 1:1–24, 25–36, 41–64; 2:1–7, 12–28, from *The Revised English Bible* (Oxford and Cambridge University Presses, 1989), pp. 155–157.

QUMRAN *COMMUNITY RULE*

Isolating themselves from despotic foreign rulers and politically driven religious leaders, the desert community of Qumran believed it was preparing for a final battle between good and evil. The following, from the Qumran's Community Rule, *describes our dual human nature as consisting of a spirit of truth and a spirit of error, the sources of proper and improper conduct, respectively. Reminiscent of Zoroastrianism, God has "established the two spirits in equal measure until the last period." Followers of truth, the Sons of Light, will ultimately wage a victorious war over followers of error, the Sons of Darkness.*

The Master shall instruct all the sons of light and shall teach them the nature of all the children of men according to the kind of spirit which they possess, the signs identifying their works during their lifetime, their visitation for chastisement, and the time of their reward.

From the God of knowledge comes all that is and shall be. Before ever they existed He established their whole design, and when, as ordained for them, they come into being, it is in accord with His glorious design that they accomplish their task without change. The laws of all things are in His hand and He provides them with all their needs.

He has created man to govern the world, and has appointed for him two spirits in which to walk until the time of His visitation: the spirits of truth and falsehood. Those born of truth spring from a fountain of light, but those born of falsehood spring from a source of darkness. All the children of righteousness are ruled by the Prince of Light and walk in the ways of light, but all the children of falsehood are ruled by the Angel of Darkness and walk in the ways of darkness.

The Angel of Darkness leads all the children of righteousness astray, and until his end, all their sin, iniquities, wickedness, and all their unlawful deeds are caused by his dominion in accordance with the mysteries of God. Every one of their chastisements, and every one of the seasons of their distress, shall be brought about by the rule of his persecution; for all his allotted spirits seek the overthrow of the sons of light.

But the God of Israel and His Angel of Truth will succor all the sons of light. For it is He who created the spirits of Light and Darkness and founded every action upon them and established every deed [upon] their [ways]. And He loves the one everlastingly and delights in its works for ever; but the counsel of the other He loathes and for ever hates its ways.

These are their ways in the world for the enlightenment of the heart of man, and that all the paths of true righteousness may be made straight before him, and that the fear of the laws of God may be instilled in his heart: a spirit of humility, patience, abundant charity, unending goodness, understanding, and intelligence; (a spirit of) mighty wisdom which trusts in all the deeds of God and leans on His great lovingkindness; a spirit of discernment in every purpose, of zeal for just laws, of holy intent with steadfastness of heart, of great charity towards all the sons of truth, of admirable purity which detests all unclean idols, of humble conduct sprung from an understanding of all things, and of faithful concealment of the mysteries of truth. These are the counsels of the spirit to the sons of truth in this world.

And as for the visitation of all who walk in this spirit, it shall be healing, great peace in a long life, and fruitfulness, together with every everlasting blessing and eternal joy in life without end, a crown of glory and a garment of majesty in unending light.

But the ways of the spirit of falsehood are these: greed, and slackness in the search for righteousness, wickedness and lies, haughtiness and pride, falseness and deceit, cruelty and abundant evil, ill-temper and much folly and brazen insolence, abominable deeds (committed) in a spirit of lust, and ways of lewdness in the service of uncleanness, a blaspheming tongue, blindness of eye and dullness of ear, stiffness of neck and heaviness of heart, so that man walks in all the ways of darkness and guile.

And the visitation of all who walk in the spirit shall be a multitude of plagues by the hand of all the destroying angels, everlasting damnation by the avenging wrath of the fury of God, eternal torment and endless disgrace together with shameful extinction in the fire of the dark regions. The times of all their generations shall be spent in sorrowful mourning and in bitter misery and in calamities of darkness until they are destroyed without remnant or survivor.

The nature of all the children of the men is ruled by these (two spirits), and during their life all the hosts of men have a portion of their divisions and walk in (both) their ways. And the whole whether each man's portion in their two divisions is great or small. For God has established the spirits in equal measure until the final age, and has set everlasting hatred between their divisions. Truth abhors the works of falsehood, and falsehood hates all the ways of truth. And their struggle is fierce in all their arguments for they do not walk together.

But in the mysteries of His understanding, and in His glorious wisdom, God has ordained an end for falsehood, and at the time of the visitation he will destroy it for ever. Then truth, which has wallowed in the ways of wickedness during the dominion of falsehood until the appointed time of judgment, shall arise in the world for ever. God will then purify every deed of man with his truth; He will refine for Himself the human frame by rooting out all spirit of falsehood from the bounds of his flesh. He will cleanse him of all wicked deeds with the spirit of holiness; like purifying waters He will shed upon him the spirit of truth (to cleanse him) of all abomination and falsehood. And he shall be plunged into the spirit of purification that he may instruct the upright in the knowledge of the Most High and teach the wisdom of the sons of heaven to the perfect of way. For God has chosen them for an everlasting Covenant and all the glory of Adam shall be theirs. There shall be no more lies and all the works of falsehood shall be put to shame.

Until now the spirits of truth and falsehood struggle in the hearts of men and they walk in both wisdom and folly. According to his portion of truth so does a man hate falsehood, and according to his inheritance in the realm of falsehood so is he wicked and so hates truth. For God has established the two spirits in equal measure until the determined end, and until the Renewal, and He knows the reward of their deeds from all eternity. He has allotted them to the children of men that they may know good [and evil, and] that the destiny of all the living may be according to the spirit within [them at the time] of the visitation.

Source: "The Community Rule," Cave 1 Copy, Column 3:13–4:26, from *The Dead Sea Scrolls in English*, 3rd ed., tr. G. Vermes (New York: Penguin Books, 1987), pp. 64–67.

RABBINIC WRITINGS

WISDOM OF THE FATHERS

The best known section of the Mishnah *is* Abot (*literally fathers*), *also called Wisdom of the Fathers. This section was considered so important that medieval copies of the Talmud have* Abot *as the conclusion of each of its six key divisions. The typical style of the* Mishnah *is a give-and-take legal debate between the* Tannaim. Abot *is different in that it is a collection of proverbs by the* Tannaim *that are not debated. The first two divisions of* Abot, *presented here, begin by listing the transmitters of the oral law from Moses to the* Tannaim *themselves.*

1. Moses received the Torah at Sinai. He conveyed it to Joshua; Joshua to the elders; the elders to the prophets; and the prophets transmitted it to the men of the Great Assembly. The latter emphasized three principles: Be deliberate in judgment; raise up many disciples; and make a fence to safeguard the Torah.
2. Simeon the Just was of the last survivors of the Great Assembly. He used to say: The world rests on three foundations: the Torah; the divine service; and the practices of lovingkindness between man and man.
3. Antigonus of Soho received the tradition from him. He was accustomed to say: Be not like servants who serve their master because of the expected reward, but be like those who serve a master without expecting a reward; and let the fear of God be upon you.
4. Yose ben Yoezer of Zeredah and Yose ben Yohanan of Jerusalem received the tradition from them. Yose ben Yoezer of Zeredah said:

Let your house be a gathering place for wise men; sit attentively at their feet, and drink of their words of wisdom with eagerness.

5. Yose ben Yohanan of Jerusalem said: Let your home be a place of hospitality to strangers; and make the poor welcome in your household; and do not indulge in gossip with women. This applies even with one's own wife, and surely so with another man's wife. The sages generalized from this: He who engages in profuse gossiping with women causes evil for himself and neglects the study of the Torah, and he will bring upon himself retributions in the hereafter.

6. Joshua ben Perahya and Nittai the Arbelite received the tradition from them. Joshua ben Perahya said: Get yourself a teacher; and acquire for yourself a companion; and judge all people favorably.

7. Nittai the Arbelite said: Avoid an evil neighbor; do not associate with the wicked; and do not surrender your faith in divine retribution.

8. Judah ben Tabbai and Simeon ben Shatah received the traditions from them. Judah ben Tabbai said: Let not the judge play the part of the counselor; when they leave after submitting to the court's decree, regard them both as guiltless.

9. Simeon ben Shatah said: Search the witnesses thoroughly and be cautious with your own words lest you give them an opening to false testimony.

10. Shemaya and Abtalyon received the traditions from them. Shemaya said: love work; hate domineering over others; and do not seek the intimacy of public officials.

11. Abtalyon said: Sages, be precise in your teachings. You may suffer exile to a place where heresy is rampant, and your inexact language may lead your disciples astray, and they will lose their faith, thus leading to a desecration of the divine name.

12. Hillel and Shammai received the tradition from them. Hillel said: Be of the disciples of Aaron. Love peace and pursue peace; love your fellow creatures and bring them near to the Torah.

13. He also said: He who strives to exalt his name will in the end destroy his name; he who does not increase his knowledge decreases it; he who does not study has undermined his right to life; and he who makes unworthy use of the crown of the Torah will perish.

14. He also said: If I am not for myself who will be? But if I am for myself only, what am I? And if not now, when?

15. Shammai said: Set a fixed time for the study of the Torah; say little and do much; and greet every person with a cheerful countenance.

16. Rabban Gamaliel said: Provide yourself with a teacher, and extricate yourself from doubt; and do not habitually contribute your tithes by rough estimates.

17. Simeon his son said: All my life I was raised among scholars and I found that no virtue becomes a man more than silence; what is more essential is not study but practice; and in the wake of many words is sin.

18. Rabban Simeon ben Gamaliel said: The world rests on three foundations: truth, justice, and peace. As it is written (Zech 8:16): "You shall administer truth, justice and peace within your gates."

Source: Mishnah, Abot, ch. 1, from *The Talmud,* tr. Ben Zion Bokser (New York: Paulist Press, 1989), pp. 219–221.

RABBINIC AUTHORITY

The chief theological paradox of the Talmud *is how collected opinions of early Rabbis can count as divine law. Although Judaism traces its oral law back to Moses, the* Mishnah *and* Talmud *are, quite obviously, only collected sayings of the* Tannaim *and* Amoraim. *Early Rabbis themselves were aware of this paradox and provide an answer. In this selection from* Baba Mezia (*one of the most famous sections of the* Talmud), *they explain that the majority position held by the carriers of oral law* becomes *the law. At that time, the sages of the* Talmud *were the carriers.*

MISHNA 8: As cheating is prohibited in buying or selling, so it is in words. (How so?) One must not ask the price of a thing when he does not intend to buy it. To a person who has repented one must not say, Remember your former acts. To a descendant from proselytes one must not say, Remember the acts of your parents. As it is written "And a stranger you shall not vex, nor shall you oppress him" (Exodus 22:20).

GEMARA: We studied in the Mishnah (Eduyot 7:7) that if a pottery stove was cut into tiles, and cemented over with sand placed between the tiles, R. Eliezer declared it unsusceptible to ritual uncleanliness, while the other Sages declared it susceptible. This was the Akhnai Stove.

Why was it called Akhnai? Said R. Judah in the name of Samuel. They surrounded it with arguments as a snake winds its body around an object, and declared it unclean. It has been taught: On that day R. Eliezer marshaled every conceivable argument, but they did not accept them. Then he said: If the law is according to my views, let this carob tree prove it. Thereupon the carob tree was thrust to a distance of a hundred cubits from its place, and some say four hundred. They replied to him: We adduce no evidence from a carob tree. Again he said to them: If the law is in accordance with my views, let the stream of water prove it, and at once the stream of water flowed in the opposite direction. But they said: We adduce no evidence from a stream of water. Again he said to them: If the law agrees with my views, let the walls of the academy prove it, and the walls of the academy began to bend and were about to fall. R. Joshua rebuked them, saying: If scholars argue on a point of law, what business is it of yours? The walls did not fall out of respect for R. Joshua, but they did not become straight again out of respect for R. Eliezer.

Thereupon he said: If the law is in accordance with my views, let them prove it from heaven. A heavenly voice came forth, saying: What have you against R. Eliezer? The law is as he propounds it in all instances.

R. Joshua then stood up and quoted: "It is not in the heavens" (Dt 30:12). What did he mean by quoting: "It is not in the heavens"? Said R. Jeremiah: That the Torah has already been given at Sinai, and we pay no attention to heavenly voices, for You have written at Sinai in the Torah: "Incline after the majority" (Ex 23:2).

R. Nathan met the prophet Elijah and he asked him: What did the Holy One, praised be He, do at that time? He replied: He laughed, and He said: My children have won over me, my chlordane have won over me!

Source: Talmud, Baba Mezia 59a–59b, from *The Talmud,* tr. Ben Zion Bokser (New York: Paulist Press, 1989), pp. 184–185.

RESURRECTION OF THE DEAD

The notion of resurrection of the dead is not readily present in the Tanakh. The book of Job, for example, poetically pronounces against it: "As a cloud breaks up and disperses, so no one who goes down to Sheol ever comes back." The idea took hold in post-exilic writings, and by the time of the Rabbinic period, it had become an important tenet of Judaism. In the selection below from the Talmud, several Rabbis debate the issue surrounding the resurrected.

MISHNA I.: All Israel has a share in the world to come. As it reads: "And thy people—they will all be righteous, for ever will they possess the land, the sprout of my planting, the work of my hands, that I may glorify myself" (Isaiah 9:21). The following have no share in the world to come: He who says that there is no allusion in the Torah concerning resurrection, and he who says that the Torah was not given by Heaven. . . .

GEMARA: Is he who does not believe that the resurrection is hinted at in the Torah such a criminal that he loses his share in the world to come? It was taught: He denies resurrection therefore he will not have a share in it, as punishment corresponds to the deed; for all retributions of the Holy One are in correspondence with man's doing. . . .

Queen Cleopatra questioned Rabbi Mair thus: I am aware that the dead will be restored. As it reads: "And men will blossom out of the city like herbs of the earth" (Psalms 72:16). My question, however, is this: When they will be restored, will they be naked or dressed? And he answered: This may be drawn by an *a fortiori* conclusion from wheat. A grain of wheat which is buried naked comes out dressed in so many garments: the upright, who are buried in their dress, so much the more will they come out dressed in many garments. . . .

Cæsar questioned Rabbon Gamaliel: You say that the dead will be restored. Does not the corpse become dust? How, then, can dust be restored? And the daughter of Cæsar said to Rabbi Gamaliel: Leave the question to me and I myself will answer it. And she said to her father: If there were two potters in our city, of whom one should make a pot from water and the other from clay, to which of them would you give preference? And he said:

Certainly to him who creates from water; for if he is able to create from water, he is undoubtedly able to create from clay. And she said: This is an answer to your question.

The school of Rabbi Ismael taught: One may learn it from glass-wares, which are made by human beings, and if they break there is a remedy for them, as they can be renewed: human beings, who are created by the spirit of the Lord, so much the more will they be restored. . . .

Antoninus said to Rabbi: The body and the soul of a human may free themselves on the day of judgment by Heaven. How so? The body may say: The soul has sinned; for since she has departed I lie in the grave like a stone. And the soul may say: The body has sinned; for since I am separated from it, I fly in the air like a bird. And he answered: I will give you a parable to which this is similar: A human king, who had an excellent garden which contained very fine figs, appointed two watchmen for it— one of whom was blind, and the other had no feet. He who was without feet said to the one who was blind: I see in the garden fine figs. Take me on your shoulders, and I shall get them, and we shall consume them. He did so, and while on his shoulders he took them off, and both consumed them. And when the owner of the garden came and did not find the figs, and questioned them what became of them, the blind one answered: Have I, then, eyes to see them, that you should suspect my taking them? And the lame one answered: Have I, then, feet to go there? The owner then put the lame one on the shoulders of the one who was blind, and punished them together. So also the Holy One puts the soul in the body and punishes them together. As it reads: "He will call to the heavens above, and to the earth beneath, to judge his people" (Psalms 1:4). "To the heavens above" means the soul, and, "to the earth beneath" means the body.

Source: Sanhedrin 11, from *New Edition of the Babylonian Talmud,* Boston, The Talmud Society, 1918.

COMING OF THE MESSIAH

During the Babylonian exile, the Jews lost hope in the ability of any present leader to return Israel to its former glory and so they placed their hopes in a future Messiah, or anointed one. The notion gained momentum and complexity during post-exilic times, and by the Rabbinic period the coming of the Messiah was linked with the culmination of human history and the establishment of God's kingdom on earth. In the following selections from the Talmud, several Rabbis debate about the events leading up to the Messiah's arrival.

The rabbis taught: In this Sabbatic period in which the son of David will appear in the first year there will be fulfilled what is written: "And I caused it to rain upon one city, and upon another city I caused it not to rain" (Amos 4:7). In the second year, arrows of famine will be sent. In the third, a great famine, from which men, women, and children, pious men and men of good deeds will die, and the Torah will be forgotten by their scholars. In the fourth there will be abundance, and not abundance. In the fifth there will be great abundance, and the people will eat, drink, and enjoy themselves, and the Torah will return to her scholars. In the sixth, voices will be heard saying that the Messiah is near. In the seventh, war will be, and at the end of the seventh, the son of David will come. Said Rabbi Joseph: Were there not many Sabbatical periods which were like this, but still he did not come? Said Abayi: Were then the above-mentioned voices heard in the sixth? And was there in the seventh war? And secondly, has it then happened in the same order as said above? . . .

Rabbi Jehudah said: The generation in which the son of David will come, the houses of assembly will be converted into houses of prostitution. Galilee will be destroyed. The place called Gablan will be astonished. Men of the borders of Palestine will travel from one city to another, but will find no favor. The wisdom of the scribes will be corrupted. Men fearing sin will be hated. The leaders of that generation will have the nature of dogs. . . .

Rabbi Nehuraia taught: The generation in which the son of David will come, young men will make pale the faces of the old, old men will rise before youth, a daughter will rebel against her mother, a daughter-in-law against her mother-in-law, the leaders of the generation will have the nature of dogs, and a son will not be ashamed when his father reproaches him.

Rabbi Nehemiah said: The generation in which the son of David will come, insolence will increase, an evil man will be honored, respect will be missed, the vine will give forth its fruit abundantly; wine, however, will be dear, and all the governments will be turned over to heretics (will embrace the religion of the heretics), and no preaching will avail. And this is as to Rabbi Itz'hak, who said that the son of David will not come unless all governments will be turned over to heretics. Where is to be found a hint to this in the Scripture? (Leviticus 13:13): "It is all turned white, he is clean."

Source: Sanhedrin 11, from *New Edition of the Babylonian Talmud.*

UNITY OF THE TEN COMMANDMENTS

In addition to debates on fine points of law and theology, Rabbis and other Jewish writers for hundreds of years had developed legends and embellishments surrounding the historical narrative in the Tanakh—from creation to the restoration. The stories are scattered throughout the Apocrypha, Pseudepigrapha, Talmud, and Midrash, and are even found in early Christian writings. The following is one such legend explaining how each of the Ten Commandments is woven together into a unified whole.

The Ten Commandments are so closely interwoven, that the breaking of one leads to the breaking of another. But there is a particularly strong bond of union between the first five commandments, which are written on one table, and the last five, which were on the other table. The first commandment: "I am the Lord, thy God," corresponds to the sixth: "Thou shalt not kill," for the murderer slays the image of God. The second: "Thou shalt have no strange gods before me," corresponds to the seventh: "Thou shalt not commit adultery," for conjugal faithlessness is as grave a sin as idolatry, which is faithlessness to God. The third commandment: "Thou shalt not take the name of the Lord in vain," corresponds to the eighth: "Thou shalt not steal," for theft leads to false oath. The fourth commandment: "Remember the Sabbath day, to keep it holy," corresponds to the ninth: "Thou shalt not bear false witness against thy neighbor," for he who bears false witness against his neighbor commits as grave a sin as if he had borne false witness against God, saying that He had not created the world in six days and rested on the seventh, the Sabbath. The fifth commandment: "Honor thy father and thy mother," corresponds to the tenth: "Covet not thy neighbor's wife," for one who indulges this lust produces children who will not honor their true father, but will consider a stranger their father.

The Ten Commandments, which God first revealed on Mount Sinai, correspond in their character to the ten words of which He had made use at the creation of the world. The first commandment: "I am the Lord, thy God," corresponds to the first word at the creation: "Let there be light," for God is the eternal light. The second commandment: "Thou shalt have no strange gods before me," corresponds to the second word: "Let there be a firmament in the midst of the waters, and let it divide the waters from the waters." For God said: "Choose between Me and the idols; between Me, the fountain of living waters, and the idols, the stagnant waters." The third commandment: "Thou shalt not take the name of thy God in vain" corresponds to the word: "Let the waters be gathered together," for as little as water can be gathered in a cracked vessel, so can a man maintain his possession which he has obtained through false oaths. The fourth commandment: "Remember to keep the Sabbath holy," corresponds to the word: "Let the earth bring forth grass," for he who truly observes the Sabbath will receive good things from God without having to labor for them, just as the earth produces grass that need not be sown. For at the creation of man it was God's intention that he be free from sin, immortal, and capable of supporting himself by the products of the soil without toil. The fifth commandment: "Honor thy father and thy mother," corresponds to the word: "Let there be lights in the firmament of the heaven," for God said to man: "I gave thee two lights, thy father and thy mother, treat them with care." The sixth commandment: "Thou shalt not kill," corresponds to the word: "Let the waters bring forth abundantly the moving creature," for God said: "Be not like the fish, among whom the great swallow the small." The seventh commandment: "Thou shalt not commit adultery," corresponds to the word: "Let the earth bring forth the living creature after his kind," for God said: "I chose for thee a spouse, abide with her." The eighth commandment: "Thou shalt not steal," corresponds to the word: "Behold, I have given you every herb-bearing seed," for none, said

God, should touch his neighbor's goods, but only that which grows free as the grass, which is the common property of all. The ninth commandment: "Thou shalt not bear false witness against thy neighbor," corresponds to the word: "Let us make man in our image." Thou, like thy neighbor, art made in My image, hence bear not false witness against thy neighbor. The tenth commandment: "Thou shalt not covet the wife of thy neighbor," corresponds to the tenth word of the creation: "It is not good for man to be alone," for God said: "I created thee a spouse, and let not one among ye covet his neighbor's wife."

Source: Louis Ginzberg, *The Legends of the Jews,* vol. 3, ch. 2, Philadelphia, The Jewish Publication Society of America, 1909.

MEDIEVAL JUDAISM

THIRTEEN PRINCIPLES OF FAITH: MAIMONIDES

Judaism has resisted the formulation of creeds or other statements of belief, perhaps in part because of the dialogical nature of the Talmud and its other principal theological works. Nevertheless, the medieval Jewish philosopher Maimonides (1135–1204) developed a list of thirteen principles of Jewish faith, which was embraced by Judaism and, in much abbreviated form, appears in most Jewish prayer books today. The following is from Maimonides' original discussion of the principles.

The First Foundation is to believe in the existence of the Creator, blessed be He. This means that there exists a Being that is complete in all ways and He is the cause of all else that exists. He is what sustains their existence and the existence of all that sustains them. It is inconceivable that He would not exist, for if He would not exist then all else would cease to exist as well, nothing would remain. And if we would imagine that everything other than He would cease to exist, this would not cause His, God's, blessed be He, existence to cease or be diminished. Independence and mastery is to Him alone, God, blessed be His Name, for He needs nothing else and is sufficient unto himself. He does not need the existence of anything else. All that exists apart from Him, the angels, the universe and all that is within it, all these things are dependent on Him for their existence. . . .

The Second Foundation is the unity of God, Blessed be His Name. In other words, to believe that this being, which is the cause of all, is one. This does not mean one as in one of a pair nor one like a species [which encompasses many individuals] nor one as in one object that is made up of many elements nor as a single simple object which is infinitely divisible. Rather, He, God, Blessed be His Name, is a unity unlike any other possible unity. . . .

The Third Foundation is that He is not physical. This means to believe that the One whom we have mentioned is not a body and His powers are not physical. The concepts of physical bodies such as movement, rest, or existence in a particular place cannot be applied to Him. Such things cannot be part of His nature nor can they happen to Him. Therefore the Sages of blessed memory stated that the concepts of combination and separation do not apply to Him and they said, "Above there is no sitting nor standing, no separation nor combination." The prophet says, *"To whom can you compare Me? To what am I equal? Says the Holy One"* (Isaiah 40:25). If He would be a physical body He would be comparable to physical bodies. . . .

The Fourth Foundation is that He is first. This means to believe that the One was the absolute first and everything else in existence is not first relative to Him. There are many proofs to this in the Holy Scriptures. . . .

The Fifth Foundation is that it is proper to serve Him, blessed be He, to ascribe to Him greatness, to make known His greatness, and to fulfill His commandments. We may not do this to any lesser being, whether it be one of the angels, the stars, the celestial spheres, the elements, or anything formed from them. For all these things have predetermined natures and have no authority or control over their actions. Rather, such authority and control is God's. Similarly, it is not proper to serve them as intermediaries in order that they should bring us closer to God. Rather, to God Himself we must direct out thoughts, and abandon anything else. . . .

The Sixth Foundation is prophecy. That is, that a person must know that there exist amongst mankind individuals who have very lofty qualities and great perfection; whose souls are prepared until their minds receive perfect intellect. After this, their human intellect can then become attached to the Active Intellect [i.e., the "mind," so to speak, of God] and have bestowed upon them an exalted state. These are the prophets and this is prophecy. . . .

The Seventh Foundation is the prophecy of Moses our Teacher, may he rest in peace. This means to believe that he is the father of all the prophets, both those that preceded him and those who arose after him; all of them were below his level. He was the chosen one from all of Mankind, for he attained a greater knowledge of the Blessed One, more than any other man ever attained or ever will attain. For he, may he rest in peace, rose up from the level of man to the level of the angels and gained the exalted status of an angel. There did not remain any screen that he did not tear and penetrate; nothing physical held him back. He was devoid of any flaw, big or small. His powers of imagination, the senses, and the perceptions were nullified; the power of desire was separated from him leaving him with pure intellect. It is for this reason that it is said on him that he could speak to God, blessed be He, without the intermediary of angels. . . .

The Eighth Foundation is that the Torah is from Heaven. This means that we must believe that this entire Torah, which was given to us from Moses Our Teacher, may he rest in peace, is entirely from the mouth of the Almighty. In other words, that it all was conveyed to him from God, blessed be He, in the manner which is called, for lack of a better term, "speech." It is not known how it was conveyed to him, except to Moshe, may he rest in peace, to whom it was given, and he was like a scribe writing from dictation, and he wrote all the incidents, the stories, and the commandments. Therefore [Moses] is called "scribe" (Numbers 21:18). . . .

The Ninth Foundation is the transcription, meaning that this Torah, and no other, was transcribed from the Creator and we may not add to it or remove from it, not in the Written Torah or in the Oral Torah, as it says, ". . . *you will not add to it, nor diminish from it"* (Deuteronomy 13:1). . . .

The Tenth Foundation is that God, blessed be He, knows the actions of mankind and does not turn His eyes from them. . . .

The Eleventh Foundation is that God, blessed be He, gives reward to one who obeys the commandments of the Torah and punishes one who violates its prohibitions. The greatest reward is the World to Come, and the greatest punishment is spiritual excision. . . .

The Twelfth Foundation is the time of the *Messiah*. This means to believe and be certain that he will come, and not to think that he is late in coming, *"if it seems slow, wait for it; [because it will surely come, it will not come late]"* (Chabakuk 2:3). You should not set a time for him, and you should not make calculations in Scripture to determine the time of his coming. The Sages say, *"Let despair come upon those who calculate endtimes."* [This foundation further includes] to believe that he [*Messiah*] will possess advantages, superiority, and honor to a greater degree than all the kings that have ever existed, as was prophesied regarding him by all the prophets, from Moses, peace be upon him, till Malachi, peace be upon him. One who doubts this or who minimizes his greatness denies the Torah that testifies explicitly to [the coming of Messiah] in the account of Balaam (Numbers 24) and in the portion of *Netzavim* (Deuteronomy 30:3–5). Included in this principle is that there is no king to the Jewish people except from the House of David and the seed of Solomon alone. Anyone who disagrees with [the status of] this family denies God and His prophets. . . .

The Thirteenth Foundation is the resurrection of the dead. . . .

Source: Maimonides, *Commentary on the Mishnah,* Sanhedrin, ch. 10, translated by Eliezer C. Abrahamson.

KABBALA: CREATION

Since the twelfth century, the most dominant school of Jewish mysticism has been Kabbala, the classic statement of which is the Book of Splendor (Sefer ha-Zohar), *written between 1280 and 1286 by Moses de Leon, a Spanish Jew from Guadalajara. The work emphasizes ten emanations—or Sefirot—of God's personality. These attributes of the divinity permeate all of creation, including our personal lives. De Leon does not systematically discuss the emanations and typically does not refer to them by their formal names. Instead, he relies heavily on metaphors, leaving it to the reader to make the association. The following is de Leon's account of creation, presented as a commentary on the first clause of the Book of Genesis, that is, "In the beginning." He describes how God (Eyn Sof, or the Infinite) created two primary emanations. The first is Hokhmah (wisdom), described below as point and Beginning, which is the primal point of God's emanation. The second is Binah (derivative wisdom), described below as palace, which is the prime mother who receives seed from Hokhmah, and gives birth to seven lower emanations.*

"In the beginning" [Gen. 1:1]—when the will of the King began to take effect, he engraved signs into the heavenly sphere [that surrounded him]. Within the most hidden recess a dark flame issued from the mystery of *eyn sof*, the Infinite, like a fog forming in the unformed—enclosed in the ring of that sphere, neither white nor black, neither red nor green, of no color whatever. Only after this flame began to assume size and dimension, did it produce radiant colors. From the innermost center of the flame sprang forth a well out of which colors issued and spread upon everything beneath, hidden in the mysterious hiddenness of *eyn sof*.

The well broke through and yet did not break through the ether [of the sphere]. It could not be recognized at all until a hidden, supernatural point shone forth under the impact of the final breaking through.

Beyond this point nothing can be known. Therefore it is called *reshit*, beginning—the first word [out of the ten] by means of which the universe has been created. When King Solomon "penetrated into the depths of the nut garden," as it is written, "I descended into the garden of nuts" [Cant. 6:11], he took up a nut shell and studying it, he saw an analogy in its layers with the spirits which motivate the sensual desires of humans, as it is written, "and the delights of the sons of men [are from] male and female demons" [Eccles. 2:8].

The Holy One, be blessed, saw that it was necessary to put into the world all of these things so as to make sure of permanence, and of having, so to speak, a brain surrounded by numerous membranes. The whole world, upper and lower, is organized on this principle, from the primary mystic center to the very outermost of all the layers. All are coverings, the one to the other, brain within brain, spirit inside of spirit, shell within shell.

The primal center is the innermost light, of translucence, subtlety, and purity beyond comprehension. That inner point extended becomes a "palace" which acts as an enclosure for the center, and is also of a radiance translucent beyond the power to know it.

The "palace" vestment for the incognizable inner point, while it is an unknowable radiance in itself, is nevertheless of a lesser subtlety and translucency than the primal point. The "palace" extends into a vestment for itself, the primal light. From then outward, there is extension upon extension, each constituting a vesture to the one before, as a membrane to the brain. Though membrane first, each extension becomes brain to the next extension.

Likewise does the process go on below; and after this design, man in the world combines brain and membrane, spirit and body, all to the more perfect ordering of the world. When the moon was conjoined with the sun, she was luminous, but when she went apart from the sun and was given governance of her own hosts, her status and her light were reduced, and shell after shell as fashioned for investing the brain, and all was for its good.

Source: Zohar, 1:49b, from *Zohar, The Book of Splendor,* ed. Gershom Scholem (New York: Schocken Books, 1949).

RECENT MOVEMENTS

HASIDISM: THE SEVEN BEGGARS

The Hasidic movement was founded by Baal Shem Tov (1700–1760) as a mystical response to disillusionment in both Messianic hope (brought on by messianic pretenders of the previous century) and Rabbinic legalism. Followers of Baal Shem Tov were preachers, rather than theologians, and thus communicated orally rather than in writing. Their homilies were eventually put in writing by their sons or disciples. The Hasids describe God pantheistically, and maintain that God can be directly accessed. Another genre of writing also emerged from the Hasidic movement: the tale. These parable-like stories draw from events in peasant life and describe God more anthropomorphically, rather than pantheistically. The most distinguished of these are by the Ukrainian Rabbi Nahman of Bratslav (1772–1810). The following selection is from his most well-known and cryptic tale, "The Seven Beggars." The story surrounds a wedding ceremony that is attended by six deformed beggars each of whom presents tales explaining his respective deformity (a seventh beggar remained in the forest). Their stories emphasize the illusory nature of the world in which we live.

. . . Today I present you a wedding gift that you should be as I am. Do you think my neck is twisted? My neck is not twisted at all. In fact, I have a straight neck, a very handsome neck. Only that there are worldly vanities (empty breaths) which are so numerous that I do not want to exhale the last breath. . . . But I really have a handsome neck, a wonderful neck because I have such a wonderful voice. I can imitate with my voice every speechless sound. . . . And I have an affidavit to that effect from a certain country.

For there is a country where everyone is skilled in the art of music. Everyone practices these arts, even little children. . . . The youngest in that country would be the wisest in another country in the art of music. And the wise men, and the king of that country and the musicians are experts in the art of music.

Once, the country's wise men sat and boasted of their expertise in the art of music. One boasted that he could play on one instrument; another, on another; and still another, on all instruments. This one boasted that he could imitate with his voice the sound of one instrument, and another boasted that he could imitate with his voice yet another instrument. . . . Another one boasted that with his voice he could make the sound of cannon firing.

I, too, was there, so I declared saying, "My Voice is better than all of yours. And here is the proof. If you are such wise men in music, see if you can save these two countries. There are two countries one thousand miles apart from each other where no one can sleep when night falls. As soon as night falls, everyone begins to wail with such anguish—men, women, and children—because they hear a certain wailing sound of mourning. Stones would melt because of this wail. . . . So if you are all so very wise in music, let us see if you can save these two countries, or at least imitate the sounds of the laments heard there."

And they all arose to go there. They left and reached one of those two countries. When they arrived, and night fell, as usual, everyone began to wail and the wise men also wailed. And so they saw that they were of no help at all to the two countries. And I said to the wise men: "Can you, at least, tell me where the sound of the wailing comes from?" They asked: "Do you know?" And I answered: "Of course I know. There are two birds, a male and a female. There was only one pair of these species on earth. The female was lost and the male roamed about seeking her. She was also seeking him. They searched for each other for such a long time that they lost their ways and realized they could no longer find one another. They remained where they were and made nests. . . . And when night fell, each one of this pair of birds began to lament with a very great wail. Each wailed for its mate. This is the wailing that is heard in these two countries, and because of the sound, everyone must wail and no one can sleep." . . .

The wise man said to me: "and you set it right?"I answered: "Yes, I can set it right, since I can imitate all the sounds of the world. I can also throw my voice, so that in the place from where I throw my voice, nobody hears, but it is heard far, far away. . . ."

But who could believe me? So I led them into a forest. They heard somebody open a door, and shut it, and lock it with a bolt. Then I shot a gun and sent my dog to retrieve what I had shot. And the dog struggled in the snow. These wise men heard it all and looked around, but they saw absolutely nothing. They heard no sound from me . . . so they understood that I could imitate all the sounds and could throw my voice and thus could set everything right.

Source: Selections from "The Seven Beggars," from *Nahman of Bratslav: The Tales* (New York: Paulist Press, 1978), pp. 274–277.

REFORM JUDAISM: DECLARATION OF PRINCIPLES

The eighteenth-century Enlightenment and its emphasis on political rights sparked a movement among Jews in Germany to reform their religious practices. Initial efforts focused on revamping the liturgy: modernizing music and integrating some components of Christian practice. This was followed by a more "scientific" approach to Judaism advocated by Abraham Geiger (1810–1875), who was influenced by the critical methodology taught at German universities. Geiger believed that the Jewish Torah was fluid, adapting to different historical contexts. Reform Judaism was brought to the United States with the immigration of German Jews, and in 1885 a conference of Rabbis was held in Pittsburgh, Pennsylvania, which explored the direction of that denomination. The outcome was the following Declaration of Principles—or the Pittsburgh Platform, as it is often called. Although the statement was modified at later conferences, Reform Judaism today still holds to these basic tenets.

1. We recognize in every religion an attempt to grasp the Infinite, and in every mode, source or book of revelation held sacred in any religious system the consciousness of the indwelling of God in man. We hold that Judaism presents the highest conception of the God-idea as taught in our Holy Scriptures and developed and spiritualized by the Jewish teachers, in accordance with the moral and philosophical progress of their respective ages. We maintain that Judaism preserved and defended midst continual struggles and trials and under enforced isolation, this God-idea as the central religious truth for the human race.

2. We recognize in the Bible the record of the consecration of the Jewish people to its mission as the priest of the one God, and value it as the most potent instrument of religious and moral instruction. We hold that the modern discoveries of scientific researches in the domain of nature and history are not antagonistic to the doctrines of Judaism, the Bible reflecting the primitive ideas of its own age, and at times clothing its conception of divine Providence and Justice dealing with men in miraculous narratives.

3. We recognize in the Mosaic legislation a system of training the Jewish people for its mission during its national life in Palestine, and today we accept as binding only its moral laws, and maintain only such ceremonies as elevate and sanctify our lives, but reject all such as are not adapted to the views and habits of modern civilization.

4. We hold that all such Mosaic and rabbinical laws as regulate diet, priestly purity, and dress originated in ages and under the influence of ideas entirely foreign to our present mental and spiritual state. They fail to impress the modern Jew with a spirit of priestly holiness; their observance in our days is apt rather to obstruct than to further modern spiritual elevation.

5. We recognize, in the modern era of universal culture of heart and intellect, the approaching of the realization of Israel's great Messianic hope for the establishment of the kingdom of truth, justice, and peace among all men. We consider ourselves no longer a nation, but a religious community, and therefore expect neither a return to Palestine, nor a sacrificial worship under the sons of Aaron, nor the restoration of any of the laws concerning the Jewish state.

6. We recognize in Judaism a progressive religion, ever striving to be in accord with the postulates of reason. We are convinced of the utmost necessity of preserving the historical identity with our great past. Christianity and Islam, being daughter religions of Judaism, we appreciate their providential mission, to aid in the spreading of monotheistic and

moral truth. We acknowledge that the spirit of broad humanity of our age is our ally in the fulfillment of our mission, and therefore we extend the hand of fellowship to all who cooperate with us in the establishment of the reign of truth and righteousness among men.

7. We reassert the doctrine of Judaism that the soul is immortal, grounding the belief on the divine nature of human spirit, which forever finds bliss in righteousness and misery in wickedness. We reject as ideas not rooted in Judaism, the beliefs both in bodily resurrection and in Gehenna and Eden (Hell and Paradise) as abodes for everlasting punishment and reward.

8. In full accordance with the spirit of the Mosaic legislation, which strives to regulate the relations between rich and poor, we deem it our duty to participate in the great task of modern times, to solve, on the basis of justice and righteousness, the problems presented by the contrasts and evils of the present organization of society.

Source: *Proceedings of the Pittsburg Rabbinical Conference, November 16, 17, 18, 1885,* Richmond, Va.: Old Dominion Press, 1923.

ZIONISM: THEODOR HERZL

"Zion" in Jewish tradition refers variously to the Temple Mount in Jerusalem, the city of Jerusalem itself, or the larger territory of Judea. Since the days of the Babylonian exile it has been the focal point in the desires of dispersed Jews to return to their native land. In the 1890s, Hungarian-born Theodor Herzl (1860–1904) founded the modern Zionist movement, which, in response to rampant anti-Semitism throughout Europe, aimed to reunite Jews in a homeland. Herzl's movement continued after his death and, in the aftermath of the Nazi Holocaust, succeeded in the creation of the modern country of Israel. The following is from Herzl's seminal book, The Jewish State, *in which he argues that Palestine, rather than Argentina, is the most suitable location for Jewish repatriation.*

No one can deny the gravity of the situation of the Jews. Wherever they live in perceptible numbers, they are more or less persecuted. Their equality before the law, granted by statute, has become practically a dead letter. They are debarred from filling even moderately high positions, either in the army, or in any public or private capacity. And attempts are made to thrust them out of business also: "Don't buy from Jews!"

Attacks in Parliaments, in assemblies, in the press, in the pulpit, in the street, on journeys—for example, their exclusion from certain hotels—even in places of recreation, become daily more numerous. The forms of persecution vary according to the countries and social circles in which they occur. In Russia, imposts are levied on Jewish villages; in Rumania, a few persons are put to death; in Germany, they get a good beating occasionally; in Austria, Anti-Semites exercise terrorism over all public life; in Algeria, there are traveling agitators; in Paris, the Jews are shut out of the so-called best social circles and excluded from clubs. Shades of anti-Jewish feeling are innumerable. But this is not to be an attempt to make out a doleful category of Jewish hardships. . . .

The whole plan is in its essence perfectly simple, as it must necessarily be if it is to come within the comprehension of all.

Let the sovereignty be granted us over a portion of the globe large enough to satisfy the rightful requirements of a nation; the rest we shall manage for ourselves.

The creation of a new State is neither ridiculous nor impossible. We have in our day witnessed the process in connection with nations which were not largely members of the middle class, but poorer, less educated, and consequently weaker than ourselves. The Governments of all countries scourged by Anti-Semitism will be keenly interested in assisting us to obtain the sovereignty we want.

The plan, simple in design, but complicated in execution, will be carried out by two agencies: The Society of Jews and the Jewish Company. . . .

Shall we choose Palestine or Argentine? We shall take what is given us, and what is selected by Jewish public opinion. The Society will determine both these points.

Argentine is one of the most fertile countries in the world, extends over a vast area, has a sparse population and a mild climate. The Argentine Republic would derive considerable profit from the cession of a portion of its territory to us. The present infiltration of Jews has certainly produced some discontent, and it would be necessary to enlighten the Republic on the intrinsic difference of our new movement.

Palestine is our ever-memorable historic home. The very name of Palestine would attract our people with a force of marvelous potency. If his Majesty the Sultan were to give us Palestine, we could in return undertake to regulate the whole finances of Turkey.

Source: Theodor Herzl, *The Jewish State,* tr. Sylvie d' Avigdor, London: D. Nutt, 1896, ch. 2, The Jewish Question.

GLOSSARY

Amoraim   Rabbinic sages from 200–500 C.E. whose comments on the *Mishnah* are in the *Talmud*.

Deuteronomistic History   The historical sequence of books in the *Tanakh* from Deuteronomy through Chronicles, connected in terms of authorship and theology.

Diaspora   Dispersion of the Jews outside of Israel.

Elohim   Hebrew for *God*.

Israelite   People of Israel until the return from the Babylonian exile.

Jew   Descendants of the Israelites from the return from the Babylonian exile to the present. *Jew* is from the Hebrew *jehudi,* meaning a descendant of Jacob's son Judah.

Judea   The name for the land of the Jews from the post-exilic period to the early Roman period.

Kabbala   Literally, "Tradition;" the largest school of Jewish mysticism, from the twelfth century C.E. to the present.

Midrash   A verse-by-verse style of commentary on the *Tanakh*, especially as used by early Rabbis.

Mishnah   The written expression of the oral law, compiled in 200 C.E. by Rabbi Judah ha-Nasi.

Saboraim   Rabbinic sages from 500–700 whose comments on the *Mishnah* were added to those of the Amoraim in the *Talmud*.

Sefirot   The ten emanations of God, as described in early Kabbalist theology.

Talmud   An extensive collection of commentaries on the *Mishnah* compiled from the sayings of Rabbis from 200–500 C.E.

Tanakh   The Hebrew Bible. The term comes from the initials of its three divisions: Torah (law), Neviim (prophets), Ketuvim (writings).

Tannaim   Rabbinic sages of the first two centuries C.E. whose sayings are compiled in the *Mishnah*.

Torah   Hebrew for *law, teaching,* or *instruction.* In the broad sense "Torah" refers to the law of Moses, both written and oral. In the narrow sense it refers to the first five books of the *Tanakh,* traditionally called the Books of Moses.

Yahweh   The personal name of God in Judaism.

FURTHER READINGS

AGUS, JACOB. *The Jewish Quest* (1983).

ALEXANDER, PHILLIP S. *Textual Sources for the Study of Judaism* Totowa, NJ: Barnes and Noble, 1986.

BAECK, LEO. *The Essence of Judaism,* rev. ed. (1987).

BLAU, JOSEPH L. *Modern Varieties of Judaism* (1966).

BLECH, B. *Understanding Judaism* (1991).

FACKENHEIM, E. L. *What Is Judaism?* (1988).

GLAZER, NATHAN. *American Judaism,* 2d ed. (1973).

GOLDBERG, D., AND RAYNER, J. *The Jewish People* (1987).

HOLTZ, BARRY. *Back to the Sources: Reading the Classic Jewish Texts.* New York: Touchstone, 1984.

MEYER, MICHAEL. *Ideas of Jewish History* (1987).

NEUSNER, JACOB. *The Life of the Torah: Readings in the Jewish Religious Experience* (1974).

SANDMEL, SAMUEL. *The Hebrew Scriptures.* Oxford: University Press, 1978.

SILVER, D., AND MARTIN, B. *A History of Judaism,* 2 vols. (1974).

STEINSALTZ, ADIN. *The Essential Talmud.* San Francisco: Harper Collins, 1976.

WIGODER, G. *Encyclopedia of Judaism* (1989).

Christianity

INTRODUCTION

Christianity is founded on the life and teachings of Jesus, a first century C.E. Jew who was executed by the Roman authorities for subversion. During its first few decades Christianity was a sect within Judaism, but quickly expanded beyond its Palestinian borders and Jewish framework, becoming an independent religion. Two elements of Christian doctrine are essentially Jewish. First, Jesus is the messiah, or anointed king, who is spoken of in Jewish prophetic writings. The term *christ* is a Greek translation of the Hebrew word *messiah,* and so Jesus is referred to as the Christ. Second, the message of Jesus is the kingdom of God. Keeping with Jewish apocalyptic notions of the messiah, early Christians expected that the kingdom would be established by cataclysmic events. A third element of Christianity departs from its Jewish heritage, namely, that Jesus is God in human form. Building on this, a fourth element is that, by his work, teachings, death, and resurrection, Jesus became the savior of the world.

The Life of Jesus

Jesus left no writings, and the knowledge we have of his life and teachings comes almost exclusively from the gospels of Matthew, Mark, and Luke. These narratives are traditionally ascribed to his disciples, but were probably written and compiled anonymously between 40 and 60 years after his death. They were also written by believers for believers, blending historical memories with early church teaching. Reconstructing an accurate picture of Jesus, then, is difficult, and, according to some theologians, impossible.

Jesus was born about 4 B.C.E. and raised in Nazareth, a small agricultural city in the Galilee region. Little is known about Jesus until he began his ministry at about age 30. Jewish territories at that time were under especially oppressive Roman rule, which caused widespread unrest. Since the times of the independent Jewish monarchies hundreds of years earlier, 90 percent of the Jewish population had consisted of agrarian peasants who supported the ruling priestly elite through taxes on their harvest. Additional taxes were imposed by the Romans, and still more to support local building projects, such as those of King Herod. By the time of Jesus, peasant taxes totaled about 40 percent of their harvest, which forced many into debt or sale of family land. Unemployment was also high. As the Romans reduced the size of Jewish territories, Jews from surrounding areas flooded into Judea and Galilee, the two principle territories of Jewish settlement. Occasional famine made economic times worse and intensified the rift between peasants and the ruling class, which supported the Romans.

Desperate peasants rallied around charismatic leaders who offered hope. Some supported social bandits who systematically robbed rich Jewish land-owners and shared the wealth with the peasants. Others found comfort in the company of prophets who, in the tradition of the old Jewish prophets, pro-nounced apocalyptic judgment against the Romans and called the people to repentance. Still others took refuge in the leadership of messiahs, that is, anointed kings. The concept of a messiah in Jewish literature did not become fixed until Rabbinic discussions after the revolt of 66 c.e. Prior to that, written discussions refer to a Davidic king, a prophet like Moses or a perfect priest, although the actual term *messiah* is rarely used. The notion of messiah in the minds of the illiterate peasants was somewhat different from that which appeared in the writings of the ruling elite. Although they retained the idea of kingship, they saw the anointing of this king as a revolutionary act of popular election. The messiah was to be a flesh-and-blood military leader, not just an apocalyptic figure waging spiritual war.

Jesus began his ministry during his association with John the Baptizer, an apocalyptic prophet, who proclaimed impending doom. John baptized Jesus, and shortly afterwards was executed by the ruler of Galilee, who feared that John's enthusiastic followers might provoke a rebellion. Jesus attracted his own followers in Galilee, who initially saw him as a popular prophet, rather more like John the Baptizer than a political messiah. Of his large following of both men and women, later Christian tradition honored 12 as having special authority (although there is disagreement on who exactly the 12 were). With his disciples, Jesus traveled around Galilee teaching, befriending outcasts, healing people, and performing exorcisms. He taught to both small gatherings in synagogues and large peasant crowds in open-air places. His ministry lasted only a couple of years until he was executed on a Roman cross. The precise reasons for his execution may never be known. For John the Baptizer, attracting large crowds in a revolutionary environment was enough to cost him his life. To the extent that Jesus appeared to be another popular prophet, Jewish and Roman leaders had reason for concern.

The Teaching of Jesus

Like the events of his life, Jesus' teachings in the gospels also blend his words with early church doctrine. Some scholars argue that less than 20 percent of the sayings attributed to Jesus in the Gospels were spoken by him. The domi-nant message that emerges, though, is the kingdom of God. The "kingdom" is never defined, but is the final state of affairs in which the world runs according to God's will. Paradoxically, some teachings proclaim that the kingdom will arrive in the near future, while others maintain that the kingdom has already begun. Although the concepts of both a future and a present kingdom of God can be found in Jewish apocalyptic literature, Jesus is unique in making the doctrine of the kingdom the basis of ethical behavior. Moral acts of repentance, love, charity, and nonviolence are God's requirements for acceptance into the kingdom. Because of the urgency in preparing for the kingdom, uncompromising behavior is required. Jesus did not see himself as the messianic ruler of the kingdom he proclaimed, especially in view of the military implications of the popular messiahs.

Along with its content, the style of Jesus' teaching is also important: the parable. Most broadly, a parable is a statement, story, or dialogue that has a metaphorical or figurative meaning. It can be as short as a single sentence, such as "It is easier for a camel to pass through the eye of a needle than for a rich man to enter the kingdom of God" (Mark 10:25), or paragraphs long. Understood this way, almost everything attributed to Jesus in the gospels of Matthew, Mark, and Luke is in the form of a parable. More narrowly, parables are extended metaphorical narratives, or figurative stories, about 30 of which appear in these first three Gospels and the Gospel of Thomas (see following). In view of their figurative nature, the parables require interpretation, and sometimes an early Christian explanation is presented within the Gospel text itself. The interpretation of virtually all of the parables, though, relates to some challenging aspect of the kingdom. Like much of Old Testament literature, Jesus' parables follow specific literary structures. For example, Luke 11:9–10 follows step parallelism:

> A   Ask, and it will be given you
>   B   Seek, and you will find
>   C   Knock, and it will be opened to you
>
> A' For everyone who asks receives
>   B' And he who seeks finds
>   C' And to him who knocks it will be opened

Even the longest narrative parables follow a combination of various parallel structures.

The Early Church

After his execution, strong leaders and apostles emerged within the Jesus movement, keeping its spirit alive and recruiting even more followers. Jesus was quickly seen as the crucified and risen messiah who would return from heaven at any moment and begin an apocalyptic (as opposed to military) reign. Old testament messianic prophecies were applied to him, bolstering the interpretation that Jesus was the Christ. Some followers sold their possessions and waited his arrival. Others, such as Paul, a former Pharisee, effectively recruited believers from among non-Jews. Early interpretations of Jesus and his message varied greatly among the new followers, and the Christian tradition we inherit was defined in reaction to and in competition with early alternatives. The New Testament canon and early church hierarchy are products of the winning tradition, whereas the losing traditions were branded as heresies along the way. An early losing interpretation was that of Judaizers who believed that Christianity was the messianic fulfillment of Judaism, and not a different religion. Thus, Christians were still bound by traditional Jewish laws, such as circumcision and food rituals. However, the Judaizers' narrow notion of Christianity did not fit the broader vision of other early church leaders.

Another unsuccessful early interpretation of Christianity was offered by Gnosticism, a diverse religious movement that flourished throughout the Near East from 100 to 400 C.E. The aim of the Gnostic religion in general was to free one's spirit from the illusions of the evil, material world and reascend to heaven. Release was to be accomplished by acquiring special knowledge (*gnosis*). In Christian Gnosticism, the material world was created by an evil demigod, and Jesus' teachings provide the knowledge that redeems us from worldly illusion. Church leaders reacted vehemently to the Gnostic interpretation, penning many polemics against it.

While theologians battled over doctrine, churches were established throughout the Roman Empire, and bishops—successors of the original Apostles—officiated in key regions. At first Roman rulers did not distinguish between Christians and Jews. But the rapid advance of Christianity soon made the distinction apparent, and, from their perspective, threatened the unity of the Empire. Christianity was outlawed and, throughout the first three centuries C.E., several emperors systematically persecuted Christians, some bent on their extinction. A decisive turning point came when emperor Constantine took the throne, and in 313 C.E. he proclaimed complete religious liberty for Christians. He sponsored a world church council, at Nicea, which determined that Christ was not subordinate to God, but substantively identical with God. The council also established the bishops of Rome, Antioch, and Alexandria as the primary officiators of the Church; later the bishop of Constantinople was added to the list. In 392 C.E. Emperor Theodosius declared Christianity the only allowable religion throughout the empire.

Christian Denominations

During the fourth century C.E., the vast Roman Empire became too difficult to manage from a single location, so it was regionally divided, with the western territory governed by Rome and the eastern territory governed by Constantinople. Now inseparably tied to empire politics, the Church too established parallel jurisdictions. The western jurisdiction, later designated *catholic*, was led by Rome's bishop, or *Pope*, and the eastern (or *orthodox*) jurisdiction looked, less formally, to Constantinople's bishop, or *Patriarch*. Differences of worship and authority further divided the regions, such as the east's use of icons, rejection of Papal authority, and emphasis on Christ's divinity above his humanity. The rift was complete in 1054 when Rome's Pope Leo IX and Constantinople's Patriarch Michael Cerularius mutually excommunicated each other. Since the great catholic-orthodox schism, the three original eastern church jurisdictions (Antioch, Alexandria, and Constantinople) have multiplied to over 20, each with its own Patriarch. Although the Orthodox jurisdictions govern independently, they are unified by shared liturgy and doctrine.

After the fall of the western Roman empire from barbarian invasions in the fifth century, missionary journeys spread Christianity throughout northern Europe. The Pope was on a par with emperors of new and primitive European states, and Christian monasteries were the default centers of learning. By the sixteenth century, growing discontentment with Catholic hierarchy erupted in the Protestant Reformation, led by the German priest Martin Luther. Luther stressed that the Bible is Christianity's exclusive authority, not the Pope, and not church traditions. Salvation, Luther declared, is achieved through God's grace, not through human achievement, and is available to all who ask. Luther was particularly successful in convincing German nobility of the benefits of breaking ties with Rome. As surrounding European countries soon followed the reformer's lead, Luther believed that the protesters would remain theologically unified because God would guide each person toward the same interpretation of the Bible. This was not to be, and five centuries later, hundreds of Protestant denominations have emerged from disputes over doctrine. The largest Protestant denominations are the Lutherans, Baptists, Presbyterians, Methodists, and Episcopalians. The large denominations are often doctrinally divided among themselves; the more conservative emphasize evangelism and Biblical inerrency, whereas the more liberal stress social concerns and metaphorical interpretations of the Bible. Pentecostal churches are part of a movement, rather than a single denomination, and stress spiritual gifts, such as prophecy and speaking in tongues.

The Bible

The primary body of scriptures in the Christian tradition is the Bible, which consists of an Old and New Testament. The Old Testament is the Jewish *Tanakh*, which makes the Christian Bible unique among world scriptures by including the canon of a different religion. The Christian Old Testament was initially based on the Septuagint, the Greek translation of the Jewish canon from 100 B.C.E. Accordingly, the Old Testament retains the book arrangement of the Septuagint. Catholic and Orthodox Christians also accept the apocryphal books from the Septuagint, although Protestants reject these, opting for what they believe are the older books as they appear in the Jewish *Tanakh*. The term *Old Testament* was coined by Paul, who used it in reference to the writings of the Mosaic covenant (2 Cor. 3:14).

By the fourth century C.E., the term *New Testament* was commonly used to refer to a collection of 27 early Christian texts composed in Greek. Traditionally they are thought to be written by the original Apostles who were Jesus' followers. Historically, though, the texts appear to have been written by second- and third-generation Christians from 50 to 150 C.E. For the first few centuries, there was no fixed New Testament canon, and manuscripts of hundreds of individual Christian texts circulated independently among the early churches. Early church fathers made recommendations as to which of these were authoritative. The first known list containing the present 27 books appears as a side comment in St. Athanasius' Easter letter of 367 C.E.

As Latin became the spoken language of the Roman Empire, Latin translations of the Old Testament and various Christian texts circulated. In 382 the Pope commissioned Jerome, a priest and scholar, to bring order to the chaotic collection of Latin texts. Returning to Hebrew and Greek language texts, Jerome produced a new Latin translation of the Old and New Testaments, referred to as the Vulgate, which, after some resistance, was accepted as definitive. Even with a more fixed canon, early theologians questioned the authority of several Old and New Testament texts and introduced a distinction between protocanonical and deuterocanonical texts: canonical writings with either primary or secondary status. In the thirteenth century the traditional chapter divisions were added to each book of the Bible by a cardinal who was preparing a biblical index. The Vulgate continued to be the official text of the Bible until the Protestant Reformation, when several modern language translations appeared, many of which removed the books of the Old Testament Apocrypha, or at least relegated them to an appendix. Verse divisions were also added at this time. As scholars today discover older manuscript copies of biblical books, passages are revised or deleted to reflect the earliest sources. For example, the well-known story from John 9 of the stoning of the adulterous woman ("Let him who is without sin cast the first stone") is now removed from many modern editions of the Bible.

The texts of the New Testament fall into five categories:

Gospels: Matthew, Mark, Luke, John

Book of Acts

Letters of Paul: Romans, 1 and 2 Corinthians, Galatians, Ephesians, Philippians, Colossians, 1 and 2 Thessalonians, 1 and 2 Timothy, Titus, Philemon, Hebrews

General letters: Letter of James; 1 and 2 Letters of Peter; 1, 2, and 3 Letters of John; Letter of Jude

Book of Revelation

The Gospels, which contain accounts of Jesus, have always been considered the most primary of all Christian texts. Scholars believe that for a few decades after Jesus' execution, the recollections of his immediate followers were transmitted orally. The first written accounts, from perhaps 50 C.E., were simply lists of his sayings with no stories. None of these have survived intact. The book of Mark appeared around 70 C.E., based on oral traditions of Jesus' life and teachings. Matthew and Luke then appeared around 85 C.E., both using information from Mark and an earlier lost list of sayings called *Quelle* (German for *source*). Matthew and Luke also contain unique stories and sayings, based on either oral traditions or earlier lost lists of sayings. Mark, Matthew, and Luke are referred to as the *synoptic gospels,* since they give very similar accounts of Jesus' life and teachings. Finally, the Gospel of John appeared in 90 C.E., Initially considered heretical by some early church fathers, it presents an account that is 90 percent different in content. All four Gospels first circulated anonymously, and were only ascribed to the apostles during the middle second century.

The Book of Acts is a continuation of Luke, penned by the same author, and discusses the spread of early Christianity immediately after Jesus. Of particular concern is the relationship of Christianity to Judaism in view of the large numbers of non-Jewish converts. More than half of Acts chronicles the conversion and missionary journeys of Paul. Of the 14 letters ascribed to Paul, only 7 are confidently traced to him (Romans, 1 and 2 Corinthians, Galatians, Philippians, 1 Thessalonians, and Philemon). His letters, composed between 50 and 60 C.E., contain encouragement and instructions to the churches he helped establish, but they did not gain a wide readership until the end of the first century. The general letters were written at the close of the first century as tracts or sermons addressing problems in early church communities. Finally, the Book of Revelation, also written at the close of the first century, describes a series of apocalyptic visions that contain instructions for Christians to remain faithful in the face of Roman persecution.

Non-Biblical Sacred Writings

Early non-canonical Christian texts are extraordinarily varied and include gospels, creeds, and writings of the Church fathers. Some collections of early sacred texts have special designations. The term *Apostolic Fathers* was coined in the seventeenth century in reference to a collection of works attributed to followers of the original apostles. The 14 texts now included under this label were popular in the early church and even included in scripture lists by early church fathers. Of particular interest in this collection is the *Didache*, or Teaching of the Twelve, which gives instructions on baptism, fasting, prayer, and the Eucharist. The expression *New Testament Apocrpha* is applied loosely to a range of early Christian texts, mostly from the second century, that are not included in the New Testament. Many of these were considered sacred by early churches and are the source of Christian beliefs, such as the assumption of Mary. Frequently they aim to fill gaps in the chronologies of Jesus' life and the early church. Paralleling the genres of New Testament texts, the writings fall into the categories of gospels, acts, epistles, and apocalypses. They are of particular value as a possible source of stray sayings of Jesus which continued to circulate into the second century.

One collection of early writings that has recently attracted scholarly attention is the Gnostic texts discovered in 1945 in Nag Hammadi, Egypt. The 45 texts are fourth- and fifth-century Coptic translations of Greek manuscripts, although the originals go back much earlier. Representing both Christian and non-Christian Gnostic ideas, they are thought to be the library of an early Gnostic Christian monastery which buried the documents in containers for protection. The texts suggest that early Christianity was more theologically diverse than initially believed. Some texts, for instance, emphasize a divine

Mother. Most important among the writings is the Gnostic Gospel of Thomas, a list of 114 sayings of Jesus. Some scholars believe that this list is based on an earlier compilation of sayings, predating the New Testament gospels, and thus, like Q represents the earliest strata of sayings attributed to Jesus.

Many early Christian creeds were the outcome of theological disputes, and represent official positions arrived at in early Church councils. They are typically short, and list the principal propositions of the official Church. The most famous of the early ones are the Apostles' Creed, Nicene Creed, and Chalcedon Creed, which even today are incorporated into worship services in many Christian traditions.

From as early as the first century, another inspirational source of Christian literature was the voluminous writings of early church fathers, saints, and mystics. The purposes and genres of these texts are quite varied, and include defenses of Christianity against heretics and pagans, stories of martyred Christians, commentaries on books of the Bible, sermons, letters, and theological treatises. Perhaps the most influential of these are the writings of St. Augustine (354–430), Bishop of the North African city of Hippo. The Orthodox, Catholic, and later Protestant traditions have a long and continuous history of mystical writings, which emphasize the importance of spiritual union with God. One such mystical work from a later period of Catholic thought is the *Interior Castle*, by Spanish Carmelite nun Teresa of Avila (1515–1582).

Since the Protestant Reformation, denominations have formed specific statements of faith, and some movements have their own special sacred texts in addition to the Bible. Protestant denominations tend to hold that the Bible is the principal, if not the exclusive, scripture of Christianity. Nevertheless, almost every Protestant group has formed some statement of faith that defines its views and distinguishes it from other denominations. Keeping with the religious freedom and pioneering spirit of nineteenth-century America, some Christian movements gave rise to new sacred texts. The distinct beliefs of the Church of Latter-Day Saints are founded on the *Book of Mormon,* a text produced by founder Joseph Smith (1805–1844). The Christian Science movement reveres *Science and Health* (1875), by founder Mary Baker Eddy (1821–1910), which emphasizes the healing aspect of Christianity. Associated with the New Age movement, American pastor Levi H. Dowling (1844–1911) produced the *Aquarian Gospel* in 1907, which recounts 18 lost years of Jesus' life as he traveled to India, Tibet, Egypt, Persia, and Greece.

JESUS' BIRTH AND MINISTRY

PRINCE OF PEACE AND SUFFERING SERVANT

The principal value of the Old Testament for Christianity is that Christ is the ultimate fulfillment of its covenants and messianic prophecies. Nowhere is that seen more clearly than in the following two selections from Isaiah on the birth of the prince of peace and the suffering servant. For Christians, these are allusions to Jesus' birth and his suffering on the cross.

9.

For to us a child is born, to us a son is given, and the government will be on his shoulders. And he will be called Wonderful Counselor, Mighty God, Everlasting Father, Prince of Peace. Of the increase of his government and peace there will be no end. He will reign on David's throne and over his kingdom, establishing and upholding it with justice and righteousness from that time on and forever. The zeal of the Lord Almighty will accomplish this.

53.

He grew up before him like a tender shoot, and like a root out of dry ground. He had no beauty or majesty to attract us to him, nothing in his appearance that we should desire him. He was despised and rejected by men, a man of sorrows, and familiar with suffering. Like one from whom men hide their faces he was despised, and we esteemed him not. Surely he took up our infirmities and carried our sorrows, yet we considered him stricken by God, smitten by him, and afflicted. But he was pierced for our transgressions, he was crushed for our iniquities; the punishment that brought us peace was upon him, and by his wounds we are healed. We all, like sheep, have gone astray, each of us has turned to his own way; and the Lord has laid on him the iniquity of us all.

He was oppressed and afflicted, yet he did not open his mouth; he was led like a lamb to the slaughter, and as a sheep before her shearers is silent, so he did not open his mouth. By oppression and judgment he was taken away. And who can speak of his descendants? For he was cut off from the land of the living; for the transgression of my people he was stricken. He was assigned a grave with the wicked, and with the rich in his death, though he had done no violence, nor was any deceit in his mouth.

Yet it was the Lord's will to crush him and cause him to suffer, and though the Lord makes his life a guilt offering, he will see his offspring and prolong his days, and the will of the Lord will prosper in his hand. After the suffering of his soul, he will see the light (of life) and be satisfied; by his knowledge my righteous servant will justify many, and he will bear their iniquities.

Source: Isaiah chs. 9:6–7, 53:2–11, from *The Holy Bible, New International Version (International Bible Society, 1984).*

BIRTH OF JESUS

Two of the four canonical gospels give accounts of the birth of Jesus, each slightly different. The following is Luke's version. The author of Luke was an educated non-Jewish Christian and, thus, his gospel reflects the broader non-Jewish implications of both Jesus' life and the Christian church. Unlike Matthew, Luke begins by placing the birth story in the context of Roman emperor Augustus' reign.

In those days it so happened that a decree was issued by Emperor Augustus that a census be taken of the whole civilized world. This first census was taken while Quirinius was governor of Syria. Everybody had to travel to their ancestral city to be counted in the census. So Joseph too went up from Galilee, from the town of Nazareth, to Judea, to the town of David called Bethlehem, because he was a descendant of David, to be counted in the census with Mary, to whom he was engaged; Mary was pregnant. It so happened while they were there that the time came for her to give birth; and she gave birth to a son, her firstborn. She wrapped him in strips of cloth and laid him in a feeding trough, because the travelers' shelter was no place for that.

Now in the same area there were shepherds living outdoors. They were keeping watch over their sheep at night, when a messenger of the Lord stood near them and the glory of the Lord shone around them. They became terrified. But the messenger said to them, "Don't be afraid: I bring you good news of a great joy, which is to benefit the whole nation; today in the city of David, the Savior was born to you—he is the Anointed, the Lord. And this will be a sign for you: you will find a baby wrapped in strips of cloth and lying in a feeding trough."

And suddenly there appeared with the messenger a whole troop of the heavenly army praising God:

> Glory to God in the highest,
> and on earth peace to people whom he has favored!

It so happened when the messengers left and returned to heaven that the shepherds said to one another, "Come on! Let's go over to Bethlehem and see what has happened, the event the Lord has told us about." And they hurried away, and found Mary, Joseph, and the baby lying in a feeding trough. And when they saw it they reported what they had been told about this child. Everyone who listened was astonished at what the shepherds told them. But Mary took all this in and reflected on it. And the shepherds returned, glorifying and praising God for all they had heard and seen; everything turned out just as they had been told.

Now eight days later, when the time came to circumcise him, they gave him the name Jesus, the name assigned him by the heavenly messenger before he was conceived in the womb.

Now when the time came for their purification according to the Law of Moses, they brought him up to Jerusalem to present him to the Lord—as it is written in the Law of the Lord, "Every male that opens the womb is to be considered holy to the Lord"—and to offer sacrifice according to what is dictated in the Law of the Lord: "A pair of turtledoves or two young pigeons." . . .

And when they had carried out everything required by the Law of the Lord, they returned to Galilee, to Nazareth, their own city. And the boy grew up and became strong, and was filled with wisdom; and God regarded him favorably.

Source: Luke, ch. 2:1–24, 39, 40, from *The Complete Gospels: Annotated Scholars Version,* ed. Robert J. Miller (Polebridge Press, Harper San Francisco, 1994).

JESUS' BAPTISM, TEMPTATION, AND FIRST DISCIPLES

The first canonical gospel to appear was Mark. Mark focuses more on activities in the life of Jesus than on teachings. His narrative is concise, matter of fact, and probably written for a non-Jewish audience in Rome about 70 C.E. Since virtually the entire content of Mark's account is included in the longer gospels of Matthew and Luke (which use Mark as one of several sources), Mark's gospel was typically not the most popular. However, as modern scholars try to identify the earliest recorded accounts of Jesus, preference is now given to Mark's narrative. The following selection, from the opening chapter of Mark, describes Jesus' baptism by John the Baptizer. This initiated his ministry, his temptation in the desert where he confronted Satan, and his acquiring of his first followers. Some scholars believe that after Jesus' death early Christians had to explain why the Jewish populace did not recognize Jesus as the messiah. Mark has an explanation which both Matthew and Luke adopt: Jesus purposefully kept word of his messiahship from circulating in order to minimize conflict with officials. Referred to as the messianic secret, *this explanation appears twice in the following passage.*

The good news of Jesus the Anointed begins with something Isaiah the prophet wrote:

> Here is my messenger,
> whom I send on ahead of you
> to prepare your way!
> A voice of someone shouting in the wilderness:
> "Make ready the way of the Lord,
> make his paths straight."

So, John the Baptizer appeared in the wilderness calling for baptism and a change of heart that led to forgiveness of sins. And everyone from the Judean countryside and all the residents of Jerusalem streamed out to him and got baptized by him in the Jordan river, admitting their sins. And John wore a mantle made of camel hair and had a leather belt around his waist and lived on locust and raw honey. And he began his proclamation by saying:

"Someone more powerful than I will succeed me, whose sandal straps I am not fit to bend down and untie. I have been baptizing you with water, but he'll baptize you with holy spirit."

During the same period Jesus came from Nazareth, Galilee, and was baptized in the Jordan by John. And just as he got up out of the water, he saw the skies torn open and the spirit coming down toward him like a dove. There was also a voice from the skies: "You are my favored son—I fully approve of you."

And right away the spirit drives him out into the wilderness, where he remained for forty days, being put to the test by Satan. While he was living there among the wild animals, the heavenly messengers looked after him.

After John was locked up, Jesus came to Galilee proclaiming God's good news. His message went:

"The time is up: God's imperial rule is closing in. Change your ways, and put your trust in the good news!"

As he was walking along by the Sea of Galilee, he spotted Simon and Andrew, Simon's brother, casting [their nets] into the sea—since they were fishermen—and Jesus said to them: "Become my followers and I'll have you fishing for people!"

And right then and there they abandoned their nets and followed him.

When he had gone a little farther, he caught sight of James, son of Zebedee, and his brother John mending their nets in the boat. Right then and there he called out to them as well, and they left their father Zebedee behind in the boat with the hired hands and accompanied him.

Then they come to Capernaum, and on the sabbath day he went right to the synagogue and started teaching. They were astonished at his teaching, since he would teach them on his own authority, unlike the scholars.

Now right there in their synagogue was a person possessed by an unclean spirit, which shouted, "Jesus! What do you want with us, you Nazarene? Have you come to get rid of us? I know you, who you are: God's holy man!"

But Jesus yelled at it, "Shut up and get out of him!"

Then the unclean spirit threw the man into convulsions, and letting out a loud shriek it came out of him. And they were all so amazed that they asked themselves, "What's this? A new kind of teaching backed by authority! He gives orders even to unclean spirits and they obey him!"

So his fame spread rapidly everywhere throughout Galilee and even beyond.

They left the synagogue right away and entered the house of Simon and Andrew along with James and John. Simon's mother-in-law was in bed with a fever, and they told him about her right away. He went up to her, took hold of her hand, raised her up, and the fever disappeared. Then she started looking after them.

In the evening, at sundown, they would bring all the sick and demon possessed to him. And the whole town would crowd around the door. On such occasions he cured many people afflicted with various diseases and drove out many demons. He would never let the demons speak, because they realized who he was.

And rising early, while it was still very dark, he went outside and stole away to an isolated place, where he started praying. Then Simon and those with him hunted him down. When they had found him they say to him, "They're all looking for you."

But he replies: "Let's go somewhere else, to the neighboring villages, so I can speak there too, since that's what I came for."

So he went all around Galilee speaking in their synagogues and driving out demons.

Then a leper comes up to him, pleads with him, falls down on his knees, and says to him, "If you want to, you can make me clean."

Although Jesus was indignant, he stretched out his hand, touched him, and says to him, "Okay—you're clean!"

And right away the leprosy disappeared, and he was made clean. And Jesus snapped at him, and dismissed him curtly with this warning: "See that you don't tell anyone anything, but go, have a priest examine [your skin]. Then offer for your cleansing what Moses commanded, as evidence [of your cure].

But after he went out, he started telling everyone and spreading the story, so that [Jesus] could no longer enter a town openly, but had to stay out in the countryside. Yet they continued to come to him from everywhere.

Source: Mark ch. 1, from *The Complete Gospels*.

SERMON ON THE MOUNT

Matthew's Gospel was written for a Jewish audience, and it continually draws parallels from the Old Testament. He incorporates Jesus' sayings into five distinct discourses, possibly representing the five books of Moses, to symbolize a new Torah. The Sermon on the Mount is the first of these and, again, the mountain motif here parallels the story of Moses receiving the Law at Mount Sinai. Many of the teachings in Matthew overlap those in Luke, suggesting that they independently drew their information from a third source (called Q by contemporary scholars). Some sayings in the Sermon on the Mount also appear in Luke in a section often called the Sermon on the Plain (6:20–49). Matthew's discourse opens with a description of how the kingdom of God will involve a dramatic reversal of conditions for the oppressed and faithful. Citizens of the kingdom must distinguish themselves through obedience to a new law, principally one of love for others, forgiveness, and trust in God.

5. Taking note of the crowds, he climbed up the mountain, and when he had sat down, his disciples came to him. He then began to speak, and this is what he would teach them:

> Congratulations to the poor in spirit!
> Heaven's domain belongs to them.
> Congratulations to those who grieve!
> They will be consoled.
> Congratulations to the gentle!
> They will inherit the earth.
> Congratulations to those who hunger and thirst for justice!
> They will have a feast.
> Congratulations to the merciful!
> They will receive mercy.
> Congratulations to those with undefiled hearts!
> They will see God.
> Congratulations to those who work for peace!
> They will be known as God's children.

Congratulations to those who have suffered persecution for the sake
of justice!
Heaven's domain belongs to them.

"Congratulations to you when they denounce you and persecute you
and spread malicious gossip about you because of me. Rejoice and be
glad! In heaven you will be more than compensated. Remember, this
is how they persecuted the prophets who preceded you.

"You are the salt of the earth. But if salt loses its zing, how will it
be made salty? It then has no further use than to be thrown out and
stomped on. You are the light of the world. A city sitting on top of a
mountain can't be concealed. Nor do people light a lamp and put it
under a bushel basket but rather on a lampstand, where it sheds light
for everyone in the house. That's how your light is to shine in the
presence of others, so they can see your good deeds and acclaim your
Father in the heavens.

"Don't imagine that I have come to annul the Law or the
Prophets. I have come not to annul but to fulfill. I swear to you, before
the world disappears, not one iota, not one serif, will disappear from
the Law, until that happens. Whoever ignores one of the most trivial
of these regulations, and teaches others to do so, will be called trivial
in Heaven's domain. But whoever acts on [these regulations] and
teaches [others to do so], will be called great in Heaven's domain. Let
me tell you: unless your religion goes beyond that of the scholars and
Pharisees, you won't set foot in Heaven's domain.

"As you know, our ancestors were told, 'You must not kill' and
'Whoever kills will be subject to judgment.' But I tell you: those who
are angry with a companion will be brought before a tribunal. And
those who say to a companion, 'You moron,' will be subject to the
sentence of the court. And whoever says, 'You idiot,' deserves the
fires of Gehenna. So, even if you happen to be offering your gift at the
altar and recall that your friend has some claim against you, leave
your gift there at the altar. First go and be reconciled with your friend,
and only then return and offer your gift. You should come to terms
quickly with your opponent while you are both on the way [to court],
or else your opponent will hand you over to the judge, and the judge
[will turn you over] to the bailiff, and you are thrown in jail. I swear to
you, you'll never get out of there until you've paid the last dime.

"As you know, we once were told, 'You are not to commit adultery.' But I tell you: Those who leer at a woman and desire her have
already committed adultery with her in their hearts. And if your right
eye gets you into trouble, rip it out and throw it away! You would be
better off to lose a part of your body, than to have your whole body
thrown into Gehenna. And if your right hand gets you into trouble,
cut it off and throw it away! You would be better off to lose a part of
your body, than to have your whole body wind up in Gehenna.

We once were told, 'Whoever divorces his wife should give her a bill of divorce.' But I tell you: Everyone who divorces his wife (except in the case of infidelity) makes her the victim of adultery; and whoever marries a divorced woman commits adultery.

Again, as you know, our ancestors were told, 'You must not break an oath,' and 'Oaths sworn in the name of God must be kept.' But I tell you: Don't swear at all. Don't invoke heaven, because it is the throne of God, and don't invoke earth, because it is God's footstool, and don't invoke Jerusalem, because it is the city of the great king. You shouldn't swear by your head either, since you aren't able to turn a single hair either white or black. Rather, your responses should be simply 'Yes' and 'No.' Anything that goes beyond this is inspired by the evil one.

As you know, we once were told, 'An eye for an eye' and 'A tooth for a tooth.' But I tell you: Don't react violently against the one who is evil: when someone slaps you on the right cheek, turn the other as well. If someone is determined to sue you for your shirt, let that person have your coat along with it. Further, when anyone conscripts you for one mile, go along an extra mile. Give to the one who begs from you; and don't turn away the one who tries to borrow from you.

As you know, we once were told, 'You are to love your neighbor' and 'You are to hate your enemy.' But I tell you: Love your enemies and pray for your persecutors. You'll then become children of your Father in the heavens. [God] causes the sun to rise on both the bad and the good, and sends rain on both the just and the unjust. Tell me, if you love those who love you, why should you be condemned for that? Even the toll collectors do as much, don't they? And if you greet only your friends, what have you done that is exceptional! Even the pagans do as much, don't they? To sum up, you are to be as liberal in your love as your heavenly Father is."

6. "Take care that you don't flaunt your religion in public to be noticed by others. Otherwise, you will have no recognition from your Father in the heavens. For example, when you give to charity, don't bother to toot your own horn as some phony pietists do in houses of worship and on the street. They are seeking human recognition. I swear to you, their grandstanding is its own reward. Instead, when you give to charity, don't let your left hand in on what your right hand is up to, so your acts of charity may remain hidden. And your Father, who has an eye for the hidden, will applaud you.

"And when you pray, don't act like phonies. They love to stand up and pray in houses of worship and on street corners, so they can show off in public. I swear to you, their prayers have been answered! When you pray, go into a room by yourself and shut the door behind you. Then pray to your Father, the hidden one. And your Father, with his eye for the hidden, will applaud you. And when you pray, you should not babble on as the pagans do. They imagine that the length of their prayers will command attention. So don't imitate them. After all, your Father knows what you need before you ask. Instead, you should pray like this:

> Our Father in the heavens,
> your name be revered.
> Impose your imperial rule,
> enact your will on earth as you have in heaven.
> Provide us with the bread we need for the day.
> Forgive our debts
> to the extent that we have forgiven those in debt to us.
> And please don't subject us to test after test,
> but rescue us from the evil one.

"For if you forgive others their failures and offenses, your heavenly Father will also forgive yours. And if you don't forgive the failures and mistakes of others, your Father won't forgive yours.

"When you fast, don't make a spectacle of your remorse as the pretenders do. As you know, they make their faces unrecognizable so their fasting may be publicly recognized. I swear to you, they have been paid in full. When you fast, comb your hair and wash your face, so your fasting may go unrecognized in public. But it will be recognized by your Father, the hidden one, and your Father, who has an eye for the hidden, will applaud you.

"Don't acquire possessions here on earth, where moths and insects eat away and where robbers break in and steal. Instead, gather your nest egg in heaven, where neither moths nor insects eat away and where no robbers break in or steal. As you know, what you treasure is your heart's true measure.

"The eye is the body's lamp. If follows that if your eye is clear, your whole body will be flooded with light. If your eye is clouded, your whole body will be shrouded in darkness. If, then, the light within you is darkness, how dark that can be!

"No one can be a slave to two masters. No doubt that slave will either hate one and love the other, or be devoted to one and disdain the other. You can't be enslaved to both God and a bank account!

"That's why I tell you: Don't fret about your life—what you're going to eat and drink—or about your body—what you're going to wear. There is more to living than food and clothing, isn't there? Take a look at the birds of the sky: they don't plant or harvest, or gather into barns. Yet your heavenly Father feeds them. You're worth more than they, aren't you? Can any of you add one hour to life by fretting about it? Why worry about clothes? Notice how the wild lilies grow: they don't slave and they never spin. Yet let me tell you, even Solomon at the height of his glory was never decked out like one of them. If God dresses up the grass in the field, which is here today and tomorrow is thrown into an oven, won't [God care for] you even more, you who don't take anything for granted? So don't fret. Don't say, 'What am I going to eat?' or 'What am I going to drink?' or 'What am I going to wear?' These are all things pagans seek. After all, our heavenly Father is aware that you need them. You are to seek [God's] domain, and his justice first, and all these things will come to you as a bonus. So don't fret about tomorrow. Let tomorrow fret about itself. The troubles that the day brings are enough.

7. "Don't pass judgment, so you won't be judged. Don't forget, the judgment you hand out will be the judgment you get back. And the standard you apply will be the standard applied to you. Why do you notice the sliver in your friend's eye, but overlook the timber in your own? How can you say to your friend, 'Let me get the sliver out of your eye,' when there is that timber in your own? You phony, first take the timber out of your own eye and then you'll see well enough to remove the sliver from your friend's eye.

"Don't offer to dogs what is sacred, and don't throw your pearls to pigs, or they'll trample them underfoot and turn and tear you to shreds.

"Ask—it'll be given to you; seek—you'll find; knock—it'll be opened for you. Rest assured: everyone who asks receives; everyone who seeks finds; and for the one who knocks it is opened. Who among you would hand a son a stone when it's bread he's asking for? Again, who would hand him a snake when it's fish he's asking for? Of course no one would! So if you, worthless as you are, know how to give your children good gifts, isn't it much more likely that your Father in the heavens will give good things to those who ask him?

"Consider this: Treat people in ways you want them to treat you. This sums up the whole of the Law and the Prophets.

Try to get in through the narrow gate. Wide and smooth is the road that leads to destruction. The majority are taking that route. Narrow and rough is the road that leads to life. Only a minority discover it.

Be on the lookout for phony prophets, who make their pitch disguised as sheep; inside they are really voracious wolves. You'll know who they are by what they produce. Since when do people pick grapes from thorns or figs from thistles? Every healthy tree produces choice fruit, but the rotten tree produces spoiled fruit. A healthy tree cannot produce spoiled fruit, any more than a rotten tree can produce choice fruit. Every tree that does not produce choice fruit gets cut down and tossed on the fire. Remember, you'll know who they are by what they produce.

Not everyone who addresses me as 'Master, master,' will get into Heaven's domain—only those who carry out the will of my Father in heaven. On that day many will address me: 'Master, master, didn't we use your name when we prophesied? Didn't we use your name when we exorcised demons? Didn't we use your name when we performed all those miracles? Then I will tell them honestly: 'I never knew you; get away from me, you subverters of the Law!'

"Everyone who pays attention to these words of mine and acts on them will be like a shrewd builder who erected a house on bedrock. Later the rain fell, and the torrents came, and the winds blew and pounded that house, yet it did not collapse, since its foundation rested on bedrock. Everyone who listens to these words of mine and doesn't act on them will be like a careless builder, who erected a house on the sand. When the rain fell, and the torrents came, and the winds blew and pounded that house, it collapsed. Its collapse was colossal."

And so, when Jesus had finished this discourse, the crowds were astonished at his teaching, since he had been teaching them on his own authority, unlike their [own] scholars.

Source: Matthew, chs. 5–7, from *The Complete Gospels*.

GOOD SAMARITAN AND PRODIGAL SON

Of the approximately 30 parables of Jesus, the two most famous appear only in Luke: the good Samaritan and the prodigal son. Luke sets both parables in a larger narrative context. The good Samaritan parable is introduced in a dialogue between Jesus and a lawyer (adapted from Mark 12:28–34) on loving one's neighbor. Jesus then explains that the notion of one's neighbor crosses religious and social boundaries, just as a Samaritan aids a battered Jew, in spite of enmity between their two ethnic groups. The prodigal son parable is one of three which Jesus gives in response to criticisms that he associates with sinners. The parable's message is one of forgiveness. The father (representing God) forgives the younger son (representing non-Jews) who squanders his inheritance, while the dutiful older brother (representing Jews) protests.

10. On one occasion, a legal expert stood up to put him to the test with a question: "Teacher, what do I have to do to inherit eternal life?"

He said to him, "How do you read what is written in the Law?"

And he answered, "You are to love the Lord your God with all your heart, with all your soul, with all your energy, and with all your mind; and your neighbor as yourself."

Jesus said to him, "You have given the correct answer; do this and you will have life."

But with a view to justifying himself, he said to Jesus, "But who is my neighbor?"

Jesus replied:

This fellow was on his way from Jerusalem down to Jericho when he fell into the hands of robbers. They stripped him, beat him up, and went off, leaving him half dead. Now by coincidence a priest was going down that road; when he caught sight of him, he went out of his way to avoid him. In the same way, when a Levite came to the place, he took one look at him and crossed the road to avoid him. But this Samaritan who was traveling that way came to where he was and was moved to pity at the sight of him. He went up to him and bandaged his wounds, pouring olive oil and wine on them. He hoisted him onto his own animal, brought him to an inn, and looked after him. The next day he took out two silver coins, which he gave to the innkeeper, and said, "Look after him, and on my way back I'll reimburse you for any extra expenses you have had."

"Which of these three, in your opinion, acted like a neighbor to the man who fell into the hands of the robbers?"

He said, "The one who showed him compassion."

Jesus said to him, "Then go and do the same yourself."

15. Now the toll collectors and sinners kept crowding around Jesus so they could hear him. But the Pharisees and the scholars would complain to each other: "This fellow welcomes sinners and eats with them."

So he told them this parable: . . .

Once there was this man who had two sons. The younger of them said to his father, "Father give me the share of the property that's coming to me." So he divided his resources between them.

Not too many days later, the younger son got all his things together and left home for a faraway country, where he squandered his property by living extravagantly. Just when he had spent it all, a serious famine swept through that country, and he began to do without. So he went and hired himself out to one of the citizens of that country, who sent him out to his farm to feed the pigs. He longed to satisfy his hunger with the carob pods, which the pigs usually ate; but no one offered him anything. Coming to his senses he said, "Lots of my father's hired hands have more than enough to eat, while here I am dying of starvation! I'll get up and go to my father and I'll say to him, 'Father, I have sinned against heaven and affronted you; I don't deserve to be called a son of yours any longer; treat me like one of your hired hands.'" And he got up and returned to his father.

But while he was still a long way off, his father caught sight of him and was moved to compassion. He went running out to him, threw his arms around his neck, and kissed him. And the son said to him, "Father, I have sinned against heaven and affronted you; I don't deserve to be called a son of yours any longer."

But the father said to his slaves, "Quick! Bring out the finest robe and put it on him; put a ring on his finger and sandals on his feet. Fetch the fat calf and slaughter it; let's have a feast and celebrate, because this son of mine was dead and has come back to life; he was lost and now is found." And they started celebrating.

Now his elder son was out in the field; and as he got closer to the house, he heard music and dancing. He called one of the servant-boys over and asked what was going on.

He said to him, "Your brother has come home and your father has slaughtered the fat calf, because he has him back safe and sound."

But he was angry and refused to go in. So his father came out and began to plead with him. But he answered his father, "See here, all these years I have slaved for you. I never once disobeyed any of your orders; yet you never once provided me with a kid goat so I could celebrate with my friends. But when this son of yours shows up, the one who has squandered your estate with prostitutes—for him you slaughter the fat calf."

But [the father] said to him, "My child, you are always at my side. Everything that's mine is yours. But we just had to celebrate and rejoice, because this brother of yours was dead, and has come back to life; he was lost, and now is found."

Source: Luke, chs. 10:25–37; 15:1–3, 11–32, from *The Complete Gospels*.

PETER RECEIVES THE KEYS

Early Christian traditions typically traced their lineage back to an original follower of Jesus. Early Gnostics viewed Jesus' brothers, James and Thomas, as their founders. For Ethiopians, the founder is the eunuch of Acts 8. For the Orthodox of Constantinople, he is Andrew the Apostle. The Catholic church, though, considers its foundation to be Peter, the first supreme Pope. The concept of the Petrine Papacy is based on two doctrines. First, the doctrine of apostolic succession maintains that the original Apostles had authority over specific regional churches, which they passed on to their successors. Peter established the church of Rome and, at his death, authority was passed to Linus. Second, the doctrine of the primacy of Peter, forged in the third through fifth centuries, maintains that Peter was given supreme authority over all church congregations. The argument for this latter claim is based on the following passage from Matthew. Drawing from a scene in Mark 8:27 in which Peter identifies Jesus as the Messiah, Matthew then recounts that Jesus rewarded Peter with keys to the kingdom of God. Although the language is metaphorical, Peter is clearly given sweeping authority, thus indicating Matthew's allegiance to the Petrine tradition. Matthew continues by foreshadowing Jesus' fate.

When Jesus came to the region of Caesarea Philippi, he started questioning his disciples, asking, "What are people saying about the son of Adam?"

They said, "Some [say, 'He is] John the Baptist,' but others, 'Elijah,' and others, 'Jeremiah or one of the prophets.'"

He says to them, "What about you, who do you say I am?"

And Simon Peter responded, "You are the Anointed, the son of the living God!"

And in response Jesus said to him, "You are to be congratulated, Simon son of Jonah, because flesh and blood did not reveal this to you but my Father who is in heaven. Let me tell you, you are Peter, 'the Rock,' and on this very rock I will build my congregation, and the gates of Hades will not be able to overpower it. I shall give you the keys of Heaven's domain, and whatever you bind on earth will be considered bound in heaven, and whatever you release on earth will be considered released in heaven."

Then he ordered the disciples to tell no one that he was the Anointed.

From that time on Jesus started to make it clear to his disciples that he was destined to go to Jerusalem, and suffer a great deal at the hands of the elders and ranking priests and scholars, and be killed and, on the third day, be raised.

And Peter took him aside and began to lecture him, saying, "May God spare you, master; this surely can't happen to you."

But he turned and said to Peter, "Get out of my sight, you Satan, you. You are dangerous to me because you are not thinking in God's terms, but in human terms."

Then Jesus said to his disciples, "If any of you wants to come after me you should deny yourself, pick up your cross, and follow me!

"Remember by trying to save your own life, you are going to lose it, but by losing your own life for my sake, you are going to find it. After all, what good will it do if you acquire the whole world but forfeit your life? Or what will you give in exchange for your life?

Remember, the son of Adam is going to come in the glory of his father with his messengers, and then he will reward everyone according to their deeds. I swear to you: Some of those standing here won't ever taste death before they see the son of Adam's imperial rule arriving."

Source: Matthew ch. 16:13–28, from *The Complete Gospels*.

LAZARUS RAISED FROM THE DEAD

The Gospel of John presents an account of Jesus that is almost entirely different from that of the synoptic gospels. In John, Jesus' ministry is three years, as opposed to one year; the subject of eternal life is emphasized, and not the kingdom of God; Jesus performs no exorcisms, refers to himself as the son of God, is the subject of his own teachings, and says little about the poor. Although Jesus performs miracles in both John and the synoptics, the purpose is different. In John, they are intentionally performed as signs indicating his divine role, whereas in the synoptics, such signs are shunned and miracles are depicted mainly as acts of compassion. In the following passage, Jesus performs his most dramatic miracle by raising a dead man to life. For John, as well as the synoptics, Jesus' supernatural powers were seen by the Jewish leaders as a threat to social and religious stability, inciting them to plot against him.

Now someone named Lazarus had fallen ill; he was from Bethany, the village of Mary and her sister Martha. (This was the Mary who anointed the Master with oil and wiped his feet with her hair; it was her brother Lazarus who was sick.) So the sisters sent for [Jesus]: "Master, the one you love is sick."

But when Jesus heard this he said, "This illness is not fatal; it is to show God's majesty, so God's son also will be honored by it."

Jesus loved Martha and her sister and Lazarus. When he heard that [Lazarus] was sick, he lingered two more days where he was; then he says to the disciples, "Let's go to Judea again."

The disciples say to him, "Rabbi, just now the Judeans were looking for the opportunity to stone you; are you really going back there?"

"Aren't there twelve hours in the day?" Jesus responded. "Those who walk during the day won't stumble; they can see by this world's light. But those who walk at night are going to stumble, because they have no light to go by."

He made these remarks, and then he tells them, "Our friend Lazarus has fallen asleep, but I am going to wake him up."

"Master, if he's only fallen asleep," said the disciples, "he'll revive." (Jesus had been speaking of death but they thought that he meant [he was] only asleep.)

Then Jesus told them plainly, "Lazarus is dead; and I'm happy for you that I wasn't there, so you can believe. Now let's go to him."

Then Thomas, called "the Twin," said to his fellow disciples, "Let's go along too, so we can die with him."

When Jesus arrived, he found that [Lazarus] had been buried four days earlier. Bethany was near Jerusalem, about two miles away, and many of the Judeans had come to Martha and Mary to console them about their brother. When Martha heard that Jesus was coming, she went to meet him; Mary stayed at home. "Master," said Martha, "if you'd been here, my brother wouldn't have died. Still I know that whatever you ask of God, God will grant you."

Jesus says to her, "Your brother will be resurrected."

Martha responds, "I know he'll be raised in the resurrection on the last day."

Jesus said to her, "I am resurrection and life; those who believe in me, even if they die, will live; but everyone who is alive and believes in me will never die. Do you believe this?"

"Yes, Master," she says, "I believe that you are the Anointed, God's son, who is to come to earth."

At this point she went to call her sister Mary, telling her privately, "The Teacher is here and is asking for you." When she heard that, she got up quickly and went to him.

Jesus hadn't yet arrived at the village; he was still where Martha had met him.

When the Judeans, who hovered about her in the house to console her, saw Mary get up and go out quickly, they followed her, thinking she was going to the tomb to grieve there. When Mary got to where Jesus was and saw him, she fell down at his feet. "Master," she said, "if you'd been here, my brother wouldn't have died."

When Jesus saw her crying, and the Judeans who accompanied her crying too, he was agitated and deeply disturbed; he said, "Where have you put him?"

"Master," they say, "come and see."

Then Jesus cried.

So the Judeans observed, "Look how much he loved him." But some wondered: "He opened the blind man's eyes; couldn't he have kept this man from dying?"

Again greatly agitated, Jesus arrives at the tomb; it was a cave, and a stone lay up against the opening. Jesus says, "Take the stone away."

Martha, sister of the dead man, replies, "But Master, by this time the body will stink; it's been four days."

Jesus says to her, "Didn't I tell you, if you believed you'll see God's majesty?" So they took the stone away, and Jesus looked upwards and said, "Father, thank you for hearing me. I know you always hear me, but I say this because of the people standing here, so they'll believe that you sent me." Then he shouted at the top of his voice, "Lazarus, come out!" The dead man came out, his hands and feet bound in strips of burying cloth, and his face covered with a cloth. Jesus says to them, "Free him [from the burying cloth] and let him go."

As a result, many of the Judeans who had come to Mary and observed what Jesus had done came to believe in him. But some of them went to the Pharisees and reported what Jesus had done.

So the ranking priests and Pharisees called the Council together and posed this question to them: "What are we going to do now that this fellow performs many miracles? If we let him go on like this, everybody will come to believe in him. Then the Romans will come and destroy our [holy] place and our nation."

Then one of them, Caiaphas, that year's high priest, addressed them as follows: "Don't you know anything? Don't you realize that it's to your advantage to have one person die for the people and not have the whole nation wiped out?"

(He didn't say this on his own authority, but since he was that year's high priest he could foresee that Jesus would die for the nation. In fact, [he would die] not only for the nation, but to gather together all God's dispersed children and make them one [people].)

Source: John, ch. 11:1–54, from *The Complete Gospels*.

JESUS' DEATH

LAST SUPPER

Jesus' final days took place in Jerusalem during the Jewish holiday of Passover. The four Gospels depict Jesus and his disciples gathering for a meal, known as the "Last Supper" (Luke describes this as the traditional meal of the passover festival). At this meal, according to the synoptic gospels, Jesus performed symbolic acts with the bread and wine. This event is the basis of the Christian sacrament of the Eucharist. In Christian doctrine, a sacrament is a visible religious rite that confers special grace. The number of sacraments has varied throughout Christian history; twelfth-century theologian Hugo of St. Victor listed 30. Baptism and the Eucharist have always been the most important.

Now it was two days until Passover and the feast of Unleavened Bread. And the ranking priests and the scholars were looking for some way to arrest him by trickery and kill him. For their slogan was "Not during the festival, otherwise the people will riot."

When he was in Bethany at the house of Simon the leper, he was just reclining there, and a woman came in carrying an alabaster jar of myrrh, of pure and expensive nard. She broke the jar and poured [the myrrh] on his head.

Now some were annoyed [and thought] to themselves: "What good purpose is served by this waste of myrrh? For she could have sold the myrrh for more than three hundred silver coins and given [the money] to the poor." And they were angry with her.

Then Jesus said, "Let her alone! Why are you bothering her? She has done me a courtesy. Remember, there will always be poor around, and whenever you want you can do good for them, but I won't always be around. She did what she could—she anticipates in anointing my body for burial. So help me, wherever the good news is announced in all the world, what she has done will also be told in memory of her!"

And Judas Iscariot, one of the twelve, went off to the ranking priests to turn him over to them. When they heard, they were delighted, and promised to pay him in silver. And he started looking for some way to turn him in at the right moment.

On the first day of Unleavened Bread, when they would sacrifice the Passover lamb, his disciples say to him, "Where do you want us to go and get things ready for you to celebrate Passover?"

He sends two of his disciples and says to them, "Go into the city, and someone carrying a waterpot will meet you. Follow him, and whatever place he enters say to the head of the house, 'The teacher asks, "Where is my guest room where I can celebrate Passover with my disciples?"' And he'll show you a large upstairs room that has been arranged. That's the place you're to get ready for us."

And the disciples left, went into the city, and found it exactly as he had told them; and they got things ready for Passover.

When evening comes, he arrives with the twelve. And as they reclined at tables and were eating, Jesus said, "So help me, one of you eating with me is going to turn me in!"

They began to fret and to say to him one after another, "I'm not the one, am I?"

But he said to them, "It's one of the twelve, the one who is dipping into the bowl with me. The son of Adam departs just as the scriptures predict, but damn the one responsible for turning the son of Adam in! It would be better for that man had he never been born!"

And as they were eating, he took a loaf, gave a blessing, broke it into pieces and offered it to them. And he said, "Take some; this is my body!"

He also took a cup, gave thanks and offered it to them, and they all drank from it. And he said to them: "This is my blood of the covenant, which has been poured out for many! So help me, I certainly won't drink it for the first time in God's domain!"

Source: Mark 14:1–25, from *The Complete Gospels*.

FATHER, SON, AND HOLY SPIRIT

In John's account of the last supper, Jesus gives a farewell discourse, presented below. Unlike the synoptic gospels, in which Jesus speaks in short, crisp sayings and parables, in John Jesus speaks in extended discourses. The discourse topic here is the relation between God the Father and Jesus the Son. The doctrine of the Trinity, central to Christianity, holds that God is a unity of three persons: the Father, Son, and Holy Spirit. Although the term "Trinity" and its technical meaning were developed by early church fathers, passages that associate the Father, Son, and Holy Spirit are the scriptural basis of the doctrine. The following is particularly important in this regard. The Holy Spirit is only briefly mentioned at the end of this passage. In the Old Testament occasional references are made to a spirit of God, but John and other New Testament writers expand on this notion and see the Holy Spirit both as a divine presence and as an agent of guidance for the church.

"Don't give in to your distress. You believe in God, then believe in me too. There are plenty of places to stay in my Father's house. If it weren't true, I would have told you; I'm on my way to make a place ready for you. And if I go to make a place ready for you, I'll return and embrace you. So where I am you can be too. You know where I'm going and you know the way."

Thomas says to him, "Master, we don't know where you're going. How can we possibly know the way?"

"I am the way, and I am truth, and I am life," replies Jesus. "No one gets to the Father unless it is through me. If you do recognize me, you will recognize my Father also. From this moment on you know him and you've even seen him."

"Let us see the Father," Philip says to him, "and we'll be satisfied."

"I've been around you all this time," Jesus replies, "and you still don't know me, do you, Philip? Anyone who has seen me has seen the Father. So how can you say, 'Let us see the Father'? Don't you believe that I'm in the Father and the Father is in me? I don't say what I say on my own. The Father is with me constantly, and I perform his labors. You ought to believe that I'm in the Father and the Father is in me. If not, at least you ought to believe these labors in and of themselves. I swear to God, anyone who believes in me will perform the works I perform and will be able to perform even greater feats, because I'm on my way to the Father. In addition, I'll do whatever you request in my name, so the Father can be honored by means of the son. If you request anything using my name, I'll do it."

"If you love me, you'll obey my instructions. At my request the Father will provide you with yet another advocate, the authentic spirit, who will be with you forever. The world is unable to accept [this spirit] because it neither perceives nor recognizes it. You recognize it because it dwells in you and will remain in you.

"I won't abandon you as orphans; I'll come to you. In a little while the world won't see me any longer, but you'll see me because I'm alive as you will be alive. At the time you will come to know that I'm in my Father and that you're in me and I'm in you. Those who accept my instructions and obey them—they love me. And those who love me will be loved by my Father; moreover, I will love them and make myself known to them."

Judas (not Iscariot) says to him, "Master, what has happened that you are about to make yourself known to us but not to the world?"

Jesus replied to him, "Those who love me will heed what I tell them, and my Father will love them, and we'll come to them and make our home there. Those who don't love me won't follow my instructions. Of course, the things you heard me say are not mine but come from the Father who sent me.

"I have told you these things while I am still here with you. Yet the advocate, the holy spirit the Father will send in my stead, will teach you everything and remind you of everything I told you. Peace is what I leave behind for you; my peace is what I give you. What I give you is not a worldly gift. Don't give in to your distress or be overcome by terror. You heard me tell you, 'I'm going away and I'm going to return to you.' If you loved me, you'd be glad that I'm going to the Father, because the Father is greater than I am. So I have now told you all this ahead of time so you will believe when it happens.

"Time does not permit me to tell you much more; you see, the ruler of this world is already on the way. However, so the world may know I love the Father, I act exactly as my Father instructed me. Come on, let's get out of here."

Source: John 14:1–26, from *The Complete Gospels.*

TRIAL, CRUCIFIXION, RESURRECTION

After the last supper, Jesus went with his disciples to a hillside graveyard to pray. There he was arrested, brought before the Jewish legal council, and accused of blasphemy. Not empowered to perform criminal executions, the council brought Jesus to the Roman governor Pilate, where they made a case for treason based on Jesus' messianic claims. Pilate pronounced the desired verdict and sentence. All four Gospels place responsibility on the Jews, first the priests and then an angry mob, although the ultimate decision rested with the governor. Jesus was then executed on a cross, in classic Roman fashion, and placed in the rock-hewn tomb of a wealthy follower. Mark's Gospel reports that after a few days the tomb was found empty, and a young man present at the tomb announced that Jesus was resurrected. The other Gospels report appearances of the resurrected Jesus.

14. And right away, while he was still speaking, Judas, one of the twelve, shows up, and with him a crowd, dispatched by the ranking priests and the scholars and the elders, wielding swords and clubs. Now the one who was to turn him in had arranged a signal with them, saying, "The one I'm going to kiss is the one you want. Arrest him and escort him safely away!" And right away he arrives, comes up to him, and says, "Rabbi," and kisses him.

And they seized him and held him fast. One of those standing around drew his sword and struck the high priest's slave and cut off his ear. In response Jesus said to them, "Have you come out to take me with swords and clubs as though you were apprehending a rebel? I was with you in the temple area day after day teaching and you didn't lift a hand against me. But the scriptures must come true!"

And they all deserted him and ran away. And a young man was following him, wearing a shroud over his nude body, and they grab him. But he dropped the shroud and ran away naked.

And they brought Jesus before the high priest, and all the ranking priests and elders and scholars assemble.

Peter followed him at a distance until he was inside the courtyard of the high priest, and was sitting with the attendants and keeping warm by the fire.

The ranking priests and the whole Council were looking for evidence against Jesus in order to issue a death sentence, but they couldn't find any. Although many gave false evidence against him, their stories didn't agree. And some people stood up and testified falsely against him: "We have heard him saying, 'I'll destroy this temple made with hands and in three days I'll build another, not made with hands!'" Yet even then their stories did not agree.

And the high priest got up and questioned Jesus: "Don't you have some answer to give? Why do these people testify against you?"

But he was silent and refused to answer.

Once again the high priest questioned him and says to him, "Are you the Anointed, the son of the Blessed One?"

Jesus replied, "I am! And you will see the son of Adam sitting at the right hand of Power and coming with the clouds of the sky!"

Then the high priest tore his vestments and says, "Why do we still need witnesses? You have heard the blasphemy! What do you think?" And they all concurred in the death penalty.

And some began to spit on him, and to put a blindfold on him, and punch him, and say to him, "Prophesy!" And the guards abused him as they took him into custody.

And while Peter was below in the courtyard, one of the high priest's slave women comes over, and sees Peter warming himself; she looks at him closely, then speaks up: "You too were with that Nazarene, Jesus!"

But he denied it, saying, "I haven't the slightest idea what you're talking about!" And he went outside into the forecourt.

And when the slave woman saw him, she once again began to say to those standing nearby, "This fellow is one of them!"

But once again he denied it.

And a little later, those standing nearby would again say to Peter, "You really are one of them, since you also are a Galilean!"

But he began to curse and swear, "I don't know the fellow you're talking about!" And just then a rooster crowed a second time, and Peter remembered what Jesus had told him: "Before a rooster crows twice you will disown me three times!" And he broke down and started to cry.

15. And right away, at daybreak, the ranking priests, after consulting with the elders and scholars and the whole Council, bound Jesus and led him away and turned him over to Pilate. And Pilate questioned him: "*You* are 'the King of the Judeans'?"

And in response he says to him, "If you say so."

And the ranking priests started a long list of accusations against him. Again Pilate tried questioning him: "Don't you have some answer to give? You see what a long list of charges they bring against you!"

But Jesus still did not respond, so Pilate was baffled.

At each festival it was the custom for him to set one prisoner free for them, whichever one they requested. And one called Barabbas was being held with the insurgents who had committed murder during the uprising. And when the crowd arrived, they began to demand that he do what he usually did for them.

And in response Pilate said to them, "Do you want me to set 'the King of the Judeans' free for you?" After all, he realized that the ranking priests had turned him over out of envy.

But the ranking priests incited the crowd to get Barabbas set free for them instead.

But in response [to their request] Pilate would again say to them, "What do you want me to do with the fellow you call 'the King of the Judeans'?"

And they in turn shouted, "Crucify him!"

Pilate kept saying to them, "Why? What has he done wrong?"

But they shouted all the louder, "Crucify him!" And because Pilate was always looking to satisfy the crowd, he set Barabbas free for them, had Jesus flogged, and then turned him over to be crucified.

And the soldiers led him away to the courtyard of the governor's residence, and they called the whole company together. And they dressed him in purple and crowned him with a garland woven of thorns. And they began to salute him: "Greetings, 'King of the

Judean'!" And they kept striking him on the head with a staff, and spitting on him; and they would get down on their knees and bow down to him. And when they had made fun of him, they stripped off the purple and put his own clothes back on him. And they lead him out to crucify him.

And they conscript someone named Simon of Cyrene, who was coming in from the country, the father of Alexander and Rufus, to carry his cross.

And they bring him to the place Golgotha (which means "Place of the Skull"). And they tried to give him wine mixed with myrrh, but he didn't take it. And they crucify him, and they divide up his garments, casting lots to see who would get what. It was 9 o'clock in the morning when they crucified him. And the inscription, which identified his crime, read, "The King of the Judeans." And with him they crucify two rebels, one on his right and one on his left.

Those passing by kept taunting him, wagging their heads, and saying, "Ha! You who would destroy the temple and rebuild it in three days, save yourself and come down from the cross!"

Likewise the ranking priests had made fun of him to one another, along with the scholars; they would say, "He saved others, but he can't save himself! 'The Anointed,' 'the King of Israel,' should come down from the cross here and now, so that we can see and trust for ourselves!"

Even those being crucified along with him would abuse him.

And when noon came, darkness blanketed the whole land until mid-afternoon. And at 3 o'clock in the afternoon Jesus shouted at the top of his voice, "*Eloi, Eloi, lema sabachthani*" (which means "My God, my God, why did you abandon me?").

And when some of those standing nearby heard, they would say, "Listen, he's calling Elijah!" And someone ran and filled a sponge with sour wine, stuck it on a pole, and offered him a drink, saying, Let's see if Elijah comes to rescue him!"

But Jesus let out a great shout and breathed his last.

And the curtain of the temple was torn in two from top to bottom! When the Roman officer standing opposite him saw that he had died like this, he said, "This man really was God's son!"

Now some women were observing this from a distance, among whom were Mary of Magdala, and Mary the mother of James the younger and Joses, and Salome. [These women] had regularly followed and assisted him when he was in Galilee, along with many other women who had come up to Jerusalem in his company.

And when it had already grown dark, since it was preparation day (the day before the sabbath), Joseph of Arimathea, a respected council member, who himself was anticipating God's imperial rule, appeared on the scene, and dared to go to Pilate to request the body of Jesus. And Pilate was surprised that he had died so soon. He summoned the Roman officer and asked him whether he had been dead for long. And when he had been briefed by the Roman officer, he granted the body to Joseph. And he brought a shroud and took him down and wrapped him in the shroud, and placed him in a tomb that had been hewn out of rock, and rolled a stone up against the opening of the tomb. And Mary of Magdala and Mary the mother of Joses noted where he had been laid to rest.

16. And when the sabbath day was over, Mary of Magdala and Mary the mother of James and Salome brought spices so they could go and embalm him. And very early on Sunday they got to the tomb just as the sun was coming up. And they had been asking themselves, "Who will help us roll the stone away from the opening of the tomb?" Then they look up and discover that the stone has been rolled away! (For in fact the stone was very large.)

And when they went into the tomb, the saw a young man sitting on the right, wearing a white robe, and they grew apprehensive.

He says to them, "Don't be alarmed! You are looking for Jesus the Nazarene who was crucified. He was raised, he is not here! Look at the spot where they put him! But go and tell his disciples, including 'Rock,' "He is going ahead of you to Galilee! There you will see him, just as he told you."

And once they got outside, they ran away from the tomb, because great fear and excitement got the better of them. And they didn't breathe a word of it to anyone: talk about terrified. . . .

Source: Mark, 14:43–16:8 from *The Complete Gospels.*

NEW TESTAMENT CHURCH

ASCENSION, PENTECOST

The book of the Acts of the Apostles, written about 85 C.E., chronicles the events of the early Church after Jesus' resurrection. The book is sometimes termed the Gospel of the Holy Spirit, since the author depicts the expansion of the early church as being guided by the Holy Spirit. The opening of Acts, appearing next, recounts Jesus' ascension into heaven and the arrival of the Holy Spirit a few days later, during the Jewish agricultural festival of Pentecost. The believers are directly affected by the presence of the Holy Spirit, as evidenced by their speaking in foreign tongues. Peter emerges as the leader of the Church, and thousands of believers are baptized.

1. After his suffering, he showed himself to these men [i.e., the Apostles] and gave many convincing proofs that he was alive. He appeared to them over a period of forty days and spoke about the kingdom of God. On one occasion, while he was eating with them, he gave them this command: "Do not leave Jerusalem, but wait for the gift my Father promised, which you have heard me speak about. For John

baptized with water, but in a few days you will be baptized with the Holy Spirit."

So when they met together, they asked him, "Lord, are you at this time going to restore the kingdom to Israel?"

He said to them: "It is not for you to know the times or dates the Father has set by his own authority. But you will receive power when the Holy Spirit comes on you; and you will be my witnesses in Jerusalem, and in all Judea and Samaria, and to the ends of the earth."

After he said this, he was taken up before their very eyes, and a cloud hid him from their sight.

They were looking intently up into the sky as he was going, when suddenly two men dressed in white stood beside them. "Men of Galilee," they said, "why do you stand here looking into the sky? This same Jesus, who has been taken from you into heaven, will come back in the same way you have seen him go into heaven."

2. When the day of Pentecost came, they were all together in one place. Suddenly a sound like the blowing of a violent wind came from heaven and filled the whole house where they were sitting. They saw what seemed to be tongues of fire that separated and came to rest on each of them. All of them were filled with the Holy Spirit and began to speak in other tongues as the Spirit enabled them.

Now there were staying in Jerusalem God-fearing Jews from every nation under heaven. When they heard this sound, a crowd came together in bewilderment, because each one heard them speaking in his own language. Utterly amazed, they asked: "Are not all these men who are speaking Galileans? Then how is it that each of us hears them in his own native language? Parthians, Medes and Elamites; residents of Mesopotamia, Judea and Cappadocia, Pontus and Asia, Phrygia and Pamphylia, Egypt and the parts of Libya near Cyrene; visitors from Rome (both Jews and converts to Judaism); Cretans and Arabs—we hear them declaring the wonders of God in our own tongues!" Amazed and perplexed, they asked one another, "What does this mean?"

Some, however, made fun of them and said, "They have had too much wine."

Then Peter stood up with the Eleven, raised his voice and addressed the crowd: "Fellow Jews and all of you who live in Jerusalem, let me explain this to you; listen carefully to what I say. These men are not drunk, as you suppose. It's only nine in the morning! No, this is what was spoken by the prophet Joel:

> In the last days, God says, I will pour out my Spirit on all people. Your sons and daughters will prophesy, your young men will see visions, your old men will dream dreams. Even on my servants, both men and women, I will pour out my Spirit in those days, and they will prophesy. I will show wonders in the heaven above and signs on the earth below, blood and fire and billows of smoke. The sun will be turned to darkness and the moon to blood before the coming of the

great and glorious day of the Lord. And everyone who calls on the name of the Lord will be saved.

"Men of Israel, listen to this: Jesus of Nazareth was a man accredited by God to you by miracles, wonders, and signs, which God did among you through him, as you yourselves know. This man was handed over to you by God's set purpose and foreknowledge; and you, with the help of wicked men, put him to death by nailing him to the cross. But God raised him from the dead, freeing him from the agony of death, because it was impossible for death to keep its hold on him. . . ."

With many other words he warned them; and he pleaded with them, "Save yourselves from this corrupt generation." Those who accepted his message were baptized, and about three thousand were added to their number that day.

They devoted themselves to the apostles' teaching and to the fellowship, to the breaking of bread and to prayer. Everyone was filled with awe, and many wonders and miraculous signs were done by the apostles. All the believers were together and had everything in common. Selling their possessions and goods, they gave to anyone as he had need. Every day they continued to meet together in the temple courts. They broke bread in their homes and ate together with glad and sincere hearts, praising God and enjoying the favor of all the people. And the Lord added to their number daily those who were being saved.

Source: Acts, chs. 1:3–11, 2:1–24, 40–47, from *The Holy Bible, New International Version.*

PAUL ON THE DISTINCTION
BETWEEN CHRISTIANITY AND JUDAISM

After a dramatic conversion experience and a period of indoctrination, Paul soon rose in the leadership to the status of an Apostle. During three missionary journeys in non-Jewish territories throughout the Mediterranean region, he established dozens of churches and corresponded with many of them. Written about 55 C.E., Paul's letter to the church of Galatia is a pivotal text in the development of early Christianity. Shortly after his visit, church members in Galatia were persuaded by Christian Judaizers that adherence to Jewish law was a prerequisite for becoming a Christian. Paul argues vehemently that obedience to Jewish law will not absolve our sins. Righteousness comes about only through faith in Christ, and this is open to Jews and non-Jews alike. The larger issue in the debate was whether Christianity was merely a Jewish sect or a distinct religion; in the first two chapters presented next, Paul describes his efforts to set Christianity apart from its Jewish framework. His account is important for its autobiographical content, and also because it is the earliest written discussion of first-century church politics.

1. I am astonished that you are so quickly deserting the one who called you by the grace of Christ and are turning to a different gospel—which is really no gospel at all. Evidently some people are throwing you into confusion and are tying to pervert the gospel of Christ. But even if we or an angel from heaven should preach a gospel other than the one we preached to you, let him be eternally condemned! As we have already said, so now I say again: If anybody is preaching to you a gospel other than what you accepted, let him be eternally condemned!

   Am I now trying to win the approval of men, or of God? Or am I trying to please men? If I were still trying to please men, I would not be a servant of Christ.

   I want you to know, brothers, that the gospel I preached is not something that man made up. I did not receive it from any man, nor was I taught it; rather, I received it by revelation from Jesus Christ.

   For you have heard of my previous way of life in Judaism, how intensely I persecuted the church of God and tried to destroy it. I was advancing in Judaism beyond many Jews of my own age and was extremely zealous for the traditions of my fathers. But when God, who set me apart from birth and called me by his grace, was pleased to reveal his Son in me so that I might preach him among the Gentiles, I did not consult any man, nor did I go up to Jerusalem to see those who were apostles before I was, but I went immediately into Arabia and later returned to Damascus.

   Then after three years, I went up to Jerusalem to get acquainted with Peter and stayed with him fifteen days. I saw none of the other apostles—only James, the Lord's brother. I assure you before God that what I am writing you is no lie. Later I went to Syria and Cilicia. I was personally unknown to the churches of Judea that are in Christ. They only heard the report: "The man who formerly persecuted us is now preaching the faith he once tried to destroy."

2. Fourteen years later I went up again to Jerusalem, this time with Barnabas. I took Titus along also. I went in response to a revelation and set before them the gospel that I preach among the Gentiles. But I did this privately to those who seemed to be leaders, for fear that I was running or had run my race in vain. Yet not even Titus, who was with me, was compelled to be circumcised, even though he was a Greek. [This matter arose] because some false brothers had infiltrated our ranks to spy on the freedom we have in Christ Jesus and to make us slaves. We did not give in to them for a moment, so that the truth of the gospel might remain with you.

   As for those who seemed to be important—whatever they were makes no difference to me; God does not judge by external appearance— those men added nothing to my message. On the contrary, they saw that I had been entrusted with the task of preaching the gospel to the Gentiles, just as Peter had been to the Jews. For God, who was at work in the ministry of Peter as an apostle to the Jews, was also at work in my ministry as an apostle to the Gentiles. James, Peter and John, those reputed to be pillars, gave me and Barnabas the right hand of fellowship when they recognized the grace given to me. They agreed that we should go to the Gentiles, and they to the Jews. All they asked was that we should continue to remember the poor, the very thing I was eager to do.

When Peter came to Antioch, I opposed him to his face, because he was clearly in the wrong. Before certain men came from James, he used to eat with the Gentiles. But when they arrived, he began to draw back and separate himself from the Gentiles because he was afraid of those who belonged to the circumcision group. The other Jews joined him in his hypocrisy, so that by their hypocrisy even Barnabas was led astray.

When I saw that they were not acting in line with the truth of the gospel, I said to Peter in front of them all, "You are a Jew, yet you live like a Gentile and not like a Jew. How is it, then, that you force Gentiles to follow Jewish customs?

"We who are Jews by birth and not 'Gentile sinners' know that a man is not justified by observing the law, but by faith in Jesus Christ. So we, too, have put our faith in Christ Jesus that we may be justified by faith in Christ and not by observing the law, because by observing the law no one will be justified.

"If, while we seek to be justified in Christ, it becomes evident that we ourselves are sinners, does that mean that Christ promotes sin? Absolutely not! If I rebuild what I destroyed, I prove that I am a lawbreaker. For through the law I died to the law so that I might live for God. I have been crucified with Christ and I no longer live, but Christ lives in me. The life I live in the body, I live by faith in the Son of God, who loved me and gave himself for me. I do not set aside the grace of God, for if righteousness could be gained through the law, Christ died for nothing!"

Source: Galatians, chs. 1:6–23, 2:1–21, from *The Holy Bible, New International Version.*

PAUL ON LIFE AFTER DEATH

An immediate theological difficulty faced by Paul was the question of how Jesus could be divine despite his criminal execution. Paul's solution was to see Jesus' death on the cross and subsequent resurrection as the end of the old Jewish law and the beginning of a new era of divine grace. Through baptism, Christians symbolically participate in the cross by dying to their old lives and reemerging anew. The crucifixion and resurrection are so central to Paul's teaching that they are the only features of the life of Jesus with which he is concerned. In the following discussion from Paul's first letter to the church of Corinth, written about 55 C.E., life after death is also linked to the resurrection: Because Christ resurrected, we are assured that we too will be. Unlike Greek writers, who construe life after death as the continuation of a bodiless, immortal soul, Christian doctrine holds to the bodily resurrection of the dead as found in post-exilic Jewish writings. Paul teaches that our new bodies will be heavenly and imperishable in nature, rather than earthly and perishable, and that all those who belong to Christ will be simultaneously resurrected when he returns.

15. But if it is preached that Christ has been raised from the dead, how can some of you say that there is no resurrection of the dead? If there is no resurrection of the dead, then not even Christ has been raised. And if Christ has not been raised, our preaching is useless and so is your faith. More than that, we are then found to be false witnesses about God, for we have testified about God that he raised Christ from the dead. But he did not raise him if in fact the dead are not raised. For if the dead are not raised, then Christ has not been raised either. And if Christ has not been raised, your faith is futile; you are still in your sins. Then those also who have fallen asleep in Christ are lost. If only for this life we have hope in Christ, we are to be pitied more than all men.

But Christ has indeed been raised from the dead, the firstfruits of those who have fallen asleep. For since death came through a man, the resurrection of the dead comes also through a man. For as in Adam all die, so in Christ all will be made alive. But each in his own turn: Christ, the firstfruits; then, when he comes, those who belong to him. Then the end will come, when he hands over the kingdom to God the Father after he has destroyed all dominion, authority and power. For he must reign until he has put all his enemies under his feet. The last enemy to be destroyed is death. For he "has put everything under his feet." Now when it says that "everything" has been put under him, it is clear that this does not include God himself, who put everything under Christ. When he has done this, then the Son himself will be made subject to him who put everything under him, so that God may be all in all.

But someone may ask, "How are the dead raised? With what kind of body will they come?" How foolish! What you sow does not come to life unless it dies. When you sow, you do not plant the body that will be, but just a seed, perhaps of wheat or of something else. But God gives it a body as he has determined, and to each kind of seed he gives its own body. All flesh is not the same: Men have one kind of flesh, animals have another, birds another and fish another. There are also heavenly bodies and there are earthly bodies; but the splendor of the heavenly bodies is one kind, and the splendor of the earthly bodies is another. The sun has one kind of splendor, the moon another and the star another; and star differs from star in splendor.

So will it be with the resurrection of the dead. The body that is sown is perishable, it is raised imperishable; it is sown in dishonor, it is raised in glory; it is sown in weakness, it is raised in power; it is sown a natural body, it is raised a spiritual body. If there is a natural body, there is also a spiritual body.

So it is written: "The first man Adam became a living being"; the last Adam, a life-giving spirit. The spiritual did not come first, but the natural, and after that the spiritual. The first man was of the dust of the earth, the second man from heaven. As was the earthly man, so are those who are of the earth; and as is the man from heaven, so also are those who are of heaven. And just as we have borne the likeness of the earthly man, so shall we bear the likeness of the man from heaven.

I declare to you, brothers, that flesh and blood cannot inherit the kingdom of God, nor does the perishable inherit the imperishable. Listen, I tell you a mystery: We will not all sleep, but we will all be changed—in a flash, in the twinkling of an eye, at the last trumpet. For the trumpet will sound, the dead will be raised imperishable, and we will be changed. For the perishable must clothe itself with the imperishable, and the mortal with immortality. When the perishable has been clothed with the imperishable, and the mortal with immortality, then the saying that is written will come true: "Death has been swallowed up in victory."

"Where, O death, is your victory?

Where, O death, is your sting?"

The sting of death is sin, and the power of sin is the law. But thanks to God! He gives us the victory through our Lord Jesus Christ.

Source: 1 Corinthians chs. 15:12–28, 35–57, from *The Holy Bible, New International Version.*

NON-CANONICAL GOSPELS

INFANCY GOSPEL OF JAMES

Early Christians were interested in accounts of Jesus' childhood, which filled the gaps in the four Gospel narratives. Many childhood gospels circulated, but most of the information in these derive from two texts written about 150 c.e.: the Infancy Gospel of James, *and the* Infancy Gospel of Thomas. *The* Infancy Gospel of James, *also called the* Protoevangelium, *or first gospel, is pseudonomously ascribed to James, the brother of Jesus, and scholars believe that its author was a non-Jewish Christian from outside of Palestine. The text presents the oldest account of the early life of Mary, including her espousal to Joseph, and describes the virgin birth of Jesus. The tradition of Mary's life-long virginity runs counter to statements in the gospels referring to Jesus' brothers. The* Infancy Gospel of James *reconciles these two traditions by presenting Joseph as a widower with children from his previous marriage. The feast of Mary's presentation in the temple (November 21) in Catholic and Orthodox traditions is based on events in the following selection.*

7. Many months passed, but when the child reached two years of age, Joachim said, "Let's take her up to the temple of the Lord, so that we can keep the promise we made, or else the Lord will be angry with us and our gift will be unacceptable."

   And Anna said, "Let's wait until she is three, so she won't miss her father or mother."

   And Joachim agreed: "Let's wait."

   When the child turned three years of age, Joachim said, "Let's send for the undefiled Hebrew daughters. Let them each take a lamp and light it, so the child won't turn back and have her heart captivated by things outside the Lord's temple." And this is what they did until the time they ascended to the Lord's temple.

   The priest welcomed her, kissed her, and blessed her: "The Lord God has exalted your name among all generations. In you the Lord will disclose his redemption to the people of Israel during the last days."

   And he sat her down on the third step of the altar, and the Lord showered favor on her. And she danced, and the whole house of Israel loved her.

8. Her parents left for home marveling and praising and glorifying the Lord God because the child did not look back at them. And Mary lived in the temple of the Lord. She was fed there like a dove, receiving her food from the hand of a heavenly messenger.

   When she turned twelve, however, there was a meeting of the priests. "Look," they said, "Mary has turned twelve in the temple of the Lord. What should we do with her so she won't pollute the sanctuary of the Lord our God?" And they said to the high priest, "You stand at the altar of the Lord. Enter and pray about her, and we'll do whatever the Lord God discloses to you."

   And so the high priest took the vestment with the twelve bells, entered the Holy of Holies, and began to pray about her. And suddenly a messenger of the Lord appeared: "Zechariah, Zechariah, go out and assemble the widowers of the people and have them each bring a staff. She will become the wife of the one to whom the Lord God shows a sign." And so heralds covered the surrounding territory of Judea. The trumpet of the Lord sounded and all the widowers came running.

9. And Joseph, too, threw down his carpenter's axe and left for the meeting. When they had all gathered, they went to the high priest with their staffs. After the high priest had collected everyone's staff, he entered the temple and began to pray. When he had finished his prayer, he took the staffs and went out and began to give them back to each man. But there was no sign of any of them. Joseph got the last staff. Suddenly a dove came out of this staff and perched on Joseph's head. "Joseph, Joseph," the high priest said, "you've been chosen by lot to take the virgin of the Lord into your care and protection."

   But Joseph objected: "I already have sons and I'm an old man; she's only a young woman. I'm afraid that I'll become the butt of jokes among the people of Israel."

13. She was in her sixth month when one day Joseph came home from his building projects, entered the house, and found her pregnant. He struck himself in the face, threw himself to the ground on sackcloth, and began to cry bitterly: "What sort of face should I present to the Lord God? What prayer can I say on her behalf since I received her as a virgin from the temple of the Lord God and didn't protect her? Who has set this trap for me? Who has done this evil deed in my house? Who has lured this virgin away from me and violated her? The story of Adam has been repeated in my case, hasn't it? For just as Adam was praying when the serpent came and found Eve alone, deceived her, and corrupted her, so the same thing has happened to me."

So Joseph got up from the sackcloth and summoned Mary and said to her, "God has taken a special interest in you—how could you have done this? Have you forgotten the Lord your God? Why have you brought shame on yourself, you who were raised in the Holy of Holies and fed by a heavenly messenger?"

But she began to cry bitter tears: "I'm innocent. I haven't had sex with any man."

And Joseph said to her, "Then where did the child you're carrying come from?"

And she replied, "As the Lord my God lives, I don't know where it came from."

14. And Joseph became very frightened and no longer spoke with her as he pondered what he was going to do with her. And Joseph said to himself, "If I try to cover up her sin, I'll end up going against the law of the Lord. And if I disclose her condition to the people of Israel, I'm afraid that the child inside her might be heaven-sent and I'll end up handing innocent blood over to a death sentence. So what should I do with her? [I know,] I'll divorce her quietly."

But when night came a messenger of the Lord suddenly appeared to him in a dream and said: "Don't be afraid of this girl, because the child in her is the holy spirit's doing. She will have a son and you will name him Jesus—the name means 'he will save his people from their sins.'" And Joseph got up from his sleep and praised the God of Israel, who had given him this favor. And so he began to protect the girl.

15. Then Annas the scholar came to him and said to him, "Joseph, why haven't you attended our assembly?"

And he replied to him, "Because I was worn out from the trip and rested my first day home."

Then Annas turned and saw that Mary was pregnant.

He left in a hurry for the high priest and said to him, "You remember Joseph, don't you—the man you yourself vouched for? Well, he has committed a serious offense."

And the high priest asked, "In what way?"

"Joseph has violated the virgin he received from the temple of the Lord," he replied. "He had his way with her and hasn't disclosed his action to the people of Israel."

And the high priest asked him, "Has Joseph really done this?"

And he replied, "Send temple assistants and you'll find the virgin pregnant."

And so the temple assistants went and found her just as Annas had reported, and then they brought her, along with Joseph, to the court.

"Mary, why have you done this?" the high priest asked her. "Why have you humiliated yourself? Have you forgotten the Lord your God, you who were raised in the Holy of the Holies and were fed by heavenly messengers? You of all people, who heard their hymns and danced for them—why have you done this?"

And she wept bitterly: "As the Lord God lives, I stand innocent before him. Believe me, I've not had sex with any man."

And the high priest said, "Joseph, why have you done this?"

And Joseph said, "As the Lord lives, I am innocent where she is concerned."

And the high priest said, "Don't perjure yourself, but tell the truth. You've had your way with her and haven't disclosed this action to the people of Israel. And you haven't humbled yourself under God's mighty hand, so that your offspring might be blessed."

But Joseph was silent.

16. Then the high priest said, "Return the virgin you received from the temple of the Lord."

And Joseph, bursting into tears . . . [said nothing]

And the high priest said, "I'm going to give you the Lord's drink test, and it will disclose your sin clearly to both of you."

And the high priest took the water and made Joseph drink it and sent him into the wilderness, but he returned unharmed. And he made the girl drink it, too, and sent her into the wilderness. She also came back unharmed. And everybody was surprised because their sin had not been revealed. And so the high priest said, "If the Lord God has not exposed your sin, then neither do I condemn you." And he dismissed them. Joseph took Mary and returned home celebrating and praising the God of Israel.

Source: Infancy Gospel of James, 7–9, 13–16, from *The Complete Gospels*.

INFANCY GOSPEL OF THOMAS

Written about 150 C.E., the Infancy Gospel of Thomas *was among the most popular apocryphal writings in the early church. The text deals with Jesus' childhood up to his twelfth year. The youthful Jesus is presented as having deadly divine powers, which he angrily uses to get his way. As he grows, though, his sense of moral responsibility progressively develops, and he uses his powers to heal rather than harm. The story provides an interesting commentary on the divine and human natures of Jesus: his power and knowledge are fully divine, but his conscience and emotions are human and require maturing. The text is reconstructed from several surviving manuscripts which vary greatly; some scholars believe that the original included sayings, although only the story lines are preserved.*

1. I, Thomas the Israelite, am reporting to you, all my non-Jewish brothers and sisters, to make known the extraordinary childhood deeds of our Lord Jesus Christ—what he did after his birth in my region. This is how it all started:

2. When this boy, Jesus, was five years old, he was playing at the ford of a rushing stream. He was collecting the flowing water into ponds and made the water instantly pure. He did this with a single command. He then made soft clay and shaped it into twelve sparrows. He did this on the sabbath day, and many other boys were playing with him.

   But when a Jew saw what Jesus was doing while playing on the sabbath day, he immediately went off and told Joseph, Jesus' father: "See here, your boy is at the ford and has taken mud and fashioned twelve birds with it, and so has violated the sabbath."

   So Joseph went there, and as soon as he spotted him he shouted, "Why are you doing what's not permitted on the sabbath?"

   But Jesus simply clapped his hands and shouted to the sparrows: "Be off, fly away, and remember me, you who are now alive!" And the sparrows took off and flew away noisily.

   The Jews watched with amazement, then left the scene to report to their leaders what they had seen Jesus doing.

3. The son of Annas the scholar, standing there with Jesus, took a willow branch and drained the water Jesus had collected. Jesus, however, saw what had happened and became angry, saying to him, "Damn you, you irreverent fool! What harm did the ponds of water do to you? From this moment you, too, will dry up like a tree, and you'll never produce leaves or root to bear fruit."

   In an instant the boy had completely withered away. Then Jesus departed and left for the house of Joseph. The parents of the boy who had withered away picked him up and were carrying him out, sad because he was so young. And they came to Joseph and accused him: "It's your fault—your boy did all this."

4. Later he was going through the village again when a boy ran by and bumped him on the shoulder. Jesus got angry and said to him, "You won't continue your journey." And all of a sudden he fell down and died.

   Some people saw what had happened and said, "Where has this boy come from? Everything he says happens instantly!"

   The parents of the dead boy came to Joseph and blamed him, saying, "Because you have such a boy, you can't live with us in the village, or else teach him to bless and not curse. He's killing our children!"

14. When Joseph saw the child's aptitude, and his great intelligence for his age, he again resolved that Jesus should not remain illiterate. So he

took him and handed him over to another teacher. The teacher said to Joseph, "First I'll teach him Greek, then Hebrew." This teacher, of course, knew of the child's previous experience [with a teacher] and was afraid of him. Still, he wrote out the alphabet and instructed him for quite a while, though Jesus was unresponsive.

Then Jesus spoke: "If you're really a teacher, and if you know the letters well, tell me the meaning of the letter alpha, and I'll tell you the meaning of beta."

The teacher became exasperated and hit him on the head. Jesus got angry and cursed him, and the teacher immediately lost consciousness and fell face down on the ground.

The child returned to Joseph's house. But Joseph was upset and gave this instruction to his mother: "Don't let him go outside, because those who annoy him end up dead."

15. After some time another teacher, a close friend of Joseph, said to him, "Send the child to my schoolroom. Perhaps with some flattery I can teach him his letters."

Joseph replied, "If you can muster the courage, brother, take him with you." And so he took him along with much fear and trepidation, but the child was happy to go.

Jesus strode boldly into the schoolroom and found a book lying on the desk. He took the book but did not read the letters in it. Rather, he opened his mouth and spoke by [the power of] the holy spirit and taught the law to those standing there.

A large crowd gathered and stood listening to him, and they marveled at the maturity of this teaching and his readiness of speech—a mere child able to say such things.

When Joseph heard about this he feared the worst and ran to the schoolroom, imagining that his teacher was having trouble with Jesus.

But the teacher said to Joseph, "Brother, please know that I accepted this child as a student, but already he's full of grace and wisdom. So I'm asking you, brother, to take him back home."

When the child heard this, he immediately smiled at him and said, "Because you have spoken and testified rightly, that other teacher who was struck down will be healed." And right away he was. Joseph took his child and went home.

16. Joseph sent his son James to tie up some wood and carry it back to the house, and the child Jesus followed. While James was gathering the firewood, a viper bit his hand. And as he lay sprawled out on the ground, dying, Jesus came and blew on the bite. Immediately the pain stopped, the animal burst apart, and James got better on the spot.

17. After this incident an infant in Joseph's neighborhood became sick and died, and his mother grieved terribly. Jesus heard the loud wailing and the uproar that was going on and quickly ran there.

When he found the child dead, he touched its chest and said, "I say to you, infant, don't die but live, and be with your mother."

And immediately the infant looked up and laughed. Jesus then said to the woman, "Take it, give it your breast, and remember me."

The crowd of onlookers marveled at this: "Truly this child was a god or a heavenly messenger of God—whatever he says instantly happens." But Jesus left and went on playing with the other children.

18. A year later, while a building was under construction, a man fell from the top of it and died. There was quite a commotion, so Jesus got up and went there. When he saw the man lying dead, he took his hand and said, "I say to you, sir, get up and go back to work." And he immediately got up and worshipped him.

The crowd saw this and marveled: "This child's from heaven—he must be, because he has saved many souls from death, and he can go on saving all his life."

Source: Infancy Gospel of Thomas, chs. 1–4, 14–18, from *The Complete Gospels*.

GNOSTIC GOSPEL OF THOMAS

The 1945 discovery of several dozen Gnostic texts has redefined the study of early Christianity. The jewel in the crown of these texts is the Gospel of Thomas, *which broadens our understanding of the historical Jesus. The text is a sayings gospel insofar as it contains no story line, and little dialogue. The 114 sayings are organized around particular catchwords, but do not systematically develop themes. Although the text was ultimately compiled in the second century, it may be based on an original core of short sayings as early as those in any other Gospel. These, in turn, come from orally transmitted accounts of Jesus' teachings. The challenge for scholars is to identify that core from embellishments penned by later writers. A Gnostic component of the text suggests that these are secret teachings of Jesus, knowledge of which will free one's spirit from the material world. Many of the sayings parallel those found in the four canonical Gospels. Some of the parables in Thomas are more concise and thus, perhaps, earlier than their canonical counterparts (8, 9, 57, 63, 64, 65). A large group of sayings is unique to this text, although it probably did not originate with Jesus (15, 17, 18, 19). Most interesting, however, are two sayings that scholars believe originated with Jesus, but which are absent from the canonical Gospels (97, 98).*

Prologue. These are the secret sayings that the living Jesus spoke and Didymos Judas Thomas recorded.

1. And he said, "Whoever discovers the interpretation of these sayings will not taste death."
2. Jesus said, "Those who seek should not stop seeking until they find. When they find, they will be disturbed. When they are disturbed, they will marvel, and will rule over all."
3. Jesus said, "If your leaders say to you, 'Look, the [Father's] imperial rule is in the sky,' then the birds of the sky will precede you. If they say to you, 'It is in the sea,' then the fish will precede you. Rather, the

[father's] imperial rule is inside you and outside you. When you know yourselves, then you will be known, and you will understand that you are children of the living Father. But if you do not know yourselves, then you live in poverty, and you are the poverty."

4. Jesus said, "The person old in days won't hesitate to ask a little child seven days old about the place of life, and that person will live. For many of the first will be last, and will become a single one."

5. Jesus said, "Know what is in front of your face, and what is hidden from you will be disclosed to you. For there is nothing hidden that won't be revealed."

6. His disciples asked him and said to him, "Do you want us to fast? How should we pray? Should we give to charity? What diet should we observe?"

   Jesus said, "Don't lie, and don't do what you hate, because all things are disclosed before heaven. After all, there is nothing hidden that won't be revealed, and there is nothing covered up that will remain undisclosed."

7. Jesus said, "Lucky is the lion that the human will eat, so that the lion becomes human. And foul is the human that the lion will eat, and the lion still will become human."

8. And he said, "The human one is like a wise fisherman who cast his net into the sea and drew it up from the sea full of little fish. Among them the wise fisherman discovered a fine large fish. He threw all the little fish back into the sea, and easily chose the large fish. Anyone here with two good ears had better listen!"

9. Jesus said,

   Look, the sower went out, took a handful (of seeds), and scattered (them). Some fell on the road, and the birds came and gathered them. Others fell on rock, and they didn't take root in the soil and didn't produce heads of grain. Others fell on thorns, and they choked the seeds and worms ate them. And others fell on good soil, and it produced a good crop: it yielded sixty per measure and one hundred twenty per measure.

10. Jesus said, "I have cast fire upon the world, and look, I'm guarding it until it blazes."

11. Jesus said, "This heaven will pass away, and the one above it will pass away. The dead are not alive, and the living will not die. During the days when you ate what is dead, you made it come alive. When you are in the light, what will you do? On the day when you were one, you became two. But when you become two, what will you do?"

12. The disciples said to Jesus, "We know that you are going to leave us. Who will be our leader?"

   Jesus said to them, "No matter where you are, you are to go to James the Just, for whose sake heaven and earth came into being."

13. Jesus said to his disciples, "Compare me to something and tell me what I am like."

Simon Peter said to him, "You are like a just angel."

Matthew said to him, "You are like a wise philosopher."

Thomas said to him, "Teacher, my mouth is utterly unable to say what you are like."

Jesus said, "I am not your teacher. Because you have drunk, you have become intoxicated from the bubbling spring that I have tended."

And he took him, and withdrew, and spoke three sayings to him.

When Thomas came back to his friends, they asked him, "What did Jesus say to you?"

Thomas said to them, "If I tell you one of the sayings he spoke to me, you will pick up rocks and stone me, and fire will come from the rocks and devour you."

14. Jesus said to them, "If you fast, you will bring sin upon yourselves, and if you pray, you will be condemned, and if you give to charity, you will harm your spirits. When you go into any region and walk about in the countryside, when people take you in, eat what they serve you and heal the sick among them. After all, what goes into your mouth won't defile you; what comes out of your mouth will."

15. Jesus said, "When you see one who was not born of woman, fall on your faces and worship. That one is your Father."

16. Jesus said, "Perhaps people think that I have come to cast peace upon the world. They do not know that I have come to cast conflicts upon the earth: fire, sword, war. For there will be five in a house: there'll be three against two and two against three, father against son and son against father, and they will stand alone."

17. Jesus said, "I will give you what no eye has seen, what no ear has heard, what no hand has touched, what has not arisen in the human heart."

18. The disciples said to Jesus, "Tell us, how will our end come?"

Jesus said, "Have you found the beginning, then, that you are looking for the end? You see, the end will be where the beginning is. Congratulations to the one who stands at the beginning: that one will know the end and will not taste death."

19. Jesus said, "Congratulations to the one who came into being before coming into being. If you become my disciples and pay attention to my sayings, these stones will serve you. For there are five trees in Paradise for you; they do not change, summer or winter, and their leaves do not fall. Whoever knows them will not taste death."

20. The disciples said to Jesus, "Tell us what Heaven's imperial rule is like."

He said to them,

It's like a mustard seed. [It's] the smallest of all seeds, but when it falls on prepared soil, it produces a large branch and becomes a shelter for birds of the sky.

57. Jesus said,

The Father's imperial rule is like a person who had [good] seed. His enemy came during the night and sowed weeds among the good seed. The person did not let the workers pull up the weeds, but said to them, "No, otherwise you might go to pull up the weeds and pull up the wheat along with them." For on the day of the harvest the weeds will be conspicuous, and will be pulled up and burned.

63. Jesus said,

There was a rich man who had a great deal of money. He said, "I shall invest my money so that I may sow, reap, plant, and fill my store-houses with produce, that I may lack nothing." These were the things he was thinking in his heart, but that very night he died. Anyone here with two ears had better listen!

64. Jesus said,

Someone was receiving guests. When he had prepared the dinner, he sent his slave to invite the guests. The slave went to the first and said, "My master invites you." The first replied, "Some merchants owe me money; they are coming to me tonight. I have to go and give them instructions. Please excuse me for dinner." The slave went to another and said, 'My master has invited you." The second said to the slave, "I have bought a house, and I have been called away for a day. I shall have no time." The slave went to another and said, "My master invites you." The third said to the slave, "My friend is to be married, and I am to arrange the banquet. I shall not be able to come. Please excuse me from dinner." The slave went to another and said, "My master invites you." The fourth said to the slave, "I have bought an estate, and I am going to collect the rent. I shall not be able to come. Please excuse me." The slave returned and said to his master, "Those whom you invited to dinner have asked to be excused." The master said to his slave, " Go out on the streets and bring back whomever you find to have dinner."
Buyers and merchants [will] not enter the places of my Father.

65. He said,

A person owned a vineyard and rented it to some farmers, so they could work it and he could collect its crops from them. He sent his slave so the farmers would give him the vineyard's crop. They grabbed him, beat him, and almost killed him, and the slave returned and told his master. His master said, "Perhaps he didn't know them." He sent another slave, and the farmers beat that one as well. Then the master sent his son and said, "Perhaps they'll show my son some respect." Because the farmers knew that he was the heir to the vineyard, they grabbed him and killed him. Anyone here with two ears had better listen!

97. Jesus said,

The [Father's] imperial rule is like a woman who was carrying a [jar] full of meal. While she was walking along [a] distant road, the handle of the jar broke and the meal spilled behind her [along] the road. She didn't know it; she hadn't noticed a problem. When she reached her house, she put the jar down and discovered that it was empty.

98. Jesus said,

> The Father's imperial rule is like a person who wanted to kill some-
> one powerful. While still at home he drew his sword and thrust it
> into the wall to find out whether his hand would go in. Then he
> killed the powerful one.

Source: Gospel of Thomas, 1–20, 57, 63, 64, 65, 97, 98, from *The Complete Gospels.*

GNOSTIC GOSPEL OF MARY

*Gnostic writings contained feminine imagery typical of ancient mythology, which was
ultimately removed from mainstream Christianity. Much of this imagery is cosmological, and it involves various layers of God's being and creative activity. Some Gnostic
texts portray God as having both a male and a female quality: God is the primal father
and the mother of all things. Others describe God as radiating divine beings or person-
alities, one of which is the female spirit of wisdom, the womb of everything. Finally,
and most interestingly, several texts depict the divine Trinity as the father, mother,
and son. In addition to their feminine theological themes, Gnostic texts defend the role
of women as teachers of divine knowledge. This is most evident in the* Gospel
of Mary *(named after Mary Magdalene), where, after Mary presents some private
teachings of Jesus, her authority is first challenged by Peter, and then defended by
Levi. Much of the* Gospel of Mary *is lost; the surviving sections are presented below.*

1. [Six manuscript pages are missing.]
2. [Jesus said] ". . . Will matter then be utterly destroyed or not?"
   The Savior replied, "Every nature, every modeled form, every
   creature, exists in and with each other. They will dissolve again into
   their own proper root. For the nature of matter is dissolved into what
   belongs to its nature. Anyone with two ears capable of hearing should
   listen!"
3. Then Peter said to him, "You have been expounding every topic to us;
   tell us one further thing. What is the sin of the world?"
   The Savior replied, "There is no such thing as sin; rather, you
   yourselves are what produces sin when you act according to the nature of adultery, which is called 'sin.' For this reason, the Good came
   among you approaching what belongs to every nature. It will set it
   within its root."
   Then he continued. He said, "This is why you get sick and die, for
   [you love] what de[c]ei[ve]s you. Anyone with a mind should use it to
   think!
   [Ma]tter gav[e bi]rth to a passion which has no [true] image because it derives from what is contrary to nature. Then a disturbing confusion occurred in the whole body. This is why I told you. 'Be content
   of heart.' And do not conform [to the body], but form yourselves in the
   presence of that other image of nature. Anyone with two ears capable
   of hearing should listen!"

4. When the Blessed One had said this, he greeted them all. "Peace be with you!" he said. "Acquire my peace within yourselves!

Be on your guard so that no one deceives you by saying, 'Look over here!' or 'Look over there!' For the seed of true humanity exists within you. Follow it! Those who search for it will find it.

Go then, preach the good news of the domain. Do not lay down any rule beyond what I ordained for you, nor promulgate law like the lawgiver, or else it will dominate you."

After he said these things, he left them.

5. But they were distressed and wept greatly. "How are we going to go out to the rest of the world to preach the good news, about the domain of the seed of true humanity?" they said. "If they didn't spare him, how will they spare us?"

Then Mary stood up. She greeted them all and addressed her brothers: "Do not weep and be distressed nor let your hearts be irresolute. For his grace will be with you all and will shelter you. Rather we should praise his greatness, for he has joined us together and made us true human beings."

When Mary said these things, she turned their minds [to]ward the Good, and they began to [as]k about the wor[d]s of the Savi[or].

6. Peter said to Mary, "Sister, we know that the Savior loved you more than any other woman. Tell us the words of the Savior that you know, but which we haven't heard."

Mary responded, "I will rep[ort to you as much as] I remember that you don't know." And she began to speak these words to them.

7. She said, "I saw the Lord in a vision and I said to him, 'Lord, I saw you today in a vision.'

"He said to me, 'Congratulations to you for not wavering at seeing me. For where the mind is, there is the treasure.'

"I said to him, 'Lord, how does a person who sees a vision see it— [with] the soul [or] with the spirit?'

"The Savior answered, 'The [visionary] does not see with the soul or with the spirit, but with the mind which exists between these two— that is [what] sees the vision and that is w[hat . . .]'

8. [Four manuscript pages are missing.]

9. . . ."And Desire said, 'I did not see you go down, yet now I see you go up. So why do you lie since you belong to me?'

"The soul answered, 'I saw you. You did not see me nor did you know me. You [mis]took the garment [I wore] for my [true] self. And you did not recognize me.'

"After it had said these things, [the soul] left rejoicing greatly.

"Again, it came to the third Power, which is called 'Ignorance.' [It] examined the soul closely, saying, 'Where are you going? You are bound by fornication. Indeed you are bound! Do not pass judgment!'

"And the soul said, 'Why do you judge me, since I have not passed judgment? I am bound, but I have not bound. They did not recognize me, but I have recognized that the universe is to be dissolved, both the things of earth and those of heaven.'

"When the soul had overcome the third Power, it went upward and it saw the fourth Power. It had seven forms. The first form is Darkness; the second, Desire; the third, Ignorance; the fourth Zeal of Death; the fifth, the Domain of the Flesh; the sixth, the Foolish Wisdom of the Flesh, and seventh is the Wisdom of the Wrathful Person. These are seven Powers of Wrath.

"They interrogated the soul, 'Where are you coming from, human-killer, and where are you going, space-conqueror?'

"The soul replied, 'What binds me has been slain, and what surrounds me has been destroyed, and my desire has been brought to an end, and my ignorance has died. In a world, I was set loose from a world and in a type, from a type which is above, and [from] the chain of forgetfulness that exists in time. For now on, for the rest of the course of the [due] measure of the time of the age, I will rest i[n] silence.' "

When Mary said these things, she fell silent, since it was up to this point that the Savior had spoken to her.

10. Andrew sai[d, "B]rothers, what is your opinion of what was just said? I for one don't believe that the S[a]vior said these things, be[cause] these opinions seem to be so different from h[is th]ought."

After reflecting on these ma[tt]ers, [Peter said], "Has the Sa[vior] spoken secretly to a wo[m]an and [not] openly so that [we] would all hear? [Surely] he did [not wish to indicate] that [she] is more worthy than we are?"

Then Mary wept and said to Peter, "Peter, my brother, what are you imagining about this? Do you think that I've made all this up secretly by myself or that I am telling lies about the Savior?"

Levi said to Peter, "Peter, you have a constant inclination to anger and you are always ready to give way to it. And even now you are doing exactly that by questioning the woman as if you're her adversary. If the Savior considered her to be worthy, who are you to disregard her? For he knew her completely [and] loved her devotedly.

"Instead, we should be ashamed and, once we clothe ourselves with perfect humanity, we should do what we were commanded. We should announce the good news as the Savior ordered, and not be laying down any rules or making laws."

After he said these things, Levi left [and] began to announce the good news.

Source: Gnostic Gospel of Mary, from *The Complete Gospels*.

EARLY STATEMENTS OF FAITH

BAPTISM, PRAYER, AND THE EUCHARIST: DIDACHE

Discovered in 1873, the Didache *is a manual of early church doctrine from the Syrian church of Antioch. Eusibius, a fourth-century Bishop, notes the high value placed on the Didache by early churches. Although the original date of the work is disputed, scholars believe that some parts are of first-century origin and contemporaneous with the gospels. The brief work can be divided into four parts. The opening lists a series of moral injunctions culled from various parts of the Bible. Instuctions concerning baptism, fasting, and prayer ritual follow. Next, instructions are given on receiving new prophets, apostles, and Christians. Finally, a warning is given concerning the return of Jesus. The following are the instructions on ritual from the second division.*

7. *Concerning Baptism.* Concerning baptism, baptize in this way: Having first said everything in these Teachings, baptize in the name of the Father, and of the Son, and of the Holy Spirit, in living water. If you have not living water, baptize in other water; and if you cannot in cold, in warm. If you do not have either, pour out water three times upon the head in the name of Father Son and Holy Spirit. Before the baptism let the baptizer fast, as well as the baptized, and whoever else can. But you shall order the baptized to fast for one or two days before.

8. *Concerning Fasting and Prayer.* But do not let your fasts be like those of the hypocrites; for they fast on the Monday and Thursday; instead, you should fast on the Wednesday and Friday. Also do not pray as the hypocrites do. Instead, pray in this way as the Lord commanded in His Gospel: "Our Father who are in heaven blessed be your name. May your kingdom come. May your will be done, as in heaven, so on earth. Give us today our daily bread, and forgive our debt as we also forgive our debtors. And bring us not into temptation, but deliver us from the evil one. For yours is the power and the glory forever." Pray this way three times a day.

9. *The Thanksgiving (Eucharist).* Now concerning the thanksgiving, give thanks in this way. First, concerning the cup: "We thank you, our Father, for the holy vine of David your servant, which you made known to us though Jesus your sevant; may you be glorified forever." And concerning the broken bread: "We thank you, our Father, for the life and knowledge which you made known to us though Jesus your servant; may you be glorified forever. Even as this broken bread was scattered over the hills, and was gathered together and became one, so let your Church be gathered together from the ends of the earth into your kingdom; for yours is the glory and the power through Jesus Christ forever." Let no one eat or drink of your Thanksgiving, except those who have been baptized to the name of the Lord; for concerning this also the Lord has said, do not give that which is holy to the dogs.

10. *Prayer after Communion.* But after you are filled, give thanks in this way: "We thank you, holy Father, for your holy name which you

caused to dwell in our hearts, and for the knowledge and faith and immortality, which you made known to us through Jesus your Servant; may you be glorified forever. You, Master almighty, created all things for your name's sake; you gave food and drink to men for enjoyment, that they might give thanks to you. You freely gave to us spiritual food and drink and life eternal through your servant. Before all things we thank you, who are mighty. May you be exalted forever. Remember, Lord, your Chruch, to deliver it from all evil and to make it perfect in your love, and gather it from the four winds, sanctified for your kingdom which you have prepared for it; may you be glorified forever. Let grace come, and let this world pass away. Hosanna to the God (Son) of David! If anyone is holy, let him come; if anyone is not so, let him repent. Maranatha. Amen."

Source: Didache 7–10, adapted from *Ante-Nicene Father* (Edinburgh: T. and T. Clark, 1867–1872), vol. 7.

APOSTLES' CREED

In the early church, many controversies erupted over fine points of Christian theology. This often resulted in the creation of some creed that distinguished acceptable theological positions from unacceptable ones. Composed around 150 C.E., the Apostles' Creed is perhaps the first of these. The controversy was gnosticism *the view that we should free our spirits from the evil material world by acquiring special knowledge. Christian Gnostics believed that God was not really the creator of the world, and Jesus could not have suffered and died since he was a spiritual being. The Apostles' Creed opposes both of these contentions.*

I believe in God the Father Almighty, maker of heaven and earth. And in Jesus Christ his only Son our Lord, who was conceived by the Holy Spirit, born of the virgin Mary. He suffered under Pontius Pilate, was crucified, died, and was buried; He descended into hell. The third day He rose again from the dead. He ascended into heaven and is seated at the right hand of God the Father Almighty. From there He shall come to judge the living and the dead. I believe in the Holy Spirit, the holy catholic church, the communion of saints, the forgiveness of sins, the resurrection of the body, and the life everlasting Amen.

Source: Apostles' Creed, from *The Book of Common Prayer* (London: Bagster, 1885).

NICENE CREED

The Nicene Creed emerged in response to the Arian controversy: a dispute involving the claims of a Christian priest named Arius (c. 250–336) that Christ was created by God, and hence was not God himself. The Council of Nicaea was called in 325 to resolve the issue, which was decidedly against Arius. The Nicene Creed's exact date of origin is a matter of dispute, and at least some components of it were added in later centuries. Nevertheless, its content reflects the Council's decision against Arianism. At a minor church council in 589 C.E., the sentence "I believe in the Holy Ghost . . . who proceeds from the father" was expanded to read "who proceeds from the father and the son (filioque)." The issue involves whether the Holy Ghost originated from the father alone, or both the father and the son. Known as the filioque *clause, its inclusion provoked discord with the Eastern Orthodox churches, and became their rallying cry in the Great Schism of 1054. The* filioque *clause was definitively added to the creed by the Catholics at the Second Council of Lyons in 1274. Today, the Nicene Creed remains the most popular confession of faith in Catholic, Orthodox, and most Protestant liturgies, although Orthodox churches omit the* filioque *clause.*

> I believe in one God, the Father Almighty, Maker of heaven and earth, of all things visible and invisible. And in one Lord Jesus Christ, the only-begotten Son of God, begotten of His Father before all worlds, God of God, Light of Light, Very God of very God, begotten, not made, being of one substance with the Father; by whom all things were made; who for us and for our salvation came down from heaven, and was incarnate by the Holy Spirit of the virgin Mary, and was made man; and was crucified also for us under Pontius Pilate; He suffered and was buried, and the third day He rose again according to the Scriptures, and ascended into heaven, and is seated at the right hand of the Father; and He shall come again, with glory, to judge both the living and the dead; whose kingdom shall have no end. And I believe in the Holy Spirit, the Lord and giver of life, who proceeds from the Father and the Son; who with the Father and the Son together is worshipped and glorified; who spoke by the Prophets; and I believe one holy catholic and apostolic church; I acknowledge one baptism for the remission of sins; and I look for the resurrection of the dead, and the life of the world to come. Amen.

Source: Nicene Creed, from *Nicene and Post-Nicene Fathers* (New York, The Christian Literature Company, 1890–1900), series 2, vol. 7.

CHALCEDON CREED

In 451 the Council of Chalcedon was called to address two controversial theological positions. A position called Nestorianism *denied the unity of Christ's divinity and humanity; in this view, Christ had two distinct personas. A contrasting position called* Monophysitism *held that Christ in fact had one nature, part of which was divine, and the other part human. Against both of these positions, the Chalcedon council held that Christ has one substance, but two natures: he is both fully human and fully God. This official view is reflected in the Chalcedon Creed.*

> Following, then, the holy fathers, we unite in teaching all men to confess the one and only Son, our Lord Jesus Christ. This selfsame one is perfect both in deity and in humanness; this selfsame one is also actually God and actually man, with a rational soul and a body. He is of the same reality as

God as far as his deity is concerned and of the same reality as we ourselves as far as his humanness is concerned; thus like us in all respects, sin only excepted. Before time began he was begotten of the Father, in respect of his deity, and now in these "last days," for us and on behalf of our salvation, this selfsame one was born of Mary the virgin, who is Godbearer in respect of his humanness.

We also teach that we apprehend this one and only Christ-Son, Lord, only-begotten—in two natures; and we do this without confusing the two natures, without transmuting one nature into the other, without dividing them into two separate categories, without contrasting them according to area or function. The distinctiveness of each nature is not nullified by the union. Instead, the "properties" of each nature are conserved and both natures concur in one "person" and in one reality. They are not divided or cut into two persons, but are together the one and only and only-begotten Word of God, the Lord Jesus Christ. Thus have the prophets of old testified; thus the Lord Jesus Christ himself taught us; thus the Symbol of Fathers has handed down to us.

Source: Chalcedon Creed, from *Nicene and Post-Nicene Fathers*, series 2, vol. 7.

CHURCH FATHERS, SAINTS, AND MYSTICS

THE MARTYRDOM OF POLYCARP

During the first three centuries, several Roman rulers systematically persecuted Christians. Some victims were outspoken leaders, and others became conspicuous for not participating in pagan religious rituals. In either case they were barbarically executed, as were Jesus and the Apostles before them. Stories of religious martyrs became an important part of early Christian writing, both to commemorate the tragic events, and also to instill a sense of religious bravery in those who might experience similar fates. The most popular of all early stories of martyrs is that of Polycarp (c. 69–c. 155) bishop of Smyrna, who was arrested during a pagan festival for failing to participate. He was burnt to death after refusing to renounce his faith.

9. As Polycarp was entering the stadium, there came to him a voice from heaven, saying, "Be strong, and show yourself a man, O Polycarp!" No one saw who it was that spoke to him; but those of our brethren who were present heard the voice. And as he was brought forward, the tumult became great when they heard that Polycarp was taken. When he came near, the proconsul asked him weather he was Polycarp. On his confessing that he was, [the proconsul] sought to persuade him to deny [Christ], saying, "Have respect for your old age," and similar things, according to their custom, [such as], "Swear by the fortune of Caesar; repent, and say, Away with the Atheists." But Polycarp, gazing with a stern countenance on all the multitude of the

wicked heathen then in the stadium, and waving his hand towards them, while with groans he looked up to heaven, said, "Away with the Atheists." The the proconsul urged him, saying, "Swear, and I will set you at liberty; reproach Christ." Polycarp declared, "Eighty and six years I have served Him, and He never did me any injury. How then can I blaspheme my King and my Savior?"

12. While he spoke these and many other like things, he was filled with confidence and joy. His countenance was full of grace, so that not merely did it not fall as if troubled by the things said to him, but, on the contrary, the proconsul was astonished. He sent his herald to proclaim in the middle of the stadium three times, "Polycarp has confessed that he is a Christian." This proclamation having been made by the herald, the whole multitude—both of the heathen and Jews who dwelt at Smyrna—cried out with uncontrollable fury, and in a loud voice, "This is the teacher of Asia, the father of the Christians, and the overthrower of our gods, he who has been teaching many not to sacrifice, or to worship the gods." Speaking this, they cried out, and besought Philip the Asiarch to let loose a lion upon Polycarp. But Philip answered that it was not lawful for him to do since the shows of wild beasts were already finished. Then it seemed good to them to cry out with one consent, that Polycarp should be burnt alive. . . .

13. This, then, was carried into effect with greater speed than it was spoken. The multitudes immediately gathering together wood and fagots out of the shops and baths; the Jews especially, according to custom, eagerly assisting them in it. . . .

15. When he had pronounced this *amen,* and finished his prayer, those who were appointed for the purpose kindled the fire. As the flame blazed in great fury, we, to whom it was given to witness it, saw a great miracle, and have been preserved that we might report to others what took place. For the fire, shaping itself into the form of an arch, like the sail of a ship when filled with the wind, encompassed the body of the martyr like a circle. And he appeared within not like flesh which is burnt, but as bread that is baked, or as gold and silver glowing in a furnace. Moreover, we perceived a sweet odor [coming from the pile], as if frankincense or some such precious spices had been smoking there.

16. Eventually, when those wicked men perceived that his body could not be consumed by the fire, they commanded an executioner to go near and pierce him through with a dagger. And on his doing this, there came forth a dove, and a great quantity of blood, so that the fire was extinguished; and all the people wondered that there should be such a difference between the unbelievers and the elect, of whom this most admirable Polycarp was one, having in our own times been an apostolic and prophetic teacher, and bishop of the Catholic Church which is in Smyrna. For every word that went out of his mouth either has been or shall yet be accomplished.

Source: *The Martyrdom of Polycarp,* adapted from *Ante-Nicene Fathers,* vol. 1.

TERTULLIAN ON HERETICS

Early Christians were forced to defend their faith against attacks by both Jewish and Roman critics, Christianity was new and comparatively distinct from more ancient religious traditions and was thus frequently ridiculed by outsiders. Even within Christianity, though, theological disputes erupted between factions, resulting in defenses on both sides of the issue. One of early Christianity's most influential defenders was Tertullian (c. 160–c. 225), who emphasized the importance of nonrational faith when confronting the more perplexing doctrines of Christianity, such as the divine incarnation and crucifixion Jesus. In the selections next we find Tertullian's most famous anti-intellectual expressions, "What indeed has Athens to do with Jerusalem?" and "It is by all means to be believed, because it is absurd."

These [pagan philosophies] are "the doctrines" of men and "of demons" produced for itching ears of the spirit of this world's wisdom. This the Lord called "foolishness," and "chose the foolish things of the world" to confound even philosophy itself. For (philosophy) it is which is the material of the world's wisdom, the rash interpreter of the nature and the dispensation of God. Indeed heresies are themselves instigated by philosophy. . . . Whence spring those "fables and endless genealogies," and "unprofitable question," and "words which spread like a cancer?" From all these, when the apostle would restrain us, he expressly names philosophy as that which he would have us be on our guard against. Writing to the Colossians, he says, "See that no one beguile you through philosophy and vain deceit, after the tradition of men, and contrary to the wisdom of the Holy Ghost." He had been at Athens, and had in his interviews (with us philosophers) become acquainted with that human wisdom which pretends to know the truth, while it only corrupts it, and is itself divided into its own manifold heresies, by the variety of its mutually repugnant sects. What indeed has Athens to do with Jerusalem? What concord is there between the Academy and the Church? What between heretics and Christians? Our instruction comes from "the porch of Solomon," who had himself taught that "the Lord should be sought in simplicity of heart." Away with all attempts to produce a mottled Christianity of Stoic, Platonic, and dialectic composition! We want no curious disputation after possessing Christ Jesus, no inquisition after enjoying the gospel! With our faith, we desire no further belief. For this is our palmary faith, that there is nothing which we ought to believe besides.

Source: Tertullian, *The Prescription Against Heretics*, ch. 7, adapted from *Ante-Nicene Fathers*, vol. 3.

There are, to be sure, other things also quite as foolish [as the birth of Christ], which have reference to the humiliations and sufferings of God. Or else, let them call a crucified God "wisdom." But Marcion will apply the knife to this doctrine [of the crucifixion] also, and even with greater reason. For which is more unworthy of God, which is more likely to raise a blush of shame, that God should be born, or that He should die? that He should bear the flesh, or the cross? Be circumcised, or be crucified? be cradled, or be coffined? be laid in a manger, or in a tomb? Talk of "wisdom" You will be more arbitrary if you refuse to believe this also. But, after all, you will not be "wise" unless you become a "fool" to the world, by believing "the foolish things of God." Have you, then, cut away all sufferings from Christ, on the ground that, as a mere phantom, He was incapable of experiencing them? . . . The Son of God was crucified; I am not ashamed because men are ashamed of it. And the Son of God died; it is by all means to be believed, because it is absurd. And He was buried, and rose again; the fact is certain, because it is impossible. But how will all this be true in Him, if He was not Himself true—if He really had not in Himself that which might be crucified, might die, might be buried, and might rise again?

Source: Tertullian, *On the Flesh of Christ*, ch. 5, adapted from *Ante-Nicene Fathers*, vol. 3.

JEROME'S PREFACE TO THE VULGATE

During the first few centuries, disorganized and conflicting Latin versions of the Christian scriptures circulated among churches. Hoping to finally put the matter in order, near the close of the fourth century Pope Damasus commissioned a scholar from Italy named Jerome (c. 342–420) to compile a definitive Latin text of the Old and New Testaments. The project took some time, but Jerome succeeded in translating most of it. His work became the foundation for the Latin Vulgate, the definitive text of the Bible in the Roman Catholic world. The following is his Preface to the four Gospels, which was addressed to Pope Damasus in 383 C.E. The issues Jerome raises here are precisely those which modern translators of the Bible must also face.

You urge me to revise the old Latin version, and, as it were, to sit in judgement on the copies of the Scriptures are now scattered throughout the whole world; and, inasmuch as they differ from one another, you would have me decide which of them agree with the Greek original. The labor is one of love, but at the same time both perilous and presumptuous; for in judging others I must be content to be judged by all. And how can I dare to change the language of the world in its hoary old age, and carry it back to the early days of its infancy? Is there a man, learned or unlearned, who will not, when he takes the volume into his hands, and perceives that what he reads not suit his settled tastes, break out immediately into violent language, and call me a forger and a profane person for having the audacity to add anything to the ancient books, or to make any changes or corrections therein? Now there are two consoling reflections which enable me to bear the odium. First is the command is given by you who are supreme bishop; and secondly, even on the showing of those who revile, readings at variance with the early copies cannot be right. For if we are to pin our faith to the Latin texts, it is for our opponents to tell us *which*; for there are almost as many forms of texts as there are copies. If, on the other hand, we are to glean the truth from a comparison of *many*, why not go back to the original

Greek and correct the mistakes introduced by inaccurate translators, and the blundering alterations of confident but ignorant critics, and, further, all that has been inserted or changed by copyists more asleep than awake? I am not discussing the Old Testament, which was turned into Greek by the Seventy elders, and has reached us by a descent of three steps. . . . I therefore promise in this short Preface the four Gospels only, which are to be taken in the following order, Matthew, Mark, Luke, John, as they have been revised by a comparison of the Greek manuscripts. Only early ones have been used. But to avoid any great divergences from the Latin which we are accustomed to read, I have used my pen with some restraint, and while I have corrected only such passages as seemed to convey a different meaning, I have allowed the rest to remain as they are.

Source: Jerome, Preface to the Four Gospels, adapted from *Nicene and Post-Nicene Fathers*, series 2, vol. 6.

AUGUSTINE'S CONFESSIONS

Perhaps the most important theologian in the history of Christianity is Augustine (354–430). Bishop of the North African city of Hippo. Like Tertullian, Augustine defended Christianity against attacks by Roman pagans and Christian heretics alike. He wrote on a range of issues of Christian doctrine, and his views helped shape the direction of the religion. His most famous work in his autobiography, the Confessions, *which describes his struggle to find spiritual contentment through hedonism, through the Manichean religious cult, and finally through Christianity.*

Book 2. . . . I will now call to mind my past foulness, and the carnal corruptions of my soul, not because I love them, but that I may love you, O my God. . . . I had a desire to commit robbery, and did so. I was compelled neither by hunger, nor poverty, but through a distaste for doing right, and a desire for wickedness. For I stole things that I already had, and much better. Nor did I desire to enjoy what I stole, but only the theft and sin itself. There was pear tree close to our vineyard, heavily loaded with fruit, which was tempting neither for its color nor its flavor. Late one night, a few of us shameless young folk went to shake and rob it, having, according to our disgraceful habit, prolonged our games in the streets until then. We carried away great loads, not to eat ourselves, but to fling to pigs, having only eaten some of them. This pleased us all the more because it was not permitted. . . .

Book 3. I came to Carthage, where a cauldron of unholy loves bubbled up all around me. . . . I contaminated the spring of friendship with the filth of sensuality, and I dimmed its luster with the hell of lustfulness. Foul and dishonorable as I was, through an excess of vanity, I nevertheless craved to be thought elegant and urbane. I fell rashly, then, into the love in which I longed to be ensured. . . . [In time] I directed my mind to the Holy Scriptures, so that I might see what they were. . . . [but] my inflated pride rejected their style, nor could the sharpness of my wit pierce their inner meaning. . . . I then fell among [Manichean] men proudly raving, very carnal, and voluble, in whose mouths were the snares of the devil—the lure being composed of a mixture of the syllables of your name, and of our Lord Jesus Christ, and of the Intercessor, the Holy Ghost, the Comforter.

Book 5. . . . For nearly the whole of those nine years during which, with unstable mind, I had followed the Manicheans, I had been looking forward with great eagerness for the arrival of [the Manichean teacher] Faustus. The other members of the sect whom I had chanced to encounter, when unable to answer the questions I raised, always directed me to look forward to his coming. By discoursing with him, these, and greater difficulties if I had them, would be most easily and amply cleared away. When at last he arrived, I found him to be a man of pleasant speech, who spoke of the very same things as they themselves did, although more fluently, and in better language. But of what profit to me was the elegance of my cup-bearer, since he failed to offer me the more precious draught for which I thirsted? . . . When it became plain to me that he was ignorant of those arts [of rhetoric] in which I had believed him to excel, I began to despair of his clearing up and explaining all the perplexities that harassed me.

I came to Milan and went to Ambrose the bishop, known to the whole world as among the best of men. . . . I studiously listened to him preaching to the people, not with the proper motive, but, as it were, trying to discover whether his eloquence matched his reputation. . . . And while I opened my heart to admit how *skilfully* he spoke, there also gradually entered with it how *truly* he spoke! These things also began to appear to me to be defensible. The Catholic faith, for which I had felt nothing could be said against the attacks of the Manichaeans, I now conceived might be maintained without presumption. . . . And so I earnestly bent my mind to see if I could possibly prove the Manichaeans guilty of falsehood. . . . Because these philosophers were without the saving name of Christ, I utterly refused to have them cure my fainting soul. I resolved, therefore, to be a catechumen in the Catholic Church, which my parents had commended to me, until something settled should manifest itself to me towards which I might steer my course.

Book 6. . . . When I had disclosed to my mother that I was now no longer a Manichaean, though not yet a Catholic Christian, she did not leap for joy. . . . She replied to me that she believed in Christ, that before she departed this life, she would see me a Catholic believer. . . . Active efforts were made to get me a wife. I wooed, I was engaged, my mother taking the greatest pains in the matter, that when I was once married, the health-giving baptism might cleanse me. . . . A maiden came forward who was two years under the marriageable age, but, as she was pleasing, I waited for her. . . . Meanwhile my sins were multiplying. My mistress was torn from my side as an impediment to my marriage, and my heart, which clung to her, was racked, and wounded, and bleeding. She went back to Africa, making a vow to you to never know another man, and leaving with me my natural son by her. But I unhappily could not imitate her and, impatient of delay, I took another mistress—since it would be two years until I was to marry my betrothed, and I was not so much a lover of marriage as a slave to lust. . . .

Book 8. The very toys of toys, and vanities of vanities, my old mistresses, still enthralled me. . . . But when a profound reflection had, from the secret depths of my soul, drawn together and heaped up all my misery before the sight of my heart, there arose a mighty storm, accompanied by as mighty a shower of tears. So that I might pour forth fully with natural expressions, I left [my friend] Alypius; for it seemed to me that solitude was fitter for the business of weeping. So I retired to such a distance that even his presence could not be oppressive to me. . . . I flung myself down, how, I do not know, under a certain fig-tree, giving free course to my tears, and the streams of my eyes gushed out, an acceptable sacrifice to you. And, not indeed in these words, yet to this effect, I spoke to you: "But you, O Lord, how long? How long, Lord? Will you be angry forever?". . .

I was saying these things and weeping in the most bitter contrition of my heart, when suddenly I heard the voice, sounding like a boy or girl—I don't know which—coming from a neighboring house, chanting, and repeating, "Take up and read; take up and read." Immediately my expression changed, and I earnestly considered whether it was usual for children in any kind of game to sing these words. Nor could I remember ever to have heard the like. So, restraining the torrent of my tears, I rose up, interpreting it no other way than as a command to me from heaven to open the book, and to read the first chapter I should light upon. For I had heard that Anthony, accidentally coming in while the gospel was being read, received the admonition as if what was read were addressed to him: "Go and sell what you have, and give to the poor, and you shall have treasure in heaven, and come and follow me." And by this oracle he was immediately converted to you. I quickly returned to the place where Alypius was sitting; for there had I put down the volume of the apostles, when I rose from there. I grasped, opened, and in silence read that paragraph on which my eyes first fell: "Not in rioting and drunkenness, not in chambering and wantonness, not in strife and envying; but put on the Lord Jesus Christ, and make no provision for the flesh, to fulfill the lusts there of." I did not read any further, nor did I need to; for instantly, as the sentence ended—by a light of security, so to speak, infused into my heart—all the gloom of doubt vanished away.

Source: Augustine, *Confessions*, adapted from *Nicene and Post-Nicene Fathers* (New York, The Christian Literature Co., 1886–1890), series 1, vol. 1.

TERESA OF AVILA ON THE PRAYER OF UNION

Teresa of Avila (1515–1582), a sixteenth-century Spanish mystic, entered a Carmelite convent at age 19. With St. John of the Cross she established the Discalced (barefoot) order, which was more strict and wore only sandals. She had visions and raptures and, in her most memorable vision, an angel pierced her heart with a flaming arrow, which, when removed, left her with a love for God. Teresa's most systematic work, the Interior Castle *(1577), uses the metaphor of seven series of mansions to represent various stages of spiritual development. The mystic enters the castle door through prayer, and then roams the mansions' millions of rooms at will. She describes the fifth series of mansions as the Prayer of Union, by which the mystic's soul is possessed by God. In the next selection, she explains the effects of this union using the analogy of a silkworm. The silkworm starts from a tiny egg which feeds on mulberry leaves, spins a cocoon, and emerges as a butterfly. The silkworm represents the soul, its nourishment is the Church, the silk house is Christ, and the spinning of the cocoon is the prayer of union. Thus, the union experience, which does not last even a half hour, transforms the mystic, and the new "butterfly" feels like a stranger in its new world.*

You will have heard of the wonderful way in which silk is made—a way which no one could invent but God—and how it comes from a kind of seed which looks like tiny peppercorns. (I have never seen this, but only heard of it, so if it is incorrect in any way the fault is not mine.) When the warm weather comes, and the mulberry-trees begin to show leaf, this seed starts to take life; until it has this sustenance, on which it feeds, it is as dead. The silkworms feed on the mulberry-leaves until they are full-grown, when people put down twigs, upon which, with their tiny mouths, they start spinning silk, making themselves very tight little cocoons, in which they bury themselves. Then, finally, the worm, which was large and ugly, comes right out of the cocoon a beautiful white butterfly. . . .

The silkworm is like the soul which takes life when, through the heat which comes from the Holy Spirit, it begins to utilize the general help which God gives to us all, and to make use of the remedies which He left in His Church—such as frequent confessions, good books and sermons, for these are the remedies for a soul dead in negligences and sins and frequently plunged into temptation. The soul begins to live and nourishes itself on this food, and on good meditations, until it is full grown—and this is what concerns me now: the rest is of little importance.

When it is full-grown, then, as I wrote at the beginning, it starts to spin its silk and to build the house in which it is to die. This house may be understood here to mean Christ. I think I read or heard somewhere that our life is hid in Christ, or in God (for that is the same thing), or that our life is Christ. (The exact form of this is little to my purpose.)

Here, then, daughters, you see what we can do, with God's favor. May His Majesty Himself be our Mansion as He is in this Prayer of Union which, as it were, we ourselves spin. When I say He will be our Mansion, and we can construct it for ourselves and hide ourselves in it, I seem to be suggesting that we can subtract from God, or add to Him. But of course we cannot possibly do that! We can neither subtract from, nor add to, but we can subtract from, and God add to, ourselves, just as these little silk-worms do. And, before we have finished doing all that we can in that respect, God will take this tiny achievement of ours, which is nothing at all, unite it with His greatness and give it such worth that its reward will be the Lord Himself. And as it is He Whom it has cost the most, so His Majesty will unite our small trials with the great trials which He suffered, and make both of them into one.

On, then, my daughters. Let us hasten to perform this task and spin this cocoon. Let us renounce our self-love and self-will, and our attachment to earthly things. Let us practice penance, prayer, mortification, obedience, and all the other good works that you know of. Let us do what we have been taught; and we have been instructed about what our duty is. Let the silkworm die—let it die, as in fact it does when it has completed the work which it was created to do. Then we shall see God and shall ourselves be as completely hidden in His greatness as is this little worm in its cocoon. Note that, when I speak of seeing God, I am referring to the way in which, as I have said, He allows Himself to be apprehended in this kind of union.

And now let us see what becomes of this silkworm, for all that I have been saying about it is leading up to this. When it is in this state of prayer, and quite dead to the world, it comes out a little white butterfly. Oh, greatness of God, that a soul should come out like this after being hidden in the greatness of God, and closely united with Him, for so short a time—never, I think, for as long as half an hour! I tell you truly, the very soul does not know itself. For think of the difference between an ugly worm and a white butterfly, it is just the same here. The soul cannot think how it can have merited such a blessing—whence such a blessing could have come to it, I meant to say, for it knows quite well that it has not merited it at all. It finds itself so anxious to praise the Lord that it would gladly be consumed and die a thousand deaths for His sake. Then it finds itself longing to suffer great trials and unable to do otherwise. It has the most vehement desires for penance, for solitude, and for all to know God. And hence, when it sees God being offended, it becomes greatly distressed. In the following Mansion we shall treat of these things further and in detail, for, although the experiences of this Mansion and of the next are almost identical, their effects come to have much greater power, for, as I have said, if after God comes to a soul here on earth it strives to progress still more, it will experience great things.

Source: Teresa of Avila, *Interior Castle*, Fifth Mansion, ch. 2, from *Interior Castle*, tr. E. Allison Peers (Garden City, N.Y.: Doubleday, 1961).

PROTESTANT STATEMENTS OF FAITH
LUTHERANS: AUGSBURG CONFESSION

As Protestant Christian Churches throughout Europe took issue with the Roman Catholic Church, they created confessions of faith that defined their principal theological tenets. Among the first of these was the Augsburg Confession, *written in part by*

Martin Luther (1483–1546) in 1530. Even today it is a foundational statement for most Lutheran denominations, and Lutheran clergy take an oath by it upon ordination. In spite of Luther's harsh attacks on core Catholic doctrine, the original 21 articles of the Augsburg Confession highlight the similarities between Lutheran Protestants and Catholics, rather than the differences. Seven articles added later discuss Catholic abuses. The selected articles below have a distinctively Lutheran tone.

Article 4. Of Justification. [Our Churches] . . . teach that men cannot be justified before God by their own strength, merits, or works, but are freely justified for Christ's sake, through faith, when they believe that they are received into favor, and that their sins are forgiven for Christ's sake, who, by His death, has made satisfaction for our sins. This faith God imputes for righteousness in His sight. Rom. 3 and 4.

Article 7. Of the Church. Also they teach that one holy Church is to continue forever. The Church is the congregation of saints, in which the Gospel is rightly taught and the Sacraments are rightly administered.

And to the true unity of the Church it is enough to agree concerning the doctrine of the Gospel and the administration of the Sacraments. Nor is it necessary that human traditions, that is, rites or ceremonies, instituted by men, should be everywhere alike. As Paul says: One faith, one Baptism, one God and Father of all, etc. Eph. 4, 5, 6.

Article 10. Of the Lord's Supper. Of the Supper of the Lord they teach that the Body and Blood of Christ are truly present, and are distributed to those who eat the Supper of the Lord; and they reject those that teach otherwise.

Article 11. Of Confession. Of Confession they teach that Private Absolution ought to be retained in the churches, although in confession an enumeration of all sins is not necessary. For it is impossible according to the Psalm: Who can understand his errors? Ps. 19, 12.

Article 21. Of the Worship of the Saints. Of the Worship of Saints they teach that the memory of saints may be set before us, that we may follow their faith and good works, according to our calling, as the Emperor may follow the example of David in making war to drive away the Turk from his country; For both are kings. But the Scripture teaches not the invocation of saints or to ask help of saints, since it sets before us the one Christ as the Mediator, Propitiation, High Priest, and Intercessor. He is to be prayed to, and has promised that He will hear our prayer; and this worship He approves above all, to wit, that in all afflictions He be called upon, 1 John 2, 1: If any man sin, we have an Advocate with the Father, etc.

Article 23. Of the Marriage of Priests. There has been common complaint concerning the examples of priests who were not chaste. For that reason also Pope Pius is reported to have said that there were certain causes why marriage was taken away from priests, but that there were far weightier ones why it ought to be given back; for so Platina writes. Since, therefore, our priests were desirous to avoid these open scandals, they married wives, and taught that it was lawful for them to contract matrimony. . . .

Source: Augsburg Confession, in *Triglot Concordia: The Symbolical Books of the Evangelical Lutheran Church.* (St. Louis: Concordia Publishing House, 1921).

ANGLICANS: 39 ARTICLES OF RELIGION

Between 1534 and 1563—a particularly volatile period of British history—the Church of England moved toward Protestantism. In 1571, during the reign of Queen Elizabeth, Parliament enacted Thirty-Nine Articles of Religion, which, influenced by Calvinist theology, defined the new denomination. Clergy today in the Church of England are required to assent to the 39 Articles, and the Articles of Religion in other Anglican churches—such as the Episcopalian Church in the United States—are based on these. Since 1784, Methodist churches have followed 24 Articles of Religion taken from these. The selections below reflect Anglican views of Church hierarchy, rejecting the papacy and establishing the British monarch as the Church's head.

Article 19: Of the Church. The visible Church of Christ is a congregation of faithful men, in which the pure word of God is preached and the sacraments be duly ministered according to Christ's ordinance in all those things that of necessity are requisite to the same. As the Church of Jerusalem, Alexandria, and Antioch have erred: so also the Church of Rome hath erred, not only in their living and manner of ceremonies, but also in matters of faith.

Article 23: Of Ministering in the Congregation. It is not lawful for any man to take upon him the office of public preaching or ministering the sacraments in the congregation, before he be lawfully called and sent to execute the same. And those we ought to judge lawfully called and sent, which be chosen and called to this work by men who have public authority given unto them in the congregation to call and send ministers into the Lord's vineyard.

Article 37: Of the Civil Magistrates. The Queen's Majesty hath the chief power in this realm of England and other her dominions, unto whom the chief government of all estates of this realm, whether they be ecclesiastical or civil, in all causes doth appertain, and is not nor ought to be subject to any foreign jurisdiction.

Where we attribute to the Queen's Majesty the chief government, by which titles we understand the minds of some slanderous folks to be offended, we give not to our princes the ministering either of God's word or of sacraments, the which thing the Injunctions also lately set forth by Elizabeth our Queen doth most plainly testify: but only that prerogative which we see to have been given always to all godly princes in Holy Scriptures by God himself, that is, that they should rule all estates and degrees committed to their charge by God, whether they be temporal, and restrain with the civil sword the stubborn and evil-doers.

The Bishop of Rome hath no jurisdiction in this realm of England. The Laws of the realm may punish Christian men with death for heinous and grievous offences.

It is lawful for Christian men at the commandment of the Magistrate to wear weapons and serve in the wars.

Source: "Articles of Religion," from *The Book of Common Prayer*, London, Bagster, 1855.

PRESBYTERIANS: WESTMINSTER CONFESSION

At the beckoning of the British Parliament, the Westminster Confession *was created in 1646 by churches in England that followed the reformed theology of John Calvin (1509–1546). Although the Anglican Church abandoned it shortly afterwards, the Confession was adopted by the Scottish Parliament in 1649, making it a cornerstone of Presbyterianism. The Confession was also adopted in modified form by other Protestant denominations throughout Europe and America. The chapters below reflect the distinctively Calvinistic points of the Confession.*

Chapter 6. Of the Fall of Man, of Sin, and of the Punishment Thereof. 1. Our first parents, being seduced by the subtlety and temptation of Satan, sinned in eating the forbidden fruit. This their sin God was pleased, according to his wise and holy counsel, to permit, having purposed to order it to his own glory. 2. By this sin they fell from their original right-eousness, and communion with God, and so became dead in sin, and wholly defiled in all the faculties and parts of soul and body. 3. They being the root of all mankind, the guilt of this sin was imputed, and the same death in sin and corrupted nature conveyed to all their posterity, descending from them by ordinary generation. 4. From this original cor-ruption, whereby we are utterly indisposed, disabled, and made opposite to all good, and wholly inclined to all evil, do proceed all actual transgres-sions. 5. This corruption of nature, during this life, doth remain in those that are regenerated: and although it be through Christ pardoned and mortified, yet both itself, and all the motions thereof, are truly and prop-erly sin. 6. Every sin, both original and actual, being a transgression of the righteous law of God, and contrary thereunto, doth, in its own nature, bring guilt upon the sinner, whereby he is bound over to the wrath of God, and curse of the law, and so made subject to death, with all miseries spiritual, temporal, and eternal.

Chapter 10. Of Effectual Calling. 1. All those whom God hath predesti-nated unto life, and those only, he is pleased, in his appointed and accepted time, effectually to call, by his Word and Spirit, out of that state of sin and death, in which they are by nature, to grace and salvation by Jesus Christ; enlightening their minds spiritually and savingly, to understand the things of God; taking away their heart of stone, and giving unto them an heart of flesh; renewing their wills, and by his almighty power determining them to that which is good, and effectually drawing them to Jesus Christ, yet so as they come most freely, being made willing by his grace. 2. This effectual call is of God's free and special grace alone, not from any thing at all foreseen in man, who is altogether passive therein, until, being quickened and renewed by the Holy Spirit, he is thereby enabled to answer this call, and to embrace the grace offered and conveyed in it. 3. Elect infants, dying in infancy, are regenerated and saved by Christ through the Spirit, who worketh when, and where, and how he pleaseth. So also are all other elect persons, who are incapable of being outwardly called by the ministry of the Word. 4. Others, not elected, although they may be called by the ministry of the Word, and may have some common operations of the Spirit, yet they never truly come to Christ, and therefore cannot be saved; much less can men, not professing the Christian religion, be saved in any other way whatsoever than by Christ, be they never so diligent to frame their lives according to the light of nature, and the law of that religion they do profess; and to assert and maintain that they may is without warrant of the World of God.

Chapter 17. Of the Perseverance of the Saints. 1. They whom God hath accepted in his Beloved, effectually called and sanctified by his Spirit, can neither totally nor finally fall away from the state of grace; but shall certainly persevere therein to the end, and be eternally saved. 2. This perseverance of the saints depends, not upon their own free will, but upon the immutability of the decree of election, flowing from the free and unchangeable love of God the Father; upon the efficacy of the merit and intercession of Jesus Christ; the abiding of the Spirit and of the seed of God within them; and the nature of the covenant of grace: from all which ariseth also the certainty and infallibility thereof. 3. Nevertheless they may, through the temptations of Satan and of the world, the prevalency of corruption remaining in them, and the neglect of the means of their preservation, fall into grievous sins; and for a time continue therein: whereby they incur God's displeasure, and grieve his Holy Spirit; come to be deprived of some measure of their graces and comforts; have their hearts hardened, and their consciences wounded; hurt and scandalize others, and bring temporal judgments upon themselves.

Source: *The Westminster Confession of Faith* (Edinburgh: T. and T. Clark, 1882).

BAPTISTS: FIRST LONDON BAPTIST CONFESSION OF FAITH

In sixteenth-century England, a group of independent churches emerged based on the conviction that local congregations should be free from the authority of larger governing bodies. By their very nature, these congregations were diverse, formulating their own practices and theology. In 1608, former Anglican minister John Smyth (1554–1612) founded the first Baptist church in Amsterdam. Smyth and his followers moved back to England, establishing Baptist churches there. After his untimely death from tuberculosis, Baptists split into two groups: General Baptists, who believed that Christ died for all people, and Particular Baptists, who held that he died only for the elect. In 1643, Particular Baptists in London created a confession of faith. Unlike later Baptist confessions, which were modifications of the Westminster Confession, *this one has a distinct content. The following selections, taken from the 1646 edition of that Confession, highlight key points of Baptist theology, and article 21 specifically articulates the position of the Particular Baptists.*

21. Jesus Christ by His death did purchase salvation for the elect that God gave unto Him: These only have interest in Him, and fellowship with

Him, for whom He makes intercession to His Father in their behalf, and to them alone doth God by His Spirit apply this redemption; as also the free gift of eternal life is given to them, and none else.

25. The preaching of the gospel to the conversion of sinners, is absolutely free; no way requiring as absolutely necessary, any qualifications, preparations, or terrors of the law, or preceding ministry of the law, but only and alone the naked soul, a sinner and ungodly, to receive Christ crucified, dead and buried, and risen again; who is made a prince and a Savior for such sinners as through the gospel shall be brought to believe on Him.

36. Being thus joined, every [local] church hath power given them from Christ, for their well-being, to choose among themselves persons for elders and deacons, being qualified according to the word, as those which Christ hath appointed in His testament, for the feeding, governing, serving, and building up of His Church; and that none have any power to impose on them either these or any other.

39. Baptism is an ordinance of the New Testament, given by Christ, to be dispensed upon persons professing faith, or that are made disciples; who upon profession of faith, ought to be baptized, and after to partake of the Lord's Supper.

42. Christ hath likewise given power to His Church to receive in, and cast out, any member that deserves it; and this power is given to every congregation, and not to one particular person, either member or officer, but in relation to the whole body, in reference to their faith and fellowship.

Source: *Confession of Faith of Seven Congregations or Churches of Christ in London* (London: 1646).

CONGREGATIONALISTS: SAVOY DECLARATION OF FAITH AND ORDER

In addition to the Baptists, another group of independent churches in England was the Congregationalists. In 1658, representatives from about 120 of these churches met in Savoy palace in an effort to unify their congregations. Modifying the Westminster Confession, *they created the* Savoy Declaration of Faith and Order. *The selection below is one of their two principal additions to the* Westminster Confession, *which asserts the right of a congregation to govern itself.*

The Institution of Churches, and the Order Appointed in Them by Jesus Christ. 1. By the appointment of the Father all power for the calling, institution, order, or government of the Church, is invested in a supreme and sovereign manner in the Lord Jesus Christ, as King and Head thereof. 2. In the execution of this power wherewith he is so entrusted, the Lord Jesus calleth out of the world unto communion with himself, those that are given unto him by his Father, that they may walk before him in all the ways of obedience, which he prescribeth to them in Word. 3. Those thus called (through the ministry of the Word by his Spirit) he commandeth to walk together in particular societies or churches, for their mutual edification, and the due performance of that public worship, which he requireth of them in this world. 4. To each of these churches thus gathered, according to his mind declared in his Word, he hath given all that power and authority, which is any way needful for their carrying on that order in worship and discipline, which he hath instituted for them to observe, with commands and rules for the due and right exerting and executing of that power. 5. These particular churches thus appointed by the authority of Christ, and entrusted with power from him for the ends before expressed, are each of them as unto those ends, the seat of that power which he is pleased to communicate to his saints or subjects in this world, so that as such they receive it immediately from himself. 6. Besides these particular churches, there is not instituted by Christ any church more extensive or catholic entrusted with power for the administration of his ordinances, or the execution of any authority in his name. 7. A particular church gathered and completed according to the mind of Christ, consists of officers and members. The Lord Christ having given to his called ones (united according to his appointment in church-order) liberty and power to choose persons fitted by the Holy Ghost for that purpose, to be over them, and to minister to them in the Lord. . . .

Source: *Declaration of Faith and Order* (London: J. P., 1659).

ASSEMBLIES OF GOD: STATEMENT OF FUNDAMENTAL TRUTHS

The Pentecostal movement began around 1900 through the ministry of Charles Parham (1873–1929), who emphasized baptism of the Holy Spirit and speaking in tongues. In 1974 several independent Pentecostal congregations formed the Assemblies of God denomination. Pentecostals initially resisted creeds, but theological disputes prompted the General Council of the Assemblies of God to create a Statement of Fundamental Truths *in 1916. Of the 17 Statements, the more uniquely Pentecostal ones are presented below.*

5. *The Promise of the Father.* All believers are entitled to, and should ardently expect, and earnestly seek the promise of the Father, the baptism in the Holy Ghost and fire, according to the command of the lord Jesus Christ. This was the normal experience of all in the early Christian church. With it comes the enduement of power for life and service. The bestowment of the gifts and their uses in the work of the ministry. Luke 24:49; Acts 1:4, 1:8; 1 Cor. 12:1–31.

6. *The Full Consummation of the Baptism in the Holy Ghost.* The full consummation of the baptism of believers in the Holy Ghost and fire,

is indicated by the initial sign of speaking in tongues, as the spirit of God gives utterance. Acts 2:4. This wonderful experience is distinct from and subsequent to the experience of the new birth. Acts 10:44–46; 15:8,9.

12. *Divine Healing.* Deliverance from sickness is provided for in the atonement, and is the privilege of all believers. Isa. 53:4,5; Matth. 8:16,17.

14. *The Blessed Hope.* The Resurrection of those who have fallen asleep in Christ. The rapture of believers, which are alive and remain, and the translation of the true church, this is the blessed hope set before all believers. 1 Thess, 4:16–17; Rom. 8:23; Tit. 2:13.

15. *The Imminent Coming and Millenial Reign of Jesus.* The premillenial and imminent coming of the Lord to gather his people unto himself, and to judge the world in righteousness while reigning on the earth for a thousand years is the expectation of the true church of Christ.

16. *The Lake of Fire.* The devil and his angles, the beast and false prophet, and whosoever is not found written in the book of Life, the fearful and unbelieving, and abominable, and murderers and whoremongers, and sorcerers, and idolators and all liars shall be consigned to everlasting punishment in the lake which burneth with fire and brimstone, which is the second death.

17. *The New Heavens and New Earth.* We look for new heaven and a new earth wherein dewelleth righteousness. 2 Pet. 3:13; Rev. 1 and 22.

RECENT SECTARIAN MOVEMENTS

UNITARIANISM: WILLIAM ELLERY CHANNING

Denominations emerging from the Protestant Reformation initially shared basic theological assumptions with the older Catholic and Orthodox traditions. Foremost among these were the notions of the Trinity and that the Bible was the unique word of God. Growing political freedom in Europe and America permitted some Christian groups to step outside these traditional theological boundaries. One of the first such groups was the Unitarians, who, as their name implies, denied the Trinity in favor of a unified conception of God. Jesus, in their view, was a divinely appointed prophet and teacher, but not God himself. In America, Unitarianism became more formally organized through the efforts of William Ellery Channing (1780–1842), a former Congregationalist pastor. Although denying the Trinity, Channing remained committed to other tenets of Christianity. Some later Unitarians departed not only from Christian theology, but from all traditional religion, adopting instead a scientific humanism. The following selections are from Channing's seminal sermon Unitarian Christianity, *delivered in 1819 at an ordination ceremony in Baltimore, Maryland.*

I. We regard the Scriptures as the records of God's successive revelations to mankind, and particularly of the last and most perfect revelation of his will by Jesus Christ. Whatever doctrines seem to us to be clearly taught in the Scriptures, we receive without reserve or exception. We do not, however, attach equal importance to all the books in this collection. Our religion, we believe, lies chiefly in the New Testament. The dispensation of Moses, compared with that of Jesus, we consider as adapted to the childhood of the human race, a preparation for a nobler system, and chiefly useful now as serving to confirm and illustrate the Christian Scriptures. Jesus Christ is the only master of Christians, and whatever he taught, either during his personal ministry, or by his inspired Apostles, we regard as of divine authority, and profess to make the rule of our lives.

This authority, which we give to the Scriptures, is a reason, we conceive, for studying them with peculiar care, and for inquiring anxiously into the principles of interpretation, by which their true meaning may be ascertained. The principles adopted by the class of Christians in whose name I speak, need to be explained, because they are often misunderstood. We are particularly accused of making an unwarrantable use of reason in the interpretation of Scripture. We are said to exalt reason above revelation, to prefer our own wisdom to God's. Loose and undefined charges of this kind are circulated so freely, that we think it due to ourselves, and to the cause of truth, to express our views with some particularity.

Our leading principle in interpreting Scripture is this, that the Bible is a book written for men, in the language of men, and that its meaning is to be sought in the same manner as that of other books. We believe that God, when he speaks to the human race, confirms, if we may also say, to the established rules of speaking and writing. How else would the Scriptures avail us more, than if communicated in an unknown tongue? . . .

II. Having thus stated the principles according to which we interpret Scripture, I now proceed to the second great head of this discourse, which is, to state some of the views which we derive from that sacred book, particularly those which distinguish us from other Christians.

1. In the first place, we believe in the doctrine of God's *unity*, or that there is one God, and one only. To this truth we give infinite importance, and we feel ourselves bound to take heed, lest any man spoil us of it by vain philosophy. The proposition, that there is one God, seems to us exceedingly plain. We understand by it, that there is one being, one mind, one person, one intelligent agent, and one only, to whom underived and infinite perfection and dominion belong. We conceive, that these words could have conveyed no other meaning to the simple and uncultivated people who were set apart to be the depositaries of this great truth, and who were utterly incapable of understanding those hair-breadth distinctions between being and person, which the sagacity of later ages has discovered. We find to intimation, that this language was to be taken in an unusual sense, or that God's unity was a quite different thing from the oneness of other intelligent beings.

We object to the doctrine of the Trinity, that, whilst acknowledging in words, it subverts in effect, the unity of God. According to this doctrine, there are three infinite and equal persons, possessing supreme divinity, called the Father, Son, and Holy Ghost. Each of these persons, as described by theologians, has his own particular consciousness, will, and perceptions. They love each other, converse with each other, and delight in each other's society. They perform different parts in man's redemption, each having his appropriate office, and neither doing the work of the other. The Son is mediator and not the Father. The Father sends the Son, and is not himself sent; nor is he conscious, like the Son, of taking flesh. Here, then, we have three intelligent agents, possessed of different consciousness, different wills, and different perceptions, performing different acts, and sustaining different relations; and if these things do not imply and constitute three minds or beings, we are utterly at a loss to know how minds or beings are to be formed. It is difference of properties, and acts, and consciousness, which leads us to the belief of different intelligent beings, and, if this mark fails us, our whole knowledge fall; we have no proof, that all the agents and persons in the universe are not one and the same mind. When we attempt to conceive of three Gods, we can do nothing more than represent to ourselves three agents, distinguished from each other by similar marks and peculiarities to those which separate the persons of the Trinity; and when common Christians hear these persons spoken of as conversing with each other, loving each other, and performing different acts, how can they help regarding them as different beings, different minds? . . .

Source: William Ellery Channing, *Unitarian Christianity,* in *The Works of William E. Channing* (Boston, American Unitarian Association, 1882).

MORMONISM: JOSEPH SMITH

Mormonism encompasses a few historically related denominations, the largest of which is the Church of Jesus Christ of Latter-Day Saints. Mormon belief is founded on the work of Joseph Smith (1805–1844), who maintained that an angelic vision revealed to him the location of gold plates buried during a previous age. Smith's translation of these plates is the Book of Mormon, *first published in 1830. The work chronicles the history and religious practices of a band of Israelites who migrated to America in 600 B.C.E. Under two leaders, two distinct conflicting cultures emerged: the civilized Nephites, and the nomadic and warring Lamanites. Ostensibly the forefathers of the native Americans, the Lamanites exterminated the Nephites. Anticipating their demise, Moroni, a Nephite chronicler, buried a golden copy of the* Book of Mormon *to preserve their story. A 20-page section of the* Book of Mormon *describes how Jesus visited the Nephites and gave them Christian Doctrine, much of which is paraphrased from the Gospels Selections from this are below.*

11.   . . . And it came to pass, as they understood they cast their eyes up again towards heaven; and behold, they saw a Man descending out of heaven; and he was clothed in a white robe; and he came down and stood in the midst of them; and the eyes of the whole multitude were

turned upon him, and they durst not open their mouths, even one to another and wist not what it meant, for they thought it was an angel that had appeared unto them. And it came to pass that he stretched forth his hand and spake unto the people, saying:

Behold, I am Jesus Christ, whom the prophets testified shall come into the world. . . .

Behold, verily, verily, I say unto you, I will declare unto you my doctrine. And this is my doctrine, and it is the doctrine which the Father hath given unto me; and I bear record of the Father, and the Father beareth record of me, and the Holy Ghost beareth record of the Father and me; and I bear record that the Father commandeth all men, everywhere, to repent and believe in me. And whoso believeth in me, and is baptized, the same shall be saved; and they are they who shall inherit the kingdom of God. And whoso believeth not in me, and is not baptized, shall be damned.

Verily, verily, I say unto you, that this is my doctrine, and I bear record of it from the Father; and whoso believeth in me believeth in the Father also; and unto him will the Father bear record of me, for he will visit him with fire and with the Holy Ghost. And thus will the Father bear record of me, and the Holy Ghost will bear record unto him of the Father and me; for the Father, and I, and the Holy Ghost are one.

And again I say unto you, ye must repent, and becomes as a little child, and be baptized in my name, or ye can in nowise receive these things. And again I say unto you, ye must repent, and be baptized in my name, and become as a little child, or ye can in nowise inherit the kingdom of God. Verily, verily, I say unto you, that this is my doctrine, and whoso buildeth upon this buildeth upon my rock, and the gates of hell shall not prevail against them. And whoso shall declare more or less than this, and establish it for my doctrine, the same cometh of evil, and is not built upon my rock; but he buildeth upon a sandy foundation, and the gates of hell stand open to receive such when the floods come and the winds beat upon them. Therefore, go forth unto this people, and declare the words which I have spoken, unto the ends of the earth.

17. Behold, now it came to pass that when Jesus had spoken these words he looked round about again on the multitude, and he said unto them: Behold, my time is at hand. I perceive that ye are weak, that ye cannot understand all my words which I am commanded of the Father to speak unto you at this time. Therefore, go ye unto your homes, and ponder upon the things which I have said, and ask of the Father, in my name, that ye may understand, and prepare your minds for the morrow, and I come unto you again. But now I go unto the Father, and also to show myself unto the lost tribes of Israel, for they are not lost unto the Father, for he knoweth whither he hath taken them.

And it came to pass that when Jesus had thus spoken, he cast his eyes round about again on the multitude, and beheld they were in tears, and did look steadfastly upon him as if they would ask him to tarry a little longer with them. And he said unto them: Behold my bowels are filled with compassion towards you. Have ye any that are sick among you? Bring them hither. Have ye any that are lame, or blind, or halt, or maimed, or leprous, or that are withered, or that are deaf, or that are afflicted in any manner? Bring them hither and I will heal them, for I have compassion upon you; my bowels are filled with mercy. . . .

18. . . . Therefore, keep these sayings which I have commanded you that ye come not under condemnation; for woe unto him whom the Father condemneth. And I give you these commandments because of the disputations which have been among you. And blessed are ye if ye have no disputations among you. And now I go unto the Father, because it is expedient that I should go unto the Father for your sakes.

And it came to pass that when Jesus had made an end of these sayings, he touched with his hand the disciples whom he had chosen, one by one, even until he had touched them all, and spake unto them as he touched them. And the multitude heard not the words which he spake, therefore they did not bear record; but the disciples bare record that he gave them power to give the Holy Ghost. And I will show unto you hereafter that this record is true. And it came to pass that when Jesus had touched them all, there came a cloud and overshadowed the multitude that they could not see Jesus. And while they were overshadowed he departed from them, and ascended into heaven. And the disciples saw and did bear record that he ascended again into heaven.

Source: *Book of Mormon*, Third Nephi, 11:8–10, 31–41; 17:1–7; 18:33–39.

JEHOVAH'S WITNESSES: CHARLES TAZE RUSSELL

The Jehovah's Witnesses denomination is based on the views of Charles Taze Russell (1852–1916), who, though not ordained, spent his life preaching about the second coming of Jesus. Russell believed that the Bible provided clues for the end times and, based on this, he made an unsuccessful prediction of Jesus' return. Attracting many followers, he formed an independent church in 1878 and the following year founded a periodical called The Watchtower, *which became a major outlet for his theological views. Since 1931 the movement he started has gone by the name Jehovah's Witnesses. In the selection below, Russell emphasizes Jesus' messianic role and the ability of the church to partake in the divine nature.*

The word Christ or *Kristos* is a Greek word, introduced into our English language, but not *translated* into it. Its translation is, ANOINTED.

'Unto us a child is born,' etc., and 'they shall call his name Jesus.' The name Jesus means Deliverer or Savior, and the child was named in view of a work he was to do; for we are told, 'he *shall* save his people from their sins.' Jesus was always his name, but from the time of his baptism, when the Holy Ghost descended upon him and *anointed* him as the High Priest, preparatory to his making 'the sin offering'on the cross, and thus accomplishing what is indicated by his *name*, his *title* has been 'The Anointed,'— Jesus 'the *Christ* (anointed) of God.'—Lu 9:20. Jesus was frequently called by this *title* instead of by his name; as English people oftenest speak of their sovereign as 'the Queen,' instead of calling her by her name— *Victoria*.

But, as Jesus was in God's plan as the *anointed one*, before the foundation of the world, so too THE CHURCH of Christ, was recognized in the same plan; that is, God purposed to take out of the world a 'little flock,' whom he purposed raising above the condition of the *perfect human* nature, to make them 'partakers of the *Divine nature*.' The relationship of Jesus toward these, is that of '*Head* over all, God blessed forever,' 'for he hath given him to head over *the church* (of the first-born) which is his body.' As Jesus was foreordained to be *the anointed one*, so we, also, were chosen to the same anointing of the Spirit, as members in his body and under him as our head. And so we read (Eph 1:3:) 'God hath blessed us with all spiritual blessings *in Christ* according as he hath chosen us *in him* before the foundation of the world, that we should be holy and without blame before him in love; having predestinated us unto the adoption of children by Jesus Christ to himself . . . wherein he hath made us accepted *in the beloved*.' (See also *vs. 20–23*.) Again, (Ro 8:29) 'Whom he did foreknow he also did predestinate to be conformed to the image of his Son, that he (head and body) might be the *first-born* (heir) among many brethren.'

God's plan of saving *the world* by a 'restitution of all things,' waits until first, this bride of Jesus—these members of the Spirit-anointed body, shall be gathered out from the world according to his purpose. . . .

Source: Charles Taze Russell, "The Christ of God," *Food for Thinking Christians*, part 5, in *Zion's Watchtower*, 1881.

CHRISTIAN SCIENCE: MARY BAKER EDDY

The Christian Science movement was founded by Mary Baker Eddy (1821–1910), who believed that the central message of Christianity is healing. In her most influenced work, Science and Health *(1875), she argues that the material world and all illness associated with it are unreal and illusory. Healing comes after prayer when God simply removes the afflicted person's false belief in the illusion.*

Chapter 2. *Healing Primary*. First in the list of Christian duties, he [i.e., Jesus] taught his followers the healing power of Truth and Love. He attached no importance to dead ceremonies. It is the living Christ, the practical Truth, which makes Jesus "the resurrection and the life" to all who follow him in deed. Obeying his precious precepts—following his demonstration so far as we apprehend it—we drink of his cup, partake of his bread, are baptized with his purity; and at last we shall rest, sit down with him, in a full understanding of the divine Principle which triumphs over death. For what says Paul? "As often as ye eat this bread, and drink this cup, ye do show the Lord's death till he come."

Healing Early Lost. The proofs of Truth, Life, and Love, which Jesus gave by casting out error and healing the sick, completed his earthly mission; but in the Christian Church this demonstration of healing was early lost, about three centuries after the crucifixion. No ancient school of philosophy, *materia media,* or scholastic theology ever taught or demonstrated the divine healing of absolute Science.

Chapter 4. *Real and Unreal Identity.* The divine Mind maintains all identities, from a blade of grass to a star, as distinct and eternal. The questions are: What are God's identities? What is Soul? Does life or soul exist in the thing formed? Nothing is real and eternal—nothing is Spirit—but God and His idea. Evil has no reality. It is neither person, place, nor thing, but is simply a belief, an illusion of material sense.

The identity, or idea, of all reality continues forever; but Spirit, or the divine Principle of all, is not in Spirit's formations. Soul is synonymous with Spirit, God, the creative, governing, infinite Principle outside of finite from, which forms only reflect.

Real Life Is God. When being is understood, Life will be recognized as neither material nor finite, but as infinite—as God, universal good; and the belief that life, or mind, was ever in a finite form, or good in evil, will be destroyed. Then it will be understood that Spirit never entered matter and was therefore never raised from matter. When advanced to spiritual being and the understanding of God, man can no longer commune with matter; neither can he return to it, any more than a tree can return to its seed. Neither will man seem to be corporeal, but he will be an individual consciousness, characterized by the divine Spirit as idea, not matter. Suffering, sinning, dying beliefs are unreal. When divine Science is universally understood, they will have no power over man, for man is immortal and lives by divine authority.

Chapter 6. *Christian Science Discovered.* In the year 1866, I discovered the Christ Science or divine laws of Life, Truth, and Love, and named my discovery Christian Science. God had been graciously preparing me during many years for the reception of this final revelation of the absolute divine Principle of scientific mental healing.

Causation Mental. Christian Science explains all cause and effect as mental, not physical. It lifts the veil of mystery from Soul and body. It shows the Scientific relation of man to God, disentangles the interlaced ambiguities of being, and sets free the imprisoned thought. In divine Science, the universe, including man, is spiritual, harmonious, and eternal.

Science shows that what is termed *matter* is but the subjective state of what is termed by the author *mortal mind.*

Mind the Only Healer. Science not only reveals the origin of all disease as mental, but it also declares that all disease is cured by divine Mind. There can be no healing except by this Mind, however much we trust a drug or any other means towards which human faith or endeavor is directed. It is mortal mind, not matter, which brings to the sick whatever good they may seem to receive from materiality. But the sick are never really healed except by means of the divine power. Only the action of Truth, Life, and Love can give harmony.

Source: Mary Baker Eddy, *Science and Health,* from chs. 2, 4, and 6 (Boston: Christian Science Publishing Company, 1875).

NEW AGE CHRISTIANITY: LEVI H. DOWLING

The New Age religious movement is based on the astrological concept that the current Piscean age is closing and will be followed by a new age of Aquarius. With the coming of this new age, a new conception of the world and religious truth will also take hold, emphasizing the unity of all things, individual freedom, and the relativity of truth. New Age religion intentionally lacks the formal institutional and doctrinal structure of the major world religions, and draws liberally from many religious sources—including astrology, Wicca, and paganism, as well as the major religions themselves. Among the influential New Age writings distinctly in the Christian tradition is the Aquarian Gospel of Jesus the Christ, *which first appeared in 1907. Its author, Levi H. Dowling (1844–1911), was a pastor and physician who claimed to have transcribed this book from the universal Akashic records. The work amplifies the account of Jesus' life and teachings in the New Testament, describing Jesus' childhood and trips to the Far East. Like the New Age movement itself, the religious views here are highly eclectic, influenced particularly by Hinduism, Buddhism, Taoism, Gnosticism, and Zoroastrianism. The New Testament book of Matthew states that Joseph fled to Egypt with Mary and the infant Jesus, thus avoiding Herod's efforts to kill the newborn king of the Jews. Developing this plot, Dowling describes Jesus' early childhood in Egypt under the tutelage of Elihu and Salome. Although the Elihu character does not appear in the New Testament, the book of Mark mentions a woman named Salome who was present at Jesus' crucifixion. In the selection below, Elihu lectures Mary and Jesus about the unity of all things, the higher and lower human selves, and the nature of God.*

Chapter 8. Again Elihu met his pupils in the sacred grove and said, No man lives unto himself; for every living thing is bound by cords to every other living thing. Blest are the pure in heart; for they will love and not demand love in return. They will not do to other men what they would not have other men do unto them. There are two selfs; the higher and the lower self. The higher self is human spirit clothed with soul, made in the form of God. The lower self, the carnal self, the body of desires, is a reflection of the higher self, distorted by the murky ethers of the flesh. The lower self is an illusion, and will pass away; the higher self is God in man, and will not pass away. The higher self is the embodiment of truth; the lower self is truth reversed, and so is falsehood manifest. The higher self is justice, mercy, love and right; the lower self is what the higher self is not. The lower self breeds hatred, slander, lewdness, murders, theft, and everything that harms; the higher self is mother of the virtues and the harmonies of life. The lower self is rich in promises, but poor in blessedness and peace; it offers pleasure, joy and satisfying gains, but gives unrest and misery and death. It gives men apples that are lovely to the eye and pleasant to the smell; their cores are full of bitterness and gall. If you would ask me what to study I would say, your selfs; and when you well had studied them, and then would ask me what to study next, I would reply, your selfs. He who knows well his lower self, knows the illusions of the world, knows of the things that pass away; and he who knows his higher self, knows God; knows well the things that cannot pass away. Thrice blessed is the man who has made purity and love his very own; he has been ransomed from the perils of the lower self and is himself his higher self. Men seek salvation from an evil that they deem a living monster of the nether world; and they have gods that are but demons in disguise; all powerful, yet full of jealousy and hate and lust; whose favors must be bought with costly sacrifice of fruits, and of the lives of birds, and animals, and human kind. And yet these gods possess no ears to hear, no eyes to see, no heart to sympathize, no power to save. This evil is myth; these gods are made of air, and clothed with shadows of a thought. The only devil from which men must be redeemed is self, the lower self. If man would find his devil he must look within; his name is self. If man would find his savior he must look within; and when the demon self has been dethroned the savior, Love, will be exulted to the throne of power. The David of the light is Purity, who slays the strong Goliath of the dark, and seats the savior, Love, upon the throne.

Source: Levi H. Dowling, *The Aquarian Gospel of Jesus the Christ*, ch. 8 (Los Angeles: Cazenove, 1908).

GLOSSARY

Apostles   Early followers of Jesus commissioned to lead the church after his death.

Bible   Fundamental Christian scripture consisting of the Old and New Testaments.

Catholic   The largest Christian denomination, which follows a church hierarchy led by the bishop of Rome (i.e., the Pope).

Disciples   Jesus' followers.

Eastern Orthodox   The church diocese originally of the eastern Roman Empire which rejects the supreme authority of the bishop of Rome.

Gnosticism The near eastern religious movement from 100 to 400 C.E., which aims to free one's spirit from the evil material world by acquiring special knowledge (gnosis).

Holy Spirit Divine presence and agent of guidance for Christians. One person of the Trinity, along with the Father and Son.

Judaizers First-century Jewish Christians who maintained that Christians were still bound by traditional Jewish laws.

Messiah Hebrew term for "anointed one," or "king" indicating that someone is set aside for a divinely appointed office, either in a religious, apocalyptic sense, or in a political, revolutionary sense.

New Age Contemporary religious movement based on the astrological view that the present Piscean age is ending and will be succeeded by a new age of Aquarius.

Pentecostal Protestant religious movement emphasizing baptism of the Holy Spirit and speaking in tongues.

Pope Head of the church and successor to the Apostle Peter according to the Roman Catholic tradition.

Protestant Christian denominations whose lineages derive from the sixteenth-century Protestant reformation.

Quelle (*or Q*) A written sayings list, no longer extant, which Matthew and Luke used as a source for Jesus' teachings.

Synoptic Gospels Gospels of Mark, Matthew, and Luke, which are similar in content, in contrast to John, which vastly differs from all three.

Trinity Doctrine that God is a unity of three persons: the Father, Son, and Holy Spirit.

FURTHER READINGS

BAINTON, R. H. *The Reformation of the Sixteenth Century*. Boston: Beacon Press, 1962.

BORG, MARCUS J. *Jesus in Contemporary Scholarship*. Valley Forge: Trinity, 1994.

CHADWICK, OWEN, ed. *The Pelican History of the Church*, 5 vols. London: Penguin, 1960–70.

CROSSAN, JOHN DOMINIC. *Jesus: A Revolutionary Biography*. San Francisco: Harper Collins, 1994.

DAVIS. STEVAN L. *The Gospel of Thomas and Christian Wisdom*. New York: Seabury, 1983.

HACKEL, S. *The Orthodox Church*. London: Ward Lock Educational, 1971.

HORSLEY, RICHARD A. *Bandits, Messiahs, and Prophets*. San Francisco: Harper Collins, 1985.

HUGHES, P. *A Short History of the Catholic Church*. London: Burns and Oates, 1978.

JACOBSON, ARLAND. *The First Gospel: An Introduction to Q*. Sonoma: Polebridge, 1992.

LATOURETTE, KENNETH S. *A History of Christianity*. 2 vols., rev. ed. San Francisco: Harper Collins, 1975.

PELIKAN, JAROSLAV. *The Christian Tradition*, 4 vols. (1971–1983).

RAHNER, K. *Foundations of Christian Faith*. New York: Seabury Press, 1978.

ROBINSON, JAMES M., ed. *The Nag Hammadi Library*. San Francisco: Harper Collins, 1990.

SCHWEITZER, ALBERT. *The Quest of the Historical Jesus*. New York: MacMillan, 1961.

WARD, KEITH. *Christianity: A Short Introduction*. Oxford: Oneworld, 2000.

Islam

INTRODUCTION

Islam's basic tenets are expressed in its most holy creed: "There is no God but Allah, and Muhammad is his messenger." *Islam* means surrender, and adherents to the religion are called *Muslims,* meaning those who surrender. Staunchly monotheistic, Islam sees Allah as the omnipotent creator God who, through a series of prophets, has called people to obedience. At the end of time, Allah will resurrect the dead, condemn the wicked to hell, and entrust believers to eternal peace in his garden. Following prophets such as Moses and Jesus, Muhammad is the final and greatest prophet, who delivered the definitive expression of Allah's voice in the Qur'an, Islam's most holy book. Drawing on Jewish narratives, Muslims trace their religious heritage from Adam, to Noah, to Abraham, and finally, to Ishmael, Abraham's first son. Muslim faith is embodied not only in religious practice but in a social order governed by Islamic law.

Time of Ingratitude

The cradle of Islam was the Arabian Peninsula, during a period which Muslims contemptuously refer to as the *time of ingratitude (al-jahiliyyah),* that is, ingratitude toward God. Economically, desert conditions of the peninsula did not allow for widespread agriculture, so inhabitants depended on trade with the surrounding empires. When the Arabs later lost their spice monopoly, trading cities such as Petra died. As a convenient stopping place on well-traveled trade routes, though, Mecca survived as the prosperous center of trading in the Arab world. Politically, Mecca was plagued by warring factions involving its two main tribes, the Quraysh and the Khuza'a, each with divisive clans.

Religiously, inhabitants believed in a range of spiritual forces and deities. Belief in polydemonism prevailed, involving supernatural *jinn,* sprites, and demons, some good and others evil, which inhabited special objects or locations. Tapping into their ancient Semitic heritage, they set up shrines to various nature gods and goddesses. Hubal, god of the moon, was the principal deity of the Meccans, and before his idol people would cast lots and divining arrows. Three chief goddesses of Mecca, Al-Lat, Al-Manat, and Al-Uzza, were worshipped. There was widespread belief in a creator deity, named Allah, who was high god of the regional pantheon. Sacred shrines with carved and uncarved stones were thought to be the dwelling places of these spirits and deities, and they became the focus of offerings and prayers. There was also a significant Jewish and Christian monotheistic presence. Large numbers of Diaspora Jews, fleeing enemies for over a thousand years, settled in Arabia's desert. The Jews interacted well with their new neighbors, and many Arabs converted to Judaism. Hermit Christian monks settled in the desert regions, along with heretical Christian sects escaping the authority of the Roman church. Muslim tradition also notes the presence of pre-Islamic monotheists, known as *Hanif,* who carried the torch of Abraham's religion through the time of ingratitude.

Festivals and pilgrimages dominated the religious activities of the Meccans. Annual festivals lasting weeks drew inhabitants from throughout the peninsula to the two cities of Mina and Ukaz. With its 365 shrines, one for each day of the year, Mecca was a constant attraction to pilgrims. Meccan religious activity centered on the Ka'bah, an austere cubical structure housing idols, murals of the gods, and the Black Stone. The stone, believed to have fallen from heaven, was the object of a special ritual in which naked pilgrims would circle it seven times and then kiss it. Muslim tradition maintains that the Ka'bah was originally built by Abraham.

Early Years of Muhammad

Even a brief survey of world religions indicates that the lives of the religious founders are shrouded in legend, often to the point that their historical lives can no longer be recovered. Although many accounts of Muhammad are also legendary, Islam has the advantage of early written sources, not just by early Muslims, but by Muhammad himself.

Born about 570 C.E., Muhammad was from the Hashimite family clan of Mecca, part of the Quraysh tribe. The clan's founder, from whom Muhammad descended, traced his lineage back to Ishmael, Abraham's first son according to Jewish legend. Muhammad's birth name is unknown, although his honorific title, *Muhammad,* means "highly praised." Tragedy marked his infant and childhood years. His father died before he was born, and as a minor under pre-Islamic law he was unable to acquire inheritance. He was entrusted to his grandfather who, according to one tradition, had him raised by a Bedouin foster mother. His natural mother died when he was six, and his grandfather two years later. Under the care of his uncle, he became involved with caravans. A story relates that the 12-year-old Muhammad accompanied his uncle to Syria on a caravan, where he met a Christian monk who recognized him as the future great prophet. Because of his reputation for honesty, Muhammad was soon entrusted with the leadership of caravans. A pivotal moment in his life arrived when, at 25, he led a caravan for a wealthy widow named Khadija. Although she was 15 years his senior, the two married, and for years she became an important source of encouragement for Muhammad. She bore him four daughters and three sons who died in infancy. Fatima, the most well-known daughter, later married his cousin Ali.

According to his tribal custom, during one month of every year Muhammad retreated for religious reflection. He reflected on the good fortune given him by Allah, in view of his family and successful caravan career. He also thought about Jews and Christians who had a *book,* the Bible, by virtue of which they were prospering more than his own people. This moved him toward monotheism. Islam was born on the *Night of Power* (Laylat al-Qadr) when, on retreat in a cave outside of Mecca, the 40-year-old Muhammad had a life-changing vision. In a voice like reverberating bells, the angel Gabriel approached him, commanding him to recite a phrase: "And the Lord is most Generous, who by the pen has taught mankind things they knew not." He went through a period of doubt for a few months, even contemplating suicide, fearing he was an ecstatic visionary, an occupation not held in high esteem in his society. He also considered that he might be mad, or that he had heard the voice of a *jinn.* Eventually his doubts dispersed and his wife became his first convert, believing that he was a prophet.

Visions and revelations of this kind continued throughout his life. They were recorded or memorized by others as they occurred, and then compiled into the text of the Qur'an. The moments of revelation began with Muhammad becoming entranced while shaking and sweating. Then, in rhymed prose, rhapsodies in Arabic flowed from his mouth. During his early prophetic career, the main points of his message were that Allah is the only God, that the dead will resurrect, and that Allah will judge all. After his wife, his next converts included his cousin Ali and a merchant named Abu Bakr, both of whom assumed leadership positions after Muhammad's death. As his following grew, the first Muslims experienced verbal attacks, threats, and later physical violence. The opposition was in part economically motivated by those whose livelihoods depended on religious pilgrimages to the Ka'bah; Muhammad's message of a single God, they assumed, threatened this. Many Meccan merchants assumed that a single god would draw fewer pilgrims than the many idols housed in their city.

For protection, Muhammad first sent a band of his followers to Ethiopia, where they were warmly received by local Christians. He and about 50 followers were then placed under siege in their Meccan neighborhood in an attempt to starve them into submission. Under pressure, Muhammad strangely reported a new revelation: Along with Allah, the three key Meccan goddesses were acknowledged. The siege was then lifted, and the exiles returned from Ethiopia. Later Muhammad announced that the new revelation was inspired by the devil, and the relevant passages were removed from his record of revelations. Hostility increased when his wife and uncle died. He tried to establish himself in an oasis town named Taif, about 60 miles southeast of Mecca, but failed.

Later Years of Muhammad

The turning point in Muhammad's mission occurred during a pilgrimage festival. He met residents of the northern city Yathrib who suggested that their people would be more receptive to him, in part because the city had many

Jews who were awaiting the arrival of a prophet. The city was in political turmoil, and the residents believed that they could benefit from Muhammad's
administrative skills. A period of negotiations followed. It was agreed that
Muhammad would be the final arbiter of all disputes and that the various religious groups, including the Jews and Muslims, would be autonomous. The
migration to Yathrib, called the *hijrah* (flight) began with around 100 of his followers' families. In 622 C.E., at age 52, Muhammad joined them, fleeing
Meccan authorities as he made the journey. This migration is so momentous
for Islam that it marks the starting point of the Muslim calendar.

Muhammad quickly became a successful administrator and statesman, an
accomplishment with which even his enemies agreed. He renamed the city
Medina, city of the prophet. Living unpretentiously in a clay house and milking
goats, he was ever available for consultation. He punished the guilty, but was
merciful toward his personal enemies. Of his several diplomatic marriages, his
primary wife, A'isha, daughter of Abu Bakr, had particular influence over him,
and is the source of many of the traditions later ascribed to him.

Although he was successful in Medina, hostilities with Mecca continued.
Believing that he had a responsibility to provide for the Meccan emigrant followers living in Medina, Muhammad intercepted a caravan to Mecca for its
booty. Attempting this a second time, his band of 300 encountered an army of
1,000 Meccans at a site called Badr. The ensuing battle was a victory for
Muhammad. Not dissuaded, a few years later the Meccans launched a military
offensive against Muhammad's army. Known as the Battle of Uhud, the
Muslims were badly outnumbered and forced to retreat, and Muhammad
himself was slightly wounded. Even so, the battle was a moral victory since the
Meccans failed to eradicate Muhammad. Two years later the Meccans attacked
Medina directly with a confederate army of surrounding cities and nomads. By
recommendation of a Persian soldier in his camp, Muhammad ordered a
trench dug around the entire city, a strategy that resulted in victory.

With each military victory (and moral victories like Uhud), his converts increased, and his control over Medina became more firm. The Jewish population,
which had attracted him to the city, ironically failed to accept him as God's
prophet. Some even aided the Meccans in their attack. Now with increased authority, Muhammad drove them out. His disappointment with the Jews had theological consequences as well. The Jewish and Christian elements of his religion
were suppressed, and the traditional Arab elements were emphasized. No longer
would Muslims pray facing Jerusalem; they would face toward Mecca. Qur'anic
passages of this period enjoined Muslims to make pilgrimages to Mecca, which
included circumambulation of the Ka'bah and kissing its Black Stone. Friday became the official day of rest, not Saturday or Sunday. During his rule in Medina,
other central Muslim doctrines were established, such as fasting, almsgiving, and
ritual prayer. Social laws involving marriage, divorce, inheritance, and treatment
of slaves and prisoners were also formalized.

In the fifth year of the migration, Muhammad and his followers approached
Mecca with the intention of making a pilgrimage, but were met with resistance
from the city leaders. The two sides reached a face-saving compromise, in

which Muhammad and his followers withdrew, with the understanding that the next year they would return and the city would be open to them for a pilgrimage. However, in the intervening year a Meccan broke the truce, and Muhammad responded by marching on the city. Realizing that they were unable to resist his force, the leaders of the city surrendered and bloodshed was avoided. Riding into the Ka'bah on his camel, with his own hands he smashed its 360 idols, declaring, "Truth has come and falsehood has vanished." Thus, he reclaimed the shrine for God. All of Mecca converted, giving no resistance. The territory around the Ka'bah was declared sacred (*haram*), and non-Muslims were prohibited from entering the area. Muhammad then returned to Medina.

In the tenth year after his migration, he made a final announcement at the Ka'bah: "Today I have completed my religion for you and I have fulfilled the extent of my favor towards you. It is my will that Islam be your religion. I have completed my mission. I have left you the Book of Allah and clear commandments. If you keep them you will never go wrong." Shortly thereafter, reporting severe headaches, he died while in A'isha's house and was buried on that spot.

The Caliphate

Muhammad founded both a new religion and a new social order. Although he believed that his mission as a religious prophet was complete at the time of his death, plans for a larger Muslim social community (*umma*) were not as yet realized. He had planned to conquer Syria and Iraq, but died too soon. Upon his death, key political decisions were made by Muhammad's early companions (*Sahaba*), many of whom were his first converts. Their first task was to appoint a successor, or Caliph, who would fill Muhammad's political leadership role, but not his prophetic role. From the start, however, there was political dissent. To the consternation of Ali, Muhammad's cousin who expected to step into the leadership role, the early companions selected Abu Bakr as the first Caliph. For the sake of unity, Ali deferred to his rival. Plans were drawn for military expansion, but the aged Caliph died only two years into his rule.

For the next ten years, the newly appointed Caliph Umar expanded Muslim territory far into the Persian and Byzantine empires. Non-Arab converts were denied equal political rights, and it would be almost a hundred years until a unified Muslim political order would emerge. Umar was stabbed to death by a Persian slave, and Uthman became the third Caliph. According to legend, trouble started for Uthman when he lost Muhammad's seal ring in a well. He prompted further negative reaction by favoring his family clan, the Umayyads, which originally opposed Muhammad in Mecca. A small rebellion erupted in Medina, in which a disaffected faction (which later became the Kharajites) laid siege to his house. Civil war later erupted and, 12 years into his rule, Uthman was assassinated by rebel Muslim troops from Egypt. The early companions finally elected Ali as the fourth Caliph, but he was immediately opposed by Syrian governor Mu'awiyah, who sought to avenge the death of Uthman, his cousin. War broke out between Ali and Mu'awiyah and, on the eve of the decisive battle, Ali was killed by a soldier from a rebel group that had split with him as a result of disagreement with his policies. The Caliphate fell to Ali's son, Husan, but he quickly ceded it to Mu'awiyah.

Under the first wave of Muslim expansion by the first four Caliphs, all of Arabia, Persia, and North Africa were conquered. For the next 90 years the Caliphate was held by the secular Umayyad Dynasty (661–750), established by Mu'awiyah. After Mu'awiyah's death, the Caliphate was passed to his unpopular son Yazid. In 680 an insurrection against Yazid was launched by Ali's son, Husayn. Husayn and his followers were massacred in what is now the Iraqi city of Kerbala (a tragedy which became the rallying cry of the Shi'i Muslims). Centered in Damascus, the Umayyads continued to push Muslim boundaries. Moving across North Africa and into Spain, expansion into Europe halted at the French borders in the Battle of Tours in 732. The Caliphate was next held by the Abbasid Dynasty (750–1285), centered in Baghdad, and then by the Ottoman Empire (1300–1922), centered in Istanbul. In 1924 the Caliphate was abolished by the Turkish National Assembly, inheritors of the Ottoman Empire. To justify this controversial decision the Assembly maintained that "The idea of a single caliph, exercising supreme religious authority over all the peoples of Islam, is an idea taken from fiction, not from reality."

Sunni and Shi'a

Just as political factions divided early Islam, so did theological differences, the key issue being whether Ali and his successors had a special spiritual status. Islam today is divided into two main groups over this issue. The Sunni, or Sunnite, attribute no special function to Ali, whereas the Shi'a, or Shi'ite, do. Sunnis make up approximately 90 percent of Muslims worldwide. Their full name is *Ahl al-Sunnah wa 'l-Hadith,* that is, followers of the path laid out by the prophet in his sayings. In addition to rejecting the special spiritual status of Ali, Sunnis recognize the first four Caliphs as political successors to Muhammad and acknowledge the political authority of the Caliphate in general. Sunnis must also follow one of the four schools of Islamic law (*madhahib*), developed in the eighth and ninth centuries.

Prior to the emergence of the four Sunni schools of law, Muslims used several guides to determine proper conduct. After the Qur'an was consulted for guidance, appeals were made to practices of Muhammad (*sunna*) as compiled by scholars into texts called *Hadith*. When these avenues failed, decisions were made in one of three ways: analogical deductions from existing laws (*qiyas*), consensus of the Muslim community or its leading scholars (*ijma*), and independent decisions of a single jurist (*ijtihad*).

The four schools of Islamic law not only systematized the above appeal routes, but developed their own codes of behavior from these. The methodological differences between the four schools are subtle, although their geographical domains are more distinct. The *Hanafite* school, which provides the greatest scope of reasoning, predominates in former Turkish empire areas (Turkey, Palestine, Egypt) and India. The *Malikite* school, which focuses more on the traditions of Muhammad's companions rather than Muhammad, is dominant in west Africa. The *Shafi'ite* school, which developed the standard hierarchy of appeals, is most prominent in Indonesia. Finally, the *Hanbalite* school, the most literalist in adhering to the letter of the Qur'an, is found in Saudi Arabia and Qatar.

Shi'a Muslims, consisting of 10 percent of the Muslim population, are located primarily in Iran. Shi'a origins are difficult to trace because of negative Sunni chronologies and biased reports by later Shi'as. However, with the assassination of Ali and the creation of the Umayyad Caliphate in 661, a faction loyal to the memory of Ali emerged. Devotion to Ali and his selected descendants became the test for true faith. Early Shi'as were in continual opposition to the ruling Caliph, some groups advocating armed resistance.

About 40 factions of Shi'as have emerged over the years. The most numerous are the Twelvers (*Ithna 'Asha-Riyyah*), who comprise about 80 percent of their number. The central Twelver doctrine is that of the Imam, or leader. Twelvers believe that Muhammad's spiritual abilities (*wilaya*) were passed on to a series of Imams, beginning with Ali. Twelver theology holds that human beings require inspired leadership in order to adhere faithfully to the dictates of Islam and that successive Imams are clearly designated by predecessors (*nass*). Imams are also thought to be guided by Allah and to be infallible (*isma*). Eleven Imams have appeared so far, and they await the appearance of the twelfth and final, named Mahdi, who is alive but hidden from view. More precisely, the Mahdi is in a state called *occultation,* in which he can see others, but others cannot see him; at age four, Allah placed him in that state for protection after the death of his father, the eleventh Imam, 873 C.E. It is believed that the Mahdi made four representations (*wakils*) between 873 and 940, a period called the *lesser occultation.* He will return at the end of time, take vengeance on unbelievers, and initiate an era of peace. Until then, leaders called the *Mujtahid* make decisions of canon law on behalf of the hidden Imam. In recent times, the Ayatollahs have this function.

Two other Shi'a factions deserve mentioning. The Fivers (*Zaydis*) split from Twelver tradition by recognizing Zaydis as the fifth Imam (as opposed to Muhammad al-Baqir). Concentrated in Yemen, they do not assert the necessity of Imams and accept some of the early Caliphs. The Seveners (*Isma'ili*) split from Twelver tradition by recognizing Isma'il as the seventh Imam (rather than Musa-l-Kazim). They see Isma'il as the final Imam, Mahdi, who will return for the day of judgment.

The Qur'an

Islam's most holy scripture, The Qur'an is the collected revelations of Muhammad, written during the last 23 years of his life. It is the primary sacred text for all sects of Islam. The work is divided into 114 sections called *surahs,* in lengths varying from three verses to almost 300 verses. The term "Qur'an" means "to recite," in the sense that Muhammad is verbally delivering Allah's message to the people. The traditional arrangement of the *surahs* is neither chronological nor topical, but according to length, beginning with the longest and ending with the shortest. *Surah* titles are derived from a prominent or recurring word, such as Cow, Abraham, Mary, Angels, Muhammad, Divorce, Infidels. Every *surah* (save one) begins with the phrase, "In the name of God, the Merciful, the Compassionate," which was probably the original indicator of the *surah* divisions.

The exact chronology of the *surahs* was forgotten even during Muhammad's life, and many short revelations from different periods were joined together to form longer *surahs*. Modern scholars have offered several chronological schemes for organizing the *surahs*, although traditional Muslims believe that such attempts compromise the inherent beauty of the nonhistorical arrangement. Nevertheless, each *surah* is associated with either the Meccan or the Medinan period of Muhammad's life. The Meccan *surahs* are the earliest and reflect Muhammad's struggle to persuade his skeptical Meccan listeners to abandon polytheism and idolatry. They are shorter and more poetic than the Medinan sections, and they are characterized by vivid imagery. Meccan *surahs* describe the world's cataclysmic end and emphasize Allah's omnipotence and active role in history.

Within the Meccan period itself the style and content of the *surahs* developed. The earliest use short sentences and particularly powerful imagery, and are the most lyrical. The later ones, by contrast, are longer, more direct and sermonizing, and less heated. Stories of the early prophets become more developed. When Muhammad and his followers migrated to Medina, political circumstances were considerably more favorable, and the *surahs* reflect the confident voice of a lawgiver concerned with social and political issues. These are the longest *surahs* in the Qur'an, and deal with the giving of the law.

Stylistically, most of the Qur'an is written in first, second, and third person, with Allah addressing believers, unbelievers, or Muhammad. The first person is used when God describes his divine attributes, and the second when describing actions in which humans participate. Passages not in the voice of Allah are prefaced by the word "say," indicating that they are to be recited by believers. Most of the Qur'an is written in rhymed prose, as opposed to poetry with meter. The latter approach was typical of poets who were thought to be guided by *jinn*, an association which Muhammad strongly resisted. Phrases are repetitive and well-suited for reciting; indeed, several traditional Qur'anic division schemes break the text into sections for daily reading. Muslims believe that the literary quality of the Qur'an itself validates Muhammad's claims of prophethood. For, although illiterate, he produced a literary work of great merit.

The initial compilation of the Qur'an is a remarkable story. After each of Muhammad's revelations, efforts were made to record their content, through either writing or memorization by specially assigned reciters. Although Muhammad may have done some editing of the earlier *surahs* when in Medina, no definitive "book" existed at the time of his death. A year after Muhammad's death, many of the original reciters were killed in battle. Fearing that the Qur'an's contents would be lost through time, the first Caliph, Abu Bakr, ordered the compilation of the first complete text of the Qur'an. The task was assigned to Zayd ibn Thabit, an aide of Muhammad, who pieced the text together from oral and written sources in Medina. Variant Qur'an fragments continued to circulate for 24 more years, until the third Caliph, Uthman, ordered the creation of a definitive text. Again Zayd supervised the compilation. He gathered all existing manuscript fragments and met with the original reciters accompanying Muhammad who had the complete contents memorized. When the compilation was finished, all previous written versions were destroyed, assuring that only one version of the Qur'an would remain. Although variant editions appeared later, the definitive text of the Qur'an we have today is the work of Zayd. Diacritical marks were later introduced to fix proper vocalization for recitation.

The content of the Qur'an covers a variety of subjects. Many stories parallel accounts in the Old Testament, and some in the New Testament, especially those of Adam, Noah, Abraham, Joseph, and Jesus. It is unlikely that Muhammad had access to Arabic translations of Jewish or Christian texts; instead, he probably relied on oral traditions of the local Jewish and Christian populace. Other narratives are of Arabian origin. Large sections of the Qur'an provide legislation for the newly formed Muslim community in Medina.

For Muslims, the Qur'an records more they believe, than the words of Muhammad; it is Allah's eternal speech. The Torah and Bible they believe, are earlier and incomplete revelations of Allah. Most Muslims believe that the Qur'an is uncreated, existing from eternity, with an original engraved tablet of the Qur'an in heaven. This eternal Qur'an is written in the Arabic language, and so authentic copies of the Qur'an will also be only in Arabic. The first unofficial translation appeared in 1141 in Latin, which was loathed by Muslims for its disparaging renderings. The physical book itself is sacred, and copies of the Qur'an are touched only after ceremonial cleansing of the handler.

The Hadith

After the Qur'an, the second most authoritative group of texts in Islam are the *Hadith* canons. The term *Hadith* means talk or speech, and it refers to collected narratives reporting actions and sayings of Muhammad recounted by his companions. These monumental collections are the principal basis for interpreting the Qur'an and were used to develop early Islamic legal systems.

While Muhammad was alive, his companions took note of his life events and his sayings. Within the first hundred years after Muhammad's death, individual sayings were transmitted both orally and in written form from teachers of *Hadith* to their students. Within the second hundred years, booklets of *Hadith* appeared on single topics, and later on several topics. The number of *Hadith* grew to about three quarters of a million, most being duplicates with only slight variations as generated by the continually growing number of teachers and students of *Hadith*. Finally, they were systematically compiled in the ninth and tenth centuries into no less than 12 multivolume collections.

The Sunnis have nine collections, six of which are particularly revered. The most widely accepted of these are referred to as the *Two Sahih* (authentic):

Sahih al-Bukhari and *Sahih Muslim*. The first of these, compiled by al-Bukhari (d. 875), is the most important. A prominent teacher of *Hadith,* al-Bukhari examined 600,000 sayings, the majority being duplicate versions, and sifted them down to 7,275 authentic ones. Of these, about 2,700 are nonrepetitious. Limited by space constraints, he remarks that he left out other sayings that he believed were authentic. The sayings are topically categorized in 97 books, with some longer sayings split and categorized into two distinct topical divisions. The second most revered collection is that by Muslim ibn al-Hajjaj (d. 875), who examined 300,000 traditions and reduced them to 4,000. A student of al-Bukhari, al-Hajjaj is thought to have been more critical in deeming a saying "authentic" and, unlike his teacher, presents the longer sayings in their integrated form. The remaining four collections (or *Sunan*) were compiled by Abu Dawud (d. 886), at-Tirmidhi (d. 892), an-Nasa'i (d. 915), and Ibn Majah (d. 886). Of the six *Hadith* collections, those by al-Bukhari, Muslim al-Hajjaj, and Dawud have been made available in English translation. Three Shi'a collections, called *akhbar* (as opposed to *Hadith*), are traditionally thought to originate with Ali and the Imams (Ja'far al-Sadiq in particular). Larger than the Sunni collections, they were compiled by al-Kafi of al-Kulini (d. 939) (whose collection is the most widely respected), al-Qummi (d. 991), and al-Tusi (d. 1067).

Hadith sayings are in two parts. First is the story itself (*matn*), and second is a list of names constituting the chain of sources which establish the story's authenticity (*isnad*). The stories themselves are of two types. The first, called sacred *Hadith* (*Hadith qudsi*), contain divine revelations similar to those in the Qur'an. The second, called noble *Hadith* (*Hadith sharif*), relate to Muhammad's personal life and nonprophetic utterances. For *Hadith* compilers, a story's authenticity rested on the integrity of each person mentioned in the chain of sources. A discipline emerged that critically scrutinized the lives of the transmitters. According to the norms of this field of study, even an otherwise authentic statement that bears a faulty chain of transmitters should be regarded as inauthentic. Muslims agree that many of the *Hadith* were invented in the early days of Islam to answer questions of law, support religious factions, or serve political needs in struggles for power. Thousands were rejected early on for this very reason. An early *Hadith* scholar was even executed for confessing he fabricated 4,000 sayings for financial gain. Critical *Hadith* scholarship is still in its infancy, however, and judgment regarding the extent of their authenticity must be postponed.

Sectarian Writings

Muslim sectarian writings are voluminous, and the lines distinguishing sacred texts from works of mere theology are often blurry. Writings from the various schools of Islamic law are particularly respected. Foundational works in the *Hanafite* school are *The Book of Roots* by Muhammad ibn al-Hasan al-Shaybani (d. 805) and the *Hidaya* by Burhan al-Din al-Marghinani (d. 1197). From the Malikite school there is the *Muwatta* by Malik ibn Anas (712–795), the school's founder. From the Shafi'ite tradition there is the *Rasala* by al-Shafi'i (767–820), founder of the school. Finally, from the Hanbalite school there is the *Musnad* by founder ibn Hanbal (780–855), and the *Kitab-al-'Umada* by Ibn Qudama (1146–1223).

There are also a number of important writings by Sufis, that is, Islamic mystics whose writings emphasize mystical union with Allah. Key writers among the Sufis include Rabi'a al-'Adawiya (717–801), a freed slave girl whose writings stress the intense love of Allah; al-Ghazali (1058–1111), a scholar of Islamic Law; and ibn-al-Arabi (1165–1240), a Spanish-born metaphysician. The most widely influential Sufi writer is Jalal ad-Din ar-Rumi (1207–1273). Rumi's six-book *Masnawi*, sometimes referred to as the "Qur'an in Persian," is a compendium of lyric poetry and stories allegorizing Sufi doctrine.

QUR'AN: MUHAMMAD IN MECCA

NIGHT OF POWER

Muhammad's first revelation occurred on the Night of Power *when on retreat in a cave near Mecca. It is recorded in the Clot (surah 96). An early sequel to this surah, called the Power (surah 97), celebrates Muhammad's call to prophethood on the Night of Power. Both appear below.*

96: Clots of Blood

Recite in the name of your Lord who created—created man from clots of blood
Recite! Your Lord is the Most Bountiful One, who by the pen taught man what he did not know.
Indeed, man transgresses in thinking himself his own master: for to your Lord all things return.
Observe the man who rebukes Our servant when he prays.
Think: does he follow the right guidance or enjoin true piety?
Think: if he denies the Truth and gives no heed, does he not know that God observes all things?
No. Let him desist, or We will drag him by the forelock, his lying, sinful forelock.
Then let him call his helpmates. We, in Our turn, will call the guards of Hell.
No, never obey him! Prostrate yourself and come nearer.

97: Qadr (Glory)

We revealed this on the Night of Qadr. Would that you knew what the Night of Qadr is like!
Better is the Night of Qadr than a thousand months.
On that night the angels and the Spirit by their Lord's leave come down with each decree.
That night is peace, till break of dawn.

Source: Surah 96, 97, from *The Koran,* tr. N. J. Dawood (London: Penguin Books, 1990).

DIVINE JUDGMENT

After his call to prophethood, Muhammad lived in Mecca for about 12 years, trying to convince his fellow citizens to worship only Allah. As illustrated in the following four early Meccan surahs, Muhammad's earliest revelations were short, poetic declamations about punishment in hell for unbelievers. Since the context of most of the Meccan revelations was quickly lost, it is not known who the specific offenders were who incited these harsh condemnations.

101: The Disaster

The disaster! What is the Disaster?

Would that you knew what the Disaster is!

On that day men shall become like scattered moths and the mountains like tufts of carded wool.

Then he whose scales are heavy shall dwell in bliss; but he whose scales are light, the Abyss shall be his home.

Would that you knew what this is like!

It is a scorching fire.

102: Worldly Gain

Your hearts are taken up with worldly gain from the cradle to the grave.

But you shall know. You shall before long come to know.

Indeed, if you knew the truth with certainty, you would see the fire of Hell: you would see it with your very eyes.

Then, on that day, you shall be questioned about your joys.

103: The Declining Day

I swear by the declining day that perdition shall be the lot of man, except for those who have faith and do good works; who exhort each other to justice and to fortitude.

104: The Slanderer

Woe to every back-biting slanderer who amasses riches and sedulously hoards them, thinking his wealth will render him immortal!

By no means! He shall be flung to the Destroying Flame.

Would that you knew what the Destroying Flame is like!

It is God's own kindled fire, which will rise up to the hearts of men. It will close upon them from every side, in towering columns.

Source: Surahs 101–104, from *The Koran*.

OPENING

The opening surah of the Qur'an is the most commonly repeated prayer in Islam and an integral part of worship. Scholars give it an early date, from about the fourth year of Muhammad's Meccan mission.

> Praise be to God, Lord of the Universe,
> The compassionate, the Merciful,
> Sovereign of the Day of Judgment!
> You alone we worship, and to You alone we turn for help.
> Guide us to the straight path,
> The path of those whom You have favoured,
> Not of those who have incurred Your wrath,
> Nor of those who have gone astray.

Source: Surah 1, from *The Koran*.

EVILS OF IDOLATRY

The overriding theme of Muhammad's message while in Mecca was commitment to Allah and the rejection of idolatry. The following selection from Jonah (surah 10), a late Meccan surah, describes how idolaters forfeit paradise and are blind to the powers of the creator.

God invites you to the Home of Peace. He guides whom He will to a straight path. Those that do good works shall have a good reward, and more besides. Neither blackness nor misery shall overcast their faces. They are the heirs of Paradise: in it they shall abide for ever.

As for those that have done evil, evil shall be rewarded with like evil. Misery will oppress them (they shall have none to protect them from God), as though patches of the night's own darkness veiled their faces. They are the heirs of Hell: in it they shall abide for ever.

On the day We assemble them all together, We shall say to the idolaters: 'Keep to your places, you had your idols!' We will separate them one from another, and then their idols will say to them: 'It was not us that you worshipped. God is our all-sufficient witness. Nor were we aware of your worship.'

Thereupon each soul will know what it has done. They shall be sent back to God, their true Lord, and the idols they invented will forsake them.

Say: 'Who provides for you from heaven and earth? Who has endowed you with sight and hearing? Who brings forth the living from the dead, and the dead from the living? Who ordains all things?'

They will reply: 'God.'

Say: 'Will you not take heed, then? Such is God, your true Lord. That which is not true must needs be false. How then can you turn away from Him?'

Thus is the Word of your Lord made good. The evil-doers have no faith.

Say: 'Can any of your idols conceive Creation, then renew it?' Say: 'God conceives Creation, then renews it. How is it that you are so misled?'

Say: 'Can any of your idols guide you to the truth?' Say: 'God can guide you to the truth. Who is more worthy to be followed: He that can guide to the truth, or he that cannot and is himself in need of guidance? What has come over you that you so judge?'

Most of them follow nothing but mere conjecture. But conjecture is in no way a substitute for truth. God is cognizant of all their actions.

Source: Surah 10:26–37, from *The Koran.*

EARLY PROPHETS

The Qur'an states that every nation has its prophet (surah 13:7). About 30 prophets who preceded Muhammad are mentioned. Most of these are also mentioned in the Bible. The prophets typically spoke to unreceptive idolatrous people, and Allah subsequently destroyed the idolaters for their continued disbelief. The hillsides are scattered with the ruins of the idolaters' cities as monuments to their recalcitrance. As Muhammad's own prophetic message was met with disbelief and hostility, he warned the Meccans of the consequences. During Muhammad's late Meccan period of revelation, detailed accounts of early prophets are prominent. Surah 11, titled Hud, recounts the stories of Noah, Hud, Salih, Abraham, Lot, Shu'aib, and Moses. Noah, Abraham, Lot, and Moses are from Jewish tradition. The Qur'an's account of these prophets differs from biblical accounts, explaining in surah 6:91 that the Jews suppressed much of Moses' revelation and that Muhammad is revealing new information. Unique to Qur'anic tradition, Hud, Salih, and Shu'aib are prophets sent by Allah to the Arabs.

[**Hud.**] To Ad We sent their compatriot Hud. He said: 'Serve God, my people; you have no god but Him. False are your inventions. I demand of you no recompense, my people, for none can reward me except my Creator. Will you not understand?'

'My people, seek forgiveness of your Lord and turn to Him in repentance. He will send from the sky abundant rain upon you; He will add strength to your strength. Do not turn away from Him with wrongdoing.'

They replied: 'Hud, you have given us no clear proof. We will not forsake our gods at your behest, nor will we believe in you. We can only suppose that our gods have afflicted you with evil.'

He said: 'God is my witness, and you are my witnesses too: I am done with your idols. Scheme against me if you will, and give me no respite. I have put my trust in God, my Lord and your Lord. There is not a living creature on the earth whose destiny He does not control. Straight is the path of my Lord.'

'If you give no heed, I have made known to you my message, and my Lord will replace you by other men. You will in no way harm Him. My Lord is watching over all things.'

And when our judgment came to pass, We delivered Hud through Our mercy, together with those who shared his faith. We delivered them from a horrifying scourge.

Such were Ad. They denied the revelations of their Lord, disobeyed His apostles, and did the bidding of every headstrong reprobate. Cursed were they in this world, and cursed they shall be on the Day of Resurrection.

Ad denied their Lord. Gone are Ad, the people of Hud.

[*Salih.*] And to Thamud We sent compatriot Salih. He said: 'Serve God, my people; you have no god but Him. It was He who brought you into being from the earth and gave you means to dwell upon it. Seek forgiveness of him, and turn to Him in repentance. My Lord is near at hand and answers all.'

'Salih,' they replied, 'great were the hopes we placed in you. Would you now forbid us to serve the gods our fathers worshipped? Truly, we strongly doubt the faith to which you call us.'

He said: 'Do but consider, my people! If my Lord has revealed to me His will and bestowed on me His grace, who would protect me from God if I rebelled against Him? You would surely aggravate my ruin.'

'My people, here is God's she-camel, a sign for you. Leave her to graze at will in God's own land, and do not molest her lest an instant scourge should fall upon you.'

Yet they slew her. He said: 'You have but three days to live in your dwellings. This prophecy shall not prove false.'

And when Our judgment came to pass, We delivered Salih through Our mercy from the ignominy of that day, together with those who shared his faith. Mighty is your Lord and all-powerful. A dreadful cry rang above the evil-doers, and when morning came they were prostrate in their dwellings, as though they had never prospered there.

[*Abraham and Lot.*] Our messengers came to Abraham with good news. They said 'Peace!' 'Peace!' he answered, and hastened to bring them a roasted calf. But when he saw their hands being withheld from it, he mistrusted them and was afraid of them. They said: 'Have no fear. We are sent forth to the people of Lot.'

His wife, who was standing by, laughed. We bade her rejoice in Isaac, and in Jacob after him.

'Alas!' she replied. 'How shall I bear a child when I am old and my husband is well-advanced in years? This is indeed a strange thing.'

They replied: 'Do you marvel at the ways of God? May God's mercy and blessings be upon you, dear hosts! Worthy of praise is He and glorious.'

And when fear left him as he pondered the good news, Abraham pleaded with Us for the people of Lot. Abraham was gracious, tender-hearted, and devout.

We said; 'Abraham, plead no more. Your Lord's will must needs be done. Irrevocable is the scourge which shall smite them.'

And when Our messengers came to Lot, he grew anxious about them, for he was powerless to offer them protection. 'This is indeed a day of woe,' he said.

His people, long addicted to evil practices, came running towards him. 'My people,' he said, 'here are my daughters: surely they are more wholesome to you. Fear God, and do not humiliate me by insulting my guests. Is there not one good man among you?'

They replied: 'You know we have no need of your daughters. You know full well what we are seeking.'

He cried: 'Would that I had strength enough to overcome you, or could find refuge in some mighty man!'

They said: 'Lot, we are the messengers of your Lord: They shall not touch you. Depart with your kinsfolk in the dead of night and let none of you turn back, except your wife. She shall suffer the fate of the others. In the morning their hour will come. Is not the morning near?'

And when Our judgment came to pass, We turned their city upside down and let loose upon it a shower of clay-stones bearing the tokens of your Lord. The punishment of the unjust was not far off.

[*Shu'aib.*] And to the people of Midian We sent their compatriot Shu'aib. He said: 'Serve God, my people; you have no god but Him. Do not give short weight or measure. Prosperous though you are, beware the torment of a fateful day!'

'My people, give just weight and measure in all fairness. Do not defraud your fellow men of their possessions, nor shall you corrupt the land with evil. Better for you is God's reward, if you are true believers. I am not your keeper.'

'Shu'aib,' they replied, 'did your prayers teach you that we should renounce the gods of our fathers and not conduct our affairs in the manner we pleased? Truly, you are a wise and gracious man!'

He said: 'Do but consider, my people! If my Lord has revealed to me His will and bestowed on me a gracious gift, should I not guide you? I do not wish to argue with you, only to practice what I forbid you. I seek only to reform you: as far as I am able. Nor can I succeed without God's help. In Him I have put my trust and to Him I turn in repentance.'

'Let your dispute with me not bring upon you the doom which overtook the peoples of Noah, Hud, and Salih; nor is it long since the tribe of Lot was punished. Seek forgiveness of your lord and turn to Him in repentance. Merciful and loving is my Lord.'

They replied: 'Shu'aib, much of what you say we cannot comprehend. We know how weak you are in our midst. But for our tribe, we should have stoned you. You shall on no account prevail against us.'

He said: 'My people, have you more regard for my tribe than for God? Dare you turn you backs upon Him? My Lord has knowledge of all your actions. Do what you will, my people, and so will I. You shall know who will be punished and held up to shame, and who is lying. Wait if you will; I too am waiting.'

And when our judgment was carried out We delivered Shu'aib through Our mercy, together with those who shared his faith. A dreadful cry overtook the evil-doers, and when morning came they were prostrate in their dwellings, as though they had never prospered there. Like Thamud, gone are the people of Midian.

[*Moses.*] We sent forth Moses with Our signs and with clear authority to Pharaoh and his nobles. But they followed the behests of their master; misguided were Pharaoh's behests. He shall stand at the head of his people on the Day of Resurrection, and shall lead them into the Fire. Dismal is the place they shall be led to.

A curse followed them in this world, and a curse shall follow them on the Day of Resurrection. Evil is the gift they shall receive.

We have recounted to you the annals of these nations: some have survived, while others have ceased to exist. We did not wrong them, but they wronged themselves. The gods they called on besides God availed them nothing: and when your Lord's will was done, they only added to their ruin.

Such was the scourge your Lord visited upon the nations while they sinned. Harrowing and relentless is His scourge.

Surely in this there is a sign for him that dreads the torment of the hereafter. On that day all men shall be assembled. That shall be a fateful day.

We shall defer it only to its appointed hour. And when that day arrives, no man shall speak but by His leave. Some shall be damned, and others shall be blessed. The damned shall abide as long as the heavens and the earth endure, unless our Lord ordain otherwise: your Lord shall accomplish what he will. As for the blessed, they shall abide in Paradise as long as the heavens and the earth endure, unless your Lord ordain otherwise. Theirs shall be an endless recompense.

Have no doubt as to what they worship. They serve the idols which their fathers served before them. We shall requite them in full measure.

We gave the Book to Moses, but differences arose about it. And but for a Word from your Lord, already decreed, their fate would have been long sealed. Yet they strongly doubt this.

Source: Surah 11:50–110, from *The Koran.*

RESURRECTION OF THE DEAD

Muhammad met with resistance concerning the concept of the bodily resurrection of the dead. In the following, from two late Meccan surahs, he makes this doctrine more palpable by offering analogies to bodily resurrection, and also by illustrating Allah's power, which implies Allah's ability to resurrect even dead bodies.

Men, if you doubt the Resurrection remember that We first created you from dust, then from a living germ, then from a clot of blood, and then from a half-formed lump of flesh, so that We might manifest to you Our power.

We cause to remain in the womb whatever We please for an appointed term, and then We bring you forth as infants, that you may grow up and reach your prime. Some die young, and some live on to abject old age when all that they once know they know no more.

You sometimes see the earth dry and barren: but no sooner do We send down rain upon it than it begins to stir and swell, putting forth every kind of radiant bloom. That is because God is Truth: He resurrects the dead and has power over all things.

The Hour of Doom is sure to come—in this there is no doubt. Those who are in the grave God will raise to life.

Some wrangle about God, though they have neither knowledge nor guidance nor divine revelation. They turn away in scorn and lead others astray from God's path. Such men shall incur disgrace in this life and taste the torment of Hell on the Day of Resurrection. 'This,' We shall say, 'is the reward of your misdeeds. God is not unjust to His servants.' . . .

We first created man from an essence of clay: then placed him, a living germ, in a safe enclosure [i.e., the womb]. The germ We made a clot of blood, and the clot a lump of flesh. This We fashioned into bones, then clothed the bones with flesh, thus bringing forth another creation. Blessed be God the noblest of creators.

You shall surely die hereafter, and be restored to life on the Day of Resurrection. We have created seven heavens above you; of Our creation We are never heedless.

We sent down water from the sky in due measure, and lodged it into the earth. But if We please, We can take it all away.

With it We caused vineyards and palm-groves to spring up, yielding abundant fruit for your sustenance. The tree which on Mount Sinai grows gives oil and a condiment for men.

In the cattle, too, you have an example of Our power. You drink of that which is in their bellies, you eat their flesh, and gain other benefits from them besides. By them, as by the ships that sail the sea, you are carried.

Source: Surahs 22:5–10; 23:12–22, from *The Koran.*

REVEALED QUR'AN

As Muhammad's revelations grew to a sizable collection within a few years, the Qur'an itself frequently became a subject of further revelation. A middle Meccan surah *recounts, "We have divided the Qur'an into sections so that you may recite it to the people with deliberation. We have imparted it by gradual revelation"* (surah *17:106). Another states, "We have revealed the Qur'an in the Arabic tongue that you may understand its meaning. It is a transcript of the eternal book in our keeping, sublime, and full of wisdom"* (surah *43:3–4). In a late Meccan* surah, *Muhammad's illiteracy is offered as proof that the Qur'an was divinely revealed (surah 29:48). The following from Jonah (surah 10), of the late Meccan period, discusses the fate of those who deny the divine authority of the Qur'an.*

. . . These are the verses of the Wise Book: Does it seem strange to mankind that We revealed Our will to a mortal from among themselves, saying: 'Give warning to mankind, and proclaim good tidings to the faithful: their endeavors shall be rewarded by their Lord'?

The unbelievers say: 'This man [i.e., Muhammad] is a skilled enchanter.' Yet your Lord is God, who in six days created the heavens and the earth and then ascended His throne, ordaining all things. None has power to intercede for you, except him who has received His sanctions. Such is God, your Lord: therefore serve Him. Will you not take heed?

To Him you shall all return: God's promise shall be fulfilled. He gives being to all His creatures, and in the end he will bring them back to life, so that he may justly reward those who have believed in Him and done good works. As for the unbelievers, they shall drink scalding water and be sternly punished for their unbelief. . . .

When Our clear revelations are recited to them, those who entertain no hope of meeting Us say to you: 'Give us a different Koran, or make some changes in it.'

Say: 'Had God pleased, I would never have recited it to you, nor would he have made you aware of it. A whole lifetime I dwelt among you before it was revealed. Will you not understand?'

Who is more wicked than the man who invents a falsehood about God or denies His revelations? Truly, the evil-doer shall not triumph. . . .

This Koran could not have been devised by any but God. It confirms what was revealed before it and fully explains the Scriptures. It is beyond doubt from the Lord of the Universe.

If they say: 'He invented it himself,' say: 'Bring me one chapter like it. Call on whom you may besides God to help you, if what you say be true!'

Indeed, they disbelieve what they cannot grasp, for they have not yet seen its prophecy fulfilled. Likewise did those who passed before them disbelieve. But see what was the end of the wrongdoers.

Some believe in it, while others do not. But your Lord best knows the evil-doers.

Source: Surah 10:2–4, 16–18, 38–41, from *The Koran*.

QUR'AN: MUHAMMAD IN MEDINA

LAWS

In 622 Muhammad and his early followers migrated to Medina, where he became the city administrator. The focus of his revelations soon shifted from that of a lone defender of monotheism to that of a lawgiver. The following selections from the Cow (surah 2) present laws concerning drinking, gambling, orphans, divorce, weaning, widows, and dowries.

They ask you about drinking and gambling. Say: 'There is great harm in both, although they have some benefits for men; but their harm is far greater than their benefits.'

They ask you what they should give in alms. Say: 'What you can spare.' Thus God makes plain to you His revelations so that you may reflect upon this world and the hereafter.

They question you concerning orphans. Say: 'To deal justly with them is best. If you mix their affairs with yours, remember they are your brothers. God knows the just from the unjust. If God pleased, he could afflict you. He is mighty and wise.'

You shall not wed pagan women, unless they embrace the Faith. A believing slave-girl is better than an idolatress, although she may please you. Nor shall you wed idolaters, unless they embrace the Faith. A believing slave is better than an idolater, although she may please you. These call you to hell-fire; but God calls you, by his will, to Paradise and forgiveness. He makes plain His revelations to Mankind, so that they may take heed.

They ask you about menstruation. Say: 'It is an indisposition. Keep aloof from women during their menstrual periods and do not touch them until they are clean again. Then have intercourse with them in the way God enjoined you. God loves those that turn to Him in repentance and strive to keep themselves clean.'

Women are your fields: go, then, into your fields whence you please. Do good works and fear God. Bear in mind that you shall meet Him. Give good tidings to the believers.

Do not make God, when you swear by Him, a means to prevent you from dealing justly, from guarding yourselves against evil, and from making peace among men. God knows all and hears all. God will not call you to account from that which is inadvertent in your oaths. But He will take you to task for that which is intended in your hearts. God is forgiving and lenient.

Those that renounce their wives on oath must wait four months. If they change their minds, God is forgiving and merciful; but if they decide to divorce them, know that God hears all and knows all.

Divorced women must wait, keeping themselves from men, three menstrual courses. It is unlawful for them, if they believe in God and the Last Day, to hide what God has created in their wombs; in which case their husbands would do well to take them back, should they desire reconciliation.

Women shall with justice have rights similar to those exercised against them, although men have a status above women. God is mighty and wise.

Divorce may be pronounced twice, and then a woman must be retained in honor or allowed to go with kindness. It is unlawful for husbands to take from them anything they have given them, unless both fear that they may not be able to keep within the bounds set by God; in which case it shall be no offense for either of them if the wife ransom herself.

These are the bounds set by God; do not transgress them. Those that transgress the bounds of God are wrongdoers.

If a man divorces his wife, he cannot remarry her until she has wedded another man and been divorced by him; in which case it shall be no offense for either of them to return to the other, if they think that they can keep within the bounds set by God.

Such are the bounds of God. He makes them plain to men of understanding.

When you have renounced your wives and they have reached the end of their waiting period, either retain them in honor or let them go with kindness. But you shall not retain them in order to harm them or to wrong them. Whoever does this wrongs his own soul.

Do not make game of God's revelations. Remember the favors God has bestowed upon you, and the book and the wisdom He has revealed for your instruction. Fear God and know God has knowledge of all things.

If a man has renounced his wife and she has reached the end of her waiting period, do not prevent her from remarrying her husband if they have come to an honorable agreement. This is enjoined on every one of you who believes in God and the Last Day; it is more honorable for you and more chaste. God knows, but you do not.

Mothers shall give suck to their children for two whole years if the father wishes the sucking to be completed. They must be maintained and clothed in a reasonable manner by the child's father. None should be charged with more than one can bear. A mother should not be allowed to suffer on account of her child, nor should a father on account of his child. The same duties devolve upon the father's heir. But if, after consultation, they choose by mutual consent to wean the child, they shall incur no guilt. Nor shall it be any offense for you if you prefer to have a nurse for your children, provided that you pay her what you promise, according to usage. Have fear of God and know that God is cognizant of all your actions.

Widows shall wait, keeping themselves apart from men, for four months and ten days after their husband's death. When they have reached the end of their waiting period, it shall be no offense for you to let them do whatever they choose for themselves, provided that it is decent. God is cognizant of all your actions.

It shall be no offense for you openly to propose marriage to such women or to cherish them in your hearts. God knows that you will remember them. Do not arrange to meet them in secret, and if you do, speak to them honorably. But you shall not consummate the marriage before the end of the waiting period. Know that God has knowledge of all your thoughts. Therefore take heed and bear in mind that God is forgiving and lenient.

It shall be no offense for you to divorce your wives before the marriage is consummated or the dowry settled. Provide for them with fairness; the rich man according to his means and the poor man according to his. This is binding on the righteous men. If you divorce them before the marriage is consummated, but after their dowry has been settled, give them the half of their dowry, unless they or the husband agree to waive it. But it is more proper that the husband should waive it. Do not forget to show kindness to each other. God observes your actions.

Attend regularly to your prayers, including the middle prayer, and stand up with all devotion before God. When you are exposed to danger pray on foot or while riding; and when you are restored to safety remember God, as He has taught you what you did not know.

You shall bequeath your widows a year's maintenance without causing them to leave their homes; but if they leave of their own accord, no blame shall be attached to you for any course they may deem fit to pursue. God is mighty and wise. Reasonable provisions shall also be made for divorced women. That is incumbent on righteous men.

Source: Surah 2:219–241, from *The Koran*.

TREATMENT OF WOMEN

In spite of contemporary criticism of the treatment of women in Muslim societies, Islam introduced women's rights where virtually none existed previously. Before Muhammad, women were essentially property, with no inheritance rights, and often were buried alive in infancy. Marriage contracts were loose, and often temporary. Muhammad condemned infanticide and required that daughters be given a share of inheritance. In matters of marriage, adultery was denounced, women were allowed the right of consent for marriage, and divorce became more difficult. Written about 626, the following selections from Women (surah 4) are laws pertaining to women and include some of these reforms.

. . . God has thus enjoined you concerning your children:

A male shall inherit twice as much as a female. If there be more than two girls, they shall have two-thirds of the inheritance; but if there be one only, she shall inherit the half. Parents shall inherit a sixth each, if the deceased have a child; but if he leave no child and his parents be his heirs, his mother shall have a third. If he have brothers, his mother shall have a sixth after payment of any legacy he may have bequeathed or any debt he may have owed.

You may wonder whether your parents or your children are more beneficial to you. But this is the law of God; God is all-knowing and wise.

You shall inherit the half of your wives' estate if they die childless. If they leave children, a quarter of their estate shall be yours after payment of any legacy they may have bequeathed or any debt they may have owed.

Your wives shall inherit one quarter of your estate if you die childless. If you leave children, they shall inherit one eighth, after payment of any legacy you may have bequeathed or any debt you may have owed.

If a man or a woman leave neither children nor parents and have a brother or a sister, they shall each inherit one sixth. If there be more, they shall equally share the third of the estate, after payment of any legacy he may have bequeathed or any debt he may have owed, without prejudice to the rights of the heirs. That is a commandment from God. God is all-knowing, and gracious.

Such are the bounds set by God. He that obeys God and His apostle shall dwell for ever in gardens watered by running streams. That is the supreme triumph. But he that defies God and His apostle and transgresses His bounds, shall be cast into a Fire wherein he will abide for ever. A shameful punishment awaits him.

If any of your women commit fornication, call in four witnesses from among yourselves against them; if they testify to their guilt confine them to their houses till death overtakes them or till God finds another way for them.

If two men among you commit indecency, punish them both. If they repent and mend their ways, let them be. God is forgiving and merciful.

God forgives those who commit evil in ignorance and then quickly turn to Him in repentance. God will pardon them. God is all-knowing and wise. But He will not forgive those who do evil and, when death comes to them, say: 'Now we repent!' Nor those who die unbelievers: for them We have prepared a woeful scourge.

Believers, it is unlawful for you to inherit the women of your deceased kinsmen against their will, or to bar them from re-marrying, in order that you may force them to give up a part of what you have given them, unless they be guilty of a proven crime. Treat them with kindness; for even if you dislike them, it may well be that you dislike a thing which God has meant for your own abundant good.

If you wish to replace a wife with another, do not take from her the dowry you have given her even if it be a talent of gold. That would be improper and grossly unjust; for how can you take it back when you have lain with each other and entered into a firm contract?

You shall not marry the women whom your fathers married: all previous such marriages excepted. That was an evil practice, indecent and abominable.

Forbidden to you are your mothers, your daughters, your sisters, your paternal and maternal aunts, the daughters of your brothers and sisters, your foster-mothers, your foster sisters, the mothers of your wives, your step-daughters who are in your charge, born of the wives with whom you have lain (it is no offense for you to marry your step-daughters if you have not consummated your marriage with their mothers), and the wives of your own begotten sons. You are also forbidden to take in marriage two sisters at one and the same time: all previous such marriages excepted. God is forgiving and merciful. Also married women, except those whom you own as slaves. Such is the decree of God. All women other than these are lawful to you, provided you seek them with your wealth in modest conduct, not in fornication. Give them their dowry for the enjoyment you have had of them as a duty; but it shall be no offense for you to make any other agreement among yourselves after you have fulfilled your duty. God is all-knowing and wise.

If any one of you cannot afford to marry a free believing woman, let him marry a slave-girl who is a believer (God best knows your faith: you are born one of another). Marry them with the permission of their masters and give them their dowry in all justice, provided they are honorable and chaste and have not entertained other men. If after marriage they commit adultery, they shall suffer half the penalty inflicted upon free adulteresses. Such is the law for those of you who fear to commit sin: but if you abstain, it will be better for you. God is forgiving and merciful. . . .

Men have authority over women because God has made the one superior to the other, and because they spend their wealth to maintain them. Good women are obedient. They guard their unseen parts because God has guarded them. As for those from whom you fear disobedience, admonish them and send them to beds apart and beat them. Then if they obey you, take no further action against them. God is high, supreme.

If you fear a breach between a man and his wife, appoint an arbiter from his people and another from hers. If they wish to be reconciled God will bring them together again. God is all-knowing and wise. . . .

They consult you concerning women. Say: 'God has instructed you about them, and so have the verses proclaimed to you in the Book, concerning the orphan girls whom you deny their lawful rights and refuse to marry; also regarding helpless children. He has instructed you to deal justly with orphans. God has knowledge of all the good you do.'

If a woman fear ill-treatment or desertion on the part of her husband, it shall be no offense for them to seek a mutual agreement, for agreement is best. Man is prone to avarice. But if you do what is right and guard yourselves against evil, know then that God is cognizant of all your actions.

Try as you may, you cannot treat all your wives impartially. Do not set yourself altogether against any of them, leaving her, as it were, in suspense. If you do what is right and guard yourselves against evil, you will find God forgiving and merciful. If they separate, God will compensate both out of His own abundance: God is munificent and wise. . . .

Source: Surah 4:11–25, 34–35, 127–130, from *The Koran.*

JESUS THE PROPHET

According to the Qur'an, Jesus is a highly exalted prophet who was born of a virgin, performed miracles, delivered God's message, and will return at the end of time. However, the Qur'an denies the reality of the crucifixion, implying either that it was an illusion or that someone else was substituted. More significantly, it denies the Trinity and the divine nature of Jesus, as seen in the following selection from the Table (surah 5), written about 629.

. . . One day God will gather all the apostles and ask them: 'How were you received?' They will reply: "We have no knowledge. You alone know what is hidden." God will say: 'Jesus, son of Mary, remember the favor I have bestowed on you and on your mother: how I strengthened you with the Holy Spirit, so that you preached to men in your cradle and in the prime of manhood; how I instructed you in the Book and in wisdom, in the Torah and in the Gospel; how by My leave you fashioned from clay the likeness of a bird and breathed into it so that, by My leave, it became a living bird; how, by My leave, you healed the blind man and the leper, and by my leave restored the dead to life; how I protected you from the Israelites when you had come to them with clear signs: when those of them who disbelieved declared: "This is but plain sorcery"; how when I enjoined the disciples to believe in Me and in My apostle they replied: "We believe; bear witness that we submit."'

'Jesus, son of Mary,' said the disciples, 'can your Lord send down to us from heaven a table spread with food?'

He replied: 'Have fear of God, if you are true believers.'

'We wish to eat of it,' they said, 'so that we may reassure our hearts and know that what you said to us is true, and that we may be witnesses of it.'

'Lord,' said Jesus, the son of Mary, 'send down to us from heaven a table spread with food, that it may mark a feast for us and for those that will come after us: a sign from You. Give us our sustenance; You are the best provider.'

God replied: 'I am sending one to you. But whoever of you disbelieves hereafter shall be punished as no man will ever be punished.'

Then God will say: "Jesus, son of Mary, did you ever say to mankind; 'Worship me and my mother as gods besides God?'"

'Glory to You,' he will answer, 'how could I ever say that to which I have no right? If I had ever said so, You would have surely known it. You know what is in my mind, but I know not what is in Yours. You alone know what is hidden. I told them only what You bade me. I said: "Serve God, my Lord and your Lord." I watched over them while living in their midst, and ever since You took me to Yourself, You have been watching over them. You are the witness of all things. If You punish them, they surely are Your servants; and if You forgive them, surely You are mighty and wise.'

God will say: 'This is the day when their truthfulness will benefit the truthful. They shall for ever dwell in gardens watered by running streams. God is pleased with them, and they are pleased with Him. That is the supreme triumph.'

God has sovereignty over the heavens and the earth and all that they contain. He has power over all things.

Source: Surah 5:109–120, from *The Koran.*

UNBELIEVING PEOPLE OF THE BOOK

According to the Qur'an, certain groups of people had received revealed scriptures prior to Muhammad. These "people of the book" include the Jews, Christians, Zoroastrians, and Sabians. The Qur'an acknowledges the legitimacy of these religions, maintaining a place for such believers in the afterlife. However, many people of the book have abandoned their revealed teachings by adopting false gods and denying God's true prophets. The following selection from the Table (surah 5) admonishes the unbelieving people of the book.

. . . We have revealed the Torah, in which there is guidance and light. By it the prophets who surrendered themselves judged the Jews, and so did the rabbis and the divines, according to God's Book which had been committed to their keeping and to which they themselves were witnesses.

Have no fear of man; fear Me, and do not sell My revelations for a paltry end. Unbelievers are those who do not judge according to God's revelations.

We decreed for them a life for a life, an eye for an eye, a nose for a nose, an ear for an ear, a tooth for a tooth, and a wound for a wound. But if a man charitably forbears from retaliation, his remission shall atone for him. Transgressors are those that do not judge according to God's revelations.

After them We sent forth Jesus, the son of Mary, confirming the Torah already revealed, and gave him the Gospel in which there is guidance and light, corroborating what was revealed before it in the Torah, a guide and an admonition to the righteous. Therefore let those who follow the Gospel judge according to what God has revealed therein. Evil-doers are those that do not base their judgments on God's revelations. . . .

Believers, take neither Jews nor Christians for your friends. They are friends with one another. Whoever of you seeks their friendship shall become one of their number. . . .

If the People of the Book accept the true faith and keep from evil, We will pardon them their sins and admit them to the gardens of delight. If they observe the Torah and the Gospel and what is revealed to them from their Lord, they shall enjoy abundance from above and from beneath.

There are some among them who are righteous men; but there are many among them who do nothing but evil.

Apostle, proclaim what is revealed to you from your Lord; if you do not, you will surely fail to convey His message. God will protect you from all men. God does not guide the unbelievers.

Say: 'People of the Book, you will attain nothing until you observe the Torah and the Gospel and that which is revealed to you from your Lord.'

That which is revealed to you from your Lord will surely increase the wickedness and unbelief of many of them. But do not grieve for the unbelievers.

Believers, Jews, Sabaeans and Christians—whoever believes in God and the Last Day and does what is right shall have nothing to fear or to regret.

We made a covenant with the Israelites and sent forth apostles among them. But whenever an apostle came to them with a message that did not suit their fancies, some they accused of lying and others they put to death. They thought no harm would follow: they were blind and deaf. God turned to them in mercy, but many again were blind and deaf. God is ever watching their actions.

Unbelievers are those that say: 'God is the messiah, the son of Mary.' For the Messiah himself said: 'Children of Israel, serve God, my Lord and your Lord.' He that worships other gods besides God, God will deny him Paradise, and Hell shall be his home. None shall help the evil-doers.

Unbelievers are those that say: 'God is one of three.' There is but one God. If they do not desist from so saying, those of them that disbelieve shall be sternly punished.

Will they not turn to God in repentance and seek forgiveness of Him? God is forgiving and merciful.

The Messiah, the son of Mary, was no more than an apostle: other apostles passed away before him. His mother was a saintly woman. They both ate earthly food.

See how We make plain to them Our revelations. See how they ignore the truth.

Say: 'Will you serve instead of God that which can neither harm nor help you? God is He who hears all and knows all.'

Say: 'People of the Book! Do not transgress the bounds of truth in your religion. Do not yield to the desires of those who have erred before; who have led many astray and have themselves strayed from the even path.'

Those of the Israelites who disbelieved were cursed by David and Jesus, the son of Mary, because they rebelled and committed evil. Nor did they censure themselves for any wrong they did. Evil were their deeds.

Source: Surah 5:44–48, 51, 65–78, from *The Koran*.

FIVE PILLARS OF ISLAM

The primary ritual requirements of Islam are known as the Five Pillars of Islam (arkan ad-din). They are (1) sincerely uttering the creed, "there is no God but Allah, and Muhammad is his messenger" (shahada), (2) praying five times a day facing Mecca (salat), (3) paying an alms tax for the needy (zakat), (4) fasting during the month of Ramadan (sawm), and (5) making a pilgrimage to Mecca once in one's life, if possible (hajj). Each of these has its foundation in the Qur'an. Elements of the first pillar, the creed, are found in surahs 37:35, 47:19, and 48:29. *The remaining four pillars are discussed in the following selections from the Cow (surah 2), from the late Medinan period.*

[*Prayer.*] Many a time have We seen you turn your face towards heaven. We will make you turn towards a *qiblah* that will please you. Turn your face towards the Holy Mosque; wherever you be, turn your faces towards it.

Those to whom the Scriptures were given know this to be the truth from their Lord. God is never heedless of what they do. But even if you gave them every proof they would not accept your *qiblah*, nor would you accept theirs; nor would any of them accept the *qiblah* of the other. If, after all the knowledge you have been given, you yield to their desires, then you will surely become an evil-doer.

Those to whom We gave the Scriptures know Our apostle as they know their own sons. But some of them deliberately conceal the truth. This is the truth from your Lord: therefore never doubt it.

Each one has a goal towards which he turns. But wherever you be, emulate one another in good works. God will bring you all before Him. God has power over all things.

Whichever way you depart, face towards the Holy Mosque. This is surely the truth from your Lord. God is never heedless of what you do.

Whichever way you depart, face towards the Holy Mosque: and wherever you are, face towards it, so that men will have no cause to reproach you, except the evil-doers among them. Have no fear of them; fear Me, so that I may perfect My favor to you and that you may be rightly guided. . . .

[*Fasting.*] Believers, fasting is decreed for you as it was decreed for those before you; perchance you will guard yourselves against evil. Fast a certain number of days, but if any one among you is ill or on a journey, let him fast a similar number of days later; and for those that cannot endure it there is a ransom: the feeding of a poor man. He that does good of his own accord shall be well rewarded; but to fast is better for you, if you but knew it.

In the month of Ramadan the Qur'an was revealed, a book of guidance with proofs of guidance distinguishing right from wrong. Therefore whoever of you is present in that month let him fast. But he who is ill or on a journey shall fast a similar number of days later on.

God desires your well-being, not your discomfort. He desires you to fast the whole month so that you may magnify Him and render thanks to Him for giving you His guidance.

When My servants question you about Me, tell them that I am near. I answer the prayer of the suppliant when he calls to Me; therefore let them answer My call and put their trust in Me, that they may be rightly guided.

It is now lawful for you to lie with your wives on the night of the fast; they are a comfort to you as you are to them. God knows that you were deceiving yourselves. He has relented towards you and pardoned you. Therefore you may now lie with them and seek what God has ordained for you. Eat and drink until you can tell a white thread from a black one in the light of the coming dawn. Then resume the fast till nightfall and do not approach them, but stay at your prayers in the mosques.

These are the bounds set by God: do not come near them. Thus he makes known His revelations to mankind that they may guard themselves against evil. . . .

[**Alms.**] Give generously for the cause of God and do not with your own hands cast yourselves into destruction. Be charitable; God loves the charitable. . . .

[**Pilgrimage.**] Make the pilgrimage and visit the Sacred House for His sake. If you cannot, send such offerings as you can afford and do not shave your heads until the offerings have reached their destination. But if any of you is ill or suffers from an ailment of the head, he must pay a ransom either by fasting or by almsgiving or by offering a sacrifice.

If in peacetime anyone among you combines the visit with the pilgrimage, he must offer such gifts as he can afford; but if he lacks the means let him fast three days during the pilgrimage and seven when he has returned; that is, ten days in all. That is incumbent on him whose family are not present at the Holy Mosque. Have fear of God: know that he is stern in retribution.

Make a pilgrimage in the appointed months. He that intends to perform it in those months must abstain from sexual intercourse, obscene language, and acrimonious disputes while on the pilgrimage. God is aware of whatever good you do. Provide well for yourselves: the best provision is piety. Fear Me, then, you that are endowed with understanding.

It shall be no offense for you to seek the bounty of our Lord. When you come running from Arafat [near Mecca] remember God as you approach the sacred monument. Remember Him that gave you guidance when you were in error. Then go out from the place whence the pilgrims will go out and implore the forgiveness of God. He is forgiving and merciful. And when you have fulfilled your sacred duties, remember God as you remember your forefathers or with deeper reverence.

Source: Surah 2:144–150, 183–187, 195–200, from *The Koran*.

JIHAD

Often called the sixth pillar of Muslim obligation, jihad, or holy war, is struggling for Allah's cause. Islam divides the world into two abodes: the abode of submission, encompassing Muslim territories (Dar al-Islam), and the abode of struggle, encompassing non-Islamic territories (Dar al-Harb). The obligation of jihad is to extend the abode of submission through missionary activities or, when necessary, through armed force. jihad aims at political control over societies, to govern them by the principles of Islam. In theory, forced conversion of individuals is not intended. It was originally the responsibility of the Caliphs. Traditionally, jihad should be undertaken only when success is likely. Although the explicit obligation of jihad first appears in the Hadith, its foundations are laid in the Qur'an. The following selection from the Women (surah 4), written just after the unsuccessful battle of Uhud, advises Muslims who fight for Allah.

Believers, show discernment when you go to fight for the cause of God, and do not say to those that offer you peace; 'You are not believers,'—

seeking the chance of booty of this world; for with God there are abundant gains. Such was your custom in days gone by, but now God has bestowed on you His grace. Therefore show discernment; God is cognizant of all your actions.

The believers who stay at home—apart from those that suffer from a grave impediment—are not equal to those who fight for the cause of God with their goods and their persons. God has given those that fight with their goods and their persons a higher rank than those who stay at home. God has promised all a good reward; but far richer is the recompense of those who fight for Him: ranks of His own bestowal, forgiveness, and mercy. God is forgiving and merciful.

The angels will ask those whom they carry off while steeped in sin; 'What were you doing?' 'We were oppressed in our land,' they will reply. They will say: 'Was not the earth of God spacious enough for you to fly for refuge?' Hell shall be their home: an evil fate.

As for the helpless men, women, and children who have neither the strength nor the means to escape, God may pardon them: God pardons and forgives.

He that flies his homeland for the cause of God shall find numerous places of refuge in the land and great abundance. He that leaves his dwelling to fight for God and His apostle and is then overtaken by death, shall be rewarded by God. God is forgiving and merciful.

It is no offense for you to shorten your prayers when traveling the road if you fear that the unbelievers may attack you. The unbelievers are your inveterate enemies.

When you (Prophet) are with the faithful, conducting their prayers, let one party of them rise up to pray with you, armed with their weapons. After making their prostrations, let them withdraw to the rear and then let another party who have not prayed come forward and pray with you; and let these also be on their guard, armed with their weapons. It would much please the unbelievers if you neglected your arms and your baggage, so that they could swoop upon you with one assault. But it is no offense for you to lay aside your arms when overtaken by heavy rain or stricken with an illness, although you must be always on your guard. God has prepared a shameful punishment for the unbelievers.

When your prayers are ended, remember God standing, sitting, and lying down. Attend regularly to your prayers so long as you are safe: for prayer is a duty incumbent on the faithful, to be conducted at appointed hours.

Seek out your enemies relentlessly. If you have suffered, they too have suffered: but you at least hope to receive from God what they cannot hope for. God is all-knowing, and wise.

Source: Surah 4:94–105, from *The Koran*.

MUHAMMAD'S WIVES

The selection below from the Clans (surah 33), revealed about 629, presents the domestic side of Muhammad in his final years. At the time he had nine wives, several previously widowed, and additional slave girls. This surah *advises his wives on proper conduct and discusses his relations with them. Recommendations are also made on etiquette when visiting Muhammad.*

. . . Wives of the Prophet! Those of you who commit a proven sin shall be doubly punished. That is easy enough for God. But those of you who obey God and His apostle and do good works shall be doubly rewarded; for them We have made a generous provision.

Wives of the Prophet, you are not like other women. If you fear God, do not be too complaisant in your speech, lest the lecherous-hearted should lust after you. Show discretion in what you say. Stay in your homes and do not display your finery as women used to do in the days of ignorance [i.e., the *time of ingratitude*]. Attend to your prayers, give alms and obey God and His apostle.

Women of the household, God seeks only to remove uncleanness from you and to purify you. Commit to memory the revelations of God and the wise sayings that are recited in your dwellings. Benignant is God and all-knowing.

Those who surrender themselves to God and accept the true Faith; who are devout, sincere, patient, humble, charitable, and chaste; who fast and are ever mindful of God—on these, both men and women, God will bestow forgiveness and a rich reward.

It is not for true believers—men or women—to take their choice in their affairs if God and His apostle strays far indeed.

You [Muhammad] said to the man [Zayd, Muhammad's adopted son] whom God and yourself have favoured: 'Keep your wife and have fear of God.' You sought to hide in your heart what God was to reveal [Muhammad's intention to marry Zayd's wife]. You were afraid of man, although it would have been more proper to fear God. And when Zayd divorced his wife, We gave her to you in marriage, so that it should become legitimate for true believers to wed the wives of their adopted sons if they divorced them. God's will must needs be done.

No blame shall be attached to the Prophet for doing what is sanctioned for him by God. Such was the way of God with the prophets who passed away before him (God's decrees are pre-ordained); who fulfilled the mission with which God had charged them, fearing God and fearing none besides Him. Sufficient is God's reckoning.

Muhammad is the father of no man among you [i.e., he left no male heirs]. He is the Apostle of God and the Seal of the Prophets. God has knowledge of all things. . . .

Prophet, We have made lawful to you the wives to whom you have granted dowries and the slave-girls whom God has given you as booty; the daughters of your paternal and maternal uncles and of your paternal and maternal aunts who fled with you; and any believing woman who gives herself to the Prophet and whom the Prophet wished to take in marriage. This privilege is yours alone, being granted to no other believer.

We well know the duties We have imposed on the faithful concerning their wives and slave-girls. We grant you this privilege so that none may blame you. God is forgiving and merciful.

You may put off any of your wives you please and take to your bed any of them you please. Nor is it unlawful for you to receive any of those whom you have temporarily set aside. That is more proper, so that they may be contented and not vexed, and may all be pleased with what you give them.

God knows what is in your [i.e., the believer's] hearts. He is all-knowing and gracious.

It shall be unlawful for you [i.e., Muhammad] to take more wives or to change your present wives for other women, though their beauty please you, except where slave-girls are concerned. God takes cognizance of all things.

Believers, do not enter the houses of the Prophet for a meal without waiting for the proper time, unless you are given leave. But if you are invited, enter; and when you have eaten, disperse. Do not engage in familiar talk, for this would annoy the Prophet and he would be ashamed to bid you go; but of the truth God is not ashamed. If you ask his wives for anything, speak to them from behind a curtain. This is more chaste for your hearts and their hearts.

You must not speak ill of God's apostle, nor shall you ever wed his wives after him; this would be a grave offense in the sight of God. Whether you hide or reveal them, God has knowledge of all things.

It shall be no offense for the Prophet's wives to be seen unveiled by their fathers, their sons, their brothers, their brothers' sons, their sisters' sons, their women, or their slave-girls. Women, have fear of God, for he observes all things.

Source: Surah 33:30–40, 50–55, from *The Koran*.

IDOLATRY ABOLISHED

By 630, the tables had clearly turned against idolatry in Mecca in favor of Islam. Muhammad rode into the Ka'bah and destroyed its idols. In the following selection from the Repentance (surah 9), a declaration of immunity is announced: Muslims would no longer be bound by obligations to idolatrous tribes which repeatedly broke agreements with Muslims. Idolaters would also be barred from the Ka'bah.

A declaration of immunity from God and His apostle to the idolaters with whom you have made agreements:

For four months you shall go unmolested in the land. But know that you shall not escape God's judgment, and that God will humble the unbelievers.

A proclamation to the people from God and His apostle on the day of the greater pilgrimage:

God and His apostle are under no obligation to the idolaters. If you repent, it shall be well with you; but if you give no heed, know that you shall not be immune from God's judgment.

Proclaim a woeful punishment to the unbelievers, except to those idolaters who have honored their treaties with you in every detail and aided none against you. With these keep faith, until their treaties have run their term. God loves the righteous.

When the sacred months are over slay the idolaters wherever you find them. Arrest them, besiege them, and lie in ambush everywhere for them. If they repent and take to prayer and render the alms levy, allow them to go their way. God is forgiving and merciful.

If an idolater seeks asylum with you, give him protection so that he may hear the Word of God, and then convey him to safety. For the idolaters are ignorant men.

God and His apostle repose no trust in idolaters, save those with whom you have made treaties at the Sacred Mosque. So long as they keep faith with you, keep faith with them. God loves the righteous.

How can you trust them? If they prevail against you they will respect neither agreements nor ties of kindred. They flatter you with their tongues, but their hearts reject you. Most of them are evil-doers.

They sell God's revelations for trifling gain and debar others from His path. Evil is what they do. They break faith with the believers and set at nought all ties of kindred. Such are the transgressors.

If they repent and take to prayer and render the alms levy, they shall become your brothers in the Faith. Thus do We make plain Our revelations for men of understanding.

But if, after coming to terms with you, they break their oaths, and revile your faith, make war on the leaders of unbelief—for no oaths are binding with them—so that they may desist.

Will you not fight against those who have broken their oaths and conspired to banish the Apostle? Surely God is more deserving of your fear, if you are true believers.

Make war on them: God will chastise them at your hands and humble them. He will grant you victory over them and heal the spirit of the faithful. He will take away all rancor from their hearts: God shows mercy to whom he pleases. God is all-knowing and wise.

Did you imagine you would be forsaken before God has had time to know those of you who have fought valiantly and served none but God, His Apostle and the faithful? God is cognizant of all your actions.

It ill becomes idolaters to visit the mosques of God, for they are self-confessed unbelievers. Vain shall be their works, and in the fire they shall abide for ever.

None should visit the mosques of God except those who believe in God and the Last Day, attend to their prayers and render the alms levy and fear none but God. These shall be rightly guided. . . .

Believers, know that the idolaters are unclean. Let them not approach the Sacred Mosque after this year is ended. If you fear poverty, God, if he pleases, will enrich you through His own bounty. God is all-knowing and wise.

Source: Surah 9:1–18, 28, from *The Koran*.

FINAL REVELATION

In 632, just months before his death, Muhammad delivered his final revelation while on pilgrimage to Mecca. Set within the context of dietary regulations, the completion of Islam is proclaimed.

Believers, be true to your obligations. It is lawful for you to eat the flesh of all beasts other than that which is hereby announced to you. Game is forbidden while you are on pilgrimage. God decrees what He will.

Believers, do not violate the rites of God, or the sacred month, or the offerings or their ornaments, or those that repair to the Sacred House seeking God's grace and pleasure. Once your pilgrimage is ended, you shall be free to go hunting.

Do not allow your hatred for those who would debar you from the Holy Mosque lead you into sin. Help one another in what is good and pious, not in what is wicked and sinful. Have fear of God; God is stern in retribution.

You are forbidden carrion, blood, and the flesh of swine; also any flesh dedicated to any other than God. You are forbidden the flesh of strangled animals and of those beaten or gored to death; of those killed by a fall or mangled by beasts of prey (unless you make it clean by giving the death-stroke yourselves); also of animals sacrificed to idols.

You are forbidden to settle disputes by consulting the Arrows. That is a pernicious practice.

The unbelievers had this day abandoned all hope of vanquishing your religion. Have no fear of them: fear Me.

This day I have perfected your religion for you and completed My favor to you. I have chosen Islam to be your faith.

He that is constrained by hunger to eat of what is forbidden, not intending to commit sin, will find God forgiving and merciful.

They ask you what is lawful to them. Say: 'All good things are lawful to you, as well as that which you have taught the birds and beasts of prey to catch, training them as God has taught you. Eat of what they catch for you, pronouncing upon it the name of God. And have fear of God: swift is God's reckoning.'

All good things have this day been made lawful to you. The food of those to whom the Book was given is lawful to you, and yours to them. . . .

Source: Surah 5:1–5, from *The Koran*.

HADITH

CALL TO PROPHETHOOD

The story of Muhammad's call to prophethood on the night of power is recorded in the following Hadith *selection.*

Narrated A'isha the mother of the faithful believers: The commencement of the Divine Inspiration to Allah's Apostle was in the form of good dreams which came true like bright day light, and then the love of seclusion was bestowed upon him. He used to go in seclusion in the cave of Hira' where he used to worship (Allah alone) continuously for many days before his desire to see his family. He used to take with him the journey food for the stay and then come back to (his wife) Khadija to take his food like-wise again till suddenly the Truth descended upon him while he was in the cave of Hira'. The angel came to him and asked him to read. The Prophet replied, "I do not know how to read."

The Prophet added, "The angel caught me (forcefully) and pressed me so hard that I could not bear it any more. He then released me and again asked me to read and I replied, 'I do not know how to read.' Thereupon he caught me again and pressed me a second time till I could not bear it any more. He then released me and again asked me to read but again I replied, 'I do not know how to read (or what shall I read?)' Thereupon he caught me for the third time and pressed me, and then released me and said, 'Read in the name of your lord, who has created (all that exists) and has created man from a clot. Read! And your Lord is the Most Generous.'" (96: 1, 2, 3) Then Allah's Apostle returned with the Inspiration and with his heart beating severely. Then he went to Khadija bint Khuwailid and said, "Cover me! Cover me!" They covered him till his fear was over and after that he told her everything that had happened and said, "I fear that something may happen to me." Khadija replied, "Never! By Allah, Allah will never disgrace you. You keep good relations with your Kith and kin, help the poor and the destitute, serve your guests generously and assist the deserving calamity-afflicted."

Khadija then accompanied him to her cousin Waraqa ibn Naufal ibn Asad ibn 'abdul 'Uzza, who, during the Pre-Islamic Period became a Christian and used to write the writing with Hebrew letters. He would write from the Gospel in Hebrew as much as Allah wished him to write. He was an old man and had lost his eyesight. Khadija said to Waraqa, "Listen to the story of your nephew, O my cousin!" Waraqa asked, "O my Nephew! What have you seen?" Allah's Apostle described whatever he had seen. Waraqa said, "This is the same one who keeps the secrets (angel Gabriel) whom Allah had sent to Moses. I wish I were young and could live up to the time when your people would turn you out." Allah's Apostle asked, "Will they drive me out?" Waraqa replied in the affirmative and said, "Anyone (man) who came with something similar to what you have brought was treated with hostility; and if I should remain alive till the day when you will be turned out then I would support you strongly." But after a few days Waraqa died and the Divine Inspiration was also paused for a while.

Source: *Sahih al-Bukhari*, 1:3, from *The Translation of the Meanings of Sahih al-Bukhari*, tr. Muhammad Muhsin Khan (Chicago: Kazi Publications, 1979), 9 vol..

NIGHT JOURNEY

Surah 17:1 of the Qur'an, written in the middle Meccan period, reads, "Glory be to him who made his servant go by night from the sacred temple [of Mecca] to the farther temple [of Jerusalem] whose surroundings we have blessed, that we might show him some of our signs." Referred to as the Night Journey, Muhammad was carried by Gabriel to the temple of Jerusalem (isra), and brought through the seven heavens to God (mi'raj). Although some Muslims interpret this as a vision, most see it as a literal journey. In commemoration of this event, a Muslim shrine called the Dome of the Rock stands on the place of Muhammad's ascent, the former site of the Jewish temple of Jerusalem. It is Islam's third most holy place, after Mecca and Medina. The story of the Night Journey from the Hadith *is recounted here.*

Narrated Anas ibn Malik from Malik ibn Sa'sa'a that Allah's Apostle described to them his Night Journey saying, While I was lying in Al-Hatim or Al-Hijr, suddenly someone came to me and cut my body open from here to here [across the chest]. He then took out my heart. Then a gold tray full of Belief was brought to me and my heart was washed and was filled (with Belief) and then returned to its original place. Then a white animal which was smaller than a mule and bigger than a donkey was brought to me. . . . The animal's step (was so wide that it) reached the nearest heaven. When he asked for the gate to be opened it was asked, "Who is it?" Gabriel answered, "Gabriel." It was asked, "Who was accompanying you?" Gabriel replied, "Muhammad." It was asked, "Has Muhammad been called?" Gabriel replied in the affirmative. Then it was said, "He is welcomed. What an excellent visit his is!" The gate was opened, and when I went over the first heaven, I saw Adam there. Gabriel said (to me), "This is your father, Adam; pay him your greetings." So I greeted him and he returned the greeting to me and said, "You are welcomed, o pious son and pious Prophet." Then Gabriel ascended with me till we reached the second heaven. . . . There I saw Yahya (i.e., John) and 'Isa (i.e., Jesus) who were cousins of each other. . . . Then Gabriel ascended with me to the third heaven and . . . there I saw Joseph. . . . Then Gabriel ascended with me to the fourth heaven and . . . there I saw Idris. . . .

Then Gabriel ascended with me to the fifth heaven and . . . there I saw Harun (i.e., Aaron). Then Gabriel ascended with me to the sixth heaven and . . . there I saw Moses. . . . When I left him (i.e., Moses) he wept. Someone asked him, "What makes you weep?" Moses said, "I weep because after me there has been sent (as Prophet) a young man whose followers will enter Paradise in greater numbers than my followers." Then Gabriel ascended with me to the seventh heaven and . . . there I saw Abraham. . . . Then I was made to ascend to Sidrat-ul-Muntaha (i.e., the Lote Tree of the farthest limit). Behold! Its fruits were like the jars of Hajr (i.e., a place near Medina) and its leaves were as big as the ears of elephants. Gabriel said, "This is the Lote Tree of the farthest limit." Behold! There ran four rivers, two were hidden and two were visible. I asked, "What are these two kinds of rivers, O Gabriel?" He replied, "As for the hidden rivers, they are two rivers in Paradise and the visible rivers are the Nile and the Euphrates." Then Al-Bait-ul-Ma'mur (i.e., the Sacred House) was shown to me and a container full of wine and another full of milk and a third full of honey were brought to me. I took the milk. Gabriel remarked, "This is the Islamic religion which you and your followers are following." Then the prayers were enjoined on me: They were fifty prayers a day.

When I returned, I passed by Moses who asked (me), "What have you been ordered to do?" I replied, "I have been ordered to offer fifty prayers a day." Moses said, "Your followers cannot bear fifty prayers a day, and by Allah, I have tested people before you, and I have tried my level best with Bani Israil (in vain). Go back to your Lord and ask for reducing your followers' burden." So I went back, and Allah reduced ten prayers for me. Then again I went back to Allah and he reduced ten more prayers. When I came back to Moses he said the same, I went back to Allah and he ordered me to observe ten prayers a day. When I came back to Moses, he repeated the same advice, so I went back to Allah and was ordered to observe five prayers a day. When I came back to Moses, he said ". . . go back to your Lord and ask for reducing your followers' burden." I said, "I have requested so much of my Lord that I feel ashamed, but I am satisfied now and surrender to Allah's Order." When I left, I heard a voice saying, "I have passed My Order and have reduced the burden of My Worshippers."

Source: *Sahih al-Bukhari*, 5:227.

JIHAD

The foundation of jihad—or holy war laid down in the Qur'an and Hadith, and refined in later legal discussions. The tradition that emerged contends that believers can fulfill jihad in four possible ways: through one's heart, tongue, hand, or sword. Jihad through one's heart—a practice sometimes called greater jihad—*involves overcoming temptation or some personal evil. Islam can next be advanced through the tongue and the hand by defending what is right and rectifying what is wrong. Finally, through the sword, Islam can be militarily advanced—a practice sometimes called* lesser jihad. *The selections below from the Hadith are often associated with different types of jihad.*

Abu Hurairah said, A man came to the Messenger of Allah and said, Guide me to a deed which is equal to jihad. He said, "I do not find it." Then he said:

"Is it in your power that when the one engaged in jihad goes forth, you should enter your mosque and stand in prayer and have no rest, and that you should fast and break it not?" He said, "Who can do it?" (Bukhari 56:1.)

Mughirah reported, The Prophet said, "Some people from among my community will remain in the ascendant, until the command of Allah comes to them and they will be triumphant." (Bukhari 61:28.)

Imran ibn Husain said, The messenger of Allah said, "A party of my community will not cease fighting for the Truth—they will be triumphant over their opponents." (Abu Dawud Mishkat 18.)

Abu Hurairah reported, The Messenger of Allah said: "Surely Allah will raise for this community at the beginning of every century one who will revive for it its faith." (Abu Dawud 36:1.)

Ibn Abbas reported, . . . And this (letter) ran as follows: "In the name of Allah, the Beneficent, the Merciful. From Muhammad, the servant of Allah and His Messenger, to Heraclius, the Chief of the Roman Empire. Peace be with him who follows the guidance. After this, I invite you with invitation to Islam. Become a Muslim and you will be in peace—Allah will give you a double reward; but it you turn away, on you will be the sin of your subjects. And, O followers of the Book! Come to an equitable proposition between us and you that we will not serve any but Allah, and that we will not associate aught with Him, and that some of us will not take others for lords besides Allah; but if they turn back, then say: Bear witness that we are Muslims." (Bukhari 1:1.)

Salamah said, "I swore allegiance to the Prophet, then I turned to the shade of a tree." When the crowd diminished, he (the Prophet) said, "O Ibn al-Akwa! Will you not swear allegiance?" He said, "I said, I have already sworn allegiance, O Messenger of Allah!" He said, "And do it again." So I swore allegiance to him a second time. I (the reporter) said to him, "O Abu Muslim! For what did you swear allegiance (to him) then?" He said, "For death." (Bukhari 56:110.)

Abd Allah ibn Aufa reported, "The Messenger of Allah said: And know that paradise is beneath the protection of the swords." (Bukhari 56:22.)

Abu Hurairah said, I heard the Prophet say, "By him in Whose hand is my soul, were it not that there are men among the believers who cannot bear to remain behind me—and I do not find that on which carry them—I would not remain behind an army that fights in the way of Allah; and by Him in whose hand is my soul. I love that I should be killed in the way of Allah then brought to life, then killed again then brought to life, then killed again then brought to life, then killed again." (Bukhari 56:7.)

Abu Hurairah said, The Messenger of Allah said, "Whom do you count to be a martyr among you?" They said, "O Messenger of Allah! Whoever is killed in the way of Allah is a martyr." He said: "In that case the martyrs of my community will be very few—he who is killed in the way of Allah is a martyr; he who dies a natural death in the way of Allah is a martyr; he who dies of the plague (in the way of Allah) is a martyr; he who dies of cholera (in the way of Allah) is a martyr." (Muslim Miskhat 18.)

Abu Allah reported, "A women was found among the killed in one of the battles of the Prophet so the Messenger of Allah forbade the killing of women and children." (Bukahri 56:147.)

Ibn Umar reported, The Messenger of Allah said: "I have been commanded that I should fight these people till they bear witness that there is no god but Allah and keep up prayer and pay zakat. When they do this, their blood and their property will be safe with me except as Islam requires, and their reckoning is with Allah." (Bukhari 2:16.)

Source: Adapted from Maulana Muhammad Ali, *A Manual of Hadith*, (Lahore, Ahmadiyya, 1944).

CHARITY

Almsgiving (zakat) *is one of the five pillars of Islam, and involves a mandatory tax upon those who can afford it. This is often contrasted with deeds of generosity* (sadaqah) *that are voluntary beyond the almsgiving tax. The spirit behind both of these is charity, which is discussed in the Hadith selections below.*

Abu Musa reported, The Prophet said: "*sadaqah* is incumbent on every Muslim." They (his companions) said, "O Prophet of Allah! And (what about him) who has not got (anything to give)?" He said: "He should work with his hand and profit himself and give in charity." They said, "What if he has nothing (in spite of this)." He said: "He should help the distressed one who is in need." They said, "What if he is unable to do this." He said: "He should do good deeds and refrain from doing evil—this is charity on his part."(Bukahri 24:31.)

Abu Hurairah reported, The Prophet said: "On every bone of the fingers charity is incumbent every day: One assists a man in riding his beast or in lifting his provisions to the back of the animal, this is charity; and a good word and every step which one takes in walking over to prayer is charity; and showing the way (to another) is charity."(Bukhari 56:72.)

Abu Hurairah reported, The Prophet said: "Removal from the way of that which is harmful is charity." (Bukhari 46:24.)

Jabir said, The Messenger of Allah said: "Every good deed is charity, and it is a good deed that you meet your brother with a cheerful countenance and that you pour water from your bucket into the vessel of your brother." (*Musnad* of Ahmad Miskhat 6:6.)

Abu Hurairah said, Then Prophet said, "The man who exerts himself on behalf of the widow and the poor one is like the one who struggles in the way of Allah, or the one who keeps awake in the night (for prayers) and fasts during the day." (Bukhari 69:1.)

Abu Hurairah said, The Messenger of Allah, "A prostitute was forgiven—she passed by a dog, panting with its tongue out, on the top of a well containing water, almost dying with thirst; so she took off her boot and tied it to her-covering and drew forth water for it; she was forgiven on account of this." It was said: Is there a reward for us in (doing good to) the beasts? He said: "In every animal having a liver fresh with life there is a reward." (Bukhari and Muslim Miskhat 6:6.)

Abu Hurairah said on the authority of the Prophet (who said): "There is a man who gives a charity and he conceals it so much so that his left does not know what his right hand spends." (Bukhari 24:11.)

Zubair reported, The Prophet said: "If one of you should take his rope and bring a bundle of fire-wood on his back and then sell it, with which Allah should save his honor, it is better for him than that he should beg of people whether give him or do not give him." (Bukhari 24:50.)

Fatimah bint Qais said, The Messenger of Allah said: "In (one's) wealth there is a due besides the zakat"; then he recited: "It is not right-eousness that you turn your faces towards the East and the West." (Tirmidhi Mishkat 6:6.)

Ibn Abbas reported, The Prophet sent Mu'adh to Yaman and said: "Invite them to bear witness that there is no god but Allah and that I am the Messenger of Allah; if they accept this, tell them that Allah has made obliga-tory on them five prayers in every day and night; if they accept this, tell them that Allah has made obligatory in their wealth a charity which is taken from the wealthy among them and given to the poor among them." (Bukhari 24:1.)

Abu Hurairah said When the Messenger of Allah died and Abu Bakr became (his successor), and those of the Arabs who would disbelieve disbe-lieved, Umar said, "How do you fight people (who profess Islam)," and the Messenger of Allah said "I have been commanded to continue fighting against people until they say, There is no god but Allah; whoever says this will have his property and his life safe unless there is a due against him and his reckoning is with Allah." (Abu Bakr) said, "By Allah! I will fight those who make a difference between prayer and zakat, for zakat is a tax on prop-erty; By Allah! If they withhold from me even a she-kid which they used to make over to the Messenger of Allah, I will fight against them for their withholding it." Umar said, "By Allah! Allah opened the heart of Abu Bakr (to receive the truth), so I know that it was true." (Bukhari 24:1.)

Source: Adapted from Maulana Muhammad Ali, *A Manual of Hadith* (Lahore, Ahmadiyya, 1944).

RECITING THE QUR'AN

Many Hadith passages indicate that the memorization and recitation of Qur'anic verses was an expected form of piety for Muslims during Muhammad's life. Muhammad him-self ritually recited its passages. Special reciters memorized the Qur'an's entirety and recited it daily. At least one function of recitation was to preserve its content, as illus-trated in the following Hadith passage: "The Prophet heard a reciter reciting the Qur'an in the mosque at night. The Prophet said, May Allah bestow his mercy on him, as he has reminded me of such-and-such verses of such-and-such surahs, which I missed!" (Sahih al-Bukhari, 6:562). *Recitation was also a daily ritual for lay people: "The Prophet said, if one recites the last two verses of surah-al-Baqara at night, it is sufficient for him (for that night)"* (Sahih al-Bukhari, 6:560). *In Qur'anic recitation, not only were the words memorized, but the tonal songlike vocalizations as well. The following describes the variety of vocalizations that were permitted.*

> Narrated Umar ibn Al-Khattab: I heard Hisham ibn Hakim reciting *surah* Al-Furqan during the lifetime of Allah's Apostle and I listened to his recitation and noticed that he recited in several different ways which Allah's Apostle had not taught me. I was about to jump over him during his prayer, but I controlled my temper, and when he had completed his prayer, I put his upper garment around his neck and seized him by it and said, "Who taught you this Surah which I heard you reciting?" He replied, "Allah's Apostle taught it to me." I said, "You have told a lie, for Allah's Apostle has taught it to me in a different way from yours." So I dragged him to Allah's Apostle and said (to Allah's Apostle), "I heard this person reciting Surah Al-Furqan in a way which you haven't taught me!" On that Allah's Apostle said, "Release him (O 'Umar)! Recite, O Hisham!" Then he recited in the same way as I heard him reciting. Then Allah's Apostle said, "It was revealed in this way," and added "Recite, O'Umar!" I recited it as he had taught me. Allah's Apostle then said, "It was revealed in this way. This Koran has been revealed to be recited in seven different ways, so recite of it whichever is easier for you."

Source: *Sahih al-Bukhari*, 6:514.

STONING OF ADULTEROUS JEWS

The Hadith *provides a narrative context for many Qur'anic passages, the meanings of which would otherwise be lost. For example,* surah 17:81 *states, "Truth has come and falsehood vanished. Falsehood is ever bound to vanish." Although the surrounding verses provide no context, the* Hadith *does: "Allah's Apostle entered Mecca (in the year of the conquest) and there were three-hundred and sixty idols around the Ka'bah. He then started hitting them with a stick in his hand and said, Truth has come and falsehood vanished. Falsehood is ever bound to vanish"* (Sahih al-Bukhari 6:244). *The following* Hadith *narrative sets the context for another equally obscure Qur'anic passage: "Bring the Torah and read it, if what you say be true"* (surah 3:93). *The* Hadith *story, from about the fourth year of the migration to Medina, highlights the interaction between the Jews and early Muslims, Muhammad's administrative function in settling legal questions, and the prohibition against adultery.*

> Narrated Abdullah ibn Umar: The Jews brought to the Prophet a man and a woman from among them who had committed illegal sexual intercourse. The Prophet said to them, "How do you usually punish the one amongst you who has committed illegal sexual intercourse?" They replied, "We blacken their faces with coal and beat them." He said, "Don't you find

the order of Ar-Rajm (i.e., stoning to death) in the Torah?" They replied, "We do not find anything in it." 'Abdullah ibn Salam (after hearing this conversation) said to them, "You have told a lie! Bring here the Torah and recite it if you are truthful." (So the Jews brought the Torah.) And the religious teacher who was teaching it to them put his hand over the Verse of Ar-Rajm and started reading what was written above and below the place hidden with his hand, but he did not read the Verse of Ar-Rajm. 'Abdullah ibn Salam removed his (i.e., the teacher's) hand from the Verse of Ar-Rajm and said, "What is this?" So when the Jews saw that Verse, they said, "This is the Verse of Ar-Rajm." So the Prophet ordered the two adulterers to be stoned to death, and they were stoned to death near the place where biers are placed near the Mosque. I saw her companion (i.e., the adulterer) bowing over her so as to protect her from the stones.

Source: *Sahih al-Bukhari,* 6:79.

DEATH OF MUHAMMAD

After complaining of severe headaches, Muhammad died in the house of his favorite wife, A'isha. The Hadith narratives surrounding his death describe his companions' concern about a possible successor to Muhammad and their fear that Muhammad might become an object of worship. The following account of Muhammad's death, attributed to A'isha, maintains that Muhammad appointed no successor.

A'isha, the wife of the Prophet said, When the ailment of Allah's Apostle became aggravated, he requested his wives to permit him to be treated in my house, and they gave him permission. He came out (to my house), walking between two men with his feet dragging on the ground. . . . When Allah's Apostle entered my house and his disease became aggravated, he said, "Pour on me the water of seven waterskins, the mouths of which have not been untied, so that I may give advice to the people." So we let him sit in a big basin . . . and then started to pour water on him from these waterskins till he started pointing to us with his hands intending to say "You have done your job". . . . Then he went out to the people and led them in prayer and preached to them. . . .

When Allah's Apostle became ill seriously, he started covering his face with his woolen sheet, and when he felt short of breath, he removed it from his face and said, "That is so! Allah's curse be on the Jews and the Christians, as they took the graves of their prophets as (places of worship)," intending to warn (the Muslims) of what they had done. . . . I argued with Allah's Apostle repeatedly about the matter (i.e., his order that Abu Bakr should lead the people in prayer in his place when he was ill), and what made me argue so much was that it never occurred to my mind that after the Prophet, the people would ever love a man who had taken his place, and I felt that anybody standing in his place would be a bad omen to the people, so I wanted Allah's Apostle to give up the idea of choosing Abu Bakr (to lead his people in prayer).

Narrated A'isha: It was one of favors towards me that Allah's Apostle expired in my house on the day of my turn while leaning against my chest and Allah made my saliva mix with his saliva at his death. 'Abdur-Rahman entered upon me with a Siwak in his hand and I was supporting (the back of) Allah's Apostle (against my chest). I saw the Prophet looking at the Siwak and I knew that he loved the Siwak, so I said (to him), "Shall I take it for you?" He nodded in agreement. So I took it and it was too stiff for him to use, so I said, "Shall I soften it for you?" He nodded his approval. So I softened it and he cleaned his teeth with it. In front to him there was a jug or a tin containing water. He started dipping his hand in the water and rubbing his face with it. He said, "None has the right to be worshipped except Allah. Death has its agonies." He then lifted his hands (towards the sky) and started saying, "With the highest companion," till he expired and his hand dropped down.

Narrated Al-Aswad: It was mentioned in the presence of A'isha that the Prophet had appointed Ali as successor by will. Thereupon she said, "Who said so? I saw the Prophet while I was supporting him against my chest. He asked for a tray, and then fell on one side and expired, and I did not feel it. So how (do the people say) he appointed Ali as his successor?"

Source: *Sahih al-Bukhari*, 5:727, 730, 736.

FIRST COMPILATION OF THE QUR'AN

During Muhammad's life, isolated Qur'anic verses were preserved in writing, but the only complete copies existed in the memories of the reciters. The following describes the circumstances surrounding the first written compilation of the Qur'an, initiated by the first Caliph, Abu Bakr, a year after Muhammad's death.

Narrated Zayd ibn Thabit: Abu Bakr As-Siddiq sent for me when the people of Yama-ma had been killed (i.e., a number of the Prophet's Companions who fought against Musailama). (I went to him) and found Umar ibn Al-Khattab sitting with him. Abu Bakr then said (to me), "Umar has come to me and said, 'Casualties were heavy among the Qurra of the Koran (i.e., those who knew the Koran by heart) on the day of the Battle of Yamama, and I am afraid that more heavy casualties may take place among the Qurra on other battlefields, whereby a large part of the Koran may be lost. Therefore I suggest you (Abu Bakr) order that the Koran be collected.' I said to Umar, 'How can you do something which Allah's Apostle did not do?' Umar said, 'By Allah, that is a good project.' Umar kept on urging me to accept his proposal till Allah opened my chest for it and I began to realize the good in the idea which Umar had realized." Then Abu Bakr said (to me), "You are a wise young man and we do not have any suspicion about you, and you used to write the Divine

Inspiration for Allah's Apostle. So you should search for (the fragmentary scripts of) the Koran and collect it (in one book)." By Allah! If they had ordered me to sift one of the mountains, it would not have been heavier for me than this ordering me to collect the Koran. . . . So I started looking for the Koran and collecting it from (what was written on) palm-leaf stalks, thin white stones and also from the men who know it by heart, till I found the last verse of Surah At-Tauba (Repentance) Abi Khuzaima Al-Ansari. . . . Then the complete manuscripts (copy) of the Koran remained with Abu Bakr till he died, then with Umar till the end of his life, and then with Hasfa, the daughter of Umar.

Source: *Sahih al-Bukhari*, 6:509.

DEFINITIVE COMPILATION OF THE QUR'AN

In spite of the existence of Abu Bakr's single written compilation of the Qur'an, the Qur'an was still principally transmitted through memorized accounts and scattered written verses. As conflicting versions arose, the third Caliph, Uthman, authorized a definitive written edition 24 years after Muhammad's death. The following recounts the story of Uthman's edition.

Narrated Anas ibn Malik: Hudhaifa ibn Al-Yaman came to 'Uthman at the time when the people of Sha'm and the people of Iraq were waging war to conquer Arminya and Adharbijan. Hudhaifa was afraid of their (the people of Sha'm and Iraq) differences in the recitation of the Koran, so he said to 'Uthman, "O the chief of the Believers! Save this nation before they differ about the Book (Koran) as Jews and the Christians did before." So 'Uthman sent a message to Hafsa saying, "Send us the manuscripts of the Koran so that we may compile the Koranic materials in perfect copies and return the manuscripts to you." Hafsa sent it to 'Uthman. 'Uthman then ordered Zayd ibn Thabit, 'Abdullah ibn Az-Zubair, Sa'id ibn Al-As and 'Abdur-Rahman ibn Harith ibn Hisham to rewrite the manuscripts in perfect copies. 'Uthman said to the three Quaishi men, "In case you disagree with Zayd ibn Thabit on any point in the Koran, then write it in the dialect of Quraish as the Koran was revealed in their tongue." They did so, and when they had written many copies, 'Uthman returned the original manuscripts to Hafsa. 'Uthman sent to every Muslim province one copy of what they had copied, and ordered that all the other Qur'anic materials, whether written in fragmentary manuscripts or whole copies, be burnt. Zayd ibn Thabit added, "A verse from Surah Ahzab was missed by me when we copied the Koran, and I used to hear Allah's Apostle reciting it. So we searched for it and found it with Khuzaima ibn Thabit Al-Ansari. (That verse was): "Among the believers are men who have been true in their covenant with Allah" (22:23).

Source: *Sahih al-Bukhari*, 6:510.

SUNNI AND SHI'I WRITINGS

SUNNI ISLAMIC LAW

Ibn Idris al-Shafi'i (767–820) was the foremost scholar of early Islamic law. He is most well known for his analysis of the "four roots of jurisprudence." That is, legal questions are resolved by appealing firstly to the Qur'an, secondly to the Sunna, thirdly to consensus, and lastly to analogical reasoning. After his death Shafi'i's disciples founded the Shafi'ite school; his penetrating analysis of the four roots was also adopted by the other schools of Islamic Law. The following from Shafi'i's Risala discusses the use of consensus, analogy, and personal reasoning in legal questions.

Chapter 11, On Consensus *(ijma)*.

480. Shafi'i said: Some asked me: I have understood your doctrine concerning God's commands and His Apostle's orders that he who obeys God obeys His Apostle, [for] God has imposed [on men] the duty of obeying His Apostle, and that the proof for what you held has been established that it would be unlawful for a Muslim who has known the Book [of God] and the sunna [i.e., Hadith tradition of the Prophet] to give an opinion at variance with either one, for I know that this [i.e., acceptance of the Book and the sunna] is a duty imposed by God. But what is your proof for accepting the consensus of the public [on matters] concerning which no explicit command of God nor any [sunna] related on the authority of the Prophet is to be found? Do you assert, with others, that the consensus of the public should always be based on an established sunna even if it were not related [on the authority of the Prophet]?

481. [Shafi'i] replied: That on which the public are agreed and which, as they assert, was related from the Apostle, that is so. As to that which the public do not relate [from the Prophet], which they may or may not relate as a tradition from the Prophet, we cannot consider it as related on the authority of the Prophet—because one may relate only what he has heard, for no one is permitted to relate [on the authority of the Prophet] information which may or may not be true. So we accept the decision of the public because we have to obey their authority, and we know that wherever there are sunnas of the Prophet, the public cannot be ignorant of them, although it is possible that some are, and we know that the public can neither agree on anything contrary to the sunna of the Prophet nor on an error.

484. He asked: What is the meaning of the Prophet's order to follow the community?

487. [Shafi'i] replied: When the community spread in the lands [of Islam], nobody was able to follow its members who had been dispersed and mixed with other believers and unbelievers, pious and impious. So it was meaningless to follow the community [as a whole], because it was

impossible [to do so], except for what the [entire] community regarded as lawful or unlawful [orders] and [the duty] to obey these [orders].

He who holds what the Muslim community holds shall be regarded as following the community, and he who holds differently shall be regarded as opposing the community he was ordered to follow. So the error comes from separation: but in the community as a whole there is no error concerning the meaning of the Qur'an, the sunna, and analogy.

Chapter 12, On Analogy *(qiyas).*

488. He asked: On what ground do you hold that [on matters] concerning which no text is to be found in the Book, nor a sunna or consensus, recourse should be had to analogy? Is there any binding text for analogical deduction?

489. [Shafi'i] replied: If analogy were [stated] in the text of the Book or the sunna, such a text should be called either God's command or the Apostle's order rather than analogy.

490. He asked: What is analogy? Is it personal reasoning [ijtihad], or are the two different?

491. [Shafi'i] replied: They are two terms with the same meaning. . . .

493. On all matters touching the [life of a] Muslim there is either a bonding decision or an indication as to the right answer. If there is a decision, it should be followed; if there is no indication as to the right answer, it should be sought by personal reasoning, and personal reasoning is analogy [qiyas].

496. [He asked]: If [legal] knowledge is derived through analogy—provided it is rightly applied—should [the scholars] who apply analogy agree on most [of the decision], although we may find them disagreeing on some?

497. [Shafi'i replied]: Analogy is of two kinds: the first, if the case in question is similar to the original meaning [of the precedent], no disagreement on this kind [is permitted]. The second, if the case in question is similar to several precedents, analogy must be applied to the precedent nearest in resemblance and most appropriate. But those who apply analogy are likely to disagree [in their answers].

Chapter 13, On Personal Reasoning *(ijtihad).*

534. He asked: On what ground do you hold that [the exercise of] personal reasoning [ijtihad] is permitted in addition to what you have already explained?

535. [Shafi'i] replied: It is on the basis of God's saying: "from whatever place thou issuest, turn thy face in the direction of the Sacred Mosque; and wherever you may be, turn your faces in its direction" [Koran. II. 145]. Regarding him who [wishes to] face the Sacred Mosque [in

prayer] and whose residence is at a distance from it, [legal] knowledge instructs [us] that he can seek the right direction through ijtihad on the basis of certain indications [guiding] toward it. For he who is under an obligation to face the Sacred House and does not know whether he is facing the right or wrong direction may be able to face the right one through certain indications known to him [which helps him] to face it as accurately as he can, just as another person may know other indications which help to orient him [in the right direction], although the direction sought by each person may be different from that sought by the other.

Source: Ibn Idris al-Shafi'i, *Risala,* 480, 481, 484, 487, 488–491, 493, 496, 497, 534, 535, from *Islamic Jurisprudence: Shafi'i's Risala,* tr. Majid Khadduri, (Baltimore: Johns Hopkins Press, 1961).

SUNNI CREED

Born in Basra, in what is now Iraq, al-Ash'ari (873–935) was a prominent theologian in the Sunni Hanbalite school of Islamic law. He argued that God's acts are utterly beyond rational comprehension and that, if God willed, he could send devout believers to hell. Al-Ash'ari is credited with having formulated the first systematic creed of Islam, which is presented below. Bracketed references are to passages in the Qur'an.

The essence of our belief is that we confess faith in Allah, His angels, His Books, His Messengers, the revelation of Allah, and what the trustworthy have handed down on the authority of Allah's Messenger, rejecting none of them.

We confess that Allah is One—There is none worthy of worship but He—unique, eternal, possessing neither consort nor child; and that Muhammad is His servant and Messenger, who He sent with the guidance and the real Religion; and that Paradise is real and Hell is real; and that there is no doubt regarding the Coming Hour; and that Allah will raise up all those who are in the graves; and that Allah is on His throne (as He has said, "The Merciful is on the Throne"—[20:4]); and that He has a face (as He has said, "but the Face of your Lord shall abide resplendent with majesty and glory"—[55:27]); and that He has two hands, bila kaifa (without asking how?) (as He has said, "I have created with my two hands,"—[38:75] and he has said, "nay! Outstretched are both His hands"—[5:69]); and that He has an eye, without asking how (as He said, "under Our eyes it floated on"—[54:14]), and that anybody who thinks that the names of Allah are other than He is in error; and that Allah has Knowledge (as He has said, "in His knowledge He sent it down,"—[4:164]), and as He said, "And no female conceives and brings forth without His knowledge"—[35:12]), we also assert that Allah has hearing and sight, and we do not deny it as the Mu'tazila, the Jahmiyyah, and the Khaarijites deny it; and we assert that Allah has Prowess (Quwwah) (as He has said, "saw they not that Allah

Who created them was mightier than they in Prowess?"—[41:14]); and we believe that the Word of Allah is uncreated, and that He has created nothing without first saying to it, "Be!," And it is as he has said, "Our word to a thing when we will it is but to say, 'Be!,' and it is"—[16:42]), and that there is no good or evil on earth save what Allah wishes: and that things exist by Allah's wish; and that not a single person has the capacity to do anything until Allah causes him to act, and we are not independent of Allah, nor can we pass beyond the range of Allah's knowledge; and that there is no creator save Allah, and the works of human beings are things created and decreed by Allah (as He had said, "Allah has created you and what you make"—[37:94]); and that human beings have not the power to create anything, but are themselves created (as He has said, "Is there a creator other than Allah?"—[35:3], and as He has said, "they create nothing, but are themselves created,"—[16:20] and as he said, "Shall He who creates be as He who creates not?,"—[16:17] and as He has said, "were they created by nothing or were they themselves the creators?,"—[52:35] for this is mentioned in Allah's Book frequently); and that Allah favors the Believers by granting them obedience to Him, is gracious to them, considers them, does what is salutary for them, guides them; whereas He causes the Disbelievers to stray, does not guide them, does not give them the grace to believe.

As the deviators and rebels think for if He were gracious to them and did what is salutary for them they would be sound; and if He guided them, they would be guided; as He has said, "He whom Allah guides is the guided and they whom he misleads will be the lost"—[7:177], and that Allah has power to do what is salutary for the infidels and be gracious to them, that they may become believers, nevertheless He wills that they be infidels, as He knows; and that He forsakes them and seals up their hearts; and that good and evil are dependent upon the general and the particular decrees of Allah, His sweet and His bitter; and we know that what passes us by was not to befall us, and what befalls us was not to pass us by; and that human beings do not control for themselves what is hurtful or what is helpful, except what Allah wishes; and that we ought to commit our affairs to Allah and assert our complete need of and dependence upon Him.

We believe, too, that the Qur'an is the uncreated word of Allah, and that he who believes that the Qur'an is created is an infidel.

We hold that Allah will be seen in the next world by sight (as the moon is seen on the night it is full, so shall the faithful see Him, as we are told in the traditions that come down on the authority of Allah's Messenger; and we believe that the infidels will be veiled from Him when the faithful see Him in Paradise (as Allah has said, "Yea, they shall be shut out as by a veil from their Lord on that day"—[83:15], and that Musa asked Allah for the sight of Him in this world, and "Allah manifested Himself to the mountain" and "turned it to dust,"—[7:139], and taught Musa by it that he should not see Him in this world.

It is opinion that we ought not to declare a single one of the people of the Qibla an infidel for a sin of which he is guilty, such as fornication or theft or the drinking of wine, as the Kharijites hold, thinking that such people are infidels; but we believe that he who commits any of these mortal sins, such as fornication or theft or the like presumptuously declaring it lawful and not acknowledging that forbidden is an infidel.

We believe that Islam is more extensive than faith, and that faith is not the whole of Islam.

We hold that Allah changes men's hearts, and that their hearts are between two of Allah's fingers, and that Allah will place the heavens on a finger and the earth on a finger, as we are told in the tradition that comes down on the authority of Allah's Messenger.

We hold that we ought not to relegate any of the Monotheists, or those who hold fast to the faith, to Paradise or to Hell, save him in whose favor the Messenger of Allah has borne witness concerning Paradise; and we hope that sinners will attain to Paradise, but we fear that they will be punished in Hell.

We believe that Allah, by the intercession of Muhammad, Allah's Messenger, will bring forth a people from Hell after they have been burned to ashes, in accordance with what we are told in the traditions related on the authority of Allah's messenger.

We believe in the punishment of the grave, and the Pool, and hold that the Scales are real, and the Bridge is real, and the resurrection after death is real, and that Allah will line up human beings at the Station, and settle the account with the faithful.

We believe that faith consists of words and deeds, and is subject to increase and decrease; and we receive the authentic traditions regarding it related on the authority of the Messenger of Allah, which the trustworthy have transmitted, one just man from another, until the tradition goes back to the Messenger of Allah.

We believe in affection towards our forebears in faith, whom Allah chose for the company of His Prophet, we praise them with the praise wherewith Allah praised them, and are attached to them all.

We believe that the excellent Imam, after the Messenger of Allah, is Abu Bakr the Veracious, and that Allah strengthened the Religion by him and gave him success against the renegades, and the Muslims promoted him to the imamate just as the Messenger of Allah made him leader of prayer, and they all named him the caliph of Allah's Messenger; then after him came 'Umar Ibn Al-Kattab; then Uthmaan bin Affaan (those who fought with him wrongfully and unrighteously); then 'Ali Ibn Abi taalib; wherefore these are the Imams after the Messenger of Allah, and their caliphate of Prophecy.

We bear witness concerning Paradise in favor of the ten in whose favour the Messenger of Allah bore witness to it, and we attached to all the Companions of the Prophet and avoid what was disputed among them.

We hold that the four Imam are orthodox, divinely guided, excellent caliphs, unmatched by others in excellence.

We accept all the traditions for which the traditionalists vouch: the descent in to the lower heavens, and the Lord's saying, "Is there any who has a request? Is there any who ask forgiveness?," and the other things they relate and vouch for; dissenting from what the deviators and followers of error assert.

We rely, in that wherein we differ, upon our Lord's book, and the sunnah of our Prophet and the unanimous consent (ijma) of the Muslims and what it signifies; and we do not introduce into Allah's religion innovations that Allah does not allow, nor do we believe of Allah what we do not know.

We believe that Allah will come in the day of resurrection (as He has said, "and thy Lord shall come and the Angels rank"—[80:23]); and that Allah is near His servants, even as He wishes (as He has said, "We are nearer to him than his Jugular vein,"—[50:15] and as He said, "He came nearer and approached and was at the distance of two bows or even closer"—[53:8,9]).

It belongs to our religion to observe the Friday Assembly, and the feasts, and the remaining prayers and public devotions under the leadership of every pious man or impious (as it is related of 'Abd Allah ibn Umar that he used to pray behind al-Hajjaj ibn-yusuf); and we believe that the wiping of the sandals is a sunnah at home and in travel, contrarily to the belief of anybody who denies it; and we approve prayer for the welfare of the imams of the Muslims, and the confession of their imamate; and we regard it as error on anybody's part to "going out" against them when they have clearly abandoned rectitude; and we believe in abstinence from "going out" against them with the sword, and abstinence from fighting in civil commotions.

We confess the going forth of Antichrist (ad-Dajjaal), as it is contained in the tradition related on the authority of Allah's Messenger.

We believe in the punishment of the grave, and in Munkar and Nakir, and their interrogation of those who are buried in the graves.

We accept the Hadith of Ascension (mi'raj) and regard as authentic many of the visions of sleep, and confess there are interpretations to them.

We approve alms on behalf of the Muslim dead, and prayer for their welfare; and we believe that Allah helps them by it.

We accept it as true that there are sorcerers and sorcery in the world, and that sorcery exists in the world.

We believe in praying for those of the people of the Qibla who are dead, the pious and the impious, and in the lawfulness of being their heirs.

We confess that Paradise and Hell are created; and that he who dies or is slain is at his appointed term; and that sustenance is from Allah who gives it to His creatures in the permitted and the forbidden; and that Satan Whispers to man and causes him to doubt and infects him, contrarily to the belief of the Mu'tazilah and the Jahmiyyahh (as Allah has said, "they who swallow down usury shall arise in the resurrection only as he arises who Satan hath infected by his touch," —[2:276] and as he has said, "against the mischief of the stealthily withdrawn whisperer, who whispers in man's breast against jinn and men."—[114:46]).

We believe that Allah can design particularly for the just signs he manifests to them.

Our belief regarding the children of the polytheists is that Allah will kindle a fire for them in the next world, and then will say to them, "rush into it!," as the tradition tells us concerning it.

We hold that Allah knows what human beings are doing, and they are going to do, what has been, what is, and what is not would have been if it had been.

We believe in obedience to the Imams and in the sincere counsel of the Muslims.

We approve separation from every innovation tendency, and the avoidance of the people of straying impulses.

Source: Islamicweb.com.

SHI'I CREED

Eighty percent of Shi'i Muslims belong to the Twelver sect (Ithna 'Asha-Riyyah). *The most distinctive feature of Twelver theology is the belief in the twelve Imams* (Ali *and eleven of his descendants*) *who intermediate between God and humans. The Imams carried both a spiritual and civil authority derived from and virtually paralleling that of Muhammad. The following selections concerning the Imam are from one of the earliest Shi'i creeds, the* Risalatu'l-I'tiqadat, *compiled by Shi'i theologian ibn Babawayhi al-Qummi (918–991). Ibn Babawayhi was also a collector of Hadith and assembled one of the Four Books of Shi'i Hadith.*

And the Prophet said: The Imams after me are twelve, the first of them is the Prince of Believers, 'Ali ibn Abi Talib, and the last of them is the Mahdi (rightly minded), the *Qa'im* (the upholder of the true religion); obedience to them is obedience to me and disobedience to them is disobedience to me; and he who denies one of them has verily denied me.

[Concerning the first eleven Imam] the Prince of Believers [Ali ibn Abi Talib, the first Imam], on whom be peace, was murdered by 'Abdu'r-Rahman ibn Muljam al-Muradi, may Allah curse him, and he was buried in Ghari. And Hasan ibn 'ali [the second Imam], on both of whom be peace,—he was poisoned by his wife Ja'da bint Ash'ath of Kinda, may Allah curse them both, and he died on account of that. And Husayn ibn 'Ali [the third Imam] was slain at Karbala. His murderer was Sinan ibn Anas an-Nakha'i, the curse of Allah on them both. And Ali ibn Husayn, the Sayyid Zaynu'l-Abidin [the fourth Imam], was poisoned by al-Walid ibn 'Abdu'l-Malik, Allah cursed him. And Muhammad al-Baqir ibn 'Ali [the fifth Imam] was poisoned by Ibrahim ibn al-Walid, may Allah curse him. And Ja'far as-Sadiq [the sixth Imam] was poisoned by Abu Ja'far al-Mansur ad-Dawaniqi, may Allah curse him. And Musa al-Kazim ibn Ja'far [the seventh Imam] was poisoned by Harunu'r-Rashid, may Allah curse him. And 'Ali ar-Rida ibn Musa [the eighth Imam] was poisoned by Ma'mun, may Allah curse him. And Abu Ja'far Muhammad at-Taqi ibn 'Ali [the ninth Imam] was poisoned by al-Mu'tasim, may Allah curse him.

And 'Ali an-Naqi ibn Muhammad [the tenth Imam] was poisoned by al-Mutawakkil, may Allah curse him. And Hasan al-Askari ibn 'Ali [the eleventh Imam] was poisoned by al-Mu'tamid, may Allah curse him.

And our belief is that these events actually occurred, and that there was no doubt in the minds of the people regarding the Imams' affairs, as some of those who exceed the bounds (of belief) allege. . . . And verily the Prophets and Imams, on whom be peace, had informed (people) that they would all be murdered.

[Concerning the twelfth Imam, Mahdi] we believe that the Proof of Allah in His earth and His vicegerent (*khalifa*) among His slaves in this age of ours is the Upholder (*al-Qa'im*). . . . He it is concerning whose name and descent the Prophet was informed by Allah the Mighty and Glorious, and he it is *who will fill the earth with justice and equity, just as now it is full of oppression and wrong.* And he it is through whom Allah will make His faith manifest "in order to supersede all religion, though the polytheists may have disliked (it)." He it is whom Allah will make victorious over the whole world until from every place the call to prayer will be heard, and all religion will belong entirely to Allah, Exalted is He above all. He it is who is the Rightly Guided (*mahdi*), about whom the Prophet gave information that when he appears, Jesus, son of Mary, will descend upon the earth and pray behind him, and he who prays behind him is like one who prays behind the Prophet of Allah, because he is his vicegerent (*khalifa*). And we believe that there can be no Qa'im other than him; he may live in the state of occultation (as long as he likes); and were he to live in the state of occultation for the space of the existence of this world, there would nevertheless be no Qa'im other than him. For, the Prophet and the Imams have indicated him by his name and descent; him they appointed as their successor, and of him they gave glad tidings—the Blessings of Allah on all of them.

Source: Ibn Babawayh al-Qummi, *Risalatu'l-I'tiqadat* 140, 142, 147, from *A Shi'ite Creed,* tr. Asaf A. A. Fyzee (London: Oxford University Press, 1942).

SUFI WRITINGS

LOVE: RABI'A

Almost as old as Islam itself, Sufism is the mystical tradition of Islam that emphasizes mystical union with God. Rabi'a al-'Adawiya (717–801) was one of the earliest and most admired Sufis and is sometimes referred to as the **Muslim St. Teresa.** *She was kidnapped as a girl, sold into slavery, and later freed because of her piety. Thereafter she lived as an ascetic with a small group of followers. Although she did not write systematic treatises on Sufism, her sayings were passed down to later generations of Sufis who recorded them and used them as sounding boards for their own mystical ideas. Her key theological contribution is the notion of unconditional love of God (mahabbah), which parallels the Hindu notion of* bhakti *or Christian notion of* agape.

Abd Allah b. Isa said: I entered Rabi'a's presence and I saw the light on her face, and she used to weep much, and a man related of her that at every mention of fire (representing the punishment of the unrepentant sinner), she swooned, and I heard the falling of her tears on the ground like the sound of water filling a vessel. . . . I came into Rabi'a's presence and she was worshipping, and when I reached my place, she raised her head, and lo, the place of her worship was like a marsh from her tears and I saluted her. Then she received me and said, "O my son, do you need anything?" and I said, "I came to you to greet you," and she wept and said, "May God censure thee!" Then she rose up for the ritual prayer and said, "I ask forgiveness of God for my lack of sincerity when I say those words "I ask forgiveness of God."

It is related that at one time she saw someone who had a bandage bound about his head. She said, "Why is this bandage bound round your head?" He said, "My head is paining me." Rabi'a asked him how old he was. "Thirty years old," he replied. She asked him, "Were you in pain and trouble for the greater part of your life?" "No," he answered. Then she said, "For thirty years (God) has kept your body fit and you have never bound upon it the bandage of gratitude, but for one night of pain in your head you bind it with the bandage of complaint."

They told us that Rabi'a al-'Adawiya once said: I praised God one night with the praises of dawn, then I slept and I saw a bright green tree, indescribable in its size and beauty, and lo, upon it were three kinds of fruit, unknown to me among the fruits of this world, like virgins' breasts, white, red and yellow, and they shone like spheres and suns in the green spaces of the tree, and I admired them and said, "Whose is this?" and one said to me, "This is yours, for your praises aforetime." Then I began to walk round it, and lo, under it were eighteen fruits on the ground, of the color of gold, and I said, "If only these fruits were with the fruits on the tree, it would surely be better." That personage said to me: "They would have been there, but that you, when you offered your praises, were thinking, 'Is the dough leavened or not?' and this fruit fell off."

Some people were speaking in Rabi'a's presence of a devotee, who was known to be holy and in the favor of God, and who lived on what he collected from the refuse-heap of one of our kings, and a man said in her hearing, "What harm would there be in this, if he is in favor with God, and he should ask of him to provide him with food by some other means?" and Rabi'a said to him, "Be silent, O worthless one, have you not realized that the saints of God are satisfied with Him, that they accept his will even if he takes from them their means of livelihood, so long as it is he who chooses this for them?

I have loved you with two loves, a selfish love and a love that is worthy of you. As for the love which is selfish, I occupy myself therein with remembrance of you to the exclusion of all others. As for that which is worthy of you, therein you raise the veil that I may see you. Yet is there no praise to me in this or that, but the praise is to you, whether in that or this.

Source: Rabi'a al-'Adawiya, selected sayings, from *Rabi'a: The Life and Work of Rabi'a,* Margaret Smith (London: Cambridge University Press, 1928).

UNVEILING THE QUR'AN'S SECRETS: SANA'I OF GHAZNI

Born in the city Ghazni, in what is now Afghanistan, Sufi poet Sana'i (d. ca. 1150) composed The Enclosed Garden of the Truth *upon his return from a pilgrimage to Mecca and Medina. In the selections below from that work, he explains the urgency of disciplining oneself to be receptive to Allah's message. He warns, though, not to confuse the words of the Qur'an with its hidden and secret meaning. As beautiful as the words themselves are, there is a deeper content that can only be grasped by the soul, and not through the intellect.*

Parable of the Schoolboy. If a boy is unable to learn his task, hear at once what it is that he wants; be kind to him and treat him tenderly; do not make him grieve in helpless expectation; at such a time give him sweetmeats in his lap to comfort him, and do not treat him harshly. But if he will not read, at once send for the strap. Take hold of his ears and rub them hard. Threaten him with the schoolmaster and say that will have strict orders to punish him—that he will shut him up in a rat-house, and the head rat will strangle him. In the path that leads to the life to come, do not be less apt than a boy to receive admonition. Eternity is your sweet-meat. Hurry, then, and you can obtain paradise for the price of two rak'ahs [i.e., a cycle in the Salah prayer ritual]. Otherwise the rat-house will for you be Hell. It will be your tomb which meets you on your way to that other mansion. Go to the writing-school of the prophets for a time. Do not choose this folly for yourself, this affliction. Read just one tablet of the religion of the prophets. Since you know nothing about this, go, read and learn, that happily you may become their friend and may happily escape from this stupidity. In this corrupt and baleful world do not think that there is anything worse than stupidity.

The Secret Qur'an. The tongue cannot tell the secret of the Qur'an, for His intimates keep it concealed. The Qur'an indeed knows its own secret; hear it from itself, for itself knows it. Except by the soul's eye no one knows the measurer of words from the true reader of the Qur'an. I will not take upon myself to say that you truly know the Qur'an though you are Uthman [the third Caliph]. The world is like the summer's heat, its people like drunkards in it, all wandering in the desert of indifference. Death is the shepherd, and men his flock. In this waste of desire and wretchedness the hot sand appears to be running water. The Qur'an is like the cool water of the Euphrates, while you are like a thirsty sinner on the plain of the Judgement. You should hold the letter and Qur'an as a cup and its water. Drink the water, but do not gaze on the vessel. . . . In a cry of anguish, the suffering of a pure heart will tell the secret of the pure Qur'an. How can reason discover its interpretation? Take a delight in it and you will discover its inmost secret. . . . The letter may be uttered by the tongue, its soul can only be read by the soul. The letter is like the shell, and the true Qur'an is the pearl; the heart of the free-born does not desire the shell. . . . when the soul recites the Qur'an it enjoys a luscious morsel. Whoever hears it, mends his ragged robe. The words, the voice, and the letters of the verses are like three stalks in bowls of vegetables. Though the husk is neither fair nor sweet, it still guards the kernel. . . . When the day of true religion dawns, the night of thought, fancy and sense will fly away. When the veiled ones of the unseen world see that you are stainless, they lead you the invisible abode and reveal to you their faces.

Disclosing to you the secret of the Qur'an, they will withdraw the veil of letters. The earthy will have a reward of earth, but the pure will see purity. An understanding of the Qur'an does not dwell in the brain where pride starts up. The ass is as dumb as a mere stone, and does not lend his ear to the secret of God's word; he turns away from hearing the Qur'an and pays no heed to the sura's secret. But if your mind is disciplined towards God, it will discover in the sura the secret of the Qur'an.

Source: Adapted from Sana'i of Ghazni, *The First Book of the Hadiquatu'l-haqiqat; or, The Enclosed Garden of the Truth*, tr. J. Stephenson, Calcutta: Baptist Mission Press, 1910.

SUFI PATH: AL-GHAZALL

Abu Hamid al-Ghazali (1058–1111) was a scholar of Islamic law and philosopher who ultimately rejected academic approaches to truth in favor of immediate mystical experience. The following is from al-Ghazali's biography, Deliverer from Error, *in which he describes his initial acquaintance with Sufism.*

When God in the abundance of his mercy had healed me of this malady, I ascertained that those who are engaged in the search for truth may be divided into three groups. (1) Scholastic theologians, who profess to follow theory and speculation. (2) The philosophers, who profess to rely upon formal logic. (3) The sufis, who call themselves the elect of God and possessors of intuition and knowledge of the truth by means of ecstasy. "The truth," I said to myself, must be found among these three classes of men who devote themselves to the search for it. If it escapes them, one must give up all hopes of attaining it. . . . Determined to follow these paths and to search out these systems to the bottom, I proceeded with my investigation in the following order: Scholastic theology; philosophical systems; and, finally Sufism. . . .

When I had finished my examination of these doctrines [of the philosophers], I applied myself to the study of Sufism. I saw that in order to understand it thoroughly one must combine theory with practice. The aim which the Sufis set before them is as follows: to free the soul from the tyrannical yoke of the passions, to deliver it from its wrong inclinations and evil instincts, in order that in the purified heart there should only remain room for God and for the invocation of his holy name.

As it was more easy to learn their doctrine than to practice it, I studied first of all those of their books which contain it. . . . I acquired a thorough knowledge of their researches, and I learned all that was possible to learn of their methods by study and oral teaching. It became clear to me that the last stage could not be reached by mere instruction, but only by transport, ecstasy, and the transformation of the moral being.

Ten years passed in this manner. During my successive periods of meditation there were revealed to me things impossible to recount. All that I shall say for the edification of the reader is this: I learned from a sure source that the Sufis are the true pioneers on the path of God. There is nothing more beautiful than their life, nor more praiseworthy than their rule of conduct, nor purer than their morality. . . . In a word, what can one criticize in them? To purge the heart of all that does not belong to God is the first step in their cathartic method. The drawing upon of the heart by prayer is the keystone of it, as the cry "God is great" is the keystone of prayer, and the last stage of being lost in God. I say the last state, with reference to what may be reached by an effort of will; but, to tell the truth, it is only the first stage in the life of contemplation, the vestibule by which the initiated enter.

From the time that they set out on this path, they begin to have revelations. They come to see in the waking state angels and souls of prophets. They hear their voices and wise counsels. By means of this contemplation of heavenly forms and images they rise by degrees to heights which human language cannot reach, which one cannot even indicate without falling into great and inevitable errors. The degree of proximity to Deity which they attain is regarded by some as intermixture of being (*haloul*), by others as identification (*ittihad*), by others as intimate union (*wasl*). But all these expressions are wrong. . . . In short, he who does not arrive at the intuition of these truths by means of ecstasy, knows only the *name* of inspiration. The miracles done by the saints are, in fact, merely the earliest forms of prophetic manifestation. Such was the state of the Apostle of God when, before receiving his commission, he retired to Mount Hira to give himself up to such intensity of prayer and meditation that the Arabs said, "Muhammad has become captivated of God."

This state, then, can be revealed to the initiated in ecstasy, and to him who is incapable of ecstasy, by obedience and attention, on condition that he frequents the society of Sufis till he arrives, so to speak, at the imitative initiation. Such is the faith which one can obtain by remaining among them, and intercourse with them is never painful.

Source: Abu Hamid al-Ghazali, *Deliverer from Error*, Sect. 78, 122–125, 132–135, adapted from *The Confessions of Al Ghazali*, tr. Claud Field (New York: E. P. Dutton and Company, 1909).

UNION AND SEPARATION: RUMI

The most widely acclaimed Sufi writer is Jalal ad-Din ar-Rumi (1207–1273), whose poetic work entitled The Masnawi *is often referred to as the Qur'an in Persian. Central to Rumi's writings are the paired notions of union and separation. That is, moments of the mystic's life consist of blissful union with God, whereas, of necessity, other moments involve separation. Separation frequently manifests itself in human pain and suffering. Rumi argues that such suffering must be understood in a larger context: The spiritual happiness we achieve in the state of union is accentuated by the suffering we experience while in separation. The following selections are from Rumi's* Masnawi *and his other epic writing, the* Diwan.

Only the imagination that has contemplated Unification, and then, after direct vision, has undergone separation;

Not a definitive separation, but one for a good purpose, since that station is secure from all separation;

In order to preserve the spiritualized body, the Sun pulls back from the snow for a moment. (*Masnawi* 6:4012–15)

At the time of union, only God knows what that Moon is! For even during separation, what incredible joy and expansion of spirit! (*Diwan* 30321)

Separation and parting from Thee is difficult, oh Beloved, especially after Thy embrace! (*Diwan* 13901)

If man should see himself at all, if he should see that his wound is deadly and gangrenous,

Then from such looking within, pain would arise, and pain would bring him out from behind the veil.

Until mothers feel the pain of childbirth, the child finds no way to be born.

The trust is within the heart and the heart is pregnant; all the exhortations of the saints act as a midwife.

The midwife says, "The woman has no pain. Pain is necessary, for it will open a way for the child."

He that is without pain is a brigand, for to be without pain is to say "I am God."

To say "I" at the wrong time is a curse, but to say it at the right time is a mercy. (*Masnawi* 2:2516–22)

The body is pregnant with the spirit, the body's suffering is the pain of childbirth—the coming of the embryo brings pain and torment for the woman.

Look not at the wine's bitterness, look at the joy of drunkards! Look not at the woman's affliction, look at the hope of the midwife! (*Diwan* 5990)

How much the Beloved made me suffer before this work settled into the eye's water and the liver's blood!

A thousand fires and smokes and heartaches—and its name is Love! A thousand pains and regrets and afflictions—and its name is Beloved!

Let every enemy of his own spirit set out to work! Welcome to the spirit's sacrifice and a pitiful death!

My heart keeps saying, "I suffer because of Him," and I keep laughing at its weak hypocrisy. (*Masnawi* 1:1773–82)

Union with this world is separation from that world. The health of this body is the sickness of the spirit.

It is hard to be separated from this caravanserai—so know that separation from that permanent abode is harder!

Since it is hard for you to be separated from the painting, think what it will be to be parted from the Painter!

Oh you who cannot bear to be without this despicable world! How can you bear to be without God, oh friend, how?

Since you cannot bear to be without this black water, how can you bear to be without God's fountain? . . .

If you should see the Beauty of the Loving God for one instant and throw your soul and existence into the fire,

Then having seen the glory and splendor of His proximity, you would see these sweet beverages as carrion. . . .

Strive quickly to find Self in selflessness—and God knows best the right course. (*Masnawi* 4:3209–13, 15–16, 18)

Source: Jalal ad-Din ar-Rumi, *Diwan* and *Masnawi* selections, from *The Sufi Path of Love: The Spiritual Teachings of Rumi*, tr. William C. Chittick (Albany: State University of New York Press, 1983), pp. 235–236.

GLOSSARY

Allah　Literally, "God"; the Muslim name for the single Deity who is creator and Judge.

Caliph　Literally, "Successor." The political successors to Muhammad according to the Sunni tradition.

Companions　*Sahaba* in Arabic; Muhammad's closest followers during his life who assumed leadership roles after his death.

Hadith　Literally, "Speech"; sacred collections of short narratives about Muhammad which are thought to have originated with his early companions.

Imam　Literally, "He" who stands before; spiritual leaders of the Shi'a tradition beginning with Ali and continuing through a line of his descendants.

Ka'bah　Literally, "Cube"; a cubelike building in the open-air Mosque of Mecca, which is the central shrine of Islam.

Qur'an　Also Qur'an, literally, to recite; Islam's most holy text, consisting of Muhammad's collected revelations.

Mahdi　Literally, "The Guided One"; the final and awaited Imam in Shi'a tradition who will establish an era of peace.

Muslim　Literally, "One Who Surrenders"; a follower of Islam.

Shi'a　Literally, "Separate Party"; branch of Islam, comprising 10 percent of all Muslims, whose members honor the spiritual leadership of Ali and the other Imams.

Sufi   Literally, "Wool Clad"; practitioners of Sufism, Islam's mystical tradition, which emphasizes the mystical union of the believer with God.

Sunni   From the Arabic *sunnah,* meaning custom; branch of Islam, comprising 90 percent of all Muslims, whose members accept the leadership role of the Caliphate.

Twelver   From the Arabic, *Ithna 'Ashariyya,* meaning followers of the twelve Imams; division of Shi'a Islam, comprising 80 percent of its number, whose members acknowledge the leadership of twelve specific Imams.

FURTHER READINGS

ABDUL-RAUF, MUHAMMAD. *Islam: Creed and Worship.* Washington: Islamic Center, 1975.

COULSON, N. A. *History of Islamic Law.* Edinburgh: University Press, 1964.

FARAH, CAESAR E. *Islam.* Hauppauge, NY: Barons, 1987.

HODGSON, G. S. *The Venture of Islam,* 3 vol. Chicago: Chicago University Press, 1974.

LEWIS, BERNARD, ed. *Islam and the Arab World.* New York: Knopf, 1976.

NIGOSIAN, S. A. *Islam: The Way of Submission.* Northants: Thorsons, 1987.

PETERS, F. E., ed. *A Reader on Classical Islam.* Princeton: Princeton University Press, 1994.

RIPPIN, ANDREW AND JAN KNAPPERT, eds. *Textual Sources for the Study of Islam.* Totowa NJ: Barnes and Noble, 1986.

SAVORY, R. M., ed. *Introduction to Islamic Civilisation.* Cambridge: Cambridge University Press, 1976.

SCHIMMEL, A. *Mystical Dimensions of Islam.* Chapel Hill: University of North Carolina Press, 1975.

SHAH, IDRIES. *The Way of the Sufi.* London: Penguin, 1968.

Baha'i Faith

INTRODUCTION

The Baha'i Faith began in middle nineteenth-century Persia, a Shi'i Islamic society. Founded by Baha'u'llah and his forerunner the Bab, developed and guided by his son, Abdu'l-Baha, and great-grandson, Shoghi Effendi, it is now widely recognized as an independent world religion. The Baha'i Faith emphasizes the unity of all religions and world peace. "To be a Baha'i," according to Abdu'l-Baha, "simply means to love all the world; to love humanity and try to serve it; to work for universal peace and universal brotherhood." Baha'i doctrine is sometimes expressed in the "three onenesses." (1) The oneness of God: There is a single and ultimately unknowable God who is given different names. The knowledge we do have of God derives from his various prophets who instruct us. (2) The oneness of humankind: There is a single human race, and we are all members of it. (3) The oneness of religion: All religions are unified insofar as they are each stages in God's revelatory plan.

Baha'i Founders

The Baha'i Faith is historically founded on the Babi religion, which in turn rests on the Shi'i Muslim doctrine of the Hidden Imam. According to this doctrine, the Mahdi, the final Imam—or spiritual successor to Ali—is alive, but was placed by God in a condition of occultation in which he can see others but others cannot see him (or at least they cannot recognize him). He will return at the end of time, take vengeance on the wicked, and initiate an era of peace. Shi'i Islam has numerous denominations and sects that have differing views of the status of the Imams in general and of the Mahdi. The nineteenth-century Shaykhi sect, founded by Shaykh (Sheik) Ahmad al-Ahsa'i (1753–1826), maintained that Imams have an almost divine status and that each generation needs a gate (Bab) as an intermediary between the Hidden Imam and believers. Although one of the Shaykhi leaders claimed to be guided by the Mahdi in his dreams, no one initially claimed to be the Bab himself.

The forerunner to the Baha'i Faith was affiliated with the Shaykhi sect—either formally or as a sympathizer. Sayyid Ali-Muhammad Shiraz (1819–1850) was born into a merchant family in south Persia; his father died soon after his birth, and he was raised by his uncle. He married at 22 and subsequently joined the Shaykhi. In 1844, while on a pilgrimage to Mecca, he claimed to be the Bab, which was a more extreme claim than his Shaykhi predecessors had made. It is this event which Baha'is designate as the beginning of their religion. Scholars believe that the Bab privately announced to his followers that he was the Mahdi himself; the public declaration of Babhood, though, was politically more safe to make. Even so, his declaration quickly attracted followers, but it also raised political concerns, and for the next six years—the remainder of his life—he was exiled or imprisoned. After his announcement, the Bab formed a religious group called the Babis. The first 18 of his followers were sent out as proselytizers. Later the Bab publicly claimed to be the Imam Mahdi himself, and in 1848, in an important work called the *Bayan,* he declared that he was a manifestation of God, superseding Muhammad. The *Bayan* also presents a constitution for the coming Babi state and a series of laws. In perhaps the most controversial section, it maintains that believers can take all possessions of nonbelievers. The severity of some of the Bab's laws dramatized his messianic role and rhetorically underscored his legislative authority. However, these laws were counterbalanced by others that prohibit harming or offending others, especially nonbelievers. In any event, only a few of the Bab's laws were ever implemented.

He summoned the Shah of Persia to acknowledge his authority, and in 1848 the Babis distanced themselves from Islam. The same year about 300 Babis set off on a march that prompted armed confrontation. They defended themselves, but were quickly crushed by the Persian government. Massive persecution of Babis followed, and the Bab was executed by a firing squad in 1850. Witnesses reported that he and a follower were suspended by rope. The first volley only severed their ropes and they dropped to the ground. Seeing this as a divine sign, the commander of the regiment withdrew the troops, but a new group of soldiers was brought in, and they finished the task. The Bab's body was secretly retrieved by his followers and, after a number of years, transported to its final resting place at the Mausoleum of the Bab in Haifa, Israel. His immediate successor as Babi leader was Mirza Yahya (Subh-i-Azal), who resided in Baghdad. Before the Bab died, he foretold of a leader, greater than himself, who would finish his work.

The Baha'i Faith's second founder was Baha'u'llah (1817–1892), an honorific title that means "Glory of God." Baha'u'llah, originally named Mirza Husayn-Ali Nur, was born in Tehran, the capital of Persia. He had no formal education and was the eldest son of a distinguished minister of state. When he was 22, his father died and he was left to manage the estate and care for his family. At age 26 (1844), he espoused Babism and became one of the Bab's earliest followers, although, as some Baha'i historians maintain, he never personally met the Bab. In 1852 a Babi named Sadiq attempted to assassinate the Iranian Shah in retaliation for the execution of the Bab. Sadiq and 80 others were killed, and many more were imprisoned or exiled. Baha'u'llah's property was confiscated and he was imprisoned for four months, after which he was exiled to Baghdad. Mirza Yahya (the Bab's provisional successor) went into hiding and made his way to Baghdad when he heard that Baha'u'llah was there. This initial period of exile lasted until 1863 and was relatively peaceful. Baha'u'llah retreated to the desert for two years (1854–1856), and when he returned he ably met challenges by the Muslim Mullahs in defense of Babism. He wrote several books while in Baghdad, the most important of these being *The Book of Certitude (Kitab-i-Iqan)*, which explained how prophets from one dispensation anticipate the prophets of the next.

In 1863 Baha'u'llah was summoned to Constantinople (Istanbul). While he was preparing for the journey, his house overflowed with well-wishers, and for 12 days he, and later his family, were compelled to camp in a garden, later named Ridvan (paradise). At this time he privately announced that he was the leader foretold by the Bab. As such, he declared himself to be the manifestation or appearance of God. This announcement is known to Baha'is as the Declaration at Ridvan, and is the basis of their most important festival, celebrated each year from April 21 to May 2. Baha'u'llah, his family, and 26 followers went to Constantinople, where they were confined to squalid conditions for four months, and then they moved to Adrianople (Edirne), Turkey, where they remained until 1868. There he attracted more followers and openly announced his mission. He wrote letters to the Shah and other world leaders, including Napoleon III, Pope Pius IX, Czar Nicholas II, and Queen Victoria. In 1868, a long-standing tension between Baha'u'llah and Mirza Yahya culminated in division, principally owing to Baha'u'llah's claim of a new dispensation and universal religion. Contrary to Baha'u'llah's wishes, their quarreling led to violence among the two factions. Mirza Yahya was deported to Cyprus, where ultimately his followers abandoned him. Baha'u'llah was deported to Acre, Palestine (then part of Syria), which was a prison city for criminals of the Turkish Empire. For two years he and 80 followers were confined to army barracks; the conditions were so harsh that several of the followers died. When the barracks were needed to house troops, Baha'u'llah was moved to a small house in the city in which he stayed for six years. During these years his followers grew substantially in number. At this time he wrote *The Most Holy Book (Kitab-i-Aqdas)*, his most important work, which lays out the basic laws and principles for his followers and establishes the basis of Baha'i administration. In 1877 he was released from the prison city, although the prison sentence was never removed. After a two-year stay in a house north of Acre, Baha'u'llah moved to a more regal estate, known as Bahji, secured through donations from his followers. He spent the remaining years of his life writing and teaching while administrative functions were taken over by his eldest son, Abdu'l-Baha (1844–1921). Upon Baha'u'llah's death in 1892 Abdu'l-Baha was appointed successor, as designated in Baha'u'llah's will. Baha'u'llah's burial site—a garden building near the main mansion at Bahji—is the most holy site for the Baha'i Faith.

Abdu'l-Baha ("servant of Baha") was born in Tehran, and was only nine when his father was first imprisoned (1852). He was a dutiful companion to his father, attending him throughout his years of exile and closely guarding him. After Baha'u'llah's death, the transition of leadership was not smooth, particularly as Abdu'l-Baha was opposed by several family members. After Baha'u'llah's death, Abdu'l-Baha built the shrine on Mount Carmel as a burial site for the Bab. Abdu'l-Baha's dissenting relatives reported to the Turkish government that he was constructing a fortress, and in 1901 he was confined to Acre for seven years. There he lived an austere life, teaching and visiting the sick. In 1907 a tribunal met to determine his fate. Coincidentally, a revolution broke out in the Ottoman Empire, and the tribunal members were called to Istanbul. The new leaders of the Empire (the Young Turks) released all political and religious prisoners in the empire. Thus, after a total of 40 years of imprisonment in Palestine, Abdu'l-Baha too was released (1908). From 1911 to 1913 he traveled to Great Britain, France, Germany, Hungary, the United States, Canada, and Egypt, where he met with religious and political leaders, scientists, and philosophers. He spoke at universities, to charitable organizations, and at institutions of various religions. Through these efforts, Abdu'l-Baha is responsible for spreading the Baha'i Faith beyond the Middle East and into the Western world. He continued adapting the Baha'i Faith to modern social ideas. In his role as a spiritual leader, he maintained exclusive authority in interpreting scripture, as appointed to him by Baha'u'llah, although he did not consider his own writings to be equally authoritative. During the years of World War I, Abdu'l-Baha and the Baha'is in Palestine were under wartime restrictions and had only limited contact with outside pilgrims. Their efforts focused on securing food supplies for the Baha'is and the surrounding poor. After the war, Palestine was occupied by the British and Abdu'l-Baha was officially honored with knighthood. He died in 1921, stating in his will that leadership should be passed to his 24-year-old grandson, Shoghi Effendi (1897–1957), whom he appointed "Guardian of the Cause."

Studying abroad at the time, Shoghi Effendi was surprised at the news of his position. During his tenure as leader, he established the administrative structure of the Baha'i Faith and became responsible for the subsequent formalized organization of Baha'is around the world. He established teaching plans to spread the Baha'i Faith worldwide, including in North America. His definitive English translations and clarifications of Baha'u'llah's writings helped secure the Baha'i Faith in non-Islamic Western countries. Perhaps most important, he arranged for the long-awaited election of members to the Universal House of Justice (Bayt al-Adl al-Azam), which would succeed him after his death by overseeing the Baha'i community and elucidating doctrine. The plan for this task was Abdu'l-Baha's Will and Testament, which, in turn, draws from the Aqdas. The first election of the members of the Universal House of Justice took place in 1963, six years after his death. Members reside in Haifa, Israel, meet almost daily, and are reelected every five years. Today, the Baha'i Faith has over five million followers in more than 230 countries worldwide, and is one of the world's fastest-growing religions. It remains the largest religious minority in Iran, the cradle of the Baha'i Faith, with more than a quarter million believers. However, since the Iranian Islamic revolution of 1979, more than 200 Baha'is have been executed, and thousands more persecuted.

Baha'i Teaching

The Baha'i Faith now reflects little of its original Imami theology, although Shi'i elements are more present in Iranian Baha'i traditions. Because of Baha'u'llah's appearance, the function of the Bab is no longer considered primary. A central tenet of Baha'i teaching holds that God's nature is unknowable. Everything around us, though, exhibits different attributes of the divine, as each is created by God and endowed with different sets of attributes. Most generally, God is a single infinite power, which implies the nonexistence of evil: Evil is only the absence of good, just as darkness is the absence of light. Neither darkness nor evil has a reality; these are only names we give to the absence of the reality in question. The most striking aspect of Baha'i theology is its notion of the unity of religions. Revelation is thought to be progressive, and prophets deliver messages appropriate to their own times. All true prophets from the various religions should be acknowledged as genuine—including Moses, Zoroaster, Jesus, Muhammad, Krishna, and Buddha. The prophets are *manifestations* of God and have special insight into the spiritual realm. Baha'i revelation is seen as the fulfillment of all previous revelations.

In its eschatological teachings, the Baha'i Faith holds that there is life after death through the continuation of a disembodied soul. However, heaven, hell, and final judgment are symbolic. Baha'u'llah is the messianic figure spoken of by previous prophets, and the "final judgment" is the appearance of each new manifestation/prophet of God. Institutionally, the Baha'i Faith has no official priests and no monastic component, and all Baha'is are expected to participate in teaching. Local spiritual assemblies assist with life cycle rites such as weddings and funerals, plan community events, counsel members, and coordinate Baha'i education programs. Nine Baha'is are elected annually by secret ballot (April 21) to help supervise the local assemblies. National spiritual assemblies oversee the local spiritual assemblies, and the Universal House of Justice oversees these. Baha'is follow a 19-month calendar, each month having 19 days with four intercalary days between the last two months. One month is designated for fasting.

In their social and moral beliefs, Baha'is teach racial and gender equality, monogamy, abstinence from alcohol and narcotics, and the voluntary sharing of property. Strong emphasis is placed on world peace and the unity of all humankind, as indicated in the statement by Baha'u'llah that "You are all fruits of one tree, the leaves of one branch, the flowers of one garden." The Baha'i founders and the Universal House of Justice have variously advocated a universal language, a universal league of nations, and an international court of arbitration. Although Baha'is believe in the doctrine of a just war, military aggression is rejected.

Baha'i Scriptures

The most sacred body of Baha'i texts is the writings of the Bab and Baha'u'llah, which are considered to be revelations. Second to those are the writings of Abdu'l-Baha, which, while not revealed, are considered to be inspired. The writings of Shoghi Effendi are not on a par with either of these groups, but are still considered authoritative. The letters of the Universal House of Justice are also authoritative, but are not scriptural either. The complete corpus of Baha'i sacred texts is perhaps two hundred volumes, although some items are still in manuscript form. The Bab, Baha'u'llah, and Abdu'l-Baha were imprisoned, and exiled for much of their lives, and, since they were prohibited from public speaking under these conditions, they devoted their time to writing.

The Bab composed about 50 volumes of writings. His most important work is the *Qayyum al-Asma'* (1844), a commentary on the Surah of Joseph in the Qur'an, which Baha'is consider to be the Bab's first revealed work. The foremost doctrinal works of the Bab are the Persian and Arabic *Bayan* ("exposition"). Although they share the same title, they are two independent works with some overlapping themes. The Persian *Bayan* (1848) is larger, although intentionally left incomplete, and is his principal doctrinal work. The Arabic *Bayan* (1850) was composed during the last few months of the Bab's life.

Baha'u'llah penned over one hundred volumes of writings, including letters to world leaders, prayers, and laws. Many of these are published as compilations. His most important writings are *The Book of Certitude (Kitab-i-Iqan), Most Holy Book (Kitab-i-Aqdas), The Hidden Words, The Seven Valleys, Tablet of the Holy Mariner,* and *Tablet of Glad-Tidings.* Abdu'l-Baha's writings include *Tablets of the Divine Plan, A Traveler's Narrative, Memorials of the Faithful,* and *Secret of Divine Civilization.* Important talks were also published, including *Promulgation of Universal Peace* and *Some Answered Questions.* Abdu'l-Baha composed about 50 volumes of text, some of which are in the form of letters to Baha'is as well as to those outside the faith. Shoghi Effendi composed about 35 volumes of text. His key works are *The Dispensation of Baha'u'llah, The Advent of Divine Justice, The Promised Day Is Come,* and *The World Order of Baha'u'llah.* His book *God Passes By* is his interpretation of Baha'i history. His writings also include letters and translations of the writings of the Bab, Baha'u'llah, and Abdu'l-Baha. *The Baha'i World,* an ongoing series of volumes founded by Shoghi Effendi (19 most recently), is a compilation of official Baha'i writings since 1925. It includes religious calendars, festival descriptions, poetry, music, administrative information, articles on theological topics, maps, bibliographies, transliterations, and definitions.

THE BAB

IMPRISONMENT

In 1844, Sayyid Ali-Muhammad Shirazi announced that he was indeed "The Bab," and for the next six years, until the end of his life, he was imprisoned or exiled. In the following selections from an "Epistle to Muhammad Shah," the Bab recounts his plight from 1844 to 1848.

God beareth Me witness, I was not a man of learning, for I was trained as a merchant. In the year sixty [i.e., 1844] God graciously infused my soul with the conclusive evidences and weighty knowledge which characterize Him Who is the Testimony of God—may peace be upon Him—until finally in that year I proclaimed God's hidden Cause and unveiled its well-guarded

Pillar, in such wise that no one could refute it. "That he who should perish might perish with a clear proof before him and he who should live might live by clear proof." [Qur'an 8:44]

In that same year I despatched a messenger and a book unto thee, that thou mightest act towards the Cause of Him Who is the Testimony of God as befitteth the station of thy sovereignty. But inasmuch as dark, dreadful and dire calamity had been irrevocably ordained by the Will of God, the book was not submitted to thy presence, through the intervention of such as regard themselves the well-wishers of the government. Up to the present, when nearly four years have passed, they have not duly presented it to Your Majesty. However, now that the fateful hour is drawing nigh, and because it is a matter of faith, not a worldly concern, therefore I have given thee a glimpse of what hath transpired.

I swear by God! Shouldst thou know the things which in the space of these four years have befallen Me at the hands of thy people and thine army, thou wouldst hold thy breath from fear of God, unless thou wouldst rise to obey the Cause of Him Who is the Testimony of God and make amends for thy shortcomings and failure.

While I was in *Shiraz* the indignities which befell Me at the hands of its wicked and depraved Governor waxed so grievous that if thou wert acquainted with but a tithe thereof, thou wouldst deal him retributive justice. For as a result of his unmitigated oppression, thy royal court hath become, until the Day of Resurrection, the object of the wrath of God. Moreover, his indulgence in alcohol had grown so excessive that he was never sober enough to make a sound judgement. Therefore, disquieted, I was obliged to set out from *Shiraz* with the aim of attaining the enlightened and exalted court of Your Majesty. The *Mu'tamidu'd-Dawlih* then became aware of the truth of the Cause and manifested exemplary servitude and devotion to His chosen ones. When some of the ignorant people in his city arose to stir up sedition, he defended the divine Truth by affording Me protection for a while in the privacy of the Governor's residence. At length, having attained the good-pleasure of God, he repaired to his habitation in the all-highest Paradise. May God reward him graciously. . . .

Following his ascension to the eternal Kingdom, the vicious *Gurgin*, resorting to all manner of treachery, false oaths and coercion, sent Me away from *Isfahan* with an escort of five guards on a journey which lasted seven days, without providing the barest necessities for My travel (Alas! Alas! for the things which have touched Me!), until eventually Your Majesty's order came, instructing Me to proceed to *Maku*. . . .

I swear by the Most Great Lord! Wert thou to be told in what place I dwell, the first person to have mercy on Me would be thyself. In the heart of a mountain is a fortress [*Maku*] . . . the inmates of which are confined to two guards and four dogs. Picture, then, My plight . . . I swear by the truth of God! Were he who hath been willing to treat Me in such a manner to know Who it is Whom he hath so treated, he, verily, would never in his life be happy. Nay—I, verily, acquaint thee with the truth of the matter—it is as if he hath imprisoned all the Prophets, and all the men of truth and all the chosen ones. . . .

When this decree was made known unto Me, I wrote to him who administereth the affairs of the kingdom, saying: "Put Me to death, I adjure thee by God, and send My head wherever thou pleasest. For surely an innocent person such as I, cannot reconcile himself to being consigned to a place reserved for criminals and let his life continue." My plea remained unanswered. Evidently His Excellency the *Haji,* is not fully aware of the truth of our Cause. It would be far more heinous a deed to sadden the hearts of the faithful, whether men or women, than to lay waste the sacred House of God. . . .

In brief, I hold within My grasp whatsoever any man might wish of the good of this world and of the next. Were I to remove the veil, all would recognize Me as their Best Beloved, and no one would deny Me. Let not this assertion astound Your Majesty; inasmuch as a true believer in the unity of God who keepeth his eyes directed towards Him alone, will regard aught else but Him as utter nothingness. I swear by God! I seek no earthly goods from thee, be it as much as a mustard seed. Indeed, to possess anything of this world or of the next would, in My estimation, be tantamount to open blasphemy. For it ill beseemeth the believer in the unity of God to turn his gaze to aught else, much less to hold it in his possession. I know of a certainty that since I have God, the Ever-Living, the Adored One, I am the possessor of all things, visible and invisible. . . .

In this mountain I have remained alone, and have come to such a pass that none of those gone before Me have suffered what I have suffered, nor any transgressor endured what I have endured! I render praise unto God and yet again praise Him. I find Myself free from sorrow, inasmuch as I abide within the good-pleasure of My Lord and Master. Methinks I am in the all-highest Paradise, rejoicing at My communion with God, the Most Great. Verily this is a bounty which God hath conferred upon Me; and He is the Lord of unbounded blessings.

Source: Ali Muhammad Shirazi, "Epistle to Muhammad Shah," from *Selections from the Writings of the Bab* (Haifa: Baha'i World Centre, 1976).

THE QAYYUMU'L-ASMA': A NEW QUR'AN

The Qayyumu'l-Asma', *a commentary on the Surah of Joseph in the Qur'an, was composed in 1844 and is the first book the Bab wrote after his Declaration. The first chapter was written in the presence of his first believer, Mulla Husayn, and, according to the Bab, the whole book was written in 40 days. Baha'is consider it his first revealed text and his most important work. He declares a new day, comparing the book itself to the Qur'an, and thereby announcing a new revelation from God. The* Qayyumu'l-Asma' *continually draws on passages and themes from the Qur'an, replicating many of its laws. It is also in the literary style of the Qur'an—even to the point that the Bab intended it to be recited like the Qur'an. The following passages establish a fundamen-*

tal theme in Baha'i faith: The Bab is a continuation in the line of the prophets acknowledged by Islam, most notably Moses, Jesus, and Muhammad.

1. ALL praise be to God Who hath, through the power of Truth, sent down this Book unto His servant, that it may serve as a shining light for all mankind. . . . Verily this is none other than the sovereign Truth; it is the Path which God hath laid out for all that are in heaven and on earth. Let him then who will, take for himself the right path unto his Lord. Verily this is the true Faith of God, and sufficient witness are God and such as are endowed with the knowledge of the Book. This is indeed the eternal Truth which God, the Ancient of Days, hath revealed unto His omnipotent Word—He Who hath been raised up from the midst of the Burning Bush. This is the Mystery which hath been hidden from all that are in heaven and on earth, and in this wondrous Revelation it hath, in very truth, been set forth in the Mother Book by the hand of God, the Exalted. . . .

61. Verily, Christ is Our Word which We communicated unto *Mary;* and let no one say what the Christians term as 'the third of three,' inasmuch as it would amount to slandering the Remembrance Who, as decreed in the Mother Book, is invested with supreme authority. Indeed God is but one God, and far be it from His glory that there should be aught else besides Him. All those who shall attain unto Him on the Day of Resurrection are but His servants, and God is, of a truth, a sufficient Protector. Verily I am none other but the servant of God and His Word, and none but the first one to bow down in supplication before God, the Most Exalted; and indeed God witnesseth all things.

62. O People of the *Qur'an!* Ye are as nothing unless ye submit unto the Remembrance of God and unto this Book. If ye follow the Cause of God, We will forgive you your sins, and if ye turn aside from Our command, We will, in truth, condemn your souls in Our Book, unto the Most Great Fire. We, verily, do not deal unjustly with men, even to the extent of a speck on a date-stone.

63. O Peoples of the earth! Verily the resplendent Light of God hath appeared in your midst, invested with this unerring Book, that ye may be guided aright to the ways of peace and, by the leave of God, step out of the darkness into the light and onto this far-extended Path of Truth. [Qur'an 5:15–18]. . . . O peoples of the earth! Verily His Remembrance is come to you from God after an interval during which there were no *Messengers,* that He may purge and purify you from uncleanliness in anticipation of the Day of the One true God; therefore seek ye whole-heartedly divine blessings from Him, inasmuch as We have, in truth, chosen Him to be the Witness and the Source of wisdom unto all that dwell on earth. . . .

Whenever the faithful hear the verses of this Book being recited, their eyes will overflow with tears and their hearts will be deeply touched by Him Who is the Most Great Remembrance for the love they cherish for God, the All-Praised. He is God, the All-Knowing, the

Eternal. They are indeed the inmates of the all-highest Paradise wherein they will abide for ever. Verily they will see naught therein save that which hath proceeded from God, nothing that will lie beyond the compass of their understanding. There they will meet the believers in Paradise, who will address them with the words "Peace, Peace" lingering on their lips. . . .

68. Say, O peoples of the world! Do ye dispute with Me about God by virtue of the names which ye and your fathers have adopted for Him at the promptings of the Evil One? God hath indeed sent down this Book unto Me with truth that ye may be enabled to recognize the true names of God, inasmuch as ye have strayed in error far from the Truth. Verily We have taken a covenant from every created thing upon its coming into being concerning the Remembrance of God, and there shall be none to avert the binding command of God for the purification of mankind, as ordained in the Book which is written by the hand of the *Bab*.

Source: Ali Muhammad Shirazi, *Qayyumu'l-Asma'*, chs. 1, 61–63, 68, from *Selections from the Writings of the Bab*.

THE *BAYAN*: A BOOK FOR A NEW DISPENSATION

The Persian Bayan *is the central book of the Babi religion insofar as it establishes a new system of laws and religious principles. The Bab here declares himself to be the independent manifestation of God, whereas in his previous writings he refers to himself as the Mahdi or the Promised One. The following selection explains the relation of the* Bayan *to previous divine books, particularly the Qur'an.*

True knowledge, therefore, is the knowledge of God, and this is none other than the recognition of His Manifestation in each Dispensation. Nor is there any wealth save in poverty in all save God and sanctity from aught else but Him—a state that can be realized only when demonstrated towards Him Who is the Dayspring of His Revelation. This doth not mean, however, that one ought not to yield praise unto former Revelations. On no account is this acceptable, inasmuch as it behooveth man, upon reaching the age of nineteen, to render thanksgiving for the day of his conception as an embryo. For had the embryo not existed, how could he have reached his present state? Likewise had the religion taught by Adam not existed, this Faith would not have attained its present stage. Thus consider thou the development of God's Faith until the end that hath no end. . . .

Twelve hundred and seventy years have elapsed since the declaration of *Muhammad*, and each year unnumbered people have circumambulated the House of God [Mecca]. In the concluding year of this period He Who is Himself the Founder of the House went on pilgrimage. Great God! There was a vast concourse of pilgrims from every sect. Yet not one recognized Him, though He recognized every one of them—souls tightly held in the grasp of His former commandment. The only person who recognized Him and performed pilgrimage with Him is the one round whom revolve eight *Vahids* [i.e., sections of the *Bayan*], in whom God hath gloried before the Concourse on high by virtue of his absolute detachment and for his being wholly devoted to the Will of God. This doth not mean that he was made the object of a special favour, nay, this is a favour which God hath vouchsafed unto all men, yet they have suffered themselves to be veiled from it. . . .

Everyone is eagerly awaiting His appearance, yet since their inner eyes are not directed towards Him sorrow must needs befall Him. In the case of the Apostle of God—may the blessings of God rest upon Him— before the revelation of the *Qur'an* everyone bore witness to His piety and noble virtues. Behold Him then after the revelation of the *Qur'an*. What outrageous insults were levelled against Him, as indeed the pen is ashamed to recount. Likewise behold the Point of the *Bayan*. His behaviour prior to the declaration of His mission is clearly evident unto those who knew Him. Now, following His manifestation, although He hath, up to the present, revealed no less than five hundred thousand verses on different subjects, behold what calumnies are uttered, so unseemly that the pen is stricken with shame at the mention of them. But if all men were to observe the ordinances of God no sadness would befall that heavenly Tree.

Source: Ali Muhammad Shirazi, *Bayan* 5:4, 18; 6:11, from *Selections from the Writings of the Bab*.

A COMING LEADER

In the Bayan, *the Bab announced the coming of a future prophet—the Sun of Truth— or, more generally described as "He Whom God Shall Manifest." The Bab depicts him in eschatological terms and notes that his nature is reflected in the* Bayan. *Baha'is believe that the Bab is foretelling the coming of Baha'u'llah.*

If at the time of the appearance of Him Whom God will make manifest all the dwellers of the earth were to bear witness unto a thing whereunto He beareth witness differently, His testimony would be like unto the sun, while theirs would be even as a false image produced in a mirror which is not facing the sun. For had it been otherwise their testimony would have proved a faithful reflection of His testimony.

I swear by the most sacred Essence of God that but one line of the Words uttered by Him is more sublime than the words uttered by all that dwell on earth. Nay, I beg forgiveness for making this comparison. How could the reflections of the sun in the mirror compare with the wondrous rays of the sun in the visible heaven? The station of one is that of nothingness, while the station of the other, by the righteousness of God— hallowed and magnified be His Name—is that of the Reality of things. . . .

If in the Day of His manifestation a king were to make mention of his own sovereignty, this would be like unto a mirror challenging the sun, saying: "The light is in me." It would be likewise, if a man of learning in His Day were to claim to be an exponent of knowledge, or if he who is possessed of riches were to display his affluence, or if a man wielding power were to assert his own authority, or if one invested with grandeur were to show forth his glory. Nay, such men would become the object of the derision of their peers, and how would they be judged by Him Who is the Sun of Truth! . . .

It is not permissible to ask questions from Him Whom God will make manifest, except that which well beseemeth Him. For His station is that of the Essence of divine Revelation. . . . Whatever evidence of bounty is witnessed in the world, is but an image of His bounty; and every thing owes its existence to His Being. . . . The *Bayan* is, from beginning to end, the repository of all of His attributes, and the treasury of both His fire and His light. Should anyone desire to ask questions, he is allowed to do so only in writing, that he may derive ample understanding from His written reply and that it may serve as a sign from his Beloved. However, let no one ask aught that may prove unworthy of His lofty station. For instance, were a person to inquire the price of straw from a merchant of rubies, how ignorant would he be and how unacceptable. Similarly unacceptable would be the questions of the highest-ranking people of the world in His presence, except such words as He Himself would utter about Himself in the Day of His manifestation.

Source: Ali Muhammad Shirazi, *Bayan* 3:12, 13, from *Selections from the Writings of the Bab.*

DAY OF RESURRECTION

The Bab believed that the resurrection, judgment, heaven, and hell were to be understood metaphorically. In the following selection, he explains that the "day of resurrection" refers to the advent of a new dispensation that "resurrects" the previous one. For example, the Qur'an is resurrected in the Bayan, *and the* Bayan *ultimately will be resurrected in the advent of "He whom God will make manifest."*

The substance of this chapter is this, that what is intended by the Day of Resurrection is the Day of the appearance of the Tree of divine Reality, but it is not seen that any one of the followers of *Shi'ih Islam* hath understood the meaning of the Day of Resurrection; rather have they fancifully imagined a thing which with God hath no reality. In the estimation of God and according to the usage of such as are initiated into divine mysteries, what is meant by the Day of Resurrection is this, that from the time of the appearance of Him Who is the Tree of divine Reality, at whatever period and under whatever name, until the moment of His disappearance, is the Day of Resurrection.

For example, from the inception of the mission of Jesus—may peace be upon Him—till the day of His ascension was the Resurrection of Moses. For during that period the Revelation of God shone forth through the appearance of that divine Reality, Who rewarded by His Word everyone who believed in Moses, and punished by His Word everyone who did not believe; inasmuch as God's Testimony for that Day was that which He had solemnly affirmed in the Gospel. And from the inception of the Revelation of the Apostle of God—may the blessings of God be upon Him—till the day of His ascension was the Resurrection of Jesus—peace be upon Him—wherein the Tree of divine Reality appeared in the person of *Muhammad*, rewarding by His Word everyone who was a believer in Jesus, and punishing by His Word everyone who was not a believer in Him. And from the moment when the Tree of the *Bayan* appeared until it disappeareth is the Resurrection of the Apostle of God, as is divinely foretold in the *Qur'an*; the beginning of which was when two hours and eleven minutes had passed on the eve of the fifth of *Jamadiyu'l-Avval*, 1260 A.H. [May 22, 1844], which is the year 1270 of the Declaration of the Mission of *Muhammad*. This was the beginning of the Day of Resurrection of the *Qur'an*, and until the disappearance of the Tree of divine Reality is the Resurrection of the *Qur'an*. The stage of perfection of everything is reached when its resurrection occurreth. The perfection of the religion of *Islam* was consummated at the beginning of this Revelation; and from the rise of this Revelation until its setting, the fruits of the Tree of *Islam*, whatever they are, will become apparent. The Resurrection of the *Bayan* will occur at the time of the appearance of Him Whom God shall make manifest. For today the *Bayan* is in the stage of seed; at the beginning of the manifestation of Him Whom God shall make manifest its ultimate perfection will become apparent. He is made manifest in order to gather the fruits of the trees He hath planted; even as the Revelation of the *Qa'im* [He Who ariseth], a descendant of *Muhammad*—may the blessings of God rest upon Him—is exactly like unto the Revelation of the Apostle of God Himself [*Muhammad*]. He appeareth not, save for the purpose of gathering the fruits of *Islam* from the *Qur'anic* verses which He [*Muhammad*] hath sown in the hearts of men. The fruits of *Islam* cannot be gathered except through allegiance unto Him [the *Qa'im*] and by believing in Him. At the present time, however, only adverse effects have resulted; for although He hath appeared in the midmost heart of *Islam*, and all people profess it by reason of their relationship to Him [the *Qa'im*], yet unjustly have they consigned Him to the Mountain of *Maku*, and this notwithstanding that in the *Qur'an* the advent of the Day of Resurrection hath been promised unto all by God. For on that Day all men will be brought before God and will attain His Presence; which meaneth appearance before Him Who is the Tree of divine Reality and attainment unto His presence; inasmuch as it is not possible to appear before the Most Holy Essence of God, nor is it conceivable to seek reunion with Him. That which is feasible in the matter of appearance before Him and of meeting Him is attainment unto the Primal Tree.

Source: Ali Muhammad Shirazi, *Bayan* 2:7, from *Selections from the Writings of the Bab*.

CALL TO BELIEF

Acceptance of the Bab's message was not as widespread as he had hoped. The Bab compared his situation to the initial disbelief Muhammad's contemporaries had demonstrated toward Muhammad—just as Muhammad had compared his situation to those of the rejected prophets from the past. The following selections are from "An Address to a Muslim Divine" (Abdu's-Sahib). And again, like Muhammad, the Bab warns of divine punishment for disbelievers.

Thy vision is obscured by the belief that divine revelation ended with the coming of *Muhammad*, and unto this We have borne witness in Our first epistle. Indeed, He Who hath revealed verses unto *Muhammad*, the Apostle of God, hath likewise revealed verses unto *Ali-Muhammad*. For who else but God can reveal to a man such clear and manifest verses as overpower all the learned? Since thou hast acknowledged the revelation of *Muhammad*, the Apostle of God, then there is no other way open before thee but to testify that whatever is revealed by the Primal Point hath also proceeded from God, the Help in Peril, the Self-Subsisting. Is it not true that the *Qur'an* hath been sent down from God and that all men are powerless before its revelation? Likewise these words have also been revealed by God, if thou dost but perceive. What is there in the *Bayan* which keepeth thee back from recognizing these verses as being sent forth by God, the Inaccessible, the Most Exalted, the All-Glorious? . . .

Thou contendest, "How can we recognize Him when we have heard naught but words which fall short of irrefutable proofs?" Yet since thou hast acknowledged and recognized *Muhammad*, the Apostle of God, through the *Qur'an*, how canst thou withhold recognition from Him Who sent thee the Book, despite thy calling thyself "His servant?" Verily He doth exercise undisputed authority over His revelations unto all mankind. . . .

We enjoin thee to save thyself and all the inhabitants of that land from the fire, then to enter the peerless and exalted Paradise of His good-pleasure. Otherwise the day is approaching when thou shalt perish and enter the fire, when thou shalt have neither patron nor helper from God. We have taken compassion on thee, as a sign of Our grace, inasmuch as thou hast related thyself unto Us. Verily We are aware of all things. We are cognizant of thy righteous deeds, though they shall avail thee nothing; for the whole object of such righteousness is but recognition of God, thy Lord, and undoubted faith in the Words revealed by Him.

Source: Ali Muhammad Shirazi, "An Address to a Muslim Divine," from *Selections from the Writings of the Bab*.

BAHA'U'LLAH

DIFFERENT MANIFESTATIONS
IN DIFFERENT DISPENSATIONS

Between 1861 and 1862, while exiled in Baghdad, Baha'u'llah composed the Kitab-i-Iqan *(The Book of Certitude), perhaps the most influential Baha'i scripture. The work explains how different periods of time had their own prophets who subtly anticipated future prophets in future dispensations. Followers of these prophets invariably misinterpreted their messages. Baha'u'llah believes that special attention to key passages in their writings and symbolic terms will show that each prophet indeed announced the coming of the next. The work was composed one or two years prior to his Declaration at Ridvan, and, thus, he does not include himself in the chain of prophets.*

Consider the past. How many, both high and low, have, at all times, yearningly awaited the advent of the Manifestations of God in the sanctified persons of His chosen Ones. How often have they expected His coming, how frequently have they prayed that the breeze of divine mercy might blow, and the promised Beauty step forth from behind the veil of concealment, and be made manifest to all the world. And whensoever the portals of grace did open, and the clouds of divine bounty did rain upon mankind, and the light of the Unseen did shine above the horizon of celestial might, they all denied Him, and turned away from His face—the face of God Himself. Refer ye, to verify this truth, to that which hath been recorded in every sacred Book.

Ponder for a moment, and reflect upon that which hath been the cause of such denial on the part of those who have searched with such earnestness and longing. Their attack hath been more fierce than tongue or pen can describe. Not one single Manifestation of Holiness hath appeared but He was afflicted by the denials, the repudiation, and the vehement opposition of the people around Him. Thus it hath been revealed: "O the misery of men! No Messenger cometh unto them but they laugh Him to scorn" [Qur'an 36:30]. . . .

Again He saith: "Each nation hath plotted darkly against their Messenger to lay violent hold on Him, and disputed with vain words to invalidate the truth." [Qur'an 40:5]. . . .

Among the Prophets was Noah. For nine hundred and fifty years He prayerfully exhorted His people and summoned them to the haven of security and peace. None, however, heeded His call. Each day they inflicted on His blessed person such pain and suffering that no one believed He could survive. How frequently they denied Him, how malevolently they hinted their suspicion against Him! . . . And after Noah the light of the countenance of *Hud* shone forth above the horizon of creation. For well-nigh seven hundred years, according to the sayings of men, He exhorted the people to turn their faces and draw nearer unto the *Ridvan* of the divine presence. What showers of afflictions rained upon Him, until at last His adjurations bore the fruit of increased rebelliousness, and His assiduous endeavours resulted in the wilful blindness of His people. . . . "And their unbelief shall only increase for the unbelievers their own perdition." [Qur'an 35:39]. . . .

And after Him there appeared from the *Ridvan* of the Eternal, the Invisible, the holy person of *Salih,* Who again summoned the people to the river of everlasting life. For over a hundred years He admonished them to hold fast unto the commandments of God and eschew that which is forbidden. His admonitions, however, yielded no fruit, and His pleading proved of no avail. Several times He retired and lived in seclusion. All this, although that eternal Beauty was summoning the people to no other than the city of God.

Later, the beauty of the countenance of the Friend of God [i.e., Abraham] appeared from behind the veil, and another standard of divine guidance was hoisted. He invited the people of the earth to the light of righteousness. The more passionately He exhorted them, the fiercer waxed the envy and waywardness of the people, except those who wholly detached themselves from all save God, and ascended on the wings of certainty to the station which God hath exalted beyond the comprehension of men. It is well known what a host of enemies besieged Him, until at last the fires of envy and rebellion were kindled against Him. And after the episode of the fire came to pass, He, the lamp of God amongst men, was, as recorded in all books and chronicles, expelled from His city.

And when His day was ended, there came the turn of Moses. Armed with the rod of celestial dominion, adorned with the white hand of divine knowledge, and proceeding from the *Paran* of the love of God, and wielding the serpent of power and everlasting majesty, He shone forth from the Sinai of light upon the world. He summoned all the peoples and kindreds of the earth to the kingdom of eternity, and invited them to partake of the fruit of the tree of faithfulness. . . .

And when the days of Moses were ended, and the light of Jesus, shining forth from the dayspring of the Spirit, encompassed the world, all the people of Israel arose in protest against Him. They clamoured that He Whose advent the Bible had foretold must needs promulgate and fulfill the laws of Moses, whereas this youthful Nazarene, who laid claim to the station of the divine Messiah, had annulled the law of divorce and of the sabbath day—the most weighty of all the laws of Moses. Moreover, what of the signs of the Manifestation yet to come? These people of Israel are even unto the present day still expecting that Manifestation which the Bible hath foretold! How many Manifestations of Holiness, how many Revealers of the light everlasting, have appeared since the time of Moses, and yet Israel, wrapt in the densest veils of satanic fancy and false imaginings, is still expectant that the idol of her own handiwork will appear with such signs as she herself hath conceived!

. . . There is yet another verse in the Gospel wherein He saith: "Heaven and earth shall pass away: but My words shall not pass away"

[Luke 21:33]. Thus it is that the adherents of Jesus maintained that the law of the Gospel shall never be annulled, and that whensoever the promised Beauty is made manifest and all the signs are revealed, He must needs re-affirm and establish the law proclaimed in the Gospel, so that there may re-main in the world no faith but His faith. This is their fundamental belief. And their conviction is such that were a person to be made manifest with all the promised signs and to promulgate that which is contrary to the let-ter of the law of the Gospel, they must assuredly renounce him, refuse to submit to his law, declare him an infidel, and laugh him to scorn. This is proved by that which came to pass when the sun of the *Muhammadan* Revelation was revealed. Had they sought with a humble mind from the Manifestations of God in every Dispensation the true meaning of these words revealed in the sacred books—words the misapprehension of which hath caused men to be deprived of the recognition of the *Sadratu'l-Muntaha*, the ultimate Purpose—they surely would have been guided to the light of the Sun of Truth, and would have discovered the mysteries of divine knowledge and wisdom.

From all that We have stated it hath become clear and manifest that be-fore the revelation of each of the Mirrors reflecting the divine Essence, the signs heralding their advent must needs be revealed in the visible heaven as well as in the invisible, wherein is the seat of the sun of knowledge, of the moon of wisdom, and of the stars of understanding and utterance. The sign of the invisible heaven must needs be revealed in the person of that perfect man who, before each Manifestation appeareth, educateth, and prepareth the souls of men for the advent of the divine Luminary, the Light of the unity of God amongst men.

Source: Baha'u'llah, *Kitab-I-Iqan* (Haifa: Baha'i World Centre, 1989).

BAHA'I LAWS

In around 1873, 10 years after his declaration at Ridvan and midway into his ministry, Baha'u'llah penned the Kitab-i-Aqdas (Most Holy Book), *which is principally a compendium of Baha'i law. Although the* Bayan *also contains laws, Baha'is believe that the* Bayan *has been superseded by the* Aqdas. *Accordingly, the* Aqdas *follows some of the* Bayan's *laws and ignores others. Section 42 below describes the function of the Universal House of Justice, which was later instituted by Shoghi Effendi as the ruling body of the Baha'i Faith.*

1. The first duty prescribed by God for His servants is the recognition of Him Who is the Dayspring of His Revelation and the Fountain of His laws, Who representeth the Godhead in both the Kingdom of His Cause and the world of creation. Whoso achieveth this duty hath attained unto all good; and whoso is deprived thereof hath gone astray, though he be the author of every righteous deed. It behoveth every one who reacheth this most sublime station, this summit of

transcendent glory, to observe every ordinance of Him Who is the Desire of the world. These twin duties are inseparable. Neither is acceptable without the other. Thus hath it been decreed by Him Who is the Source of Divine inspiration.

12. It hath been ordained that obligatory prayer is to be performed by each of you individually. Save in the Prayer for the Dead, the practice of congregational prayer hath been annulled. He, of a truth, is the Ordainer, the All-Wise.

13. God hath exempted women who are in their courses from obligatory prayer and fasting. Let them, instead, after performance of their ablutions, give praise unto God, repeating ninety-five times between the noon of one day and the next "Glorified be God, the Lord of Splendour and Beauty." Thus hath it been decreed in the Book, if ye be of them that comprehend.

14. When travelling, if ye should stop and rest in some safe spot, perform ye—men and women alike—a single prostration in place of each unsaid Obligatory Prayer, and while prostrating say "Glorified be God, the Lord of Might and Majesty, of Grace and Bounty." Whoso is unable to do this, let him say only "Glorified be God"; this shall assuredly suffice him. He is, of a truth, the all-sufficing, the ever-abiding, the forgiving, compassionate God. Upon completing your prostrations, seat yourselves cross-legged—men and women alike—and eighteen times repeat "Glorified be God, the Lord of the kingdoms of earth and heaven." Thus doth the Lord make plain the ways of truth and guidance, ways that lead to one way, which is this Straight Path. Render thanks unto God for this most gracious favour; offer praise unto Him for this bounty that hath encompassed the heavens and the earth; extol Him for this mercy that hath pervaded all creation.

16. O Pen of the Most High! Say: O people of the world! We have enjoined upon you fasting during a brief period, and at its close have designated for you *Naw-Ruz* as a feast. Thus hath the Day-Star of Utterance shone forth above the horizon of the Book as decreed by Him Who is the Lord of the beginning and the end. Let the days in excess of the months be placed before the month of fasting. We have ordained that these, amid all nights and days, shall be the manifestations of the letter *Ha*, and thus they have not been bounded by the limits of the year and its months. It behoveth the people of *Baha*, throughout these days, to provide good cheer for themselves, their kindred and, beyond them, the poor and needy, and with joy and exultation to hail and glorify their Lord, to sing His praise and magnify His Name; and when they end—these days of giving that precede the season of restraint—let them enter upon the Fast. Thus hath it been ordained by Him Who is the Lord of all mankind. The traveler, the ailing, those who are with child or giving suck, are not bound by the Fast; they have been exempted by God as a token of His grace. He, verily, is the Almighty, the Most Generous.

30. The Lord hath ordained that in every city a House of Justice be established wherein shall gather counsellors to the number of *Baha*, and should it exceed this number it doth not matter. They should consider themselves as entering the Court of the presence of God, the Exalted, the Most High, and as beholding Him Who is the Unseen. It behoveth them to be the trusted ones of the Merciful among men and to regard themselves as the guardians appointed of God for all that dwell on earth. It is incumbent upon them to take counsel together and to have regard for the interests of the servants of God, for His sake, even as they regard their own interests, and to choose that which is meet and seemly. Thus hath the Lord your God commanded you. Beware lest ye put away that which is clearly revealed in His Tablet. Fear God, O ye that perceive.

31. O people of the world! Build ye houses of worship throughout the lands in the name of Him Who is the Lord of all religions. Make them as perfect as is possible in the world of being, and adorn them with that which befitteth them, not with images and effigies. Then, with radiance and joy, celebrate therein the praise of your Lord, the Most Compassionate. Verily, by His remembrance the eye is cheered and the heart is filled with light.

32. The Lord hath ordained that those of you who are able shall make pilgrimage to the sacred House, and from this He hath exempted women as a mercy on His part. He, of a truth, is the All-Bountiful, the Most Generous.

33. O people of *Baha*! It is incumbent upon each one of you to engage in some occupation—such as a craft, a trade or the like. We have exalted your engagement in such work to the rank of worship of the one true God. Reflect, O people, on the grace and blessings of your Lord, and yield Him thanks at eventide and dawn. Waste not your hours in idleness and sloth, but occupy yourselves with what will profit you and others. Thus hath it been decreed in this Tablet from whose horizon hath shone the day-star of wisdom and utterance. The most despised of men in the sight of God are they who sit and beg. Hold ye fast unto the cord of means and place your trust in God, the Provider of all means.

37. Whoso layeth claim to a Revelation direct from God, ere the expiration of a full thousand years, such a man is assuredly a lying impostor. We pray God that He may graciously assist him to retract and repudiate such claim. Should he repent, God will, no doubt, forgive him. If, however, he persisteth in his error, God will, assuredly, send down one who will deal mercilessly with him. Terrible, indeed, is God in punishing! Whosoever interpreteth this verse otherwise than its obvious meaning is deprived of the Spirit of God and of His mercy which encompasseth all created things. Fear God, and follow not your idle fancies. Nay, rather, follow the bidding of your Lord, the Almighty, the All-Wise. Erelong shall clamorous voices be raised in most lands. Shun them, O My people, and follow not the iniquitous

and evil-hearted. This is that of which We gave you forewarning when We were dwelling in *Iraq*, then later while in the Land of Mystery, and now from this Resplendent Spot.

42. Endowments dedicated to charity revert to God, the Revealer of Signs. None hath the right to dispose of them without leave from Him Who is the Dawning-place of Revelation. After Him, this authority shall pass to the *Aghsan*, and after them to the House of Justice—should it be established in the world by then—that they may use these endowments for the benefit of the Places which have been exalted in this Cause, and for whatsoever hath been enjoined upon them by Him Who is the God of might and power. Otherwise, the endowments shall revert to the people of *Baha* who speak not except by His leave and judge not save in accordance with what God hath decreed in this Tablet—lo, they are the champions of victory betwixt heaven and earth—that they may use them in the manner that hath been laid down in the Book by God, the Mighty, the Bountiful.

49. God hath imposed a fine on every adulterer and adulteress, to be paid to the House of Justice: nine *mithqals* of gold, to be doubled if they should repeat the offence. Such is the penalty which He Who is the Lord of Names hath assigned them in this world; and in the world to come He hath ordained for them a humiliating torment. Should anyone be afflicted by a sin, it behoveth him to repent thereof and return unto his Lord. He, verily, granteth forgiveness unto whomsoever He willeth, and none may question that which it pleaseth Him to ordain. He is, in truth, the Ever-Forgiving, the Almighty, the All-Praised.

63. God hath prescribed matrimony unto you. Beware that ye take not unto yourselves more wives than two. Whoso contenteth himself with a single partner from among the maidservants of God, both he and she shall live in tranquillity. And he who would take into his service a maid may do so with propriety. Such is the ordinance which, in truth and justice, hath been recorded by the Pen of Revelation. Enter into wedlock, O people, that ye may bring forth one who will make mention of Me amid My servants. This is My bidding unto you; hold fast to it as an assistance to yourselves.

65. It hath been laid down in the *Bayan* that marriage is dependent upon the consent of both parties. Desiring to establish love, unity and harmony amidst Our servants, We have conditioned it, once the couple's wish is known, upon the permission of their parents, lest enmity and rancour should arise amongst them. And in this We have yet other purposes. Thus hath Our commandment been ordained.

149. Recite ye the verses of God every morn and eventide. Whoso faileth to recite them hath not been faithful to the Covenant of God and His Testament, and whoso turneth away from these holy verses in this Day is of those who throughout eternity have turned away from God. Fear ye God, O My servants, one and all. Pride not yourselves on much reading of the verses or on a multitude of pious acts by night and day; for were a man to read a single verse with joy and radiance it

would be better for him than to read with lassitude all the Holy Books of God, the Help in Peril, the Self-Subsisting. Read ye the sacred verses in such measure that ye be not overcome by languor and despondency. Lay not upon your souls that which will weary them and weigh them down, but rather what will lighten and uplift them, so that they may soar on the wings of the Divine verses towards the Dawning-place of His manifest signs; this will draw you nearer to God, did ye but comprehend.

155. Gambling and the use of opium have been forbidden unto you. Eschew them both, O people, and be not of those who transgress. Beware of using any substance that induceth sluggishness and torpor in the human temple and inflicteth harm upon the body. We, verily, desire for you naught save what shall profit you, and to this bear witness all created things, had ye but ears to hear.

Source: Baha'u'llah, *Kitab-I-Aqdas*, 1, 12–14, 16, 30–33, 37, 42, 49, 63, 65, 149, 155 (Haifa: Baha'i World Centre, 1992).

PROMOTING PEACE

Many of Baha'u'llah's writings focus on the place of the Baha'i Faith in God's scheme of revelation, and also on laws which govern the Baha'i community. Some writings, though, focus on the larger issue of world peace—a distinguishing feature of the Baha'i Faith. Such themes are seen in the following from the Lawh-i-Dunya (Tablet of the World).

Whilst in the Prison of *Akka,* We revealed in the *Crimson Book* that which is conducive to the advancement of mankind and to the reconstruction of the world. The utterances set forth therein by the Pen of the Lord of creation include the following which constitute the fundamental principles for the administration of the affairs of men:

First: It is incumbent upon the ministers of the House of Justice to promote the Lesser Peace so that the people of the earth may be relieved from the burden of exorbitant expenditures. This matter is imperative and absolutely essential, inasmuch as hostilities and conflict lie at the root of affliction and calamity. Second: Languages must be reduced to one common language to be taught in all the schools of the world. Third: It behoveth man to adhere tenaciously unto that which will promote fellowship, kindliness and unity. Fourth: Everyone, whether man or woman, should hand over to a trusted person a portion of what he or she earneth through trade, agriculture or other occupation, for the training and education of children, to be spent for this purpose with the knowledge of the Trustees of the House of Justice. Fifth: Special regard must be paid to agriculture. Although it hath been mentioned in the fifth place, unquestionably it precedeth the others. Agriculture is highly developed in foreign lands, however in Persia it hath so far been grievously neglected. It is hoped that His Majesty the *Shah*—may God assist him by His grace—will turn his attention to this vital and important matter.

Were men to strictly observe that which the Pen of the Most High hath revealed in the Crimson Book, they could then well afford to dispense with the regulations which prevail in the world. Certain exhortations have repeatedly streamed forth from the Pen of the Most High that perchance the manifestations of power and the dawning-places of might may, sometime, be enabled to enforce them. Indeed, were sincere seekers to be found, every emanation of God's pervasive and irresistible Will would, for the sake of His love, be revealed. But where are to be found earnest seekers and inquiring minds? Whither are gone the equitable and the fair-minded? At present no day passeth without the fire of a fresh tyranny blazing fiercely, or the sword of a new aggression being unsheathed. Gracious God! The great and the noble in Persia glory in acts of such savagery that one is lost in amazement at the tales thereof.

Source: Baha'u'llah, *Lawh-I-Dunya*, from *Tablets of Baha'u'llah Revealed after The Kitab-i-Aqdas* (Haifa: Baha'i World Centre, 1978).

PARADISE

Just as the Bab reinterpreted the traditional notion of the "Day of Judgment," so too does Baha'u'llah give a broader interpretation to the notion of "paradise" and "hell." They are partly experienced here on earth, although they are more vast in the afterlife. The following selection is from the Suriy-i-Vafa (Tablet to Vafa).

As to Paradise: It is a reality and there can be no doubt about it, and now in this world it is realized through love of Me and My good-pleasure. Whosoever attaineth unto it God will aid him in this world below, and after death He will enable him to gain admittance into Paradise whose vastness is as that of heaven and earth. Therein the Maids of glory and holiness will wait upon him in the daytime and in the night season, while the day-star of the unfading beauty of his Lord will at all times shed its radiance upon him and he will shine so brightly that no one shall bear to gaze at him. Such is the dispensation of Providence, yet the people are shut out by a grievous veil. Likewise apprehend thou the nature of hell-fire and be of them that truly believe. For every act performed there shall be a recompense according to the estimate of God, and unto this the very ordinances and prohibitions prescribed by the Almighty amply bear witness. For surely if deeds were not rewarded and yielded no fruit, then the Cause of God—exalted is He—would prove futile. Immeasurably high is He exalted above such blasphemies! However, unto them that are rid of all attachments a deed is, verily, its own reward. Were We to enlarge upon this theme numerous Tablets would need to be written.

Source: Baha'u'llah, *Suriy-I-Vafa*, from *Tablets of Baha'u'llah Revealed after The Kitab-i-Aqdas*.

ABDU'L-BAHA

BAHA'U'LLAH'S TEACHINGS

Several of Abdu'l-Baha's writings are formal religious texts and resemble the style of the Bayan *or* Kitab-i-Iqan. *Other texts, though, are more informal in nature, such as those based on public lectures. The effect of these is the communication of Baha'i doctrine to a wider circle of people. Such is the case with the following summary of Baha'u'llah's teachings from Abdu'l-Baha's "Discourse at the London Theosophical Headquarters," September 30, 1911.*

[Baha'u'llah] declared the most human virtues; He manifested the Spiritual powers, and put them into practice in the world around Him.

Firstly: He lays stress on the search for Truth. This is most important, because the people are too easily led by tradition. It is because of this that they are often antagonistic to each other, and dispute with one another. But the manifesting of Truth discovers the darkness and becomes the cause of Oneness of faith and belief: because Truth cannot be two! That is not possible.

Secondly: *Baha'u'llah* taught the Oneness of humanity; that is to say, all the children of men are under the mercy of the Great God. They are the sons of one God; they are trained by God. He has placed the crown of humanity on the head of every one of the servants of God. Therefore all nations and peoples must consider themselves brethren. They are all descendants from Adam. They are the branches, leaves, flowers and fruits of One Tree. They are pearls from one shell. But the children of men are in need of education and civilization, and they require to be polished, till they become bright and shining. Man and woman both should be educated equally and equally regarded. It is racial, patriotic, religious and class prejudice, that has been the cause of the destruction of Humanity.

Thirdly: *Baha'u'llah* taught, that Religion is the chief foundation of Love and Unity and the cause of Oneness. If a religion become the cause of hatred and disharmony, it would be better that it should not exist. To be without such a religion is better than to be with it.

Fourthly: Religion and Science are inter-twined with each other and cannot be separated. These are the two wings with which humanity must fly. One wing is not enough. Every religion which does not concern itself with Science is mere tradition, and that is not the essential. Therefore science, education and civilization are most important necessities for the full religious life.

Fifthly: The Reality of the divine Religions is one, because the Reality is one and cannot be two. All the prophets are united in their message, and unshaken. They are like the sun; in different seasons they ascend from different rising points on the horizon. Therefore every ancient prophet gave the glad tidings of the future, and every future has accepted the past.

Sixthly: Equality and Brotherhood must be established among all members of mankind. This is according to Justice. The general rights of mankind must be guarded and preserved. All men must be treated equally. This is inherent in the very nature of humanity.

Seventhly: The arrangements of the circumstances of the people must be such that poverty shall disappear, and that every one as far as possible, according to his position and rank, shall be comfortable. Whilst the nobles and others in high rank are in easy circumstances, the poor also should be able to get their daily food and not be brought to the extremities of hunger.

Eighthly: *Baha'u'llah* declared the coming of the Most Great Peace. All the nations and peoples will come under the shadow of the Tent of the Great Peace and Harmony—that is to say, by general election a Great Board of Arbitration shall be established, to settle all differences and quarrels between the Powers; so that disputes shall not end in war.

Ninthly: *Baha'u'llah* taught that hearts must receive the Bounty of the Holy Spirit, so that Spiritual civilization may be established. For material civilization is not adequate for the needs of mankind and cannot be the cause of its happiness. Material civilization is like the body and spiritual civilization is like the soul. Body without soul cannot live.

This is a short summary of the Teachings of *Baha'u'llah*. To establish this *Baha'u'llah* underwent great difficulties and hardships. He was in constant confinement and He suffered great persecution. But in the fortress (*Akka*) He reared a spiritual palace and from the darkness of His prison He sent out a great light to the world. It is the ardent desire of the *Baha'is* to put these teachings into common practice: and they will strive with soul and heart to give up their lives for this purpose, until the heavenly light brightens the whole world of humanity.

Source: Abdu'l-Baha, "Discourse at the London Theosophical Head Quarters," from *Abdu'l-Baha in London* (London: Baha'i Publishing, 1982).

PANTHEISM

In another informal work, Some Answered Questions *(written between 1904 and 1906), Abdu'l-Baha considers the issue of pantheism—the theological position that God is identical to the universe as a whole. He distinguishes between two types of pantheism: that of the Sufis and that of the prophets. The pantheism of the Sufis maintains that individual beings (people, animals) are subcomponents of God's essence. This he rejects, since it implies that God becomes a lower form of existence. The pantheism of the prophets sees the world as an emanation of God, distinct from, yet illuminated by God's being. This maintains the immanence of God's attributes, while still conserving God's transcendence. Baha'u'llah endorses this view as true Pantheism.*

Question—How do the Theosophists and the *Sufis* understand the question of pantheism? What does it mean, and how nearly does it approximate to the truth?

Answer—Know that the subject of pantheism is ancient. It is a belief not restricted to the Theosophists and the *Sufis*; on the contrary, some of the sages of Greece believed in it, like Aristotle, who said, "The simple truth is all things, but it is not any one of them." In this case, "simple" is the opposite of "composed"; it is the isolated Reality, which is purified and sanctified from composition and division, and which resolves Itself into innumerable forms. Therefore, Real Existence is all things, but It is not one of the things. Briefly, the believers in pantheism think that Real Existence can be compared to the sea, and that beings are like the waves of the sea. These waves, which signify the beings, are innumerable forms of that Real Existence; therefore, the Holy Reality is the Sea of Preexistence, and the innumerable forms of the creatures are the waves which appear.

. . . The *Sufis* admit God and the creature, and say that God resolves Himself into the infinite forms of the creatures, and manifests like the sea, which appears in the infinite forms of the waves. These phenomenal and imperfect waves are the same thing as the Preexistent Sea, which is the sum of all the divine perfections. The Prophets, on the contrary, believe that there is the world of God, the world of the Kingdom, and the world of Creation: three things. The first emanation from God is the bounty of the Kingdom, which emanates and is reflected in the reality of the creatures, like the light which emanates from the sun and is resplendent in creatures; and this bounty, which is the light, is reflected in infinite forms in the reality of all things, and specifies and individualizes itself according to the capacity, the worthiness and the intrinsic value of things. But the affirmation of the *Sufis* requires that the Independent Wealth should descend to the degree of poverty, that the Preexistent should confine itself to phenomenal forms, and that Pure Power should be restricted to the state of weakness, according to the limitations of contingent beings. And this is an evident error. Observe that the reality of man, who is the most noble of creatures, does not descend to the reality of the animal, that the essence of the animal, which is endowed with the powers of sensation, does not abase itself to the degree of the vegetable, and that the reality of the vegetable, which is the power of growth, does not descend to the reality of the mineral.

Briefly, the superior reality does not descend nor abase itself to inferior states; then how could it be that the Universal Reality of God, which is freed from all descriptions and qualifications, notwithstanding Its absolute sanctity and purity, should resolve Itself into the forms of the realities of the creatures, which are the source of imperfections? This is a pure imagination which one cannot conceive. On the contrary, this Holy Essence is the sum of the divine perfections; and all creatures are favored by the bounty of resplendency through emanation, and receive the lights, the perfection and the beauty of Its Kingdom, in the same way that all earthly creatures obtain the bounty of the light of the rays of the sun, but the sun does not descend and does not abase itself to the favored realities of earthly beings.

Source: Abdu'l-Baha, *Some Answered Questions* (Wilmette, Ill.: Bahá'i Publishing Committee, 1982).

UNIVERSAL LOVE

A key theme in the Baha'i religion is a love of humanity. One of the most dramatic state-ments of this doctrine is from Abdu'l-Baha's public talk in Paris, October 24, 1911, on the subject of "The Universal Love."

An Indian said to *Abdu'l-Baha:* "My aim in life is to transmit as far as in me lies the message of Krishna to the world."

Abdu'l-Baha said: The Message of Krishna is the message of love. All God's prophets have brought the message of love. None has ever thought that war and hate are good. Every one agrees in saying that love and kind-ness are best. Love manifests its reality in deeds, not only in words—these alone are without effect. In order that love may manifest its power there must be an object, an instrument, a motive. There are many ways of ex-pressing the love principle; there is love for the family, for the country, for the race, there is political enthusiasm, there is also the love of community of interest in service. These are all ways and means of showing the power of love. Without any such means, love would be unseen, unheard, unfelt—altogether unexpressed, unmanifested! Water shows its power in various ways, in quenching thirst, causing seed to grow, etc. Coal expresses one of its principles in gas-light, while one of the powers of electricity is shown in the electric light. If there were neither gas nor electricity, the nights of the world would be darkness! So, it is necessary to have an instrument, a mo-tive for love's manifestation, an object, a mode of expression.

We must find a way of spreading love among the sons of humanity. Love is unlimited, boundless, infinite! Material things are limited, circum-scribed, finite. You cannot adequately express infinite love by limited means. The perfect love needs an unselfish instrument, absolutely freed from fetters of every kind. The love of family is limited; the tie of blood re-lationship is not the strongest bond. Frequently members of the same fam-ily disagree, and even hate each other. Patriotic love is finite; the love of one's country causing hatred of all others, is not perfect love! Compatriots also are not free from quarrels amongst themselves. The love of race is limited; there is some union here, but that is insufficient. Love must be free from boundaries! To love our own race may mean hatred of all others, and even people of the same race often dislike each other. Political love also is much bound up with hatred of one party for another; this love is very limited and uncertain. The love of community of interest in service is likewise fluctuating; frequently competitions arise, which lead to jealousy, and at length hatred replaces love. A few years ago, Turkey and Italy had a friendly political understanding; now they are at war! All these ties of love are imperfect. It is clear that limited material ties are insufficient to adequately express the universal love.

The great unselfish love for humanity is bounded by none of these imperfect, semi-selfish bonds; this is the one perfect love, possible to all mankind, and can only be achieved by the power of the Divine Spirit. No worldly power can accomplish the universal love. Let all be united in this Divine power of love! Let all strive to grow in the light of the Sun of Truth, and reflecting this luminous love on all men, may their hearts become so united that they may dwell evermore in the radiance of the limitless love. . . . The animal creation is captive to matter, God has given freedom to man. The animal cannot escape the law of nature, whereas man may control it, for he, containing nature, can rise above it. The power of the Holy Spirit, enlightening man's intelligence, has enabled him to discover means of bending many natural laws to his will. He flies through the air, floats on the sea, and even moves under the waters. All this proves how man's intelligence has been enabled to free him from the limitations of nature, and to solve many of her mysteries. Man, to a certain extent, has broken the chains of matter. The Holy Spirit will give to man greater powers than these, if only he will strive after the things of the spirit and endeavour to attune his heart to the Divine infinite love.

When you love a member of your family or a compatriot, let it be with a ray of the Infinite Love! Let it be in God, and for God! Wherever you find the attributes of God love that person, whether he be of your family or of another. Shed the light of a boundless love on every human being whom you meet, whether of your country, your race, your political party, or of any other nation, colour or shade of political opinion. Heaven will support you while you work in this in-gathering of the scattered peoples of the world beneath the shadow of the almighty tent of unity. You will be servants of God, who are dwelling near to Him, His divine helpers in the service, ministering to all Humanity. All Humanity! Every human being! never forget this! Do not say, he is an Italian, or a Frenchman, or an American, or an Englishman, remember only that he is a son of God, a servant of the Most High, a man! All are men! Forget nationalities; all are equal in the sight of God!

Source: Abdu'l-Baha, "The Universal Love," *Paris Talks* (London: Baha'i Publishing Trust, 1979).

ABDU'L-BAHA'S WILL

Abdu'l-Baha died in 1921, and in his will he appointed Shoghi Effendi to succeed him as the Guardian of the Cause of the Baha'i Faith. The following selections, from the conclusion of his will, describe this appointment.

O ye the faithful loved ones of *Abdu'l-Baha*! It is incumbent upon you to take the greatest care of Shoghi Effendi, the twig that hath branched from and the fruit given forth by the two hallowed and Divine Lote-Trees, that no dust of despondency and sorrow may stain his radiant nature, that day by day he may wax greater in happiness, in joy and spirituality, and may grow to become even as a fruitful tree.

For he is, after *Abdu'l-Baha*, the Guardian of the Cause of God, the *Afnan*, the Hands (pillars) of the Cause and the beloved of the Lord must obey him and turn unto him. He that obeyeth him not, hath not obeyed God; he that turneth away from him, hath turned away from God and he that denieth him, hath denied the True One. Beware lest anyone falsely interpret these words, and like unto them that have broken the Covenant after the Day of Ascension (of *Baha'u'llah*) advance a pretext, raise the standard of revolt, wax stubborn and open wide the door of false interpretation. To none is given the right to put forth his own opinion or express his particular conviction. All must seek guidance and turn unto the Center of the Cause and the House of Justice. And he that turneth unto whatsoever else is indeed in grievous error.

Source: Abdu'l-Baha, *The Will And Testament Of Abdu'l-Baha* (Wilmette, Ill.: Baha'i Publishing Trust, 1971).

SHOGHI EFFENDI

POSSIBILITIES FOR THE FUTURE

A principal achievement of Shoghi Effendi's leadership was the establishment of the formal Baha'i administrative structure. As a visionary, in many of his writings and talks he mapped out achievement goals and multiyear plans to accomplish these. Some of his goals, such as the establishment of the Universal House of Justice, did not come into being until after his death. The following selection from The Advent of Divine Justice, a December 25, 1938, address to American and Canadian Baha'is, lists goals for the future.

I can only for the moment cite at random certain of these opportunities which stand out preeminently, in any attempt to survey the possibilities of the future: The election of the International House of Justice and its establishment in the Holy Land, the spiritual and administrative center of the *Baha'i* world, together with the formation of its auxiliary branches and subsidiary institutions; the gradual erection of the various dependencies of the first *Mashriqu'l-Adhkar* of the West, and the intricate issues involving the establishment and the extension of the structural basis of *Baha'i* community life; the codification and promulgation of the ordinances of the *Most Holy Book* [*Kitab-i-Aqdas*], necessitating the formation, in certain countries of the East, of properly constituted and officially recognized courts of *Baha'i* law; the building of the third *Mashriqu'l-Adhkar* of the *Baha'i* world in the outskirts of the city of *Tihran*, to be followed by the rise of a similar

House of Worship in the Holy Land itself; the deliverance of *Baha'i* communities from the fetters of religious orthodoxy in such Islamic countries as Persia, *Iraq,* and Egypt, and the consequent recognition, by the civil authorities in those states, of the independent status and religious character of *Baha'i* National and Local Assemblies; the precautionary and defensive measures to be devised, coordinated, and carried out to counteract the full force of the inescapable attacks which the organized efforts of ecclesiastical organizations of various denominations will progressively launch and relentlessly pursue; and, last but not least, the multitudinous issues that must be faced, the obstacles that must be overcome, and the responsibilities that must be assumed, to enable a sore-tried Faith to pass through the successive stages of unmitigated obscurity, of active repression, and of complete emancipation, leading in turn to its being acknowledged as an independent Faith, enjoying the status of full equality with its sister religions, to be followed by its establishment and recognition as a State religion, which in turn must give way to its assumption of the rights and prerogatives associated with the *Baha'i* state, functioning in the plenitude of its powers, a stage which must ultimately culminate in the emergence of the worldwide *Baha'i* Commonwealth, animated wholly by the spirit, and operating solely in direct conformity with the laws and principles of *Baha'u'llah.*

Source: Shoghi Effendi, *The Advent of Divine Justice* (Wilmette, Ill.: Baha'i Publishing Trust, 1990).

UNITY OF RELIGIONS, RACES, AND GOD

The writings of the Bab and Baha'u'llah reflect the fact that their initial audience was Muslim. The unity of religions, races, and God are indeed pervasive themes of their writings; however, these themes are often presented in contexts that defend the Bab's and Baha'u'llah's roles as legitimate prophets in the line of Moses, Jesus, and Muhammad. In Shoghi Effendi's writings, the Muslim context is less important and the themes of unity are brought to the fore on their own merits. This is evident in the following selections from the Preface to The Promised Day Is Come *(1941).*

The fundamental principle enunciated by *Baha'u'llah* . . . is that religious truth is not absolute but relative, that Divine Revelation is a continuous and progressive process, that all the great religions of the world are divine in origin, that their basic principles are in complete harmony, that their aims and purposes are one and the same, that their teachings are but facets of one truth, that their functions are complementary, that they differ only in the nonessential aspects of their doctrines, and that their missions represent successive stages in the spiritual evolution of human society. . . .

. . . His mission is to proclaim that the ages of the infancy and of the childhood of the human race are past, that the convulsions associated with the present stage of its adolescence are slowly and painfully preparing it to attain the stage of manhood, and are heralding the approach of that

Age of Ages when swords will be beaten into plowshares, when the Kingdom promised by Jesus Christ will have been established, and the peace of the planet definitely and permanently ensured. Nor does *Baha'u'llah* claim finality for His own Revelation, but rather stipulates that a fuller measure of the truth He has been commissioned by the Almighty to vouchsafe to humanity, at so critical a juncture in its fortunes, must needs be disclosed at future stages in the constant and limitless evolution of mankind.

The *Baha'i* Faith upholds the unity of God, recognizes the unity of His Prophets, and inculcates the principle of the oneness and wholeness of the entire human race. It proclaims the necessity and the inevitability of the unification of mankind, asserts that it is gradually approaching, and claims that nothing short of the transmuting spirit of God, working through His chosen Mouthpiece in this day, can ultimately succeed in bringing it about. It, moreover, enjoins upon its followers the primary duty of an unfettered search after truth, condemns all manner of prejudice and superstition, declares the purpose of religion to be the promotion of amity and concord, proclaims its essential harmony with science, and recognizes it as the foremost agency for the pacification and the orderly progress of human society. . . .

Mirza Husayn-'Ali, surnamed *Baha'u'llah* (the Glory of God), a native of *Mazindaran,* whose advent the *Bab* [Herald and Forerunner of *Baha'u'llah*] had foretold, . . . was imprisoned in *Tihran,* was banished, in 1852, from His native land to *Baghdad,* and thence to Constantinople and Adrianople, and finally to the prison city of *Akka,* where He remained incarcerated for no less than twenty-four years, and in whose neighborhood He passed away in 1892. In the course of His banishment, and particularly in Adrianople and *Akka,* He formulated the laws and ordinances of His Dispensation, expounded, in over a hundred volumes, the principles of His Faith, proclaimed His Message to the kings and rulers of both the East and the West, both Christian and Muslim, addressed the Pope, the Caliph of *Islam,* the Chief Magistrates of the Republics of the American continent, the entire Christian sacerdotal order, the leaders of *Shi'ih* and *Sunni Islam,* and the high priests of the Zoroastrian religion. In these writings He proclaimed His Revelation, summoned those whom He addressed to heed His call and espouse His Faith, warned them of the consequences of their refusal, and denounced, in some cases, their arrogance and tyranny. . . .

The Faith which this order serves, safeguards and promotes is . . . essentially supernatural, supranational, entirely non-political, non-partisan, and diametrically opposed to any policy or school of thought that seeks to exalt any particular race, class or nation. It is free from any form of ecclesiasticism, has neither priesthood nor rituals, and is supported exclusively by voluntary contributions made by its avowed adherents. Though loyal to their respective governments, though imbued with the love of their own country, and anxious to promote at all times, its best interests, the followers of the *Baha'i* Faith, nevertheless, viewing mankind as one entity, and profoundly attached to its vital interests, will not hesitate to subordinate every particular interest, be it personal, regional or national, to the over-riding interests of the generality of mankind, knowing full well that in a world of interdependent peoples and nations the advantage of the part is best to be reached by the advantage of the whole, and that no lasting result can be achieved by any of the component parts if the general interests of the entity itself are neglected. . . .

Source: Shoghi Effendi, *The Promised Day Is Come* (Wilmette, Ill.: Baha'i Publishing Trust, 1980).

THE UNIVERSAL HOUSE OF JUSTICE

PROMISE OF WORLD PEACE

Shoghi Effendi died in 1957. One of his principal concerns was to establish the Universal House of Justice to succeed him when he died. The Universal House of Justice was officially elected in 1963, and since then has overseen Baha'i administration, interpreted Baha'i scripture, and produced its own authoritative Baha'i texts. The following selections are from one such text, The Promise of World Peace, *addressed to the world on October 1985.*

The Great Peace towards which people of good will throughout the centuries have inclined their hearts, of which seers and poets for countless generations have expressed their vision, and for which from age to age the sacred scriptures of mankind have constantly held the promise, is now at long last within the reach of the nations. For the first time in history it is possible for everyone to view the entire planet, with all its myriad diversified peoples, in one perspective. World peace is not only possible but inevitable. It is the next stage in the evolution of this planet—in the words of one great thinker, "the planetization of mankind." . . .

A candid acknowledgement that prejudice, war and exploitation have been the expression of immature stages in a vast historical process and that the human race is today experiencing the unavoidable tumult which marks its collective coming of age is not a reason for despair but a prerequisite to undertaking the stupendous enterprise of building a peaceful world. That such an enterprise is possible, that the necessary constructive forces do exist, that unifying social structures can be erected, is the theme we urge you to examine. . . .

No serious attempt to set human affairs aright, to achieve world peace, can ignore religion. Man's perception and practice of it are largely the stuff of history. An eminent historian described religion as a "faculty of human nature." That the perversion of this faculty has contributed to much of the confusion in society and the conflicts in and between individuals can hardly be denied. But neither can any fair-minded observer discount the preponderating influence exerted by religion on the vital expressions of civilization. Furthermore, its indispensability to social order has repeatedly been demonstrated by its direct effect on laws and morality. . . .

Banning nuclear weapons, prohibiting the use of poison gases, or outlawing germ warfare will not remove the root causes of war. However important such practical measures obviously are as elements of the peace process, they are in themselves too superficial to exert enduring influence. Peoples are ingenious enough to invent yet other forms of warfare, and to use food, raw materials, finance, industrial power, ideology, and terrorism to subvert one another in an endless quest for supremacy and dominion. Nor can the present massive dislocation in the affairs of humanity be resolved through the settlement of specific conflicts or disagreements among nations. A genuine universal framework must be adopted. . . .

The emancipation of women, the achievement of full equality between the sexes, is one of the most important, though less acknowledged prerequisites of peace. The denial of such equality perpetrates an injustice against one half of the world's population and promotes in men harmful attitudes and habits that are carried from the family to the workplace, to political life, and ultimately to international relations. There are no grounds, moral, practical, or biological, upon which such denial can be justified. Only as women are welcomed into full partnership in all fields of human endeavour will the moral and psychological climate be created in which international peace can emerge.

Source: Universal House of Justice, *The Promise of World Peace, to the Peoples of the World, a Statement* (Wilmette, Ill.: Baha'i Pubishing Trust, 1985).

GLOSSARY

Bab   Arabic for "gate"; the term refers to a person who is an intermediary between the Hidden Imam and believers. This is the title adopted by Sayyid Ali-Muhammad Shiraz (d. 1850), who declared himself to be the Bab.

Babi religion   (babism)   The religion founded by the Bab (Sayyid Ali-Muhammad Shirazi), which was the precursor to the Baha'i Faith.

Baha   Literally "Glory" or "Splendor"; a title that designates Baha'u'llah. The phrase "People of Baha" refers to followers of Baha'u'llah (superseding People of the Bayan). This designation of *Baha'i* as a follower of Baha'u'llah became current during the later years of Baha'u'llah's residence in Adrianople.

Baha'u'llah   Literally "Glory of God." Founder of the Baha'i Faith, born Mirza Huasayn-Ali Nur (d. 1892). Baha'is believe him to be the *Manifestation of God*, commissioned by God to unify the modern world through a theory and practice of unity.

Bayan   Literally "exposition"; the title of two distinct books by the Bab (one in Persian, the other in Arabic); the term "Bayan" is also used by the Bab as a reference to the whole of his revelation in a generic sense.

Dispensation   A divinely appointed age in which God reveals himself through a prophet.

House of Justice   **(Bayt al-Adl al-Azam)** Internationally elected Baha'i administrative institution which oversees the Baha'i community. First described by Baha'u'llah and officially elected in 1963.

Manifestation   Appearance of God; a prophet of God's revelation in a given dispensation.

Point, Primal   Symbol of the Bab. In Persian mysticism, all knowledge originates from a single dot, or point.

Qa'im   Literally, "He who shall arise" from a descendant of Muhammad; also known as the the Mahdi, "The Guided One."

FURTHER READINGS

BAHA'U'LLAH. *The Summons of the Lord of Hosts*. Haifa: Baha'i World Centre, 2002.

BUCK, CHRISTOPHER. *Paradise and Paradigm: Key Symbols in Persian Christianity and the Baha'i Faith*. Albany: State University of New York Press, 1999.

BUCK, CHRISTOPHER. *Symbol and Secret: Qur'an Commentary in Baha'u'llah's Kitab-i Iqan*, in *Studies in the Babi and Baha'i Religions*, vol. 7. Los Angeles: Kalimat Press, 1995.

ESSLEMONT, JOHN EBENEZER. *Baha'u'llah and the New Era*. Wilmette, Ill., Baha'i Pub. Committee, 1950.

GOUVION, COLETTE AND PHILIPPE JOUVIONS. *The Gardeners of God: An Encounter with Five Million Baha'is*. Oxford: Oneworld, 1993.

HATCHER, WILLIAM S. AND MARTIN, J. DOUGLAS. *The Baha'i Faith*. San Francisco: Harper Collins, 1958.

HATCHER, WILLIAM S. AND MARTIN, J. DOUGLAS. *The Baha'i Faith: The Emerging Global Religion*. Wilmette, IL: Baha'i Publishing, 2003.

McMULLEN, MICHAEL. *The Baha'i: The Religious Constuction of a the Global Identity*. Piscataway, NJ: Rutgers University Press, 2000.

MOMEN, WENDI. *A Basic Baha'i Dictionary*. Oxford: George Ronald, 1989.

SMITH, PETER. *A Concise Encyclopedia of the Baha'i Faith*. Oxford: Oneworld, 1999.

SMITH, PETER. *A Short History of the Baha'i Faith*. Oxford; Rockport, MA: Oneworld Publications, 1996.

Indigenous Religions
of the West

INTRODUCTION

Like other indigenous religions around the world, those from Africa and America are as varied as the hundreds of native tribes within those regions. It is also typical of indigenous religions in general that our knowledge of those from Africa and America rest largely on the work of social scientists, rather than on documents composed by religious practitioners themselves. Because of both the uniqueness of various tribal practices and the rarity of firsthand documents, religions from these regions lack the kind of official sacred texts that we find in major world religions such as Hinduism or Judaism. Nevertheless, tribal religions have perpetuated an oral tradition, often passed from generation to generation, some of which has been recorded by researchers. These include myths about spirits and gods, hymns to spiritual beings, legends containing moral wisdom, and sacred utterances for special events and life passage rituals.

African Religion

Africa is a large and culturally diverse continent, which makes it difficult to generalize about its religious practices. About one-third of the African people follow traditional African religion, and the remaining two-thirds are Muslim or Christian. Traditional African religions are restricted to specific tribal regions; there are as many as 700 languages in Africa, and each represents a different cultural group and religion. The various traditional religions are unique insofar as they developed from within their respective cultures, and no attempt was made to send out missionaries or to convert people of other tribal religions to their own. Nevertheless, these tribal religions have some shared features. First, many African religions hold a common belief in a high god—a supreme being in the sky and creator of all. However, since they believe that the high god is remote, religious rituals often focus on specialized tutelary gods, ancestral spirits, and animal spirits. Second, African religions have dramatic rituals involving ecstatic dances, chants, the wearing of masks, and the use of other fetish objects. So prominent are these visual worship practices in African religion that, for some time, the term "fetishism" designated African religion in general. Third, although African religions have some belief in the

490

afterlife, their primary concern is with living well in this life. Fourth, African religions frequently hold that individual people are composed of numerous souls of their ancestors, which were handed on to them by their parents. The ancestral spirits inhabit all parts of a person's body, such as her blood or bones, and make their wishes known. The ancestral spirits are particularly offended when with living family members quarrel with each other or are immoral. This might prompt a particular ancestral spirit to rise up from within a living family member, take possession of her, and make her vocalize the ancestral spirit's discontent. Spirit possession and trances of this type, they believe, are important for helping heal and integrate an individual.

For more distinct features of African religions, we must look to regional tribal practices. For simplicity, we can divide the African continent into four geographical regions, which designate distinct cultural and religious traditions. One region is the northern portion, dominated by the Sahara desert. This area has seen much Christian and Muslim missionary activity, especially along the well-traveled trade routes; thus, when scholars speak of traditional African religion, they typically refer to the remaining three sub-Saharan areas. A second geographical area is east Africa, which contains 200 distinct tribal societies. The religious practices of the Nuer–herds-people from the grasslands and swamps of southern Sudan–have attracted special attention. A third area is central and southern Africa, which is marked off by its regionally shared language group called *Bantu*. A fourth and final area is West Africa, which accounts for half of Africa's total population.

Native American Religion

The term "Native American" designates the indigenous people of the Western Hemisphere, including the peoples of both North and South America. Unlike African religion, which does contain some common themes, few generalizations can be made about indigenous American religion beyond what is central to most religions—namely, belief in the supernatural, the use of religious symbols, and ritual practices. There is no single concept of a High God or nature Gods. In some tribes religious symbols are sometimes modeled after natural objects, and in others they tend to be abstract. Religious practices are sometimes formalized, and other times integrated into daily activity. When Europeans first arrived in the Americas, there were around 240 tribal groups in North America alone. Anthropologists have classified these into the following nine groups based on geographical location and language; the most recognizable tribal names are from the last five categories:

Subarctic (Alaska to Labrador)

Northwest Coast (Alaska to north California)

California

Western Plateau (Western Canada)

Western Great Basin (east of California): Shoshoni, Comanche

Southwest (Arizona, New Mexico, Texas, Northern Mexico): Pueblo, Navajo, Apache

Plains (north of Texas): Cheyenne, Arapaho, Sioux, Pawnee

Eastern Woodlands (East of Mississippi): Seneca, Delaware, Chippewa, Shawnee, Winnebago

Southeast (Louisiana to Florida): Creek, Choctaw, Cherokee, Chickasaw, Seminoles

Though Mexico and South America were no less varied in their regional tribes, these areas are most distinguished by major empires. Among the oldest of these is the *Maya*, which flourished between 250 and 900 C.E. in Meso-America (Southern Mexico, Guatemala, and Belize). They developed a complex calendar and a hieroglyphic form of writing that has recently been translated. Their religion focused on a collection of nature gods, such as the sun, moon, rain, corn, and double-headed snake. For reasons not entirely clear, the civilization went into decline, its major cities being overtaken with jungle growth. Following on the heels of the Maya, just to the north in central Mexico, there arose the *Toltec* Empire, which peaked from the tenth to the twelfth centuries C.E. They practiced human sacrifice in religious ceremonies, and, drawing on earlier mythology, they developed a cult of *Quetzalcoatl*, the "Feathered Serpent." They declined with the invasion of northern Mexican tribes into this region, thus giving rise to the Aztec Empire. The Aztecs perpetuated both the practice of human sacrifice and the cult of Quetzalcoatl. Like the Maya, they too developed a system of writing, which gives us a direct avenue to understanding their religion. By the fifteenth century the Aztecs ruled central and southern Mexico; they were finally halted in 1521 by Spanish explorers. During the rise of the Aztecs in Mexico, Peru saw the emergence of the Inca Empire, which, like the Aztecs, was crushed by Spanish conquest in 1532. With the Spanish invasion came Roman Catholic Christianity, which was quickly imposed on the conquered people. In rural areas, though, vestiges of the ancient religions remain, often intermingled with Catholic elements.

The selections below sample the religious mythology of African and Native American tribes. They explore the cause of death, the structure of the spiritual realm, the creation of the world, and the source of human suffering. In each case the myths express anguish about the human predicament and offer some statement about our place in the spiritual nature of things.

AFRICA

CAUSE OF DEATH

One of the most distinctive and pervasive themes in African religious myth is that death is unnatural: God originally intended humans to live forever, but there was some misunderstanding which prevented this. The plots, human characters, and Gods

differ, but there is an unmistakable thread tying these myths together throughout Africa's diverse regions. Three such stories are presented here.

Unkulunkulu [the High God of the Zulu people of the Bantu] sent a chameleon; he said to it, "Go, chameleon, go and say, 'Let not men die!'" The chameleon set out; it went slowly, it loitered in the way; and as it went it ate of the fruit of a bush which is called Ubukwebezane. At length Unkulunkulu sent a lizard after the chameleon, when it had already set out for some time. The lizard went; it ran and made great haste, for Unkulunkulu had said, "Lizard, when you have arrived say, 'Let men die!'" So the lizard went, and said, "I tell you, it is said, 'Let men die!'" The lizard came back again to Unkulunkulu before the chameleon had reached his destination, the chameleon, which was sent first—which was sent and told to go and say, "Let not men die!" At length it arrived and shouted, saying, "It is said, 'Let not men die!'" But men answered, "Oh, we have accepted the word of the lizard; it has told us the word," It is said "Let men die!'" We cannot hear your word. Through the word of the lizard men will die."

Imana [the High God of the Bantu tribes in Rwanda] used to talk with men. One day he said to a man, "Do not go to sleep to-night; I am coming to give you some good news." There was a serpent hidden in the hut, who overheard these words. The man kept awake till cockcrow, after which he was overpowered by sleep, and did not hear when Imana came and called him. The serpent was on the watch and answered the call. Imana thought the man was speaking, and said, "You will die, but you will rise again; you will grow old, but you will get a new skin, you, your children, and your grandchildren." Next morning the man went to see Imana, and complained that he had not received any message. Imana asked, "It was not you, then, to whom I spoke in the night?" "No." "Then it must have been the snake, who is for ever accursed. If a Tusi ever comes across that snake let him kill it—likewise the Hutu and the Twa. Let them kill one wherever they find it. But as for you, you will die, you and your children and your children's children."

Source: Adapted from Alice Werner, *Myths and Legends of the Bantu*, London: G. G. Harrap and Co., Ltd., 1933, chs. 2 and 3.

In the beginning of the world when the Creator had made men and women and the animals, they all lived together in the creation land. The Creator was a big chief, past all men, and being very kindhearted, was very sorry whenever any one died. So one day he sent for the dog, who was his head messenger, and told him to go out into the world and give his word to all people that for the future whenever any one died the body was to be placed in the compound, and wood ashes were to be thrown over it; that the dead body was to be left on the ground, and in twenty-four hours it would become alive again.

When the dog had traveled for half a day he began to get tired; so as he was near an old woman's house he looked in, and seeing a bone with some meat on it he made a meal of it, and then went to sleep, entirely forgetting the message which had been given him to deliver.

After a time, when the dog did not return, the Creator called for a sheep, and sent him out with the same message. But the sheep was a very foolish one, and being hungry, began eating the sweet grasses by the wayside. After a time, however, he remembered that he had a message to deliver, but forgot what it was exactly. So as he went about among the people, he told them that the message the Creator had given him to tell the people, was that whenever any one died they should be buried underneath the ground.

A little time afterwards the dog remembered his message, so he ran into the town and told the people that they were to place wood ashes on the dead bodies and leave them in the compound, and that they would come to life again after twenty-four hours. But the people would not believe him, and said, "We have already received the word from the Creator by the sheep, that all dead bodies should be buried." In consequence of this the dead bodies are now always buried, and the dog is much disliked and not trusted as a messenger. If he had not found the bone in the old woman's house and forgotten his message, the dead people might still be alive.

Source: Elphinstone Dayrell, *Folk Stories from Southern Nigeria, West Africa*, London, New York: Longmans, Green and Co., 1910.

KING OF DEATH: ANGOLAN MYTH

The above myths about the cause of death express a frustration with the boundaries that separate the living from the dead. This theme plays out in a variety of myths in which a dejected person attempts to cross over this boundary. The following legend from the Bantu Ambundu tribe of Angola describes a heartbroken king's efforts to retrieve his dead wife from the realm of death–which is presided over by Lord Kalunga-ngombe. The king enlists the aid of a medicine man that makes the journey.

Kitamba was a chief who lived at Kasanji. He lost his head-wife, Queen Muhongo, and mourned for her many days. Not only did he mourn himself, but he insisted on his people sharing his grief. "In my village, too, no man will do anything. The young people will not shout; the women will not pound; no one will speak in the village." His headmen argued with him, but Kitamba was inflexible, and declared that he would neither speak nor eat nor allow anyone else to do so till his queen was restored to him. The headmen consulted together, and called in a medicine man. Having received his fee—first a gun, and then a cow—hearing their statement of the case, he said, "All right," and set off to gather herbs. He pounded these in a medicine-mortar, and, having prepared a potion, ordered the king and all the people to wash themselves with it. He next directed some men to dig a grave in his guest-hut at the fireplace, which they did. He entered it with his little boy, giving two last instructions to his wife: to leave off her girdle [*i.e.*, to dress negligently, as if in mourning] and to pour water every day on the fireplace. Then the men filled in the grave.

The medicine man saw a road open before him. He walked along it with his boy till he came to a village, where he found Queen Muhongo sitting, sewing a basket. She saw him approaching, and asked, "Where do you come from?" He answered, in the usual form demanded by native politeness, "I have sought you, yourself. Since you have been dead, King Kitamba will not eat, drink, or speak. In the village they do not pound food; they do not speak. He says, 'fetch my head-wife and I will talk and eat.' That is what brought me here. I have spoken." The queen then pointed out a man seated a little way off, and asked the doctor who he was. As he could not say, she told him, "He is the King of Death, Lord Kalunga-ngombe. He is always consuming us, us all." Directing his attention to another man who was chained, she asked if he knew him, and he answered, "He looks like King Kitamba, whom I left where I came from." It was indeed Kitamba, and the queen further informed the messenger that her husband had not many years to live, and also that "anyone who comes here in the realm of Death never returns again." She gave him the armlet which had been buried with her, to show to Kitamba as a proof that he had really visited the abode of the dead. She urged him, though, not to tell the king that he had seen him there. And he must not eat anything in Kalunga; otherwise he would never be permitted to return to earth.

Meanwhile, the medicine man's wife had kept pouring water on the grave. One day she saw the earth beginning to crack; the cracks opened wider, and, finally, her husband's head appeared. He gradually made his way out, and pulled his small son up after him. The child fainted when he came out into the sunlight, but his father washed him with some herbal medicine, and soon brought him to.

Next day the medicine a man went to the headmen and presented his report; he was repaid with two slaves and returned to his home. The headmen told Kitamba what he had said, and produced the token. The only comment he is recorded to have made, on looking at the armlet, is "Truth, it is the same." We do not hear whether he countermanded the official mourning, but it is to be presumed he did so, for he made no further difficulty about eating or drinking. Then, after a few years, he died. They wailed at the funeral, then dispersed.

Source: Adapted from Alice Werner, *Myths and Legends of the Bantu*, 1933, ch. 2.

WOMAN'S SEARCH FOR THE HIGH GOD: ZAMBIAN MYTH

Religious traditions around the world struggle with explaining why God allows human suffering. The next story from a Bantu tribe of Zambia is about an old woman who, having suffered miserably through her life, attempts to find the High God and have him explain the meaning of her ordeal. Her efforts, though, fail.

An old woman, whose parents had died when she was a child, lost all her sons and daughters, one after another, and was left with no one belonging to her. When she was very old and weary she thought she must be about to follow them. But instead of that she found herself growing younger, and was seized with a strong desire to find Leza [the High God] and ask him the meaning of it all. Thinking that he had his abode in the sky, she began to cut down trees and make a scaffolding by which she could climb up.

But when she had built it up to a considerable height, the lower poles rotted away, and the whole fell down, she falling with it. She was not hurt, and tried again, but with no better success. At last she gave up in despair, and set out to reach the place where, as she believed, the sky joins the earth. So she wandered through one country after another, and when the people asked her what she wanted she said, "I am seeking Leza." "What do you want of him?" "My brothers, you ask me? Here in the nations is there one who has suffered as I have suffered? I am alone. As you see me, a solitary old woman, that is how I am!"

The people answered, "Yes, we see! That is how you are! Bereaved of friends and kindred? In what do you differ from others? Shikakunamo [High God of the Baila tribe] sits on the back of every one of us, and we cannot shake him off!"

Source: Adapted from Alice Werner, *Myths and Legends of the Bantu,* 1933, ch. 3.

TREE TO THE UPPER WORLD: TANZANIAN MYTH

The above myth expresses the belief that the spiritual realm is located physically above the world in which we live. Just as the old woman attempts to build a scaffolding to breach the gulf, other myths describe similar mechanisms for climbing up to the heavens. The following myth from the Wachagga people of Tanzania's Kilimanjaro region describes a mysterious tree that leads to the world above.

A girl named Kichalundu went out one day to cut grass. Finding it growing very luxuriantly in a certain place, she stepped on the spot and sank into a quagmire. Her companions took hold of her hands and tried to pull her out, but in vain; she vanished from their sight. They heard her singing, "The ghosts have taken me. Go and tell my father and mother," and they ran to call the parents. The whole countryside gathered about the place, and a diviner advised the father to sacrifice a cow and a sheep. This was done, and they heard the girl's voice again, but growing fainter and fainter, till at last it was silent, and they gave her up for lost. But after a time a tree grew up on the spot where she had disappeared. It went on growing, until at last it reached the sky. The herd-boys, during the heat of the day, used to drive their cattle into its shade, and themselves climbed up into the spreading branches. One day two of them ventured higher than the rest, and called out, "Can you see us still?" The others answered, "No, come down again!" but the two daring fellows refused. "We are going on into the sky to *Wuhu,* the World Above!" Those were their last words, for they were never seen again. And the tree was called *Mdi Msumu*, "the Story-tree."

Source: Alice Werner, *Myths and Legends of the Bantu*, 1933, ch. 5.

DEAD PEOPLE BECOME CLOUDS: SAN MYTH

The San—or Bushmen—are an indigenous people of Southern Africa. Their social composition consists of autonomous groups of families totaling around 50 people, typically with no dominant leader. Though at one point they occupied about one-third of the African continent, their numbers now are greatly diminished and total less than 100,000. The following San myth describes how, upon death, nature covers over the footprints that we made while alive, and then carries us away to become clouds. Unlike the above myths, which are presented in a somewhat stylized form, the one here conveys the unedited utterances of a specific tribesperson.

The wind does thus when we die, our (own) wind blows; for we, who are human beings, we possess wind; we make clouds when we die. Therefore, the wind does thus when we die, the wind makes dust, because it intends to blow, taking away our footprints, with which we had walked about while we still had nothing the matter with us. And our footprints, which the wind intends to blow away, would (otherwise still) lie plainly visible. For, the thing would seem as if we still lived. Therefore, the wind intends to blow, taking away our footprints. And, our gall, when we die, sits in the sky; it sits green in the sky, when we are dead.

Therefore, mother was wont to do thus when the moon lying down came, (when) the moon stood hollow. Mother spoke, she said: "The moon is carrying people who are dead. For, you are those who see that it lies in this manner; and it lies hollow, because it is killing itself (by) carrying people who are dead. This is why it lies hollow. It is not threatening; for, it is a moon of badness? You may (expect to) hear something, when the moon lies in this manner. A person is the one who has died, he whom the moon carries. Therefore, you may (expect to) hear what has happened, when the moon is like this."

The hair of our head will resemble clouds when we die, when we in this manner make clouds. These things are those which resemble clouds; and we think that (they) are clouds. We, who do not know, we are those who think in this manner, that (they) are clouds. We, who know, when we see that they are like this, we know that (they) are a person's clouds; (that they) are the hair of his head. We, who know, we are those who think thus, while we feel that we seeing recognize the clouds, how the clouds do in this manner form themselves.

Source: Wilhelm Heinrich Immanuel Bleek, et al., *Specimens of Bushman Folklore* (London, G. Allen and Company, 1911).

AMERICA

CREATION: MAYAN MYTH

The Popol Vuh *is one of the more important documents of pre-Columbian Mayan religion. Composed around 1550 by a Mayan author, it was written in the Quiché language of Mayan Guatemala, using Spanish letters. In the early 1700s it was translated into Spanish by a Catholic priest, and, though the original Quiché has since been lost, the translation survives. The work chronicles the formation of the world of the Quiché people, and lists their kings up to the year 1550. The selection below is the account of creation, which describes the gods' efforts to create humans; dissatisfied with their early productions, though, they resolve to destroy the immoral and arrogant creatures.*

Over a universe wrapped in the gloom of a dense and primeval night passed the god Hurakan, the mighty wind. He called out "earth," and the solid land appeared. The chief gods took counsel; they were Hurakan, Gucumatz, the serpent covered with green feathers, and Xpiyacoc and Xmucane, the mother and father gods. As the result of their deliberations animals were created. But as yet man was not. To supply the deficiency the divine beings resolved to create manikins carved out of wood. But these soon incurred the displeasure of the gods, who, irritated by their lack of reverence, resolved to destroy them. Then by the will of Hurakan, the Heart of Heaven, the waters were swollen, and a great flood came upon the manikins of wood. They were drowned and a thick resin fell from heaven. The bird Xecotcovach tore out their eyes; the bird Camulatz cut off their heads; the bird Cotzbalam devoured their flesh; the bird Tecumbalam broke their bones and sinews and ground them into powder. Because they had not thought on Hurakan, therefore the face of the earth grew dark, and a pouring rain commenced, raining by day and by night. Then all sorts of beings, great and small, gathered together to abuse the men to their faces. The very household utensils and animals jeered at them, their mill-stones, their plates, their cups, their dogs, their hens. Said the dogs and hens, "Very badly have you treated us, and you have bitten us. Now we bite you in turn." Said the mill-stones, "Very much were we tormented by you, and daily, daily, night and day, it was *squeak, screech, screech,* for your sake. Now you will feel our strength, and we will grind your flesh and make meal of your bodies." And the dogs upbraided the manikins because they had not been fed, and tore the unhappy images with their teeth. And the cups and dishes said, "Pain and misery you gave us, smoking our tops and sides, cooking us over the fire burning and hurting us as if we had no feeling. Now it is your turn, and you will burn." Then ran the manikins hither and thither in despair. They climbed to the roofs of the houses, but the houses crumbled under their feet; they tried to mount to the tops of the trees, but the trees hurled them from them; they sought refuge in the caverns, but the caverns closed before them. Thus was accomplished the ruin of this race, destined to be overthrown. And it is said that their posterity are the little monkeys who live in the woods.

After this catastrophe, before the earth was yet quite recovered from the wrath of the gods, there existed a man "full of pride," whose name was Vukub-Cakix. The name signifies "Seven-times-the-color-of-fire," or "Very brilliant," and was justified by the fact that its owner's eyes were of silver, his teeth of emerald, and other parts of his anatomy of precious metals. In his own opinion Vukub-Cakix's existence rendered unnecessary that of the sun and the moon, and this egoism so disgusted the gods that they resolved upon his overthrow. His two sons, Zipacna and Cabrakan (earth-heaper and earthquake), were daily employed, the one in heaping up mountains, and the other in demolishing them, and these also incurred the wrath of the immortals. Shortly after the decision of the deities the twin hero-gods Hun-Ahpu and Xbalanque came to earth with the intention of chastising the arrogance of Vukub-Cakix and his progeny.

Now Vukub-Cakix had a great tree of the variety known in Central America as "nanze" or "tapal," bearing a fruit round, yellow, and aromatic, and upon this fruit he depended for his daily sustenance. One day on going to partake of it for his morning meal he mounted to its summit in order to seek out the choicest fruits, when to his great indignation he discovered that Hun-Ahpu and Xbalanque had been before him, and had almost stripped the tree of its produce. The hero-gods, who lay concealed within the foliage, now added injury to theft by hurling at Vukub-Cakix a dart from a blowpipe, which had the effect of precipitating him from the summit of the tree to the earth. He arose in great wrath, bleeding profusely from a severe wound in the jaw. Hun-Ahpu then threw himself upon Vukub-Cakix, who in terrible anger seized the god by the arm and wrenched it from the body. He then proceeded to his dwelling, where he was met and anxiously interrogated by his spouse Chimalmat. Tortured by the pain in his teeth and jaw he, in an access of spite, hung Hun-Ahpu's arm over a blazing fire, and then threw himself down to bemoan his injuries, consoling himself, however, with the idea that he had adequately avenged himself upon the interlopers who had dared to disturb his peace.

But Hun-Ahpu and Xbalanque were in no mind that he should escape so easily, and the recovery of Hun-Ahpu's arm must be made at all hazards. With this end in view they consulted two venerable beings in whom we readily recognize the father-mother divinities, Xpiyacoc and Xmucane, disguised for the nonce as sorcerers. These personages accompanied Hun-Ahpu and Xbalanque to the abode of Vukub-Cakix, whom they found in a state of intense agony. The ancients persuaded him to be operated upon in order to relieve his sufferings, and for his glittering teeth they substituted grains of maize. Next they removed his eyes of emerald, upon which his death speedily followed, as did that of his wife Chimalmat. Hun-Ahpu's arm was recovered, re-affixed to his shoulder, and all ended satisfactorily for the hero-gods.

But their mission was not yet complete. The sons of Vukub-Cakix, Zipacna and Cabrakan, remained to be accounted for. Zipacana consented, at the entreaty of four hundred youths, incited by the hero-gods, to assist them in transporting a huge tree which was destined for the roof-tree of a house they were building. While assisting them, he was beguiled by them into entering a great ditch which they had dug for the purpose of destroying him, and when once he descended was overwhelmed by tree-trunks by his treacherous acquaintances, who imagined him to be slain. But he took refuge in a side-tunnel of the excavation, cut of his hair and nails for the ants to carry up to his enemies as a sign of his death, waited until the youths had become intoxicated with pulque because of joy at his supposed demise, and then, emerging from the pit, shook the house that the youths had built over his body about their heads, so that all were destroyed in its ruins.

But Hun-Ahpu and Xbalanque were grieved that the four hundred had perished, and laid a more efficacious trap for Zipacna. The mountain-bearer, carrying the mountains by night, sought his sustenance by day by the shore of the river, where he lived upon fish and crabs. The hero-gods constructed an artifical crab which they placed in a cavern at the bottom of a deep ravine. The hungry titan descended to the cave, which he entered on all fours. But a neighboring mountain had been undermined by the divine brothers, and its bulk was cast upon him. Thus at the foot of Mount Meavan perished the proud "Mountain Maker," whose corpse was turned into stone by the catastrophe.

Of the family of boasters only Cabrakan remained. Discovered by the hero-gods at his favourite pastime of overturning the hills, they enticed him in an easterly direction, challenging him to overthrow a particularly high mountain. On the way they shot a bird with their blow-pipes, and poisoned it with earth. This they gave to Cabrakan to eat. After partaking of the poisoned fare his strength deserted him, and failing to move the mountain he was bound and buried by the victorious hero-gods.

Source: *The Popol Vuh,* Book I, from Lewis Spence, *The Popol Vuh, the Mythic and Heroic Sagas of the Kichés of Central America* (London: David Nutt, 1908).

QUETZALCOATL AND TEZCATLIPOCA: MEXICAN MYTH

Quetzalcoatl and Tezcatlipoca were major rival deities in pre-Columbian Meso-America. Quetzalcoatl, the feathered serpent, was the subject of a religious cult among the Toltec people of central Mexico in the tenth to twelfth centuries C.E. Several myths depict Quetzalcoatl as a priest-king of Tollan, the urban center of the Toltec region. Sacrificing only animals, he runs into conflict with the evil wizard Tezcatlipoca, who prefers human sacrifice. Tezcatlipoca then expels Quetzalcoatl. In the myth below, Tezcatlipoca tricks Quetzalcoatl and usurps his power. The dejected Quetzalcoatl then leaves for his homeland.

In the days of Quetzalcoatl there was abundance of everything necessary for subsistence. The maize was plentiful, the calabashes were as thick as one's arm, and cotton grew in all colors without having to be dyed. A variety of birds of rich plumage filled the air with their songs, and gold, silver, and precious stones were abundant. In the reign of Quetzalcoatl there was peace and plenty for all men.

But this blissful state was too fortunate, too happy to endure. Envious of the calm enjoyment of the god and his people the Toltecs, there wicked "necromancers" plotted their downfall—the deities Huitzilopochtli, Tezcatlipoca, and Tlacahuepan. These laid evil enchantments upon the city of Tollan, and Tezcatlipoca in particular took the lead in these envious conspiracies. Disguised as an aged man with white hair, he presented himself at the palace of Quetzalcoatl, where he said to the pages in-waiting: "Pray present me to your master the king. I desire to speak with him."

The pages advised him to retire, as Quetzalcoatl was indisposed and could see no one. He requested them, however, to tell the god that he was waiting outside. They did so, and procured his admittance.

On entering the chamber of Quetzalcoatl the wily Tezcatlipoca simulated much sympathy with the suffering god-king. "How are you, my son?" he asked. "I have brought you a drug which you should drink, and which will put an end to the course of your malady."

"You are welcome, old man," replied Quetzalcoatl. "I have known for many days that you would come. I am exceedingly indisposed. The malady affects my entire system, and I can use neither my hands not feet."

Tezcatlipoca assured him that if he partook of the medicine which he had brought him he would immediately experience a great improvement in health. Quetzalcoatl drank the potion, and at once felt much revived. The cunning Tezcatlipoca pressed another and still another cup of the potion upon him, and as it was nothing but *pulque,* the wine of the country, he speedily became intoxicated, and was as wax in the hands of his adversary. . . .

The Toltecs were so tormented by the enchantments of Tezcatlipoca that it was soon apparent to them that their fortunes were on the wane and that the end of their empire was at hand. Quetzalcoatl, chagrined at the turn things had taken, resolved to leave Tollan and go to the country of Tlapallan, from which he had come on his civilizing mission to Mexico. He burned all the houses which he had built, and buried his treasure of gold and precious stones in the deep valleys between the mountains. He changed the cacao-trees into mesquites, and he ordered all the birds of rich plumage and song to quit the valley of Anahuac and to follow him to a distance of more than a hundred leagues. On the road from Tollan he discovered a great tree at a point called Quauhtitlan. He rested there, and requested his pages to hand him a mirror. Regarding himself in the polished surface, he exclaimed, "I am old," and from that circumstance the spot was named Old Quauhtitlan. Proceeding on his way accompanied by musicians who played the flute, he walked until fatigue arrested his steps, and he seated himself upon a stone, on which he left the imprint of his hands. This place is called Temacpalco (The Impress of the Hands). At Coaapan he was met by the Nahua gods, who were inimical to him and to the Toltecs.

"Where do you go?" they asked him. "Why do you leave your capital?"
"I go to Tlapallan," replied Quetzalcoatl, "from which I came."
"For what reason?" persisted the enchanters.
"My father the Sun has called me thence," replied Quetzalcoatl.
"Go, then, happily," they said, "but leave us the secret of your art, the secret of founding in silver, of working in precious stones and woods, of painting, and of feather-working, and other matters."

But Quetzalcoatl refused, and cast all his treasures into the fountain of Cozcaapa (Water of Precious Stones). At Cochtan he was met by another enchanter, who asked him where he was bound, and on learning his destination proffered him a draught of wine. On tasting the vintage Quetzalcoatl was overcome with sleep. Continuing his journey in the morning, the god passed between a volcano and the Sierra Nevada (Mountain of Snow), where all the pages who accompanied him died of cold. He regretted this misfortune exceedingly, and wept, lamenting their fate with most bitter tears and mournful songs. On reaching the summit of Mount Poyauhtecatl he slid to the base. Arriving at the sea-shore, he embarked upon a raft of serpents, and was wafted away toward the land of Tlapallan.

Source: Lewis Spence, *The Myths of Mexico and Peru* (New York, T.Y. Crowell Co., 1913).

CREATION: HOPI MYTH

The Hopi people of North America are part of the Pueblo Indian group, located in what is now the southwest United States. Their villages were often cliff dwellings and contained at least two dominant kivas—underground social chambers. The most well-known of their rituals is the Snake Dance, in which performers danced with live snakes in their mouths. The Hopi creation myth below describes how two principal goddesses—the Hard-Being Women of the east and west—dried the land, created animals, and then created one race of people. Another goddess—Spider Woman—created other races, which introduced discord into society.

A very long time ago there was nothing but water. In the east, the Hard-Being Woman [Huruing Wuhti], the deity of all hard substances, lived in the ocean. Her house was a kiva like the kivas of the Hopi of to-day. To the ladder leading into the kiva were usually tied a skin of a gray fox and one of a yellow fox. Another Hard-Being Woman lived in the ocean in the west in a similar kiva, but to her ladder was attached a turtle-shell rattle.

The Sun also existed at that time. Shortly before rising in the east, the Sun would dress up in the skin of the gray fox, whereupon it would begin to dawn—the so-called white dawn of the Hopi. After a little while the Sun would lay off the gray skin and put on the yellow fox skin, whereupon the bright dawn of the morning—the so-called yellow dawn of the Hopi—would appear. The Sun would then rise, that is, emerge from an opening in the north end of the kiva in which the Hard-Being Woman lived. When arriving in the west again, the sun would first announce his arrival by fastening the rattle on the point of the ladder beam, whereupon he would enter the kiva, pass through an opening in the north end of the kiva, and continue his course eastward under the water, and so on.

By and by these two deities caused some dry land to appear in the midst of the water, the waters receding eastward and westward. The Sun passing over this dry land constantly took notice of the fact that no living being of any kind could be seen anywhere, and mentioned this fact to the two deities. So one time the Hard-Being Woman of the west sent word through the Sun to the Hard-Being Woman in the east to come over to her as she wanted to talk over this matter. The Hard-Being Woman of the east complied with this request and proceeded to the West over a rainbow. After consulting each other on this point the two concluded that they would create a little bird; so the deity of the east made a wren of clay, and covered it up with a piece of native cloth. Hereupon they sang a song over it, and after a little while the little bird showed signs of life. Uncovering it, a live bird came forth, saying: "Why do you want me so quickly?" "Yes," they said, "we want you to fly all over this dry place and see whether you can find anything living." They thought that as the Sun always passed over the middle of the earth, he might have failed to notice any living beings that might exist in the north or the south. So the little Wren flew all over the earth, but upon its return reported that no living being existed anywhere. Tradition says, however, that by this time Spider Woman [Kohk'ang Wuhti], lived somewhere in the south-west at the edge of the water, also in a kiva, but this the little bird had failed to notice.

Hereupon the deity of the west proceeded to make very many birds of different kinds and form, placing them again under the same cover under which the Wren had been brought to life. They again sang a song over them. Presently the birds began to move under the cover. The goddess removed the cover and found under it all kinds of birds and fowls. "Why do you want us so quickly?" the latter asked. "Yes, we want you to inhabit this world." Hereupon the two deities taught every kind of bird the sound that it should make, and then the birds scattered out in all directions.

Hereupon the Hard-Being Woman of the west made of clay all different kinds of animals, and they were brought to life in the same manner as the birds. They also asked the same question: "Why do you want us so quickly?" "We want you to inhabit this earth," was the reply given them, whereupon they were taught by their creators their different sounds or languages, after which they proceeded forth to inhabit the different parts of the earth. They now concluded that they would create people. The deity of the east made of clay first a woman and then a man, who were brought to life in exactly the same manner as the birds and animals before them. They asked the same question, and were told that they should live upon this earth and should understand everything. Hereupon the Hard-Being Woman of the east made two tablets of some hard substance, whether stone or clay tradition does not say, and drew upon them with the wooden stick certain characters, handing these tablets to the newly created man and woman, who looked at them, but did not know what they meant. So the deity of the east rubbed with the palms of her hands, first the palms of the woman and then the palms of the man, by which they were enlightened so that they understood the writing on the tablets. Hereupon the deities taught these two a language. After they had taught them the language, the goddess of the east took them out of the kiva and led them over a rainbow, to her home in the east. There they stayed four days, after which the Hard-Being Woman told them to go now and select for themselves a place and live there. The two proceeded forth saying that they would travel around a while and wherever they would find a good field they would remain. Finding a nice place at last, they built a small, simple house, similar to the old houses of the Hopi. Soon the Hard-Being Woman of the west began to think of the matter again, and said to herself: "This is not the way yet that it should be. We are not done yet," and communicated her thoughts to the Hard-Being Woman of the east. By this time Spider Woman had heard about all this matter and she concluded to anticipate the others and also create some beings. So she also made a man and woman of clay, covered them up, sang over them, and brought to life her handiwork. But these two proved to be Spaniards. She taught them the Spanish language, also giving them similar tablets and imparting knowledge to them by rubbing their hands in the same manner as the woman of the East had done with the "White Men." Hereupon she created two burros, which she gave to the Spanish man and woman. The latter settled down close by. After this, Spider Woman continued to create people in the same manner as she had created the Spaniards, always a man and a woman, giving a different language to each pair. But all at once she found that she had forgotten to create a woman for a certain man, and that is the reason why now there are always some single men.

She continued the creating of people in the same manner, giving new languages as the pairs were formed. All at once she found that she had failed to create a man for a certain woman, in other words, it was found that there was one more woman than there were men. "Oh my!" she said, "How is this?" and then addressing the single woman she said: "There is a single man somewhere, who went away from here. You try to find him and if he accepts you, you live with him. If not, both of you will have to remain single. You do the best you can about that." The two finally found each other, and the woman said, "Where will we live?" The man answered: "Why here, anywhere. We will remain together." So he went to work and built a house for them in which they lived. But it did not take very long before they commenced to quarrel with each other. "I want to live here alone," the woman said. "I can prepare food for myself." "Yes, but who will get the wood for you? Who will work the fields?" the man said. "We had better remain together." They made up with each other, but peace did not last. They soon quarreled again, separated for while, came together again, separated again, and so on. Had these people not lived in that way, all the other Hopi would now live in peace, but others learned it from them, and that is the reason why there are so many contentions between the men and their wives. These were the kind of people that Spider Woman had created. The Hard-Being Woman of the west heard about this and commenced to meditate upon it. Soon she called the goddess from the east to come over again, which the latter did. "I do not want to live here alone," the deity of the west said, "I also want some good people to live here." So she also created a number of other people, but always a man and a wife. They were created in the same manner as the deity of the east had created hers. They lived in the west. Only wherever the people that Spider Woman had created came in contact with these good people there was trouble. The people at that time led a nomadic life, living mostly on game. Wherever they found rabbits or antelope or deer they would kill the game and eat it. This led to a good many contentions among the people. Finally the Woman of the west said to her people: "You remain here; I am going to live, after this, in the midst of the ocean in the west. When you want anything from me, you pray to me there." Her people regretted this very much, but she left them. The Hard-Being Woman of the east did exactly the same thing, and that is the reason why at the present day the places where these two live are never seen.

Those Hopi who now want something from them deposit their prayer offerings in the village. When they say their wishes and prayers they think of those two who live in the far distance, but of whom the Hopi believe that they still remember them.

The Spanish were angry at the Hard-Being Woman and two of them took their guns and proceeded to the abiding place of the deity. The Spaniards are very skillful and they found a way to get there. When they arrived at the house of the Hard-Being Woman the latter at once surmised what their intentions were. "You have come to kill me," she said; "don't do that; lay down your weapons and I will show you something; I am not going to hurt you." They laid down their arms, whereupon she went to the rear end of the kiva and brought out a white lump like a stone and laid it before the two men, asking them to lift it up. One tried it, but could not lift it up, and what was worse, his hands adhered to the stone. The other man tried to assist him, but his hands also adhered to the stone, and thus they were both prisoners. Hereupon the Hard-Being Woman took the two guns and said: "These do not amount to anything," and then rubbed them between her hands to powder. She then said to them: "You people ought to live in peace with one another. You people of Spider Woman know many things, and the people whom we have made also know many, but different, things. You ought not to quarrel about these things, but learn from one another; if one has or knows a good thing he should exchange it with others for other good things that they know and have. If you will agree to this I will release you." They said they did, and that they would no more try to kill the deity. Then the latter went to the rear end of the kiva where she disappeared through an opening in the floor, from where she exerted a secret influence upon the stone and thus released the two men. They departed, but the Hard-Being Woman did not fully trust them, thinking that they would return, but they never did.

Source: H. R. Voth, *The Traditions of The Hopi,* in *Field Columbian Museum, Publication, Anthropological Series* (Chicago: The Museum, 1895–1905, vol. 8).

CREATION: CHEROKEE MYTH

The Cherokee people of North America are of the Iroquois language group and lived in what is now the southeastern United States. In the 1830s the United States government forced them to relocate to Oklahoma. The Cherokee creation myth below emphasizes the role of animals in the creation process. While the world was covered with water, they existed in a realm above the earth, slowly inhabiting it as it became dry. Vegetation followed, and finally humans appeared.

The earth is a great island floating in a sea of water, and suspended at each of the four cardinal points by a cord hanging down from the sky vault, which is of solid rock. When the world grows old and worn out, the people will die and the cords will break and let the earth sink down into the ocean, and all will be water again. The Indians are afraid of this.

When all was water, the animals were above, in the place Beyond the Arch; but it was very much crowded, and they were wanting more room. They wondered what was below the water, and at last "Beaver's Grandchild," the little Water-beetle, offered to go and see if it could learn. It darted in every direction over the surface of the water, but could find no firm place to rest. Then it dived to the bottom and came up with some soft mud, which began to grow and spread on every side until it became the island which we call the earth. It was afterward fastened to the sky with four cords, but no one remembers who did this.

At first the earth was flat and very soft and wet. The animals were anxious to get down, and sent out different birds to see if it was yet dry, but they found no place to land and came back again to the place Beyond the Arch. At last it seemed to be time, and they sent out the Buzzard and told him to go and make ready for them. This was the Great Buzzard, the father of all the buzzards we see now. He flew all over the earth, low down near the ground, and it was still soft. When he reached the Cherokee country, he was very tired, and his wings began to flap and strike the ground, and wherever they struck the earth there was a valley, and where they turned up again there was a mountain. When the animals above saw this, they were afraid that the whole world would be mountains, so they called him back, but the Cherokee country remains full of mountains to this day.

When the earth was dry and the animals came down, it was still dark, so they got the sun and set it in a track to go every day across the island from east to west, just overhead. It was too hot this way, and the "Red

Crawfish" had his shell scorched a bright red, so that his meat was spoiled; and the Cherokee do not eat it. The conjurers put the sun another hand-breadth higher in the air, but it was still too hot. They raised it another, until it was seven handbreadths high and just under the sky arch. Then it was right, and they left it so. This is why the conjurers call the highest place "The Seventh Height," because it is seven hand-breadths above the earth. Every day the sun goes along under this arch, and returns at night on the upper side to the starting place.

There is another world under this, and it is like ours in everything—animals, plants, and people—save that the seasons are different. The streams that come down from the mountains are the trails by which we reach this underworld, and the springs at their heads are the doorways by which we enter it, but to do this one must fast and go to water, and have one of the underground people for a guide. We know that the seasons in the underworld are different from ours, because the water in the springs is always warmer in winter and cooler in summer than the outer air.

When the animals and plants were first made—we do not know by whom—they were told to watch and keep awake for seven nights, just as young men now fast and keep awake when they pray to their medicine. They tried to do this, and nearly all were awake through the first night, but the next night several dropped off to sleep, and the third night others were asleep, and then others, until, on the seventh night, of all the animals only the owl, the panther, and one or two more were still awake. To these were given the power to see and to go about in the dark, and to make prey of the birds and animals which must sleep at night. Of the trees only the cedar, the pine, the spruce, the holly, and the laurel were awake to the end, and to them it was given to be always green and to be greatest for medicine, but to the others it was said: "Because you have not endured to the end you will lose your hair every winter."

Men came after the animals and plants. At first there were only a brother and sister until he struck her with a fish and told her to multiply, and so it was. In seven days a child was born to her, and thereafter every seven days another, and they increased very fast until there was danger that the world could not keep them. Then it was made that a woman should have only one child in a year, and it has been so ever since.

Source: James Mooney, *Myths of the Cherokee,* from *Nineteenth Annual Report of the Bureau of American Ethnology: To the Secretary of the Smithsonian Institution, 1897–98* (Washington, D.C.: Government Printing Office, 1900).

ORIGIN OF DISEASE AND MEDICINE: CHEROKEE MYTH

The myth below illustrates the exceptionally close relationship that the Cherokee people had to their natural surroundings. According to the myth, as the human population increased and became insensitive toward the animal world, the animals rose up against them. They inflicted humans with rheumatism, fears, nightmares and diseases. Only the plants were sympathetic to the humans, and thus provided cures for their ailments.

In the old days the beasts, birds, fishes, insects, and plants could all talk, and they and the people lived together in peace and friendship. But as time went on the people increased so rapidly that their settlements spread over the whole earth, and the poor animals found themselves beginning to be cramped for room. This was bad enough, but to make it worse humans invented bows, knives, blowguns, spears, and hooks, and began to slaughter the larger animals, birds, and fishes for their flesh or their skins, while the smaller creatures, such as the frogs and worms, were crushed and trodden upon without thought, out of pure carelessness or contempt. So the animals resolved to consult upon measures for their common safety.

The Bears were the first to meet in council in their townhouse under Kuwahi Mountain, the "Mulberry Place," and the old White Bear chief presided. After each in turn had complained of the way in which humans killed their friends, ate their flesh, and used their skins for their own purposes, it was decided to begin war at once against them. Someone asked what weapons humans used to destroy them. "Bows and arrows, of course," cried all the Bears in chorus. "And what are they made of?" was the next question. "The bow of wood, and the string of our entrails," replied one of the Bears. It was then proposed that they make a bow and some arrows and see if they could not use the same weapons against humans themselves. So one Bear got a nice piece of locust wood and another sacrificed himself for the good of the rest in order to furnish a piece of his entrails for the string. But when everything was ready and the first Bear stepped up to make the trial, it was found that in letting the arrow fly after drawing back the bow, his long claws caught the string and spoiled the shot. This was annoying, but some one suggested that they might trim his claws, which was accordingly done, and on a second trial it was found that the arrow went straight to the mark. But here the chief, the old White Bear, objected, saying it was necessary that they should have long claws in order to be able to climb trees. "One of us has already died to furnish the bowstring, and if we now cut off our claws we must all starve together. It is better to trust to the teeth and claws that nature gave us, for it is plain that human weapons were not intended for us."

No one could think of any better plan, so the old chief dismissed the council and the Bears dispersed to the woods and thickets without having concerted any way to prevent the increase of the human race. Had the result of the council been otherwise, we should now be at war with the Bears, but as it is, the hunter does not even ask the Bear's pardon when he kills one.

The Deer next held a council under their chief, the Little Deer, and after some talk decided to send rheumatism to every hunter who should kill one of them unless he took care to ask their pardon for the offense. They sent notice of their decision to the nearest settlement of Indians and told them at the same time what to do when necessity forced them to kill one of the Deer tribe. Now, whenever the hunter shoots a Deer, the Little Deer, who is swift as the wind and can not be wounded, runs quickly up to the spot and, bending over the blood-stains, asks the spirit of the Deer if it has heard the prayer of the hunter for pardon. If the reply be "Yes," all is well, and the Little Deer goes on his way; but if the reply be "No," he follows on the trail of the hunter, guided by the drops of blood on the ground, until he arrives at his cabin in the settlement, when the Little Deer enters invisibly and strikes the hunter with rheumatism, so that he becomes at once a helpless cripple. No hunter who has regard for his health ever fails to ask pardon of the Deer for killing it, although some hunters who have not learned the prayer may try to turn aside the Little Deer from his pursuit by building a fire behind them in the trail.

Next came the Fishes and Reptiles, who had their own complaints against humans. They held their council together and determined to make their victims dream of snakes coiling about them in slimy folds and blowing foul breath in their faces, or to make them dream of eating raw or decaying fish, so that they would lose appetite, sicken, and die. This is why people dream about snakes and fish.

Finally the Birds, Insects, and smaller animals came together for the same purpose, and the Grubworm was chief of the council. It was decided that each in turn should give an opinion, and then they would vote on the question as to whether or not humans were guilty. Seven votes should be enough to condemn them. One after another denounced human cruelty and injustice toward the other animals and voted in favor of their death. The Frog spoke first, saying: "We must do something to check the increase of the race, or people will become so numerous that we will be crowded from off the earth. See how they have kicked me about because I'm ugly, as they say, until my back is covered with sores"; and here he showed the spots on his skin. Next came the Bird—no one remembers now which one it was—who condemned humans "because he burns my feet off," meaning the way in which the hunter barbecues birds by impaling them on a stick set over the fire, so that their feathers and tender feet are singed off. Others followed in the same strain. The Ground-squirrel alone ventured to say a good word for humans, who seldom hurt him because he was so small, but this made the others so angry that they fell upon the Ground-squirrel and tore him with their claws, and the stripes are on his back to this day.

They began then to devise and name so many new diseases, one after another, that had not their invention at last failed them, no one of the human race would have been able to survive. The Grubworm grew constantly more pleased as the name of each disease was called off, until at last they reached the end of the list, when some one proposed to make menstruation sometimes fatal to women. On this he rose up in his place and cried: "Thanks! I'm glad some more of them will die, for they are getting so thick that they tread on me." The thought fairly made him shake with joy, so that he fell over backward and could not get on his feet again, but had to wriggle off on his back, as the Grubworm has done ever since.

When the Plants, who were friendly to humans, heard what had been done by the animals, they determined to defeat the latter's evil designs. Each Tree, Shrub, and Herb, down even to the Grasses and Mosses, agreed to furnish a cure for some one of the diseases named, and each said: "I will appear to help humans when they call upon me in their needs." Thus came medicine; and the plants, every one of which has its use if we only knew it, furnish the remedy to counteract the evil wrought by the revengeful animals. Even weeds were made for some good purpose, which we must find out for ourselves. When the medicine man does not know what medicine to use for a sick person the spirit of the plant tells him.

Source: James Mooney, *Myths of the Cherokee*.

GLOSSARY

Bantu   Region and language group of central and Southern Africa.

Cherokee   Indigenous North American people of the Iroquois Indian group from southeastern United States.

Fetishism   Use in worship practices of special objects that contain spiritual power, such as masks.

High God   A supreme being in the sky and creator of all.

Hopi   Indigenous North American people of the Pueblo Indian group in southwest United States.

Maya   Indigenous pre-Columbian people and civilization of southern Mexico and Guatemala.

Popol Vuh   Mayan religious text composed around 1550.

Quetzalcoatl   Mythical priest-king of the Toltec people.

San   Indigenous people of Southern Africa, also called Bushmen; prior to and distinct from Bantu inhabitants.

Tezcatlipoca   Mythical evil wizard of the Toltec people.

Toltec   Indigenous pre-Columbian people and civilization of central Mexico in the tenth to twelfth centuries C.E.

FURTHER READINGS

BLACK ELK, WALLACE H. *Black Elk: The Sacred Ways of a Lakota*. San Francisco: Harper San Francisco: 1991.

BROWN, JOSEPH EPES. *Teaching Spirits: Understanding Native American Religious Traditions*. Oxford: Oxford University Press, 2001.

FLORESCANO, ENRIQUE. *The Myth of Quetzalcoatl*. Baltimore: Johns Hopkins University Press, 1999.

GILL, SAM D. *Native American Religions*. Belmont, California: Wadsworth Publishing Company, 1982.

KING, NOEL QUINTON. *African Cosmos: An Introduction to Religion in Africa*. Belmont, California: Wadsworth Publishing Company, 1986.

LEON-PORTILLA, MIGUEL, ED. *Native Mesoamerican Spirituality*, New York: Paulist Press, 1980.

MAGESA, LAURENTI. *African Religion: The Moral Traditions of Abundant Life*. Maryknoll, New York: Orbis Books, 1997.

MBITI, JOHN S. *African Religions and Philosophy*. Oxford: Heinemann Educational, 1990.

MBITI, JOHN S. *Introduction to African Religion*. Oxford: Heinemann Educational, 1991.

RAY, BENJAMIN C. *African Religions: Symbol, Ritual, and Community*. Englewood Cliffs, New Jersey: Prentice Hall, 1999.

TORRANCE, ROBERT MITCHELL. *The Spiritual Quest: Transcendence in Myth, Religion, and Science*. Berkeley: University of California Press, 1994.

YOUNG, WILLIAM A. *Quest for Harmony: Native American Spiritual Traditions*. New York: Seven Bridges Press, 2002.

ZIMMERMAN, LARRY J. *Native North America*. Norman: University of Oklahoma Press, 2000.

Acknowledgments

HINDUISM

Translation of excerpts from Hindu texts, by John Powers. Reprinted by permission.

Excerpts from *The Rig Veda,* tr. Wendy Doniger O'Flaherty (New York: Penguin, 1981). Reproduced by permission of Frederick Warne & Co.

Excerpts from *Shankara's Crest-Jewel of Discrimination,* tr. Swami Prabhavananda and Christopher Isherwood (Hollywood: Vedanta Press, 1975). Used by permission.

Excerpts from *The Bhagavad-gita: Krishna's Counsel in Time of War,* translated by Barbara Stoler Miller. Copyright © 1986 by Columbia University Press. Reprinted with permission of the publisher.

Excerpts reprinted from *Encountering the Goddess,* tr. Thomas B. Coburn (Albany: State University of New York Press, 1991). Used by permission.

Excerpts from *Saundaryalahari,* attributed to Shankara, translated by W. N. Brown. Copyright © 1958 by the President and Fellows of Harvard College. Reprinted by permission of Harvard University Press.

Excerpts from *Speaking of Siva,* tr. A. K. Ramanujan (Baltimore: Penguin Books, 1973). Reproduced by permission of Frederick Warne & Co.

JAINISM

Translation of excerpts from Jaina texts, by John Powers. Reprinted by permission.

Translation of excerpts from Jaina texts, by Royce Wilies. Reprinted by permission.

BUDDHISM

Translation of excerpts from Buddhist texts, by John Powers. Reprinted by permission.

Translation of excerpts from Buddhist texts, by David Moore. Reprinted by permission.

Excerpts from *Indo-Tibetan Buddhism: Indian Buddhists and Their Tibetan Successors* by David Snellgrove. Copyright © 1987. Reprinted by arrangement with Shambhala Publications, Inc., 300 Massachusetts Avenue, Boston, MA. 02115

Excerpts from *The Garland of Mahamudra Practices* (Ithaca: Snow Lion, 1986). Used by permission.

Excerpts from *The Hevajra Tantra: A Critical Study,* David Snellgrove (London: Oxford University Press, 1959). By permission of Oxford University Press.

Excerpts from *Bar do thos grol: The Tibetan Book of the Dead: Liberation through Understanding in the Between,* tr. Robert A. F. Thurman. Copyright © 1994. Used by permission of Bantam Books, a division of Bantam Doubleday Dell Publishing Group, Inc.

Excerpts from *The Beautiful Ornament of the Three Visions* (Ithaca: Snow Lion, 1991). Used by permission.

Excerpts from *The Platform Sutra of the Sixth Patriarch* by Philip Yampolsky. Copyright © 1967 by Columbia University Press. Reprinted with permission of the publisher.

Excerpts from *Kukai's Petition to Supplement the Annual Reading of Sutra in the Imperial Palace with Special Esoteric Buddhist (Shingon) Rites,* translated by David Gardiner. Reprinted by permission of David Gardiner.

Excerpts from *Dogen's Manual of Zen Meditation,* tr. Carl Bielefeldt (Berkeley: University of California Press, 1988). Used by permission.

Excerpts from *Nichiren: Selected Writings,* tr. Laurel Rodd (Honolulu: University of Hawaii Press, 1980). Copyright Laurel Rasplica Rodd. Reprinted by permission.

SIKHISM

Translation of excerpts from Sikh texts, by John Powers. Reprinted by permission.

Excerpts from *Adi Granth: Guru Nanak and the Sikh Religion,* tr. W. H. McLeod (Oxford: Clarendon Press, 1968). By permission of Oxford University Press.

CONFUCIANISM

Translation of excerpts from Confucian texts, by Kurt Vall. Reprinted by permission.

Translation of excerpts from Confucian texts, by John Powers. Reprinted by permission.

Excerpts from *Sources of Chinese Tradition,* by William Theodore deBary. Copyright © 1964 by Columbia University Press. Reprinted with permission of the publisher.

Excerpts from *Mencius,* tr. D. C. Lau (Hong Kong: The Chinese University Press, 1979). Reproduced by permission of Frederick Warne & Co.

Excerpts from *Xunzi: A Translation and Study of the Complete Works,* vol. III, tr. John Knoblock (Stanford: Stanford University Press, 1994). Used by permission.

Excerpts from *Instructions for Practical Living and Other Neo-Confucian Writings* By Wang Yang-Ming, translated by Wing-tsit Chan. Copyright © 1963 by Columbia University Press. Reprinted with permission of the publisher.

DAOISM

Translation of excerpts from Daoist texts, by John Powers. Reprinted by permission.

Excerpts from *Early Chinese Mysticism: Philosophy and Soteriology in the Daoist Tradition,* Livia Kohn. Copyright © 1992 by Princeton University Press. Reprinted by permission of Princeton University Press.

Excerpts from *Chuang-tzu: Basic Writings,* translated by Burton Watson, Copyright © 1964 by Columbia University Press. Reprinted with permission of the publisher.

Excerpts reprinted from *Daoist Mystical Philosophy: The Scripture of the Western Ascension,* tr. Livia Kohn (Albany: State University of New York Press, 1991). Used by permission.

Reprint from *Immortal Sisters,* by Thomas Cleary. Copyright © 1990 by Thomas Cleary. Reprinted by arrangement with North Atlantic Books, P.O. Box 12327, Berkeley, CA 94712.

SHINTO

Translation of Shinto texts, by Meredith McKinney. Reprinted by permission.

Excerpts from *Kojiki,* Records of Ancient Matters in The Great Asian Religions: An Anthology (New York: Macmillan, 1969). Reprinted by permission of Evelyn Kitagawa.

Excerpts from *Interior Castle,* tr. E. Allison Peers. Reprinted with permission of Sheed & Ward, 115 E. Armour Blvd., Kansas City, MO 64111.

ISLAM

Excerpts from *The Koran,* tr. N. J. Dawood (London: Penguin Books, 1990). Reproduced by permission of Frederick Warne & Co.

Selections from *The Translation of the Meanings of Sahih al-Bukhari,* tr. Muhammad Muhsin Khan. Copyright © Kazi Publications Inc. Used by permission.

Excerpts from *Islamic Jurisprudence: Shafi'i's Risala,* tr. Majid Khadduri. Copyright © 1961. Johns Hopkins University Press.

Excerpts reprinted from *A Shi'ite Creed,* Ibn Babawayh al-Qummi, tr. Asaf A. A. Fyzee (London: Oxford University Press, 1942). Reprinted by permission of Oxford University Press.

Excerpts from *Rabi'a: The Life and Work of Rabi'a and Other Women Mystics in Islam,* Margaret Smith (Oxford: Oneworld Publications, 1994).

Excerpts reprinted from *The Sufi Path of Love: The Spiritual Teachings of Rumi,* tr. William C. Chittick (Albany: State University of New York Press, 1983). Used by permission.

BAHA'I FAITH

Extracts from Baha'i scriptures reprinted by permission from the National Spiritual Assembly of the Bahais of the United States.